Financing the Entrepreneurial Venture

Financing the Entrepreneurial Venture

A Casebook

Paul A. Gompers

ANTHEM PRESS

Anthem Press
An imprint of Wimbledon Publishing Company
www.anthempress.com

This edition first published in UK and USA 2024
by ANTHEM PRESS
75–76 Blackfriars Road, London SE1 8HA, UK
or PO Box 9779, London SW19 7ZG, UK
and
244 Madison Ave #116, New York, NY 10016, USA

British Library Cataloguing-in-Publication Data
A catalogue record for this book is available from the British Library.

Library of Congress Cataloging-in-Publication Data: 2023923836
A catalog record for this book has been requested.

ISBN-13: 978-1-83999-148-6 (Hbk)
ISBN-10: 1-83999-148-8 (Hbk)

This title is also available as an e-book.

CONTENTS

ACKNOWLEDGMENTS

Over the course of my academic career, entrepreneurial firms have been at the center of my research and teaching. During this period, I have written more than 100 case studies and more than 50 notes that knit together the insights of that career. This book represents the combination of my research and writings that I hope can provide foundational insights to entrepreneurs and investors.

The implications of this research are wide-ranging. For entrepreneurs, understanding the nuances of venture capital financing, governance mechanisms, and the broader financial landscape can be crucial for success. For venture capitalists and other investors, my findings offer strategies for investment and portfolio management, emphasizing the importance of active involvement in guiding portfolio companies. For policymakers, the insights highlight the significance of creating a favorable regulatory and economic environment that supports innovation, entrepreneurship, and the flow of venture capital.

The decade of the 2010s has been called an entrepreneurial decade because many new products and services were introduced by new and fast-growing companies. The number of start-ups exploded and entrepreneurial ecosystems sprang up around the world. And while it is true that employment growth in small firms fueled nearly all job creation over the past decade and a half, the real nature of entrepreneurship can only be understood within the context of the global opportunity that entrepreneurial firms will continue to drive.

This book would not have been possible without the advice and mentorship of colleagues, including Andrei Shleifer, Richard Ruback, and Bill Sahlman. More than 30 years ago, these three scholars guided me on this path. My many coauthors over the years have also been a constant source of inspiration and motivation. Josh Lerner, Andrew Metrick, Steve Kaplan, Alon Brav, Joy Ishii, David Scharfstein, Anna Kovner, Malcolm Baker, Henry Chen, Vladimir Mukharlyamov, Sophie Calder-Wang, Kevin Huang, Ilya Strebulaev, Will Gornall, Natee Amornsiripanitch, George Hu, and Will Levinson deserve special acknowledgment.

I also need to thank more than a dozen research associates who have helped in the writing of these cases, traveling everywhere to interview entrepreneurs and investors. Their names appear as coauthors on these case studies, and they all deserve tremendous credit. Additionally, more than 100 case protagonists were willing to share their life's journey to educate the next generation of founders and venture capitalists. I have always been amazed at how open and candid these individuals are. They have formed the backbone of the lessons in this book.

Finally, my family has been a constant source of support, always willing to engage in discussions of ideas that affect the world. Jody Dushay, my wife, and my three daughters—Sivan, Annika, and Zoe—have always been there and encouraged me to dig deeper. I could not have completed this book without their constant presence in my life.

SECTION 1

Introduction

CHAPTER 1.1

Introduction to Entrepreneurial Finance – 2020: Course Overview Note

Paul Gompers

This note presents an overview of the structure and material that will be covered in Entrepreneurial Finance. In addition to presenting the outline and themes of the course, this note provides resources from the academic literature to use as reference material. The listing of articles, while not exhaustive, covers a broad range of topics in entrepreneurial finance at various technical levels.

When looking through the course description, many of you may have asked, "What is entrepreneurial finance?" The best way to understand it is to define the individual terms. Finance is easier to define. Finance is the study of value and resource allocation. Cash is central to any working definition of finance. The value of any cash stream is influenced by its magnitude, timing, and riskiness. Finance is also concerned with the cost of capital and determining the least expensive source of funds for an investment project. This issue is especially important for start-up and growing firms that may face internal financial constraints and have different costs of debt and equity capital.

Entrepreneurship has had many definitions over the past two and one half centuries since Richard Cantillon first used the term in the early 18th century. Some have focused on the risk-bearing nature of entrepreneurship, while others have focused on the innovations that entrepreneurs create. Both are important elements of what entrepreneurs do, but neither is entrepreneurship. Entrepreneurship focuses on a way of thinking, managing a career, business, or anything else. While most of us associate entrepreneurship with small, startup companies, large firms can also be "entrepreneurial." The important element of entrepreneurship is the relentless pursuit of opportunity without regard to resources currently controlled.[1]

Introduction to Entrepreneurial Finance – 2020: Course Overview Note
by PAUL GOMPERS, case number 9-220-050 DECEMBER 10, 2019

Entrepreneurial Finance will focus on financial management within entrepreneurial firms. Most of these will be young firms, although some are more established. The course will examine these firms at all phases of their life cycle, from the initial idea generation to the ultimate harvesting of the venture. The course will cover firms in a diverse set of industries including high technology, low technology, and services. A significant fraction of the cases will focus on non-U.S. ventures.

Financial management in entrepreneurial firms entails understanding both sides of the balance sheet. Consequently, we will look at issues related to both sides as well. The first section of the course will explore how to evaluate entrepreneurial business opportunities, i.e., the asset side of the balance sheet. The skills necessary to make good investment decisions include developing a framework of analysis for business opportunities. The process also entails reinforcing and enhancing valuation skills. With these tools, you will be able to qualitatively and quantitatively assess markets and opportunities.

The second section of the course examines how entrepreneurial investments are financed. An emphasis will be placed on understanding financial institutions and deal terms. We then examine how entrepreneurial firms which have succeeded need to continually finance the scaling of their operations. What are the financial issues that affect this types of firms? How do the sources and terms of financing change? This transition to the second product or opportunity is often the most difficult time for the entrepreneurial enterprise. The course then concludes with an examination of harvesting. Unless an entrepreneur plans for the future realization on investment, he or she could get left holding the bag with little value having been created.

Finally, we will make use of notes throughout the course. These notes provide background information about industry facts and figures. They are meant to be references that you can use often, both during the course and as you start your venture.

MODULE 1: IDENTIFICATION OF OPPORTUNITY

The first module explores the structural model of entrepreneurship. We will use it as a framework for evaluation. The behavioral model defines entrepreneurship as the pursuit of opportunity without regard to resources currently controlled.[2] The four stages of entrepreneurship include: identifying opportunities; acquiring the financial, professional, and productive resources to exploit the opportunity; implementing a plan of action; and harvesting the rewards.[3] Entrepreneurship should not, however, be seen as a linear process. True entrepreneurship involves any or all the elements at any one particular time and should be viewed as a constantly repeating cycle.

William Sahlman had developed a framework that identifies four critical success factors for entrepreneurial ventures: people, opportunity, deal, and context.[4] The cases in this course are selected to highlight how these various factors influence success and failure for firms in various industries. Each element is dynamic and can change over time, and the entrepreneur must constantly reevaluate the four factors that are critical to entrepreneurial value creation. Three questions can help center your analysis as you go forward:

What can go right?
What can go wrong?
What actions can be taken to increase the probability that things will go right or minimize the chances that things will go wrong?

People

An important task in each case is to identify the key players. What is their experience? How does this experience prepare or not prepare them for the opportunity that exists? What are the strengths and weaknesses of the people involved on all sides of the transaction? Are there key individuals that the company should add or replace?

Opportunity

The opportunity that arises may be a new product or service, a new method of delivery, or a new production technique that provides a cost advantage. The entrepreneur must answer many questions before he or she commits to the venture. What is the nature of the opportunity? Is there a sustainable competitive advantage or is the idea easily replicated? Must the opportunity be exploited immediately or is there the possibility of delaying investment until further information is available? Are there intermediate milestones that can be used to assess the success of the project?

Deal

Once the people and opportunity pass some litmus test, a proper deal just be structured. Throwing money at good projects and good people will not guarantee success. Incentives and contingencies are important considerations. The proper deal structure can minimize moral hazard and adverse selection problems. From whom should the firm raise money: wealthy individuals (angels), banks, venture capitalists? What is the proper financing instrument: debt, equity, convertible securities, or a combination? Is a "no-compete" clause important? Can the deal create stakeholders that increase the probability of success? Who bears the downside (upside) risk?

Context

Often the most difficult part of the analysis is identifying contextual issues that are relevant to the success or failure of the project. Potential competitors may not be easily identified, but will always be waiting to enter potentially profitable markets. The government is important because regulations and restrictions can aid or harm the firm's profitability. The entrepreneur must attempt to forecast what policies the government might pursue in response to political pressure. The opening of markets and the collapse of foreign regimes may be important in creating a favorable environment for new ideas. Economic conditions and trends will also influence a particular market and should be analyzed and understood.

The Concept of "FIT"

While most of the analysis may be divided into the four areas discussed above, it is important to understand the big picture. In other words, how do the four elements relate to each other? Do the people have the requisite skills and experience to exploit the opportunity? Does the deal provide the proper incentive to all players given the necessity of their input and the level of their skills? Will the context change the nature of the opportunity?

MODULE 2: VALUATION

The second module of the course will address valuation techniques. Value is one of the fundamental concepts of finance and should be familiar to you from your first year. To make proper investment decisions, it is always necessary to undertake a valuation. Stating that the uncertainty is too great to "value" a given project or company misses the point. Uncertainty affects the distribution of possible values, not the ability to undertake a valuation. Valuation in finance is a way to ask the right questions and understand what important assumptions determine the ultimate value. In fact, if the range of potential outcomes is quite high, i.e., there is high uncertainty, a thorough valuation can give information about when to invest, when to discontinue a project, or when to investigate further. The sole purpose of valuation is not the production of a single number.

The first set of valuation problems are discounted cash flow valuation models. While we discuss various discounted cash flow models, under the right assumptions, they should all give similar answers. The most important lesson is to fully understand the assumptions made in the process. We analyze discounted cash flow models in the case of both mature leveraged buyout situations as well as young, startup ventures. The analysis emphasizes both the strengths and weaknesses of such models. In fact, for many young firms, simple discounted cash flow models can give misleading values.

We will explore issues of valuation that are specific to entrepreneurial firms. First, our common models of valuation assume that the person performing the valuation is a diversified investor, i.e., they hold the market portfolio. In that setting, they only care about systematic risk because idiosyncratic risk is diversified away. That is almost universally not true for an entrepreneur. Their entire wealth is likely tied up in their company. This lack of diversification means that traditional cost of capital approaches used for assessing discount rates are wholly inappropriate. Entrepreneurial finance will explore how we need to adjust those approaches to deal with the reality of entrepreneurs whose entire wealth may be tied up in their ventures.

Entrepreneurial finance will also explore other sources of risk that may need to be considered in valuing a company. Emerging markets have become hot beds of entrepreneurship. Country-specific sources of risk need to be examined and, in specific circumstances, included in the calculation of discount rates. We will explore the foundations for adjustments to discount rates that stem from an entrepreneurial firm operating in an emerging market.

Those of you have worked in the venture capital world know that few venture capitalists use typical discounted cash flow analysis. The relationship between the DCF methods that you learn in finance and the hurdle rate approaches used by venture capital practitioners is important to understand. We will draw a connection between both methods to assess "value" and how such industry rules of thumb are employed.

The shortcomings of standard discounted cash flow models often stem the inability to account real option value. Many projects have embedded optionality. A project that requires a small investment today to allow for information gathering and a possible future investment is like a financial option. The ability to delay investment until the acquisition of more information is a real option. The ability to halt a project creates an option to abandon. The payoff curve is similar to a call option where the only downside is the price of the option, but the upside is substantial. If the entrepreneur does not understand the value of these options, he or she may make improper investment decisions.

Entrepreneurial Finance will also examine real options in entrepreneurial firms. We will discuss their importance in the decisions of young, emerging companies. The course will develop tractable methods to deal with real option value and use it in the planning and structuring of investments.

MODULE 3: FINANCING THE ENTREPRENEURIAL FIRM

Once the entrepreneur identifies an investment opportunity, a financing strategy needs to be outlined. The opportunity may be a new firm, a new project, an expansion of a plant, or even the hiring of new employees. Any of these types of investments present particular financing problems. An entrepreneur who cannot raise the required resources will not succeed. A firm needs cash to survive.

Discussion will identify financial institutions and players that actively provide resources to entrepreneurial firms. We will also examine the nature of contracting between investors and entrepreneurial firms. Understanding the terms and conditions of financing is important for all entrepreneurs to determine payoffs and incentives. Similarly, terms and conditions determine who controls the firm under various circumstances. Control rights such as board membership, information rights, covenants and restrictions are often employed in the financing of entrepreneurial firms. Careful crafting of the financing document often increases the likelihood of success. Various factors drive firms to seek capital from a multitude of capital providers. Four primary factors that influence the source of funds can be identified.

The Four Factors

Uncertainty is a measure of the array of potential outcomes for a company or project. The greater the uncertainty, the wider the dispersion of potential outcomes. By their very nature, young companies are associated with significant levels of uncertainty. Uncertainty may exist about whether the research program or new product will succeed. Uncertainty may also exist about the response of rival firms to the introduction of a new product. High uncertainty means that investors and entrepreneurs cannot confidently predict how the firm will perform, what investment opportunities the company will identify, or what resources the firm will require.

Uncertainty affects the willingness of investors to contribute capital, the desire of suppliers to extend credit, and the decisions of a firm's manager. If managers are risk averse, it may be difficult to induce them to make the right decisions. Conversely, if entrepreneurs are overoptimistic, then investors want to curtail various actions. Uncertainty and the revelation of new information also affect the timing of investment. Should an investor contribute all the capital at the beginning or should he stage the investment through time? Investors need to know how information-gathering activities can address these concerns and when to undertake them.

Asymmetric information is distinct from uncertainty. Due to her day-to-day involvement with the firm, an entrepreneur knows more about her company's prospects than investors, suppliers, or strategic partners. Similarly, investors may know more about their resources or ability to add value than the entrepreneur. Various problems develop in settings where asymmetric information is prevalent. Moral hazard can result when the entrepreneur takes potentially detrimental actions that investors cannot observe. For example, the entrepreneur may undertake a riskier strategy than initially suggested or may not work as hard as the investor expects. The entrepreneur might also invest in projects that build up her reputation at the investors' expense.

Asymmetric information can also lead to adverse selection problems when the entrepreneur knows more about the project or his abilities than investors do. Investors may find it difficult to distinguish between competent entrepreneurs and incompetent ones. Without the ability to screen out unacceptable projects and entrepreneurs, investors are unable to make efficient and appropriate decisions.

The third factor dynamically affecting a firm's corporate and financial strategy is the nature of its assets. Firms that have tangible assets—e.g., machines, buildings, land, or physical inventory—may find financing easier to obtain or may be able to obtain more favorable terms. The ability to abscond with the firm's source of value is more difficult when it relies on physical assets. When the most important assets are intangible, such as trade secrets, raising outside financing is often more challenging.

Market conditions also play a key role in shaping a firm's evolution. The supply of capital from public and private investors and the price at which this capital is available may vary dramatically. These changes may be a response to regulatory edicts or shifts in investors' perceptions of future profitability. Similarly, the nature of product markets may vary dramatically due to shifts in the intensity of competition or in the nature of the customers.

The ability of young companies to grow rapidly and respond swiftly to the changing competitive environment is a key source of competitive advantage, but also a major problem for those who provide resources to these firms. The key characteristics of the firm—uncertainty, asymmetric information, the nature of its assets, and market conditions—will change dramatically over time. Because the firm may be different in the future, investors and entrepreneurs need to be able to anticipate change.

The combination of case studies and notes in this course develops recommendations for optimal capital raising and ownership structures in entrepreneurial firms. The materials demonstrate that careful crafting of financing strategies and contracts can alleviate many potential roadblocks. For instance, the best source of capital is not always obvious. Each source may be appropriate for a firm at different points in its life. The various factors identified above play a critical role in determining the optimal decision.

In addition, the form of financing (e.g., debt, equity, or convertible security) plays a critical role in reducing potential conflicts. Financing can be simple debt or equity, or involve hybrid securities like convertible preferred equity or convertible debt. These financial structures can potentially screen out overconfident or under-qualified entrepreneurs because they have very different payoffs for the entrepreneur in good and bad outcomes. The structure and timing of financing can also reduce the impact of uncertainty on future returns.

Another important element is the division of the profits between entrepreneurs and investors. Compensation contracts can be written that align the incentives of managers and investors. Incentive compensation can be in the form of cash, stock, or options. Performance can be tied to several measures and compared to various benchmarks. Carefully designed incentive schemes can avert destructive behavior.

Firms can also alter the nature of their assets and thus obtain greater financial flexibility. Patents, trademarks, and copyrights are all mechanisms to protect firm assets. Understanding the advantages and limitations of various forms of intellectual property protection, and coordinating financial and intellectual property strategies are essential to ensuring a young firm's growth. Firms can also affect the nature of their assets through strategic decisions, such as encouraging the creation of a set of "locked-in" users who rely on its products.

Monitoring and evaluation are also critical elements of the relationship between entrepreneurs and investors. Both parties must ensure that proper actions are taken and that appropriate progress is being made. Critical control mechanisms--e.g., active and qualified boards of directors, the right to approve important decisions, and the ability to fire and recruit key managers--need to be effectively allocated in any relationship between an entrepreneur and investors. By examining theory and evidence, this course makes both descriptive and prescriptive comments on the effective use of monitoring, evaluation, and control.

MODULE 4: FINANCING THE SCALING VENTURE

In the fourth module of the course, we discuss the financing issues that scaling ventures face. The issues that these firms face differ from those that early stage ventures must deal with. First, the ecosystem of late stage investors has rapidly changed in recent years. These investors are often driven by the desire to deploy capital that can affect the late stage valuations. Such cycles in late stage financing can affect the underlying discipline and strategy of the firms raising that capital. For example, the time to exit has increased markedly as the availability of late stage financing has expanded. Similarly, the focus on achieving profitability may be adversely affected by firms that are "flush" with cash.

We will examine the types of investors approached and types of strategies followed by late scaling ventures. Industry and geographic considerations will be a key element of this module. Finally, we will assess the value implications of terms in this late stage rounds for the implied valuations of scaling companies. Terms like preferences and ratchets can dramatically affect that total implied enterprise value in late stage rounds. We will develop methods to analytically (and intuitively) adjust the "post-money" valuations for the myriad terms in late stage financing rounds.

MODULE 5: HARVESTING THE ENTREPRENEURIAL VENTURE

Every entrepreneur needs to consider harvesting at some point. Harvesting can take many forms. Successfully planning for harvesting of the entrepreneurial venture is critical to maximizing the value of your input. We will explore various modes of harvesting like initial public offerings (IPOs) and acquisitions. The emphasis is on assessing whether the entrepreneurial firm is "ready" for harvesting. In addition, we will emphasize the structural, legal, and dynamic issues of various modes of harvest.

The public markets are a significant source of capital for emerging companies. For many firms, accessing the public market is just the next phase of their dynamic capital process. For others, it represents the beginning of the ability to receive the fruits of their labors. We explore the various motivations for "going public" and the advantages and disadvantages of being a public company. Structural and legal issues will be discussed. In addition, we explore the impact that the cyclical nature of the initial public offering market has on firms' access to capital. The role of various intermediaries will be examined and the motivations of various parties discussed.

The course then covers acquisitions. Most firms will never be large enough for the public market and will therefore need to find one specific buyer. The ability to find the best buyer and negotiate the best deal terms of the deal for the entrepreneur is critical. We emphasize the role of bargaining and auctions in the context of acquisitions. The motivations of buyers and sellers must be understood to ensure the conclusion of a successful deal.

Finally, we will explore how to "shut down" a venture that has not met milestones and will run out of cash. Liquidating failing ventures is a common occurrence, even for venture capital-financed firms. At least 50% of venture capital-backed companies fail. Failure rates for angel-backed and boot-strapped are even higher. The process of liquidation is critical to maintaining ones reputation in the face of company failure.

CONCLUSION

Entrepreneurial Finance is a course that examines the issues confronting entrepreneurial firms at all stages of their existence. The course presents various frameworks and builds new skills needed to identify important business ideas, raise and structure financing, and ultimately harvest the project. The knowledge and skills learned are invaluable for all students, whether they find a job in an entrepreneurial enterprise, a fund that finances entrepreneurial companies, work in a traditional firm, or start a company of their own.

NOTES

1 Howard H. Stevenson and William A. Sahlman, *"The Importance of Entrepreneurship,"* Entrepreneurship, Intrapreneurship, and Venture Capital, (Robert D. Hisrich, ed.), Lexington books; Lexington, MA (1986).
2 Ibid.
3 William A. Sahlman, *"Entrepreneurial Finance,"* Harvard Business School Case No. 288-004 (1987).
4 Ibid.

REFERENCES

Aghion, Philippe, and Peter Howitt. 1992. "A Model of Growth through Creative Destruction." *Econometrica* 60 (2): 323–51.

Akcigit, Ufuk, and William Kerr. 2018. "Growth through Heterogeneous Innovations." *Journal of Political Economy* 126 (4): 1374–1443.

Akerlof, George, 1970, "The market for 'lemons': Qualitative uncertainty and the market mechanism,: *Quarterly Journal of Economics* 84, 488–500.

Amit, Raphael, James Brander, and Christoph Zott. 1998. "Why Do Venture Capital Firms Exist? Theory and Canadian Evidence." *Journal of Business Venturing* 13 (6): 441–66.

Barry, Chris, Chris Muscarella, John Peavy, and Michael Vetsuypens, "The role of venture capital in the creation of public companies: evidence from the going-going public process," *Journal of Financial Economics* 27, 447–472.

Berger, Allen, and Greg Udell, 1995, "Relationship lending and lines of credit in small firm finance," *Journal of Business* 65, 351–381.

Berger, Allen, and Greg Udell, 1996, "Universal banking and the future of small business lending," in A. Saunders and I. Walters eds, *Financial System Design: The Case for Universal Banking*, Irwin Publishing, Homewood, IL.

Berk, Jonathan, and Peter DeMarzo. 2016. *Corporate Finance.* Fourth Edition. Boston, MA: Pearson. *April 15th, 2019* Chapter 1:

Bernstein, Shai, Arthur Korteweg, and Kevin Laws. 2017. "Attracting Early-Stage Investors: Evidence from a Randomized Field Experiment." *The Journal of Finance* 72 (2): 509–38.

Bottazzi, Laura, Marco Da Rin, and Thomas Hellmann. 2008. "Who Are the Active Investors?: Evidence from Venture Capital." *Journal of Financial Economics* 89 (3): 488–512.

Brav, Alon, and Paul Gompers. 1997. "Myth or Reality? The Long-Run Underperformance of Initial Public Offerings: Evidence from Venture and Nonventure Capital-Backed Companies." *The Journal of Finance* 52 (5): 1791–1821.

Bygrave, William and M. Stein, 1989, "A time to buy and a time to sell: a study of 77 venture capital investments in companies that went public," *Frontiers of Entrepreneurship Research* 1989.

Carter, Richard and Steven Manaster, 1990, "Initial public offerings and underwriter reputation," *Journal of Finance* 45, 1045–1067.

Casamatta, Catherine. 2003. "Financing and Advising: Optimal Financial Contracts with Venture Capitalists." *The Journal of Finance* 58 (5): 2059–85.

Chemmanur, Thomas, Karthik Krishnan, and Debarshi Nandy. 2011. "How Does Venture Capital Financing Improve Efficiency in Private Firms? A Look Beneath the Surface." *The Review of Financial Studies* 24 (12): 4037–90.

Da Rin, Marco, Thomas Hellmann, and Manju Puri. 2013. "A Survey of Venture Capital Research." In *Handbook of the Economics of Finance*, edited by George Constantinides, Milton Harris, and René Stulz, 2:573–648. Amsterdam, North Holland: Elsevier.

Decker, Ryan, John Haltiwanger, Ron Jarmin, and Javier Miranda. 2014. "The Role of Entrepreneurship in US Job Creation and Economic Dynamism." *Journal of Economic Perspectives* 28 (3): 3–24.

Diamond, Doug, 1989, "Reputation acquisition in debt markets," *Journal of Political Economy* 97, 828–862.

Dimov, Dimo, and Dean Shepherd. 2005. "Human Capital Theory and Venture Capital Firms: Exploring 'Home Runs' and 'Strike Outs.'"" *Journal of Business Venturing* 20 (1): 1–21.

Fazzari, Steve, R. Glen Hubbard, and B. Petersen, 1988, "Investment and finance reconsidered," *Brookings Papers on Economic Activity*, 141–195.

Gompers, Paul, 1994, "The rise of venture capital," *Business and Economic History* 23, 1–24.

Gompers, Paul, 1995, "Optimal investment, monitoring, and the staging of venture capital", *Journal of Finance* 50, 1461–1489. December 1995.

Gompers, Paul, 1996, "Grandstanding in the venture capital industry," *Journal of Financial Economics* 42, 133–156.

Gompers, Paul, 1997, "Resource allocation, incentives, and control: The importance of venture capital in financing entrepreneurial firms," *Entrepreneurship, SMEs, and the Macroeconomy.*

Gompers, Paul, and Josh Lerner, 1996, "The Use of Covenants: An Empirical Analysis of Venture Partnership Agreements," *Journal of Law and Economics* 39 463–498.

Gompers, Paul, and Josh Lerner, 1997, "Risk and Reward in Private Equity Investments: The Challenge of Performance Assessment," *Journal of Private Equity.*

Gompers, Paul, and Josh Lerner, 1997, "Venture Capitalists and the Creation of Public Companies," *Journal of Private Equity.*

Gompers, Paul, and Josh Lerner, 1998, "What Drives Venture Capital Fundraising?," the *Brookings Proceedings on Microeconomic Activity.*

Gompers, Paul, and Josh Lerner. 1999. "Conflict of Interest in the Issuance of Public Securities: Evidence from Venture Capital." *The Journal of Law and Economics* 42 (1): 1–28.

Gompers, Paul, William Gornall, Steven Kaplan, and Ilya Strebulaev. 2019. "How Do Venture Capitalists Make Decisions?"

Gorman, Michael, and William Sahlman. 1989. "What Do Venture Capitalists Do?" *Journal of Business Venturing* 4 (4): 231–48.

Gornall, Will, and Ilya Strebulaev. 2015. "The Economic Impact of Venture Capital: Evidence from Public Companies." Scholarly Paper 2681841. SSRN.

Greenwald, Bruce, Joseph Stiglitz, and Andrew Weiss, 1984, "Information imperfections in the capital market and macroeconomic fluctuations," *American Economic Review Papers and Proceedings* 74, 194–199.

Hall, Robert, and Susan Woodward. 2010. "The Burden of the Nondiversifiable Risk of Entrepreneurship." *American Economic Review* 100 (3): 1163–94.

Haltiwanger, John, Ron Jarmin, and Javier Miranda. 2013. "Who Creates Jobs? Small versus Large versus Young." *The Review of Economics and Statistics* 95 (2): 347–61.

Harris, Milton and Artur Raviv, 1989, "The design of securities," *Journal of Financial Economics* 24, 255–287.

Hart, Oliver and Bengt Holmstrom, 1987, "The Theory of Contracts," in T. Bewly (ed), *Advances in Economic Theory*, Fifth World Congress, Cambridge, Cambridge University Press.

Hart, Oliver and John Moore, 1990, "Property rights and the nature of the firm," *Journal of Political Economy* 98, 1119–1158.

Hart, Oliver, and John Moore, 1994, "A theory of debt based on the inalienability of human capital," *Quarterly Journal of Economics*, 841–880.

Hegde, Deepak, and Justin Tumlinson. 2014. "Does Social Proximity Enhance Business Partnerships? Theory and Evidence from Ethnicity's Role in U.S. Venture Capital." *Management Science* 60 (9): 2355–80.

Hellmann, Thomas, and Manju Puri. 2002. "Venture Capital and the Professionalization of Start-Up Firms: Empirical Evidence." *The Journal of Finance* 57 (1): 169–97.

Hermalin, Benjamin, and Michael Weisbach, 1988, "The determinants of board composition," *Rand Journal of Economics* 19, 589–606.

Hochberg, Yael, Alexander Ljungqvist, and Yang Lu. 2007. "Whom You Know Matters: Venture Capital Networks and Investment Performance." *The Journal of Finance* 62 (1): 251–301.

Holmstrom, Bengt and Ricarti-I-Costa, 1986, "Managerial incentives and capital management," *Quarterly Journal of Economics*, 839–860.

Hoshi, T., Anil Kashyap, and David Scharfstein, 1991, "Corporate structure, liquidity, and investment," *Quarterly Journal of Economics* 106, 33–60.

Hsu, David, and Martin Kenney. 2005. "Organizing Venture Capital: The Rise and Demise of American Research & Development Corporation, 1946–1973." *Industrial and Corporate Change* 14 (4): 579–616.

Hurst, Erik, and Benjamin Pugsley. 2011. "What Do Small Businesses Do?" *Brookings Papers on Economic Activity* 43 (2): 73–142.

Hvide, Hans, and Georgios Panos. 2014. "Risk Tolerance and Entrepreneurship." *Journal of Financial Economics* 111 (1): 200–223.

James, Christopher, 1987, "Some evidence on the uniqueness of bank loans: A comparison of bank borrowing, private placements, and public offerings," *Journal of Financial Economics* 19, 217–235.

James, Christopher, and Peggy Weir, 1990, "Borrowing relationships, intermediation, and the cost of issuing public securities," *Journal of Financial Economics* 28, 149–171.

Jensen, Michael and William Meckling, 1976, "Theory of the firm: managerial behavior, agency costs, and capital structure," *Journal of Financial Economics* 3, 305–360.

Jensen, Michael, 1986, "Agency cost of free cash flow, corporate finance and takeovers," *AER Papers and Proceedings* 76, 323–329.

Jensen, Michael, 1989, "Eclipse of the public corporation," *Harvard Business Review* 5, 61–74.

Kaplan, Steven, and Per Strömberg. 2003. "Financial Contracting Theory Meets the Real World: An Empirical Analysis of Venture Capital Contacts." *The Review of Economic Studies* 70 (2): 281–315.

Kaplan, Steven, and Per Strömberg. 2004. "Characteristics, Contracts, and Actions: Evidence from Venture Capitalist Analyses." *The Journal of Finance* 59 (5): 2177–2210.

Kaplan, Steven, and Per Strömberg. 2016. "The Importance of Trust for Investment: Evidence from Venture Capital." *The Review of Financial Studies* 29 (9): 2283–2318.

Kerr, William, and Ramana Nanda. 2015. "Financing Innovation." *Annual Review of Financial Economics* 7 (1): 445–62.

Kerr, William, Josh Lerner, and Antoinette Schoar. 2014. "The Consequences of Entrepreneurial Finance: Evidence from Angel Financings." *The Review of Financial Studies* 27 (1): 20–55.

Kerr, William, Ramana Nanda, and Matthew Rhodes-Kropf. 2014. "Entrepreneurship as Experimentation." *Journal of Economic Perspectives* 28 (3): 25–48.

Kihlstrom, Richard, and Jean-Jacques Laffont. 1979. "A General Equilibrium Entrepreneurial Theory of Firm Formation Based on Risk Aversion." *Journal of Political Economy* 87 (4): 719–48.

Koellinger, Philipp, and Roy Thurik. 2012. "Entrepreneurship and the Business Cycle." *The Review of Economics and Statistics* 94 (4): 1143–56.

Kortum, Samuel, and Josh Lerner. 2000. "Assessing the Contribution of Venture Capital to Innovation." *The RAND Journal of Economics* 31 (4): 674–92.

Lerner, Josh, 1994, "The syndication of venture capital investments," *Financial Management* 23 (Autumn) 16–27.

Lerner, Josh, 1995, "Venture capital and the oversight of privately-held firms," *Journal of Finance* 50, 301–318.

Lerner, Josh, Antoinette Schoar, Stanislav Sokolinski, and Karen Wilson. 2018. "The Globalization of Angel Investments: Evidence across Countries." *Journal of Financial Economics* 127 (1): 1–20.

Lerner, Josh. 1994. "Venture Capitalists and the Decision to Go Public." *Journal of Financial Economics* 35 (3): 293–316.

Lucas, Robert. 1988. "On the Mechanics of Economic Development." *Journal of Monetary Economics* 22 (1): 3–42.

Megginson, William and Kathleen Weiss, 1991, "Venture capitalist certification in initial public offerings," *Journal of Finance* 46, 879–903.

Metrick, Andrew, and Ayako Yasuda. 2010. "The Economics of Private Equity Funds." *The Review of Financial Studies* 23 (6): 2303–41.

Modigliani, Franco and Merton Miller, 1958, "The cost of capital, corporation finance, and the theory of investment," *American Economic Review* 48, 261–297.

Myers, Stewart and N. Majluf, 1984, "Corporate financing and investment decisions when firms have information that investors do not have," *Journal of Financial Economics* 13, 187–221.

Myers, Stewart, 1984, "The capital structure puzzle," *Journal of Finance* 39, 575–592.

Patel, Jay, Richard Zeckhauser, and D. Hendricks, 1991, "The rationality struggle: Illustrations from financial markets," *American Economic Review* 81, 232–236.

Peterson, Mitchell and Raghu Rajan, 1994, "The benefits of lending relationships: Evidence from small business data," *Journal of Finance* 99, 3–37.

Peterson, Mitchell and Raghu Rajan, 1995, "The benefits of firm-creditor relationships: a study of small business financings," *Quarterly Journal of Economics* 110, 407–443.

Puri, Manju, and Rebecca Zarutskie. 2012. "On the Life Cycle Dynamics of Venture-Capital- and Non-Venture-Capital-Financed Firms." *The Journal of Finance* 67 (6): 2247–93.

Ritter, Jay, 1987, "The cost of going public," *Journal of Financial Economics*, 269–281.

Ritter, Jay, 1991, "The long run performance of initial public offerings," *Journal of Finance* 46. 3¬28.

Ritter, Jay, "The 'hot issue' market of 1980," *Journal of Business* 57, 215–241.

Robb, Alicia, and David Robinson. 2012. "The Capital Structure Decisions of New Firms." *The Review of Financial Studies* 27 (1): 153–79.

Sahlman, William. 1990. "The Structure and Governance of Venture-Capital Organizations." *Journal of Financial Economics* 27 (2): 473–521.

Samila, Sampsa, and Olav Sorenson. 2011. "Venture Capital, Entrepreneurship, and Economic Growth." *The Review of Economics and Statistics* 93 (1): 338–49.

Sapienza, Harry, "When do venture capitalists add value," *Journal of Business Venturing*, 1992, 9–27.

Stiglitz, Joseph and Andrew Weiss, 1981, "Credit rationing in markets with incomplete information," *American Economic Review* 71, 393–409.

Stiglitz, Joseph and Andrew Weiss, 1983, "Incentive effects of terminations: Applications to the credit and labor markets," *American Economic Review* 73, 919–927.

Titman, Sheridan and R. Wessels, 1988, "The determinants of capital structure choice," *Journal of Finance* 43, 1–19.

Townsend, Robert, 1979, "Optimal contracts and competitive markets with costly state verification," *Journal of Economic Theory* 21, 265–293.

Wetzel, William, 1987, "The informal venture capital market," *Journal of Business Venturing* 2, 299–314.

Williamson, Oliver, 1988, "Corporate finance and corporate governance," *Journal of Finance* 43, 567–591.

CHAPTER 1.2

Entrepreneurial Finance Vignettes: 2022

Paul Gompers

BROOKLYN BAGEL: HUNGARY APRIL 2014[1]

Gathered in the vaulted cellar office of Brooklyn Bagel (BB) shop in Budapest, Taylor and his staff were jubilant, having posted another day of record revenue. His partner, Sara Cohen, was meanwhile meeting with contractors at the site of BB's upcoming 3,000 square foot shop. Taylor, Co-founder and Co-CEO of BB, stepped over to his fax machine and read line by line the incoming term sheet. This was the last round of a long-negotiated deal with Spartan-Hungary Ventures (SHV), that Taylor and Cohen hoped would finally help them realize their dream of a multi-unit chain of bagel shops. The terms from the venture capital fund were much worse than he had expected.

Taylor had to once again remind himself where the business stood. Their first shop, despite its out of the way location, experienced a growing base of regular customers, not to mention a flurry of local and international press intrigued by the reintroduction of bagels to Hungary after centuries of absence. He and his partner realized that the fixed costs of pioneering the market could not be recouped in a single store, so they prepared for expansion, which included installing multi-unit retail systems, building a real estate development team, and securing a lease on a prime urban location. These measures were complete; all the partners needed was capital to finance the expansion.

However, cash was a serious problem. Until the new store opened, the business would continue to post operating losses. Taylor had not paid himself a salary for the past three months, and funds trickling in from the US, thanks to the fund raising efforts of their third partner, Tomas Szabo,

Entrepreneurial Finance Vignettes: 2022
by PAUL GOMPERS, case number 9-222-056 Rev. AUGUST 10, 2023

would not last long. Taylor and Cohen would have to raise institutional money if they wanted to survive.

"Project Bagel"

John Taylor and Sara Cohen became friends as students in the Class of 1999 at Swarthmore College. Taylor, with a degree in Economics, went into investment banking where he was initially an analyst, then moved to a marketing and operations function. Cohen, after a year at a boutique M&A firm, decided to go to law school, where he met Tomas Szabo, a second generation Hungarian-American who had worked for an investment bank in Budapest.

When the allure of corporate life lost its glow in 2012, the three decided to explore opportunities in Eastern Europe. The bagel business was chosen for several reasons. The partners figured that the bagel's reputation for healthiness and freshness would set it apart from the other fast food concepts and traditional Hungarian cuisine, which often called for fat-laden goose lard. They also had a sense of bringing the bagel "home". Folklore suggests that the bagel was developed in the Austro-Hungarian Empire in 1683 to celebrate the banishment of the despised Turks. The round-shaped bread with the hole in the middle was named after the stirrups of the victorious cavalry; the German word for stirrup is "bugel". Fortunately, the word had dropped out of the Hungarian language, enabling the partners to trademark the word "bagel" in Hungary. The large captive market of American expatriates in the Hungarian capital, longing for the tastes of home, would also provide an initial customer base.

The decision to open a bagel store in Budapest - "Project Bagel" - had come about quickly. Taylor, Cohen, and Szabo had already collected some money into a fund to search for opportunities in Hungary. In order to reach the initial starting capital of $200,000 projected for opening a bagel shop, the partners raised capital from individuals in the United States, mostly family and friends. Recognizing the comfort for investors of investing in a U.S. company, the partners set up a Delaware-based holding company, Brooklyn Brookside Ventures, Inc., which would own 100% of Brooklyn Bagel Corp. in Hungary. This way, investors would be protected by U.S. laws.

Driven to acquire hands-on experience of the bagel business, Taylor took several part-time jobs at bagel stores in the Boston area while still at Lehman Brothers. His new employers were suspicious, noticing that Taylor showed up to work in a suit and tie before changing to perform the nightly cleanup. On weekends, his responsibilities alternated between tending the bagel boiler, cleaning, and serving customers. Once Taylor announced his departure plans, though, his boss was supportive and even invested personally in the bagel venture.

"What's a Bagel?"

The first store was launched in June 2013. Taylor and Cohen considered this first store their "beta-test!" Everything was brand new to the Hungarian employees, customers, and the American owners. "To create a concept we had to jump through eighteen regulatory hoops and spent extensive time training staff to adopt a 'customer first' attitude." Even with Taylor's bagel experience, the partners felt that they needed an expert at the helm, at least in the start-up stage of the store. Stuart Kaplan, whose family had been making bagels in New Jersey for three generations, went to Hungary to help start the company. His services entitled him to buy shares in BB at a discounted price.

Revenues for the first store were between $13,000 and $20,000 per month. (see **Exhibits 1-2**) Despite the enthusiasm which greeted the bagel enterprise, operational losses for the first six months were approximately $10-20,000 per month. A number of factors contributed to the losses. For one, BB employed a full-time purchasing manager and two people responsible for new store development. The partners figured that they needed a core group of employees willing to work long hours to get the business off the ground. Fortunately, the BB team coalesced well, resulting in a store opening in less than six months, but the partners were well aware of the cash drain of the core team, not to mention the partners' salaries, plus the expense of installing retail management systems. If financing would not be forthcoming, Taylor and Cohen considered a "no expansion" scenario whereby the core team would be dismantled and Taylor and Cohen would return to the U.S.; even then the shop would have a hard time making money due to the large fixed costs of producing bagels. On the other end of the spectrum, the partners felt they had the capability and could generate sizeable returns for investors by developing a bagel production commissary serving up to 20 stores. This would lower costs by spreading the fixed costs out among as many stores as possible.

BB's Second Store

BB started to look for second store within three months of opening the first. In September 2013 they found a location in the city's prime office district and right across the street from a subway station packed full with commuters. In the auction for the property, BB submitted a bid of $200,000 in

December 1993. Although they did not have enough capital at the time of the auction, they felt that they could not forgo the opportunity of the location. They only had $150,000 of the $400,000 they estimated was needed to pay for the rental right and refurbish the store. They also wanted to have adequate funds available to set up more stores after the second store was up and running. (see **Exhibits 3-4** for store projections)

The BB bid won the auction on December 17, 2013, but the partners still did not have adequate funds to refurbish the store. Even with possession of the rental right, they could not use it as collateral for a bank loan. They wondered if they should risk investors' money on a second store. The location of the store was critical to the success of the future chain and it would take another three to six months to find a similarly situated property, by which time the business would probably run out of cash. They did not want any further delay in opening the second store.

Financing Decisions

Taylor and Cohen looked at their options for raising more capital. They could continue to get funds from individual investors, go to institutional investors, or approach venture capital firms. They had raised $200,000 between December 2, 2013 and mid-January 2014 from several individual investors. The two partners wondered about raising institutional venture capital. The advantages of obtaining funds from venture capital firms were obvious. The partners of BB would no longer have to raise funds from individual investors, allowing them to spend more time running the company.

J2 AND OURA RING

Alex Harstrick and Jon Bronson, co-founders of J2 Ventures, an early stage venture capital firm with a focus on companies with applications in the military, looked at their investment recommendation memo for a potential investment in the series C round for Oura Ring, a fitness wearable company with a revolutionary ring capable of measuring heart rate, body temperature, resting heart rate, heart rate variability, respiratory rate, duration and timing of physical activity, calories burned, inactivity, and metabolic equivalents (METs). (See **Exhibit 5** for an image of the Oura Ring wearable and **Exhibit 6** for bios of Harstrick and Bronson.) The size and sophistication of the device was intriguing to Harstrick and Bronson.

Moreover, the product was attracting attention from a highly unusual confluence of users: the quantified-self community liked fidelity of data resulting from the long battery life and convenient form-factor; celebrities such as the Kardashians and Jennifer Aniston liked the aesthetic enough to provide unpaid endorsements; communities looking for patient monitoring, ranging from couples trying to conceive to the NBA to the US military, liked the medically rigorous approach the company was taking to help users monitor sleep, fertility, fitness to operate heavy machinery and, most importantly, early COVID detection. The decision they were about to make for their young venture capital firm would surely set the tone for future opportunities.

Investment Decision

Harstrick and Bronson were considering investing in Oura's $800M series C secondary offering ($800 million post-money valuation). The company had recently raised an $80M series C led by Bedford Ridge Capital and based upon Harstrick's relationship with the company, J2 was offered the opportunity to invest in an extension of the Series C, at the same terms as the primary offering. The investment would be part of a secondary offering of a $100M to cash out early employees and early angel investors and better position the company for growth minded investors who could help the company expand. (See **Exhibit 7** for an overview of the Series C term sheet.)

Oura was founded in 2013 in Oulu Finland and had 2020 gross revenue of approximately $80 million USD. In 2020, the company employed 225 people. Oura sold a combination wearable and software application that measured human biometrics information and translated insights related to the user's sleep, activity, readiness and predictions of disease onset. Historically, the biometrics wearables space had focused on the wrist, but the company believed its patented ring form factor was clinically proven to provide superior detection through infrared LED's. The multiple biometric markers were processed in the ring's software application allowing for measurement and processing of information related to recovery, sleep stages and activity recommendations. The smaller size also allowed the ring to be charged in 40-80 minutes with an average battery life of five to seven days. This increased user adherence and the reliability of trending information collected. Most impressively, the average consumer satisfaction score was 91.2. Of note, the technology had been used in a number of peer-reviewed publications, including the prestigious scientific journal *Nature*.

Notable healthcare clients included University of California San Francisco (UCSF) with whom Oura partnered for a national COVID-19 prediction study and West Virginia Rockefeller Neuroscience Institute. Oura had also successfully reached initial deployments across the Army,

Navy, Air Force and Marine Corps in a joint study sponsored by the Defense Threat Reduction Agency (DTRA) named Rapid Analysis of Threat Exposure (RATE). J2 believed there was significant interest from the DOD to expand their contracts with Oura. The company had successfully won a US Air Force Direct to Phase II SBIR and was in negotiations to provide an additional 10,000 rings to the Air Force as part of a COVID-19 response effort. Harstrick was actively guiding management through military and health insurance procurement conversations even prior to the proposed investment.

Harstrick and Bronson's investment thesis was based upon several important considerations. First, the company had more than doubled revenue every year since 2017. (See **Exhibit 8** for historical revenues.) The company had raised over $140 million across four rounds of financing (See **Exhibit 9** for historical financing information.) Wearables were a $27 billion industry in 2020 and growing, with some estimates suggesting 15% growth per year through 2027[2]. (See **Exhibit 10** for an overview on the wearables market leaders.) Oura had entered into several high-profile partnerships including with the NBA, UFC, NASCAR and Redbull Racing. The company was seeing growth from diversified channels, most notably consumer, healthcare, and defense. Oura had also recently decided to move from a hardware-only revenue model to hardware + SaaS, where publicly-traded comps traded at higher multiples. With approximately $80 million USD in gross revenue last year, the post-money valuation of roughly 10x revenue LTM revenue was believed to be attractive for a company at this stage.

Conclusion

Hastrick and Bronson looked at each other and pondered the implications of their choice. They both had dreamed of establishing their own venture capital firm and now the rubber was hitting the road. Was Oura an attractive investment? Could Hastrick and Bronson add value? Were the terms reasonable? Bronson noticed his heart rate had just spiked to over 100 beats per minute. "Okay, Alex, what is your vote?"

CAR WASH PARTNERS[3]

Tom Curtis had already been a successful entrepreneur in the service industry when he proposed the investment in Car Wash Partners to Bill Burgin and Cabot Brown. Curtis received his undergraduate degree from the University of North Carolina as well as his J.D. from the University of Pennsylvania Law School and his MBA from Harvard Business

School. In 1969, Curtis founded Executive Air Fleet Corporation which provided comprehensive management services for corporate aircraft around the world. In 1982 he sold Executive Air Fleet to PHH, Inc. Curtis had built the firm from no revenues in 1969 to over $50 million in sales in 1982. After the sale of his firm, Curtis taught Entrepreneurship at a well-known business school. After retiring from teaching in 1987, Curtis became an advisor to several venture capital firms and startup companies.

By 1995, however, Curtis was beginning to feel the entrepreneurial itch. He researched several ideas within the service industry before finding the opportunity to consolidate within the car wash market. As he surveyed the market, he became more convinced that the idea made sense. Over the course of 1996, Curtis visited over fifty car wash units and had started acquisition discussions with several leading car wash chains.

Car Wash Partners' Strategy

Curtis had outlined a strategy with which he hoped to build the leading provider of car wash and related services in the U.S. Car Wash Partners would focus on the conveyor segment of the market. Curtis felt that a reputation for service excellence would be most effective in the full-service and exterior-only segments of the industry. Self-service and hand-wash units generally did not attract sufficient volumes to allow for scale economies or premium pricing.

Car Wash Partners would also focus on growth via acquisition. The construction and opening of a new exterior-only center generally took from 18 to 24 months, of which the first nine to twelve months were required to obtain the necessary governmental approvals. As such, growth through new sites would require not only large amounts of capital and real estate expertise, but it would dramatically slow the rate at which Car Wash Partners could expand.

Financial Projections

Curtis had already identified two acquisition candidates that he wished to finance using the proceeds from the offering, one in Bakersfield, CA and the other in Boise, ID. The Bakersfield company had three sites, all with detailing, merchandise, lubrication, and gas. The operations were well run and highly profitable. Similarly, the Boise, ID operations were operating smoothly, although none of the sites in Boise offered lubrication services and only one offered gasoline.

Car Wash Partners would start from modest beginnings. In 1996, Curtis projected to have only two cities in operation. (See **Exhibit 11** for detailed plan on the number of planned cities and sites. **Exhibits 11-14** have financial projections.) By 2000, Curtis expected Car Wash Partners to be the nation's leading provider of car washing services with operations in 13 cities, 115 units in operation, and more than twelve millions cars washed. Curtis was convinced that these numbers were reasonable given the large and fragmented market. After all, this was less than 1% of the car wash units across the country. (See **Exhibit 15** for data on public comparables and **Exhibit 16** for macroeconomic data.)

With these modest assumptions, however, Car Wash Partners would grow into a substantial company. (See **Exhibits 11-14** for financial projections.) If projections were met, the firm would generate more than $330 million in revenue in 2000 and earn more than $18 million after tax. Curtis's plan, however, called for substantial investment in acquisitions as well as capital expenditure building new sites and renovating existing ones. While the company would be profitable by 1998 according to his projections, the required investments would create extremely large funding needs. (See **Exhibit 14** for detailed financing plan.) Curtis's estimate placed the required need for outside capital at $283 million. Because of the large amount of real estate and fixed assets, he believed that Car Wash Partners could take on substantial amounts of debt. He conservatively felt that the company could obtain at least half of this financing from debt, with the remaining coming from private equity.

According to his business plan, Curtis would use the small initial equity financing to acquire the properties in Bakersfield and Boise. These cities were to serve as beta sites for the firm. Once he proved the Car Wash Partners value proposition, he felt that he could attract substantial amounts of capital for the roll-up of existing operators. It was not unheard of for large private equity organizations to provide $50 to $100 million to acquire small retail and service providers. Once these small players were rolled up into a larger entity, Curtis felt the company could access the public markets to finance the remaining acquisitions. Having a public company might also allow him to provide stock instead of cash to do the acquisitions. In the interim, however, Curtis felt that he would need to finance most of the acquisition in cash. Current car wash operators had little interest holding the equity of an illiquid private company. Curtis worried, however, how he might provide the right incentives for the local partners. After all, he would be in Boston and needed local management to run the properties. Structuring the acquisitions would take some careful crafting.

NOTES

1 Based upon Paul A. Gompers and Catherine Coneely, "New York Bagel" Harvard Business School Case 297-078.
2 Grand View Research, "Wearable Technology Market Size, Share & Trends Analysis Report By Product (Wrist-Wear, Eye-Wear & Head-Wear, Foot-Wear, Neck-Wear, Body-wear), By Application, By Region, And Segment Forecasts, 2021 – 2028," October 21, 2021, https://www.grandviewresearch.com/industry-analysis/wearable-technology-market, accessed December 2021.
3 Excerpted from Gompers, Paul A. "Car Wash Partners, Inc." Harvard Business School Case 299-034, February 1999.

EXHIBIT 1 Detailed Income Statement Brooklyn Bagel, Q1 2014

	January	February	March
Revenues	$20,228	$20,025	$20,882
Costs			
Overhead			
Management	9,563	9,257	6,285
Travel, Setup, & Benefits	2,944	2,351	1940.67
Office & Related	2,892	1,761	2,146
Marketing	749	773	8
Professional Services	1,112	937	877
Total Overhead	$17,260	$15,079	$11,257
Ferenc Korut Store			
Labor	$5,798	$5,159	$5,293
Food Costs	5,243	4,874	4,795
Supply Costs	2,636	2,001	2,213
Rent	2,000	2,000	2,000
Leasehold Improvements	0	0	0
Equipment	4,915	4,500	5,039
Maintenance, Utilities, Insurance	1,264	1,271	1,104
Taxes and Fees	2,242	2,222	2,350
Total Costs - Ferenc Korut	$24,098	$22,027	$22,794
Bajcsy-Zsilinszky Store			
Labor	$0	$0	$0
Food Costs	0	0	0
Supply Costs	0	0	0
Property (Purchase & Rent)	510	510	510
Leasehold Improvements	0	65,919	110,867
Equipment	0	2,679	62,489
Maintenance, Utilities, Insurance	0	18	2,615
Taxes and Fees	0	10,103	25,877
Total Costs - Bajcsy-Zsilinszky Store	$510	$79,229	$202,358
Operating Cash Flow	($21,641)	($96,311)	($215,527)
Interest Payments	0	5,403	0
Total Cash Flow	($21,641)	($101,714)	($215,527)

Source: Company documents.

EXHIBIT 2 Cash Flow Statement for Brooklyn Bagel 2013-2014 (Thousands of US Dollars)

	93Q1	93Q2	93Q3	93Q4	94Q1
Revenues	$389	$2,169	$55,628	$53,494	$61,135
Costs					
Overhead					
Management	0	5,050	6,750	31,351	25,106
Travel, Setup, & Benefits	4,429	7,794	37,226	20,628	7,235
Office & Related	2,285	5,681	12,358	11,715	6,799
Marketing	0	15,446	18,927	9,556	1,531
Professional Services	4,671	1,975	4,697	28,452	2,925
Total Overhead	$11,385	$35,946	$79,958	$101,702	$43,596
Ferenc Korut Store					
Labor	$0	$851	$31,109	$28,252	$16,249
Food Costs	0	5,740	21,376	19,382	14,912
Supply Costs	0	5,201	23,488	10,446	6,850
Rent	0	10,130	9,721	9,280	6,000
Leasehold Improvements	0	86,251	15,235	1,221	0
Equipment	0	73,726	25,897	108,477	14,455
Maintenance, Utilities, Insurance	0	254	3,586	3,980	3,639
Taxes and Fees	0	43,833	47,667	7,504	6,815
Total Costs - Ferenc Korut	$0	$225,986	$178,079	$188,542	$68,920

(*continued*)

EXHIBIT 2 *(continued)*

	93Q1	93Q2	93Q3	93Q4	94Q1
Bajcsy-Zsilinszky Store					
Labor	$0	$0	$0	$0	$0
Food Costs	0	0	0	0	0
Supply Costs	0	0	0	0	0
Property (Purchase & Rent)	0	0	0	178,704	1,531
Leasehold Improvements	0	0	0	1,547	176,786
Equipment	0	0	8,900	11,155	65,168
Maintenance, Utilities, Insurance	0	0	0	0	2,633
Taxes and Fees	0	0	0	2,725	35,980
Total Costs - Bajcsy-Zsilinszky	$0	$0	$8,900	$194,131	$282,098
Operating Cash Flow	($10,996)	($259,763)	($211,309)	($430,881)	($333,479)
Interest Payments	1,000	100	0	10,675	5,403
Total Cash Flow	($11,996)	($259,863)	($211,309)	($441,556)	($338,882)

Source: Company documents.

EXHIBIT 3 Projections of Profit and Loss and Cash Flow Statements for Brooklyn Bagel (2013-2018) Thousands of US Dollars

		2013	2014	2015	2016	2017	2018
Budapest							
Store 1	Sales	$113	$165	$353	$353	$353	$353
	EBIT	-40	-40	87	87	87	87
Core Store 2	Sales		329	1044	1063	1370	1446
	EBIT		118	375	382	492	520
Store 3	Sales		59	353	353	353	353
	EBIT		15	87	87	87	87
Store 4	Sales			176	353	353	353
	EBIT			41	87	87	87
Store 5	Sales			88	353	353	353
	EBIT			22	87	87	87
Pecs							
Core Store	Sales			44	353	353	353
	EBIT			11	87	87	87
Store 2	Sales				264	353	353
	EBIT				65	87	87
Store 3	Sales				176	353	353
	EBIT				44	87	87
Debrecen							
Core Store	Sales				44	353	353
	EBIT				11	87	87
Store 2	Sales					323	353
	EBIT					80	87
Szeged							
Core Store	Sales					264	353
	EBIT					65	87
Store 2	Sales					176	353
	EBIT					44	87
Gyor							
Core Store	Sales						264
	EBIT						65
Store 2	Sales						44
	EBIT						11
Franchise	Sales			57	162	247	332
	EBIT			47	152	237	322
Total Sales		$113	$553	$2,114	$3,471	$5,200	$5,963
Total EBIT Contributed by Stores		-40	93	670	1,089	1,614	1,875
Overhead		69	102	192	244	254	291
Commissary		19	34	24	32	40	40
Non-capital Startup Expense		303	137	163	146	108	70

(continued)

EXHIBIT 3 *(continued)*

	2013	2014	2015	2016	2017	2018
Depreciation	10	61	137	227	317	397
EBIT	($421)	($241)	$153	$440	$896	$1,077
Interest - Investors	8	26	21	21	21	21
Interest - Bank	0	0	22	0	0	0
Pretax Profit	-449	-267	111	419	875	1,057
Income Tax	0	0	0	0	-241	-370
Profit After Tax	-449	-267	111	419	634	687

Source: Company documents.

EXHIBIT 4 Cash Flow Projections for Brooklyn Bagel – 2013-2018 (Thousands of US Dollars)

	2013	2014	2015	2016	2017	2018
Operations						
Profit after Tax	($449)	($267)	$128	$419	$628	$687
Depreciation	10	61	137	227	317	397
Capital	-100	-522	-450	-450	-450	-300
Total	($539)	($727)	($185)	$196	$495	$784
Financing						
Equity	$603	$560	$0	$0	$0	$0
Debt						
Hungarian Ventures, Inc.	147	0	0	0	0	-147
Secured Financing	0	200	0	0	0	0
Bank	0	0	40	-40	0	0
Total	$750	$760	$40	($40)	$0	($147)
Net Cash Flow	211	33	-145	156	495	637
Cumulative Cash	211	244	99	255	750	1,387

Source: Company documents.

EXHIBIT 5 Oura Ring's Wearable
Source: J2 company documents.

EXHIBIT 6 J2 Ventures Bios

Alexander Hastrick – Prior to forming J2 Ventures, Hastrick was the defense contracting at Office of the Secretary of the Defense. During his time as the defense contracting officer he invested over $2 Billion of strategic military contracts. Earlier Hastrick served as an Army Intelligence Officer and was a special operations officer in Iraq and Afghanistan special ops. He spent seven years in venture capital investing in aspects of dual-use companies and defense startups, managing over $400M in venture capital. Hastrick holds an MBA from Harvard Business School and a BA from Columbia University.

Jonathan Bronson, Ph.D. – Prior to forming J2 Ventures, Bronson was a Director at D.E. Shaw Private Equity and helped invest more than $750 million of equity and debt. Bronson also served as COO of Backpack Health (acquired) and was a Project Leader at the Boston Consulting Group. Bronson holds a BS from the University of Pennsylvania and a Ph.D. in Chemistry with a focus on AI / ML applied to chemical systems. He has published peer reviewed articles and open-source software with nearly 1,000 citations. Bronson was also a National Science fellow.

Source: J2 company documents.

EXHIBIT 7 Summary Series C Term Sheet

- US $99.6334 / share; 8,027,913 fully diluted shares post-money (same as the primary)
- Seniority in a liquidation above Series Seed and Common. The Series C is Pari Passu with the Series B and Series A
- Consent rights (e.g., create new share classes, issue new stock, purchase / redeem equities, pay dividends, sell the company, etc.)
- Drag-along and tag-along rights
- Anti-dilution provisions

Source: J2 company documents.

EXHIBIT 8 Oura Historic Revenue and Growth
Source: J2 company documents.

EXHIBIT 9 Oura Ring Historical Fundraising

Date	Round	Amount	Select Investors
November 11, 2015	Seed	$2.3 million	Lifeline Ventures,
September 30, 2016	Series A	$18 million	Bold Capital Partners, Tesi, MSD Capital, Will Smith, Shaquille O'Neal
December 27, 2019	Series B	$28 million	Gradient Ventures, Square, Alumni Ventures, Marc Benioff, Able Partners
May 4, 2021	Series C	$100 million	Bedford Ridge Capital, Roosh Ventures, Jazz Venture Partners, Pau Gasol, Elysian Park Ventures

Source: Compiled from Crunchbase.

EXHIBIT 10 Consumer Wearables Market Volumes

	Est. 2019 Volume	Implied Unit Market Share	Est. ASP	Implied Industry Revenue	Implied. Revenue Market Share	Estimated Gross Margin	Implied Industry Gross Profit	Implied. Revenue Market Share
Apple	35,000,000	23.3%	$400	14,000,000,000	51.1%	65%	9,100,000,000	60.8%
Garmin	10,000,000	6.7%	$400	4,000,000,000	14.6%	65%	2,600,000,000	17.4%
Fitbit high end	5,000,000	3.3%	$200	1,000,000,000	3.6%	65%	650,000,000	4.3%
Fitbit low end	11,000,000	7.3%	$80	880,000,000	3.2%	30%	264,000,000	1.8%
Samsung	6,000,000	4.0%	$150	900,000,000	3.3%	40%	360,000,000	2.4%
Other	83,000,000	55.3%	$80	6,640,000,000	24.2%	30%	1,992,000,000	13.3%
Total	**150,000,000**	**100.0%**		**27,420,000,000**	**100.0%**		**14,966,000,000**	**0.0%**

Source: J2 company documents.

EXHIBIT 11 Car Wash Partners Projected Operations

Car Wash Partners, Inc.

Consolidated Operation Projections

	1996	*1997*	*1998*	*1999*	*2000*
Cities of Operation					
Existing	0	2	4	7	10
New	2	2	3	3	3
Total	2	4	7	10	13
Master Units					
Beginning Units	0	0	7	14	21
Units Acquired	0	7	7	7	7
Ending Units	0	7	14	21	28
Full-Service/Super Center Units					
Beginning Units	0	4	10	23	38
Units Acquired	4	6	8	10	12
Units Opened	0	0	5	5	5
Ending Units	4	10	23	38	55
Express/Mini-Super Center Units					
Beginning Units	0	3	6	12	22
Units Acquired	3	3	3	3	3
Units Opened	0	0	3	7	7
Ending Units	3	6	12	22	32

Total Ending Units	7	23	49	81	115
Total Units Under Construction	8	20	24	24	24
Total Cars					
Washed	420,000	1,710,000	4,800,000	8,410,125	12,589,631
Fueled	420,000	1,578,750	5,293,125	10,323,844	16,120,473
Express Waxed	16,500	74,250	261,750	510,056	801,112
Lubricated	-	52,500	294,000	569,138	881,001

Source: Company documents.

EXHIBIT 12 Car Wash Projected Income Statement

Car Wash Partners, Inc.

CONSOLIDATED INCOME STATEMENT ($000)	*1996*	*1997*	*1998*	*1999*	*2000*
Revenues					
Car Wash Services	$3,120	$13,410	$38,989	$75,320	$118,881
Merchandise	315	1,330	5,370	12,256	21,580
Express Wax	412	1,853	6,076	12,424	20,429
Express Lubrication	-	1,835	8,506	18,833	30,309
Total Services and Merchandise	3,847	18,427	58,942	118,833	191,199
Gasoline	3,614	13,526	42,870	89,359	147,266
Total Revenues	7,461	31,953	101,812	208,192	338,465
Cost of Sales					
Car Wash Services	468	1,788	4,851	9,293	14,791
Merchandise	211	891	3,598	8,355	14,459
Express Wax	41	185	608	1,257	2,081
Express Lubrication	-	525	2,434	5,138	8,304
Total Services and Merchandise	720	3,390	11,491	24,090	39,634
Gasoline	3,281	12,278	38,913	81,111	133,672
Total Cost of Sales	4,001	15,667	50,404	105,201	173,306
Gross Profit	3,460	16,286	51,408	102,991	165,159
Gross Margin - %	46.4%	51.0%	50.5%	49.5%	48.8%

Operating Expenses					
Corporate Overhead	$1,164	$2,998	$3,715	$4,216	$4,607
Unit Salaries & Bonuses	1,397	6,577	20,936	41,850	64,307
Maintenance	201	901	2,865	5,785	9,333
Advertising	149	639	2,036	4,150	6,744
Corporate Marketing Programs	37	160	509	1,041	1,692
Rent	416	1,995	4,485	7,190	10,014
Other	631	2,907	7,995	14,551	22,877
Total Operating Expenses	2,831	13,179	38,826	74,566	114,967
EBITDA	$629	$3,107	$12,582	$28,426	$50,192
EBITDA/Revenues - %	8.4%	9.7%	12.4%	13.7%	14.8%
Depreciation	45	946	2,724	4,683	6,774
Amortization	154	825	1,914	3,113	4,421
EBIT	$431	$1,336	$7,944	$20,630	$38,997
EBIT/Revenues - %	5.8%	4.2%	7.8%	9.9%	11.5%
Interest Expense	364	2,011	4,564	6,927	8,855
Interest Income (a)	-	-	-	-	-
Pre-Tax Income	$67	($674)	$3,380	$13,702	$30,142
Pre-Tax Margin - %	0.9%	-2.1%	3.3%	6.6%	8.9%
Income Taxes	50	-	1,518	5,341	11,323
Net Income	$16	($674)	$1,862	$8,362	$18,819
Net Margin - %	0.2%	-2.1%	1.8%	4.0%	5.6%

Source: Company documents.

EXHIBIT 13 Car Wash Partners Projected Balance Sheet

SUMMARY BALANCE SHEET ($000)	1996	1997	1998	1999	2000
Assets					
Current Assets					
Excess Cash	$263	$620	$780	$406	$7,909
Operating Cash	410	1,731	5,354	10,786	17,296
Accounts Receivable	207	888	2,828	5,783	9,402
Inventories	267	1,044	3,360	7,013	11,554
Other	252	594	382	2,759	2,779
Total	$1,399	$4,877	$12,704	$26,747	$48,940
Fixed Assets					
Real property improvements	$1,738	$14,624	$30,550	$47,316	$64,885
Equipment	1,633	13,641	25,512	38,054	49,481
Land	6,950	19,987	34,181	49,533	66,043
Total	$10,321	$48,251	$90,242	$134,904	$180,409
Goodwill	4,452	19,262	34,892	51,343	68,614
Total Assets	$16,172	$72,389	$137,839	$212,993	$297,963
Liabilities and Shareholder's Equity					
Current Liabilities					
Accounts Payable & Deferred Expenses	$569	$2,404	$7,436	$14,981	$24,023
Long-term Debt					
Mortgage	$4,355	$18,070	$33,442	$49,292	$65,554
Bank Debt	2,484	10,146	16,350	17,063	12,377
Supplier Financing	879	6,522	11,910	18,760	25,541
Seller Note	-	-	-	-	-
Subordinated Debt	-	-	-	-	-
Total	$7,718	$34,738	$61,702	$85,115	$103,472
Shareholders' Equity					
Preferred & Common Equity	$7,868	$35,905	$67,497	$103,332	$142,083
Retained Earnings	16	-658	1,204	9,566	28,384
Total Shareholder's Equity	$7,885	$35,247	$68,701	$112,898	$170,468
Total Long-term Liab. & Shareholder's Equity	$16,172	$72,389	$137,839	$212,993	$297,963

Source: Company documents.

EXHIBIT 14 Car Wash Partners Projected Cash Flow Statements

SUMMARY STATEMENT OF CASH FLOWS ($000)	1996	1997	1998	1999	2000
Operations					
Net Income	$16	($674)	$1,862	$8,362	$18,819
Depreciation	45	946	2,724	4,683	6,774
Amortization	154	825	1,914	3,113	4,421
Additions (Reductions in Working Capital	315	944	2,847	4,496	5,627
Capital Expenditures	5,100	21,233	24,668	29,478	31,638
Cash Flow From Operations	($5,200)	($21,080)	($21,016)	($17,815)	($7,251)
Investment Activities					
Acquisitions	($10,336)	($34,842)	($38,516)	($42,191)	($37,464)
Financing Activities					
Issuance of Debt	7,718	28,037	31,592	35,834	38,752
Repayment of Debt	-	(1,017)	(4,843)	(13,517)	(26,894)
Issuance of Equity	7,718	28,037	31,592	35,834	38,752
Cash Flow from Financing Activities	$15,436	$55,057	$58,341	$58,151	$50,609
Financing (Shortfall) Surplus	($100)	($865)	($1,191)	($1,855)	$5,694
Net Cash Added from Acquisitions	$363	$1,222	$1,351	$1,480	$1,609
Net Financing (Shortfall) Surplus	$263	$357	$160	($375)	$7,504
Cumulative	$263	$620	$780	$406	$7,909

Source: Company documents.

EXHIBIT 15 Valuation of Public Companies

Envirotest, Inc.

	1992	1993	1994	1995
Sales	$53.3	$88.5	$96.4	$104.8
SG&A	$6.3	$13.3	$19.1	$24.9
Cap Ex	$5.7	$3.1	$69.3	$118.9
Op Inc Bef Dep	$19.6	$28.7	$27.1	$19.5
Net Income	$2.5	-$4.7	$2.2	-$14.9
Total Assets	$144.5	$200.7	$418.2	$457.3
Current Assets	$22.0	$88.8	$218.7	$31.6
Current Liab.	$26.2	$17.0	$35.3	$29.8
Debt	$108.8	$130.2	$328.6	$388.4
Net Worth	$18.4	$50.6	$52.9	$38.0
Beta				0.82
P/E Ratio	NA	35.0	110.4	NM

Grease Monkey Holdings, Inc.

	1992	1993	1994	1995
Sales	$17.6	$20.1	$18.8	$18.5
SG&A	$4.1	$4.0	$4.0	$4.3
Cap Ex	$0.3	$0.3	$0.3	$0.2
Op Inc Bef Dep	-$0.1	-$0.2	$0.8	$1.4
Net Income	-$1.1	-$1.5	$0.1	$0.2
Total Assets	$16.0	$16.9	$13.3	$13.1
Current Assets	$2.7	$3.7	$2.8	$2.7
Current Liab.	$3.1	$4.0	$2.4	$2.0
Debt	$11.9	$12.2	$8.8	$9.4
Net Worth	$0.7	$1.2	$1.7	$1.9
Beta				0.55
P/E Ratio	NM	NM	NM	33.3

Monroe Muffler, Inc.

	1992	1993	1994	1995
Sales	$78.5	$93.6	$109.1	$117.1
SG&A	$23.6	$28.1	$32.3	$35.3
Cap Ex	$14.8	$14.4	$20.3	$25.6
Op Inc Bef Dep	$16.1	$19.1	$22.6	$22.3
Net Income	$6.2	$7.4	$9.1	$7.6
Total Assets	$63.5	$77.0	$93.0	$120.1
Current Assets	$17.6	$21.1	$22.1	$26.5
Current Liab.	$9.5	$13.2	$15.3	$17.7
Debt	$23.4	$27.2	$31.7	$48.6
Net Worth	$31.4	$38.8	$48.2	$55.9
Beta				0.35
P/E Ratio	13.3	15.6	14.9	16.2

Earl Scheib, Inc.

	1992	1993	1994	1995
Sales	$53.6	$48.5	$47.3	$44.0
SG&A	$13.8	$13.3	$12.7	$12.3
Cap Ex	$1.4	$1.2	$0.9	$5.2
Op Inc Bef Dep	$0.3	-$2.0	-$6.4	-$0.1
Net Income	-$0.1	-$1.8	-$5.6	$0.9
Total Assets	$34.8	$34.1	$29.5	$28.5
Current Assets	$11.4	$12.4	$12.8	$7.4
Current Liab.	$6.6	$8.0	$8.7	$6.6
Debt	$0.0	$0.0	$0.0	$0.0
Net Worth	$24.9	$22.7	$17.2	$18.1
Beta				0.6-3
P/E Ratio	NM	NM	NM	38.5

Source: Company documents.

EXHIBIT 16 General Macroeconomic Conditions

Year	Real GDP (1992 $ Billions)	Inflation	12 Month Treasury Bill Rate	5 Year Government Bond	10 Year Government Bond
1990	$6,079.0	5.3%	6.4%	7.7%	8.1%
1991	$6,105.3	2.6%	3.9%	5.9%	6.7%
1992	$6,327.1	2.9%	3.5%	6.0%	6.7%
1993	$6,476.9	2.5%	3.5%	5.2%	5.8%
1994	$6,688.6	2.7%	6.8%	7.8%	7.8%
1995	$6,796.5	2.3%	4.9%	5.4%	5.6%
1996	$7,017.4	2.9%	5.3%	6.2%	6.4%

Source: Compiled from Citibase.

SECTION 2

Defining the Entrepreneurial Business Model and Cash Flow Implications

CHAPTER 2.1

Simplifyy

Paul A. Gompers and Alicia Dadlani

On a crisp November evening in 2021, Simplifyy co-Founders Jake Lisby and Paul Worcester and COO Evan Conway huddled over steaming mugs of coffee at their office in Kansas City, Missouri. The trio at the helm of the property technology startup were both exhausted and exhilarated by the flurry of activity since their recent decision to pivot the business model. Worcester rubbed his temples. Due to downsizing the team, he had just released one of his longest-standing employees with a hug and well wishes to each other's families. Lisby and Conway were also disheartened by the terminations, yet were energized and eager to share their latest updates. Lisby just hired a new software engineer in Pakistan, and Conway had secured the company's largest customer to date.

Together Lisby, a software engineer, and Worcester, a property management veteran, founded Simplifyy in 2019. They saw an opportunity to apply technology to the traditional, labor-intensive property management business, thereby reducing operating costs for property management. Simplifyy had taken an unusual approach. Rather than developing the property management software alone, they initially also provided multifamily building owners with full property management services. The idea was to provide a one-stop-shop solution for property owners that offered a lower-cost solution for all their property management needs. Their software handled leasing, billing, and communication functions, among other things.

Growing the business during the COVID-19 pandemic proved challenging, but by early 2021 they secured $5 million in a Series A financing. By mid-2021, they employed 80 people, earned $1 million in annual recurring revenue, and managed 3,500 rental properties in Kansas City, Indianapolis, Dallas, and Columbia, South Carolina.

However, in November 2021, the three leaders decided to pivot. The company found building out and operating a property management

Simplifyy
by PAUL A. GOMPERS, ALICIA DADLANI, case number 9-222-050 Rev. SEPTEMBER 8, 2023

company to be more time-consuming and challenging than anticipated, leading to lower than expected profitability. Attracting and retaining customers and employees was difficult. After much soul-searching, the trio decided to exit the property management side of the business in order to focus on selling the software in a subscription SaaS model, where they felt there was more upside.

The company's goal was to grow its user base to one million multifamily residential units and reach a $1 billion valuation by 2030. To achieve these aggressive targets, Simplifyy needed to attract both sales and engineering talent, improve the functionality of its software, and attract new customers - all of which might require additional funding. While the trio were proud of the company's Missouri roots, they also acknowledged the challenges of starting a software business in Kansas City, which lacked the entrepreneurial ecosystem of other tech hubs such as Silicon Valley, Austin, and New York. The team needed to determine the best way to work within their geographical constraints to attract the necessary talent, customers, and funding to grow the business.

MULTIFAMILY PROPERTY INDUSTRY

In 2018, there were approximately 29 million multifamily residences in the U.S., representing 20% of the housing market. These included condominiums, apartments, townhouses, and mixed-use developments that combined homes with retail and other commercial spaces. From 2008 to 2018, the number of multifamily units grew from 26 to 29 million, with complexes of over 20 units driving over 80% of that growth.[1] Since the end of 2018, demand for multifamily housing continued to be strong, due to a combination of changing demographics, job growth, a nationwide shortage of housing, COVID-19-related federal stimulus payments, and more local economies reopening following pandemic restrictions.[2]

In Kansas City, multifamily housing development remained stable. Total inventory of multifamily units reached 184,000 in 2018 and had grown at an annual average rate of 1.1% over the last ten years, with 45% of growth originating from large multifamily complexes.[3] Occupancy rates remained near or above 95% for over six years.[4]

In 2020, during the pandemic, the federal government enacted the federal eviction moratorium, which prevented housing owners from evicting tenants for nonpayment of rent, charging fees for nonpayment of rent, or issuing notices to vacate due to unpaid rent or fees. The moratorium ran for four months in 2020 but was extended multiple times in 2021.[5] However, the U.S. Supreme Court struck down the October 2021 extension, leaving millions of renters across the country without federal protection against eviction from unpaid rent.[6]

Property Management

With over 300,000 property management companies in the U.S., the property management industry was highly fragmented.[7] The largest property management company, Greystar, operated 500,000 units, representing a 2% share of the multifamily market. The second-largest property manager, Lincoln Property Company, managed less than half the number of units as Greystar (See **Exhibit 1a**).[8] Large property owners (more than 4,000 units) typically self-managed their properties; those with fewer units generally outsourced management to third parties. Some large self-managed properties were publicly traded as REITs (see **Exhibit 1b** for financials).

Property management companies provided essential services to the buildings they managed and to owners and residents. Management companies oversaw all tasks related to owning and running properties such as leasing, collecting and managing rents, tenants, property repairs and maintenance activities, taxes, and property records and accounting. Generally, management companies had three to seven onsite employees at multifamily housing complexes that handled maintenance, leasing, and tenant communications.

According to a 2020 survey, property managers' most pressing challenges were inefficiencies, stagnant revenue growth, and burdensome maintenance. These needs created tensions between the demands for more efficient business processes through technology adoption and human-centric customer service. Many tenants increasingly expected real-time responses and were disgruntled when property managers did not have the technology or staff to provide quick solutions.[9]

APPLYING TECHNOLOGY TO REAL ESTATE

A wave of real estate technology, or "PropTech," ushered in a new era of managing real estate. These innovations changed the way people researched, rented, bought, sold, and managed properties. Online real estate companies such as Zillow and Opendoor streamlined traditional real estate models, improving flexibility and transparency for buyers and sellers. Airbnb created an online marketplace for lodging. Latch expanded the use of smart locks in multifamily buildings. Over time, industry consolidation picked up pace. In 2014, there were roughly 25 mergers and acquisitions completed in the U.S. in real estate technology.[10] Five years later, that number had increased to more than 100.[11]

Funding to venture-backed real estate technology companies accelerated in the early 2010s. From 2011 to 2018, venture capital investments in PropTech worldwide grew from $500 million to over $8 billion.[12] With more than 2,000 real estate technology companies, or 60% of worldwide total, many analysts considered the U.S. to be the hub of PropTech innovation.[13] Within the U.S., New York, San Francisco, and Boston housed more than 30% of U.S. PropTech companies.[14]

Property Management Tech Solutions

Property management was a fairly hands-on industry, and some industry participants characterized the field as slow to adopt technology. Yet, a host of new tech tools and applications became standard across the industry starting in the 2000s. Developments arose allowing 3D virtual property tours, virtual leasing, online rent collection, online property management, online financial management, AI-enabled tenant communications, and automated property valuations.[15] Popular technology solutions included accounting, rent payment, and maintenance requests (See **Exhibit 2** for use cases). The COVID-19 pandemic accelerated the pace at which property managers implemented technology in other areas of their business, such as virtual leasing and self-guided tours.[16]

By 2021, hundreds of property management software companies existed throughout the U.S. Some companies focused on a specific area of property management like accounting or tenant communications. But many others, including larger, established companies, such as Yardi, RealPage, and AppFolio, offered a full array of property management software for management companies.

Yardi. Started in 1984, Yardi, a private California-based company, offered comprehensive property management software for residential and commercial property owners. Yardi offered multiple platforms to meet varying customer needs. Yardi Voyager was a fully integrated central database that offered advanced services, allowing customers to run specialized reports. Yardi Breeze was a simpler property management software that offered a range of services such as accounting, online rent collection, online lease execution, email and text communications, and live chat support. In 2021, Yardi acquired Forge, a software company that specialized in smart access control and visitor management.[17]

RealPage. Founded in 1998 and headquartered in Texas, RealPage developed multifamily property management software, which included payment processing, accounting and financial reporting, and document management. In recent years, the company acquired several PropTech software companies. In 2018, the company acquired LeaseLabs, a digital marketing software and services company, and ClickPay, an electronic payment platform company. The following year RealPage acquired SimpleBills, a utility management company, and Buildium, a property management software company. In 2020, the company continued acquisitions, buying Stratis IoT, an energy automation software company that enabled residents to control doors, thermostats, and lighting, and Modern Message, a resident rewards program. RealPage was a publicly-traded company until April 2021, when it was acquired by a private equity firm for $10.2 billion.[18]

AppFolio. Publicly traded on NASDAQ, AppFolio was founded in 2006. The company was located in California and had $310 million in revenues in 2020 and over 1,300 employees. AppFolio offered SaaS applications for residential and commercial property management companies and priced on a per-unit per-month basis. Over 5 million units were under management on its platform. The company offered comprehensive software solutions in marketing, leasing, accounting, reporting, and tenant communications.[19] AppFolio also ventured into the legal software market, acquiring a case management software company in 2012 that is subsequently sold for nearly $200 million in 2020 (See **Exhibit 3** for AppFolio historical financials).[20]

THE FOUNDERS' JOURNEYS

Although from different geographic regions, Lisby and Worcester shared common threads in terms of upbringing and professional interests.

Jake Lisby

Lisby grew up in a small rural town on the Missouri-Arkansas border. The son of a police officer and an entrepreneur, Lisby knew at an early age he wanted to launch his own business. As a teenager, Lisby started a lawn mowing company and taught himself how to code after his father bought his first laptop. Lisby reflected, "After high school, I started a web design company. I built a website for my uncle's company, and he later connected me with other people, and I just kept building my portfolio. I did this all the way through school."

In 2003, Lisby enrolled in William Jewell College in Liberty, Missouri, a suburb of Kansas City, to pursue a degree in Entrepreneurial Leadership. He recalled, "I went to college, played basketball, had a full-time job, and ran my own company doing web design and development. Having a side hustle was just something ingrained in me."

Following graduation in 2007, Lisby joined Cerner Corporation, a large healthcare IT company in Kansas City. Lisby worked on the company's first web team and created a web-based healthcare application. As a side job, Lisby started a software development company, Rain Tomorrow. "I was working 80 hours in my full-time job and then running a four-person software development firm with a handful of clients," Lisby recalled.

Over the next several years, Lisby worked for multiple small startups in the Kansas City area while continuing to operate Rain Tomorrow, which served as an idea engine for consulting projects. Lisby remained focused on developing software that improved operational efficiency. He commented, "My focus has always been on automating human effort, writing software that can replace manual work."

Paul Worcester

Worcester came from a humble background in Oregon; his father was a pastor, and his mother was a third-grade school teacher. In 2008, Worcester graduated from Northwest Christian University in Eugene, Oregon, with a degree in biblical studies.

Inspired by reading *Rich Dad Poor Dad* by Robert Kiyosaki, Worcester, his siblings, and his father decided to go into business together, buying and operating small multifamily properties. Lacking funds needed to purchase properties, his father took out a $200,000 second mortgage on his home and founded Worcester Investments in 2006. The family bought their first fourplex property in Salem, Oregon, from a man who moved to Kansas City.[21]

Worcester visited the former property owner in Kansas City and quickly realized the allure of the city for real estate investors. There the family could afford to buy two to three times as much property as they could in Eugene, Oregon, while only taking a 15 to 25% reduction in total rental income. Together the family moved to Kansas City and grew their business over the next decade, and by 2021 the company owned and operated more than 3,000 rental units in the greater Kansas City area.[22]

Together, Worcester and his brother managed Worcester Investments as co-CEOs. For years the partnership worked well, but a decade into the property management business, Worcester had grown increasingly dissatisfied with the lack of innovation and disruption in the multifamily property industry. Tenants communicated needed repairs by physically visiting the onsite manager's office. A few large property managers began to adopt technology, but many small to medium-sized property managers still manually input monthly financial information into Excel spreadsheets, just as they had done for years. Property maintenance and repair records were manually maintained. Financial reports were often issued 30 to 45 days after month-end because of time delays gathering information. "Other industries were getting disrupted and improved in positive ways. This industry was antiquated and broken," Worcester summarized.

Starting Simplifyy

Worcester and Lisby were introduced socially by their wives. Soon Worcester hired Lisby's software company to help solve the problem of late rent payments they were facing at Worcester Investments. Lisby built an app that rewarded renters for on-time payment by accruing points towards upgrades in their units, such as new lighting or oven fans. Yet tenant feedback expressed in a focus group was lukewarm; instead, what they really wanted was to be able to easily communicate with property managers when maintenance problems arose after business hours. These insights led Lisby to craft new solutions. He commented, "We wrote four different technology solutions that reduced manual effort. I felt we could really advance this industry, so I put together a plan and presented it to Paul."

Between 2018 and 2019, Lisby beta tested software for the property management industry that would replace physical visits and voicemails from tenants with online communication. Lisby piloted the software on a small number of properties that Worcester owned and operated in Kansas City. Beta testing went well and tenant feedback was positive, but the software development costs were high, and Worcester Investments did not have the appetite to continue to pay for more testing.

It became clear that Worcester and his brother had different visions for technological innovation in their industry, and these divergent opinions led to a rift. Worcester made the difficult decision to separate from the family business so he could go "all in" on developing property management technology. Investing $2 million of his own funds and helping to raise an additional $2.8 million of outside seed capital, Worcester co-founded Simplifyy with Lisby in October 2019.

Simplifyy 1.0: The Early Product

At the outset, Simplifyy offered a full-service property management solution for multifamily property owners. The company developed an end-to-end software product, and in addition, provided property management services. In essence, Simplifyy replaced the role of the traditional property manager.

Lisby felt Simplifyy offered three primary competitive advantages. First, Simplifyy offered remote property management services, replacing the need for high-cost, onsite property managers. Second, the enterprise software was specifically built to streamline or "simplify" operations. Most established solutions were initially created for accounting departments and did not serve other functions well. Simplifyy's product focused on operations first and then rolled in an industry-standard accounting package. It was user-friendly, operationally oriented, and met the accounting department's needs. Third, Simplifyy was small and nimble. Simplifyy could swiftly tailor its product to meet customer needs, something large incumbent software companies could not do. The software automated many labor-intensive, repetitive processes, focusing on leasing, resident retention, property care, and finance (See **Exhibit** 4).

Leasing AI software allowed for contactless tours for potential residents 24/7 using smartphones. The software verified potential applicants' identities through uploading driver's licenses and selfies and communicated with smart locks to allow prospects access to units. Using AI, the company then followed up after every tour to convert prospects into residents.

Resident Retention Using AI, Simplifyy's software enabled 24/7 communications with residents. All conversations with residents were logged and available to the Simplifyy team to serve residents better. The AI software could predict the likelihood of tenants vacating the property based on data gathered from late rent payments and the number and frequency of maintenance visits, thereby enabling Simplifyy team members to proactively communicate with residents to resolve problems before they became larger issues. The company offered online rent payments and promoted community-building activities with residents.

Property Care Necessary repairs could be communicated to property managers in real-time. Simplifyy employed smart technology such as water leak sensors to detect property maintenance issues, which allowed maintenance workers to address problems quickly. All repairs and maintenance were documented and tracked to provide accountability and transparency. The AI system could predict the useful life of appliances and fixtures, which enabled property managers to plan and allocate budgets for future expenses.

Finance Account information could be accessed through the owner's app anytime, from anywhere, and contained real-time financial data. Vendor invoices were mailed or electronically sent to Simplifyy, and the AI system would extract the data, perform accounting entries and prepare invoices for review and payment. Operational costs were forecasted based on real-time data, which enabled greater accuracy than traditional budgeting methods.

Under the initial pricing model, customers paid a flat monthly fee to Simplifyy based on the number of units under management (See **Exhibit 5**). Simplifyy expected that by automating and centralizing traditionally labor-intensive leasing and management services, the company could capture value for owners and itself by reducing or eliminating the need for onsite labor. Simplifyy at first expected it could achieve 60% margins adopting this remote labor model, a significant improvement from the three to 10% margins they believed property management companies typically earned.

What the company did not anticipate was that some states and lenders required property managers to be onsite, which impacted profitability. For example, California state housing law required apartment buildings with more than 16 units to have an on-premise manager.[23] Fannie Mae and Freddie Mac (two of the largest lenders in the multifamily industry) had similar regulations, making the fully-remote labor model impractical to implement.

CHALLENGES OF THE EARLY BUSINESS MODEL

Sitting on Missouri's western border, Kansas City was located almost exactly in the middle of the United States. With a steadily growing population of 508,000, the city had a reputation for friendly people, affordable living, and a relaxed pace of life.[24] In 2020, the average price of a home sold in Kansas City was $273,000, roughly 30% less than the national average.[25,26] For many, Kansas City was an attractive place to live. Conversely, its central U.S. location created unique challenges for attracting labor, customers, and capital.

Attracting Initial Customers

Initially, Simplifyy targeted third-party property managers of small multifamily properties, those defined as owning less than 4,000 units. The company first focused on the Kansas City area, then sought to expand regionally and nationally. The theory was that Simplifyy could have a competitive advantage by bundling property management software and services to provide an enterprise solution to a highly fragmented industry, reducing the cost and hassle of servicing properties for property owners. Worcester reflected on how the COVID-19 pandemic, which began right after the company launched operations, impacted the business, "Covid accelerated the industry's adoption of tech by three to seven years in a one-year period. Before Covid, we would meet with an owner of 12,000 multifamily units to talk about self-touring and get *laughed* at. Fast forward a few months and it's illegal to physically show a unit. The timing of our product was very good."

But the company soon learned that attracting new customers during the COVID-19 pandemic was harder than imagined as face-to-face meetings critical to the sales process were simply not an option. The geographical location of Kansas City presented an additional hurdle in attracting new customers. In 2020, New York City had almost 9 million people in approximately 300 square miles, while Kansas City had about 500,000 in roughly the same land area.[27,28] As Kansas City had a lower population density, it was necessary to travel farther to reach the same number of multifamily units as its urban counterparts.

Convincing companies to switch software, which had sometimes been in place for years, from established software players to an unknown startup that offered novel remote property management services was tough. Zoom meetings were effective but not nearly as effective as in-person meetings when trying to sell new concepts to new customers. Keeping existing customers happy on the property management side also proved difficult. Not having a full staff of maintenance workers onsite caused delays in needed repairs, frustrating some property owners and tenants.

Early Labor Issues

Of the 80 initial employees working at Simplifyy, about 15 people worked in technology. The Midwest had a number of top computer science and engineering schools, common degrees for software developers. *U.S. News and World Report* ranked Carnegie Mellon, located in Pittsburg, Pennsylvania, the number one school in the country for computer science.[29] Many other Midwestern schools such as University of Illinois, University of Michigan, Purdue University, University of Wisconsin, Ohio State University, University of Minnesota, and Boise State University had strong computer engineering programs, providing an annual supply of graduates entering the technology workforce.

At first, the attractiveness of the relatively low cost of living and housing of the Midwest was compelling to prospective Simplifyy employees. In addition, from inception Simplifyy had offered remote work options, a policy ahead of its time. However, as firms nationwide shifted to remote work during the pandemic, Simplifyy's competitive advantage diminished. Lisby recalled:

> Before Covid, we were actively recruiting against the coasts with success. But Covid led to startups on the coasts allowing employees to work from home, and people started to realize that they could work

for a coastal firm and make a coastal salary but live in the Midwest. We just couldn't compete with that.

Within months it became clear that attracting and retaining technology talent would be difficult, and many industry analysts expected that hybrid work would represent a new normal. The demand for talented software developers was strong and expected to increase 22% over the next decade, far outpacing the 8% growth rate for all occupations.[30]

In 2021, the average salary for a software developer in San Francisco was $125,000, nearly 50% more than the average salary of $84,000 for a developer in Kansas City.[31] In comparison, the average annual salary of a developer in Pakistan was $5,100.[32] Having difficulty procuring affordable talent, Lisby decided to expand his geographical search, hiring talented developers across the United States and internationally.

The remainder of initial employees were property managers and maintenance technicians, who also became increasingly difficult to hire. According to the National Center for Housing Management, trade workers such as electricians, carpenters, and plumbers were aging and retiring at increasing rates, and the number of new, mechanically-skilled workers was not keeping up with demand. Furthermore, there was a cultural shift across the country towards encouraging more high school students to seek college educations rather than technical training.[33] Simplifyy relied on its novel startup culture to attract maintenance workers, but leadership knew that retaining and replacing the turnover of these employees would remain difficult in the current macroeconomic environment.

Raising Capital in Missouri

By the end of 2020, Simplifyy had spent over $3 million on software development and had annual recurring revenue of nearly $1 million. However, the company had a monthly cash burn approaching $200,000 and only $500,000 cash on hand. The company needed to raise capital (See **Exhibit 6** for historical financials).

Trends in Venture Capital Between 2012 and 2020, the compound annual growth rate for venture capital assets under management (AUM) was 10%. Nearly 2,000 venture capital firms managed over 3,500 venture capital funds and had approximately $548 billion AUM at the end of 2020, including $150 billion in unallocated capital. Despite facing headwinds from the COVID-19 pandemic and the worst economic downturn since the Great Depression, the venture capital industry remained strong. Venture capital firms raised a record $74 billion in 2020.[34]

Venture capital funds continued to be geographically concentrated. Three states – California, Massachusetts, and New York – were home to funds that managed 85% of total venture capital AUM in 2020. With $1.9 billion in venture capital AUM, Missouri represented just 0.3% of total U.S. venture capital AUM. Venture capital funds invested $164 billion in 2020 into more than 10,000 portfolio companies. Consistent with previous years, the software sector received the most capital, with roughly 30% of investments flowing into such startups.[35]

Despite travel restrictions during the pandemic limiting face-to-face meetings between entrepreneurs and investors, venture capital still managed to reach startup companies in all 50 states. Many venture capital firms shifted meetings, due diligence, and closings online. Still, capital deployed to startups remained concentrated in coastal areas. The established hubs of California, Massachusetts, and New York continued to see the most deal activity, accounting for 54% of total deal count and 73% of total capital invested. Missouri accounted for 7% of total deals and 0.3% of total capital invested. (See **Exhibit** 7)[36]

Access to Venture Capital In venture capital, networks mattered. Based on a recent Harvard Business Review study, it was estimated that more than 30% of deals originated from leads from venture capitalists' former work colleagues or work acquaintances, while 20% of deals came from referrals from other investors. Only 10% came from cold email pitches. Accessing venture capital money could be challenging if entrepreneurs were not connected to the right networks of people. As Silicon Valley investor Jim Breyer, founder of Breyer Capital, commented, "I've found that the best deals often come from my network of trusted investors, entrepreneurs, and professors."[37]

Even entrepreneurs who were able to access venture capital firms often found that the odds of receiving funding were extraordinarily low. Survey results found that for every "101 opportunities, 28 of those opportunities will lead to a meeting with management; 10 will be reviewed at a partner meeting; 4.8 will proceed to due diligence; 1.7 will move on to the negotiation of a term sheet with the startup, and only one will actually be funded."[38]

Lisby and Worcester found fundraising more challenging than expected. Kansas City was approximately 1,800 miles from San Francisco and 1,200 miles from New York City. The geographical isolation of Kansas City meant networks and connections were of heightened importance, and neither of them had deep venture capital connections. Lisby reflected, "One of the hardest things about the Midwest is fundraising. Raising money, especially in Missouri, is *tough*." He continued, "In the Kansas City area, investors want to make early-stage, low dollar investments. Anytime you are talking about a Series A, you're probably not going to raise it in the Midwest. Midwestern firms don't write big enough checks, and they don't want high risk."

The capital raise became the primary focus for Lisby and Worcester. "We pitched small investors, big investors, and family office networks. We pitched and pitched and pitched," Lisby lamented. Worcester had similar sentiments, "It was tenuous. I was spending my days doing pitches, and I really wasn't sure it was going to happen until the very end."

After several months of nonstop fundraising meetings and pitches, the two finally found a lead investor, Unit Leader, in San Diego, California. A venture capital firm with over a dozen portfolio companies, Unit Leader was led by Dana Zeff, who had over 35 years of experience in the multifamily industry. Prior to starting Unit Leader, Zeff was the founder and CEO of LeaseLabs, which sold in 2018 for over $100 million.[39] Unit Leader was joined by investors in Dallas and Chicago to close out a $5 million Series A round in March 2021. Zeff commented, "We are excited to be a part of an organization that provides property owners a solution that is more effective, more efficient, and more transparent than anything else on the market today."[40]

SIMPLIFYY 2.0: A NEW MODEL

In May 2021, Kansas City-based Evan Conway signed on as COO of Simplifyy. Conway, a graduate of both Cornell undergraduate and graduate schools, was an experienced executive who had worked for multiple technology startup companies, many of which had been acquired. He commented on Simplifyy's initial strategy, "We had a good technology product and believed we had a competitive advantage by providing both technology and property management in a tough, fragmented industry. By combining these two things, we thought we could win business quickly and go from zero to several thousand units in one year."

During his first 100 days, Conway sorted through call center requests to better understand the allocation of tasks and which activities could be done remotely. He commented, "The initial vision was to centralize functions and have remote property managers, reducing labor costs by 50%. We weren't able to execute a fully remote model, so we only achieved about 20% of the labor savings."

There were other issues. As CEO responsible for both technology and property management, Lisby soon found that he spent most of his days fighting fires, addressing urgent call center issues like fixing residents' heating systems and unclogging sinks, as well as managing the maintenance staff.

Lisby was spending almost all of his time on property management issues and no longer had much time to spend on the technology side of the business.

While Simplifyy reached $1 million in annual recurring revenue, the company was still losing money, and some Simplifyy customers had grown unhappy with the quality of its property management services and terminated contracts. By late October 2021, the company was servicing less than 2,000 units and anticipated that number might fall further.

The Decision to Adapt and a New Revenue Stream

In November 2021, the leaders decided to steer the company in a new direction. The new model would reshape Simplifyy into a more traditional software company and fully exit the property management business. Simplifyy would license software to property managers on a per-unit per-month basis, similar to a typical SaaS model. Lisby commented, "I know that I can beat a lot of the software companies out there. We may not excel at property management, but we are top class on software."

Lisby realized that the true value to Simplifyy was not only the subscription revenue but also the volume of currency running through the platform. Simplifyy locked in a partnership with Stripe, an online payment processing platform that allowed for swift, secure processing of funds via credit or debit card, bank transfers, or paper checks. All currency, such as rental payments coming in, payments to vendors, or distributions to owners, would travel on the Stripe platform. Simplifyy would pass all Stripe fees on to customers while adding a small service fee for Simplifyy on every transaction. In addition, Simplifyy would charge a fee for value-added reselling of services from service partners on its platform. Under the previous business model, Simplifyy did not charge fees on payments received or remitted; revenue was solely based on amounts charged for property management services. Total fee-based revenue was anticipated to be larger than subscription revenue. The company believed this new business model would be more scalable and profitable than the previous one (See **Exhibit 8** for an illustrative example). Additionally, the time to scale would be considerably faster. Lisby estimated that Simplifyy could reach 100,000 units within two years. Under the previous model, he felt it would take more than a decade to reach that number.

Customer Base Broadens

Shifting to the new operating model allowed Simplifyy to cast a significantly wider customer net. The company could now sell enterprise solutions to large self-managed property owners as well as third-party operators. Central to its success would be to secure roughly ten anchor partners, large operators of multifamily housing units, to start serving at the 100,000-unit level and build credibility in the marketplace. After reaching critical mass through strategic partners, Simplifyy planned to sell its software to smaller mom-and-pop operators on its website.

In mid-November 2021, Simplifyy signed its first cornerstone partner, a large multifamily property company that owned and operated over 10,000 geographically diverse units across the Southeast. The partner planned to start using Simplifyy software in late November. Lisby expected to close another cornerstone partner that operated 20,000 units before year-end and two or three additional partners that operated between 2,000 and 6,000 units.

Conway would lead the new salesforce, which would need to be built as the company grew. The first salesperson had deep property management knowledge and would be retrained in sales. The company planned to hire an additional experienced salesperson in April 2022. The key was finding the right person. This new salesperson could be located outside Kansas City and would be compensated on a base plus commission structure, consistent with industry standards.

Labor Needs Shift

Shifting to a SaaS model had implications for the team since most of the 80 initial employees at Simplifyy had been property managers and maintenance workers—many of whom had been long-term employees at Worcester Investment. As the company exited the property management business, Simplifyy expected the total number of employees to decrease from 80 to 20 people. Only a handful of employees would remain in Kansas City, and the remainder would be offsite, including all software developers. The company handled separations delicately, adhering to what Lisby described as its Midwestern ethos. "It's being done in person. It's conversations," said Worcester.

Unlike many startups, the three leaders worked tirelessly to find displaced workers new employment. Lisby articulated, "It has been very difficult to lay people off right before the holidays. It's a difficult balance to care for the people during the transition to ensure that they have good landings while continuing to push the business forward."

As Simplifyy focused on its core software development business, the need for great product developers was even more pressing. Conway believed that product excellence was crucial for the company's success. He mused, "In a very stodgy industry with high switching costs, can we convince property management companies to give up what they're accustomed to? If our software is ten times better, everybody will switch. If just eight times better, they might not. We need to get to ten."

While the company may have had success in the past attracting local tech talent, the recent national shift to remote work meant that many of the top local developers were working for higher-paying coastal firms. The company needed to find talent elsewhere and extended its talent search nationally and internationally. Lisby commented, "We just weren't able to find great local developers. Half of our developers will be based internationally, and the rest will be working remotely from other Midwestern cities. We needed to widen our labor pool, and right now, the biggest pool is overseas." Lisby compensated the international developers the same as U.S.-based developers, significantly more than they would earn locally, gave them equity, and treated them the same as full-time domestic employees, an attractive proposition for many located overseas.

Building Options for Capital

Simplifyy had enough cash to operate the next 12 to 18 months. Securing a Series A round had taken valuable time, and the next round of financing was not anticipated to be any less challenging. In the short term, Lisby did not want to hunt a growth round of financing. "I'm laser-focused on creating sustainable growth right now," he commented, "That kind of stability creates choices, and in turn, having options is liberating. For example, we could fundraise to pursue rapid growth, we could become an attractive acquisition target, or we could manage as-is on our own and seek non-dilutive funding. I don't want to chase capital continuously."

Lisby considered his mentality to be different than that of a typical startup. "Startup magazines write stories about companies that raised $100 million, but they don't write stories about companies that generated $100 million or even $1 million in profit. It makes me wonder if the goal is to deploy capital or to build successful companies," he commented.

LOOKING FORWARD

Settling in for another late evening, Lisby, Conway, and Worcester focused on the future. The last several months had been a whirlwind, and yet there was no time to spare. The company had aggressive long-term goals: 1 million doors and a $1 billion valuation within the next decade. With a strong strategic customer on board, Lisby welcomed the opportunity to refocus Simplifyy on the core software product, but he knew there were challenges ahead with customer acquisition, hiring talent, and fundraising from their Kansas City headquarters.

Yet, they were confident that the company would find a way forward. The company had always espoused a trailblazer attitude, and it was about finding the right set of people. Worcester commented, "We embrace the discomfort, fear, opportunity, and adventure that come with being a pioneer. The culture is such that if you're not comfortable with that, it's not going to be a great place to be. But if you embrace the challenges that come with it, it's fun to be in a startup."

Finally, as a SaaS company, Simplifyy would now be competing against large, established software companies and many new startups. Fundraising would likely be key to growth and gaining market share. How could the company grow its customer base? How could Simplifyy best attract and retain talent from the U.S. and abroad? How could Simplifyy open the doors to a wider group of investors to secure capital over the long term? Lisby knew that not only to survive but to thrive, they had to get this right.

NOTES

1 "Single-Family and Large Multifamily Properties Drove Rental Growth in the Last Decade | Joint Center for Housing Studies" (Harvard Joint Center for Housing Studies, 2021), https://www.jchs.harvard.edu/single-family-and-large-multifamily-properties-drove-rental-growth-last-decade.

2 "2021 Multifamily Market Mid-Year Outlook – Demand Improving | Fannie Mae Multifamily," accessed November 8, 2021, https://multifamily.fanniemae.com/news-insights/multifamily-market-commentary/2021-multifamily-market-mid-year-outlook-demand.

3 "Single-Family and Large Multifamily Properties Drove Rental Growth in the Last Decade | Joint Center for Housing Studies."

4 Maguire, Martin et al., "Kansas City Multifamily 21Q1" (Colliers, June 2021), https://www.colliers.com/en/research/kansas-city/2021-q1-multifamily-trends.

5 "How Does the Federal Eviction Moratorium Impact the Emergency Solutions Grant and Continuum of Care Program?" (U.S. Department of Housing and Urban Development, 2020).

6 "Supreme Court Strikes down CDC Eviction Moratorium despite Delta's Rise," *Washington Post*, accessed November 8, 2021, https://www.washingtonpost.com/politics/courts_law/supreme-court-eviction-ban-struck-down/2021/08/26/46bce3e2-0511-11ec-a654-900a78538242_story.html.

7 Jaleesa Bustamante, "Property Management Industry Statistics" (iPropertyManagement, 2021), https://ipropertymanagement.com/research/property-management-industry-statistics.

8 "NHMC 50 Largest Apartment Managers" (National Multifamily Housing Council, 2020), https://www.nmhc.org/research-insight/the-nmhc-50/top-50-lists/2020-top-managers-list/.
9 "2020-Industry-Report-Digital.Pdf," accessed December 1, 2021, https://3jt0l76j0a937x1bk3li34iw-wpengine.netdna-ssl.com/wp-content/uploads/2019/10/2020-Industry-Report-Digital.pdf.
10 "Volume of Real Estate Tech Merger and Acquisition Activity in the United States from 2013 to 2nd Quarter 2021" (Statista Research Department, September 2021), https://www-statista-com.ezp-prod1.hul.harvard.edu/statistics/972337/merger-acquisition-proptech-deals-worldwide/.
11 "Volume of Real Estate Tech Merger and Acquisition Activity in the United States from 2013 to 2nd Quarter 2021."
12 "Value of Venture Capital Investments in PropTech Companies Worldwide From 2008 to 2018" (Statista Research Department, September 2021), https://www-statista-com.ezp-prod1.hul.harvard.edu/statistics/1060470/global-proptech-venture-capital-investment-value/.
13 "Real Estate Technology (ReTech) And PropTech In The USA - Overview" (Unissu, May 2021), https://www.unissu.com/proptech-resources/proptech-retech-in-the-usa.
14 "Real Estate Technology (ReTech) And PropTech In The USA - Overview."
15 Emilio Matthaei and Micha-Manuel Bues, "What Is Proptech? A Brief History," *European PropTech Initiative* (blog), August 2016, http://epti.eu/?p=153.
16 Wasila Rehman, "Property Management Industry Trends 2021" (lethub, September 2021), https://www.lethub.co/blog/property-management-industry-trends-2021.
17 "Yardi - Crunchbase Company Profile & Funding," Crunchbase, accessed November 9, 2021, https://www.crunchbase.com/organization/yardi-systems.
18 "RealPage - Crunchbase Company Profile & Funding," Crunchbase, accessed November 9, 2021, https://www.crunchbase.com/organization/realpage.
19 "Property Management Software | AppFolio Property Management," AppFolio, accessed November 9, 2021, https://www.appfolio.com/.
20 RTTNews, "AppFolio To Sell 100% Interest In Subsidiary MyCase To Apax Partners - Quick Facts" (Nasdaq, September 2020), https://www.nasdaq.com/articles/appfolio-to-sell-100-interest-in-subsidiary-mycase-to-apax-partners-quick-facts-2020-09-08.
21 The Real Estate Syndication Show, *The Uber of Property Management with Paul Worcester*, 2020, https://www.youtube.com/watch?v=S1eOuRZ1eTg.
22 The Real Estate Syndication Show.
23 "California Health and Safety Code Division 13, Part 1.5 Regulations of Buildings Used For Human Habitation," accessed November 22, 2021, https://nchh.org/resource-library/HH_Codes_CA_9-9-07.pdf.
24 "U.S. Census Bureau QuickFacts: Kansas City, Missouri" (U.S. Census Bureau, 2020), https://www.census.gov/quickfacts/kansascitycitymissouri.
25 Marco Santarelli, "Kansas City Housing Market: Prices | Trends | Forecasts 2021" (Norada Real Estate Investments, September 2021), https://www.noradarealestate.com/blog/kansas-city-real-estate/.

26 U.S. Census Bureau and U.S. Department of Housing and Urban Development, "Average Sales Price of Houses Sold for the United States" (FRED Economic Data, 2020), https://fred.stlouisfed.org/series/ASPUS.
27 "U.S. Census Bureau QuickFacts: New York City, New York" (U.S. Census Bureau, 2020), https://www.census.gov/quickfacts/newyorkcitynewyork.
28 "U.S. Census Bureau QuickFacts," 2020.
29 "The Best Undergraduate Computer Science Programs" (U.S. News & World Report, 2021), https://usnews.com/best-colleges/rankings/computer-science-overall.
30 "Software Developers, Quality Assurance Analysts, and Testers : Occupational Outlook Handbook: : U.S. Bureau of Labor Statistics" (U.S. Bureau of Labor Statistics, September 2021), https://www.bls.gov/ooh/computer-and-information-technology/software-developers.htm.
31 "Software Developer Search | Glassdoor," accessed November 21, 2021, https://www.glassdoor.com/Search/results.htm?keyword=software%20developer&locId=1131040&locT=C&locName=Kansas%20City%2C%20MO.
32 "Software Developer Search | Glassdoor."
33 Paul Votto, "Why It's Getting Harder To Hire Maintenance Staff" (National Center for Housing Management, July 2016), https://www.nchm.org/why-its-getting-harder-to-hire-maintenance-staff/.
34 National Venture Capital Association, "NVCA 2021 Yearbook," March 2021, https://nvca.org/wp-content/uploads/2021/08/NVCA-2021-Yearbook.pdf.
35 National Venture Capital Association.
36 National Venture Capital Association.
37 Paul Gompers et al., "How Venture Capitalists Make Decisions," *Harvard Business Review*, March 1, 2021, https://hbr.org/2021/03/how-venture-capitalists-make-decisions.
38 Gompers et al.
39 "Bio on Dana Zeff," https://unitleader.com/, November 2021, https://unitleader.com/.
40 Startland News Staff, "KC Proptech Startup Simplifyy Gets $5M Series A Boost toward Expansion Plans; next up: DFW," *Startland News*, March 31, 2021, sec. Funding, https://www.startlandnews.com/2021/03/simplifyy-series-a/.

EXHIBIT 1A Top 20 Property Managers in 2020

Rank	Company Name	Units Managed	Share of Market
1	Greystar Real Estate Partners	492,967	1.5%
2	Lincoln Property Company	203,342	0.6%
3	Pinnacle	169,002	0.5%
4	Alliance Residential	138,650	0.4%
5	FPI Management, Inc.	122,479	0.4%
6	WinnCompanies	105,214	0.3%
7	MAA	100,031	0.3%
8	Apartment Management Consultants, LLC	92,978	0.3%
9	BH Management, LLC	92,747	0.3%
10	Equity Residential	80,624	0.2%
11	AvalonBay Communities, Inc.	78,367	0.2%
12	Morgan Properties	76,831	0.2%
13	Bozzuto	75,095	0.2%
14	Asset Living	71,679	0.2%
15	Avenue5 Residential, LLC	67,858	0.2%
16	Edward Rose Building Enterprise	65,600	0.2%
17	Related Companies	64,238	0.2%
18	The Irvine Company	62,254	0.2%
19	Hunt/Envolve Communities	61,673	0.2%
20	Essex Property Trust, Inc.	60,040	0.2%

Source: Casewriter, based on data from "NHMC 50 Largest Apartment Managers" (National Multifamily Housing Council, 2020), https://www.nmhc.org/research-insight/the-nmhc-50/top-50-lists/2020-top-managers-list/.

EXHIBIT 1B 2020 Annual Income Statements for Publicly Traded REITs With Large Property Management Companies

(USD millions)

	MAA	Equity Residential	AvalonBay Communities	Essex Property Trust
Rental Revenue	1,678.0	2,571.7	2,297.4	1,486.2
Property Management Fee	-	-	3.8	9.6
Other Revenue	-	-	1.3	61.2
Total Revenue	**1,678.0**	**2,571.7**	**2,302.5**	**1,556.9**
Property Expenses	692.8	916.4	823.2	472.5
Gross Profit	**985.2**	**1,655.3**	**1,479.3**	**1,084.5**
Selling General & Admin Expenses	46.9	48.3	57.8	65.4
Depreciation & Amortization	510.8	820.8	707.3	525.5
Total Operating Exp.	**557.7**	**869.1**	**765.1**	**590.9**
Operating Income	**427.5**	**786.2**	**714.2**	**493.6**
Interest Income (Expense)	(167.6)	(374.0)	(214.2)	(220.6)
Other Investment Income (Expense)	-	5.9	-	6.5
Net Interest Income (Expense)	**(167.6)**	**(368.1)**	**(214.2)**	**(214.2)**
Income/(Loss) from Affiliates	7.1	(3.3)	-	-
Other Non-Operating Income (Expense)	3.6	(17.5)	-	11.5
EBT Excluding Unusual Items	**270.6**	**397.3**	**500.1**	**291.0**
Gain (Loss) on Sale of Invest	-	-	5.2	272.2
Gain (Loss) on Sale of Assets	1.0	566.0	340.9	65.0
Asset Writedown	-	-	(12.3)	(1.8)
Other Unusual Items	(4.4)	-	(9.3)	(27.0)
EBT Including Unusual Items	**267.3**	**963.4**	**824.5**	**599.3**
Income Tax Expense	3.3	0.9	(3.2)	-
Earnings After Taxes	**264.0**	**962.5**	**827.7**	**599.3**
Minority Interest Earnings (Loss)	(9.1)	(48.9)	(0.1)	(30.5)
Net Income	**255.0**	**913.6**	**827.6**	**568.9**

Valuation Multiples	MAA	Equity Residential	AvalonBay Communities	Essex Property Trust
Total Enterprise Value/Total Revenue	11.4	12.6	13.6	14.8
Total Enterprise Value/EBITDA	20.1	20.1	22.6	23.7
Price/Earnings before Unusual Items	44.0	21.9	16.5	40.4
Price/Book	2.5	2.1	2.1	2.6

Source: Casewriter, based on data from Annual Reports.

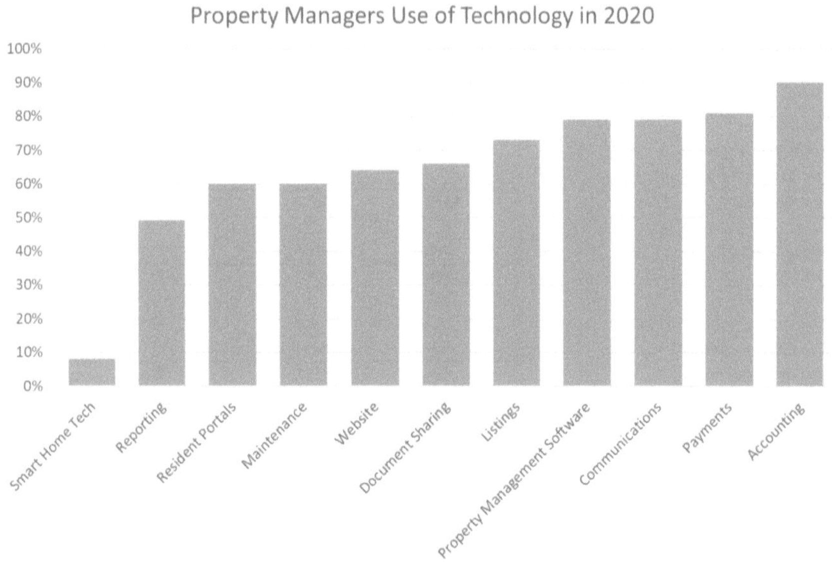

EXHIBIT 2 How Property Managers Use Technology
Source: Casewriter, based on data from Wasila Rehman, "Property Management Industry Trends 2021" (lethub, September 2021), https://www.lethub.co/blog/property-management-industry-trends-2021.

EXHIBIT 3 AppFolio Historical Annual Income Statements and Valuation Multiples

(USD thousands)

	2016	2017	2018	2019	2020
Total Revenue	**105,586**	**143,803**	**190,071**	**256,012**	**310,056**
Cost of Revenues	44,630	55,283	73,549	101,642	119,029
Gross Profit	**60,956**	**88,520**	**116,522**	**154,370**	**191,027**
Sales and Marketing	28,827	28,709	33,288	51,528	58,445
General and Administrative	17,979	21,199	24,891	34,478	47,480
Research and Product Development	12,638	16,578	24,111	39,508	48,529
Depreciation and Amortization	9,935	12,699	14,576	22,395	26,790
Total Operating Expenses	**69,379**	**79,185**	**96,866**	**147,909**	**181,244**
Operating Income	**(8,423)**	**9,335**	**19,656**	**6,461**	**9,783**
Interest Income (Expense), Net	246	535	787	(1,654)	(1,849)
Other Income (Expense), Net	(37)	(96)	(56)	16	188,897
Income Before Taxes	**(8,214)**	**9,774**	**20,387**	**4,823**	**196,831**
Provision for Income Taxes	67	58	420	(31,459)	38,428
Net Income	(8,281)	9,716	19,967	36,282	158,403

Valuation Multiples	
Market-Value Capitalization	6,480,170
EBITDA, Adjusted	22,973
Total Enterprise Value/Total Revenue	20.9
Total Enterprise Value/EBITDA	282.1
Price/Earnings before Unusual Items	n/a
Price/Book	21.7

Source: Casewriter, based on data from Annual Reports.

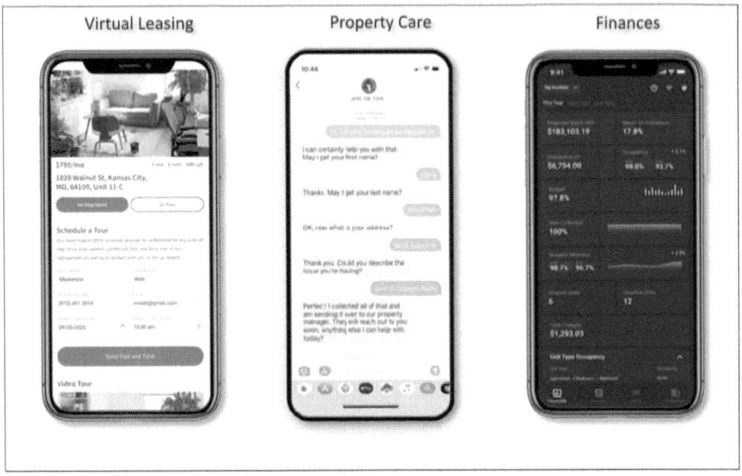

EXHIBIT 4 Simplifyy Screen Snapshots
Source: Company documents and website

Monthly Pricing Comparison

200 Units

	simplifyy.	Traditional Management*
OFFICE PAYROLL	$0	$12,000
MANAGEMENT / BOOKKEEPING	$0	$7,000
ADMIN/IT	$0	$5,000
ADVERTISING	$0	$3,000
TOTAL	$20,000	$27,000

$7,000 Monthly Profit Increase

*Per unit per month data via - National Apartment Association, Yardi Matrix, RentCafe Apartment List

EXHIBIT 5 Initial Pricing Model
Source: Company documents

EXHIBIT 6 Simplifyy Historical Income Statements

	(USD) Year Ended 12/31/2020	10 Months Ended 10/31/21
Subscription Fees	391,185	1,526,626
Other Income (Maintenance Services)	324,470	6,273
Total Revenues	**715,655**	**1,532,899**
Payroll Expense	1,352,710	3,322,159
Contract Labor	-	436,297
Administrative	422,475	303,768
Advertising & Marketing	207,898	279,868
New Market Entry	-	87,041
Consulting	609,334	205,479
Dues & Subscriptions	121,799	239,136
Legal & Professional Services & Fees	244,471	174,473
Insurance & Workers Comp	49,754	86,910
Utilities	10,964	16,004
Repairs & Maintenance	67,320	39,608
Total Expenses	**3,086,727**	**5,190,743**
Net Operating Income	**(2,371,072)**	**(3,657,844)**
Depreciation & Amortization	60,293	303,648
Interest Expense	8,733	42,732
Other (Income) Expenses	(246,212)	11,630
Total Non-Operating Expenses	**(177,186)**	**358,011**
Net Income	**(2,193,886)**	**(4,015,855)**

Source: Company documents

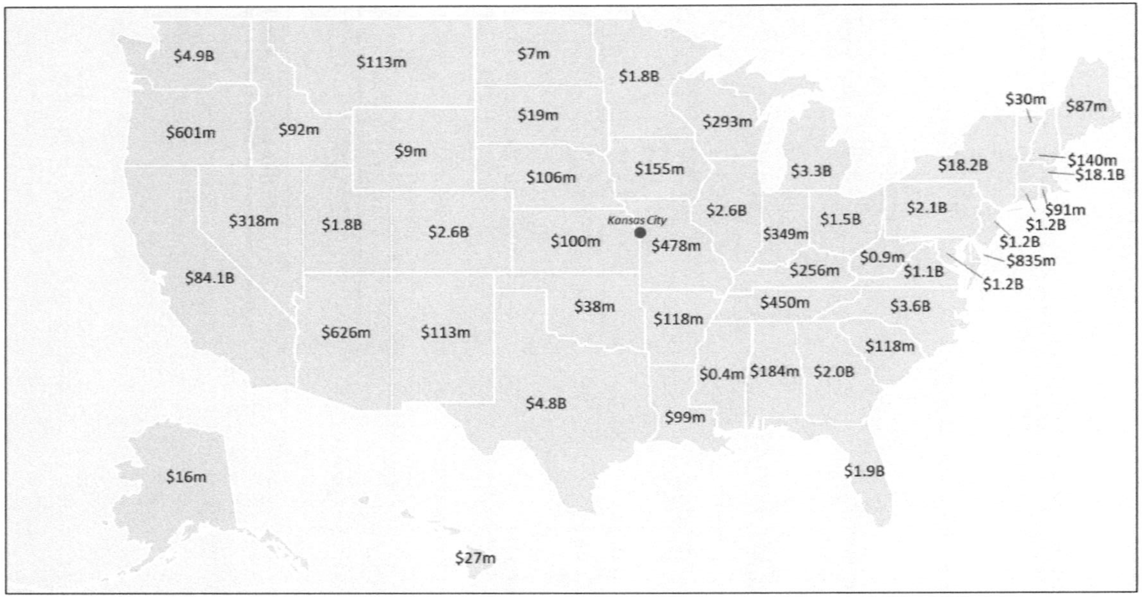

EXHIBIT 7 2020 Venture Capital Investment in the United States
Source: Casewriter, based on data from National Venture Capital Association, "NVCA 2021 Yearbook," March 2021, https://nvca.org/wp-content/uploads/2021/08/NVCA-2021-Yearbook.pdf.

EXHIBIT 8 Illustrative Example of Monthly Financial Impact of Changing Business Model

(USD, Monthly)	1,000 Units		100,000 Units	
	Old Model	New Model	Old Model	New Model
Revenue				
Property Management Fees	80,000		8,000,000	
Base Software Subscription	-	4,000	-	400,000
Software Upgrades	-	1,500	-	150,000
Value-Added Reselling	-	2,500	-	250,000
Transaction Revenue	-	5,000	-	810,000
Total Revenue	**80,000**	**13,000**	**8,000,000**	**1,610,000**
Cost of Revenue				
Customer Support & Onboarding Roles	110,000	10,000	5,600,000	30,000
Hosting and Delivery (Hard Cost of Operating Software)	15,000	6,000	800,000	230,000
Gross Profit	**(45,000)**	**(3,000)**	**1,600,000**	**1,350,000**
Gross Proft Margin			**20%**	**84%**
Expenses				
Engineering	60,000	60,000	120,000	120,000
General & Administrative	10,000	10,000	600,000	35,000
Sales & Marketing	8,000	8,000	210,000	160,000
Total Operating Costs	**78,000**	**78,000**	**930,000**	**315,000**
Net Income	**(123,000)**	**(81,000)**	**670,000**	**1,035,000**

Source: Company documents

CHAPTER 2.2

Evaluating Start Up Ventures

William A. Sahlman, Ramana Nanda and Robert White

INTRODUCTION

This note summarizes a fundamental framework used to evaluate start up ventures. It draws heavily from the HBS note Some Thoughts on Business Plans written by Professor William Sahlman, 897-101. It provides a conceptual framework for understanding entrepreneurial venture creation and is called the POCD framework.

There are four key areas that are worth considering when evaluating or managing a startup venture: the People, the Opportunity, the External Context and Deals.

- The **People** are the individuals who will have an important impact on a venture, whether or not they are actual employees. This category includes founders and employees, of course, as well as advisors, investors, lawyers, and key suppliers. In some cases, even customers can be considered part of the team.
- The **Opportunity** is an intended product or service for which customers will pay more than it costs the venture to provide it. In economic terms, an opportunity is a positive net present value project where the value of customer inflows exceeds the value of outflows to all resource providers. To create and capture value, a company must have a differentiated product or service and/or a sustainable cost advantage. They must have benefits of scale, including scale economies and/or network effects. And they must build barriers to competition.
- The Context represents those factors that affect the outcome of the opportunity but that are generally outside management's direct control. This category includes interest rates, regulations, macroeconomic

Evaluating Start Up Ventures
by WILLIAM A.SAHLMAN, RAMANA NANDA, ROBERT WHITE, case number 9-819-039 AUGUST 29, 2018

activity, technology, and some industry variables like the competition or relative business bargaining power.

- The **Deals** are the implicit and explicit contractual relationships between the venture and all resource providers. Deals allocate cash and risk and therefore affect the venture's value. Examples of deals range from investment contracts to the terms of employment for managers. Ventures also strike important deals with customers and vendors.

The fundamental insight gained from studying hundreds of successful and unsuccessful ventures is the concept of integration, referred to as "**fit**," which is defined as the degree to which the people, the opportunity, the deal, and the context together influence the potential for success. Phrased differently, the degree of fit is the answer to the following questions:

- To what degree do the people have the right experience, skills and attitudes, given the nature of the opportunity, the context and the deals struck?
- To what degree does the opportunity make sense, given the people involved, the context and the deals struck?
- To what degree is the context favorable for the venture, given the people involved, the nature of the opportunity and the deals struck?
- To what degree do the deals involved in the venture make sense, given the people involved, the nature of the opportunity, and the context?

These questions focus attention on the fact that excellence in any single dimension is not sufficient: the proper perspective from which to make an evaluation takes into account all of the elements simultaneously. A diagram of the basic framework is provided in Appendix 1.

Nor is it sufficient to focus on these elements and their relationship from a static perspective. The people, opportunity, context and deal (and the relationship among them) are all likely to change over time as a company goes from identification of opportunity to harvest. To focus attention on the dynamic aspects of the entrepreneurial process, three related questions can be asked to guide the analysis of any business venture:

- What can go wrong?
- What can go right?
- What decisions can management make today and in the future to ensure that "what can go right" does go right, and "what can go

wrong" is avoided, or failing that, is prevented from critically damaging the enterprise? Phrased another way, what decisions can be made to tilt the reward to risk ratio in favor of the venture?

This framework and set of questions are extremely powerful in understanding how ventures evolve over time and how managers can affect outcomes. The balanced emphasis on anticipating (as opposed to predicting) good and bad news is a distinctive feature of the framework. Most people are adept at identifying risks, far fewer are practiced at foretelling the good news, and even fewer have thought systematically about how they can manage the reward to risk ratio. Yet, there are some recurrent themes in the world of venturing. That projects often take more time and money than originally estimated should not surprise people.

These questions described above concerning potential good and bad news also shed light on the fact that current decisions affect future decisions: some decisions open up or preserve options for future action while others destroy options. Managers must be cognizant of this relationship between current and future decisions.

According to this framework, great businesses have some easily identifiable (but hard to assemble) attributes. They have a world class managerial team in all dimensions, from the top to the bottom, and across all relevant functions. The teams have directly relevant skills and experiences for the opportunity they are pursuing. Ideally, the team has worked successfully together in the past. The opportunity has an attractive, sustainable business model: it offers a low cost or asset light alternative to current offerings, it displays network effects and scale economies and it is possible to create a competitive edge and to defend it through creation of barriers to entry. There are multiple options for expanding the scale and scope of the business and these options are unique to the enterprise and its team. There are a number of ways to extract value from the business either in a positive harvest event or in a scale down or liquidation mode. The context is favorable both with respect to the regulatory environment and the macroeconomic situation. The deals binding the people to the opportunity are sensible and robust: they provide the right incentives under a wide range of scenarios. The venture is financed by individuals or firms who add value in addition to their capital, thereby increasing the likelihood of success. The financing terms provide the right incentives for the provider and the recipient. There is access to additional capital on an as-warranted basis. In short, the venture is characterized by a high degree of dynamic **fit** (see Appendix 2 for a diagram of the expanded fit management framework). The role of management is to continuously adapt a business to improve the degree of fit: doing so does not guarantee success, but it does increase the odds.

People

When assessing any business venture, one should start by assessing the people involved.

- Who are the founders?
- What have they accomplished in the past?
- What is their relationship? Have they worked together previously?
- What directly relevant experience do they have for the opportunity they are pursuing?
- What knowledge and skills do they have?
- Whom do they know and who knows them?
- What is their reputation?
- How realistic are they?
- Can they design and execute efficient and effective experiments or tests?
- Can they adapt as circumstances warrant?
- Who else needs to be on the team?
- Are the founders prepared to recruit high quality people?
- How will the team respond to adversity?
- Can they make the inevitable hard choices that have to be made?
- What are their motivations?
- How committed are they to this venture?
- How can I gain objective information about each member of the team including how they will work together?
- What are the possible consequences if one or more of the team members leaves?

The model in venture capital is to back teams with great (directly relevant) track records who are pursuing attractive opportunities. The old adage in venture capital circles is: "I'd rather back an 'A' team with a 'B' idea than a 'B' team with an 'A' idea." Of course, the goal is to only back high-quality teams with high quality opportunities, but that is not always feasible.

The concept of an A team is different from a collection of A people. It's like a sports team that collectively does very well even when the individuals are not necessarily the best in each position. Successful entrepreneurial ventures have great teams who create and capture customer value.

Opportunity

An opportunity is a proposed venture to sell a product or service for which customers are willing to pay more than the required investments and operating costs. Resources include people, money, distributors and suppliers. The opportunity can be measured in terms of net present value – the present value of all potential cash inflows from customers less the present value of all required resources. Value is a function of cash, risk and time. In simple terms, more cash is preferred to less cash, cash sooner is preferred to cash later, and less risky cash is preferred to more risky cash.

An informative way to depict an opportunity is to draw a cash flow curve with cash flow on the Y axis and time on the X axis:

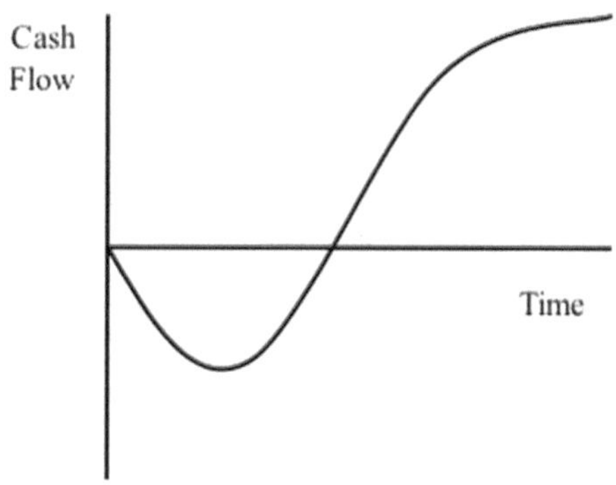

Typically, ventures have negative cash flow in the beginning – successful ventures have high positive cash flows later. A great opportunity is one in which it doesn't take much time or investment to generate high cash flows.

Entrepreneurs (individuals or teams) scan the environment for situations in which customers might be willing, over time, to pay more than all the costs and investments required. Entrepreneurs form hypotheses about what customers want or need and how they can deliver that. They structure a test, an experiment, in which they try to figure out if their idea is going to work. Typically, they recruit some people and invest some money to determine if customers will indeed value the product and if they can produce it and deliver it at an acceptable cost.[1]

It is useful to depict the experimentation process by adding perceived value as a second vertical axis and by showing the investments in each successive test that change perceived value of future cash flows from that point on:

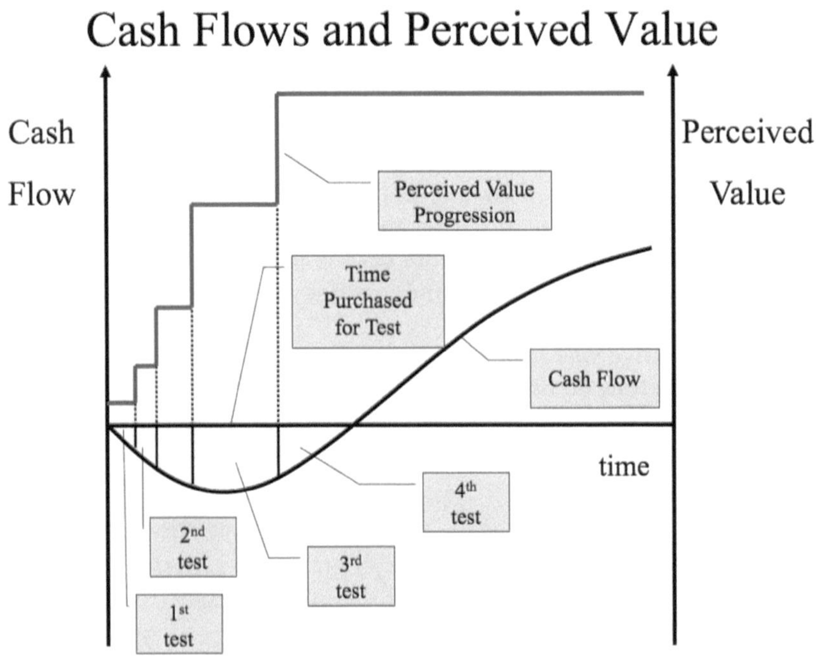

In words, a team raises money or uses personal savings – say $50,000 – that supports a 3-month test that enables them to create a prototype and test consumer feedback. If that test is encouraging the value assigned for the company might increase dramatically – say from $100,000 to $2 million – because expected cash flows are higher (amount and/or probability).

Based on the positive feedback, the team raises enough money – say $500,000 – to build a functional product that can be sold. That money might last for 9 months at which point the team and external investors will know more about customer willingness to pay, product function and durability, and costs, as well as the team's ability to execute.

As shown in the graphic, this process keeps repeating until the company fails, goes public, or has some other terminal event. At each point, based on previous tests, investors decide whether to keep backing the team or abandon the project. Members of the team – and customers, suppliers, etc. – also decide if it makes sense to continue or if they must modify the plan.

This is the fundamental nature of entrepreneurship – identifying a possible opportunity and then testing until the team and resource suppliers are confident they are on the right path. Often, an original venture idea is quickly abandoned or substantially modified. Often the team changes dramatically to match the evolving nature of the opportunity.

The graph used above is a stylized version – most real companies have curves that resemble roller coasters rather than rocket ships. To illustrate, a company like Federal Express almost went bankrupt after "Test 1" and again after "Test 2." In share price terms, the first round of financing was at $200, the second at $7 and the third at $1. By then, Federal Express had figured out how to deliver a package profitably from Los Angeles to San Francisco by going through Memphis, TN. Amazing!

Many entrepreneurial efforts aren't so lucky (or skilled). Sometimes the hypothesis about customer need or desire turns out to be wrong. Or it costs too much to develop or deliver the product or service. Sometimes, a competitor has a better plan or better execution and wins the day. Or the venture can't raise enough money to buy enough time to find a viable path.

The next major issue is the nature of the opportunity, starting first with an assessment of the potential Customer Value Proposition. Key questions are:

- What unmet needs will the venture address, and for which customer segments?
- Will the venture emphasize differentiation or cost savings? Is it an asset light disruptive business?
- What will be its product's key features? How will customers' willingness to pay for the venture's product compare to total cost of ownership?

Then one must assess the overall market potential and its characteristics. Obviously, all markets are not created equal: some are more attractive than others. One must look at the five factors when assessing the industry as described by HBS Professor Michael Porter (buyer power, supplier power, competitive rivalry, threat of new entry and threat of substitution). The goal is to pick industries that have lots of potential to create and protect value. Growth in sales is not equivalent to growth in value. Key initial questions are:

- Is the total addressable market for the venture's product or service large and/or rapidly growing?
- Is the industry one that is now or can become structurally attractive?

Finally, key elements of the business model must be assessed:[2]

- **Technology and Operations Management.** What activities will be required to develop and produce the venture's core offering? Which of those activities will be performed in-house? Who will perform outsourced activities, and under what terms? Will the venture create valuable intellectual property?

- **Go-To-Market Plan.** Through what mix of direct and indirect channels will the venture educate prospective customers, deliver its product, and provide after-sale service? Given the expected lifetime value of a customer, how much can the venture afford to spend to acquire a typical new customer? What mix of free and paid demand generation methods will it employ?
- **Cash Flow Formula.** What contribution margin will the venture earn per unit of product sold? Given expected fixed costs, what will be the breakeven sales volume, and what share of the total addressable market does this represent? How much investment in working capital and property, plant & equipment will be required per dollar of revenue? Given projected growth, how much cash will be required from external sources?

The other way to shed light on the riskiness of a project is to assign probabilities to different outcomes for returns on investment. The following diagram shows the payoff structure for an investment in a new software company:

PROBABILITY DISTRIBUTION FOR A HIGH RISK/HIGH REWARD FINTECH

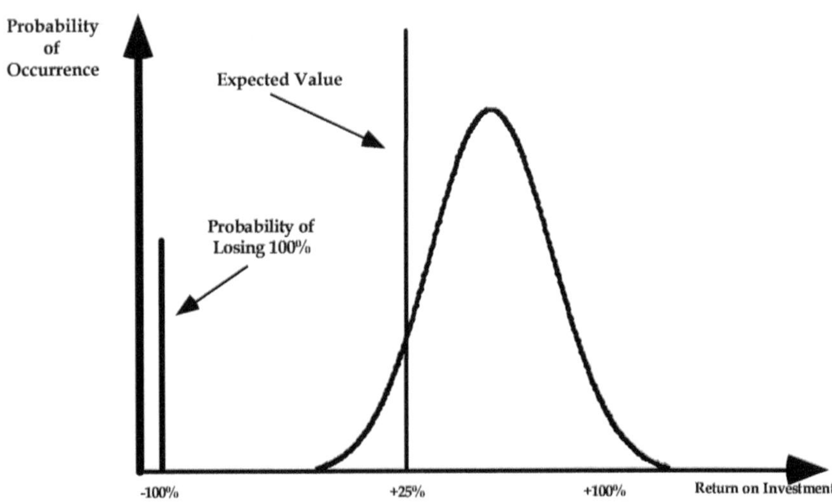

There is some considerable risk that you will lose all of your money. At the same time, I might well invest in the next Uber or Airbnb, in which case you will have very high returns, perhaps in excess of 100% per year. The picture above suggests that there is a small, perhaps even negligible probability of earning a small rate of return on an investment in a Fintech company. The rationale is that most small Fintech companies are not very profitable and are therefore not worth much very much. Unless the venture reaches escape velocity, it probably won't succeed.

In general, these types of graphical tools can be used to describe investment opportunities. Investments involve different combinations of capital requirements and payoffs. They involve differing degrees of uncertainty. To reiterate the obvious, you want opportunities that offer the prospect of high, safe returns on modest investment, with lots of attractive and proprietary growth options -- a simple rule to describe, but one that is almost impossible to follow in the real world.

Context

Opportunities exist in a context. At one level, there is the macroeconomic environment, including the level of economic activity, inflation, exchange rates, and interest rates. There are also a wide range of rules and regulations that affect opportunity and how resources are marshaled to exploit it. Examples range from tax policy to the rules concerning raising capital for a private or public company. Then, there are factors like technology, which affect what a business or its competitors can accomplish.

When assessing start up ventures, look for two pieces of evidence related to context. First, see that the entrepreneurial team is aware of the context and how it helps or hinders their specific proposal. Second, and more importantly, look for sensitivity to the fact that the context will inevitably change. If so, how might the changes affect the business? And, what can management do in the event the context worsens? Finally, are there ways in which management can affect context in a positive way? For example, can management have an impact on regulation or on setting industry standards?

Deals

Most people think of valuation and terms when considering deals. What share of the company will they have to give to the investors to raise capital? What are the terms of the financing? These are the prominent questions. Equally important is how much money is being raise and from whom.

Ventures are inherently risky. Most ventures end up taking more time and more money than the entrepreneur ever imagined. The name of the game, then, is not to minimize dilution at each stage of a company's existence but rather to maximize the value of your share at the end of the process.

When the inevitable bad news arrives, inexperienced investors often panic and get angry. They refuse to advance the company more money. They are surprised that results are disappointing. In such situations, it is often difficult to recruit new investors. The new investor has to worry about the old investor group -- if they're not putting up more money, what's wrong? The old investors are also reticent to accept the valuation proposed by the new investor. Picking the right investors who can add value and are experienced when things don't go right are critical.

An old saying is "time is money." In entrepreneurial finance, the expression gets turned around: "money is time." - money buys time for a venture to find the right combination of people, strategy, and tactics to succeed. Each chunk of money buys an additional chunk of time.

Sensible deals have the following characteristics:

- They are simple
- They are fair
- They reflect trust rather than legalese
- They are robust - they do not blow apart if actual differs slightly from plan
- They do not provide perverse incentives that will cause one or both parties to behave in destructive ways
- They do not foreclose valuable options
- The papers used to describe the deal are no greater than one-quarter inch

No discussion of deals would be complete without a section on valuation. How are ventures valued, particularly ones for which there is massive uncertainty? The venture investor knows from hard-earned experience that few if any ventures come anywhere close to meeting their projections. Only 10% to 20% of the deals in which they invest will do really well. Some 30% will actually result in losses, in some cases complete loss. What seasoned investors do, therefore, is base their valuations on the overall experience they have had.

In closing, this section on deals has been implicitly based on a simple set of structured questions, which are listed below:

- From whom should the money be raised?
- How much money is needed and for what purpose?
- What deal terms are fair and provide the appropriate incentives for each side under a wide range of scenarios?

Risk/Reward Management

One fascinating aspect of business is the degree to which the future is hard to predict. It is certainly possible to write down a detailed description of a bright future, but hard to make it happen. The notion above that there is a known probability distribution for outcomes is useful but slightly misleading. There are no immutable distributions of outcomes. It is ultimately the responsibility of management to change the distribution, to increase the likelihood and consequences of success and decrease the likelihood and implications of problems.

RISK/REWARD MANAGEMENT

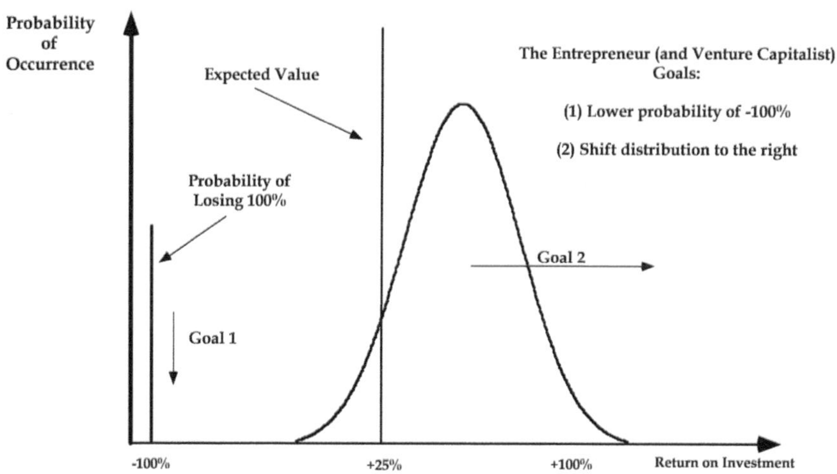

Summary and Conclusion

In summary, when evaluating a new venture you must provide reasonable answers to the following questions:

- Who are the **people** involved? What have they done in the past that would lead one to believe that they will be successful in the future? Who is missing from the team and how will they be attracted?
- What is the nature of the **opportunity**? How will the company create and capture value? Can the company develop a differentiated product or service and/or can it create an enduring cost advantage? How is the opportunity likely to evolve? Are there benefits of scale, including network effects? Can entry barriers be built and maintained? What are the key characteristics of its business model?
- What **contextual factors** will affect the venture? What contextual changes are likely to occur, and how can management respond to those changes?
- What **deals** have been or are likely to be struck inside and outside the venture? Do the deals struck increase the likelihood of success? How will those deals and the implicit incentives evolve over time?
- What decisions have been made (or can be made) to increase the ratio of reward to risk?

In thinking through the answers to these questions, a deeper understanding of the Opportunity and the Context will provide a robust sense of the venture's cash flow potential if it is successful, as well as a sense of the transition path to achieve those cash flows prior to generating revenue and achieving scale. A deeper understanding of the People and Deals will provide a sense of how likely it is that the venture will succeed and what the probability distribution of outcomes is likely to look like. Taking these components together, this framework allows investors to evaluate and assess the potential of startup ventures without access to detailed data.

APPENDIX 1

THE CONCEPT OF FIT

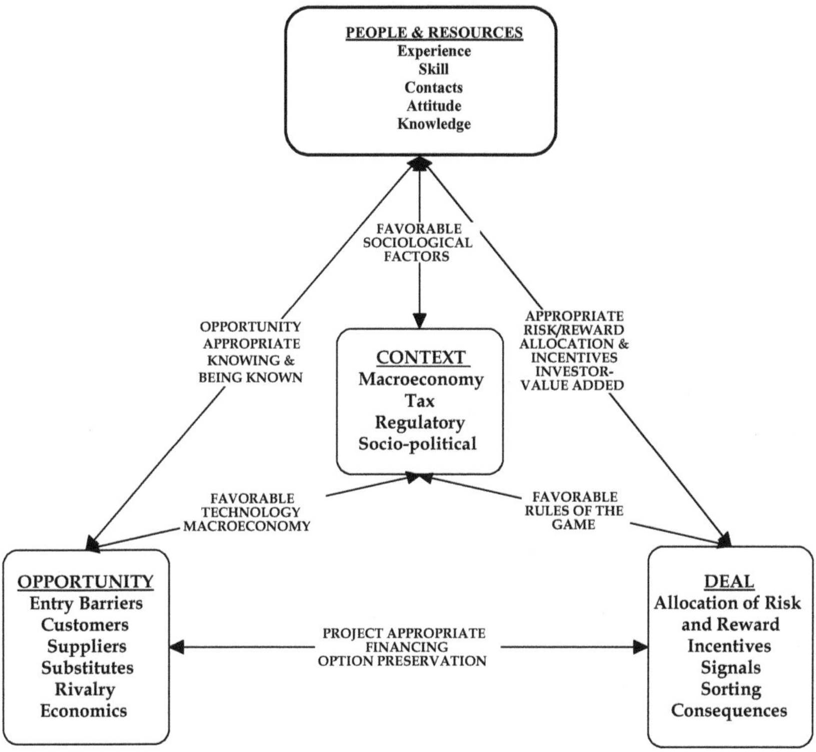

Source: Casewriters.

APPENDIX 2

DYNAMIC FIT MANAGEMENT

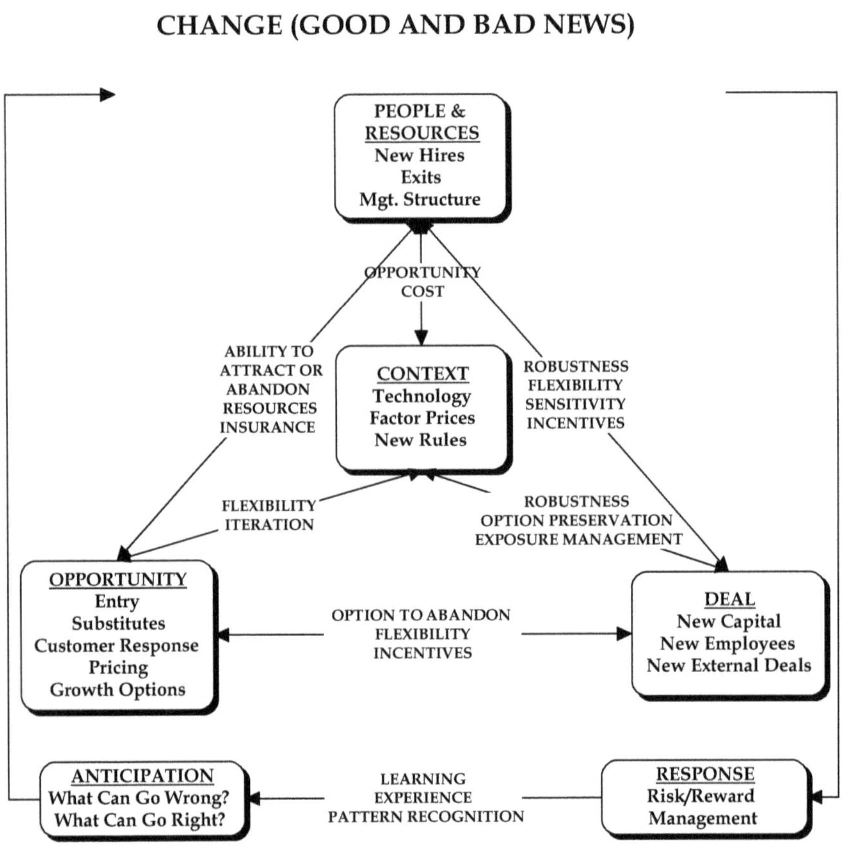

Source: Casewriters.

NOTES

1 Many essays focus on the "lean startup" methodology for discovery, as in works by Eric Ries and Steve Blank. The methodology entails creating products, getting customer feedback, and iterating, all in the least amount of time and at the lowest cost. This note focuses on the process of creating a successful venture, as distinct from a product, and also note that the nature of competition will play an important role in determining the speed and capital required for the business to succeed.

2 Drawn from Kerr, William R., and Mark Roberge. "The Entrepreneurial Manager, Module I: Defining and Developing the Business Model." HBS No. 817-108 (2017).

CHAPTER 2.3

SRS and the Defense Innovation Unit: Rethinking Procurement

Paul A. Gompers and David Lane

In January 2015, Jesse Rodocker and his wife Tracey[a] co-founded Strategic Robotic Systems (SRS) to build the "next generation" submersible remote-operated vehicle (ROV), the SRS FUSION (see **Exhibit 1**). With 15 years of experience in the ROV business, including previous sales to the U.S. Navy, Rodocker designed the FUSION with features and capabilities that he knew appealed to military needs. Given the complexities of winning a major government procurement contract, he also structured SRS carefully to ensure it could sustain a procurement process of up to seven years.

In January 2018, Rodocker proposed the FUSION in response to a U.S. Department of Defense (DoD) invitation for submissions that had been posted by the DoD's Defense Innovation Unit (DIU). Headquartered in Silicon Valley, the DIU aimed to accelerate the military's acquisition of commercial technologies. It assessed company offerings for their relevance to DoD program objectives and purchased prototypes of the most promising for DoD testing. For the vendors—many of them early-stage entrepreneurial ventures—this generated revenues, validated sometimes-nascent products and approaches, and could lead directly, after DoD testing, to production contracts. For DoD clients, DIU prototype agreements provided the chance to test and purchase promising commercial technologies that could materially address DoD challenges and get solutions into the hands of its end users within three years.

a For the purpose of the case, Jesse will be referred to by his last name, his wife by her first name.

SRS and the Defense Innovation Unit: Rethinking Procurement
by PAUL A. GOMPERS, DAVID LANE, case number 9-220-047 MARCH 18, 2020

THE DEFENSE ACQUISITIONS PROCESS

Getting new products into the military typically was a long and complex process. Navigating this process often took deep institutional knowledge, persistence, and the ability to clear multiple hurdles. Three years represented unprecedented speed for DoD acquisitions, which could be staggeringly complicated (see **Exhibit 2** for a generic flowchart). Like almost every other executive-branch agency, the DoD normally acquired weaponry and equipment via the U.S. government's Federal Acquisition Regulation (FAR) process. The process was described in a document that ran over 1,900 pages, excluding a DoD supplement of nearly 1,500 more pages[1] and multiple DoD-specific guidebooks.[2] Among FAR's more unusual provisions were protocols governing interaction between the DoD and contractors in an effort to mitigate potential bias and favoritism, and the opportunity for contractors to protest and have contracts re-awarded if either the DoD or the contract winner violated project solicitation terms.[3]

The contracting process alone could consume 18 months or more,[4] and pre-acquisition technology development, proposals, and contract negotiations collectively delayed the start of production for between two and five years.[5] An average of seven more years passed before major weapons systems were available for use in the field.[6]

Moreover, no FAR contract could proceed unless and until funded by Congress. This meant including DoD statements and funding requests for every program objective in the annual congressional National Defense Authorization bill, whose eventual passage authorized spending requests for final appropriation.[7] In practice, therefore, DoD acquisitions officials needed to time and submit requests for funds two years in advance of their expected use.

THE DEFENSE INNOVATION UNIT

The DIU was created in 2015 as an alternative to this onerous process. Central to the DIU mission was the acquisition of commercial technologies by the armed forces at commercial speeds, thereby boosting military capabilities while supporting U.S. innovation in products and services related to national security—what the DIU termed "strengthening the national security innovation base" (NSIB). The commercial focus reflected the increasing availability and relevance of commercial technologies for military uses. It was also recognition that businesses other than government labs or military contractors had conducted an ever-growing share of U.S. research and development (R&D) over the post-World War II period. The combined R&D spending of the five dominant U.S. military contractors in 2018 barely exceeded one-third of Amazon's $22.6 billion in R&D spending that year.[8] Over the five years through 2018, moreover, private start-ups had raised $48 billion to invest in artificial intelligence (AI) and machine learning, and $16 billion for driverless vehicles, drones, and robotics.[9] These areas represented important areas for the military, and civilian-developed technologies could potentially bolster the military's capabilities.

THE DIU PROCESS

To these ends, the DIU benefited from an alternative contracting approach to FAR that was made permanent in 2016. This approach, called Other Transaction Authority (OTA), was designed to fund the research, prototyping, and production of dual-use technologies by either small businesses or non-traditional military contractors.[10,b]

In tandem, the DIU developed a rapid contracting process to validate requests from DoD clients within its service arms to determine the potential ability of commercial vendors to deliver impactful solutions, and solicit and evaluate bids for prototype systems. Successful vendors were offered OTA agreements to supply prototypes for evaluation and testing by the DoD client, with the ultimate aim of transitioning from prototype agreement to production contract (see **Exhibit 3**). To take just one example, successful prototyping of commercial AI software showed that predictive rather than time-based maintenance could cut up to $5 billion per year from the DoD's annual $45 billion aircraft maintenance bill and boost available flying time.[11]

Companies also benefited from the fact that the DIU was not dedicated to a specific DoD service arm, unlike some of the other roughly 70 DoD innovation organizations. One such organization was SOFWERX, which supported innovation by engaging industry and academia to address challenges germane to Special Forces needs via hackathons, crowdsourcing contests, and funding for hardware and software prototypes.[c] One of the most active of these organizations was AFWERX, an Air Force effort launched in 2017 to catalyze innovation by supporting private R&D via Small Business

---

b Non-traditional companies included defense contractors that had not done business with the DoD for a year or longer.

c For additional information, see Herman Leonard, Mitchell Weiss, Jin Hyun Paik, and Kerry Herman, "SOFWERX: Innovation at U.S. Special Forces Command," HBS No. 819-004 (Boston: Harvard Business Publishing, 2018).

Innovation Research (SBIR) grants and contracts.[d] Each year, the federal government awarded nearly $2.5 billion in SBIR funding, nearly half of which went to companies with fewer than 25 employees. These grants were for the development of technologies that met specific needs. Roughly half of the annual grants fell under one of the DoD's branches. Phase I SBIR grants were typically up to $150,000 while follow-on Phase II grants might reach $750,000. Only at Phase III, however, did recipient companies pursue commercialization of the technologies supported with earlier funding. To encourage the transition toward commercialization, the Air Force had launched Strategic Phase 2 SBIR awards, which required 25% combined government contribution (from organizations such as AFWERX), 25% Air Force contribution, and 50% company investor contribution.[12] As a DIU manager related, "This signals to private investors that a market exists for the start-up's technology and encourages them to match it."

The DIU differentiated itself by working only with individuals and companies able to demonstrate a viable product, and by attempting to locate DoD customers for that technology in as many as possible of the 50-60 purchasing offices throughout the Army, Navy, Air Force, and Marine Corps. The DIU's OTA budget authority also created a clear pathway to follow prototype agreements with production contracts under either OTA or FAR conditions.

While the DIU supported each service arm, it focused on projects within five portfolios: AI applications; autonomy (drones and unmanned vehicles); cyber (both warfare and security); human systems (to improve battlefield survivability); and space (to benefit from growing commercial investment).[13] To develop and execute on these projects, the DIU employed roughly 125 people at headquarters in Silicon Valley and offices in Austin, Texas; Boston, Massachusetts; and Washington, DC. Roughly 90% were active-duty or retired military personnel. DIU defense engagement teams focused on DoD customers to hone and curate DoD project requirements. After market research to confirm the existence of private sector suppliers of potential solutions, the DIU project decision board—akin to an investment firm's investment committee—met to decide which projects DIU project managers would take forward into a three-phase competitive sourcing process that covered the following steps (see **Exhibit 4** for details):

d For a description of SBIR funding available across U.S. executive agencies, see Karim Lakhani, Peter Barrett, and Noubar Afeyan, "Note on Funding Deep Tech Startups," HBS No. 620-029 (Boston: Harvard Business Publishing, 2019).

Phase 1 Translating DoD needs into actionable project statements posted to the DIU website and RSS feed to solicit interest from commercial vendors; evaluating vendor submissions for relevance, technical merit, business viability, and innovation;

Phase 2 Hosting vendor pitches, demonstrations, and evaluations of the most promising vendor products and services submitted in phase 1, with input from DoD customer representatives; and

Phase 3 Selecting the best vendor solutions from phase 2 and negotiating prototype agreements enabling equipment purchases sufficient for subsequent months of DoD testing and evaluation.

Phase 1: Solution Briefs

Interested parties had two weeks to respond to a DIU project statement with proposed solutions. Unlike the substantial submissions the FAR process required, the DIU preferred to limit the burden on submitters and evaluators alike to short briefs. Crafting effective program statements (which the DIU called AOIs) quickly became a critical skill for project managers, as DIU Project Manager Eddie Brown explained:

> Once the AOI is posted, it becomes the one immovable object in the entire process and the basis of our decision-making. Everything else is negotiable. The process is designed to generate learning from commercial firms at every stage. The AOI states the problem, and industry presents their solutions. We avoid stating specifications and requirements, if possible. Because we define the problem and not the solution space, invariably we are surprised with novel answers and unexpected approaches.

Phase 2: Vendor Pitches

Within 30 days of initial submissions, the DIU invited several of the most promising vendors to a government facility to explain and demonstrate their solutions to a team that typically included a DIU project manager, a representative from the DoD program office behind the initial request, and one or more DoD technical experts. The evaluating team sought specifics on how vendor solutions worked, how much each cost, and the time needed to deliver a prototype. (DoD-requested modifications normally lengthened prototype delivery time and cost.) Brown elaborated: "We want to see if they can do what they say they can do and whether their engineering and technical teams can get to where they need to be. We are not evaluating for the best prototype. Their pitches and the product demonstrations can reveal companies that overextend themselves or can't perform. That itself educates us further." He scheduled phase 2 discussions during the mornings: one hour for the company's pitch, one for company dialog with the evaluating team, and a final hour limited to the evaluating team's assessment. Product demonstrations followed in the afternoon.

Brown particularly valued the final morning hour, which offered a window into the priorities and views of the DoD user base. The opportunity for vendors to sit down with DoD representatives provided useful insights to all parties as well, not least to the companies. By contrast, the FAR process featured double-blind procedures that prohibited interaction between vendors and the DoD customer. Instead, FAR imposed source selection panels that were isolated from the DoD, much like a sequestered jury, with no opportunity to interact directly with companies or DoD customers. Brown explained:

> Under the FAR process, companies submit proposals, and if evaluators have questions, they have to guess at the answers by attempting to interpret the language of the proposals. There are a limited number of rounds in which evaluators can write out a question and have it approved and submitted to the vendor. Sometimes those questions need to be shared publicly with rival respondents, all before an answer comes back. It's like a weird game of Telephone.[e] It is difficult to get clarification, or to get questions asked and answered.

Phase 3: Negotiating Prototype Agreements

In phase 3, DIU project managers negotiated prototype agreements with two or more of the best performers from phase 2. The agreements covered cost, schedule, performance, and property rights. To inform negotiations, DIU project managers often teamed with DoD funding officers and representatives from the DoD program office responsible for the relevant equipment type. Also discussed were DoD field testing plans for each firm's product, which typically consumed multiple months after prototype delivery. Brown explained:

e The game of "Telephone" ("Chinese Whispers" in England and "Quiet Post" in Germany) asked players to repeat a message down a chain of participants. The message at the end often barely resembles the original message.

> We ask if company representatives can come out and observe the testing at their own expense. That's unusual for the government, but doing so leads them to make adjustments on the fly that strengthen their application if they see a chance to do better. The companies are willing to do it at no cost to gain frontline access to users of their equipment as they test and grade it. We permit a great deal of cooperation that is not captured in the text of the prototyping agreement. That too is very unusual compared to the FAR process.

The DIU also differed from FAR by negotiating rather than appropriating companies' intellectual property rights. From the start of every DIU project, companies were asked to identify any IP assets they shared with the DIU. Thereafter, companies normally retained ownership of IP created during the project but licensed it to the DoD for limited purposes in conformance with negotiated rights to its use, disclosure, and reproduction.[14] Typically this allowed basic engineering, maintenance, and training on the equipment the DoD purchased. Flexibility went a long way, Brown explained:

> Issues of IP control can alarm companies and subvert deals. The government sometimes doesn't understand what it takes to run a business, and companies don't understand what government needs. The DIU approach is about trying to bridge this gap. We will talk about what we want to do with a piece of technology and why IP rights should be written a certain way, and you as a company can come back and tell us where we may be wrong, redefine your submission, or have us redefine ours.

Progress, Potential, and Pathways to Production

The DIU aimed to award prototype agreements within 60 days of posting a solicitation of interest on its website. In practice, the figure was closer to 90-100 days, but even this pace was unrivaled for DoD program officers accustomed to the lengthy FAR process. Between June 2016 and December 2018, the DIU signed 104 prototype agreements totaling $354 million with 87 non-traditional vendors, 43 of which had never previously worked with the DoD.[15] Because each prototype had been competitively sourced, suppliers under OTA rules could transition directly to production contracts.[16] Even so, testing and production contract timing meant that products successfully prototyped by the DIU process were only starting to reach DoD end users in 2019.

Nevertheless, the DIU process did offer early-stage start-ups access to a potentially massive and undiscovered market, and it could potentially offer a source of revenue to help bring products to market. A DIU prototype contract also alerted investors to market interest in a company's products, technology, and capabilities. DIU Director Michael Brown stated, "Prototype revenue is not exactly financing for entrepreneurial ventures, but we have found that every $1 we spend generates up to $10 in equity investment from venture capital backers."

STRATEGIC ROBOTIC SYSTEMS

In some ways, DIU's objectives and approach seemed a perfect fit for SRS. Rodocker had designed the FUSION to supersede existing ROVs, with particular focus on military applications. He and his father had previously co-founded and led the ROV maker SeaBotix for a decade, selling it late in 2010 to Connecticut-based Bolt Technology Group for an initial cash payment of $11.5 million.[17] SeaBotix ROVs were used in the oil and gas, aquaculture, and hydropower and nuclear energy industries, as well as for underwater search and recovery, scientific research, and maritime security.[18] The U.S. Navy was a SeaBotix customer, and many hours of field observation revealed to Rodocker the operational limitations of existing ROVs. At the end of a rewarding four-year earn-out period with Bolt, Rodocker founded SRS in January 2015 to deliver a new ROV with unparalleled capabilities and ease of use.

ROVs normally comprised an underwater vehicle to which various off-the-shelf sensors and payloads were attached. The vehicle was controlled and powered via a tether, which also conveyed video and sensor feed to operators at the surface. The habit of purchasing sensors and payloads gave ROV makers the flexibility to offer products for specific use cases, and at one point SeaBotix sold 12 different ROV models. To Rodocker, however, this approach "lacked integration, came at the expense of an intuitive user experience, and made ROV delivery and development dependent on supplier responsiveness." The FUSION was different, seamlessly integrating functionality with superior performance. Rodocker likened it to Apple's iPhone:

> We have the first smartphone of the underwater robotics industry. Like Apple, we control both hardware and software. My previous firm makes ROVs, equivalent to the cell phone. Other firms make autonomous underwater vehicles, equivalent to iPods. Still others make navigation devices and sensors—think Palm Pilots or GPS. Every other

> ROV is mounted with third-party sensors. We combine them into a single product with a unique user interface that uses the most integrated, cleanest software of any, bar none.

While at SeaBotix, Rodocker had gotten to know the industry's sensor and component makers. In designing the FUSION, he approached what he felt was the best company for each technology and invited them to partner with SRS on a bespoke version of their existing products. He also offered them sweat equity in order to create a vested interest in the FUSION's success:

> We brought together strategic partners to develop the product as if built from the ground up. Some were more favorably disposed to cash payment than to equity—depending on how well they knew me, my track record, and if they knew the industry well enough to grasp the potential of the product concept. All received some cash, if only to cover the costs of the development needed to supply the upgraded components. The benefit wasn't the cash. That would come from the equity. SRS is the only company in the industry like this.

This arrangement allowed SRS to reduce its Series A capital needs to $2 million over five years, which it raised from accredited investors first in the form of restricted shares that paid interest, and then from raising preferred shares. Capital was drawn down as needed in order to limit the interest expense incurred by unused balances. Roughly 25% of the firm's equity went to "sweat equity" partners. Several owners of these firms later invested personal funds in SRS too. **Exhibit 5** describes SRS partners and core SRS staff. This approach brought several other benefits, as Rodocker explained:

> We knew from experience that starting with a complete team to do everything yourself imposes a much higher initial cost. The partnerships allowed us to tap into engineering expertise and production capabilities. Our U.K. partner works on acoustic imaging sensors and the electronics rack. Our Norwegian partner makes an acoustic positioning system for us. Our Australian partner produces cameras, arms, and lights to our specifications, while our Portuguese partner wrote critical software code. We put the onus on them to build it, test it, and configure it just as we wanted it. As a result, we don't need our own staff to do so.

> The components arrive already certified for conformity; we do final assembly and testing. We use contract manufacturers and mold rather than machine some parts for further economies. The result is a base system that integrates the best available sensors and capabilities, everything the operator needs in the field. All functionality is built-in; operating any add-on modules requires no modification.

Targeting Military Customers

Rodocker designed the FUSION to address specific mine clearing and disposal of explosive ordinance (EOD) needs. This assumed that the FUSION would significantly outperform all other options, but prior experience gave him room for optimism, he said: "For some time, the military has needed to be able to get ROVs farther away from the boats that operate them to do things like blow things up underwater. Traditionally you can't do that with a small boat because the attached cable creates too much drag. Our tether is thinner, and comes in lengths of up to two kilometers. We are the only firm with a cable that allows functional operation." This was because the FUSION was designed to be battery-powered—the FUSION tether could be thinner because it was used only for sensor data and telemetry, and not as the vehicle's power supply. Eventually Rodocker added the ability to operate the FUSION untethered for roughly three hours at a time, using an onboard acoustic navigation system.

Rodocker also preferred military clients to commercial clients. Government customers purchased ROVs in greater quantities than commercial clients did, and the military represented a larger potential market than commercial customers. "ROVs are built with a one-off approach that commercial customers try to adapt to various scenarios. Commercial clients will buy one or two units and usually expect FUSION to do something that only more expensive systems can," he observed. "The military specifies what task needs to be done and wants equipment that performs that task well. In my view, clients are a company's largest consumer of labor, and 15 military clients are much easier to manage than 100 commercial clients."

The Rodockers wrote their business plan anticipating spending five to seven years to develop the FUSION and to solicit for and receive a major production contract. This posed risks, he recounted:

> Knowing that it would take longer, the biggest piece of the gamble was the need for more funding upfront, which meant more to repay investors. But what if the military contract took even longer? What if we did not win it? We hedged risk by keeping the company small, with a very low breakeven in unit terms, both to avoid overhead and to weather

that storm. Low breakeven also gave us the fallback option of commercial sales at lower volumes.

Designing the FUSION to excel at the relatively narrow tasks of locating and clearing mines was a further gamble, Rodocker noted: "We would need to sustain the business without cash flow for a specific set of customers. But we had built a military product without a military price tag—the base system costs $250,000—and we believed that if we could satisfy hard-to-please EOD customers, we would satisfy others too." Although SRS remained lean to keep risk low, production of the FUSION could be scaled quickly, both up and down. "Typically," he noted, "in bootstrapping operations you can't afford everything you want in the early days, so you plan to build them five years out. When that time comes, it's often still hard to devote resources to them. Instead, we started with all the pieces in place with an easily scalable operating model."

Until its first sale in July 2017, SRS employed only four people: the Rodockers, a mechanical designer, and a fourth developer focused on prototype development. Tracey ran commercial management, finances, and accounting; Rodocker focused on business development. SRS first sold a few FUSION units commercially, then placed others with foreign search and rescue organizations. There were FUSION operators within the DoD too, who acquired the ROV through the Defense Logistics Agency. "That *just* sustained us while we worked for bigger government contracts," Rodocker said. Over six to eight months, these sales led SRS to double its technical and administrative staff while tripling production capacity. As he explained:

> We kept it very lean until we needed it, adding assembly technicians and an inventory storage person to the production team, so that the business remained easily scalable based on order volumes and without material overhead costs tied directly to revenue. Our overhead flatlines very quickly as revenues grow. Our profit margin gets very high once we break even. It's hard to be definite about the market size—we think growth will be several billion dollars over a five-year period, but our business plan was based on selling 250 systems in that time. Our crew can build approximately 50 systems a year. If we want to build 75 systems a year, we only need to add one technician.

APPLYING THE DIU PROCESS

In January 2018, the DIU posted a program statement seeking an unmanned solution to the dangerous task of disarming naval mines. Eddie Brown explained: "For years, the Navy assigned highly trained people, who are expensive and hard to replace, to swim up to and disarm live mines. Having a human in the water as the first choice for explosive ordnance demolition seemed illogical, if not ludicrous. We decided to do what we could to end this situation." The effort was sponsored by the Navy's EOD program management office, with technical support from a San Diego Naval engineering center. The program statement requested tethered ROVs that could operate to depths of 600 feet but weighed no more than 88 pounds in order to be deployed from inflatable boats. Companies submitting successful proposals would be asked to demonstrate their product within a matter of weeks (see **Exhibit 6**). Mention of the product demonstration was included to reduce the number of submissions that did not have an active company behind them.

Four firms submitted solution briefs, fewer than Brown had hoped: "We were underwhelmed by the number of responses, but we were a relatively unknown organization, and companies were more interested in traditional Navy acquisition channels." The submissions came from SRS, from Rodocker's previous company, from a third ROV maker, and from a fourth, more software-oriented company that was not brought forward to phase 2.

The Rodockers were comfortable with the initial phase: Tracey appreciated that the project statement did not call for the lengthy submissions that FAR solicitations imposed. Jesse was pleased to learn that his rivals included the two firms he had expected, both of which he knew well. He added:

> We quickly realized that this was a more commercial approach: it was more open, and DIU removed lot of existing barriers. We found that we could ask very specific and pointed questions about DIU and DoD goals and expectations There were no guarantees we would win, but they did communicate what they were looking for.
>
> We had been going down an existing path, and their guidance allowed us to calculate how—if we deviated to accommodate their requests in some area—we could still meet their interests. Following the traditional process, we would never know what they actually wanted. We would offer something, thinking, "Hopefully that's good enough," throw the submission paper over the wall, and get some Navy assessment back over the wall. The open discussion we had through DIU was very refreshing.

As project manager, Brown was quickly impressed by SRS. Unlike the other firms, SRS was represented solely by Rodocker, who transported and demonstrated the FUSION himself. "He was an expert on it," Brown recalled. "It became very evident that Jesse's approach was incredibly tight and well-integrated, that he had a deep understanding both of the mission space and of users' pain points." The DoD representatives Brown invited to evaluate the pitches and demonstrations were split, however. There were two evaluator groups—engineers, to ensure technical soundness, and the actual end users. The engineers preferred a different ROV, Brown said:

> It could do heavy lifting under the waves, to the point that its power requirements at depth taxed the generators on hand. It was made by an older company and had a less refined user interface. This required greater piloting skill and consumed more power. Each excelled at a different purpose, but the users clearly preferred the look, feel, and intuitive operation of the red one, to the point that pressure was put on the engineers, temporarily disrupting our evaluation process.

All three ROVs advanced to phase 3 and each firm signed prototype agreements to supply two ROVs. In the process, Rodocker learned that his was the least expensive of the three. "To be frank, we did not expect to be," he said. "We were designed to be the best performer at a good price, and it turned out we were better *and* cheaper." Given the Navy's budget for each firm's prototypes, the price advantage gave SRS additional leverage during the subsequent nine months of prototype testing, Rodocker explained: "For $600,000, the Navy bought two FUSION systems from us plus the dual, multi-function arms that we offer for $80,000 and our acoustic positioning system for $25,000. For the other two companies, that sum covered only the cost of two basic systems, with no arms or positioning system."

Although the Navy viewed the FUSION as a superior product, it expressed doubt that a firm as small as SRS could scale up rapidly enough to deliver quality production on schedule. Brown explained:

> The issue was not in Jesse's supply chain or his partners. The issue was that the Navy did not believe that a company with just a handful of workers could do it. The government does not necessarily understand managing commercial risk or how entrepreneurial ventures are run. The assumption was that only a large organization could deliver. A lot of government workers also think that businesses are flush with cash and can operate for years without being paid. There can be a lot of misinterpretation.

Brown successfully overcame Navy concerns and dove into the prototype testing process: "Once we had three performing ROV prototypes, we stuck them in the water together and tested them side by side. FAR would prohibit exposing vendors to each other's products, but it's informative and really engages the companies. They improve the ROVs on the spot at their own cost because they want to win this." SRS, for instance, added new features to the FUSION, including optional side-scanning sonar and the ability to operate untethered.

Independently, Rodocker confirmed Brown's conclusion: "A U.S. Navy contract is the Holy Grail to us. It was an open contest with potential for a great number of units sold, and we knew there were a very limited number of players, so we went after it. The U.S. Navy is regarded as one of the best in the world, so plenty of others will opt for the same suppliers. We knew that winning a Navy production contract would open other doors."

During prototype testing, Brown shocked the EOD sponsoring office with a photo of the ROVs in the water (see **Exhibit** 7). Three things prompted their surprise, he explained:

> First was simply seeing all three products side by side and allowing the vendors to see who they are and how they are doing. Second, the ROVs were holding still in the water and not tangled in each others' tethers. Ordinarily there's a high risk that putting them together would mean that a small amount of mis-piloting would result in them becoming tangled up together and require a diver to go untangle them. Finally, we had a photo available of all three products being compared within months of the initial request for proposals. That was much faster than the typical acquisition process.

BUILDING DIU CAPACITY

The EOD reaction suggested that the DIU could take pride in having successfully delivered on its mission. Yet larger questions remained. SRS was hardly a generic small business—Rodocker had designed the FUSION specifically for EOD needs and structured SRS leanly around the goal of securing government customers. His extensive prior experience with both ROV manufacturing and Navy operations were uncommon among early-stage ventures. Awarding a production contract to SRS might very well be the best choice for Navy users. It also could materially boost the Rodockers' business, rewarding their judicious planning and careful execution. But what benefits would the Navy receive other than to hasten a logical outcome? Was an easy test of the DIU process adequate validation of its efficacy? What stretch goals would best build additional DIU capacity?

Events in 2019 suggested an expanded vision for the organization. That year, the DIU absorbed two other DoD efforts focused on early-stage ventures. The National Security Innovation Capital (NSIC) aimed to invest in start-ups making dual-use hardware that were "either underserved or deemed too risky by private investors."[19] The DIU had observed that over 90% of U.S. venture capital funding supported software rather than hardware manufacturers. By helping to create entirely new dual-use hardware vendors, the NSIC would support the broader DIU mission of strengthening the NSIB. This would include high-cost, high-risk ventures in such areas as commercial space, quantum sensing, and rare-earth distillation.[20] NSIC investments would be informed by relationships the DoD formed with venture capital firms, hardware incubators, and private research laboratories.[21] This opportunity potentially gave DIU the ability to dramatically accelerate the development of technologies that the DoD could field. The DIU also absorbed the National Security Innovation Network (NSIN), an organization tasked—like SOFWERX for the Special Forces—with supporting collaboration among early-stage private ventures, academia, and military laboratories to generate innovative solutions to varied national security challenges.[22] Collectively, the core DIU prototyping business, plus NSIC and NSIN, would cover multiple stages of technology development, from advanced conceptual development to production (see **Exhibit 8**).

The opportunity to invest directly into start-ups was new for DIU, but Rodocker expressed skepticism:

> The DIU stayed agnostic or neutral toward the three companies competing for the EOD project. DIU equity ownership in SRS would have created a conflict of interest, particularly if the others were left out. Accepting government funds will drive you in their direction. Not doing so preserves the freedom to accept input from multiple sources. Successful examples exist though. The U.S. Navy has funded some projects heavily, and can represent a viable customer for companies that are willing to sell to just one customer. But doing so will discourage you from pursuing other paths.

Other federal sources of funding, such as the SBIR process, did not restrict development results exclusively to the government, he noted. Indeed, SBIR had made awards for little more than a product concept. Over time, moreover, SBIR funding could grow and deepen in step with progress made by the awardee, making it a relatively low-risk source of support.

As the DIU deepened its exposure to early-stage technology, its managers would need to consider whether and how equity investments would best align private and public interests. How would the deals be sourced? Who would make the investment decisions? How would the investment managers be compensated? How could the power to invest help build scale for the

DIU? There were clearly other sources of funding for start-ups available from the DoD, and other funding approaches might yield better results for firms at other stages of development. For that matter, tools other than funding might contribute more effectively to increased DIU capacity. For the foreseeable future, DIU projects would remain a fraction of overall DoD procurement spending. What leverage might propel the DIU beyond experimental scale? How could it have a material impact on attracting firms able to enhance military capabilities while also deepening the U.S. national security infrastructure base? Some of the answers surely lay in the learning that would flow from projects yet to come. DIU Director Michael Brown wondered how to navigate the next chapter of DIU's mission.

NOTES

1 Bret Boyd, "Defense Acquisition Reform Is a National Security Issue," Grayline Capital LLC, 2016-2019, https://graylinegroup.com/defense-acquisition-reform-is-a-national-security-issue/, accessed March 2020.
2 For examples, see http://acqnotes.com/dod-guides-handbooks, accessed March 2020.
3 Federal Acquisition Regulation, "Part 15: Contracting by Negotiation," and "Part 33: Protests, Disputes, and Appeals," FAC 2020-04, January 15, 2020, respectively https://www.acquisition.gov/content/part-15-contracting-negotiation and https://www.acquisition.gov/content/part-33-protests-disputes-and-appeals, accessed March 2020.
4 Defense Innovation Unit, "Who We Are/Our Mission," undated, https://www.diu.mil/about, accessed March 2020.
5 Bret Boyd, "Defense Acquisition Reform Is a National Security Issue," Grayline Capital LLC, 2016-2019, https://graylinegroup.com/defense-acquisition-reform-is-a-national-security-issue/, accessed March 2020.
6 Calculated from 2007-2015 data. Under Secretary of Defense, Acquisition, Technology, and Logistics, "Performance of the Defense Acquisition System: 2016 Annual Report" (Washington, DC: Department of Defense, 2016), p. xvi, https://www.govexec.com/media/gbc/docs/pdfs_edit/performance-of-defense-acquisition-system-2016.pdf, accessed March 2020.
7 Valerie Heitshusen and Brendan W. McGarry, "Defense Primer: The NDAA Process," Congressional Budget Office, January 8, 2020, https://fas.org/sgp/crs/natsec/IF10515.pdf, accessed March 2020.
8 Statista, "Private Sector Outspends Defense Contractors in R&D," October 1, 2019, https://www.statista.com/chart/19515/defense-spending-research-development/, accessed March 2020.
9 PitchBook data, cited in Defense Innovation Unit, "Report to Congress," April 2019, p. 5.
10 AcqNotes, "Contracts and Legal: Other Transaction Authority," August 15, 2019, http://acqnotes.com/acqnote/careerfields/other-transaction-authority

-ota, accessed March 2020. Also see Moshe Schwartz and Heidi M. Peters, "Department of Defense Use of Other Transaction Authority: Background, Analysis, and Issues for Congress, February 22, 2019, https://fas.org/sgp/crs /natsec/R45521.pdf, accessed March 2020.

11 Defense Innovation Unit, "Annual Report 2018," 2019, p. 7, https://assets .ctfassets.net/3nanhbfkr0pc/26OECgBCK7AZ2XhkbLyyMQ/3a64bb03255 0e3f0b9086b00d60f012c/DIU_2018_Annual_Report_FINAL.pdf, accessed March 2020.

12 AFWERX, "Air Force (AF) 19.2 Small Business Innovation Research Direct to Phase II Proposal Instructions," 2019, pp. AF DP II-2, II-16, https://www.afwerx.af.mil/resources/SBIR-USAF-Direct-to-Phase-II-Instructions.pdf, accessed May 2020.

13 Defense Innovation Unit, "Annual Report 2018," 2019, p. 3.

14 Defense Innovation Unit, "Common Questions," undated, https://www.diu .mil/work-with-us/commercial, accessed March 2020.

15 Defense Innovation Unit, "Annual Report 2018," 2019, p. 6.

16 As the DIU website described, "In accordance with 10 U.S.C. § 2371b(f), and upon a determination that the prototype project has successfully been completed, any competitively awarded prototype-OT contract or agreement may result in the award of a follow-on production contract or agreement without the use of additional competitive procedures." Defense Innovation Unit, "Common Questions," undated, https://www.diu.mil/work-with-us/commercial, accessed March 2020.

17 Cash paid by Bolt Technology for SeaBotix Inc. through March 2011: Bolt Technology Group, June 30, 2011 Form 10-K, p. F-11, http://www.annualreports.com/HostedData/AnnualReportArchive/b/NASDAQ_BOLT_2011 .pdf, accessed March 2020.

18 "Bolt Technology Announces Acquisition of SeaBotix, Inc.," Businesswire.com, January 6, 2011, https://www.businesswire.com/news/home/20110106007121 /en/Bolt-Technology-Announces-Acquisition-SeaBotix, accessed March 2020.

19 Defense Innovation Unit, National Security Innovation Capital, "Report to Congress," June 2019, p. 5.

20 Defense Innovation Unit, National Security Innovation Capital, "Report to Congress," June 2019, p. 5.

21 Defense Innovation Unit, National Security Innovation Capital, "Report to Congress," June 2019, p. 4.

22 Defense Innovation Unit, National Security Innovation Capital, "Report to Congress," June 2019, p. 6.

Features

- Forward-scanning sonar and video
- Multiple navigation sensors
- Gigabit LAN data transfer
- Rechargeable, easily swapped batteries
- Payload bay

Additional options

- Two-function grabber
- Dual, five-function manipulator package
- AUV (untethered) mode
- Side-scanning sonar
- Acoustic underwater positioning system w/ 1km radius
- 2,000m (1.2 mile) tether

EXHIBIT 1 The SRS FUSION
Source: Compiled from SRS documents.

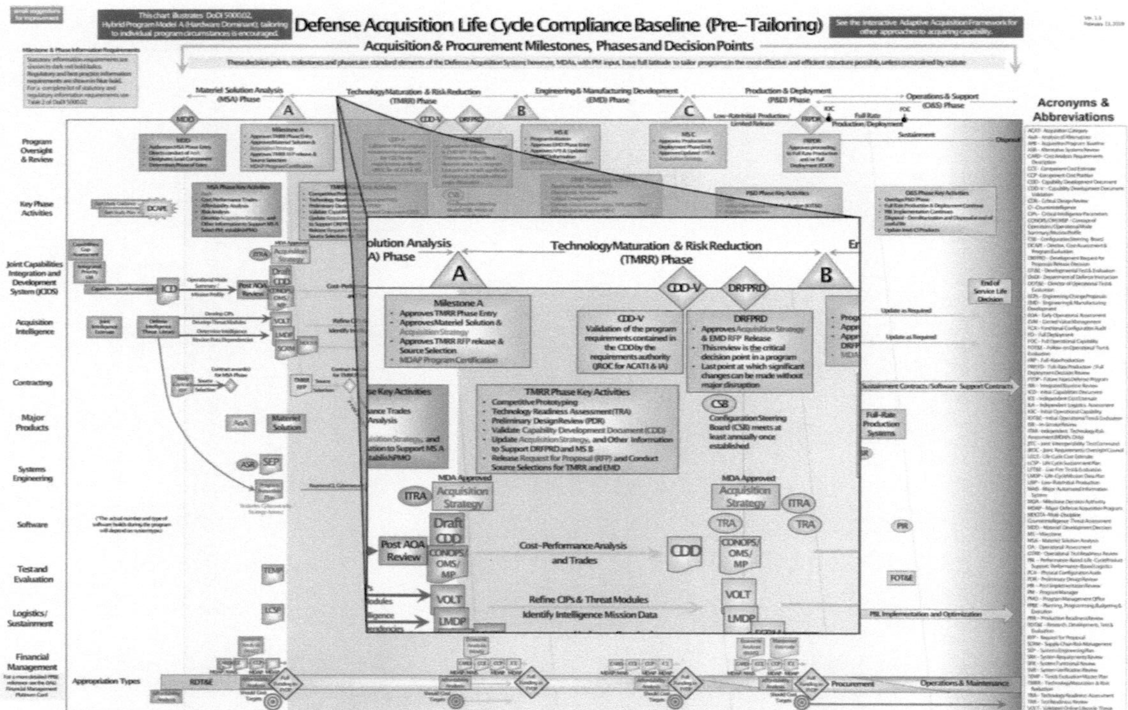

EXHIBIT 2 The U.S. Defense Acquisition Process, Flow Chart with Enlarged Detail, 2019
Source: Adapted from Defense Acquisition University, "Defense Acquisition Life Cycle Wall Chart," February 13, 2019, p. 1, https://www.dau.edu/tools/t/Department-of-Defense-Acquisition-Life-Cycle-Chart, accessed March 2020.

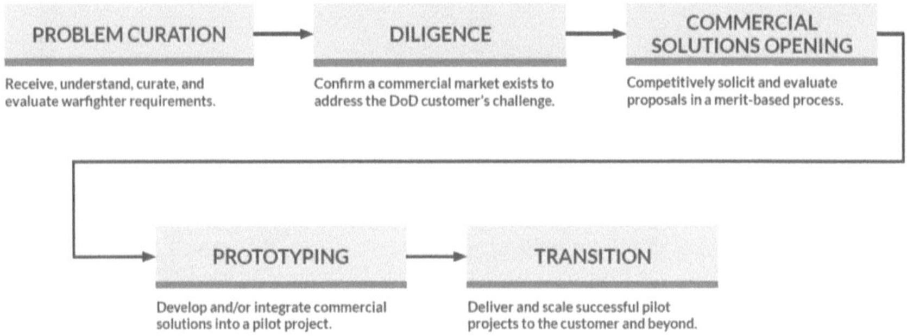

EXHIBIT 3 The DIU Process
Source: DIU.

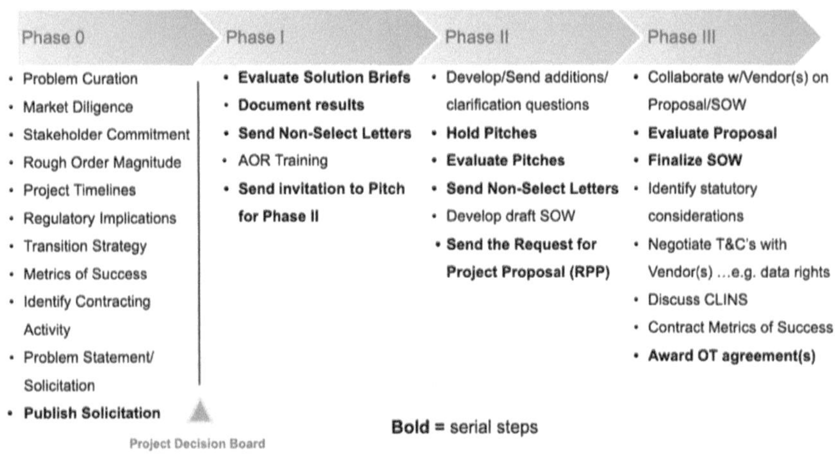

EXHIBIT 4 Summary of DIU Contracting Process
Source: DIU.
Notes: AOR: area of responsibility; SOW: statement of work; T&Cs: terms and conditions; CLINS: contract line item numbers; OT: Other Transaction—contracting authority outside the FAR process.

EXHIBIT 5 Core Strategic Robotic Systems Team Members and Partners

STRATEGIC ROBOTIC SYSTEMS

Co-Founder and President—Jesse Rodocker

Jesse is the founder of SRS and the key visionary behind its product focus. As the co-founder of SeaBotix, Jesse spent 15 years in the unmanned underwater vehicle. At SeaBotix, he managed sales, marketing, and distribution. Working with clients in the field generated thousands of hours of operational experience with UUVs that was unique to few people in the world. Jesse conceptualized or developed every SeaBotix product sold. All key business decisions were made collectively with co-founder Don Rodocker. Jesse's experience is critical to understanding how a UUV manufacturing company succeeds.

Co-Founder and Commercial/Office Manager—Tracey Rodocker

Tracey has over 20 years' experience as office manager, including for two diving firms. As Commercial/Office Manager, Tracey oversees day-to-day operations including accounting, materials management, human resources, and compliance requirements.

Mechanical Design—Tony Llerandi

Tony was the Senior Mechanical Designer at SeaBotix for seven years, where he worked closely with Jesse Rodocker to develop industry-leading ROV systems and accessories. Tony has over 20 years of experience as a mechanical designer, specializing in machining, molding, and materials.

Software—Rafe Montgomery

Rafe is a specialist in the real-time visualization of subsea activities, with 20 years' experience developing software for the offshore mining industry.

EXHIBIT 5 *(continued)*

PARTNERS

Sensors and Electronics Team— Blueprint Subsea (United Kingdom)

Founded in 2006, Blueprint is responsible for developing the key sensors and electronics for the SRS FUSION, including its multi-beam sonar, side-scan sonar, USBL positioning system, GPS, and main electronics.

- James Barratt, director and co-owner—mechanical design
- Robin Sharphouse, director and co-owner—electronic and software design
- John Smith—sonar system design

Control and Navigation Team—Instituto Superior Tecnico (Portugal)

- Antonio Pascoal—design and development of autonomous marine and air vehicles
- Luis Sebastiao—design and development of advanced marine robotics systems and instrumentation

Source: Compiled from SRS documents.
Note: Data as of 2015.

EXHIBIT 6 Defense Innovation Unit EOD ROV Problem Statement, January 2017

Problem Statement: The Department of Defense is seeking a demonstration-ready, remotely-operated system to detect at distance, accurately navigate to and reacquire based on a geo-reference, and optically and acoustically inspect explosive threats located in maritime and littoral environments at sea, and in ports and harbors. The system must be man-portable, deployable from a small rubber/inflatable boat within one-half of the available deck space with a minimal setup time, and operable for extended periods in an expeditionary environment. The system must have automated control capabilities, and a physical and operating architecture capable of hosting compatibly designed third party payloads and autonomy engines that can be reconfigured in the field.

For the purpose of this solicitation: a) maritime and littoral environments represent the area from the high water mark of coastal regions, ports

EXHIBIT 6 (*continued*)

and harbors, out to blue water regions of approximately 600 feet in depth, b) static weight for man-portable is considered 88 pounds (in air), and c) expeditionary environments are operations that require the system operators to be essentially self-sustaining with an organic logistics capability. Offerers that provide solutions that meet the government's needs will be provided an opportunity to demonstrate a current variant of their system.

Demonstrations will take place in a government-owned deepwater pool in San Diego, CA. The government will provide support equipment (table, chairs, and shade tent) and one 2kW portable gas generator for the demonstrations. The current window for demonstrations is planned for February 26, 2018 to March 2, 2018. Demonstrations will allow the government to validate the information provided in offerers' submitted solution briefs about their current technology.

Responses should address, at a minimum, the information identified below and provide a top-level diagram of the system architecture. Proprietary information, if any, should be kept to minimum and MUST BE CLEARLY MARKED. Responses will be reviewed by government and approved DoD contractor personnel only.

Source: DIU.

EXHIBIT 7 EOD Project Entrants
Source: DIU.

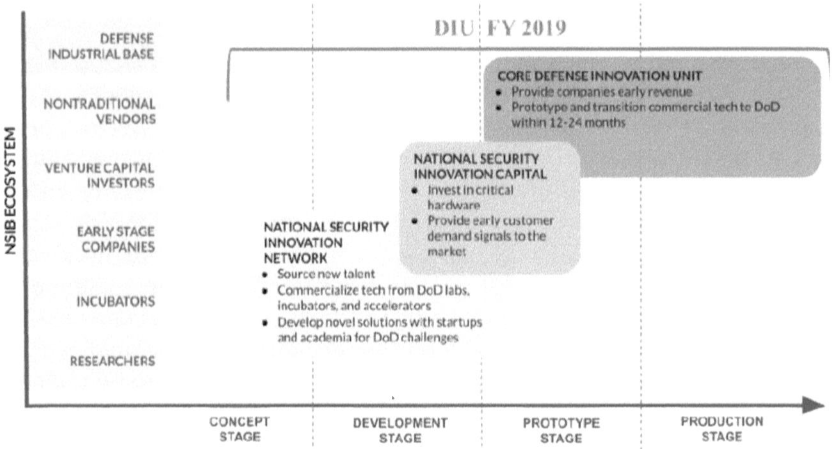

EXHIBIT 8 DIU Coverage of the Technology Development Process
Source: DIU.
Note: NBIS: National security innovation base.
Fiscal 2019 began on October 1, 2018.

CHAPTER 2.4

Loma Vista Medical

Paul Gompers and Silpa Kovvali

Alex Tilson reached the peak of the Sweeney Ridge Trail in San Bruno, California, a community adjacent to Silicon Valley. The steep grades and cool fog helped to make it the training ground-of-choice for Tilson during his pursuit of the American 50 kilometer record and a spot in the US Olympic Marathon trials. But today, Alex was not training for a race, but to find clarity and inspiration for a critical decision for his current endurance event, growing a life science start-up. Alex was in a tough spot. Again. He was preparing for a meeting with his venture capital investors at DeNovo Ventures, and he knew everything had to be just right; he had to give off an air of stability, decisiveness, and, most importantly, confidence. He was, after all, asking them to approve the company's second major pivot in just three years.

In many respects, the meeting should have been a triumphant one for Tilson, not an added stressor. When Tilson founded Loma Vista Medical (LVM) in 2006, he'd intended to apply his engineering background to create a superior product for performing colonoscopies, a diagnostic procedure performed many millions of times annually. A year later, in 2007, he returned to his lead investor at DeNovo, Joe Mandato, empty-handed. LVM didn't have a product that worked. But, Tilson had stayed true to his company's biggest promise and what he considered the core of its identity: the lean model. The company was young, its burn rate was low, and he had plenty of new, exciting ideas.

Mandato agreed to let Tilson steer LVM in a new direction, into kyphoplasty [ˈkīfōplastē], a large market focused on vertebral compression fractures and dominated by a single vendor. LVM was to focus on novel materials and manufacturing to create medical balloons for use in the spine. This time, Tilson and his team at LVM were able to deliver a working product. In fact, they had successfully manufactured a device that they were confident was superior to anything else in the market. And the

Loma Vista Medical
by PAUL GOMPERS, SILPA KOVVALI, case number 9-819-050 Rev. FEBRUARY 1, 2021

market was large, with a recent, profitable exit that Tilson could point to as a future path for LVM's success.

Instead, he intended to approach Mandato with yet another ask, one that had the potential to spook any investor. He wanted LVM to pivot again, this time to creating medical balloons for use with heart valves. It was now 2009, and he could no longer gesture at LVM's relative youth to justify the significant pivot. Instead, he hoped to convince Mandato and his colleagues at DeNovo that the comparably miniscule market for transcatheter aortic valve replacement (TAVR [ˈtavər]) was a rapidly growing, high-potential space, that if LVM could present the right product at the right time, it could be enormously successful, and that the company should make that leap.

Tilson only hoped he could convey this sense of certainty to his investors. Was he right to propose this pivot to DeNovo? Would they suggest that they pack up their bags and move on? Would they suggest LVM stay the course? Would they instead agree with Tilson, and approve his proposed pivot? Should they?

BACKGROUND

Tilson's decisions at Loma Vista, including the decision to found the company in the first place, were driven largely by his background—since his childhood in Oregon, he'd considered himself first and foremost a builder, and was a competitor at heart. Tilson graduated from Stanford in 1992, where he ran cross country and track and studied mechanical engineering. He also participated in the Stanford Solar Car Project, designing and racing solar powered vehicles twice across the United States and once across Australia. He continued his athletic pursuits after graduation, cycling across the United States and Asia and pursuing competitive distance running as an Olympic Trials marathoner and as the American 50 kilometer record holder.[1]

Tilson initially applied his engineering background at Edge Innovations, a film animatronics special effects company, where he worked on the robots used in *Free Willy II* and *Anaconda*, amongst others. The work was a great opportunity to hone and refine his technical skills, working on ambitious projects with talented coworkers, but he ultimately found it unfulfilling. He hoped instead to apply those skills to work with greater purpose. "Long term, it seemed like Moore's law would win, that computer special effects would get better and better, destining robotic special effects to be less relevant. I worked on one movie that went direct-to-video," he recalled. "It got me thinking if the incredible engineering could perhaps be redirected to something more meaningful."

Tilson took a breather, mulling over his future paths during a six-week bicycle tour of the Caucasus. When he returned, he found himself faced with the opportunity he was looking for. On its face, the company he left wound up bearing striking similarities to the company he considered departing it for. At Edge, a team of twenty-five made robotic whales for movies, and less than a mile down the same street, a similarly sized group at Intuitive Surgical was utilizing similar technology to develop medical robotics. As Tilson weighed his offer to join Intuitive, talent wasn't a concern: he felt both companies had comparably intelligent and dedicated engineers, and that both had leaders who were brave, bright, and charismatic.

Still, Tilson accepted the position at Intuitive, which allowed him to transition from robotics for movies to robotics with surgical applications. Intuitive Surgical was borne out of a license to DARPA technology. The company's original goal was to create a robotic system that could perform remote surgery on soldiers wounded in the battlefield during the so-called "golden hour" following the injury. Proof-of-concept was achieved when a team successfully tele-robotically operated on a pig in the back of a Bradley fighting vehicle using inputs delivered wirelessly from a doctor in a second location.

As a venture-funded startup, Intuitive was working to create a robotic surgical platform initially intended for heart bypass surgery. But it wasn't yet obvious to Alex that the company would be successful. Indeed, Intuitive struggled with the challenges of its first application, and briefly teetered on the edge of irrelevance. It was only in 2001— six years after its founding, and after Tilson had already departed— that it pivoted, quite accidentally, to prostate surgery. The pivot proved a sound and lucrative decision, leading to an impressive valuation and niche market dominance. The soundness of Tilson's own personal pivot were also confirmed. Though Edge Innovations continued to do cutting edge work for the film and gaming industries, and on key elements of James Cameron's submarine expedition in the Mariana Trench, the company was unable to scale or grow.

After his brief tenure at Intuitive, Tilson decided to return to school, and graduated from Harvard Business School in 1999.[2] The experience confirmed his decision to stay in the medical device space. "In healthcare you can build companies that make products that really matter, directly affecting people's health. These companies can be of remarkably enduring value. You can do this with a small team. There is an established pathway for raising money and exiting, and it has a core of invention." He came to perceive himself as, yes, an MBA, but HBS reaffirmed the core of his identity as an engineer and inventor. He had found an arena in which he could use his skills and the skill set of people he knew.

After leaving HBS, Tilson did short stints at two Silicon Valley medical device firms— the publicly traded Guidant and the small startup Converge

Medical— before accepting a role as Director of Product Development at InSound Medical in October of 2004.[3] Also a startup based in Silicon Valley, InSound was working to develop and commercialize an extended wear, invisible hearing aid partially financed by DeNovo Ventures. The then-struggling company often found itself the setting for some heated political battles, and in January of 2006, two weeks before the birth of his daughter, Tilson was let go. Though the turn of events was anxiety-inducing, Tilson still suspected it was for the best, giving him the push he needed to get to work on a deferred dream of starting his own company. Furthermore, his experience at InSound would serve as a good example for the cultural pitfalls he hoped to avoid in building his own firm. He wanted to create a company with a positive and effective culture, one where his employees would look forward to coming to work each day. He set out to assemble a team to solve a problem that desperately needed solving.

STARTING LOMA VISTA

The Company

Tilson founded Loma Vista in April of 2006, shortly after leaving InSound. The company was initially funded by personal savings and credit card debt, in addition to opportunity cost— Tilson paid himself no salary. He sought out investments from family and friends, who pitched in a modest amount. Rather than investing in costly office space, Tilson pushed his car out of his garage to create Loma Vista's worldwide headquarters. Several initial consultants he hired were happy to accept stock rather than cash.

One of these consultants was Mark Scheeff, a classmate of Tilson's from Stanford and close friend.[4] During their four years together, Scheeff and Tilson had worked closely on the Stanford Solar Project, lived together, and traveled together on a bicycling trip from Oregon to the Arctic Ocean, and then back to California. His time as a consultant demonstrated that working together was as enjoyable and productive an experience for the duo as it had been in college, and he soon became Loma Vista's first hire.

The Problem

Loma Vista decided to focus its efforts on improving the device used to perform colonoscopies. In Tilson's assessment, the process was ripe for refinement and full of unmet needs. When a colonoscopy was performed, a five-foot-long flexible endoscope was inserted into the body. (See **Exhibit 4.**) Complications with the procedure primarily arose from looping— the endoscope could buckle and bend at intermediate points, stretching the anatomy and failing to advance. Because this looping caused significant pain, the procedure necessitated anesthesia, meaning it could only be performed in a set of specific facilities, had greater cost, and presented opportunity cost for transport and requisite assistance from family and friends. Tilson felt that he and his team were well-equipped to produce a viable alternative to the endoscopes that dominated the market: an endoscope that resisted buckling and looping and could thus significantly decrease patient discomfort and inconvenience.

Apart from the appeal of the problem from an engineering perspective, the procedural volume and costs were key initial motivators. In 2001, the mean professional fees associated with colonoscopy performance were $199 for Medicare reimbursements and $272 for commercial payments.[5] However, the elevated needs for colonoscopy facilities, due largely to the use of anesthesia, meant total colonoscopy charges could range from $700 to $1500. Complications and add-ons like biopsies and therapeutic procedures could increase costs further still. A whole 40% of this total cost was due to the need for anesthesia,[6] expenses a better endoscope would eliminate.

Despite these expenses, the frequency and widespread nature of the screening test left the exact procedural volume unclear. Perhaps the most-cited work on U.S. procedural volume was performed by the Center for Disease Control (CDC.) A 2004 study[7] estimated a volume of 14.2 million colonoscopies performed domestically in 2002. Industry analysts repeatedly pronounced high volume procedural growth in the mid-to-high single digits, but Tilson was content to conservatively assume a modest 3% CAGR. He also assumed total world-wide volumes of 2 to 2.5x these numbers.

Despite the commonality of the procedure, one that left a great deal to be desired, no major improvements had occurred in many years. Tilson posited that the stagnant innovation was attributable to a market oligopoly. At the time of Loma Vista's founding, three major, established players controlled virtually the entire market for flexible endoscopes: Olympus, Pentax, and Fuji. Olympus alone commanded a 75% market share in gastrointestinal (GI) endoscopy.

All of this waste was caused by a kinematic, mechanical issue that Tilson and his team of engineers at Loma Vista thought they could solve. They set out to invent a solution. However, there were not alone. Several other emerging players also had their sights set on the colonoscopy market, including Neoguide, Invendo, Endonav, GI View, USGI, and Avantis.

Lean Model

Tilson had drawn certain lessons from Intuitive. He'd come to view business plans as a best initial hypothesis, but something that would inevitably evolve. The startup wasn't there to execute a static plan, but to rapidly, efficiently, and honestly execute a series of experiments. The company was, in Tilson's view, a laboratory. Some of their assumptions might be proven right—the medical world needed their devices—and some might be proven wrong—the best application of Intuitive's technology was far from what they initially thought. Tilson internalized this philosophy and resolved to apply it in his own ventures going forward.

Though Tilson was determined to maintain the lean experimentation foundation he'd committed to, he recognized that it posed unique challenges in the medical technology space. Where software companies could create a product and run inexpensive AB testing on the very same day, Loma Vista crafted tangible products, which in their case involved a minimum investment of $100,000 and required a far longer time frame. Meaningful data usually required animal or cadaveric testing, expensive and imperfect models. Getting a prototype to work was difficult enough, but transforming that into a truly reliable and clinically-robust product that was market-ready usually took at least another year. A submission to the Food and Drug Administration (FDA) was rarely approved in less than four months. Medical devices often involved exotic materials or specialized manufacturing, with extended lead-times and a number of iterative design loops. The end-to-end process could easily take four to eight years. Significantly reducing these timeframes would be a notable challenge.

Still, Tilson's commitment was a reaction to a venture capital-centric funding model that he strongly believed wasn't working in the medical device space. VC firms mitigated their risks through portfolios, but entrepreneurs, on the other hand, were forced to throw themselves all-in to their startups. Tilson reflected:

> VCs can take a bet that there's a 5% or 10% chance of a company working out, and if they sprinkle their money around enough and get a high enough multiple on one investment, that works out. An individual has one bet, and that bet is their career. They're doing one thing at a time.
>
> In software, if you're an engineer, you can go from dot-com to dot-com with eighteen-month tenures and assemble a portfolio of stock. But you can't really do that in the life sciences, and it is very difficult to do that as a founder and operator. In medical devices, it takes a minimum of five years, and often more like ten. I don't want a 5% chance of being successful in each five to ten year cycle. That math would doom me, statistically, to a career of futility.

Beyond time frames and success rates, the financials of medical devices made, Tilson believed, a company like Loma Vista ill-suited to the typical

VC funding model. Where software companies might rise to be worth tens of billions of dollars, scaling to 100x their initial valuations, and thus justifying a low hit rate, medical device multiples were too low to pay off as a portfolio strategy. When high initial valuations persisted, Tilson observed that the massive expectations required bigger clinical requirements, which drove longer time frames, expensive team hires, and highly diluted cap tables. The end result, and Tilson's fear, was a corporate culture gone astray and the loss of a company's initial founding vision.

To a degree, VC firms had begun to catch on to the unique challenges posed by the medical device sector: valuations lowered and available funding dried up commensurate with mediocre returns. (See **Exhibit 3**.) Still, Tilson wanted to take things further, lowering his ideal valuation considerably, and sought to raise funding in such a way that allowed for a more entrepreneur-friendly model. In this vein, rather than exclusively seeking funding from Silicon Valley VC firms, Tilson sought out a group of investors who were eclectic and diverse, based in California, Oregon, Virginia, and Texas.

DeNovo Ventures was the sole VC firm included in this fundraising round. The basis for DeNovo's investment was quite simple. Mandato had led the DeNovo investment in InSound Medical. He was involved in the hiring of Tilson and was aware of the rationale for his brief tenure at the company. Mandato observed, "Alex is an extremely smart guy, smarter than 99.9% of the people out there. However, they outnumber him. Alex was not meant to be a good soldier in a large organization. He needed to be in an environment which would allow him to blossom and uphold his high standards in an environment he invariably would lead. He would set extreme standards, expect 24x7 devotion, and be results-driven." Loma Vista was an inexpensive way for Mandato to test his assumptions.

Though DeNovo's investment was a modest sum of $200,000 in convertible debt, it was also an important signaler that allowed Tilson to more efficiently fundraise from angel investors: family members, former co-workers, and friends from cycling, medicine, and business school, all of whom felt more comfortable contributing given DeNovo's involvement. Collectively, these eight individual investors provided the remaining funds. In its October 2007 Seed 1 round, Loma Vista raised a total of $422,000 in convertible debt from these eight individual investors and DeNovo Ventures combined.[8]

Beyond flexibility in product and target market, the fundraising strategy granted Loma Vista flexibility surrounding hiring and other spending decisions, where their approach would again differ substantially from that of the software companies that typically dominated a VC portfolio. First, Tilson strongly felt there was a great return on investment (ROI) for engineers, though he acknowledged that his own background might be biasing his thinking. Tilson characterized a typical VC launch as focused heavily on sales, hiring, say, ten salespeople right out of the gate. But for a medical device company going through an iterative process of finding product/market fit process, investing too heavily in salespeople upfront could prove disastrous if the initial product needed to be refined.

Tilson similarly looked to cut back on general and administrative expenses, particularly managerial ones. All but one of the company's first sixteen employees were hands-on contributing engineers or technicians. (See **Exhibit 8** for organization chart.) Tilson rebalanced these funds to invest heavily in product development and manufacturing, which he believed to be the core, driving force of the company. (See **Exhibits 9-11** for income statements.)

Tilson crafted a list of lean methodology elements guiding principles that all essentially amounted to rules against rules: stop thinking you have the answers, or that they can be contained in a ten-year business plan; start thinking you are running experiments; go down one path until you find a better one. He knew that even decisions which he didn't view as experiments at the time might wind up needing to be reconsidered, and he wanted to ingrain a culture of humility into the company so that it could pivot when needed.

The Problem With The Problem

One-and-a-half years into Loma Vista's founding, and just two months after DeNovo's investment, the results of their testing left Tilson grappling with an inescapable fact: their product wasn't good enough, and wasn't accomplishing what it needed to do. To determine the efficacy of their endoscope, the Loma Vista engineers used a crude but effective test: laying out animal intestines on a bench, inserting their device, and attempting to navigate through the tract. Their product had shortcomings on both speed and effectiveness; it simply couldn't navigate as deeply or quickly as was required to be commercially viable.

"What do we do here?" Tilson wondered. "Part of the challenge is that successful people are really persistent: they'll beat their heads against the wall again and again and again, and that can often lead to a real breakthrough. But sometimes, being successful is about having an understanding of when it might be necessary to move on."

THE FIRST PIVOT

Tilson directed his Loma Vista team to take a step back and answer a simple question: what is our core competency? Upon examining the technology they'd developed, Tilson stumbled upon a surprising answer: they were really good at using sophisticated materials and manufacturing for the creation of advanced medical balloons.

During his time at Edge Innovations, Tilson had worked on developing hydraulics for *Anaconda* and *Free Willy*. He had also worked with composite materials while at Stanford, both during the solar car competition and during a summer he spent working on one of the America's Cup boats, and liked the technology. Scheeff had worked extensively with mechantronics, which could form the genesis of the necessary manufacturing automation:

> We decided to manufacture and design another company. The inflatable stuff was really special, so what if we called ourselves a balloon company instead of a colonoscopy company? (See **Exhibit 12**.) We knew there were applications that would be a really good fit for our flexible composite balloon technology. Though we had failed at colonoscopy, that experience had allowed us to work with the companies and materials used in medical inflatables. It became clear to us that the companies were stuck in the past, and that few people in the world really understood the opportunity like we did. We believed that our vision, successfully implemented, could significantly advance therapies for patients.

The pivot, however, would mean some hoop-jumping. "We went back to our VCs in December of 2007 and said, 'Remember all this stuff you funded? We're not doing that anymore,'" Tilson said. "It took them a while to understand that the colonoscopy effort was over, and that we intended to now focus on balloons in the spine." However, Tilson was able to get their VC investors on board by constructing a compelling narrative.

Rather than framing the pivot as the result of a failure, Tilson instead approached the board by touting a success. "If we could become world-class at high performance medical balloons," his slides read, "What are other applications?" He spent a month surveying a range of opportunities and comparing them to the company's current and potential capabilities. From the exercise he began to focus on one possible appealing application: kyphoplasty. The procedure, developed by a Bay area device company called Kyphon, was used to treat vertebral compression fractures by inflating a balloon inside a vertebrae and filling the resultant space with bone cement. (See **Exhibit 5**.) His slides also highlighted where their technology might exceed current market offerings. He quoted one potential collaborator who expressed interest in "a balloon that follows its own shape and not the shape of the hole in the vertebrae. We have been working on a product for 2.5 years but have not yet succeeded. If it was successful it would be a mainstream product for us, with $500 million potential." In fact, Tilson suspected the market was even larger. He highlighted the sale of Kyphon, just five months before, to the giant Medtronic for $3.9 billion.[9]

In making the decision to pivot, and attempting to sell Loma Vista's investors on this shift, Tilson also researched successful pivots of the past. He was surprised to find that pivots were far, far more common than he realized, perhaps because he, like most people, associated iconic companies with the product that eventually produced their success rather than their original mission. The Gap, for example, began as a record store but was eventually known for its jeans. Twitter started out as an audio podcasting company and YouTube initially had video dating applications.

In the medical devices space, the company Conceptus created devices for gynecology. They utilized catheters that were initially developed for use in the brain, instead using them to promote fertility, then pivoting to use the technology to promote infertility. Eventually, the company produced the only device that could be used for minimally invasive female sterilization, and sold for $2.5 billion. Much like his list of expensive, failed ventures, Tilson produced a contrasting list of successful companies that had started out with one focus and wound up with another. "We told a story about opportunity and fit," Tilson says. "They understood that story."

Mandato remembers the story about opportunity and fit, and largely agrees, but qualifies:

> As with any VC firm, we have many choices. Demand for our product, cash, exceeds supply. And, importantly, decision making is not unilateral. While we respect failure, I certainly had to sell my four partners. I picked them off one by one, beginning with the most thoughtful. Jay Watkins, who knew and respected Alex and understood the extent of the opportunity. He supported the pivot. Perhaps more importantly, the amount at stake was insignificant and, most importantly, we believed in the leader.

The group went along with the recommendation to move ahead and Mandato was able to present a united front to Tilson when approving the pivot.

KYKOPHLASTY TRANSITION

Tilson and his team found that the developments they'd made in flexible composites (multiple materials utilized in multiple layers), particularly balloons, would be applicable to the kyphoplasty process once they developed new, supplementary technology. Here, his hiring strategy had paid off. Because Loma Vista had initially recruited generalist engineers, they were able to take on this new challenge, and he was able to avoid wasting time, effort, and other resources on firing and hiring a new team. Perhaps more importantly, morale remained decent, and the pivot didn't seem to shake his team's confidence in management.

Further, from a development perspective, Tilson's lean governing philosophy had ensured that the pivot was a gradual transition and not an abrupt switch. The goal had always been to continually create new assets and shed others. The colonoscopy procedure had required the development of automation, which LVM performed in-house, and partnering with another device company called Cubic Tech to develop the requisite flexible composite. But sensing a potential pivot on the horizon as early as October of 2007, Tilson moved the flexible composite manufacturing in-house as well. By the time LVM definitively stopped pursuing the colonoscopy market altogether in 2009, they had already created a working kyphoplasty product.

Tilson and his team were able to develop a highly flexible balloon of unique geometries that couldn't be achieved with standard balloon manufacturing techniques. Importantly, the balloon was also non-compliant. In other words, it didn't stretch. In addition to offering the advantages they'd set out to— namely, that it retained its shape rather than conforming to that of the fracture—this also meant that it could reach a higher pressure and required a smaller surgical incision. They'd developed a product superior to that offered by a $3.9 billion company, and not just reached, but exceeded their goal.

PIVOT NUMBER TWO?

But several things didn't sit right with Tilson, who suspected an upcoming downturn in the kyphoplasty market. It began with the publication of two articles in the authoritative New England Journal of Medicine (NEJM), which cast doubt on the value proposition of kyphoplasty: that it was cheaper, faster, and easier than the alternatives. The NEJM article cast doubt on this conventional wisdom by presenting the results of a randomized clinical trial that found no meaningful difference in the efficacy of vertebroplasties and the traditional alternatives.[10] Because kyphoplasties were similar enough to the procedure, the studies were enough to cast a dark shadow over the entire space. Though Kyphon firmly disputed the controversial findings, Tilson worried the debate was enough to dampen enthusiasm.

Tilson was confident LVM could avoid getting caught in the headwinds with a second pivot, this time to heart valves. Tilson hoped to enter the market for transcatheter aortic valve replacement (TAVR), a procedure used to treat calcified heart valves. The traditional treatment required the old, damaged heart valves be removed, which could only be done with a sternotomy: an open heart surgical procedure which required surgically separating the chest while circulating blood through an artificial circuit. The TAVR procedure was far less risky, invasive, and debilitating, delivering a collapsed replacement valve through another artery and expanding it once it entered the chest.[11] (See **Exhibit 6.**)

However, even given Tilson's dim projections in the kyphoplasty space, it was noteworthy that the TAVR market was drastically smaller. 2008 had essentially been the dawn of the TAVR industry's sales, at the time occupied entirely by a dedicated spin-off of an established, fifty-year-old company focused on structural heart disease. This company, Edwards Lifesciences[12], had seen annual revenues of $53 million in 2008 for transcatheter heart valves (THV) alone, with an average sales price of approximately $25,000 per procedure. Loma Vista intended to sell an accessory for the surgery, with an estimated revenue of $800 per procedure. Where Tilson saw potential was not in these numbers, but in the prospect of getting in on the ground floor of a rapidly growing market: optimistic projections placed Edwards' 2017 THV revenues at $1.7 billion.

Tilson met with his investors and literally sketched out his projections. (See **Exhibit 7.**) While he understood the disparity in the market size, he instead made an effort to emphasize the differing slopes. A declining market meant a more crowded environment, and Tilson felt investors would find a rapidly growing market appealing. He played to their desire to get in on the ground floor.

One board member, Charles Love, shared Tilson's bullishness on the TAVR. "Chuck said this was going to be the biggest, most important medical device in decades. But he is also one of the most optimistic people I know, so I was torn about how to view the opportunity. In this case, he had deep clinical knowledge of the clinical area, so was arguably one of a handful of people with this combination of wisdom and insight into the market. But other board members weren't sure if they could take his optimism at face value." Tilson was well aware that a pivot into a miniscule market was a tough sell, heightened by the fact that they had a well-working product in their current space. "With our first pivot," Tilson laid out, "we liked our market, but at the core our product didn't do what we needed to. When we considered our second pivot, we were concerned about a market failure, not a technical one."

Mandato's initial reaction was,

> Why me? The fact that a stone headed engineer like Alex who thinks he can solve any engineering problem took it upon himself to pivot once was really significant. I gave him a ton of credit for that, since many engineers will not do it. For the second pivot, that was no longer valid. Now we had an issue, especially with the other partners, a nagging sense that he might not know what he was doing. This time *I* was

the one who was having to go out on a limb, and that was challenging, especially in an environment that had become a partnership in name only.

Tilson always maintained that a company should be persistent and focused while also honestly examining its adjacencies, which he termed "peripheral vision." "If you're not focused and relentless, you're in trouble. But if you don't have peripheral vision, you're also in trouble," he said. "Part of pivoting is having the courage to throw things aside, including developed assets you've spent time and money on, to whittle down to a core you can build around that is useful."

The question before Tilson, and Mandato, was what exactly comprised Loma Vista's core. Had the growing market on the periphery just distracted Tilson from their core competency, and the best opportunity for Loma Vista to pursue? Did LVM risk eroding the trust of their investors if they pivoted again? Or would a second pivot help them achieve the kind of multiple that made their investments worthwhile?

NOTES

1 "Alex Tilson," *LinkedIn*, accessed in October 2018, https://www.linkedin.com/in/alex-tilson-6753281/. http://www.hogue.com/svclassic/index2002.html.
2 LinkedIn.
3 LinkedIn.
4 Anderson, Evan. "Loma Vista is Hard to Kill," *Stanford Biodesign Alumni Association*, March 25, 2014, https://biodesignalumni.com/2014/03/25/loma-vista-is-hard-to-kill/.
5 http://www.solucient.com/docs/OutpatientView_WP.pdf.
6 "Sedation and the Technical Performance of Colonoscopy," by Douglas Rex et. Al. Gastrointestinal Endoscopy Clinics of N. America. 15 (2005) 661-672.
7 Seeff L, Richards T, Shapiro J, et al. "How Many Endoscopies are Performed for Colorectal Cancer Screening? Results From CDC's Survey of Endoscopic Capacity." Gastroenterology . 2004; 127: number 6, 1670-7. http://www.ncbi.nlm.nih.gov/entrez/query.fcgi?cmd=Retrieve&db=pubmed&dopt=Abstract&list_uids=15578503
8 Anderson, Evan.
9 https://www.forbes.com/2007/07/27/medtronic-kyphon-kyphoplasty-biz-sci-cx_mh_0727kyphon.html#1b301cc2831b.
10 https://www.nejm.org/doi/full/10.1056/NEJMoa0900563, https://www.nejm.org/doi/full/10.1056/NEJMoa0900429.
11 https://www.forbes.com/2007/07/27/medtronic-kyphon-kyphoplasty-biz-sci-cx_mh_0727kyphon.html#1b301cc2831b.
12 http://www.heart.org/en/health-topics/heart-valve-problems-and-disease/understanding-your-heart-valve-treatment-options/what-is-tavr.

EXHIBIT 1 Loma Vista Management Team

Alex Tilson Founder & CEO

Alex founded Loma Vista Medical in 2006, where he also serves as CEO. Prior to starting the company, Alex was Director of Product Development for Insound Medical, a start-up focused on creating the world's first extended wear hearing aid. Alex previously worked as Director of Product Development for Converge Medical, a start-up developing a nitinol-based anastomotic device for coronary bypass surgery.

Earlier in his career, Alex worked in strategic product development for a division of Guidant Corporation. His previous medical device positions include roles for Act Medical and Intuitive Surgical. Alex earned his BS degree in Mechanical Engineering from Stanford University and his MBA from Harvard Business School.

Mark Scheeff VP of Product Development

Mark joined Loma Vista Medical in 2007 as Vice President of Product Development. Prior to that, he co-founded Hummingbird Scientific, a company building tools for electron and ion microscopes, where he also served as Director of Engineering. Mark served as an engineer for the Lawrence Berkeley National Lab where he worked for an internal consulting group specializing in small-to-medium sized projects.

He has held a variety of engineering and management positions for organizations including Interval Research Company, Stanford Linear Accelerator Center, and the Stanford Solar Car Project. Mark earned both his BS and MS in Mechanical Engineering from Stanford University.

Source: Company documents.

EXHIBIT 2 Loma Vista Board of Directors

Joe Mandato

Joe has served as a Loma Vista Medical board member since 2007. He joined DeNovo Ventures as a Managing Director in March 2003. Prior to that, Joe served as Chair of Confer Software, a software developer of tools to create efficiencies and streamline processes in healthcare. He also served as President/CEO of Origin Medsystems, a developer of minimally invasive surgical devices for use in general, cardio-thoracic, and ob-gyn surgery, which was acquired by Eli Lilly & Company and spun out as one of the five units that formed Guidant. At Guidant, Mr. Mandato served as a member

EXHIBIT 2 (*continued*)

of the founding management committee and CEO of two of its five operating units, Origin and Heart Rhythm Technology. He also co-founded and served as CEO of Gynecare, a women's health spin-out of Guidant, which was acquired by Johnson & Johnson.

Subsequent to his tenure at Guidant, he served as an Entrepreneur-in-Residence at Mayfield Fund, a venture capital firm. Earlier in his career, he was CEO of Ioptex Research, a developer of intraocular lenses used in cataract surgery, acquired by Smith & Nephew PLC. He joined Ioptex from Cilco AG in Zug, Switzerland, the Europe, Middle East, and Africa headquarters of a unit of Rorer Group, where he was founder/CEO. He began his career in healthcare as a Captain in the U.S. Army Medical Service Corps. Joe received his Doctor of Management from Case Western Reserve University and serves on its Board of Trustees. He serves on the adjunct faculty of The University of San Francisco's Graduate School of Management and co-teaches the course Medical Device Innovation at Stanford University. He also serves on the board of Save the Children.

In addition to Loma Vista Medical, Joe sits or has sat on a number of boards including Avedro, Axogen (NASDAQ: AXGN), Hansen Medical (HNSN), InSound Medical, Align Technology (ALGN), Tear Science, Valeritas (VTAS), and WaveTec Vision Systems.

Charles Love

Charles Love has served on the Loma Vista board since 2007. He has over 24 issued patents in his name, and over 20 years of experience with implantable medical devices, with a diverse background in product development, regulatory approval and clinical trials, business development, and strategy. Charles is principal consultant of Spot On Medical, a Santa Barbara based consulting firm focused on the medical device industry.

Prior to launching Spot On Medical, Charles served a Vice President of Regulatory & Clinical Affairs for Ventracor Limited, a company developing a third-generation left ventricular assist device, where he established a global regulatory and clinical affairs department. Before Ventracor, Charles was Vice President of R&D and Regulatory Clinical at Converge Medical, where he led efforts to develop a nitinol based anastomotic device for coronary bypass surgery. Earlier in his career, Charles founded Ramus Medical Technologies, where he served as President & CEO. Other positions include COO at Autogenics, Research Engineer at MiniMed Technologies, and management positions at Symbion and Symetrics.

Charles earned his degree in Biology from Westmont College.

EXHIBIT 2 *(continued)*

Carter Meyer

Carter Meyer has served on the Loma Vista Medical board since 2007. He is the CEO of SHD (Scientific Health Development), a Texas-based healthcare-focused venture capital firm, since its formation in February 2006. He is a General Partner of SHD II. Prior to joining SHD, he was an attorney in private practice for over 12 years, most recently with the Dallas office of the Vinson & Elkins L.L.P. As an attorney, Mr. Meyer focused on commercial transactions with substantial experience buying, selling, financing and making investments in both public and private entities. Mr. Meyer has a B.B.A. in finance from Texas Christian University and a J.D. from St. Mary's University School of Law. Mr. Meyer is a director of all SHD portfolio companies.

Jay Watkins

Jay has served as a Loma Vista Medical board member since 2007. He joined DeNovo Ventures in 2002 as a Managing Director. Prior to that, Jay was a co-founder of Origin Medsystems, a venture-funded medical technology start-up that was purchased by Eli Lilly & Company. When Eli Lilly divested its medical device businesses to form Guidant, he became a member of the corporation's management committee. During this time, he served as president of numerous divisions, including the Minimally Invasive Surgery Group.

In addition, Jay was the President of Compass, Guidant Corporation's corporate business development and new ventures group. Prior to founding Origin, Jay held management positions in several start-ups, including Microgenics Corporation, and was a consultant with the international consulting firm of McKinsey & Company. He has been a member of the board of directors of several public companies, including Gynecare, Cardiogenesis, and Rita Medical. Jay received his MBA from Harvard University and his undergraduate degree from Stanford University. In addition to Loma Vista Medical, Jay sits on the boards of EBR Systems, PhotoThera, Pulmonx, Sierra Surgical, Synergeyes and Ventus Medical. He also represented DeNovo on investments in Lumend and Hansen Medical.

Source: Company documents.

EXHIBIT 3 Venture Capital Investments in Medical Sector

Median Premoney Valuation, by Industry Group ($M)

		1999	2000	2001	2002	2003	2004	2005		
Industry Group	**Industry Segment**	Total	Total	Total	Total	Total	Total	1Q	2Q	Total
Healthcare	Biopharmaceuticals	$16.0	$25.2	$18.2	$15.6	$20.9	$19.4	$16.4	$17.1	$17.1
	Healthcare Services	$13.6	$13.5	$14.8	$11.0	$9.9	$12.0	NS	$17.3	$12.5
	Medical Devices	$13.4	$17.2	$17.7	$22.3	$14.9	$16.4	$35.5	$27.4	$27.9
	Medical Information Systems	$15.0	$22.0	$13.0	$11.0	$9.9	$16.5	NS	$6.9	$9.7
Health-care Total		**$14.0**	**$20.0**	**$16.5**	**$15.0**	**$15.7**	**$16.5**	**$17.8**	**$18.1**	**$18.1**
Information Technology	Communications & Networking	$35.5	$42.0	$27.3	$13.5	$14.3	$17.6	$17.5	$23.5	$20.3
	Electronics & Computer Hardware	$13.1	$30.0	$18.8	$9.8	$7.3	$14.0	$25.3	$14.9	$18.5
	Information Services	$28.0	$25.5	$10.3	$7.3	$11.5	$9.9	NS	NS	$23.6
	Semiconductors	$18.1	$40.0	$25.0	$13.9	$13.8	$16.5	$21.8	$14.0	$14.0
	Software	$22.5	$24.5	$13.0	$8.8	$7.5	$9.6	$15.0	$15.0	$15.0
Information Technology Total		**$25.0**	**$29.3**	**$16.7**	**$10.0**	**$9.5**	**$12.0**	**$18.3**	**$15.2**	**$17.0**
Products & Services	Consumer & Business Products	$10.5	$10.7	$5.1	$5.6	$4.5	$10.8	NS	NS	$6.2
	Consumer & Business Services	$19.5	$24.0	$15.0	$8.0	$9.9	$11.8	$17.2	$15.8	$16.6
	Retailers	$37.8	$33.9	$49.8	$16.1	$7.2	$23.0	NS	NS	NS
Products & Services Total		**$20.0**	**$24.0**	**$15.0**	**$8.0**	**$8.5**	**$12.0**	**$13.5**	**$8.7**	**$12.0**
Other Total		$24.4	$19.0	$10.4	$8.0	$6.2	$6.2	$7.0	NS	$7.0
Grand Total		**$21.1**	**$25.5**	**$16.0**	**$10.8**	**$10.0**	**$13.0**	**$15.5**	**$15.6**	**$15.6**

Median Premoney Valuation, by Development Stage ($M)

	1999	2000	2001	2002	2003	2004	2005		
Stage of Development	Total	Total	Total	Total	Total	Total	1Q	2Q	Total
Startup	$5.3	$7.0	$5.0	$4.8	$3.8	$2.6	NS	NS	$9.2
Product Development	$12.2	$16.2	$14.6	$9.5	$9.5	$11.9	$9.0	$15.6	$13.5
Shipping Product	$31.9	$40.0	$19.0	$12.5	$10.5	$14.5	$18.5	$15.4	$17.0
Profitable	$35.1	$40.0	$21.5	$10.9	$16.8	$16.5	$19.4	$19.5	$19.5
Restart	$5.3	NS	NS	$1.5	NS	NS	NS	NS	NS

Median Premoney Valuation, by Round Class ($M)

	1999	2000	2001	2002	2003	2004	2005		
Round Class	Total	Total	Total	Total	Total	Total	1Q	2Q	Total
Seed Round	$4.0	$5.0	$3.4	$2.8	$2.4	$1.6	NS	NS	$1.7
First Round	$9.8	$12.4	$8.0	$6.0	$4.8	$5.5	$7.0	$5.0	$5.5
Second Round	$30.0	$40.0	$18.0	$13.0	$13.0	$12.3	$13.2	$14.0	$14.0
Later Round	$65.0	$89.8	$40.0	$24.0	$20.0	$29.0	$30.5	$29.5	$30.2
Restart	$13.4	$21.0	$17.5	$8.0	$10.0	$11.8	$24.0	$16.0	$19.3

*NS = Not Significant

Source: Created by casewriter using data from Dow Jones Venture One.

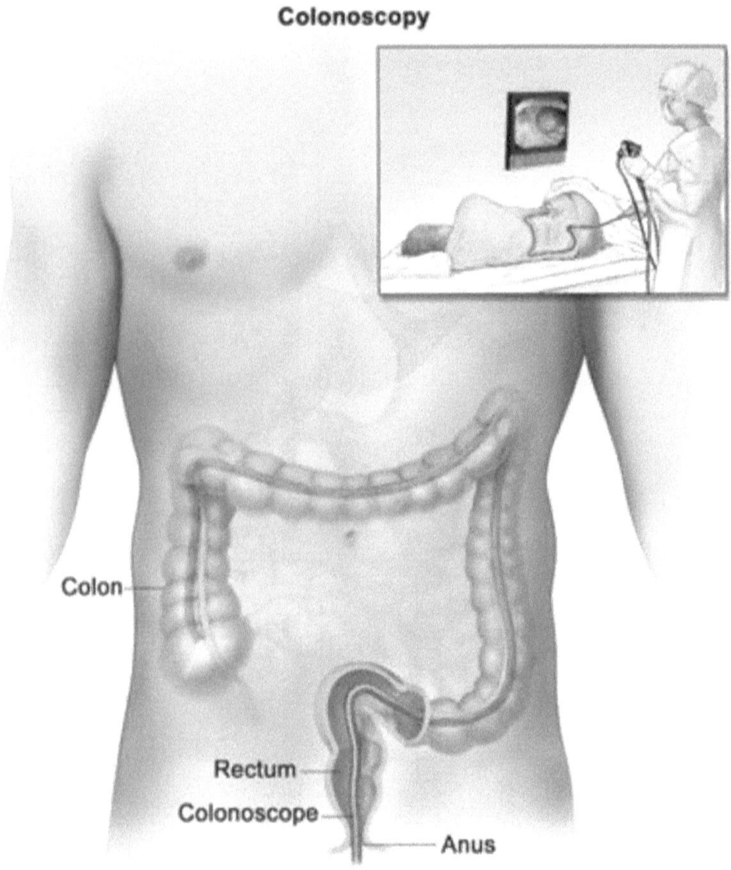

EXHIBIT 4 Colonoscopy Diagram
Source: Company documents.

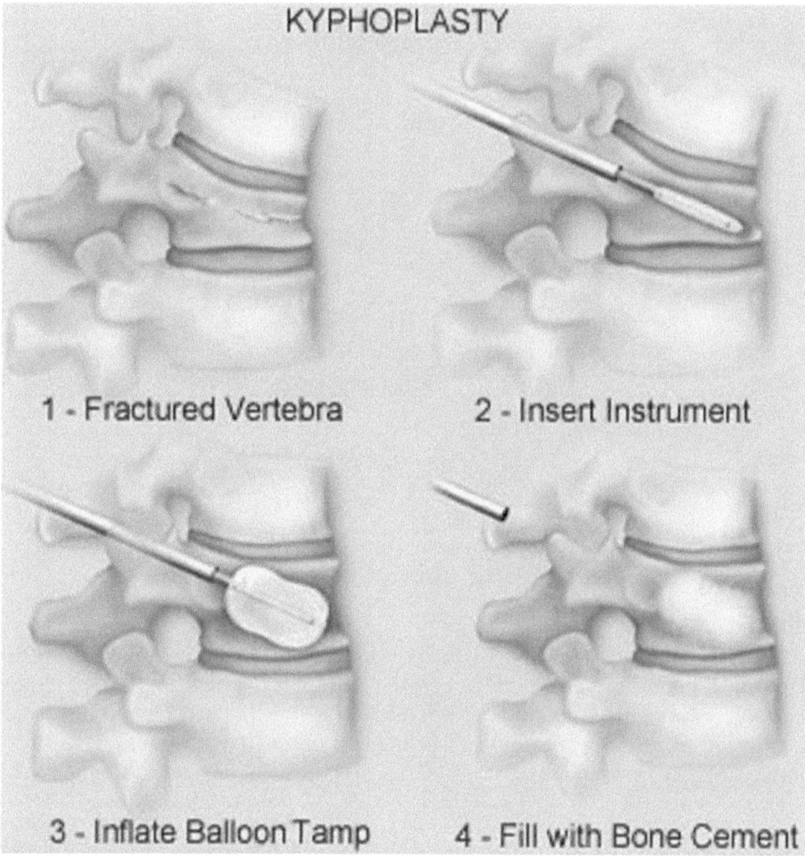

EXHIBIT 5 Kyphoplasty Diagram
Source: Company documents.

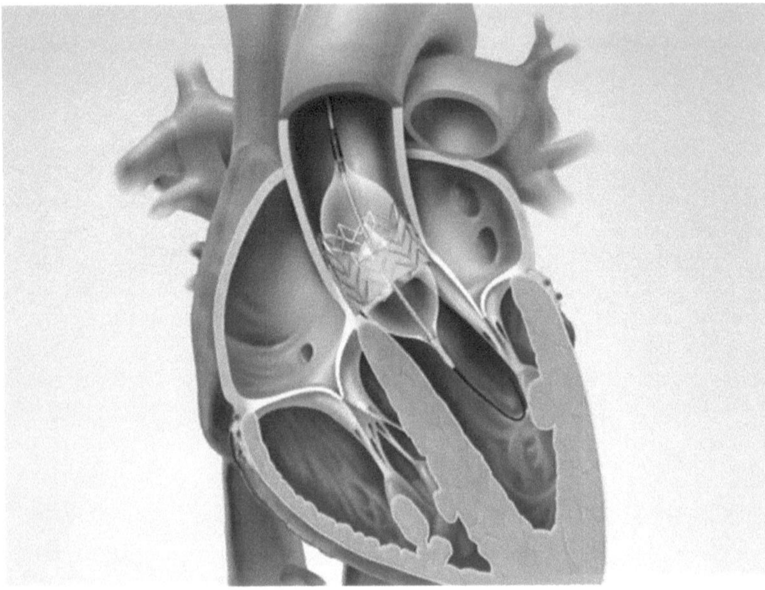

EXHIBIT 6 TAVR Diagram
A transcatheter valve delivered by balloon expansion. Balloons are used for pre-dilatation (dilating the native valve before the implant is delivered) and for post-dilatation (dilating the implant once it has been deployed). Post-dilatation enhances the valve opening and serves to 'seat' the implant in the native annulus.
Source: Company documents.

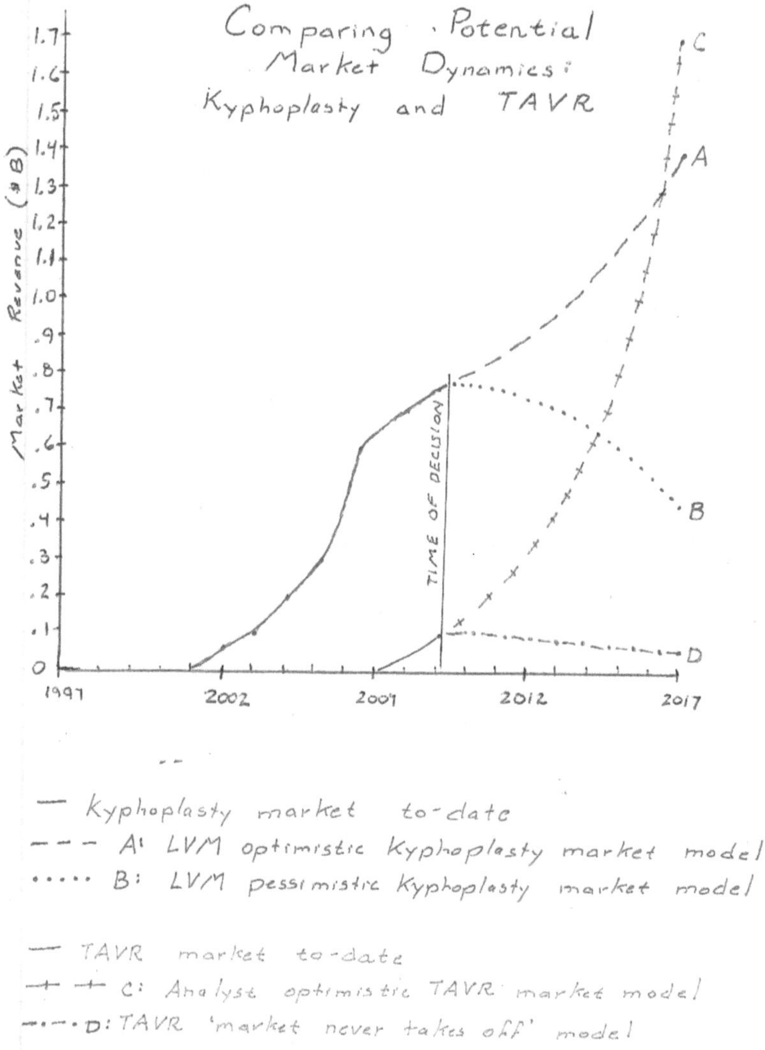

EXHIBIT 7 Tilson's Projections
Source: Alex Tilson.

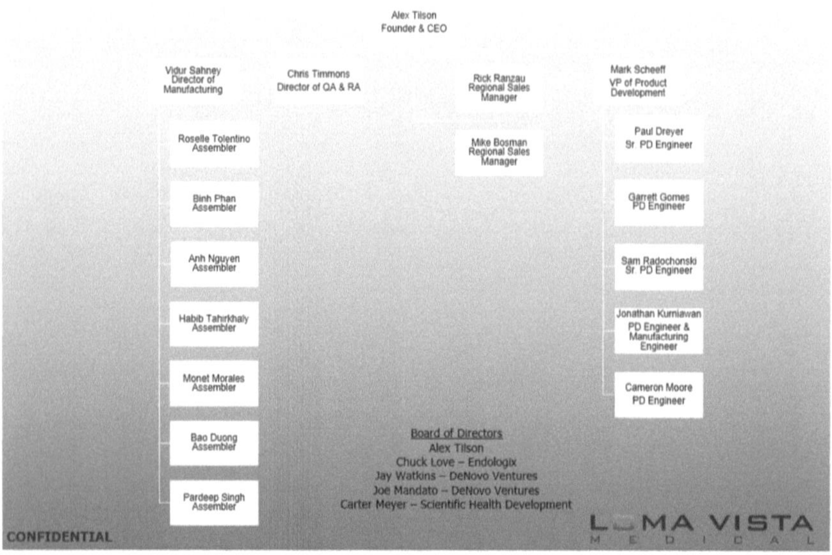

EXHIBIT 8 Loma Vista Org Chart
Source: Alex Tilson.

EXHIBIT 9 2007 Income Statement

Loma Vista Medical Income Statement For the Twelve Months Ending December 31, 2007	
	Year to Date
Revenues	
Total Revenues	0.00
Cost of Sales	
Total Cost of Sales	0.00
Gross Profit	0.00
Operating Expenses	
Travel - Non Air	$ 297.77
Entertainment/EE's activities	39.18
Consultants - General	595.00
Consultants - Engineering	75,862.11
Consultants - Medical	5,979.00
Legal - General	13,471.01
Legal - Patents/Trademarks	50,732.37
Material - Prototype	34,514.28
Outside services	36,320.00
Expensed Lab Supply/Tools/Equi	1,575.56
Expensed Computer Equip/Repair	195.44
Dues/Books/Subscriptions	416.60
Telecommunications	104.95
Bank Charges	112.00
Office Supplies	1,353.88
Shipping and Postage	1,329.29
Print and Copies	116.43
Total Expenses	223,014.87
Interest Income/Expenses	(1,244.51)
Net Income	($ 221,770.36)

Legal & IP	64,203
Clinical & Preclinical	5,979
R&D	149,062
Other	2,526

Source: Alex Tilson.

EXHIBIT 10 2008 Income Statement

Loma Vista Medical
Income Statement
For the Twelve Months Ending December 31, 2008

	Year to Date
Revenues	
Income	$ 3,200.00
Consulting Income	9,794.00
Total Revenues	12,994.00
Cost of Sales	
Total Cost of Sales	0.00
Gross Profit	12,994.00
Operating Expenses	
Travel - Air	10,367.47
Travel - Non Air	4,261.57
Lodging	3,449.95
Meals	2,212.95
Entertainment/EE's activities	173.27
Consultants - General	11,985.00
Consultants - Engineering	241,493.19
Consultants - Medical	7,125.00
Legal - General	10,040.40
Legal - Patents/Trademarks	80,852.07
Aminal Studies	14,341.56
Training/Recruiting	75.00
Meetings/Trade Shows	1,195.00
Material - Prototype	99,496.93
Outside services	57,923.68
Depreciation Expenses	590.34
Expensed Lab Supply/Tools/Equi	9,248.53
Experimental Materials	1,800.00
Expensed Computer Equip/Repair	80.01
Expensed Software/sw maintenan	26.80
Dues/Books/Subscriptions	803.06
Telecommunications	1,517.88
Bank Charges	411.90
Office Supplies	337.20
Shipping and Postage	8,504.11
Utilities	269.70
Total Expenses	568,582.57
Interest/Dividends Income	(1,243.21)
Interest Expenses	45,652.67
FED, DE and CA State Taxes	1,037.70
Interest Income/Expenses	45,447.16
Net Income	($601,035.73)

Legal & IP	90,892
Clinical & Preclinical	21,467
Engineering	422,985
Other	78,686

Source: Alex Tilson.

EXHIBIT 11 2009 Income Statement

Loma Vista Medical Income Statement For the Twelve Months Ending December 31, 2009	
Revenues	
Consulting Income	$ 19,598.20
Total Revenues	19,598.20
Cost of Sales	
Payroll - Employees	318,666.63
Payroll Taxes	21,129.15
Employee Benefits	4,393.00
Workers Compensation Insurance	2,312.52
Temp Help	9,841.43
Total Cost of Sales	356,342.73
Gross Profit	(336,744.53)
Operating Expenses	
Payroll Fee	191.94
Travel - Air	5,684.08
Travel - Non Air	2,814.56
Lodging	475.55
Meals	929.25
Entertainment/EE's Activities	1,585.81
Consultants - General	43,345.00
Consultants - QA	9,144.67
Consultants - Engineering	120,262.85
Consultants - Medical	7,084.00
Legal - General	27,494.76
Legal - Patents/Trademarks	145,379.85
Aminal Studies	5,999.90
Training/Recruiting	75.00
Meetings/Trade Shows	1,395.00
Material - Prototype	171,267.54
Outside Services	11,143.53
Expensed Lab Supply/Tools/Equipment	21,209.75
Experimental Materials	35.28
Expensed Computer Equip/Repair	1,576.20
Expensed Software/Sw Maintenan	385.87
Expensed Furniture	332.14
Fees and Licenses	2,142.54
Dues/Books/Subscriptions	185.54
Telecommunications	4,163.20
Bank Charges	607.00

Legal & IP	172,875
Clinical & Preclinical	14,659
Engineering	735,705
Other	68,571

EXHIBIT 11 (*continued*)

Office Supplies	1,589.11
Shipping and Postage	7,287.37
Print and Copies	210.51
Building Rent	16,840.00
Utilities	975.00
Other Facilities Expenses	582.64
Clinical Studies - Documents	1,575.00
Total Expenses	613,970.44
Interest/Dividends Income	(124.86)
Interest Expenses	20,821.99
FED, DE and CA State Taxes	800.00
Interest Income/Expenses	21,497.13
Net Income	($972,212.10)

Source: Alex Tilson.

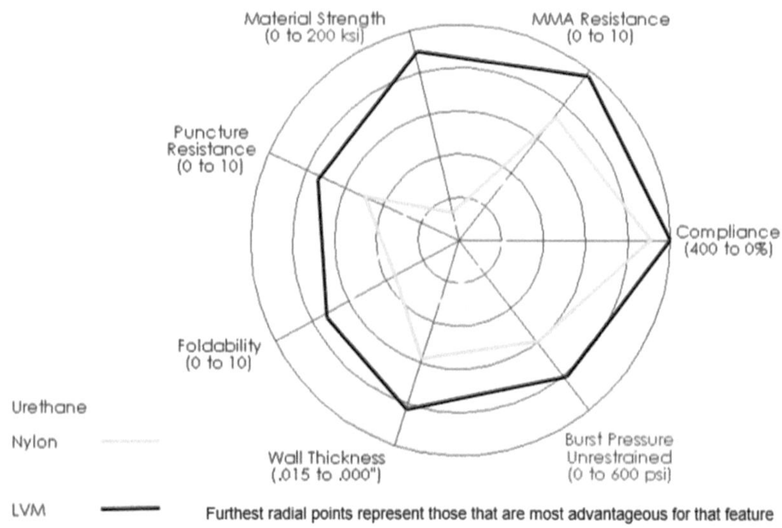

EXHIBIT 12 Comparing Material Properties
Source: Alex Tilson.

CHAPTER 2.5

Vueling Airlines

Paul A. Gompers and Kristin A. Perry

It was November 2003 when Carlos Muñoz's start-up – a low-cost airline poised for a spring 2004 launch in Barcelona, Spain – came to a screeching halt. Careful market studies indicated that Barcelona was an attractive base of operations for a low-cost airline in Spain, but Muñoz had just met with the airport's slot coordinator and learned that Vueling would obtain landing and take-off rights for only 6 of the 20 slots necessary for full operations. The airport expansion plan had suffered a delay, and new capacity was put on hold. Worse yet, this devastating blow could potentially have been avoided if Muñoz and his team had had a better understanding of how the industry distributed landing rights.

Muñoz exited his meeting and made his way through the airport. The sound of Barcelona's bustling travelers was reduced to a quiet hum as his mind raced to identify viable alternatives. Of course, his lead investors could refuse to fund Vueling without the Barcelona slots and effectively squash any alternative solution. Muñoz didn't want to chalk this past year up as a mere learning experience and was convinced that if he didn't create a low-cost Spanish airline, then someone else would. Had he missed the window of opportunity? Slower growth through a smaller, middle-market hub might work, but it would imply a lower value potential and higher launch risk. Alternatively, Vueling could launch in 2005 after gathering more slots in Barcelona. Muñoz's next steps would not only impact the company's survival, but also the lives of the team he had built over the past year – some of whom had young families and could not work indefinitely on an unfunded project. It was clear that he needed a plan, that he needed to contact his lead investors, and that he had no time to waste.

Vueling Airlines
by PAUL A. GOMPERS, KRISTIN A. PERRY, case number 9-808-077 Rev. AUGUST 8, 2023

BACKGROUND: AN IDEA TAKES FLIGHT

Upon graduation from Harvard Business School (HBS) in 1998, Carlos Muñoz had every intention of returning home to Murcia, Spain to run his family's business, AMC, a fourth-generation, €250 million company in the fruit and juice business. After an 18 month stint with the management consulting firm of McKinsey & Company in California, he did return for three years to AMC and served as general manager, working together with his father and two older brothers. However, Muñoz's business interests had expanded during graduate school, and he quickly began to realize that he wanted to follow his own path. Though he had little experience outside of the food industry, he had worked on several low-cost operational models during his McKinsey internship.

The idea took hold in November of 2002. David Long, a former juice industry business partner, introduced Muñoz to Eduardo Fairen and Sue Smith, a pilot and an airport manager, who had been discussing the "pie in the sky" notion of a low-cost carrier that would fly between Spain and the UK. Muñoz quickly recognized the cost-advantage of simple, efficient operations and the potentially large business opportunity of starting a low-cost carrier (LCC) in southern Europe, a market currently un-served by this model. Muñoz recalled his early excitement about the opportunity,

> David knew I had left my family business with the intention to start my own company, and he thought I could be interested in the idea of starting an airline, which was admittedly a long shot at the time. I liked the fact that the LCC model was so solid and well-tested in other countries, such as the US and the UK, and that air fares were still very high in Spain, France, and Italy. I also liked the simplicity of the business, and I felt very capable of leading the project from the get-go.

Low-Cost Carrier Industry

In the wake of the September 11, 2001 terrorist attacks in the United States, the airline industry was experiencing historic declines in profitability and revenues worldwide (see **Exhibit 1**). Low-cost carriers in the United States and Europe, however, appeared to have weathered the upheaval quite well. This was inherent to the low-cost model – low-cost carriers like Southwest and JetBlue had historically continued to yield stable profits and high valuation even in the midst of high fuel prices, recessions, wars, and plane crashes (see **Exhibit 2**).

Southwest Airlines pioneered the low-cost carrier model in the 1970s when it offered direct, short haul flights at a 60-70% discount on market fares with limited in-flight services.[1] Two main factors drove the success of Southwest Airlines: sustainable cost advantage over traditional carriers and market stimulation. More seats per plane and greater flight frequencies ensured higher utilization rates. The carrier's "no frills" services, lower labor costs, airport choice, and higher asset utilization drove its cost advantages. The U.S. Department of Transportation coined the phrase "the Southwest effect"[2] in 1993 to describe the airline's stimulation on the market when entering a new geographic area. When Southwest announced a new route at their discounted rate, traditional carriers also dropped prices and increased their flight frequencies. Fares typically sustained a lasting 65% reduction, and passenger traffic tended to increase 200-500%.[3]

Several new startups in both the United States and Europe were following Southwest's lead, showing strong revenue per passenger growth and financial success (see **Exhibit 3**). JetBlue Airlines was profitable just six months after its founding in 2000 and went public 18 months after it began operations. The European market was served by two dominant LCCs, Ryanair and easyJet, which industry analysts expected to capture roughly 14% of the European air travel market by 2007 and 28% of the market by 2010 (see **Exhibit 4**).[4]

Spanish Context and Opportunity

Muñoz was certain that the Spanish market was ripe for the entry of a low-cost carrier. "The market was the decisive factor," Muñoz recalled. "It was evident low-cost was going to continue to grow—and there was a vacuum in southwest Europe."[5] With a population of 40.8 million,[6] Spain was large by European standards and continued to demonstrate robust growth. It had the second largest European market in the airline industry, with 144.6 million passengers in 2001, and exhibited strong growth with 7.5% passenger CAGR[a] from 1995-2001.[7] Furthermore, Spanish travelers were particularly price sensitive. Eighty percent of the Spanish market was comprised of business travel from small and mid-sized companies, as well as leisure budget travelers.[8] No low-cost incumbents were based in Spain, and none were serving southwestern Europe at all. The two large European LCCs, Ryanair and easyJet, were focused on north-south traffic, carrying British and German tourists to Spain or Italy. Two existing local LCCs, France's Aeris and Italy's Volare Airlines, were weak players based

a CAGR = compound annual growth rate.

on previous charter airlines, with higher-cost bases, no direct-distribution (i.e., Internet) skills, and a low probability of survival against LCCs. The three major Spanish carriers, Iberia, Spanair, and Air Europa, had a 95.2% share of the domestic market and were all positioned as traditional "full service" carriers.[9] The potential for market stimulation in Spain, however, was evident in early low-cost routes originating from the UK. For example, prior to 1998, Barcelona-Liverpool was served only by Iberia, with 50,000 passengers traveling per year. EasyJet started serving the route in 1998. From 1998-2001, total passengers grew 480% to 240,000 per year.[10]

The more Muñoz learned, the more convinced he was that he should seize this opportunity before someone else did. It was also clear that he didn't need to reinvent the wheel. In January 2003, after several business and philosophical discussions with his wife (who was fully supportive of his plans), Muñoz decided to quit his job, borrow the standard LCC business model, and begin forming his company in earnest. He invited Fairen and Smith to invest, but both declined, instead committing to helping informally on their free time. He started the company as sole investor, committing half of his savings as seed capital for the venture.

PEOPLE, PARTNERSHIPS, AND PLANES (OR, HOW DOES A 33-YEAR-OLD CREATE AN AIRLINE?)

Although Muñoz was very comfortable with his assessment of the business opportunity at hand, he was also acutely aware that he knew nothing about running an airline. He had no experience in the industry and certainly couldn't invest on the scale required by such an asset-intensive business. Fairen and Smith were good supporters, but each only knew their part of airline operations. The success of Vueling would clearly hinge on Muñoz's ability to assemble the right group of people and resources.

Building the Team

At the forefront of Muñoz's mind was his need to recruit a partner as Chief Operational Officer (COO) for the company. Muñoz recalled, "I needed a partner whom I could trust and who displayed a high degree of integrity. I also wanted someone who knew the business well and had grown an airline from a top executive position, yet who had not been 'polluted' with a large, high-cost, traditional carrier mentality." In the following weeks, Muñoz began attending industry conferences and meeting with industry executives. He cast a wide net and conducted thorough interviews with interested parties – for both the partnership role and other key positions.

In late January 2003, Muñoz attended an aviation seminar in Madrid. Two people he met at the seminar began advising him informally about partner candidates, and a shortlist soon emerged for the position. After a professional background check and a five hour interview, Lazaro Ros signed on as Muñoz's COO. Ros was COO of a growing charter airline in his previous position, and fortuitously, his non-compete agreement had just expired. Muñoz recalled their initial meeting:

> We discussed the project´s basics, our careers, and management, people and life at large. Ros was much more experienced in the airline industry, and his calm, controlled management style stood in contrast with my bolder executive style. We immediately recognized our complementary management skills – a unique combination of 'experience and innovation'. We felt good about each other, and decided to take the project forward together.

A handshake sealed their agreement, and a few days later Ros bought 15% of the founder's share in the company. Ros and Muñoz agreed to increase Ros' participation when the company needed more capital.

A selection process for the management team then began in earnest. The process was thorough and professional, including numerous skill and "fit" interviews, tests, and reference checks. Muñoz and Ros required a financial commitment from everyone who signed on to the team. Many candidates were rejected, and some who received offers decided not to join, typically judging the project to be "too risky." However, most were attracted to the business opportunity and to the equity upside potential offered to the team upon the launch of the airline.

By June, Muñoz and Ros had assembled a 9-person team with 220 years of combined airline experience (see **Exhibit 5**). Muñoz was very excited about the experience and knowledge the team added to the business – a quality that would prove valuable when talking with Boeing, Airbus, and the airport authority. "I felt very strongly that this was a business that must be treated with great respect, given the risks involved with air travel. I placed a high priority on operational expertise. After assembling our management team, the Vueling business plan went from being a really good idea, to a compelling business opportunity by the summer of 2003."

Initially, Muñoz and Ros were the only shareholders. The rest of the management team agreed to partial commitment at this point – to helping out on nights and weekends, with a share in the upside when the company launched. No team members drew a salary during this early phase, including Muñoz and Ros.

Despite his confidence in his team, Muñoz continued to seek advisors in the industry. In May of 2003, he decided to take a shot at contacting Kim Clark, who was the Dean of Harvard Business School at the time and also a member of JetBlue's board of directors. He had met Clark twice before during school events when he as a student but assumed that the Dean's busy calendar left little time to respond to young graduates' emails. Muñoz also recalled that "informal opinion had it that he would not care to reply to alumni under the age of 50, or to alumni who had donated less than $100,000 to the school!" To his delight, informal opinion proved wrong, and Muñoz received a very prompt reply from Clark as well as an introduction to the CEO of JetBlue, David Neeleman. Over the next months, Muñoz had several invaluable meetings with both Neeleman and David Barger, JetBlue's President and COO.

Honing the Business Plan

Muñoz invested the initial €150,000 in equity to fund market studies and administrative costs. [See **Exhibit 6** for start-up financial projections and operational forecasts.] Muñoz and Ros focused intently on sharpening the business plan as they shopped for professional investors.

Base of Operations and Route Development

Muñoz recognized that perhaps the most critical decision for a low-cost airline was its choice of base operations. Operationally, crews, aircraft, and all basic support groups centered around the base to achieve optimal efficiency. LCCs also concentrated their advertising budgets very intensely in the local market.

Muñoz hired Leoncio Vadillo, a recently retired Iberia Airlines pricing director whom he had met at an industry seminar, to help identify the optimal route network and location for Vueling's initial base of operations. Vadillo recommended El Prat Airport in Barcelona. [See **Exhibit 7** for base selection data.] El Prat was located in Spain's top tourist region, Catalonia, which offered a variety of cultural and business attractions. The region accounted for 19% of Spain's GDP, boasted Spain's second highest GDP per capita of $21,000, and its local economy was largely comprised of mid-sized family owned businesses, a cost-conscious and trade-oriented group.[11] While Barcelona enjoyed a large, growing air travel market, with over 20 million passengers in 2001, it currently offered very limited connections – only 13% of travelers connected to other flights.[12] Furthermore, prospects for future growth in the air travel market were promising. El Prat planned to double its operations by 2006, and the regional government was actively seeking to attract new airlines and increased air traffic.[13]

Vueling focused first on building a Barcelona market by serving routes from Barcelona to mid-sized cities and the islands, a few smaller routes to Bilbao and Alicante, and weekly flights to Paris and Milan. [See **Exhibit 8** for a map of the region.] Early on, Muñoz discarded the UK and German markets due to excessive competition from incumbents Ryanair and easyJet. Muñoz planned the second phase of operations, 6-12 months after Vueling's launch, to focus on service from Barcelona to southern Europe (Paris, Milan, Brussels, and Rome) as well as more frequent flights to and from mid-size cities. Finally, phase three would establish a base in Madrid, contingent on the development of new runways at the Madrid airport, to serve Madrid-to-southern Europe traffic. Muñoz also planned to initiate southern Europe service from mid-size Spanish cities, for example, Valencia to Milan. Graduation to the second and third phases of development would hinge on Vueling's ability to execute the low-cost model, as well as proven success with mid-size cities and southern Europe traffic.

Positioning, Branding and Marketing Strategy

Consumer focus groups soon pointed to the strong need to adapt the existing LCC model to the idiosyncrasy of the local market. For example, Spanish consumers' willingness to drive far away to secondary, cheaper airports was minimal, in sharp contrast to British or German consumers, who were willing to drive up to 100km in order to get a "good deal." Since industry research pointed to the same preference on the part of French and Italian consumers, Vueling decided to serve only major airports. Also, the business travelers segment targeted by Vueling showed little tolerance for non-assigned seating, as found on Southwest and major European LCC airlines. Vueling assigned seating from day one, as did JetBlue, with minimal operational impact.

Muñoz would position Vueling as an alternative, business-friendly LCC product, targeting not only leisure travelers, but also the more lucrative business segment, especially small-to-mid-sized businesses that comprised a large part of the economies of southern European countries. He hoped that scheduling 3 to 4 daily trips per route would help attract travelers in both of these market segments. Advertising would target business and leisure travelers in the existing market by emphasizing Vueling's best price for air travel. Muñoz decided to concentrate spending via local media and corporate discount programs for small businesses (see **Exhibit 9**).

Muñoz pursued a branding strategy for Vueling that was hip, fresh, and exciting. There had not been anything new in Spanish air travel for decades. A top branding firm, Saffron, agreed to develop the brand and complete the "look and feel" of the company for a small fee and a "success payment" at the time of the launch. The Vueling name itself came from a twist on the Spanish word Vuelo – to fly – as well as a nod to a fashionable Spanish habit of adding the "ing" suffix to a root in order to create a stylish, though incorrect, new word. For example, "footing" was the popular term for "jogging" in Spain.[14]

Pricing System

Traditional airlines typically offered many discounted fares (often between six and ten different fare classes on a single flight), oversold their flights at 5-10% capacity, and had a large percentage of passengers (20-40%) who connected via a central hub.[15] This resulted in a complex pricing system with limited low fares and high operational costs when passengers were denied boarding or missed connecting flights. By comparison, Vueling´s low cost model would offer only 3-5 fare types (based on booking time and demand patterns), no connector flights, and limited overbooking scenarios (only 2-5% for high demand flights). This simple pricing model, which was easily understood through an Internet pricing grid based on dates booked, would guarantee low fares and would not incur additional operational costs or loss of goodwill due to lost connections or denied boarding.

Vueling's dynamic pricing model was based on the number of seats sold and speed of sale according to the following ranges: 20-35% of seats allocated to the lowest advertised fare (€25); 20-35% of seats allocated to a mid-priced fare when low fare was not available, or for bookings made less than 7 days in advance; and 30-60% of seats allocated to the full-priced fare when other fares were not available, for bookings less than 3 days in advance, or for the same day return (business travel).

Sales and Distribution

Like Ryanair and easyJet, Vueling's sales and distribution efforts would focus on the Internet. Ticketless reservations helped avoid logistical issues. Distribution costs would be kept low by employing direct sales methods and no commissions on tickets sold by travel agents. To generate ancillary revenue, the confirmation page would link directly to preferred partners in hotels and car rentals. (This represented an additional 10-15% revenue for Ryanair and easyJet). Vueling would also offer call center support for online users and clients without access to the Internet. Fares booked through the center would have an additional €5 charge, to help push users to Internet bookings.

IT Systems were to be based on those of existing LCCs, which typically used the same simple, inexpensive reservation system called Navitaire, originally designed by Neeleman for JetBlue. The system purposely avoided all complexity and "whistles" of traditional carriers systems, and allowed – almost imposed – operational efficiency as the highest priority. For example, no passenger connections, or airline "interlining" (different airlines sharing passengers) were possible with the system. All other systems, especially those related to the Operations Control Center (OCC), which constitute the basic structure of an airline, were also kept very simple and scalable, with sights on a fast growth pace in the years to come.

Ground Handling and Maintenance

Quality, speed, and cost-efficiency were the planned hallmarks of Vueling's ground handling and maintenance priorities. Light maintenance, which was required every 500 block hours/60 days/350 segments, would occur overnight by the line engineers. For heavy plane maintenance (which required 8 days out of schedule per plane, approximately every 50 weeks), Muñoz and Ros planned to hire an outside contractor. The operational base was designed to support an entire team of human resources – 12 ticket agents, 3 flight coordinators, 9 bag loaders and material resources (ticket sales office, buses, ground power units, steps, luggage trucks, radios, car, and a motorcycle). During phase one, Vueling would use third party handling companies in other airports due to the lack in critical mass of flights.

Customer Service

Customer service on the ground and via ticketing sales was a top priority for Muñoz, especially with the business traveler in mind, and given that large traditional carriers were receiving a record number of complaints regarding punctuality, lost bags, and poor client service. Muñoz felt strongly that Vueling's commitment to customer service needed to be comprehensive and meticulous, as well as cost effective (see **Exhibit 10**). Vueling would measure and publish simple, key service statistics on a monthly basis. JetBlue provided a good role model in this regard, successfully combining the lowest cost-base among US carriers with high client satisfaction ratings.

Assembling Resources

Efficient execution of the LCC model was essential in order to compete with traditional, established carriers. Although Muñoz had created a solid business plan, assembled an experienced management team, and had begun courting a group of interested investors, Vueling was still a long way from its maiden voyage. Meeting a thirty-minute turn-around standard was a high order, and would require all components to be in place and operating efficiently (see **Exhibit 11**). There was not much room for learning curves and Muñoz recognized the need for the swift assembly of several key resources.

Fleet Acquisition

With an experienced management team in place, the prospect of purchasing or leasing an actual airplane was a bit less daunting than it had seemed six months ago. Operating leases typically offered monthly fixed rate payments for 3-6 year terms. Muñoz was convinced that an all-leased fleet would ensure greater flexibility in fleet management as well as lower capital commitment. On the other hand, purchasing aircraft directly from manufacturers could minimize per annum aircraft costs. EasyJet and Ryanair both owned a significant portion of their fleets in 2003. Ryanair began its operations by purchasing older, discounted planes, while easyJet began by leasing its fleet and only later purchased aircraft directly from manufacturers.[16]

The fleet size and type of plane would likely be less influenced by the preference of the team and more so by which manufacturers would even talk to Vueling. Muñoz knew the General Electric (GE) country manager through his family's business and had exploratory meetings with GE Commercial Aviation Services (GECAS), the largest aircraft leasing company in the world. After September 11, 2001, planes were parked by the hundreds and available to lease. The uncertainty in the global air travel market combined with order cancellations from traditional airlines[b] had resulted in a large pool of unused planes – approximately 13% of 30,000 commercial passenger planes.

Boeing was hungry to cut a deal, but it was difficult to get the attention of Airbus' commercial management team in Spain – they did not seem to understand the growing success of low-cost carriers. Muñoz recalled the difficulties the team encountered while navigating this terrain,

> The trade-off between convincing suppliers to do business with us by sharing much company information and the confidentiality risk of doing so was a major issue. We did not want the airline community – especially future competitors like Iberia or easyJet – to find out about

b At the time of the case, Delta and Continental had recently canceled orders for 45 Boeing 737s.

our plans. We navigated this with as much legal protection as possible, and by using common sense on a case-by-case basis to decide how much information to release.

Muñoz hoped his team would find a way through Airbus' disinterest so that Vueling could choose among the best of all available planes, based on their age, cost and performance. Fleet choice was clearly a key decision point for the company, given safety concerns and the asset-intensive nature of this business. Both Southwest and Ryanair had fleets exclusively made up of Boeing 737s. Airbus was used by both JetBlue and easyJet. Talks with Boeing and GECAS suggested that brand new aircraft could be leased for roughly $50,000 per month more than slightly used aircraft. Older planes (10-20 years old) were available at a significant discount, but higher maintenance and fuel costs, as well as higher incidence rates, and the subsequent operational disruption and public image costs, would have to be factored into Vueling's analysis (See **Exhibit 12**).

Regulatory Processes

As the industry veteran, Ros led all work with Civil Aviation and other regulatory bodies to obtain Vueling's airline operating certificate (AOC) and airline license. Muñoz recalled that "this was a fairly straight forward process; we just needed to be knowledgeable and work through the system." Through official presentations and consistent communications, Ros introduced regulatory authorities to the team, the business plan and investors in order to establish Vueling's safety credentials and secure a favorable, smooth reception at the time of Vueling's launch. Ros kept his efforts closely synchronized with the company launch timeline, as the process was dependent upon such items as aircraft import and registration, third-party contracts, safety management systems, and the publication of operational and maintenance manuals.

Given the importance of the operational base, and the fact that the team had decided to operate out of major congested airports, Muñoz set out to secure landing and take-off rights at El Prat immediately after identifying it as a preferable headquarters. The process for securing these landing rights "slots" was conducted through the International Air Transportation Association (IATA) Scheduling Conference, which met two times per year for three full days of meetings.[c] Only major airports were "coordinated" or

c In the United States, most airports did not allocate take-off and landing slots, instead operating on a "first come, first serve" basis, which often led to long runway taxiing queues.

slot-driven, but all airlines – incumbents and newcomers alike – attended these conferences to vie for available slots. About three weeks prior to the conference, airlines sent requests for preferred arrival and departure times to airport coordinators. Having identified areas where demand exceeded airport capacity, coordinators would open the conference by offering alternative schedules for those requests determined to be of 'lower priority.' During the rest of the conference, schedules were adjusted either though discussions between airlines and slot coordinators, or through airlines exchanging slots with each other.[17] Muñoz and Ros were acutely aware that this global system favored incumbent airlines through "grandfathering rights." Muñoz explained,

> This meant carriers that had operated a given slot one season, got to keep it for the next one, effectively closing the entrance to new carriers. In practice, a carrier never gave up a slot in a congested airport at a valuable time. If a given flight did not work well, say Barcelona-to-Milan with a daily 8am departure, carriers would use the slot to try another route, say Barcelona-to-Madrid, but would never return the slot to the 'slot pool' and let someone else take it.
>
> The European Union, in an attempt to increase competition, passed legislation in the late 1990s giving new airlines a preferential right for half of any new slots available (the other half being distributed equally among all carriers). We planned to use this to our advantage so that we could obtain more slots – because Barcelona was planning to expand its capacity over the following seasons.

Many local politicians were very excited about the prospects of a Barcelona-based low-cost carrier and assured Muñoz that they could help the company secure landing rights at El Prat by promoting Vueling to local slot coordinators and the local business community at large. As a result, Muñoz and his team began logging many hours talking with local leaders about Vueling's operational plans.

Crew Management

Vueling's low-cost model relied heavily on crew management practices to keep unit labor costs 60-80% lower than Iberia's. This would be achieved mainly through higher productivity (total hours flown in the year), and in part through somewhat lower compensation. Muñoz expected to hire 30 pilots at approximately €85,000 per pilot with limited union activism and a willingness to fly the maximum legal amount of 900 flight hours per year. The pilot crew would be comprised of experienced captains and young co-pilots, providing an attractive career path for new pilots and a pipeline for future expansion. Cabin crews would cost €27,000 per full-time employee. Muñoz wanted to hire 15 managers with experience and 30 junior crew members, made up of students and young people wanting to travel. Limited union affiliation and seniority benefits would ensure flexible hiring and work rules. Muñoz would assign three crew members to each flight, scheduled for regular, short flights and ending the day at home to minimize per diem costs. The company's light overhead would ensure a small operational staff, comprised of youthful, multi-tasking employees.

Though the logistical aspects of hiring and training the requisite personnel to get Vueling in the air could be daunting, Muñoz did not expect any difficulties in attracting people. He recalled that "the industry was still in 'recovery mode' from 9/11, and crews, especially pilots, were largely available." Led by captain Fairen, they also applied an innovative approach to hiring pilots: they would recruit across all European nationalities to reach a much wider and more diverse candidate pool. This contrasted with traditional carriers, which only recruited Spanish pilots. Muñoz, Ros, and other members of the executive team would be directly involved in both the hiring and training process of all employees in order to develop and preserve a homogeneous culture, characterized by safety, client-orientation, caring and a "can-do" attitude. Muñoz explained,

> Our salaries were competitive but not high, so we complemented this with 'social salary,' meaning a fun, team-spirited work atmosphere, parties, dinners, etc. The choice of Barcelona also helped – it was an attractive city to foreign people, and it was an opportunity for locals to work in their hometown (since Barcelona did not have a real airline before us.

On the flipside, Muñoz was aware that Barcelona may not help when it came to hiring technical, highly skilled employees, and that they would likely need to go abroad to fill those positions.

Funding the Venture

While Muñoz conducted interviews and sharpened his business plan, he also spent a great deal of time trying to connect to venture capitalists who may be interested in funding the company. The HBS network proved a very valuable resource in this regard. During the early phase of the idea formation in Christmas 2002, Muñoz consulted a friend and mentor from McKinsey – Andreas Stavropoulos (HBS '97), who worked for Draper Fisher Jurvetson, a venture capital firm in Palo Alto. Over the course of several conversations with Stavropoulos, the strategy for fundraising and operations took sharper focus. The first investor meetings were not very successful. In March 2003, after several working sessions with two large European potential investors, both companies turned the investment down on the same day. At that point another classmate, Allen Custard (HBS ´98), who worked in a Dallas-based investment bank, helped polish the financial model and presentations, and set up meetings with US investors. He thought that US private equity firms might be interested in funding Vueling and introduced Muñoz to the Texas Pacific Group (TPG), a private equity backer that had invested successfully in many airlines before. They showed some interest in Vueling – much more so than the European firms – but did not make an immediate offer.

In April, Muñoz attended a Harvard/Georgetown alumni dinner chaired by the Prince of Spain, and found himself at a table with Oriol Pinya, an HBS '99 alum who was working for Apax Partners, a global private equity group. They spoke at length about the Vueling model and Muñoz was subsequently invited to present his plan to Apax. Apax was very impressed with Muñoz's business plan and thought the opportunity was both thought-provoking and exciting. In exchange for a leading percentage of the company, Apax suggested that they would be willing to invest between €10 and €15 million in the start-up. Muñoz agreed to give preference to the investors and to concentrate Vueling's financing with them. They became very strong supporters over the coming months, adding financial discipline and a value focus, helping with introduction to other potential investors, and even providing input on management team selection- to the point that the initial CFO candidate was replaced largely at their request.

Having identified Barcelona as Vueling's operational base, Muñoz sought a local investor. Apax recommended a subsidiary of Grupo Planeta, a publishing and media company that was very well known in Barcelona and capable of investing upwards of another €10 million in the company. Two similarly sized Catalan investors also wanted to participate. On the US side, TPG had been dragging its feet, and Muñoz feared that TPG's investment in Ryanair would cause Vueling too much trouble. Although Muñoz had looked to Barger solely as a valuable advisor over the past several months, he decided to invite him to invest in the company as well. Barger was interested and suggested that he may be willing to contribute a million euros or more. Custard also wanted to invest a similar amount, and together with Barger would form a "US investor group" in Vueling.

By the end of his capital raising efforts, Muñoz had approached fifteen potential investors and had identified six interested parties. He recalled, "private equity investors had three major concerns: understanding the risks of LCCs, the exit options, and the solidness of the team – including my youth!" Muñoz had hoped to diversify the funding base and raise money from at least five of the six interested investors, but Apax recommended that he choose only three, in order to keep corporate governance more manageable.

TURBULENCE

Muñoz was starting to feel the pressure of time. He had yet to acquire aircraft, crew, and landing rights for the late Spring launch, all of which would require substantial capital. [See **Exhibit 13** for the launch timeline.] Vueling's seed capital had been exhausted, and despite the uncertainty about closing dates, Muñoz and Ros had had to invest a further €150,000 to pay for steep legal and financial fees associated with the negotiation and closing of funding.

At the global International Air Transportation Association (IATA) Scheduling Conference in late October 2003, it became frighteningly clear that they had been wasting their time with local authorities who had been over-promising slots that they could not deliver. Barcelona had delayed its expansion plans and Vueling would receive only 6 of the 20 slots they'd requested. As Muñoz recalled:

> The Spanish slot coordinator told us: 'Father Christmas may have promised you landing rights, but here is how it works: you get in line.' While Ros and I knew that the formal process happened through airport authority, perhaps we chose to believe that 'political clout' carried more weight than it really did. We found out that whilst being well-connected did not hurt us – it certainly helped us with local PR and acceptance into the local business community – it did not produce slots where there were none available. The delay of the Barcelona airport expansion proved more important for the slot coordinator than any politician's wishes.

After meeting with Barcelona's slot coordinator, it was clear that they were not going to be able to base the airline there, at least not for all fleet and commercial flights.

What should Muñoz do now? He knew he had to tell Apax. He hoped they would remain supportive. Was a late Spring launch date completely out of the question now? Could they succeed via a different base? If so, which one and how would they go about securing landing rights at this late date? Furthermore, Vueling's fleet negotiations had to be finalized soon, the lease to its headquarters was being signed, and its personnel were being hired and trained. Muñoz wondered how a shift in venue or a suspension of operations would affect the milestones his team had been striving for, the contracts he'd signed, and the people who'd invested their time, money, and faith in the company. Could this venture survive such a blow?

NOTES

1 Company documents compiled from *No Frills: The Truth Behind the Low Cost Revolution in the Skies*, by Simon Calder (London 2002), http://www.southwest.com, and 2001 Southwest annual report.
2 Rogelio Oliva, Jody Hoffer Gittell, and David Lane "Southwest Airlines in Baltimore," HBS Case No. 602-154, p.3.
3 Ibid.
4 Company documents compiled from Morgan Stanley and Mercer Management reports.
5 Cathy Buyck, "¿Habas LCC?," *Air Transport World*, February 26, 2006.
6 Economist Intelligence Unit Data Service, http://www.alacra.com/eiu, accessed November 2007.
7 Company documents compiled from The Economist Country Briefings, AENA, SAS (parent company of Spanair) 2001 Annual Report.
8 Company documents compiled from Aeropuertos Espanoles y Navegacion Aerea (Spanish Airports and Air Navigation) and Booz Allen analysis.
9 Company documents compiled from Aeropuertos Espanoles y Navegacion Aerea (Spanish Airports and Air Navigation) and Booz Allen analysis.
10 Company documents compiled from Briston International Airport, Ferrovial Aeropuertos, and an interview with easyJet country manager, Rafael Aragones.
11 Company documents compiled from Aeropuertos Espanoles y Navegacion Aerea (AENA), National Institute of Statistics (INE), and the Ministerio de Fomento (Ministry for Infrastructures).
12 Company documents compiled from Aeropuertos Espanoles y Navegacion Aerea (AENA), National Institute of Statistics (INE), and the Ministerio de Fomento (Ministry for Infrastructures).
13 Company documents compiled from Aeropuertos Espanoles y Navegacion Aerea (AENA), National Institute of Statistics (INE), and the Ministerio de Fomento (Ministry for Infrastructures).
14 Http://spainforvisitors.com/Article179.htm, accessed November 2007.
15 Company documents compiled from interviews with easyJet and AirNostrum management and "Yield Management at American Airlines," HBS case 2-698-034.
16 Christopher Avery, *JP Morgan Analyst Report*, January 16, 2007, p. 31.
17 International Air Travel Association, http://www.iata.org/whatwedo/passenger/scheduling/how.htm, accessed March 2008.

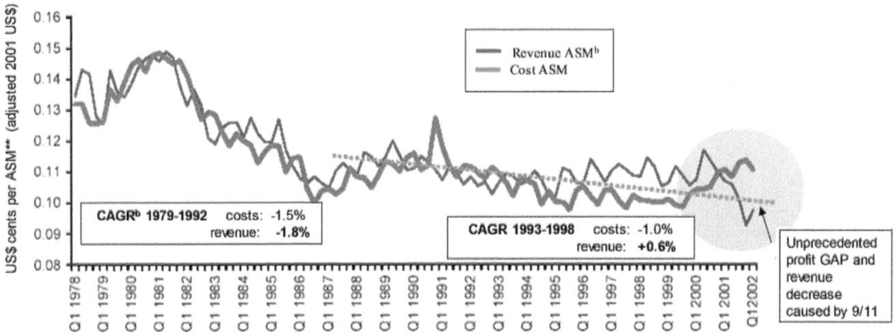

EXHIBIT 1 Comparison of Unit Revenue and Unit Cost in Airline Industry[a]
Source: Company documents. (Data compiled from International Air Transportation Association (IATA), company financial statements, and Booz Allen.)

[a] Data covers Alaska, American, America West, Continental, Delta, Eastern, Northwest, Pam Am, Piedmont, Southwest, TWA, United, US Airways

[b] ASM = available seat mile; CAGR is "compounded annual growth rate"

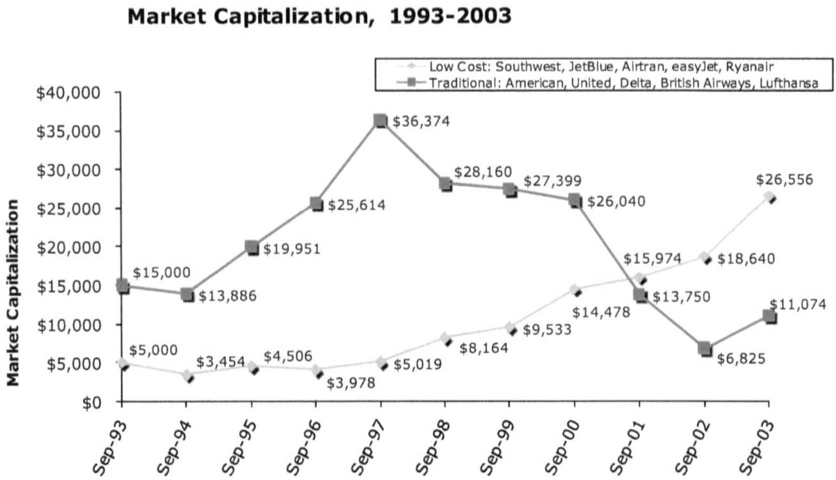

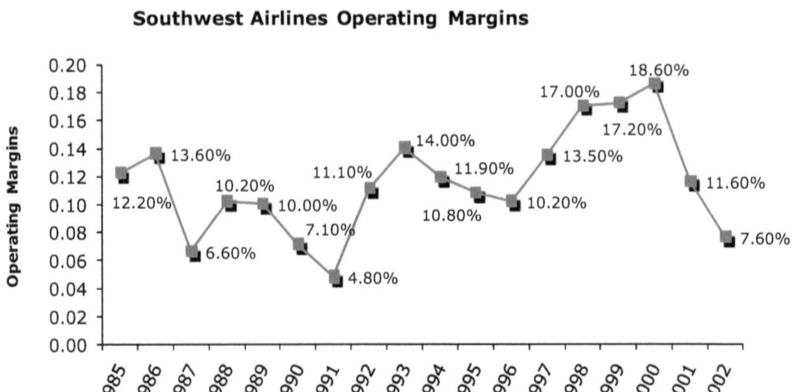

EXHIBIT 2 Low-Cost Carriers Withstand Industry Upheaval
Source: Company documents. (Data compiled from IATA, company financial statements, and Bloomberg.)

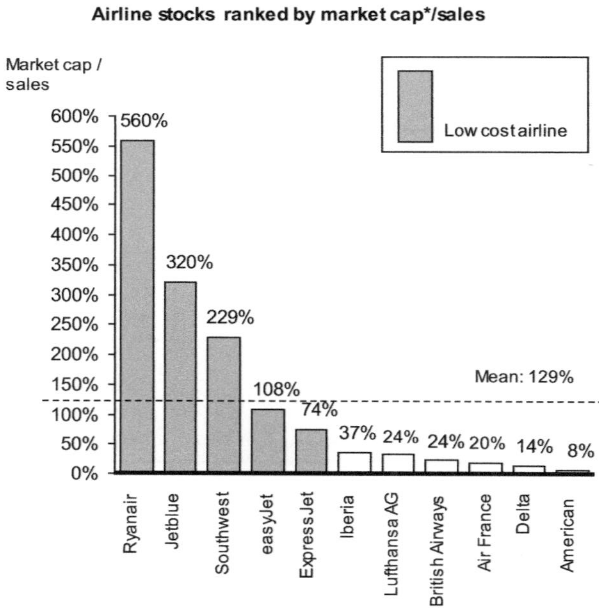

Top 5 North American Airlines (by market cap)*

Company	Traditional, LowCost	Market Cap ($million)	Revenue (LTM, $million)	Net Profit Margin (LTM)	Passengers (2002 thousand)	$ Value / Passenger
Southwest	LC	$ 12,875	$ 5,616	4.3%	63,100	$ 204.0
Jetblue	LC	$ 2,298	$ 719	8.2%	5,800	$ 396.2
Delta	TRAD	$ 1,805	$ 13,357	-10.0%	107,100	$ 16.9
American	TRAD	$ 1,425	$ 17,256	-17.3%	94,100	$ 15.1
ExpressJet	Hybrid	$ 832	$ 1,130	7.9%	9,200	$ 90.4

Top 5 European Airlines (by market cap)*

Company	Traditional, LowCost	Market Cap ($millions)	Revenue (2002, $million)	Net Profit Margin (latest)	Passengers (2002 thousand)	$ Value / Passenger
Ryanair	LC	$ 5,513	$ 985	28.4%	14,500	$ 380.2
Lufthansa AG	TRAD	$ 4,529	$ 13,883	4.0%	43,900	$ 103.2
British Airways	TRAD	$ 3042	$ 12,771	0.9%	40,000	$76.1
easyJet	LC	$ 1,304	$ 1,213	0.2%	11,400	$ 114.4
Iberia	TRAD	$ 1,911	$ 5,149	2.7%	25,000	$ 76.4

EXHIBIT 3 Low-Cost Airline Performance, United States and Europe

Source: Company documents. (Data compiled from Bloomberg and recent company public filings.)

* As of 6/06/03

			Start-up Phase					Growth (CAGR)		
Company	Year Start	First Base / Market	Initial Equity	Sources	Planes	Years to break-even	Market Cap (6/06/03)	Rev	EBIT	Founder/Significant Milestones
Ryanair	1991 [a]	Ireland/UK (Dublin, Stansted) to Continental Europe	€ 1.4M	• Tony Ryan	6 BAE 1-11s (leased)	2.0[a]	$5.5 bn	35%	37%	• Founded by Dr. Ryan, aviation entrepreneur • Transformed into LC by Michael O'Leary, then 30 years old • IPO in 1997 • Bought Buzz in January 2003
JetBlue	2000	USA (JKF) Coast to coast	$130M[b]	• Chase • George Soros • Weston Presidio	2 Airbus A320s (bought)	0.5	$2.3 bn	90%	37%	• Founded by David Neeleman, former CEO and founder of Morris Air at Age 23 • IPO April 2002 raised additional $180 M • Today #2 US airline by value
easyJet	1995	UK (Luton) to Continental Europe	€ 7.5M	• Founder Family	2 Boeing 737-300 (leased)	3.0	$1.3 bn	40%	52%	• Founded by Stelios Haji, a 28 year-old greek entrepreneur • IPO in 2000 for $2.2 billion • Bought rival GO in 2002
GO	1997	UK to Continental Europe	€ 35M	• British Airways	Boeing 737-300 (leased)	2.5	NA	44%	51%	• Founded by Barbra Cassani, 36 years-old, formerly in BA sales • MBO in 2001 for € 160 M (25% management, 75% Fund 3i) • Sold to easyJet in 2002 for € 600M

EXHIBIT 3 *(continued)*

Source: Company documents. (Data compiled from "JetBlue Airways" (Gittell and O'Reilly, HBS No. 801-354), *No Frills: The Truth Behind the Low Cost Revolution in the Skies* (Simon Calder 2002), and Morgan Stanley, Goldman Sachs and JP Morgan analysis.)

[a] Ryanair started operations in 1985, originally as a regional airline out of Dublin- O´Leary, decided to grow into a Low Cost after a week-long visit to Southwest.

[b] David Neeleman business plan called for $30M funding needs, but he decided to raise $130M in order to preserve his independence on timing for an IPO.

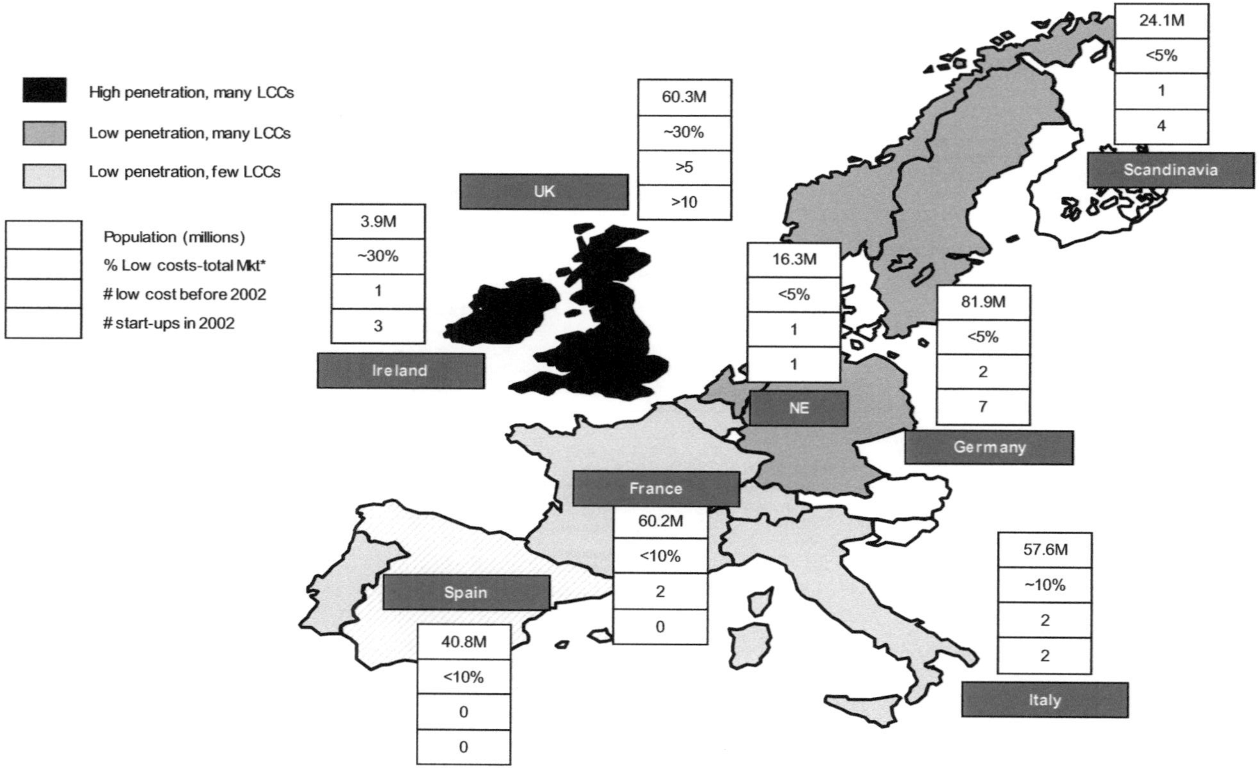

EXHIBIT 4 Low-cost carriers in Europe
Source: Company documents. (Data compiled from Boston Consulting Group, Lowcost.org, and The Economist World in 2003.)

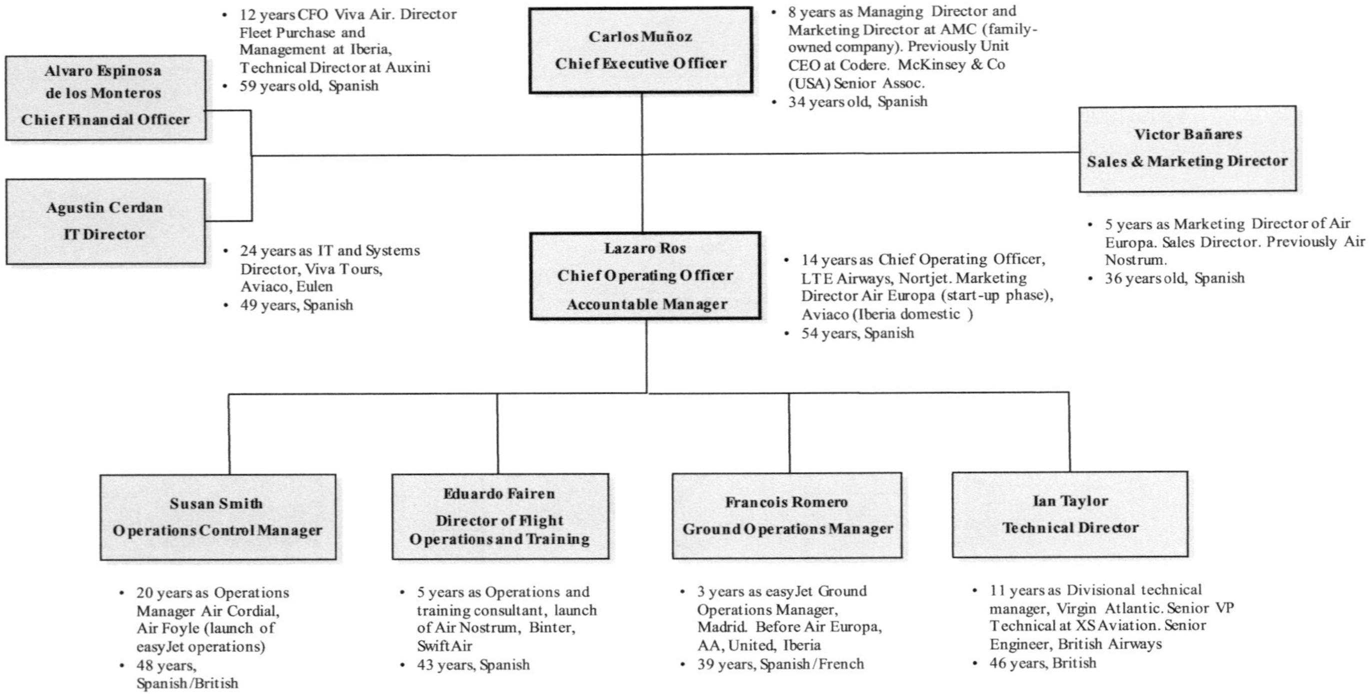

EXHIBIT 5 Vueling Management Team
Source: Company documents.

In thousands of Euros

START-UP BUDGET	
Pre-launch (Months 1-3)	
3 Plane leasing deposit	€ 1,116
Advertising	€ 800
IT platform	€ 650
Auto-handling at base	€ 590
Other deposits	€ 363
Crew salaries & training	€ 300
Management & admin.	€ 299
Other[a]	€ 210
Brand development	€ 110
Route research	€ 50
TOTAL (1)	**€ 4,488**

OTHER USES OF CASH	
Launch operations (Months 4-14)	
1 Plane leasing deposit	€ 1,116
Advertising	€ 2,000
Operating cash flow defecit[b]	€ 886
TOTAL (2)	**€ 4,002**
Predatory pricing fund[c]	
Iberia	€ 4,000
Others	€ 1,000
TOTAL (3)	**€ 5,000**
Cash reserve[d]	€ 11,510

TOTAL CASH NEEDS	**€ 25,000**
(1) = (2) + (3) + Cash reserve	

EXHIBIT 6 Financial Projections
Source: Company documents.

[a] Includes travel, maintenance, communications, accommodation, AOC license, uniforms, stationary and miscellaneous.

[b] Not including items above and in start-up phase. Total estimated maximum cash deficit is €16,368,000 occurring in month 13.

[c] From risk analysis, "worst case scenario" competitive response.

[d] Based on average one-month total expense rate, for the period 6-18 months after launch.

EXHIBIT 6 (*continued*)

Revenue Overview

	YEAR 1							
	Q1	Q2	Q3	Q4	YR2	YR3	YR4	YR5
Total passengers (thousands)	0	83.9	98.7	156.9	1,588.60	2,800	4,481	5,974
Total revenues	**0**	**€ 3.6M**	**€5.2M**	**€9.1M**	**€100.7M**	**€194.8M**	**€338.7M**	**€451.7M**
Key components to passenger revenue								
• Number of planes operating (average)	0	2	2	3	5.7	10	15	20
• Seats/ plane	149	149	149	149	149	149	149	149
• Days of operation per plane[a]	0	360	360	360	358	358	358	358
• Number sectors per plane daily[b]	0	8	8	8	7.5	7	7	7
• % Seat load	0.0%	38.3%	45.0%	58.3%	70.0%	75.0%	80.0%	80.0%
• Average price per passenger	0	42	50	55	60	65	70	70
Total passenger revenue	**0**	**€ 3.6M**	**€ 4.9M**	**€ 8.6M**	**€ 95.0M**	**€ 182.0M**	**€ 313.6M**	**€ 418.2M**
Ancillary revenue[c]	**0**	**0**	**€ 0.3M**	**€ 0.4M**	**€ 5.7M**	**€ 12.7M**	**€ 25.1M**	**€ 33.5M**

Source: Company documents.

[a] Net of heavy maintenance days (7 per plane per year, considering that additional leased planes only need heavy maintenance after their first year).

[b] Decreases after introduction of longer sectors to other destinations in France, Portugal and Italy.

[c] Includes on-board sales and 3rd party booking fees through web site (car-rental, hotels).

EXHIBIT 6 *(continued)*

In thousands of euros	YEAR 1				YEAR 2	YEAR 3	YEAR 4	YEAR 5
	QTR 1	QTR 2	QTR 3	QTR 4				
Passenger Revenue	€ 0	€ 3,568	€ 4,935	€ 8,628	€ 95,040	€ 182,030	€ 313,651	€ 418,201
Ancillary Revenue	-	-	247	431	5,702	12,742	25,092	33,456
Total Revenue	-	3,568	5,182	9,059	100,742	194,772	338,743	451,657
Expenses								
Ground Handling Charges	-	1,329	1,329	1,618	13,686	23,813	37,001	51,207
Airport Charges	-	528	528	643	5,435	9,345	14,578	20,215
Fuel	-	1,775	1,775	2,161	20,568	35,363	55,167	76,498
Navigation Charges	-	864	864	1,052	10,013	17,217	26,858	37,243
Crew Costs, incl. Training	65	605	605	785	6,383	11,509	17,814	24,606
Maintenance, incl. Reserves	64	283	283	356	2,739	4,823	7,385	10,144
Advertising	800	800	450	450	4,000	6,240	7,571	8,999
G&A and Other Costs	341	912	896	1,109	8,577	14,623	20,953	27,198
Total Expenses	1,270	7,097	6,730	8,175	71,401	122,933	187,328	256,110
Initial Start Up Costs	605							
EBITDAR	**(1,875)**	**(3,530)**	**(1,549)**	**884**	**29,341**	**71,839**	**151,415**	**195,548**
Aircraft Dry Lease Costs	-	1,116	1,116	1,488	12,648	23,213	36,212	50,214
EBITDA	**(1,875)**	**(4,646)**	**(2,665)**	**(604)**	**16,693**	**48,626**	**115,203**	**145,334**
Depreciation and Amortization	57	57	57	57	211	251	336	471
EBIT Operating Profit / (Loss)	**(1,933)**	**(4,703)**	**(2,722)**	**(661)**	**16,481**	**48,375**	**114,867**	**144,863**
Net Interest Expense	(186)	(132)	(115)	(109)	(746)	(1,412)	(2,990)	(5,433)
Taxation Expense	(611)	(1,600)	(912)	(193)	6,030	17,426	41,250	52,603
Net Profit	**(€ 1,135)**	**(€ 2,971)**	**(€ 1,694)**	**(€ 359)**	**€ 11,198**	**€ 32,362**	**€ 76,607**	**€ 97,692**
OTHER FINANCIAL DATA								
Cash	€ 21,042	€ 19,659	€ 17,205	€ 18,202	€ 37,187	€ 75,809	€ 163,396	€ 271,205
Total Assets	25,364	26,110	24,557	27,422	48,860	94,064	190,495	306,150
Retained Earnings	(1,135)	(4,106)	(5,801)	(6,160)	5,038	37,400	114,008	211,700
Total Capex	-	(50)	-	-	(690)	(1,090)	(1,680)	(1,680)
Net Cashflow	(€ 1,058)	(€ 1,037)	(€ 741)	€ 50	€ 22,425	€ 38,622	€ 87,587	€ 107,809

Source: Company documents.

EXHIBIT 7 Base selection data

Major Spanish Airports, 2001

	Airport	Passenger Traffic 2001 (000s)	Population (000s)	GDP (base 100= Spain)	Main traffic focus	Local pricing	# flight connect	Base to airline	Appeal as destination	Estimated Impact High Speed Train[b]	Political support for newcomer
1	Madrid	33,800	5,370	118	Leisure/ Business	Low[a]	High	Iberia	High	Very high (~68%)	Indifferent
2	Barcelona	20,500	5,580	120	Leisure/ Business	Mid	Mid	No	Very high	Limited to Madrid (~30%)	Very favorable
3	Palma	19,100	830	119	Leisure	Mid	Mid	Spanair, Air Europa	Very high	None	Favorable
4	Malaga	9,800	1,300	75	Leisure	Mid	Mid	No	Very high	Limited to Madrid (~48%)	Indifferent
5	Tenerife	8,900	785	92	Leisure	High	Mid	No	Very high	None	Very favorable
6	Alicante	6,500	2,800	83	Leisure	Mid	Low	No	Very high	Limited to Madrid (~48%)	Favorable
7	Bilbao	2,500	1,930	123	Leisure/ Business	Very High	Low	No	Mid	Limited to Madrid (~40%)	Very favorable[c]
8	Valencia	2,300	2,245	100	Leisure/ Business	Mid	Low	Air Nostrum	Mid	Very High	Favorable

Source: Company documents. (Data compiled from Aeropuertos Espanoles y Navegacion Aerea (Spanish Airports and Air Navigation), INE (National Institute of Statistics), Despegar.com, and Ministerio de Fomento (Ministry for Infrastructures)).

Note: Political support levels estimated by Vueling team after informal discussions with regulators.

[a] Madrid pricing is 30-35% below on average for the top 8 Spanish mid-size cities and island destinations (on absolute terms, not adjusted by distance).

[b] Estimated as % of traffic that falls within less than 3 hours ride with High Speed Train.

[c] The Basque government financed the creation of Euskal Air in 1985. It went bankrupt in 1989, after much political interference in routes and management decisions.

EXHIBIT 7 (*continued*)

Slot Availability in Major Spanish Airports

○ = No slots available

● = Full slot availability

	Airport	No. of runways (2003)	No. of runways (2005)	Slot availability 2003/2004: Peak morning (7-10 am)	Slot availability 2003/2004: Mid-day (10 am-6 pm)	Slot availability 2003/2004: Peak evening (6-10 pm)	Climate (#non operational days/year[c])
1	Madrid	3	4	○	◑	○	2d (fog)
2	Barcelona	2	3	◔ →[a] ◑	◕	◔ →[a] ◑	3-4 d (storms)
3	Palma	2	2	● →[b] ◔	●	◕ →[b] ◔	O-1d
4	Malaga	1	1	● →[b] ◑	●	◕ →[b] ◑	10d (storms, wind)
5	Tenerife	1	1	●	●	●	15-20d (winds, fog)
6	Alicante	1	1	● →[b] ◔	●	◕ →[b] ◔	0d
7	Bilbao	2	2	●	●	●	20d (winds)
8	Valencia	1[b]	1	●	●	●	10d (storms, fog)

Source: Company documents. Data compiled from Aeropuertos Espanoles y Navegacion Aerea (Spanish Airports and Air Navigation) and Ministerio de Fomento (Ministry for Infrastructures).

[a] Through local political support.

[b] Winter (first moon) and Summer (second moon) presented very different situations in tourist-focused airports.

[c] Team estimates (3 Vueling captains) based on last 10 years average.

EXHIBIT 8 Map of Europe, Including Potential Base and Destination Cities
Source: Adapted from company documents.

EXHIBIT 9 Vueling Marketing plan

ADVERTISING PLAN (€ 2,500,000 year 1) – PER MARKET

Market	Total market	Target (round trip passengers)	Allocation spend
Barcelona	5.6M	150,000	**€ 1,850,000**
Alicante	2.8M	20,000	**€ 200,000**
Bilbao	1.9M	20,000	**€ 200,000**
Mallorca	0.8M	10,000	**€ 50,000**
Tenerife	0.8M	5,000	**€ 50,000**
Other	5.1M	10,000	**€ 150,000**

ADVERTISING PLAN (€ 2,500,000 year 1) – PER CHANNEL

Channel	Activity	Cost (unit)	% total
Local press	Full-1/4 page ads	€ 1,200-3,000	**40%**
Radio	Local Spots	€ 600-900	**15%**
Billboards	City, airport	€ 1,200/week	**20%**
Flyers, handouts	Travel locations	€ 40/1,000unit	**15%**
Internet	Travel sites	€ 10/1,000hits	**10%**

Source: Company documents.

EXHIBIT 10 Vueling's "Seven Commitments to Customer Service"

1. Sell lowest fares at all times
2. Deliver #1 on-time performance >80% (vs. Iberia's 67%)
3. Guarantee no cancellation policy
4. Eliminate overbooking
5. Lowest bag damage or loss ratios
6. Courteous, full information to passengers (in case of delays, lost bags, etc.)
7. Prompt complaint response (>99% within one week)

Source: Company documents.

	Start passenger check-in	Prepare gate contact plane	Empty incoming flight	Load outgoing flight	Finish checks / close doors	Depart!!
What it is	• Check-in passengers at counter • Close 30 minutes before ETD and do weight calculations (passengers, cargo, luggage)	• Contact incoming plane – Confirm ETA – Inform "load chit" • Prepare gate/parking – Scales – Buses, wheel chairs – Luggage equipment – Fuel	• "Aircraft is serviceable" – Descent passengers – Empty bags • Toilet dump • Plane clean-up • Start refueling • Call outgoing passengers (boarding)	• Take passengers and luggage out to aircraft • End fueling	• Finalize "load sheet" – Passengers – Luggage, cargo • Captain signs off after passenger and luggage count • Confirm fuel level • OK plane, motors, wheels => "Go" by captain	
Responsible	• Check-in manager	• Handling coordinator ("mobile")	• Mobile	• Mobile / check-in manager	• Mobile	
Time	• 2 hours to 30 minutes before ETD[a]	• 45 to 30 minutes before ETD	• 30 to 20 minutes before ETD	• 25 to 10 minutes before ETD	• 10 minutes to ETD	
KSF's[b]	• Non assigned seating (allow faster check-in and weight calculations) • Charge for overweight luggage	• Inform captain of next flight details (allows time for calculations) • Run fuel trailers in advance	• Cabin crew do manual clean-up (no third party) • No catering to load • Captain decides and communicates fuel volume in advance	• No "late-comers" allowed on board • Cabin crew actively help with seating • Cabin crew start counts while seating is ending	• Discipline of doors closing is key (no exceptions) • Find "no-show" passenger bags before loading into plane • Review "end of week" issues	

EXHIBIT 11 Process Steps and key success factors for 30-minute plane turnaround
Source: Company documents.

[a] ETD (estimated time of departure) defined as block time, from the moment "chalks" are removed.

[b] KSF = Key Success Factor.

EXHIBIT 12 Fleet selection matrix

	BOEING 737-300[a]	BOEING 737-700[a]	MD-83	AIRBUS A319	AIRBUS A320-200
Number of seats	149	149	172	134	164
Likely age (yrs)	5-8	<4	10+	<3	<3
Availability for leasing	High	Mid	High	High	Low
Lease cost monthly (US$)	150,000	200,000 - 260,000	100,000	200,000 - 250,000	200,000
Cabin crew	3	3	3	3	4-6
Fuel consumption (kgs/hr)	3,550	3,300	4,100	3,300	2,450
Cruise Speed (mph)	506	506	504	530	530
Suitability for LC	Highly reliable	Highly reliable	Poor performance (wet, ice)	Highly reliable, issues with fast loading	Highly reliable
Installed base	Southwest, Ryanair, easyJet	Southwest, Ryanair, easyJet	No Low cost	easyJet (2003)	JetBlue

Source: Company documents. (Data compiled from GE Capital Aviation Services, Airbus Commercial Director Spain & Latam, manufacturers web sites, maintenance from ATC Lasham)

[a] Ryanair Annual Report stated that the 737s performed much better than Boeing's initial estimates on maintenance, fuel consumption and reliability.

EXHIBIT 13 Proposed Vueling Timeline: May 1, 2004 Launch

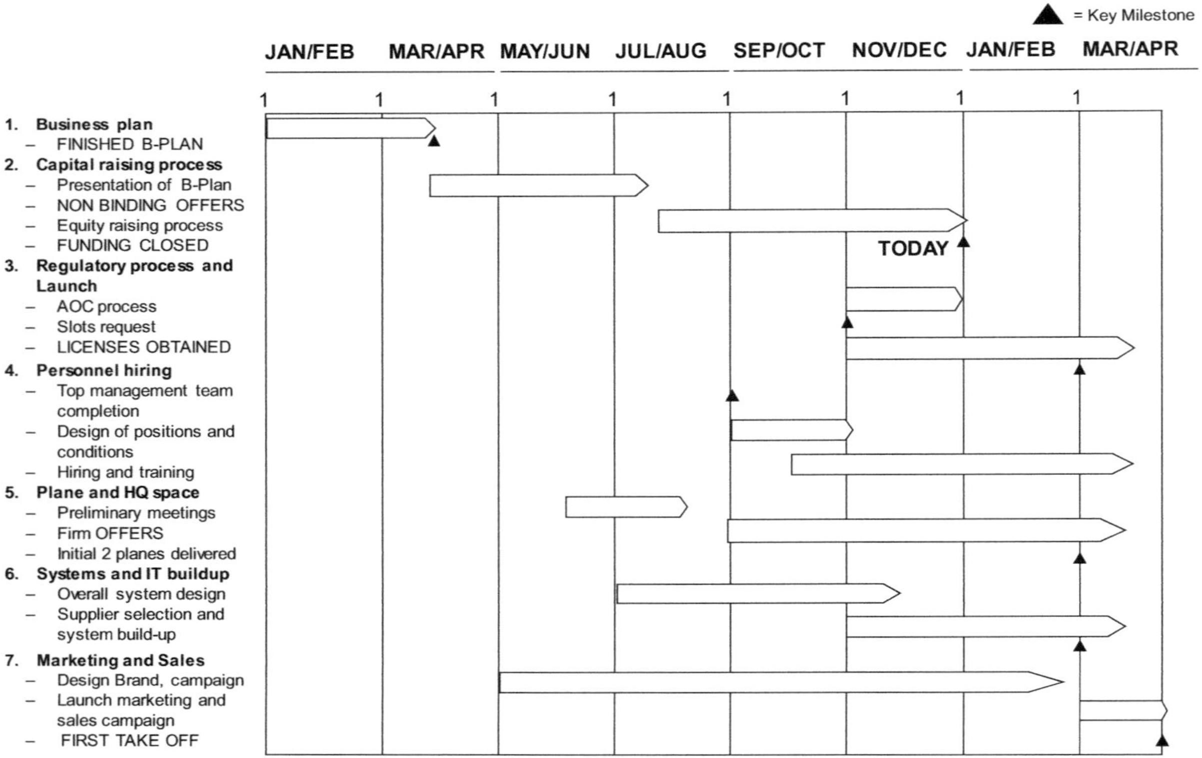

Source: Company documents.

CHAPTER 2.6

Ginkgo Bioworks: The Cell as a Factory

Paul A. Gompers, Amitabh Chandra and Matthew Wozny

INTRODUCTION

One early morning, Jason Kelly, the co-founder and CEO of Ginkgo Bioworks, looked over Boston's Seaport from his company's 100,000 square foot facility, lost in thought. He had founded his fledgling start-up in 2008 with four other co-founders on the cutting edge of a field today known as synthetic biology It had grown slowly at first as they developed their core technology. Yet by 2019, Ginkgo was valued at $4.2 billion and was called "the most valuable venture-backed startup in Boston {...} and the second-most- valuable VC-backed biotech startup in the country.[1] But the rapid growth in a new industry that Kelly and his team felt had limitless potential led to new business model opportunities and challenges. One in particular was on Kelly's mind. His team had made the decision to take equity from early-stage startups instead of cash. As he stared at the cranes and construction work outside, Kelly wondered: had they made the right decision, and how would they make it work?

SYNTHETIC BIOLOGY: A PRIMER

Synthetic biology is a multidisciplinary field spanning biology, engineering, and computer science. Its goal is to engineer living organisms to do useful things at scale and according to specification.[2] The major insight of synthetic biology is that cells, the basic building blocks of life, are "programmable" – they run on DNA "code." DNA stores and transfers genetic information, coding for the amino acids that make the proteins that perform the functions of the cell. This "operating system" informs all biological growth and behavior. Synthetic biologists leverage this process by

Ginkgo Bioworks: The Cell as a Factory
by PAUL A. GOMPERS, AMITABH CHANDRA, MATTHEW WOZNY, case number 9-220-069 APRIL 9, 2020

synthesizing DNA and inserting it into an organism's genome, thus altering the cell's program to. For example, produce a desired product or action in the cells. These synthesized pieces of DNA could be genes found in other organisms, or they could be entirely novel.[3] As cells grow and duplicate, desired molecules are manufactured at scale.

Bioengineering is not new. Fermentation, the process where microorganisms like yeast use enzymes to break carbohydrates into simpler compounds like alcohols, has been used by humans to make leavened bread, wine, and beer for at least the past 9,000 years.[4] Similarly, humans have selectively bred crops and livestock for thousands of years. Advancements in technology and understanding of genetics, however, have propelled bioengineering capability. While the cost of the project to sequence the full human genome was $2.7 billion in 2001, the cost of sequencing a human genome today has dropped to under $1000, falling at a speed faster than Moore's Law (see **Exhibit 1**.) New genome editing technologies, like CRISPR have increased the precision of genetic edits at a fraction of the cost of incumbents (see **Exhibit 2** for a more granular history.)

These rapid advancements greatly expanded the potential applications of synthetic biology. Companies like Impossible Foods leveraged engineered yeast to produce hemoglobin, enabling them to create innovative meat alternatives, while others like Bolt Threads grew spider silk from yeast to make high performance fabrics. Others have worked to create new biofuels, new foods, new biomaterials, sustainable plastics, as well as new drugs and therapies. (See **Exhibit 3** for a representative list of synthetic biology businesses.) The promise of synthetic biology is that the ability to read and write DNA will drive the next stage in engineering advancement, ushering in the biological age for manufacturing. Anything leveraging biology at any point in its supply chain, many synthetic biologists believe, will be at risk for disruption as this new field harnesses engineering principles to grow organisms that produce tailored products. Problems as diverse as expensive manufacturing, scalable drug development, climate change, and sustainable supply chains might be addressed through synthetic biology. Media attention and venture capital investment in the sector have recently exploded, with invested capital in the industry growing from 1.5 billion in 2015 to $4 billion in 2018. (See **Exhibit 4** for industry growth.) Analysts sized the potential of the bioeconomy market – i.e., products synthesized via biotechnology – as approximately $350 billion to $2 trillion in the United States.[5]

COMPANY HISTORY

Ginkgo was founded in 2008 at the Massachusetts Institute of Technology (MIT) by Tom Knight and four Ph.D. students, Jason Kelly, Reshma Shetty,

Barry Canton, and Austin Che. (See **Exhibit 5** for a list of Ginkgo's senior team members.) Knight was a computer science professor who began programming cells like computers and set up a biology lab in the computer-science building in the 1990s. Shetty and Che worked in Knight's lab, while Kelly and Canton worked in the laboratory of Drew Endy, then an Assistant Professor in Biological Engineering at MIT.[6] These were the early days of synthetic biology, and the application of computer science and engineering principles to the biological world did not have much traction in academia. Nevertheless, Knight's core group of students were drawn to the promise of making biology easier to engineer. After finishing their studies, they started Ginkgo with grants, a $100K loan, and the vision to make bioengineering faster, cheaper, and easier.[7]

At first, Ginkgo focused on developing their technology platform, struggling to find a viable business model. They relied on non-dilutive grants from the National Science Foundation (NSF), the Defense Advanced Research Projects Agency (DARPA), and the Department of Health and Human Services, which funded R&D work into the core platform for engineering cells, investing in the long term vision for synthetic biology at scale while focusing on a number of different potential applications of engineered biology. (See **Exhibit 6** for Ginkgo's full financing history.) Grants for $3.25 million funded research to build tools that would reduce fermentation costs in metabolic engineering, fermenting plant-inspired fragrances, engineering microbes that cost-efficiently produce L-Threonine, an amino acid used in animal feed, and reducing antibiotic resistance of bacterial populations by inserting engineered mobile genetic elements into bacteria. While Ginkgo grew the platform, the grants kept them afloat. They kept their burn rate low, renting office space in the underdeveloped Seaport area and purchasing only approximately $100,000 of laboratory equipment through second hand sales from academic labs.

Between 2008 and 2014, the team built out its capabilities. By 2013, they were adding organism engineering product companies as customers and growing quickly. Yet, they realized that as five PhDs they lacked the level of credibility and access they needed to supercharge their company. They began to consider joining Y Combinator (YC), an accelerator for start-ups founded by Paul Graham in Cambridge, MA in 2005, which by 2014 had become the most prestigious and well-known accelerator in the world. That YC had never admitted a biotech start-up did not deter the team.

FINANCING HISTORY

After the accelerator program, the team raised a $9 million Series A round in 2015 with OS Fund, Data Collective, and Felicis Ventures, venture capital firms who believed in the new bioeconomy. The team selected the investors because they shared in Ginkgo's vision to make biology more accessible. Despite pressures from these West Coast investors to relocate to the Bay Area, Kelly and his team felt the best source of talent was in Boston. Determining it would be a competitive advantage to stay, they did.

Unlike many mature biotechnology companies, Ginkgo never took on significant debt. Nor did it follow the most common life sciences path of raising from conventional venture capital firms until reaching a liquidity event. Four months after completing its Series A, the team raised a substantially larger $45 million round in July 2015, adding Viking Global Investors, a Greenwich-based hedge fund with $30 billion assets under management. In June 2016, Ginkgo again added new investors to a $100 million Series C round – this time Cascade Investment, Bill Gates' family office, Baillie Gifford, a large asset management firm headquartered in Edinburgh, and Allen and Company, a New York investment bank. Ginkgo's Series D in December 2017 brought $275 million in new capital from existing investors and General Atlantic, a private equity firm. And in July 2019, the Ginkgo team raised another $290 million in a Series E round, adding T. Rowe Price as an investor and Marijn Dekkers, Chairman of Unilever and former CEO of Bayer AG and Thermo Fisher Scientific, to its Board of Directors. (See **Exhibit** 7 for a partial list of Ginkgo's Board Members.)

On the process of fundraising, Che reflected:

> Fundraising at the end of the day is stochastic. At the end of each round, you look at the options and see who's there. When you're raising you try to take the best money you find. Fundraising also requires a crystal-clear story—what is synthetic biology? Why will it matter? What do we envision for the future? There's a great feedback loop with this kind of storytelling, where we learned how to tell a clearer story about who we are, learning a lot about ourselves and getting got a lot of clarity about the business opportunity in the process as we learned what was resonating with investors.

After the Ginkgo team completed its Series E round, the company was valued at $4.2 billion and was the most valuable venture-backed startup in Boston.

BUSINESS MODEL

Synthetic biology companies follow a similar high-level process for organism engineering. First, they agree on specifications, or what the organism must be able to do to, say, produce a fragrance oil for a customer. Then, the synthetic biology company takes genetic DNA sequences from nature that it knows would, or believes might, give the particular desired scent, inserting it usually into a microbe such as *Escherichia coli* (E. coli) bacterium or brewer's yeast by editing its genome. To do this, often it first means sequencing entire genomes of species that exhibit the required traits. Each genetic variant of a virus, bacterium, or fungus created is called a strain. One strain may contain minor distinguishable differences from another in its genetic code that have large differences in how it behaves.[8] Very many strains are typically grown in petri dishes and tested before an organism that sufficiently meets requirements is successfully designed. Once an organism to secrete the fragrance oil is achieved, the business gradually scales up its manufacturing, first in a small bioreactor, then a large pilot, and finally for commercial production.

Ginkgo Bioworks branded itself as an organism design company. It brought biology to industrial engineering and developed organisms specific to the agriculture, food, healthcare, and energy sectors. The team built four foundries, or factories, where laboratory operations were systematized into an engineering process of design, build, test, ferment, and repeat to further optimize the strains. These foundries leveraged automation and data analytics to greatly augment the team's ability to engineer new organisms at scale. In addition, Ginkgo collected and centralized its codebase of engineered strains. As it completed more projects and developed more strains, Ginkgo anticipated over time it could leverage this codebase to more efficiently design organisms that satisfy customer requirements, just as a software engineer uses a software codebase to start a new project rather than coding a new application from scratch. The team expected this collected data would create network effects, making biological success easier to achieve internally and turning biology into a more mature engineering discipline.

The core metric the team focused on reducing was the unit cost. The unit cost in traditional genetic engineering environments had historically stayed linear to the number of PhDs executing a manual discovery process. Given the high cost and relative low productivity of human capital, only drug discovery could absorb those economics. The team reasoned that if Ginkgo could dramatically lower the cost to engineer a new strain, customers could get more work done for the same amount of dollars, leading to a higher probability of success and expanding the sectors that biotechnology could touch. By leveraging software, focusing on automating and scaling their foundries, the Ginkgo team was consistently halving unit costs each year, believing it could reach massive reductions compared to the traditional industry unit cost.

After engineering a cell that acted according to a customers' specifications, Ginkgo transferred the microbe to partners for full scale-up and commercial production.[9] In areas where the team felt the industry could benefit from a more consolidated approach, it spun out businesses that would focus on product and applications. A notable example was Motif Foodworks, a food ingredients innovation company which develops and supplies animal- and dairy-free proteins to the food industry. Ginkgo spun out Motif and helped it raise over $115 million in 2019, taking a minority stake in it as well.

CUSTOMERS

While most companies spending money on cell engineering were in the pharmaceutical sector, its low unit costs gave Ginkgo the ability to engineer different types of microbes and serve a diverse set of clients and industries. (See **Exhibit 8** for a representative list of Ginkgo customers.) Cronos, a global cannabinoid company, enlisted Ginkgo to develop microorganisms that produced cannabinoids in a scalable and efficient manner. The company paid $22 million in cash for a deal with an aggregate value of $100 million if all milestones were met.[10] Cargill, a company with interests in agriculture, food, and industrial production, tasked Ginkgo to enhance its bioindustrial fermentation processes.[11] Ginkgo designed new flavors and fragrances with Robertet, the world's leading source of natural ingredients.[12] The team signed a $100 million joint venture with Bayer, a German life sciences company, to design organisms that reduce the amount of traditional chemical fertilizer needed to grow crops.[13]

Matthew F. McKnight (MBA 2012), Ginkgo's Chief Commercial Officer, described the team's complex sales process:

> The commercial challenge is that, first and foremost, we have to convince Fortune 1000 companies that biotech is a critical part of their discovery innovation agenda and product portfolio. Whether that's a biopharmaceutical or a giant consumer packaged goods company that has built their business on chemistry for the past 100 years, the first step is evangelizing biotech, convincing *every* CEO that the 21st century is the century of biology. Second, after we've done that, we have to convince them that they shouldn't do it themselves, that they shouldn't do it with someone else, and that Ginkgo is the best place for them to do their research and discovery work. And then third, we have to figure out how to convert them into a deal structure that allows them to get the best leverage out of their $10 to $100 million investment. And

> so, you think about what our commercial task is, it's: (1) biotech, (2) Ginkgo is the best partner, and (3) then financial structuring.
>
> We've designed our commercial organization around that process. We've got the sales team – the business development (BD) team – which is the consulting, relationship-building and problem-solving segment of the company. The BD team has about 10 people today. If you include corporate development, which looks at creative deal structures, call it 12 people. We're a $4+ billion company with essentially a 12-person sales team. We're not scaling our sales team super-fast. But being cautious because it's hard and we haven't figured all the applications that will resonate.

By 2019, the team had over two dozen customers and 50 active development programs.

EQUITY-AS-PAYMENT MODEL

As Ginkgo assessed the market of potential customers, it realized that there were many incubators and accelerators that provided services for early-stage synthetic biology start-ups that needed help with research and development. The team at Ginkgo felt it could provide a lot more value than the existing support platforms or in-house capability. Early-stage startups wanted to work with Ginkgo because they could not otherwise build the technology platform equivalent and believed their best probability of success per dollar used would be with Ginkgo. The team wondered if it was leaving a lot of value on the table by not finding a way to engage with those earlier stage companies. Che reasoned:

> There are smaller companies which we believe can grow to be big future customers and can also serve as current customers. Unlike other bigger customers, these companies often already believe in the power of biotech and that Ginkgo is the best partner to accelerate their products to market. But given they are small, they are often cash-strapped, and the commercial challenge comes down to financial structuring. We could choose to wait and only work with companies once they have the resources to pay us cash, or we could choose to take equity or some other form of non-cash consideration. Having the flexibility to take equity is an opportunity for us to work with startups, or businesses without much cash, in a nascent but growing industry.

There was some precedence to Silicon Valley law firms and real estate firms occasionally accepting equity as payment from early-stage start-ups.

For Ginkgo, the total amount would be far larger. Nevertheless, the team felt it was a model worth experimenting with in deal structures with customers that aligned on Ginkgo's value proposition but did not necessarily have the required cash.

The team wrestled with how to structure the transactions. At first, it experimented with a simple model of taking equity in lieu of *any* cash. They realized that on its own, it would not be viable: the projects all would have 6-to-10 year exit horizons, and investor worries about reaching near term cash-flow break-even would be crippling. While the team believed in the value of its own platform, it also believed that capital markets would not have the patience required to make the model possible. Instead, the team members evolved the model to charge cash to cover R&D costs and take equity on the upside. McKnight reflected on the team's internal decision-making process:

> Our general philosophy has been that we want to open our platform to people who are trying to build applications leveraging cells as a manufacturing platform. We generally seek partners who are (1) organizations with significant demand and critical value propositions in their business that rely on a microbial or cellular solution and (2) structured such that Ginkgo's platform can enable better utilization of their risk capital. This generally appeals to C-suites of big companies or investors supporting companies whose value proposition has cell engineering as a core feature.
>
> Then we ask: "Are we willing to trade what we normally would ask for in cash for at-risk equity? Are we willing forego our normal upside in royalty per kilogram of molecule produced?" In the royalty model, we are aligning directly with the success or failure of the program. In the equity model, we are aligning directly with the success or failure of the company. If we believe our performance on a program is highly correlated with the outcome of that company, the answer, we think, should be 'Yes.
>
> Where we've evolved to today is to take cash to cover R&D expenses and sharing in the company's upside by taking equity. There are core reasons why we've evolved to this model. First, in theory, we are different from a financial investor in that we are closer to the science and are involved in the R&D program, so can understand and assess the likelihood of a technology being successful. Second, our aspiration is to be a major platform for cell engineering. We believe that all human output – $92 trillion in GDP – that has biology in its manufacturing and supply chain process should have cell engineering in its manufacturing process. Thus, by definition there's not enough capital in the world that Ginkgo could raise to finance that ecosystem.

> So, we need to move to a model where we cover costs and then share in the upside over time. We can't be the financial vehicle for the growth of biology in all sectors. From a macro perspective, it is impossible and, more importantly, not our mission. There were other reasons to consider pursuing the new equity/cash-cover model.

The industry was experiencing a Series A crunch. Prices were attractive. Furthermore, the team felt it could make informed bets. McKnight reflected:

> We will have solid data about what is possible and what is not possible and the different risk levels when looking at companies and their technologies. We'll be well positioned to select good projects and help advise our partners on the risk level of different technical objectives. We do not have all the data we need yet in all areas, but in 3 years, we will.

On top of that, the team felt the services and intellectual property it provided companies it worked with, otherwise unavailable to those startups, made them more likely to succeed. In addition, it was beneficial for Ginkgo's business model to work with additional synthetic biology startups. Che noted: "Even if those companies fail, the work itself is valuable. We're building experience and developing our platform. So how we think about the value of work we do with the startups where we take equity is different than an investor."

The Ginkgo team wondered what mix of their future customers should be large companies that pay in cash or start-ups whose upside is captured through increases in equity value after R&D costs were paid for. McKnight reflected: "That's the existential debate we have inside the company all the time. And then you know what happens? Reality hits and you realize selling biotech as a platform is very hard. As a result, we constantly refine ideal models but then, ultimately, when we see an opportunity to partner, we figure out what the best possible structure is and go with that."

SUCCESS FACTORS IN VENTURE CAPITAL

In order to successfully execute an equity-based deal model, Ginkgo would have to develop the ability to identify and work with the most promising startups. Recent research on success factors in venture capital explored how investors made decisions across eight areas: deal sourcing; investment selection; valuation, deal structure; post-investment value-added; exits; internal firm organization; and relationships with limited partners.[14] The survey of 885 institutional venture capitalists at 681 firms found that venture capitalists viewed the management team, rather than business-related characteristics like product or technology, as the single most important attribute to the ultimate success or failure of any investments they made. While they found that venture capitalists looked to provide their portfolio companies with a large number of services post-investment – including providing strategic or operational guidance, making connections to future investors or customers, and hiring board members or employees – those services did not play a major role in the ultimate investment success or failure. Instead, the most important success factors were deal selection followed by proprietary deal flow.

CONCLUSION

This deal strategy was effective in explaining Ginkgo's future growth and untapped potential to new investors. The Ginkgo team partnered with Y Combinator and Petri, a new synthetic biology focused accelerator in Boston, to provide to the accelerators' portfolio companies access to Ginkgo's platform and intellectual property in exchange for equity and a steady pipeline. However, the team now needed to determine how to operationalize their dealmaking experiment. McKnight reflected:

> What we're trying to answer is 'What's the team that you would need to hire if you wanted to design the optimal business team on top of Ginkgo's platform?' Is it company formation model, because we're bringing a step-change to biotech-lead discovery and creating cutting-edge around that intellectual property? Or is it a consulting firm model, because selling to the C-suite of a giant company feels a lot more like the McKinsey or BCG partner model where you're building relationships and designing strategy on their behalf. Or are we a CRO salesforce and we're trying to sell in a transactional fashion to companies already doing cell engineering? We constantly ask: are we company creation, are we a consulting firm, or are we enterprise sales? Perhaps we're all three for different markets.

Kelly thought carefully about these issues. How would they value the future value of the equity into their forecasts, and how would they prioritize their team's time between start-ups and large corporations? How would they diversify and how would they incorporate liquidity events in their forecasts? What new team members and what new capabilities would they need to build? The team was experimenting with a payment model that had no precedent. As Kelly reflected on Ginkgo's long journey, he could not help but wonder: how could he make it work?

NOTES

1 Saltzman, Jonathan. "Ginkgo, a Boston biotech venture, is a magnet for VC money." *Boston Globe*, September 19, 2019. www.bostonglobe.com/business/2019/09/19/ginkgo-boston-biotech-venture-magnet-for-money/aPAdgud0oAU4JYAGHyReMP/story.html, accessed January 2020.
2 Natalie Kuldell, Rachel Bernstein, Karen Ingram, and Kathryn Hart. *BioBuilder: Synthetic Biology in the Lab.* 1st Edition. O'Reilly Media Lag: 2015, 1-10.
3 National Human Genome Institute www.genome.gov, accessed March 2020.
4 Feldman, Amy. "Synthetic Biology Company Ginkgo Bioworks Tops $4 Billion Valuation, Pushing Its Ph.D. Founders' Stakes to Some $250 Million Each." *Forbes*. September 19, 2019. www.forbes.com/sites/amyfeldman/2019/09/19/synthetic-biology-company-ginkgo-bioworks-tops-4-billion-valuation-with-t-rowe-investment-pushin-its-phd-founders-stakes-to-some-250-million-each/#2c2945b74b0c, accessed January 2020.
5 Cumbers, John and Karl Schmieder. *What's Your Bio Strategy? How to Prepare Your Business for the Age of Biology*. Pulp Bio Books: 2017. 1-4.
6 Feldman, Amy. "Synthetic Biology Company Ginkgo Bioworks Tops $4 Billion Valuation, Pushing Its Ph.D. Founders' Stakes to Some $250 Million Each." *Forbes*. September 19, 2019. www.forbes.com/sites/amyfeldman/2019/09/19/synthetic-biology-company-ginkgo-bioworks-tops-4-billion-valuation-with-t-rowe-investment-pushin-its-phd-founders-stakes-to-some-250-million-each/#2c2945b74b0c, accessed January 2020.
7 Ginkgo Bioworks, www.ginkgobioworks.com/our-work/scaling-bioprocesses/, accessed January 2020.
8 Biology Dictionary. www.biology-online.org/dictionary/Strain. accessed January 2020.
9 Ginkgo Bioworks, www.ginkgobioworks.com/our-work/scaling-bioprocesses/, accessed January 2020.
10 PRNewswire. www.prnewswire.com/news-releases/cronos-group-and-ginkgo-bioworks-announce-a-landmark-partnership-to-produce-cultured-cannabinoids-300706085.html, accessed February 2020.
11 PRNewswire. www.prnewswire.com/news-releases/ginkgo-bioworks-is-tapped-by-cargill-to-help-enhance-its-bioindustrial-fermentation-processes-300332706.html, accessed February 2020.
12 PRNewswire. www.prenewswire.com/news-releases/ginkgo-bioworks-and-robertet-announce-successful-commercial-scale-fermentation-of-flavor-and-fragrance-cultured-ingredient-300459584.html, accessed February 2020.

13 Cosgrove, Emma. "The $100m Bayer, Ginkgo Bioworks Joint Venture Has a Name, a CEO, and a Plan." *AGFunder News*. March 20, 2018. agfundernews.com/joyn-bio-bayer-gingko-bioworks-joint-venture.html, accessed March 2020.

14 Gompers, Paul A., Will Gornall, Steven N. Kaplan, and Ilya A. Strebulaev. 2020. "How Do Venture Capitalists Make Decisions?" *Journal of Financial Economics*, 135. 169-190, www.sciencedirect.com/science/article/pii/S0304405X19301680, accessed March 2020.

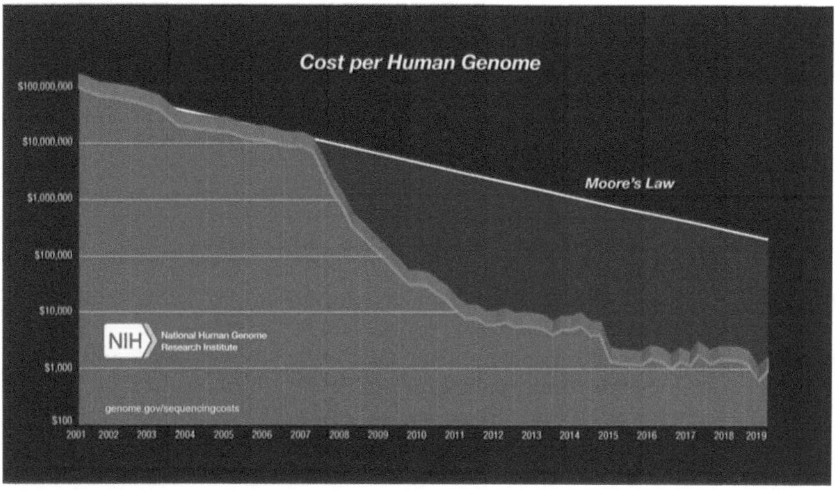

EXHIBIT 1 Moore's Law in Genome Sequencing Cost
Source: National Human Genome Research Institute, "DNA Sequencing Costs: Data," https://www.genome.gov/about-genomics/fact-sheets/DNA-Sequencing-Costs-Data, accessed February 2020.

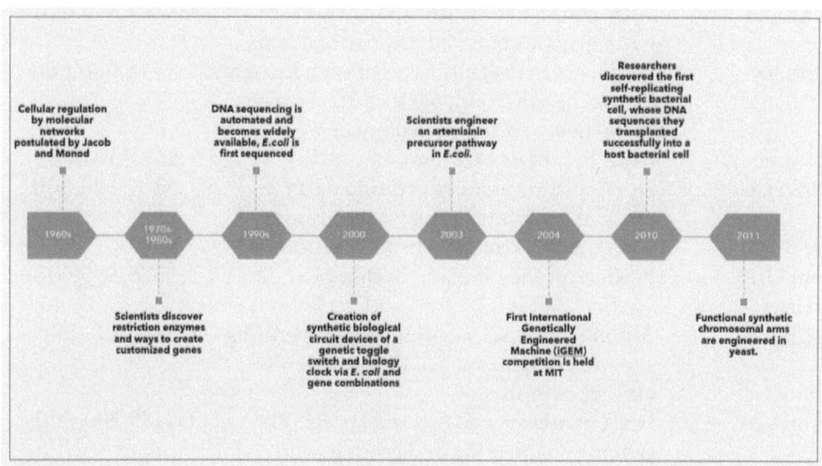

EXHIBIT 2 A brief history of synthetic biology
Source: Casewriters, from Gibson, DG, "Creation of a bacterial cell controlled by a chemically synthesized genome," *Science*, July 2010, accessed March 2020; V.J. Martin, "Engineering a Mevalonate Pathway in Escherichia coli for production of terpenoids," *Nature Biotech*, 2003, accessed March 2020; MB Elowitz, "A synthetic oscillatory network of transcriptional regulators," *Nature*, January 2000, accessed March 2020, iGEM timeline, www.igem.org/timeline, accessed March 2020.

EXHIBIT 3 List of Representative Synthetic Biology Companies

Name	Description	Total Financing
Amyris	Makes useful molecules using synthetic biology methods. Focuses on creating products supporting biopharmaceutical drug discovery and production, cosmetics emollients and fragrances, fuels, solvents and nutraceuticals	$551,900,000
Benchling	Life science research and development cloud-based software for the lab	$61,900,000
Berkeley Lights	Digital cell biology company that commercializes platforms for the acceleration of discovery and development of cell-based products and therapies	$191,500,000
Bolt Threads	Material solutions company engineering sustainable fashion biomaterials and fabrics	$213,000,000
Ecovative	Biotech designing mycelium materials	$30,100,000
eGenesis	Growing human transplantable organs from pig cells	$140,000,000
Impossible Foods	Develops plant-based substitutes for meat products	$675,500,000
Inscripta	Fully automated benchtop instrument to write genetic code and create organisms	$259,500,000
Intrexon	Engineers living cells focused on human and animal health, food, agriculture, energy, chemicals, and the environment.	$344,000,000
Origene	DNA Synthesis provider	$69,400,000
Perfect Day	Develops processes of creating dairy proteins by fermentation in microflora rather than extraction from bovine milk	$201,500,000
Sapphire Energy	Produce crude oil made from algae	$376,500,000
Synthace	Automate life sciences labs with operating system, computer-aided design software, and other tools	$46,000,000
Synthego	DNA Synthesis and full stack CRISPR genome engineering and editing tools	$159,700,000
Twist Bioscience	DNA Synthesis Manufacturer	$253,100,000

Source: Casewriters from www.Crunchbase.com, accessed January 2020.

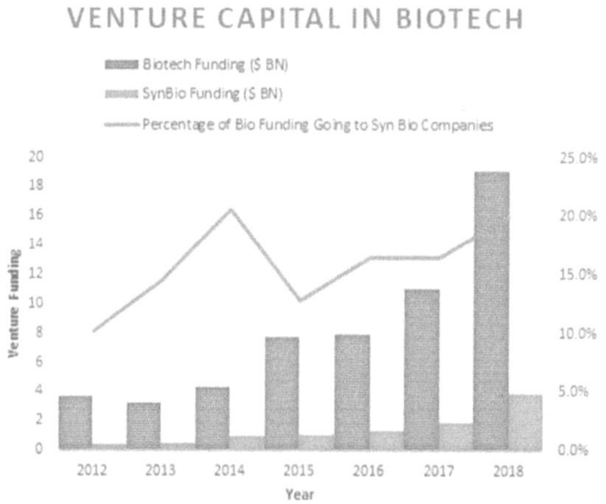

EXHIBIT 4 Time Series of Venture Capital in Biotech and Synthetic Biology
Sources: Casewriters, based on CB Insights (https://www.cbinsights.com/research/synthetic-biology-startup-funding/) accessed January 2020, Pitchbook (https://pitchbook.com/news/articles/is-vcs-insatiable-appetite-for-biotech-sustainable) accessed January 2020, SynBioBeta (https://synbiobeta.com/these-33-synthetic-biology-companies-just-raised-925-million/), accessed January 2020.

EXHIBIT 5 Senior Team Bios

Barry Canton - Barry is the co-founder and CTO of Ginkgo Bioworks. At Ginkgo, Barry is responsible for the development of the foundry, a centralized facility for organism engineering. In this role he oversees the development of hardware, software, and wetware technologies. Earlier, he led the development of new methods for assembling DNA from standard parts. He holds a PhD in Biological Engineering from MIT, where his thesis focused on refinement of standard biological parts and the interactions between a host cell and an engineered genetic circuit. At MIT, he was involved with the Synthetic Biology Working Group that was instrumental in catalyzing the new field. He also holds an MEngSc in Mechanical Engineering from University College Dublin.

Austin Che - Austin is a co-founder of Ginkgo Bioworks. At Ginkgo, he has worn many hats from leading software development, organism engineering, managing the physical infrastructure, finance, and strategic decision making. Prior to Ginkgo, Austin received dual undergraduate degrees from Stanford in Computer Science and Psychology and was awarded the departmental best honors thesis. He then completed a PhD at MIT in

EXHIBIT 5 (*continued*)

synthetic biology where he switched from programming silicon to carbon. He has been involved in the field of synthetic biology for many years. He was an organizer of Synthetic Biology 1.0, the first international conference in synthetic biology in 2004, wrote the first registry for standard biological parts, and was a founder of OpenWetWare, a wiki promoting open science and collaboration for life science researchers.

Jason Kelly - Jason is the co-founder and CEO of Ginkgo Bioworks. Jason earned his PhD from MIT in Biological Engineering in 2008, under Professor Drew Endy, and his BS in Chemical Engineering and Biology in 2003. His doctoral research included the development of a widely adopted measurement standard for characterizing transcriptional elements.

Tom Knight - Tom is a co-founder of Ginkgo Bioworks. Tom spent most of his career teaching computer science and electrical engineering at MIT, before playing the major role in creating the engineering discipline of synthetic biology. In 1996 he seeded interest in the field at DARPA, and built a molecular biology laboratory in the MIT computer science department. He developed important standards for engineering biological systems, specifically Biobricks, the first standard assembly technique for functional DNA components, and in establishing the MIT Registry of Standard Biological Parts. He was one of four founders of IGEM, an international competition between undergraduate teams to design and build biological systems, now hosting 300 teams across the globe. In 2008, he co-founded Ginkgo Bioworks, where he remains a full-time researcher. His interests include minimal organisms, origins of life, and predictive models of biological systems. He is a Fellow of the American Association for the Advancement of Science, a director of the IGEM Foundation, and member of the International Committee on the Taxonomy of the Mollicutes.

Matthew McKnight - Matt is the Chief Commercial Officer of Ginkgo Bioworks. Prior to Ginkgo, he spent 7 years as an investor at IndUS Growth Partners and was the President and COO of Decision Resources Group. Matt has worked supporting business development at Palantir Technologies and is an active seed stage venture investor. Early in his career, he served as an officer in the United States Marine Corps. Matt completed a degree in History at Dartmouth College and is a graduate of the joint degree program at the Harvard Business School and the Harvard Kennedy School of Government where he was a Zuckerman Fellow.

Reshma Shetty – Reshma is the co-founder, President, and COO of Ginkgo Bioworks. Reshma has a B.S. degree in Computer Science from the University of Utah and a Ph.D. in Biological Engineering from MIT. As a graduate student, Reshma's research was supported by the National

EXHIBIT 5 (*continued*)

Science Foundation Graduate Research Fellowship, the Whitaker Graduate Fellowship in Biological Engineering and the Andrew and Edna Viterbi Fellowship in Computational Biology. As an undergraduate, Reshma was supported by the Barry M. Goldwater Scholarship, the Beckman Undergraduate Research Fellowship, the Pfizer Undergraduate Research Fellowship and the University of Utah Presidential Scholarship.

Source: Internal company documents.

EXHIBIT 6 Ginkgo Bioworks Financing Rounds

Round	Date	Funding	Investors
Series E	July '19	$290.0 MN	T. Rowe Price, Viking Global Investors, Y Combinator, Cascade Investment, General Atlantic
Series D	December '17	$275.0 MN	Viking Global Investors, Y Combinator, Cascade Investment, General Atlantic
Series C	June '16	$100.0 MN	Viking Global Investors, Y Combinator, Senator Investment Group, Baillie Gifford, Allen and Company
Series B	July '15	$45.0 MN	Viking Global Investors, OS Fund, Felicis Ventures, 11.2 Capital
Series A	March '15	$9.0 MN	Vast Ventures, OS Fund, Felicis Ventures, iGlobe Partners, Data Collective
Seed	July '14	$0.12 MN	Y Combinator, TSVC, CRCM Ventures, 11.2 Capital
Awards & Grants	2011-2014	$3.1 MN - $15 MN	Department of Health, National Science Foundation, DARPA, Department of Defense, ARPA-E
Loan	2009	$100,000	Tom Knight

Source: Internal company documents.

EXHIBIT 7 Abbreviated List of Board of Directors and Brief Bios

Christian Henry - EVP and CCO of Illumina

Mr. Henry is Executive Vice President and Chief Commercial Officer of Illumina. With over 20 years of business leadership experience, including more than 10 years at Illumina, Mr. Henry has a broad background in finance, management, and strategy. While at Illumina, Mr. Henry has held a number of roles, including Chief Commercial Officer, Chief Financial Officer, General Manager of Life Sciences and Senior Vice President of Corporate Development. Prior to Illumina, he served as the Chief Financial Officer of Tickets.com and the Vice President of Finance of Affymetrix, Inc. Today he sits on a number of boards across the genomics and broader biotech industries.

Marijn Dekkers - Chairman of Unilever

Born on September 22, 1957, in Tilburg, Netherlands, Dekkers studied chemistry and chemical engineering. He began his professional career in 1985 as a scientist at the corporate research center of General Electric in the United States, gaining experience in various units of the company before joining AlliedSignal (subsequently Honeywell International Inc.) in 1995. In 2000, Dekkers became Chief Operating Officer of Thermo Electron Corporation, the world's leading manufacturer of laboratory instruments (later renamed Thermo Fisher Scientific Inc. following the acquisition of laboratory supplier Fisher Scientific). As of 2002, he served as this company's President and CEO. After spending 25 years of his career in the United States, Marijn Dekkers joined Bayer on January 1, 2010. From October 1, 2010 to April 30, 2016 he was Chairman of the Board of Management (CEO) of Bayer AG. In this function Dekkers took over the two-year presidency of the German Chemical Industry Association (VCI), Frankfurt.

Dekkers is a member of the Board of Directors at General Electric in the United States and Chairman of the Dutch consumer goods group Unilever.

Source: Internal company documents.

Note: Jason Kelly - CEO and Co-Founder of Ginkgo Bioworks
See senior team bios.
Reshma Shetty – President, COO, and Co-Founder of Ginkgo Bioworks
See senior team bios.

EXHIBIT 8 Representative Ginkgo Customers

Name	Application
Bayer	Design beneficial microbes that focus on nitrogen fixation and enhance agricultural sustainability
Roche	Discover new classes of customized antibiotics
Cronos	Produce cultured cannabinoids at scale
Glycosyn	Production of human milk oligosaccharides
Kerry	Efficient production of specialty enzymes in food
Cargill	Designs organisms that enhance company's bioindustrial fermentation processes
Robertet	Commercial-scale fermentation of flavor and fragrance cultured ingredients
Swissaustral	Produce industrial enzymes at scale
Genomatica	Bioproduction of chemicals
Synlogic	Engineered microbes as therapeutics

Source: Internal company documents.

EXHIBIT 9 Representative Ginkgo Customers

Illustrative deal 1 - early stage biotech company

	Q1	Q2	Q3	Q4	Q5	Q6	Q7	Q8	Q9+
Cash*	100%	100%	100%	100%	100%	100%	100%	100%	0%
Equity grant+	0%	0%	0%	0%	0%	0%	0%	10%	0%

Illustrative deal 2 - established industry player

	Q1	Q2	Q3	Q4	Q5	Q6	Q7	Q8	Q9+
Cash*	130%	130%	130%	130%	130%	130%	130%	130%	0%
Royalties[1]	0%	0%	0%	0%	0%	0%	0%	0%	2%

Source: Internal company documents.

Note: * % of Ginkgo's incurred R&D costs

+ % of customer total

1 % of customer product sales; contingent upon success

SECTION 3

Valuation in Entrepreneurial Settings

CHAPTER 3.1

Car Wash Partners, Inc.

Paul Gompers

Cabot Brown pulled out of his garage and onto the street outside his home in San Francisco. A steady autumn rain fell and he switched on his wipers. He dialed his cellular phone in the hopes of reaching Bill Burgin, a partner at Bessemer Venture Partners (Bessemer), to discuss their potential investment in Car Wash Partners, Inc. (CWP), a business being formed by a successful service company entrepreneur to acquire and manage car washes across the U.S. Brown had just completed a final draft of an investment memorandum calling for a $5.6 million investment by his firm in the CWP. He hoped to complete his final assessment of CWP by the end of the month, October 1996.

Over the previous nine months, Brown and Burgin had helped Tom Curtis, CWP's founder, put his business plan together. They both had a lot riding on the investment. CWP would be the first transaction sponsored by Brown's new firm, Brown, McMillan & Co. ("BMC"), a private equity firm he had co-founded earlier in 1996. Brown and his partner, Peter McMillan, were staking their reputation on this deal. And though Burgin planned to invest only $1 million, he and Curtis had been friends and business associates for many years. If he were to press too hard, his friendship might be compromised.

In the coming week, Brown and Burgin would seek to hammer out a final term sheet with Curtis for the financing. Many elements of the deal still needed to be worked out. At the same time, Brown was beginning to question certain basic tenets of the transaction. The car wash industry had a number of characteristics that Brown believed made a roll-up strategy attractive, but no national car wash company had ever been created. Brown was concerned about the amount of capital BMC and Bessemer would have to invest over time to build a company with sufficient size and scale to pursue a public offering, the exit for the investment Curtis thought most likely. Brown had also just read an article in a trade magazine about another

Car Wash Partners, Inc.
by PAUL GOMPERS, case number 9-299-034 Rev. JUNE 25, 2010

consolidator, reportedly well-capitalized and already doing acquisitions. This company represented competition that Brown had not anticipated. Given the size of the industry, he was not sure if it mattered. He wheeled toward the Golden Gate Bridge as Burgin's secretary picked up the phone.

CAR WASH INDUSTRY

In 1994, U.S. consumers spent approximately $100 billion on automotive-related car services such as car washing, detailing, lubrication, fluid replacement, and general repairs. The automated car wash market was estimated to be $3.2 billion, excluding the sale of gas and other ancillary products, and was growing by 3% to 5% annually.

The car wash industry could be divided into six segments. First, individuals could wash their cars themselves using their own cleaning supplies and implements. Second, car-owners could utilize "self-service" washes consisting of coin-operated bays. By inserting coins into automatic equipment, customers washed their cars using water, soap, and wax supplied by the operator. Third, consumers could use "roll-over" car washes, 10- to 20-foot enclosures usually located behind gas stations in which car washing machinery moved over a stationary car. Fourth, car-owners could bring their cars to "exterior-only" washes, generally housed in stand-alone structures housing 50- to 200-foot long tunnels through which cars were moved by conveyor past various pieces of washing and drying equipment. Fifth, they could use "full-service" car washes, offering similar conveyor car wash systems and a variety of other services to maintain the appearance and operating condition of their vehicles, including interior cleaning, detailing, windshield repair, smog checks, gasoline, and oil changes. Finally, high-end consumers could utilize hand-washes, offering a manual wash of their vehicles, both exterior and interior.

In building CWP, Curtis planned to focus on exterior-only and full-service car washes, which represented the largest portion of the professional car washing market. Though sizable, these segments of the industry were also extremely fragmented. Only 1.2% of exterior-only and full-service operators owned 10 or more locations and 8.7% owned four to nine locations. The 50 largest operators controlled only 625 of nearly 14,000 conveyor car wash sites across the country. (See **Exhibit 1** for statistics on car wash operators, **Exhibit 2** for statistics on the operating characteristics of full-service and exterior-only car washes, and **Exhibit 3** for industry pricing information.)

The majority of the car washes targeted by CWP were family-owned businesses controlled by either first or second generation owners. Many of these owners were reaching retirement age, and often the next generation showed little desire in taking over the business. Nonetheless, even moderately successful operators of full-service and exterior-only car washes were frequently able to generate high and predictable levels of cash flow and profit at the unit level. Gross margins ranged from 70% to 90%, and EBITDA margins were typically between 15% and 25%. Working capital requirements were extremely low, because customers generally paid cash at the time of sale. Ongoing capital expenditures also were low, averaging approximately $75,000 per year for most owners to maintain an acceptable appearance for their sites.

In many towns and cities across the country, zoning restrictions made it extremely difficult to build a new car wash to compete with a successful operation already in existence. Lack of competition allowed owners of many full-service and exterior-only car washes to prosper without making investments in their businesses that were typical in other consumer service businesses, such as restaurants and retailing. Car wash operators rarely invested meaningful amounts of money in advertising and marketing programs. Few operators develop human resources programs, even though labor costs represented by far their largest category of expense. Operators typically utilized local pools of highly marginal workers that were hired and discharged daily, even hourly, depending on weather conditions and other factors affecting demand. Turnover rates at many car washes exceeded 300% per annum.

Studies commissioned by the International Car Wash Association indicated that only 50% of car owners in the U.S. used- professional car washes, and the average customer only washed his or her car twice per year. However, industry sources predicted that demographic shifts would lead to increases in demand for professional car wash services through the 1990s. The growing incidence of dual-income households was driving increased demand for personal services of all kinds, such as laundry, house cleaning, and meal preparation, due to work and other demands on free time. There was an emerging awareness among consumers that professional car washes were better for car finishes and, as importantly, far more environmentally friendly than self-washes at home. The aging of the population meant that fewer consumers would be willing or able to wash their own cars. Finally, industry observers believed that the rapidly rising prices of new cars, whether purchased or leased, would cause car owners to own their cars for longer periods of time, and thus pay more attention to car care and maintenance.

The ownership and operation of car washes carried several risks. Professional car washes used chemicals that could be detrimental to the environment. The use of these chemicals and their disposal was widely regulated by Federal, state, and local authorities. Lubrication centers and gasoline pumping systems that often were key components of full-service car wash sites were highly regulated by the same agencies. Under federal law, owners of car washes were liable for all damages associated with any required environmental clean-up, even if the contamination occurred prior to their ownership of a site.

If car wash operators employed immigrant workers as part of their labor force, they were required to ensure that these workers carried with them proper documentation as a condition of their employment, even if on a temporary basis. Over the past 10 years, federal penalties for non-compliance had increased dramatically. Inspectors from the Immigration and Naturalization Service frequently visited car wash sites unannounced to ensure compliance with these laws. Penalties for improper documentation included seizure of the operation.

Car wash sites were also favorite targets for inspectors from state and federal Occupational Safety and Health Administration ("OSHA") agencies. On-the-job injuries at car washes were common, generally resulting from the handling of caustic chemicals, falls on wet and slippery floor surfaces, accidents during the operation of washing machinery, and car collisions on site. Violators of OSHA laws were subject to fines or temporary shutdowns.

TOM CURTIS

Before conceiving CWP, Tom Curtis had enjoyed a successful career as an entrepreneur, teacher, and business consultant. Upon receiving his law degree from the University of Pennsylvania in 1969, Curtis chose not to enter law and instead founded Executive Air Fleet Corporation ("EAF"), a pioneering company in the emerging field of aviation management services. He sold EAF at a substantial profit in 1982 when it reached more than $50 million in sales. After the sale of EAF, Curtis taught entrepreneurship at a well-known business school for three years and became an advisor to numerous venture capital firms and start-up companies.

By 1995, Curtis was beginning to feel the entrepreneurial itch again. He researched several ideas within service industries before deciding that a consolidation play in the car wash market represented the most attractive opportunity for him to build his second successful service company. Over the course of 1996, as he refined his business plan, Curtis visited more than 50 car wash units and started acquisition discussions with several leading car wash chains.

CWP'S STRATEGY

When he approached Brown and Burgin about funding, Curtis had outlined a plan to build the leading provider of car wash and related services in the U.S. CWP would implement a "buy and build" strategy to enter target markets around the country, then consolidate appropriate operational functions in regional and national headquarters, and dominate each of its markets by re-defining the standard of service. The markets targeted by the Company would be carefully selected on the basis of several factors, including population, wealth, climate, zoning requirements, and existing competition. The Company would focus on the full-service and exterior-only segments of the market, where Curtis felt that a reputation for service excellence would provide the greatest competitive advantage. Self-service and hand-wash units generally did not attract sufficient volumes to allow for scale economies or premium pricing.

The Company would enter a target market by purchasing an existing operator and then build market share through follow-on acquisitions and, as appropriate, the construction of new sites. The construction and opening of a new car wash generally took from 18 to 24 months, of which the first nine to 12 months were required to obtain governmental approvals. As such, growth exclusively through new sites would require large amounts of capital and real estate expertise, while dramatically slowing the rate at which CWP could expand.

Based on his industry research and prior experiences at EAF, Curtis believed that the financial performance of existing units could be improved significantly along several dimensions. First, he hoped to expand revenues by developing basic marketing and advertising programs not typically utilized in the industry. These programs would be designed to increase patronage by existing customers and to attract the estimated 50% of car-owners not currently utilizing the services of a professional car wash. Few operators spent any time tracking customer satisfaction or usage. Curtis planned to build strong brand awareness through a focused, well-articulated marketing strategy, directed at consumers as well as potential high volume purchasers of CWP's services, such as car dealers, city governments, and owners of large car fleets.

Curtis believed he could increase unit revenues by expanding the array of services and products offered for sale. Curtis believed that broader service and product offerings would enhance the overall experience of a customer visit, increase revenue per car washed, and attract non-car wash customers to a site, generating traffic independent of weather conditions that affect car wash demand. Standard services to be offered at CWP sites included express waxing and lubrication services, each of which had equivalent gross margins to car washing itself. Retail programs Curtis sought to develop involved the sale of gas, fast food, and sundry goods such as greeting cards, gift items, and car care products.

Curtis also hoped to institute industry-leading production practices at all of CWP's facilities as a means to speed throughput and thus lower operating costs and improve customer satisfaction. The conveyor car washes targeted by CWP were essentially small, automated manufacturing plants. Curtis believed that a key cause of customer dissatisfaction with professional car washes were delays in service resulting from production bottlenecks. He was not sure what investment was necessary to identify and remedy production problems, but he felt he could find someone to oversee the implementation of the improved systems he envisioned.

Curtis was particularly interested in improving human resource systems as a source of competitive advantage. Curtis found current industry practices unacceptable. He strongly believed that human resource programs designed to reduce turnover would result in substantially lower labor costs and much improved levels of service to the customer. Curtis wanted to invest $250,000 to $500,000 in developing proprietary screening and recruiting tools and organizational design programs. As part of this effort, Curtis intended to establish a national training program to develop and provide training to current and prospective general and unit managers. In addition, he planned to develop a comprehensive training curriculum for production staff.

Curtis believed he would rely on incentive compensation for local managers to implement best practices. Local managers would be given a significant degree of autonomy to encourage prompt and effective responses to local market demands. Curtis felt that on-site managers were critical for maintaining quality.

While the day-to-day operations would be very decentralized, Curtis was convinced that local operators would benefit from being part of a national operation. They would have access to human resource development expertise, marketing, merchandising, training, and sophisticated financial systems that a small, independent operator could not afford. A central office would also be able to monitor the quality of service in various markets. The collection of financial and customer data in the central office through the use of information technology would allow CWP to respond effectively to shifts in both local and national markets.

FINANCIAL PROJECTIONS

Curtis had already identified two acquisition candidates in Bakersfield, CA and in Boise, ID that he proposed to purchase using proceeds from the offering. (See **Exhibit 4** for details on the acquisition targets.) The Bakersfield company had three sites, all with detailing, merchandise, lubrication, and gas. The operations were well run and consistently profitable. The Boise, ID operations, also comprising three sites, were smaller in scope but similarly prosperous.

CWP would start from modest beginnings. In 1997, Curtis projected to have only two cities in operation. (See **Exhibit 5** for detailed plan on the number of planned cities and sites.) By 2001, Curtis expected CWP to be the nation's leading provider of car washing services with operations in 13 cities, 115 units in operation, and more than 12 million cars washed. Curtis was convinced that these projections were reasonable given the large and fragmented market. After all, an operation reaching this size was less than 1% of the car wash units across the country.

With these modest assumptions, however, CWP would grow into a substantial company. (See **Exhibits 6-8** for financial projections.) If unit projections were met, the Company would generate more than $330 million in revenue in 2001 and earn more than $18 million in after-tax profit. Curtis's plan called for substantial investment in acquisitions as well as capital expenditures related to building new sites and renovating existing ones. (See **Exhibit 9** for detailed financing plan.) Curtis placed the required need for outside capital at $283 million. Because of the Company's large amount of real estate and fixed assets, he believed that CWP could take on substantial amounts of debt. He conservatively felt that the Company could obtain at least half of this financing from debt, with the remaining coming from private equity.

According to his business plan, Curtis would use the small initial equity financing to acquire the properties in Bakersfield and Boise. These cities were to serve as beta sites for the Company's various initiatives to create value. Once he proved the efficacy of these programs, Curtis felt he could attract substantial amounts of capital for the roll-up of existing operators. Then, Curtis felt CWP could access the public markets to finance the remaining acquisitions. Having a public company might also allow him to provide stock instead of cash to do acquisitions. In the interim, however, Curtis felt that he would need to finance most acquisitions with cash. Current car wash operators had little interest holding the equity of an illiquid private company. Curtis worried about how to provide the right incentives for the local partners once they had been bought out. After all, he would be in Boston and needed local management to run the properties. Structuring the acquisitions would take some careful crafting.

BROWN, MCMILLAN & CO.

Three months before Curtis approached Brown about CWP, Brown had co-founded BMC with his partner, Peter McMillan. Curtis and Brown had become acquainted over the prior three years, when Brown had served as an investment banker to a healthcare products company on whose board of directors Curtis served. Curtis thought that Brown's knowledge of consolidation strategies, corporate finance, and mergers and acquisition techniques would be useful to him as CWP was launched. For Brown, CWP represented exactly the sort of transaction he and McMillan wanted to pursue when they formed BMC. (See **Exhibit 10** for biographies of Cabot Brown and Peter McMillan.)

BMC was founded to sponsor investments involving highly promising entrepreneurial enterprises that fell between the traditional mandates of large buy-out firms and venture capital funds. The firm targeted buy-outs, consolidation transactions, recapitalizations, and negotiated purchases of equity-related securities in which BMC could commit $5 to $10 million. The firm sought to make investments in circumstances where the principals believed the potential returns were attractive and the risk of losing capital was low. In analyzing investments, BMC thought it critical that a potential portfolio company demonstrate a realistic ability to generate superior levels of profitability, return on equity, and revenue growth.

While opportunistic in their investment approach, BMC's principals wanted to concentrate their endeavors in industries in which (i) they had direct experience or knowledge; and (ii) they believed smaller, entrepreneurial companies would be the beneficiaries of important structural shifts in regulatory, demographic, or competitive forces. Industries of particular interest to them included consumer products and services, where CWP fit; healthcare services; financial and business services; and media and publishing.

BMC sponsored its investments pursuant to an arrangement it established with a select group of participating investors who paid the firm annual management fees in exchange for the right to participate in BMC-sponsored transactions on a case-by-case basis. Many of the firm's investors had extensive experience in private equity investments like the proposed transaction involving CWP.

While BMC's principals had made numerous private investments over their careers, CWP represented their first commitment on behalf of their new investor group. Brown felt that even though his investors had sufficient resources to fund the entire deal, syndicating the investment with the right partner might be an attractive way to proceed, especially in light of the Company's potential funding needs going forward. Because Bessemer had been active in other successful service company investments and Curtis was close friends with Burgin and several other Bessemer partners, Brown thought Bessemer represented an ideal candidate to become a co-sponsor of CWP. Bessemer could bring not only its extensive network to bear on the deal, but the certification benefit of having the Bessemer name attached to CWP would increase the companies recognition and chance of success.

BESSEMER VENTURE PARTNERS

Bessemer was one of the oldest venture capital organizations in the country. In 1911, Henry Phipps established what was to become Bessemer Securities Corporation (Bessemer's principal limited partner) as an investment firm for the benefit of his descendants, starting with his share of the proceeds from the sale of Carnegie Steel. Since its inception, a central component of Bessemer Securities' charter had been to invest in and help build innovative, high-growth companies. Some of the companies that Bessemer helped establish or build in the early days included W.R. Grace, International Paper, and Ingersoll-Rand.

In 1996, Bessemer Venture Partners carried forward this tradition and invested between $50 and $60 million each year, while other Bessemer entities managed more than $1 billion of investments in public and private non-venture capital assets. Bessemer Venture Partners was an autonomous entity of 12 professionals with investing offices in Menlo Park, CA and Wellesley Hills, MA and an administrative office on Long Island in New York. (See **Exhibit 11** for biographies of Bessemer investment professionals.) The firm's efforts were entirely devoted to financing and building young companies. Bessemer had a reputation of working with potential entrepreneurs before the concept for a new company had been charted and continued to be active shareholders and partners through their growth, even to their entry into the Fortune 500. Bessemer typically participated in early-stage financings and later-stage financings where venture capital had not previously been raised. The industries in which Bessemer had invested ranged from healthcare to information systems to telecommunications to retailing.

More than 30 of Bessemer's portfolio companies had completed initial public offerings since 1991. (See **Exhibit 12** for Bessemer-financed public companies.) Bessemer individuals sought to play an active role in partnering with entrepreneurs to build companies that dominated their sectors. After decades of investing, Bessemer had cultivated a network of successful entrepreneurs, bankers and industry experts who helped recruit business partners, highly talented employees, and experienced directors for the companies they financed. With more than 100 years of collective venture capital experience, Bessemer investors had assisted with virtually every aspect of growing a successful enterprise. They had proven experience in helping companies develop business and organizational strategies, establish corporate alliances, execute business and product line acquisitions, and close follow-on rounds of private and public financing.

DEAL TERMS

Brown was looking to negotiate a preliminary term sheet with Curtis in which BMC would invest $5.6 million into CWP. Bessemer would invest $1 million on the same terms that he negotiated. Burgin had wanted Brown to negotiate the term sheet because of Burgin's friendship with Curtis. Brown wondered, however, how much of the Company BMC and Bessemer should get? What should the valuation of CWP be?

Brown had prepared information on some comparable firms. (See **Exhibit 13** for information on car care service firms.) Brown thought the most relevant of these companies were Earl Scheib, Inc., which owned and operated more than 160 automobile paint and repair centers throughout the US; Monro Muffler and Brakes, which operated more than 550 automotive repair shops providing a full range of brake, tire, exhaust system, and suspension services; and Envirotest, a chain of car inspection centers. Brown wondered which of the firms were truly comparable to CWP. Similarly, Brown also had prepared a list of recent public offerings by roll-up players. (See **Exhibit 14**.)

Brown also wondered about the structure of the financing. Should he purchase equity or some hybrid mix of equity and debt? Should the investment be made in one installment or in stages, triggered by the execution of definitive acquisition agreements or other milestones? How much debt should be used to fund the acquisitions? Should the amount of debt depend on the assets being acquired? He noted that some car wash operators owned the real estate underneath their car washes, but others leased all of their property and leasehold improvements. What about board seats, covenants, and other control mechanisms? And how, if at all, would the inclusion of Bessemer affect the terms of the deal?

ISSUES TO CONSIDER

As Brown pondered the investment, he worried that Curtis had not yet built up a management team. Brown was essentially acting as the Company's chief financial officer in the development of CWP's budgets and in the negotiations concerning the acquisitions in Bakersfield and Boise. Curtis had promised to focus on hiring a finance and marketing person as soon as the financing was complete, but no candidates had been identified. Brown hoped that his contacts and those of Burgin could help Curtis recruit the right team members. Bessemer had built many companies from ground zero and Burgin's experience in doing so would be critical.

Brown also wondered how easily Curtis would be able to utilize his prior experiences to become an effective leader and manager in the car wash industry. At the core of the investment thesis in this transaction was an assumption that CWP management, led by Curtis, could determine best practices in the industry and then get local managers to adopt them.

A larger issue related to future financings. Brown knew that if CWP were to be successful, it would need substantial amounts of financing, perhaps in excess of $100 million in private equity. Clearly, BMC and Bessemer could not provide that type of funding. New investors would need to be identified soon to maintain momentum. How would the addition of these new investors affect BMC and Bessemer's returns?

In examining the successes and failures among other roll-up companies, Brown was not certain how management should prioritize its efforts to generate the highest returns over the next three years. How would CWP be able to develop into an industry leader if it did not quickly become one of the largest companies in the car wash business? He was concerned that the first two targets identified by Curtis were too small. He wondered if the investment in the marketing and human resource programs Curtis proposed should be delayed until the Company reached critical mass, which he and Burgin thought was about $100 million in revenues.

Brown turned off his windshield wipers as the sky began to clear. He and Peter McMillan already had plenty of experience driving through automated car washes with Curtis. In some ways, the simplicity of Curtis's idea is what made it so appealing. Any investor would know what a car wash was. There was no complicated technology to decipher to understand the essence of this opportunity. Burgin's secretary told Brown to wait as she transferred his call to Burgin's office.

EXHIBIT 1 Car Wash Site Statistics

Top 100 Companies

Company Ranking	Total Units Controlled
1-20	319
21-40	139
41-60	101
61-80	80
81-100	61

Top Ten Companies

Company	Number of Locations
A	40
B	36
C	33
D	27
E	20
F	14
G	14
H	12
I	12
J	12

Source: Company Documents

EXHIBIT 2 Car Wash Operator Statistics in 1996

Advertising Method	Percent of Car Wash Operators Using:
Direct Mail	47.3%
Yellow Pages	48.9%
Radio	39.1%
TV	16.4%
Newspaper	45.7%
Other	28.3%
No Advertising	7.6%
Full Service Car Washes	
Operator Profiles	
Experience in car washing	12.0 years
Number of conveyors owned	1.6
Number of locations (all types)	1.9
Number of competitors	4.4
Labor and Compensation	
Starting hourly wage	\$5.01
Average hourly wage	\$5.68
Crew size	17.9
Annual turnover	10.1
Exterior-Only Car Washes	
Operator Profiles	
Experience in car washing	13.5 years
Number of conveyors owned	1.8
Number of locations (all types)	1.9
Number of competitors	3.7
Labor and Compensation	
Starting hourly wage	\$5.45
Average hourly wage	\$6.29
Crew size	7.0
Annual turnover	5.1

Source: Compiled from Professional Car Washing and Detailing 1996 Automatic Car Wash Survey.

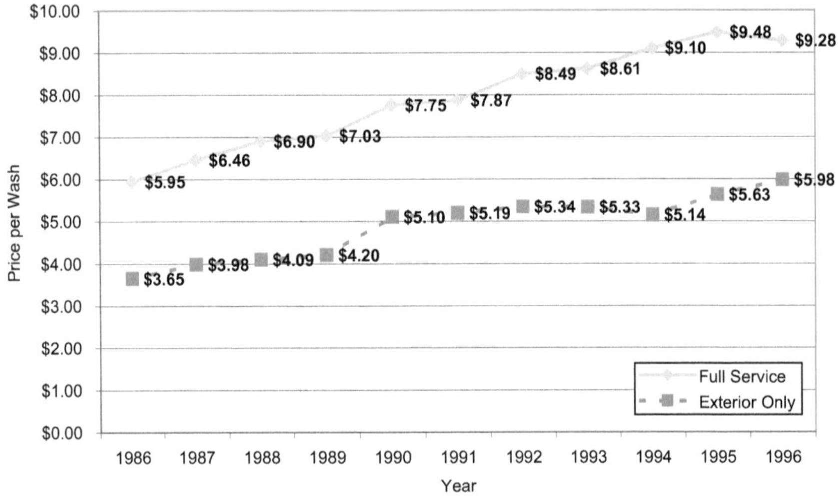

EXHIBIT 3 Car Wash Industry Pricing
Source: Compiled from Professional Car Washing and Detailing 1996 Automatic Car Wash Survey.

EXHIBIT 4 CWP Potential Acquisitions Targets

Potential Acquisition Target in Bakersfield, CA

Profit Center Overview:

Service	Unit #1 Stine Rd.	Unit #2 Downtown	Unit #3 White Ln.
Car Count - Car Wash	157,270	258,209	180,348
Car Count - Detail	11,665	N/A	12,321
Car Wash			
LTM Revenues	$1,201,691	$2,124,751	$1,409,616
LTM Gross Margin	1,047,191	1,931,000	1,158,000
Gross Margin %	87.1%	90.9%	82.2%
Revenues per car washed	$7.64	$8.23	$7.82
Detailing			
LTM Revenues	$309,834	$284,290	$207,106
LTM Gross Margin	258,533	244,000	171,800
Gross Margin %	83.4%	85.8%	83.0%
Revenues per car detailed	$26.56	N/A	$16.81
Merchandise/Deli			
LTM Revenues	$197,442	$267,800	$188,500
LTM Gross Margin	63,642	100,800	45,400
Gross Margin %	32.2%	37.6%	24.1%
Revenues per car washed	$1.26	$1.04	$0.39
Lubrication			
LTM Revenues	$543,649	$835,294	$610,082
LTM Gross Margin	337,654	533,000	370,900
Gross Margin %	62.1%	63.8%	60.8%
Revenues per car washed	$3.45	$3.24	$3.38
Gasoline			
LTM Revenues	$497,544	$868,437	$680,614
LTM Gross Margin	30,844	61,600	36,500
Gross Margin %	6.2%	7.1%	5.4%
Revenues per car washed	$3.16	$3.36	$3.77

EXHIBIT 4 (*continued*)

Potential Acquisition Target in Bakersfield, CA

Financial Profile:	1996	1997E	1998E
Income Statement			
Revenues	$10,226,636	$11,063,564	$13,195,706
Gross Margin	6,390,864	6,883,021	8,327,333
Adjusted EBITDA[1]	2,022,021	2,015,595	2,462,464
Balance Sheet			
Total Assets	6,834,700	13,024,354	12,403,177
Total Long Term Debt	5,862,300	9,385,059	8,161,480
Total Equity	571,400	3,528,860	4,109,939
Other			
Rent	920,100	966,105	1,014,410
Capital Exp.	250,000	900,000	0
Maintenance	213,544	219,905	226,502
Depreciation	414,100	445,052	445,052
Amortization	0	242,089	242,089

Notes:

[1]Adjusted for excess salary to family members.

EXHIBIT 4 (*continued*)

Potential Acquisition Target in Boise, ID

Profit Center Overview:

Service	Unit #1 Fairview	Unit #2 Broadway	Unit #3 Express
Car Count - Car Wash	182,682	148,200	90,974
Car Count - Detailing	13,977	15,015	-
Car Wash			
LTM Revenues	$1,578,500	$1,238,500	$347,500
LTM Gross Margin	$1,291,000	$1,110,000	$280,000
Gross Margin %	81.8%	89.6%	80.6%
Revenues per car washed	$8.64	$8.36	$3.82
Express Detailing			
LTM Revenues	$313,500	$428,500	-
LTM Gross Margin	$294,000	$296,500	-
Gross Margin %	93.8%	69.2%	-
Revenues per car detailed	$22.43	$28.54	-
Express Lubrication			
LTM Revenues	-	-	-
Gross Margin	-	-	-
Gross Margin %	-	-	-
Revenues per car washed	-	-	-
Gasoline			
LTM Gallonage	89,079	-	-
LTM Revenues	$118,000	-	-
LTM Gross Margin	$8,000	-	-
Gross Margin %	6.8%	-	-
Revenues per car washed	$0.65	-	-
Merchandise			
LTM Revenues	$83,000	$129,000	-
LTM Gross Margin	$41,500	$64,500	-
Gross Margin %	50%	50%	-
Revenues per car washed	$0.45	$0.87	-

EXHIBIT 4 (*continued*)

Potential Acquisition Target in Boise, ID

Financial Profile:	1995	1996E	1997E	1998E
Income Statement				
Revenues	$4,389	$4,450	$5,731	$7,578
Gross margin	3,585	3,706	4,764	6,231
EBITDA	627	606	713	972
Adjusted EBITDA[1]	927	906	1,013	1,275
Balance Sheet				
Total Assets	,234	N/A	N/A	N/A
Total Debt	779	N/A	N/A	N/A
Total Equity	455	N/A	N/A	N/A
Other				
Rent	204	N/A	N/A	N/A
Capital Exp.	150	N/A	N/A	N/A
Maintenance	220	N/A	N/A	N/A
Depreciation	148	N/A	N/A	N/A
Amortization	-	N/A	N/A	N/A

Notes:

[1]Adjusted for excess owner's salary.

Source: Company documents.

EXHIBIT 5 CWP Projected Operations

CWP, Inc.

Consolidated Operation Projections

	1997	1998	1999	2000	2001
Cities of Operation					
Existing	0	2	4	7	10
New	2	2	3	3	3
Total	2	4	7	10	13
Master Units					
Beginning Units	0	0	7	14	21
Units Acquired	0	7	7	7	7
Ending Units	0	7	14	21	28
Full-Service/Super Center Units					
Beginning Units	0	4	10	23	38
Units Acquired	4	6	8	10	12
Units Opened	0	0	5	5	5
Ending Units	4	10	23	38	55
Express/Mini-Super Center Units					
Beginning Units	0	3	6	12	22
Units Acquired	3	3	3	3	3
Units Opened	0	0	3	7	7
Ending Units	3	6	12	22	32
Total Ending Units	7	23	49	81	115
Total Units Under Construction	8	20	24	24	24
Total Cars					
Washed	420,000	1,710,000	4,800,000	8,410,125	12,589,631
Fueled	420,000	1,578,750	5,293,125	10,323,844	16,120,473
Express Waxed	16,500	74,250	261,750	510,056	801,112
Lubricated	-	52,500	294,000	569,138	881,001

Source: Company Documents.

EXHIBIT 6 CWP Projected Income Statement

CONSOLIDATED INCOME STATEMENT ($000)	1997	1998	1999	2000	2001
Revenues					
Car Wash Services	$3,120	$13,410	$38,989	$75,320	$118,881
Merchandise	315	1,330	5,370	12,256	21,580
Express Wax	412	1,853	6,076	12,424	20,429
Express Lubrication	-	1,835	8,506	18,833	30,309
Total Services and Merchandise	3,847	18,427	58,942	118,833	191,199
Gasoline	3,614	13,526	42,870	89,359	147,266
Total Revenues	7,461	31,953	101,812	208,192	338,465
Cost of Sales					
Car Wash Services	468	1,788	4,851	9,293	14,791
Merchandise	211	891	3,598	8,355	14,459
Express Wax	41	185	608	1,257	2,081
Express Lubrication	-	525	2,434	5,138	8,304
Total Services and Merchandise	720	3,390	11,491	24,090	39,634
Gasoline	3,281	12,278	38,913	81,111	133,672
Total Cost of Sales	4,001	15,667	50,404	105,201	173,306
Gross Profit	3,460	16,286	51,408	102,991	165,159
Gross Margin - %	46.4%	51.0%	50.5%	49.5%	48.8%
Operating Expenses					
Corporate Overhead	$1,164	$2,998	$3,715	$4,216	$4,607
Unit Salaries & Bonuses	1,397	6,577	20,936	41,850	64,307
Maintenance	201	901	2,865	5,785	9,333
Advertising	149	639	2,036	4,150	6,744
Corporate Marketing Programs	37	160	509	1,041	1,692
Rent	416	1,995	4,485	7,190	10,014
Other	631	2,907	7,995	14,551	22,877
Total Operating Expenses	3,995	13,179	38,826	74,566	114,967
EBITDA	$629	$3,107	$12,582	$28,426	$50,192
EBITDA/Revenues - %	8.4%	9.7%	12.4%	13.7%	14.8%
Depreciation	45	946	2,724	4,683	6,774
Amortization	154	825	1,914	3,113	4,421
EBIT	$431	$1,336	$7,944	$20,630	$38,997
EBIT/Revenues - %	5.8%	4.2%	7.8%	9.9%	11.5%
Interest Expense	364	2,011	4,564	6,927	8,855
Interest Income (a)	-	-	-	-	-
Pre-Tax Income	$67	($674)	$3,380	$13,702	$30,142
Pre-Tax Margin - %	0.9%	-2.1%	3.3%	6.6%	8.9%
Income Taxes	50	-	1,518	5,341	11,323
Net Income	$16	($674)	$1,862	$8,362	$18,819
Net Margin - %	0.2%	-2.1%	1.8%	4.0%	5.6%

Source: Company Documents.

EXHIBIT 7 CWP Projected Balance Sheet

SUMMARY BALANCE SHEET ($000)	1997	1998	1999	2000	2001
Assets					
Current Assets					
Excess Cash	$263	$620	$780	$406	$7,909
Operating Cash	410	1,731	5,354	10,786	17,296
Accounts Receivable	207	888	2,828	5,783	9,402
Inventories	267	1,044	3,360	7,013	11,554
Other	252	594	382	2,759	2,779
Total	$1,399	$4,877	$12,704	$26,747	$48,940
Fixed Assets					
Real property improvements	$1,738	$14,624	$30,550	$47,316	$64,885
Equipment	1,633	13,641	25,512	38,054	49,481
Land	6,950	19,987	34,181	49,533	66,043
Total	$10,321	$48,251	$90,242	$134,904	$180,409
Goodwill	4,452	19,262	34,892	51,343	68,614
Total Assets	$16,172	$72,389	$137,839	$212,993	$297,963
Liabilities and Shareholder's Equity					
Current Liabilities					
Accounts Payable & Deferred Expenses	$ 569	$ 2,404	$ 7,436	$ 14,981	$ 24,023
Long-term Debt					
Mortgage	$4,355	$18,070	$33,442	$49,292	$65,554
Bank Debt	2,484	10,146	16,350	17,063	12,377
Supplier Financing	879	6,522	11,910	18,760	25,541
Seller Note	-	-	-	-	-
Subordinated Debt	-	-	-	-	-
Total	$7,718	$34,738	$61,702	$85,115	$103,472
Shareholders' Equity					
Preferred & Common Equity	$7,868	$35,905	$67,497	$103,332	$142,083
Retained Earnings	16	(658)	1,204	9,566	28,384
Total Shareholder's Equity	$7,885	$35,247	$68,701	$112,898	$170,468
Total Long-term Liab. & Shareholder's Equity	$16,172	$72,389	$137,839	$212,993	$297,963

Source: Company Documents.

EXHIBIT 8 CWP Projected Cash Flow Statement

SUMMARY STATEMENT OF CASH FLOWS ($000)	1997	1998	1999	2000	2001
Operations					
Net Income	$16	($674)	$1,862	$8,362	$18,819
Depreciation	45	946	2,724	4,683	6,774
Amortization	154	825	1,914	3,113	4,421
Additions	315	944	2,847	4,496	5,627
(Reductions in Working Capital					
Capital Expenditures	5,100	21,233	24,668	29,478	31,638
Cash Flow From Operations	($5,200)	($21,080)	($21,016)	($17,815)	($7,251)
Investment Activities					
Acquisitions	($10,336)	($34,842)	($38,516)	($42,191)	($37,464)
Financing Activities					
Issuance of Debt	7,718	28,037	31,592	35,834	38,752
Repayment of Debt	-	(1,017)	(4,843)	(13,517)	(26,894)
Issuance of Equity	7,718	28,037	31,592	35,834	38,752
Cash Flow from Financing Activities	$15,436	$55,057	$58,341	$58,151	$50,609
Financing (Shortfall) Surplus	($100)	($865)	($1,191)	($1,855)	$5,694
Net Cash Added from Acquisitions	$363	$1,222	$1,351	$1,480	$1,609
Net Financing (Shortfall) Surplus	$263	$357	$160	($375)	$7,504
Cumulative	$263	$620	$780	$406	$7,909

Source: Company Documents

EXHIBIT 9 CWP Projected Financing Plan

Car Wash Partners, Inc.

Financing Analysis

	Acquisitions Master	Full	Express	Total Acquisitions
1997	-	$7,349	$2,987	$10,336
1998	$20,831	$11,024	$2,987	$34,842
1999	$20,831	$14,699	$2,987	$38,516
2000	$20,831	$18,373	$2,987	$42,191
2001	$20,831	$22,048	$2,987	$45,866
			Grand Total	$171,751

	Cap. Exp. Master	Full	Express	Total Cap. Exp.
1997	$2,750	$1,000	$1,350	$5,100
1998	$8,463	$4,700	$8,070	$21,233
1999	$8,988	$6,980	$8,701	$24,668
2000	$8,988	$9,140	$11,350	$29,478
2001	$8,988	$11,300	$11,350	$31,638
			Grand Total	$112,116

	Financing Supplier	Bank	Subordin.	Mortgage	Total Debt	Equity	Total Financing
1997	$879	$2,484	-	$4,355	$7,718	$7,718	$15,436
1998	$5,731	$8,374	-	$13,933	$28,037	$28,037	$56,074
1999	$6,049	$9,257	-	$16,287	$31,592	$31,592	$63,184
2000	$8,116	$10,140	-	$17,578	$35,834	$35,834	$71,668
2001	$8,859	$11,023	-	$18,870	$38,752	$38,752	$77,503
			Grand Total		$141,933	$141,933	$283,866

Source: Company Documents.

EXHIBIT 10 Biographies of Cabot Brown and Peter McMillan

Cabot Brown and Peter McMillan co-founded Brown, McMillan & Co., LLC in 1996. BMC is a private investment firm that sponsors buy-outs of and equity investments in highly promising entrepreneurial enterprises. The Firm concentrated its investment activities on transactions involving businesses with $10 million to $100 million of revenues and significant growth potential that fell between the traditional mandates of venture capital funds and buy-out funds.

Before co-founding BMC, **Mr. Brown** worked for 10 as an investment banker, most recently at Volpe, Welty & Company. At Volpe Welty, Mr. Brown was the first person to join the investment banking department after the firm's founding in 1987, became a general partner in 1989, co-founded the firm's industry practice in healthcare in 1990, and served as a member of its Executive Committee from 1992 to 1995. Previously, Mr. Brown served in the corporate finance and merger and acquisition departments of The First Boston Corporation and Lehman Brothers. Before becoming involved in finance, Mr. Brown worked as a journalist with such publications as the Los Angeles Times and Rolling Stone magazine. Mr. Brown received his M.B.A. from Harvard Business School with high distinction as a George F. Baker Scholar and his A.B. cum laude in Government from Harvard College

Mr. McMillan spent 12 years in finance before co-founding BMC. From 1983 to 1994, Mr. McMillan worked at Montgomery Securities, an investment banking firm, where he served in the institutional sales department, ultimately as a special limited partner and director of U.K. sales. Mr. McMillan worked extensively with clients in transactions involving both public and private securities. Previously, Mr. McMillan served as a foreign country risk analyst at European American Bank. From 1994 until 1996, Mr. McMillan worked as an author, television producer, and lecturer for The National Geographic Society in connection with a project he led to recreate the record-setting 1919 flight which was the first aerial voyage from England to Australia. Mr. McMillan supervised the construction of a replica of this plane, the Vickers Vimy, and co-piloted it on this 16,000-mile expedition. Mr. McMillan received a B.S. in Business Administration from the University of North Carolina, Chapel Hill.

Source: Company documents

EXHIBIT 11 Biographies of Partners at Bessemer Venture Partners

Bill Burgin Burgin joined Bessemer Venture Partners in 1970. He has invested in a broad range of industrial and technology companies, including Domain, Galileo Electro Optics, GMIS, Horizon Cellular, James River Corporation (now Fort James), Midway Airlines, and Numerax (acquired by McGraw Hill). He served on the board of the National Venture Capital Association from 1978 to 1983 and on the board of the New England Venture Capital Association from 1987 to 1991. He holds a B.A. and an M.B.A. from Harvard University.

Felda Hardymon Hardymon joined Bessemer Venture Partners in 1981. He invested in many young companies in the software, communications and retail sectors, including American Superconductor, Cascade Communications (acquired by Ascend), Celcore (acquired by DSC), Parametric Technologies, the Sports Authority, Staples and VideoServer. Previously Hardymon worked at BDSI, the original venture subsidiary of General Electric Corporation, where he was an investor in Ungermann-Bass, Stratus Computer and Western Digital. Prior to that time he taught mathematics and served as Director of Systems & Research at Duke University. He received his undergraduate degree from Rose Polytechnic Institute, a Ph.D. in Mathematics from Duke University and an M.B.A. from Harvard. Hardymon is on the board of the National Venture Capital Association.

Christopher Gabrieli Gabrieli was a partner who joined Bessemer Venture Partners in 1986. Previously he founded GMIS, a publicly traded healthcare information systems company. Gabrieli's investments spanned the gamut of healthcare, from biotechnology to medical devices to healthcare services. Among his portfolio companies are Alkermes, Centocor, EPIX Medical, GMIS, ImmuLogic, Isis Pharmaceuticals, Millennium Pharmaceuticals and OPTA Food Ingredients. He graduated from Harvard College with an A.B. in History & Science.

David Cowan Cowan joined Bessemer Venture Partners in 1992. His communications investments include CellAccess (acquired by Fore), Ciena, Data Labs (acquired by Lucent), Netsys (acquired by Cisco), ON Technology, P-Com and Worldtalk. Cowan specialized in e-commerce investments, including BabyCenter, eToys, Flycast, Keynote, Mothernature.com, PSI-Net, Tumbleweed and VeriSign. He received his B.S. in computer science and M.B.A. degrees from Harvard University.

Bruce Graham Graham joined Bessemer Venture Partners in 1996. His investments include GenOA, ISR Global Telecom, Lightwave Microsystems,

EXHIBIT 11 *(continued)*

Obsidian, QED, Smart Machines, Stream Machines and Summit Microelectronics. Previously, he spent five years with Vertex Management investing in information technology product companies such as Premisys, Proxim and SCM Microsystems. Graham has held operational roles with Intel and Siemens AG and a management consulting role with the Boston Consulting Group. Graham holds a B.S. in chemical engineering from Princeton University and an M.B.A. from Stanford University.

Rob Soni Soni joined Bessemer Venture Partners in 1994. He specializes in communications, and his portfolio includes Altiga Networks, Aptis Communications (acquired by Nortel), Castle Networks, C-Port Corporation, InformationView Software Solutions, ITC^DeltaCom, Maker Communications, MindSpring, NBX Corporation, Omnia Communications, Oresis Communications, Powertel, Sahara Networks (acquired by Cascade) and Sirocco Systems, among others. Previously, Soni worked for The Boston Consulting Group. He graduated from Harvard College with an A.B. in social studies.

Source: Compiled from company Web Page.

EXHIBIT 12 Bessemer Portfolio Companies Which Had Gone Public

Company	Location	Industry
American Superconductor	Watertown, MA	General-Purpose Integrated Circuits
Bright Horizons	Cambridge, MA	Educational and Training Services
Cascade Communications	Westford, MA	Connectivity Products
Cerplex Group	Tustin, CA	Business Services (not Financial)
Ciena	Hanover, MD	Fiberoptic Equipment; Photonics
Community First Bankshares	Fargo, ND	Financial Institutions and Services
Davox Communications	Westford, MA	Computer Systems
DSP Group	Santa Clara, CA	Application-Specific Integrated Circuits
Eagle Hardware & Garden	Tukwila, WA	Construction Products
Echelon	Palo Alto, CA	Connectivity Products
EPIX Medical	Cambridge, MA	Biotechnology
Factory Card Outlet	Bensonville, IL	Specialty Retail
Gmis	Malvern, PA	Enterprise Systems
Hometown Buffet	San Diego, CA	Restaurants and Food Service
Immulogic Pharmaceutical	Cambridge, MA	Pharmaceutical
Isis Pharmaceuticals	Carlsbad, CA	Biopharmaceuticals: Other
ITC Deltacom	West Point, GA	Telecommunications Service Providers
Lam Research	Fremont, CA	Integrated Circuit Production
Maxim Integrated Products	Sunnyvale, CA	General-Purpose Integrated Circuits
Multiple Zones International	Bellevue, WA	Specialty Retail
Netframe Systems	Milpitas, CA	Data Storage
On Technology Corporation	Cambridge, MA	Network/Systems Mgt Tools
Opta Food Ingredients	Cambridge, MA	Food Products
P-Com	Campbell, CA	Wireless Communications Equipment
Parametric Technology	Waltham, MA	Design-Automation Software
Performance Systems Internat.	Herndon, VA	Internet Service Providers

(*continued*)

EXHIBIT 12 *(continued)*

Company	Location	Industry
Perseptive Biosystems	Cambridge, MA	Automated Manufacturing
Programmer's Paradise	Shrewsbury, NJ	Specialty Retail
Promedco	Fort Worth, TX	Physician Practice Management
Stant	Richmond, IN	Consumer Electronics
Staples	Newton, MA	Broadlines Retailing; Mass Merchandizing
Summagraphics	Seymour, CT	Computer Peripherals
Syquest Technology	Fremont, CA	Data Storage
Systemsoft	Natick, MA	Business Applications Software
Verio	Englewood, CO	Internet Service Providers
VeriSign	Mountain View, CA	Other Online Services
Veritas Software	Santa Clara, CA	Design-Automation Software
Versant Object Technology	Menlo Park, CA	Database Software
Videoserver	Lexington, MA	Videoconferencing Equipment and Services
Worldtalk Communications	Santa Clara, CA	Software: Other

Source: Compiled from VentureOne - Venture Source database.

EXHIBIT 13 Valuation of Comparable Public Companies

Envirotest, Inc.

	1992	1993	1994	1995
Sales	$53.3	$88.5	$96.4	$104.8
SG&A	$6.3	$13.3	$19.1	$24.9
Cap Ex	$5.7	$3.1	$69.3	$118.9
Op Inc Bef Dep	$19.6	$28.7	$27.1	$19.5
Net Income	$2.5	-$4.7	$2.2	-$14.9
Total Assets	$144.5	$200.7	$418.2	$457.3
Current Assets	$22.0	$88.8	$218.7	$31.6
Current Liab.	$26.2	$17.0	$35.3	$29.8
Debt	$108.8	$130.2	$328.6	$388.4
Net Worth	$18.4	$50.6	$52.9	$38.0
Beta				0.82
P/E Ratio	NA	35.0	110.4	NM

Grease Monkey Holdings, Inc.

	1992	1993	1994	1995
Sales	$17.6	$20.1	$18.8	$18.5
SG&A	$4.1	$4.0	$4.0	$4.3
Cap Ex	$0.3	$0.3	$0.3	$0.2
Op Inc Bef Dep	-$0.1	-$0.2	$0.8	$1.4
Net Income	-$1.1	-$1.5	$0.1	$0.2
Total Assets	$16.0	$16.9	$13.3	$13.1
Current Assets	$2.7	$3.7	$2.8	$2.7
Current Liab.	$3.1	$4.0	$2.4	$2.0
Debt	$11.9	$12.2	$8.8	$9.4
Net Worth	$0.7	$1.2	$1.7	$1.9
Beta				0.55
P/E Ratio	NM	NM	NM	33.3

Monroe Muffler, Inc.

	1992	1993	1994	1995
Sales	$78.5	$93.6	$109.1	$117.1
SG&A	$23.6	$28.1	$32.3	$35.3
Cap Ex	$14.8	$14.4	$20.3	$25.6
Op Inc Bef Dep	$16.1	$19.1	$22.6	$22.3
Net Income	$6.2	$7.4	$9.1	$7.6
Total Assets	$63.5	$77.0	$93.0	$120.1
Current Assets	$17.6	$21.1	$22.1	$26.5
Current Liab.	$9.5	$13.2	$15.3	$17.7
Debt	$23.4	$27.2	$31.7	$48.6
Net Worth	$31.4	$38.8	$48.2	$55.9
Beta				0.35
P/E Ratio	13.3	15.6	14.9	16.2

Earl Scheib, Inc.

	1992	1993	1994	1995
Sales	$53.6	$48.5	$47.3	$44.0
SG&A	$13.8	$13.3	$12.7	$12.3
Cap Ex	$1.4	$1.2	$0.9	$5.2
Op Inc Bef Dep	$0.3	-$2.0	-$6.4	-$0.1
Net Income	-$0.1	-$1.8	-$5.6	$0.9
Total Assets	$34.8	$34.1	$29.5	$28.5
Current Assets	$11.4	$12.4	$12.8	$7.4
Current Liab.	$6.6	$8.0	$8.7	$6.6
Debt	$0.0	$0.0	$0.0	$0.0
Net Worth	$24.9	$22.7	$17.2	$18.1
Beta				0.63
P/E Ratio	NM	NM	NM	38.5

Source: Company Documents.

EXHIBIT 14 Valuation of Public Roll-Ups

.Selected "Roll-Up" IPOs 1990-1996

Date of IPO	Company	Industry	IPO Price	Current Price (10/4/96)
April 1990	Sanifill	Garbage Collection	$9.50	$47.00
August 1992	American Medical Response	Ambulance Services	8.50	36.50
May 1994	US Delivery	Local Package Delivery	10.00	35.00
September 1994	Corporate Express	Document/Supplies Delivery	14.00	36.25
February 1995	US Office Products	Wholesale Office Supplies	10.00	37.00
June 1995	Physicians Resource	Healthcare	13.00	22.13
January 1996	FYI	Document Storage	13.00	22.50
June 1996	Coach USA	Regional Bus Lines	17.00	32.00
July 1996	Telespectrum	Telemarketing	15.00	20.00
September 1996	American Residential Services	Heating/Air Conditioning Services	15.00	18.75

Source: Company Documents.

EXHIBIT 15 General Macroeconomic Conditions

Year	Real GDP (1992 $ Billions)	Inflation	Unemployment Rate	12 Month Treasury Bill Rate	5 Year Government Bond	10 Year Government Bond	Prime Rate	S&P 500 Index
1990	$6,079.0	5.3%	6.3%	6.4%	7.7%	8.1%	10.0%	330.2
1991	$6,105.3	2.6%	7.3%	3.9%	5.9%	6.7%	7.2%	417.1
1992	$6,327.1	2.9%	7.4%	3.5%	6.0%	6.7%	6.0%	435.7
1993	$6,476.9	2.5%	6.5%	3.5%	5.2%	5.8%	6.0%	466.5
1994	$6,688.6	2.7%	5.4%	6.8%	7.8%	7.8%	8.5%	459.3
1995	$6,796.5	2.3%	5.6%	4.9%	5.4%	5.6%	8.7%	615.9
1996	$7,017.4	2.9%	5.3%	5.3%	6.2%	6.4%	8.3%	740.7

Source: Compiled from Citibase.

CHAPTER 3.2

Valuation in Entrepreneurial Settings

Paul Gompers

INTRODUCTION

Valuation is the central concept in finance. While investors believe that the process of valuation is difficult and fraught with error and assumptions, in the context of entrepreneurial settings, valuation is approached with rigor and care. Without methods to assess value, capital budgeting becomes impossible. While elements of valuation remain an "art," finance theory and its implementation through valuation methodologies has important implications for private equity practice. When reasonable assumptions are made, the techniques discussed in this note can lead to better investment decision-making in whatever setting you work. The margin for error in entrepreneurial settings, however, is much smaller than it is in other contexts. The goal of proper valuation methodologies is to maximize the probability that the "right" investment decision is made.

Valuation methodologies can be widely applied to analyze many of the decisions that a firm faces. Anything that might affect the size or the timing of a firm's cash flow or changes its riskiness affects the firm's value. Whether it is an existing public company or division, an expanding young company, a new research project, a new production facility, an acquisition target, or a new product launch, value is the fundamental currency that compares all of an investor's potential decisions. The ability to make value-increasing decisions is clearly enhanced by a thorough understanding of the material in this note. In addition, a well thought out valuation will provide important information that is useful in managing the firm and monitoring its progress.

I would like to highlight several important points up front. Thinking about discount rates is important. Not because we can precisely estimate

Valuation in Entrepreneurial Settings
by PAUL GOMPERS, case number 9-220-057 JANUARY 27, 2020

discount rates for young, entrepreneurial firms. Thinking about discount rates allows us to understand the behavior of entrepreneurs and investors in their companies. This note discusses how an undiversified entrepreneur views their personal discount rate. It also explores the types of hurdle rates that venture capitalists use when deciding whether to invest in a young companies. Understanding the underlying "theory" about how each of them views risk and value will improve decision-making. While there will always be tremendous uncertainty with estimates of value for young companies, this note will provide critical intuition and frameworks that will inform entrepreneurs and investors in their companies.

This note will discuss various valuation techniques and when they are appropriate. Investment professionals employ many (if not all) of these valuation methodologies during the course of evaluating an investment opportunity. The theory behind much of this discussion will be glossed over in order to keep this note to a reasonable length. A detailed analysis and discussion of these issues would occupy a large book. The reference section of this note contains a detailed list of texts and articles that explore these issues in more detail. Many of the references are highly specialized and can provide a deep understanding of the theory behind the methodologies. This note is intended to present the reason for and the mechanics of several approaches to valuation and to give you a sense of when the various techniques are appropriate. The interested student should refer to the appropriate source for further reading.

The rest of this note is divided into three sections. The note starts by discussing two approaches to discounted cash flow analysis, capital cash flows (CCF) and weighted average cost of capital (WACC). These methods form the basis of other techniques that are applied and should be understood fully. While much of this should be familiar from your first year finance course, this overview provides a quick refresher and provides a foundation for much of the rest of the note and the course in general.

Second, the note examines "venture capital" valuation models. These models are employed by most venture capital organizations in their investment decision-making. They can best be viewed as an internal rate of return (IRR) or multiple on invested capital (MOIC) analysis. They start by projecting a certain equity investment upfront (as well as likely future equity investments), assume growth in earnings/cash flow over some time horizon (typically five years), then assume some sale or exit from the company at a pre-determined exit multiple or value. The IRR or MOIC of these entry and exit values is then compared to the firms hurdle rate, i.e., the return it desires on its successful investments. The note will discuss a variety of factors that influence a firm's hurdle rate.

Finally, the note discusses comparable companies' valuation methodologies which for entrepreneurial companies entail looking at pre- or post-money valuation of companies in the same industry at a similar stage who have received financing recently. These methods are quick and dirty approaches to assessing value. They often do not reflect the "core" underlying value of a company and may lead to signification over (or under) valuation of an opportunity. This note will help you take into consideration what those implicit assumptions when doing a comparables valuation.

DISCOUNTED CASH FLOW VALUATION: CASH FLOWS

Both the CCF and WACC methods of valuation start by determining cash flows from operations. These cash flows are pre-financing, i.e., they are independent of the capital structure of the firm. One common mistake that students make when calculating cash flows for CCF or WACC is to take out interest payments from the cash flows and call that number cash flow to equity holders. While this approach has merit (it is referred to as equity cash flow valuation), it does not easily allow an individual to calculate the value of the firm independent of financing and under various financing scenarios. Equation (1) gives a quick refresher on how to calculate cash flows. Subscripts denote time periods.

$$CF_t = EBIT_t * (1-\tau) + DEPR_t - CAPEX_t - \Delta WK_t + other_t \quad (1)$$

CF = Cash Flow
EBIT= Earnings Before Interest and Taxes
τ = Corporate Tax Rate
DEPR = Depreciation
CAPEX = Capital Expenditures
ΔWK = Increases in Working Capital
other = Increases in Taxes Payable, Wages Payable, etc.

These cash flows are what are economically significant to the firm and to an investor. As will be discussed below, estimating cash flows is far more important than determining the discount rate. People valuing risky projects have a tendency to increase the discount rate if they feel that the project's returns are uncertain. This "fudge" factor addition to the discount rate should always be avoided. The critical element of CCF and WACC analysis is to have unbiased estimates of free cash flows. One way to approach this estimation is scenario analysis.

Valuing Cash Flows with the CCF Method

The capital cash flows (CCF) method of valuation takes cash flows estimates and calculates the value of an unlevered (all equity) firm. The value of the debt tax shield is added to the present value of future cash flows in an unlevered firm. CCF also adds other elements of value enhancement if they are present (e.g., present value of investment tax credits, etc.). In order to calculate the value of the firm, the first order of business is to forecast cash flows from Equation (1). After cash flows for periods 1 to T are obtained, a terminal value (TV) is calculated. The firm is assumed to grow forever at the rate g and the appropriate discount rate for the unlevered firm (more below) is determined by the riskiness of the firm's assets, r_a.

$$TV_T = \frac{CF_T * (1+g)}{r_a - g} \tag{2}$$

Other methods of calculating a TV are possible. Most of you should be familiar with salvage value analysis from your introductory finance course. In the salvage value method, the TV is just the sum of recoverable value in the final year, making sure to take tax considerations into account. A brief comment on growth rates is appropriate. First, always check the reality of your growth rate assumption. Remember that if you are using nominal discount rates, your terminal growth rate should reflect your beliefs about inflation. Real growth is the nominal growth rate minus the expected inflation rate. If you get large negative or large positive numbers, what does that imply? Is the business going to shrink in real terms? Is it going to grow in real terms forever? We often assume a growth rate slightly larger than the expected inflation rate to compensate for faster growth now but zero real growth in the future. In the long-run (when the "long-run" starts is dependent upon industry maturity, firm strategy, etc.), most firms will probably grow at a rate between that of inflation and the overall growth rate of the economy (nominal GDP). Be aware that if your cash flow estimates are over a short period of time (three years or less), then the terminal value will drive your estimates of net present value. Valuation in which the terminal value represents a substantial majority of the value are likely to be very sensitive to small changes in growth rate assumptions.

Once the terminal value is calculated, the net present value of future cash flows is given by Equation (3):

$$PV^U = \frac{CF_1}{1+r_a} + \frac{CF_2}{(1+r_a)^2} + \ldots + \frac{CF_T + TV_T}{(1+r_a)^T} \tag{3}$$

The debt taken on by the firm provides tax advantages because the interest payments are tax deductible. The value of the tax shield, TS, in period t from debt level D paying interest at a rate of r_d is given by (4):

$$TS_t = \tau * r_d * D \tag{4}$$

These tax shields need to be discounted at a rate appropriate to their riskiness. If firms set debt at a level proportional to firm value, then the tax shields are as risky as the firm's assets, so the proper discount rate is r_a. In that case, the present value of the tax shield for the firm, PVTS, having debt of D_t and a long-run equilibrium debt level of D_{eq} is given by Equation (5):

$$PVTS = \frac{\tau * r_d * D_1}{(1+r_a)} + \frac{\tau * r_d * D_2}{(1+r_a)^2} + \frac{\tau * r_d * D_3}{(1+r_a)^3} + \ldots + \frac{\frac{\tau * r_d * D_{eq}}{r_a}}{(1+r_a)^T}$$
$$= \frac{\tau * r_d * D_1}{(1+r_a)} + \frac{\tau * r_d * D_2}{(1+r_a)^2} + \frac{\tau * r_d * D_3}{(1+r_a)^3} + \ldots + \frac{\tau * r_d * D_{eq}}{r_a(1+r_a)^T} \quad (5)$$

If D is the constant level of debt, then (5) implies that the debt tax shield is just (τ*rd*D)/ra. The adjusted present value of the project is now given by Equation (6):

$$PV_{CCF} = PV^U + PVTS$$
$$= \frac{CF_1}{(1+r_a)} + \frac{\tau * r_d * D_1}{(1+r_a)} + \frac{CF_2}{(1+r_a)^2} + \frac{\tau * r_d * D_2}{(1+r_a)^2} \quad (6)$$
$$+ \ldots + \frac{\frac{(1+g)CF_T}{r_a - g}}{(1+r_a)^T} + \frac{\tau * r_d * D_{eq}}{r_a(1+r_a)^T}$$

This value is then compared with the investment cost to determine whether or not the firm or individual should undertake the project. CCF minus the cost of the investment, I, yields a much talked about term, net present value (NPV).

$$NPV_{CCF} = PV_{CCF} - I \quad (7)$$

Discount Rates

Estimation of discount rates should be familiar to most people from earlier course work. Simple formulas provide a guide to appropriate rates.

$$r_a^U = r_f + \beta^U * (r_m - r_f) \quad (8)$$

r^U_a = discount rate for the firm's assets, i.e., the rate on unlevered equity
r_f = risk free rate
β^U = unlevered β
r_m= market rate of return on common stocks
(r_m-r_f)= market risk premium

The underlying basis for (8) is the Capital Asset Pricing Model and its implications have been extensively discussed in the academic and practitioners' literature. I will discuss some of the potential caveats to the use of βs in estimating cost of capital, but given that we have no better alternative, you should use it with caution.

The first question that (8) brings up is what are the appropriate rates to use? r_f is the risk free rate. When determining the appropriate risk free rate, you should attempt to match the maturity of the investment project with that of rf. For example, if you are valuing a long-term investment project, r_f would be the yield on long-term Treasury. For shorter-term investment projects you should use the short-term Treasury rate.

The market risk premium used can vary. Some evidence indicates that the risk premium has decreased over time to around 5-6% today. For example, Siegel (2005) estimated that a historical equity risk premium over the 1871–2004 period was equal to (approximately) 5.2 percent. In a 2011 update, Siegel (2011) estimated a historical equity risk premium over the 1870–2011 period as 4.9 percent. Welch (2009) surveyed financial economists in January 2009 and found that the median equity risk premium over short-term Treasury bills reported by survey responders constituted 6 percent. Ibbotson (2012) calculated that the forward-looking equity risk premium as of 2011 was 6.14 percent. Ibbotson and Chen (2003) calculated that the forward-looking, long-term equity risk premium based on data from 1926–2000 was 5.9 percent. Fernandez et al (2013) surveyed finance and economics professors, analysts and managers of companies in May and June 2012 and asked them about the market risk premium that they use to calculate the required return to equity. According to their findings, the average and median equity risk premium for the U.S. was equal to 5.5 and 5.4 percent, respectively. As a general rule, we will utilize a risk premium of 6% in Entrepreneurial Finance, but a risk premium of anywhere between 5 and 6% would be a reasonable choice.

Choosing an estimate of β^U is more difficult than the market risk premium. β^U is the systematic risk of the investment being evaluated assuming that it is 100% equity financed. For public companies, estimates of β^U can be obtained from a regression of stock returns for that company on the market return. Typically, it is best to use as much data as possible to estimate β. The first question is how long of a time period one should use. The answer is that as long as there are no structural changes in the company, you should use as long a time series as possible. Two to five years might be typical. Similarly, given issues with bid-ask bounce and daily returns, it is typical to use weekly returns when estimating data. The next question is, what day of the week to use in your weekly regression? Services like Bloomberg typically default to using Friday-to-Friday returns. Recent research, however, has shown that there are issues with weekends and stock returns that make Friday and Monday problematic. A better approach is to potentially calculate the β across all five days (i.e., run five regressions), then average your estimates. In that way, you won't be throwing out any data and are likely to get a better estimate of β for a particular company. The β estimates obtained from stock returns are, however, equity βs for levered firms, β^L. To go from the equity β to the unlevered β, we need to "unlever" the β.

$$\beta^U = \frac{\beta^L}{\left[1+\left(\frac{D^i}{E^i}\right)\right]} \tag{9}$$

D^i = total debt of company i.
E^i = market value of equity for company i.
τ = tax rate.

If the project is substantially different from the firm's existing assets or the firm is privately held, then you should search for comparable firms that have assets and activities that are similar to the investment project. As the discussion below will make clear, the more firms you can find that are similar to the project being evaluated, the more confidence you will have in your estimate of β.

Historical β^L are defined as β^L derived from a regression of a firm's stock return on the market excess return estimated on historical stock return data. They can typically be found for most public companies from services like Bloomberg or ValueLine. Because β^L tends to be mean reverting towards 1 over time, services like Bloomberg will often also provide an Adjusted β^L measure. The Adjusted β^L is typically just a weighted average of both the Historical β^L and 1 to reflect that extreme values of β^L are likely to move towards 1 over time.

Additionally, investors are concerned with an investment's future returns. Therefore, an estimate of systematic risk, such as β^L, should be used in a forward-looking context because β^L is an approximation of what investors perceive the sensitivity of that firm's value to changes in the economy will be going forward. Many external factors can be expected to affect a stock's systematic risk (or β^L) over time. However, the expected β is unobservable in the market and, therefore, must be estimated. While there are a number of approaches to calculating the expected β, academic studies have opined that models that incorporate fundamental risk factors in addition to stock market movements provide reliable predictors of the expected risk of a company on a looking-forward basis. Barra, a well-known data provider, estimates predicted βs using such a model. Barra's predicted β L are frequently relied upon by academics and investment professionals for equity valuation. Barra defines its predicted β as:

> [A] forecast of a stock's sensitivity to the market. It is also known as fundamental β, because it is derived from fundamental risk factors. In the BARRA model these risk factors include 13 attributes—such as size, yield, and price/earnings ratio... Because we reestimate these risk factors monthly, the predicted β reflects changes in the company's underlying risk structure in a timely manner.[1]

A question often arises when there are no comparable companies. This often occurs in entrepreneurial or venture capital settings. The firm may be doing something new or have a totally new project. In this case you need to use a little common sense to get "ballpark" estimates of the systematic risk of the firm. If you have accounting data on the firm, you can try to use "earnings βs" which have some correlation with equity βs. You should also try to think about how cyclical the firm is. Is the risk systematic or can it be diversified away? How does the firm fair in booms and busts? These types of questions will get you close to an appropriate discount rate when trying to do valuation. Remember, however, that you should always see how sensitive the value is to various discount rates. It is also important to worry more about cash flow estimation.

Some Thoughts about Discount Rates

When you calculate a β for a firm, you should not regard this as the discount rate. Considerable controversy exists about the validity of the Capital Asset Pricing Model that underlies the calculation of costs of capital in this way. Without going into the academic debate, I just warn you that you should not think that βs somehow represent facts that will exactly estimate value.

The first caution is to note that βs are measured with a significant amount of error. The βs of companies that do very similar things often appear to be quite different. If one looks, however, at the standard errors of the estimate (i.e., the potential range of values), the precision of β estimates for any one company are quite low. For this reason, it is usually useful to try to triangulate the discount rate of a target firm with a number of comparable companies in the search for a proper β. Using a greater number of firms can average out the noise in the estimation of β. Using all five days of the week (via five weekly returns regressions) can also help. There is usually a trade-off between picking many comparable firms or only a few. The greater the number of comparables, the greater the reduction in estimation error. At the same time, however, you run the risk of including firms that are not truly comparable.

Even trying to find comparables may prove troublesome. One should try to find companies that are as close to the project or acquisition target as possible. This might entail a detailed analysis of what the comparables actually do and the various weights these activities have within the firm.

Finally, the patterns of βs vary over time even for one particular company. If one looks at the β for an individual company, the β can change from year to year. The systematic risk of the firm may vary, the capital structure may vary, or both. This fact should provide some caution about using βs estimated over long time periods.

These points are not intended to dissuade you from using discounted cash flow methods for valuing firms and projects. Alternatives have little justification in most cases. You should remember, however, that considerable care needs to be taken when applying the simple formulas. Think about which firms are closest to the firm being valued. Think about the underlying economics of the firm.

Cost of Capital for an Undiversified Entrepreneur

One critical assumption of our use of a CAPM β to derive a discount rate is that the person doing the valuation is completely diversified.

$$\beta_i = \frac{\rho_{im}\sigma_i}{\sigma_m} \tag{10}$$

Equation (10) is just the regression coefficience from a regression of the return of firm i on the market which is how we estimate β. The numerator ($\rho_{im}\sigma_i$) is just the portion of the firm's standard deviation of returns that is non-diversifiable, i.e., how much does this firm's risk increase the riskiness of a diversified portfolio. σ_m is the standard deviation of the market returns while σ_I is the standard deviation of firm i's returns. You can see from this that a firm's cost of capital derived from its β is dependent about the correlation of a firm's return with the market return, ρ_{im}.

Now when an entrepreneur is undiversified, they care about the total risk of their investment, i.e., their wealth moves one for one with the movements in the value of their company. Hence, ρ_{im} is equal to 1. To estimate the β of an undiversified entrepreneur, you should set the

$$\beta_i^{ENT} = \frac{\sigma_i}{\sigma_m} \tag{11}$$

$$\beta_i^{ENT} = \frac{\beta_i}{\rho_{im}} \tag{12}$$

You can therefore benchmark the β for an entrepreneur who is undiversified by setting β equal to the ratio of the standard deviation of the firm's return relative to the market return or dividing the CAPM β of firm i by the correlation of firm i with the market. While there is great uncertainty about how precise these estimates will be, they will at least give you a sense about how much higher the discount rate of an undiversified entrepreneur will be. For example, if we assume that σ_m, the standard deviation of the market returns, is 15% while σ_I, the standard deviation of the firm's returns are 100%, then we can get a β_i of 6.67. With an equity risk premium of 6.0% and assuming a risk free rate 3%, we get a discount rate for the undiversified entrepreneur of 43%.

How does one go about estimating the standard deviation of the entrepreneur's company? One can look to small, public companies in the startups industry to get a rough estimate. The thing to remember is that any estimate of this volatility will be only approximate. The critical lesson is to understand that because most entrepreneurs are undiversified, they care about total risk, not just systematic risk. This implies that their discount rates will be substantially higher than those used by diversified outside investors.

What are the implications of these high discount rates for entrepreneurs? First, the high discount rates for entrepreneurs may affect their exit strategy. Entrepreneurs may sell out in an acquisition too early relative to what investors would want because they care about total risk. Venture capitalists have increasingly been willing to "partially cash out" entrepreneurs in later rounds. By cashing out the entrepreneur, they are more willing to continue building their company in order to exit later at a higher value. This aligns the incentives of the entrepreneur with the incentives of the venture capital investors.

Partially offsetting the higher cost of capital for an undiversified entrepreneur is their over-optimism. Typically, entrepreneurs tend to be over-optimistic about their startups. Even though nearly 60% of startups fail, most entrepreneurs believe the likelihood of their success is virtually certain. Therefore, in early rounds, the effects of the entrepreneur's high discount rates on firm strategy are unlikely to be important. It is likely only later, when offers to acquire the company come in our the firm receives later rounds of financing that the high discount rates of undiversified entrepreneurs become important to consider.

Weighted Average Cost of Capital (WACC)

Estimation using weighted average cost of capital starts with the same cash flows and asset βs with which CCF starts. The difference between the two methods is where the tax advantages of debt comes into the calculation. In CCF the value of the debt tax shield is calculated each year. Therefore, the value of debt and interest payment can be changing over time. With WACC the debt tax advantage affects the discount rate applied to the cash flows. This implies that we either use some long-run debt-to-equity ratio or some average debt-to-equity ratio for the firm. If debt changes a lot over time, then WACC can be somewhat cumbersome.

The first step in WACC is to determine the appropriate discount rate. Using the same inputs as in the CCF method, the discount rate for WACC, r_{WACC} is given by Equation (13):

$$r_{WACC} = \frac{r_e^L * E + r_d * (1-\tau) * D}{D+E} \tag{13}$$

To estimate the cost of equity, r_a^L, you need to relever β assuming the appropriate debt to equity ratio.

$$\beta^L = \beta^U * \left[1 + \frac{D}{E}\right] \tag{14}$$

The levered cost of equity is then given by Equation (13):

$$r_e^L = r_f + \beta^L * (r_m - r_f) \tag{15}$$

The appropriate net present value of the firm is then calculated by discounting the pre-interest payment cash flows by the appropriate weighted average cost of capital. Equation (14) gives that calculation

$$PV_{WACC} = \sum_{t=1}^{T}\left[\frac{CF_t}{(1+r_{WACC})^t}\right] + \frac{\left[\frac{CF_T}{r_{WACC}-g}\right]}{(1+r_{WACC})^T} \tag{16}$$

The net present value of the project is then given by Equation (12):

$$NPV_{WACC} = PV_{WACC} - I \tag{17}$$

The values you obtain with WACC and CCF should give you very close answers. Appendix 1 gives an example of both CCF and WACC valuations of a certain hypothetical firm. The values obtained in each are very close to the other, which is comforting.

The advice of this section is to employ the method that you feel most comfortable using. The CCF method is perhaps easier to use and allows you to explicitly calculate the net present value of the tax shield effects of debt financing. WACC may be easier to implement if the numbers are presented with an equilibrium debt-to-equity ratio. Remember that whichever method you use, the values you get are only as good as what you put in. Garbage in, garbage out! Make reasonable and justifiable assumptions when you attempt to value firms.

VENTURE CAPITAL VALUATION/INVESTMENT MODELS

Many venture capital investors in practice utilize the "venture capital" method of valuing investments and making investment decisions. This method has developed to compensate for various patterns in early stage investments and utilizes rules of thumb by which they seek to assess whether the investment "makes sense." I will discuss how the venture capital method works and how it is related to the discounted cash flow methodologies that we discussed earlier.

The method starts in a similar manner to a discounted cash flow analysis by projecting a company's revenues and net income over several years. Five years is the most common. Typically, interim revenue, earnings, and cash flows will be ignored although most firms model additional dilution when the firm needs to raise cash in future investment rounds. Venture capitalists will then take some performance measure in the terminal year (say year 5) and use that to generate an exit value. The exit value may be determined using EBITDA multiples, revenue multiples, etc. The critical element is that the venture capitalist seeks to determine the value that they believe they can exit their investment. The exit value is typically an enterprise value. From this number, any outstanding debt (if it exists) in the exit year is subtracted to arrive at an exit equity value. An IRR or MOIC is the calculated for the equity in and the equity out.

Selecting the right exit multiple requires judgment. Current industry multiples may be helpful, but if the industry is growing more quickly today (because it is a young industry or is in an expansion phase), then exit multiples might be lower in the future than they are today. In any case, it is typical for the venture capitalist to utilize a range of exit values in their VC model.

The venture capitalist then models an IRR or MOIC based upon the equity that they invest up front today and what they believe they will receive for their equity ownership at exit in five years. In essence, the venture capitalists is assessing equity in-equity out.

The investor then compares the IRR of their equity investment to their "hurdle rate." Hurdle rates vary from firm to firm and also depend upon the size, stage, and industry of the investment. Typically venture capital hurdle rates may be 25 to 50% whereas seed stage hurdle rates may be in the 75% range, although these ranges can vary substantially across firms and across investments. Venture capital firms will typically adjust their hurdle rate depending upon geography, leverage, industry risk, etc.

Where do these hurdle rates come from? Many are derived from industry rules of thumb. If a firm is doing an investment with substantial risk and a high probability of failure, then the model essentially looks to what the venture capitalist hopes to earn if the investment is successful, i.e., doesn't fail. The high return on winners compensates for those that fail. We know that roughly two thirds of all venture capital investments fail. Similarly, riskier industries may require higher returns to compensate for the underlying risk of the investment. In addition, the return that the venture capital firm models is the gross investment return. It does not represent the net return to investors. From the gross return management fees and carried interest are subtracted to derive the net return for limited partners. These fees and carry can reduce a gross return number by 5 percent or more when the limited partners ultimately get their net return. Because venture capital firms market their funds as having returns in excess of the public market and often tout target returns in the high teens and low twenty percentages, these high hurdle rates may be necessary to generate attractive returns for their investors.

MULTIPLES VALUATION METHODOLOGY

A common method for valuation that is often utilized in addition to discounted cash flow is the comparable company valuation method. For mature companies, this method is utilized by investment bankers, private equity investors, and investment analysts and looks at various multiples of financial metrics to estimate value. This method entails finding a comparable company or set of companies. The comparable company valuation method is often used as a complement to discounted cash flow analyses. In this method, the value of a company or set of companies is used to estimate the value of another company or project. The comparable companies are chosen to be as similar as possible to the company that is to be valued. Typical dimensions that are utilized to gauge comparability include industry, past performance, size, growth rates, and business model. In the venture capital industry, comparable company valuations typically entail looking for similar stage company, in a similar industry, that received financing in the recent past. These "comparables" provide the venture capitalist with a benchmark for how they might value their investment.

The comparable company valuation is done by calculating "multiples" for the benchmark company, or companies, and then applying the multiple to the company that is to be valued. A multiple is generally the ratio of company value (measured in different ways) to a performance measure. The calculated multiple is adjusted (if appropriate) and then multiplied by the utilized performance measure for the company of interest in order to derive a valuation of that company. This performance measure can be revenues, EBITDA, earnings, etc.

If a person valuing a particular firm only has one comparable company, then it is imperative to adjust the multiple of the comparison company for any differences in factors that may affect the multiple of the firm. Close scrutiny of the growth rates, riskiness, and cash flow generation of the firms needs to be undertaken.

The use of these metrics to pick comparable firms is a way to match firms that are similar to the firm of interest in terms of growth rates and discount rates. In fact, the critical dimensions of a comparable company are expected cash flow generation, future growth, and the riskiness of the firm.

The use of multiples is really just a variation on the use of a terminal value as discussed above. Terminal values are typically calculated by multiplying cash flow in some terminal year by one plus the growth rate and dividing that number by the discount rate of the assets minus the long-run expected growth rate, i.e., the growth rate that is expected to last forever.

A multiple just provides a summary statistic for how the market capitalizes (or values) the long-run stream of future cash flows. In fact, if one knows the long-run growth rate of a firm and its discount rate (cost of capital), one can then calculate the appropriate multiple to apply. That formula, which is the same formula that is used to calculate the terminal value in a DCF, is captured in equation (16):

$$CF\,Multiple = \frac{CF * (1+g)}{r_a - g} \tag{16}$$

where:
CF= cash flow in the current period.
g = long-run growth rate
r_a = cost of capital for the firm's assets.

Equation (16) is nothing more than a cash flow multiple that gives the value of a firm that is expected to grow at a rate of g forever. Other multiples are sometimes used in practice. For example, EBITDA, revenue, and net asset multiples are often utilized in practice.

In equation (17), the EBITDA multiple is expressed as some function "F" that transforms EBITDA into cash flows and then multiplies this cash flow times one plus the long-run growth rate and divides by the discount rate on assets minus the long-run growth rate.

$$EBITDA\,Multiple = \frac{F(EBITDA)*(1+g)}{r_a - g} \tag{17}$$

Implicit in every multiple is the relationship between the chosen metric (EBITDA, Net Income, EPS, Revenues, etc.) and cash flows. A cash flow multiple is typically better than other multiples because investors value the cash that a firm generates. A person valuing a firm does not need to make an implicit assumption about how that cash is transformed into cash flows. Typically, EBITDA multiples will be more appropriate than net income, EPS, or Revenue multiples because EBTIDA is close to cash flow. It is still necessary, however, to compare how much cash is generated for each dollar of EBITDA, or net income, or revenue.

For example, if two firms have the exact same revenues, but one firm has twice the cash flow margin as the other, the firm with the higher cash flow margin will have a higher value. If one uses the revenue multiple from the firm that is more profitable to value the less profitable firm, one would overvalue the less profitable firm.

A simple rule to follow when valuing a company using a multiples method is to use a multiple that is derived from a performance measure that is as close to cash flow as possible. For example, the relationship between revenues and cash flow is less tight than the one between net income and cash flow. In other words, net income is closer to cash flow and more related to cash flow than is revenue.

It is also important to benchmark the expected long-run growth and the discount rates of the comparable firms to those of the firm that is being valued. Equation (13) makes it clear that the higher the growth rate of the firm, the higher the value of the multiple, all else being equal. Therefore, if the comparable firm that is chosen to value a particular firm is actually expected to grow faster than the firm to be valued, the comparable company method will overvalue the firm of interest. In essence, the multiple implies a future growth rate for the firm that is too high.

For this reason, it is almost always preferable to do a comparable company valuation using forward-looking multiples. While trailing multiples (i.e., multiples based upon past performance) are sometimes used and may be the only multiples if projections are not available, they are less precise than using forward-looking multiples.

Similarly, the riskiness of the comparable firms and the firm to be valued need to be compared. As equation (13) makes clear, as the discount rate of a particular firm goes up, the multiple that applies to that firm will be lower. Riskier streams of cash are worth less than less risky streams of cash.

If someone is trying to value a particular company by using a comparable firm, but that comparable firm has a lower discount rate (cost of capital) than the firm to be valued, any comparable company multiple would have to be reduced accordingly to compensate for the greater risk.

It should be easy to see from the above discussion that implicit in every multiple of a financial metric, the method is a one-step discounted cash flow. As such, comparable company valuations should typically be utilized as a check to other methods. A well-specified and thoughtful discounted cash flow analysis will typically provide more insights than a quick and dirty comparable companies valuation.

VENTURE CAPITAL COMPARABLE COMPANY METHODS

Venture capitalists often use comparable company valuation techniques as well, although they typically do not use financial metrics. It is quite common for venture capital investors and entrepreneurs to look at the implied valuation of previous investment rounds for similar companies, in a similar industry, in a similar geography. One often hears that "SaaS companies in the Valley are receiving pre-money valuations on Series A rounds of $10 million." Essentially, venture capitalists are looking at these transactions as benchmarks for what they are willing to pay for an investment. Venture capitalists will often adjust their "valuation" based upon relative attributes. If the company has a better team, they will increase the value. If the company is further along, they will increase the value. If there are currently holes in the management team, they may decrease the value.

It is important to remember, however, that these valuations are the product of supply and demand. When there is a glut of capital looking for opportunity, valuations get driven up. At times when capital is scarce, valuations get driven down. The implied valuations based on financing rounds may not be tethered in reality. As such, significant over- and under-valuation may persist. Remember that the valuations from investment rounds are nothing more than "implied valuations" that were set to determine how much equity the company gives up for a certain amount of capital. They may not represent the actual valuation of future cash flows from the business.

RECOMMENDATION

When should you use which method? That depends upon the problem. If you are estimating the value of a firm with positive cash flows or you believe will soon have positive cash flows, then the standard CCF or WACC is appropriate. Each will give you roughly the same answer. Venture capitalists who have target fund returns almost universally employ a venture capital valuation model. Finally, the reasonableness of each of these approaches can be assessed using a thoughtful comparable companies valuation, whether that is looking at comparable investments by venture capitalists in similar companies or the use of market multiples to calculate a comparable value.

This note is meant to provide a review of the valuation material. The references contained in the back of this note are intended to provide an initial source of further data and information. It is important to understand how the methods differ and when to utilize the various methods. The marginal value of this thoughtful analysis is probably substantially higher for private equity investors than it is for public corporations. One clear lesson from Entrepreneurial Finance should be that analysis pays.

APPENDIX 1: VALUATION EXAMPLE USING CCF AND WACC

Pro Formas

	Year 1	Year 2	Year 3	Year 4
EBIT	5.5	6.2	7.0	7.2
Depreciation	2.5	2.4	2.3	2.2
Capital Expenditure	2.0	3.0	3.0	3.1
Working Capital Investment	1.3	1.9	1.9	1.5
Interest Expense	0.36	0.36	0.36	0.36

Tax Rate	40%
Current Book Value of Debt	3.0
Equity B of Comparable Firm	1.90
Debt to Equity Ratio of Comparable Firm	40%
Target Debt to Total Capital Ratio	40%
Long-term T-Bond Rate	9%
Long-term Debt Rate	11%
Long-term Growth Rate	2%

Calculating Free Cash Flows

FCF=EBIT(1-τ)+ Depreciation-Capital Expenditure-Change in Working Capital

	Year 1	Year 2	Year 3	Year 4
FCF	2.5	1.22	1.6	1.92

Discount Rate

If we assume an equity risk premium of 8%, we get the following:

$\beta^{U} = \beta^{L} / [1 + (D / E)]$
$\beta^{U} = 1.90 / [\ 1 + (0.40/0.60)] = 1.14$
$r_a = r_f + \beta^{U} * 8$
$r_a = (9) + 1.19*8 = 18.12\%$

For CCF we will use a discount rate of 18.12%.

In order to calculate the discount rate for WACC, we need to assume some equilibrium debt to equity ratio. I will assume that the firm is financed by 40% debt and 60% equity. If we use our formulas from above, we get:

$\beta^{L} = \beta^{U} * [1 + (D / E)]$
$\beta^{L} = 1.19 * [\ 1 + 0.40/ 0.60)] = 1.90$
$r^{L}_e = r_f + \beta^{L} * 8$
$r^{L}_e = (9) + 1.90 *8 = 24.2\%$
$r_{WACC} = E / (D+E) * r^{L}_e + D / (D+E) * (1 - \tau)* r_d$
$r_{WACC} = 0.60 * 24.2\% + 0.40 * (1\text{-}0.40) * 11.00\% = 17.16\%$

Therefore, for WACC we will use a discount rate of 17.16%.

Terminal Value

We take the cash flow in year 4, 1.92 and we assume that this cash flow will grow at 2% forever. The terminal values are:

$TV_{CCF} = 1.92 * (1.02) / (0.1812 - 0.02) = 12.15$
$TV_{WACC} = 1.92 * (1.02) / (0.1716 - 0.02) = 12.92$

Present Value

Discounting the cash flows and terminal value in year four at 18.12% for the CCF and 17.16% for WACC cases yields:

$PVCF_{CCF} = 4.95$
$PVCF_{WACC} = 5.04$

$PVTV_{CCF} = 6.24$
$PVTV_{WACC} = 6.86$

Now we need to calculate the present value of the tax shield for the CCF method. If we assume that the debt level is held constant at 3, then we get:

$PVTS_{CCF} = (\tau^*r_d^*D)/r_a=(.4^*.11^*3)/.1812=0.73$

Summing the present values gives us:

$PV_{CCF} = PVCF + PVTV + PVTS = 4.95 + 6.24 + 0.73 = 11.92$
$PV_{WACC} = PVCF + PVTV = 5.04 + 6.86 = 11.90$

Source: Casewriter.

NOTE

1 Barra Inc. (2000), "Predicted B," p. 1. Retrieved from http://www.barra.com/support/library/predictedβ.pdf. Accessed 1/2020.

REFERENCES

Baldwin, C., 1982, "Optimal Sequential Investment when Capital is Not Readily Reversible," *Journal of Finance* 37, 763–782.
Brealey, R., S. Myers, and F. Allen, Principles of Corporate Finance, 9th edition, Boston, MA: McGraw-Hill Irwin, 2008.
Bruner, R., K. Eades, R. Harris, and R. Higgins, "Best Practices in Estimating the Cost of Capital: Survey and Synthesis," Financial Practice and Education, Spring/Summer 1998, pp. 13–28.
Connor, G., "Three Types of Factor Models: A Comparison of Their Explanatory Power," Financial Analysts Journal, Vol. 51, No. 3, May/June 1995, pp. 42–46.
Copeland, T., T. Koller, and J. Murrin, 1991, Valuation: Measuring and Managing the Value of Companies, (John Wiley & Sons, New York, NY.)
Damodaran, A., Damodaran On Valuation, New York, NY: John Wiley & Sons, 1994.
Damodaran, A., Investment Valuation, 2nd edition, New York: John Wiley & Sons, 2002.
Dixit, A. 1992, "Investment and Hysteresis," *Journal of Economic Perspective*, 107–132.

Dixit, A. and R. Pindyck, 1994, Investment under Uncertainty, (Princeton University Press, Princeton, NJ.)

Fabozzi, F. and H. Markowitz, The Theory and Practice of Investment Management: Asset Allocation, Valuation, Portfolio Construction, and Strategies, 2nd edition, Hoboken, NJ: John Wiley & Sons, 2011.

Fama, E., 1977, "Risk-Adjusted Discount Rates and Capital Budgeting under Uncertainty," *Journal of Financial Economics* 5, 3–24.

Fernandez, Pablo, Javier Aguirreamalloa, and Luis Corres, 2013, "Market Risk Premium used in 82 countries in 2012: A survey with 7,192 answers," IESE Business School, University of Navarra.

Grenadier, S., and A. Weiss, 1997, "Investment in Technological Innovations: An Option Pricing Approach," *Journal of Financial Economics* 44, 397–416.

Hoffman, W., W. Raabe, J. Smith, and D. Maloney, Corporations, Partnerships, Estates, and Trusts, 2001 edition, Cincinnati, OH: South-Western College Publishing, 2001.

Ibbotson "Market Results for Stocks, Bonds, Bills, and Inflation 1926–2011," Valuation Yearbook, Chicago, IL: pp. 53–69 at p. 66.

Ibbotson, Roger G. and Peng Chen, 2003, "Long-Run Stock Returns: Participating in the Real Economy", *Financial Analysts Journal*, 59(1), 88–98.

Ibbotson, R. and P. Chen, "Long-Run Stock Returns: Participating in the Real Economy," Financial Analysts Journal, Vol. 59, No. 1, January/February 2003, pp. 88–98.

Kaplan, S. and R. Ruback, "The Valuation of Cash Flow Forecasts: An Empirical Analysis," The Journal of Finance, Vol. 50, No. 4, September 1995, pp. 1059–93.

Koller, T., M. Goedhardt, and D. Wessels, Valuation: Measuring and Managing the Value of Companies, 4th edition, Hoboken, NJ: John Wiley & Sons, 2005.

Luehrman, T., 1997, "Using APV: A Better Tool for Valuing Operations," *Harvard Business Review* 145–154.

Majd, S. and R. Pindyck, 1987, "Time to Build, Option Value, and Investment Decisions," *Journal of Financial Economics* 18, 7–27.

Meulbroek, L., "The Efficiency of Equity-Linked Compensation: Understanding the Full Cost of Awarding Executive Stock Options," Financial Management, Vol. 30, Summer 2001, pp. 5–44.

Modigliani, F. and M. Miller, 1958, "The Cost of Capital, Corporation Finance, and the Theory of Investment," *American Economic Review* 48, 261–287.

Mullins, D., 1982, "Does the Capital Asset Pricing Model Work?," *Harvard Business Review*, 105–114.

Myers, S. and S. Turnbull, 1977, "Capital Budgeting and the Capital Asset Pricing Model: Good News and Bad News," *Journal of Finance* 21, 727–730.

Nichols, N. 1994, "Scientific Management at Merck: An Interview with CFO Judy Lewent" *Harvard Business Review*, 88–99.

Pindyck, R., 1993, "Investment under Uncertain Cost," *Journal of Financial Economics* 34, 53–76.

Pindyck, R., 1991, "Irreversibility, Uncertainty, and Investment," *Journal of Economic Literature* 29, 1110–1152.

Quigg, L., 1993, "Empirical Testing of Real Option-Pricing Models," *Journal of Finance* 48, 621–639.

Roberts, K. and M. Weitzman, 1981, "Funding Criteria for Research, Development, and Exploration Projects," *Econometrica* 49, 1261–1288.

Rosenberg, B., "Prediction of common stock βs," The Journal of Portfolio Management, Vol. 11, No. 2, Winter 1985, pp. 5–14

Ruback, R., 1986, "Calculating the Market Value of Riskless Cash Flows," *Journal of Financial Economics* 15, 323–339.

Siegel, D., J. Smith, and J. Paddock, 1987, "Valuing Offshore Oil Properties with Option Pricing Models," *Midland Corporate Finance Journal* 5, 22–30.

Siegel, Jeremy J., 2005, "Perspectives on the Equity Risk Premium," *Financial Analysts Journal*, 61(6), 61–73.

Siegel, Jeremy J., 2011, "Long-Term Stock Returns Unshaken by Bear Markets," in Rethinking the Equity Risk Premium (eds. P. Brett Hammond, Martin L. Leibowitz, and Laurence B. Siegel), Research Foundation of CFA Institute.

Taggart, R., 1991, "Consistent Valuation and Cost of Capital Expressions with Corporate and Personal Taxes," *Financial Management* 20, 8–20.

Triantis, A. and James Hodder, 1990, "Valuing Flexibility as a Complex Option," *Journal of Finance* 45, 549–565.

Trigeorgis, L. and S. Mason, 1987, "Valuing Managerial Flexibility," *Midland Corporate Finance Journal* 5, 14–21.

Weitzman, M., W. Newey, and M. Rabin, 1981, "Sequential R&D Strategy for Synfuels," *Bell Journal of Economics* 12, 574–590.

Welch, I., "Views of Financial Economists on the Equity Premium and on Professional Controversies," Journal of Business, Vol. 73, No. 4, 2000, pp. 501–37.

Widen, R. S., "Delaware Law, Financial Theory and Investment Banking Valuation Practice," N.Y.U. Journal of Law and Business, Vol. 4

CHAPTER 3.3

United Capital Partners (A)

Paul A. Gompers, J. Daniel Kim and Vladimir Mukharlyamov

It was another brisk day in Moscow in January of 2007, but Ilya Sherbovich marveled at the enervating snowfall somehow with excitement. Sherbovich, then the president of Deutsche Bank's investment banking group in Russia, just received internal compliance from the bank's senior leadership; he was officially allowed to leave his post a year earlier than his contract's expiration date. After years of assisting myriad Russian companies reach their next level of growth, Sherbovich had contemplated a transition from advisor to investor. He was glad to achieve the move's first step of amicably convincing his employer to let him go early. In fact, Deutsche Bank considered it a mutually beneficial deal with the hopes that the two parties would provide deal flow to each other. Sherbovich sat down, wanting to thoroughly finish his task as the president of the group, and began facilitating the transition of his duties to his replacement.

Meanwhile Victoria Lazareva, a colleague at the investment bank who planned to join Sherbovich on his move, called and enthusiastically talked about a Russian fashion retail company. The idea of institutional investing was nice, but it was only an idea to Sherbovich who had yet to make a full-time transition from Deutsche Bank. Lazareva, also calling from her office at Deutsche Bank, strongly recommended that Sherbovich's new investment firm, United Capital Partners, purchase a 15% stake in the fashion retail company – now.

MASS PRIVATIZATION

Rooted in the Russian Revolution of 1917, the Soviet Union became the first country to adopt a centrally planned economy. The government centralized the country's production and distribution of goods. Gosplan, the

United Capital Partners (A)
by PAUL A. GOMPERS, J. DANIEL KIM, VLADIMIR MUKHARLYAMOV, case number 9-213-044
SEPTEMBER 18, 2012

committee responsible for the Soviet Union's economy, planned the entire economy in 5-year blocks, appropriately allocating resources and making key economic decisions. As a consequence, the government effectively built the manufacturing, heavy industry, and defense sectors, and provided state-funded services such as education and healthcare for its citizens. In contrast, the production of consumer goods was strikingly inferior and inefficient because consumer demand in command economies carried no effect on the price and supply of goods.

In response, Mikhail Gorbachev attempted to reform the economy through his program of perestroika. Gorbachev's goal was not to end the centrally planned economy, but rather to improve it in order to more efficiently meet the needs of Soviet consumers. However, the program incited much social unrest and ultimately failed. Despite the disappointing results, many considered perestroika the harbinger of Russia's privatization.

Following the dissolution of the Soviet Union in 1991, privatization reforms swept the country under President Boris Yeltsin. In order to transition from a centrally planned economy to a market-driven economy, Russia had to dispose of thousands of state-owned enterprises. In response, the Russian government issued vouchers to its citizens that they could use to bid for shares of privatized companies – a model that the Czech Republic implemented in 1991.[1]

Overall, the privatization program was a successful piece of Russian economic reform. By January of 1993, all 147 million Russian citizens were given an opportunity to pick up a voucher for a fee of only 25 rubles – equivalent to 10 cents under then-current exchange rate. While the Czech government charged a much higher fee to discourage marginally interested citizens from participating, Russia undertook a populist approach by charging a nominal fee. Consequently, 98% of the issued vouchers were picked up. Within twenty months of privatization, over 14,000 companies went through the auction process.[2]

However, the rapid mass privatization of state-owned enterprises in Russia came with several unintended consequences, engendering a new class of entrepreneurs. A small number of industrial tycoons – dubbed as the "oligarchs" – profited from the process by purchasing important Russian companies at bargain prices. Among many other factors, the design of the auction process empowered the oligarchs to rise in immense wealth. Essentially, shares of the company auctioned off were distributed in proportion to the number of vouchers offered in the bid.[3,4] [1,2] Therefore, fewer vouchers that were bid for a company's shares meant that more shares would be distributed per voucher. Insiders thus tried to discourage others from participating in the auction process in order to maximize their stake in the company.

There were several ways to discourage – and even prevent – broad participation. Most commonly, auctions occurred in extremely inconvenient locations in remote areas with severely limited transportation infrastructure. Often, auctions were announced or changed at the last minute. And in some cases, armed guards outside the auction room fended off unwanted bidders. Not surprisingly, the oligarchs used these tactics to mainly capture large, important companies.

In addition to the auction design, the voucher's marketability contributed to Russian privatization's shortcomings. Vouchers were publicly tradeable in Russia, fostering a liquid voucher market. This allowed citizens to cash out, albeit at a modest sum of money, or even diversify their holdings. In many cases, however, managers of the company coerced stakeholders – often employees – to sell their shares and pushed them out. This allowed oligarchs and managers to forcefully retain their companies.

Corruption also played a conspicuous role in the privatization of Russian enterprises. Many oligarchs were well connected with governmental officials and were thus able to secure the best companies at favorable prices. Some claim that more than 8% of the 15,000 mass-privatized firms in Russia benefitted from special deals with the government.[5] More specifically, it was a common belief that these oligarchs massively profited from "loans-for-shares" schemes that government officials devised. In the classical "loans-for-shares" situation, the government assigned a commercial banker to oversee an auction in which the government sold a controlling stake of a large natural resources company for a loan that was not expected to be repaid. Of course, the auctioneer purchased the shares at a very low price since he would be the sole bidder in the room.

Although it is unclear how much government corruption contributed to the rise of oligarchs, this new coterie of Russian tycoons certainly shaped the country's economic landscape. Oligarchs controlled several key sectors in the Russian economy. For instance, one study conducted in 2005 suggested that oil – the largest sector in Russia with 1.3 trillion rubles in annual sales – was controlled by oligarchs with a 72% market share.[6]

SHERBOVICH'S JOURNEY

Ilya Sherbovich, the founder of United Capital Partners, was only in his second year of undergraduate studies at Plekhanov Economics Academy when he was offered a job from the International Finance Corporation in 1992. At the time, the International Finance Corporation advised the Russian government on the privatization process. Searching for Russian talent with excellent English speaking skills, the group found and hired Sherbovich at just eighteen years of age.

After a year, Sherbovich moved to Price Waterhouse, all while he attended school. Although Russian economic reforms rapidly progressed, the general public found it difficult to keep up with the changes. Even the experts seemed to be lost. Sherbovich explained that "even after the government formed laws that allowed Russian business owners to register joint-stock companies and hence issue shares, no one in the securities commission knew how to actually register companies under the new set of rules." Consequently, the Russian government hired Price Waterhouse along with other major accounting firms to develop Russia's securities and exchange commission. At Price Waterhouse, Sherbovich led a small team that monitored Russian companies' issuances of new shares and registration of ownership rights.

Then Sherbovich was introduced by his former IFC colleague to Charles Ryan who later introduced him to Boris Fyodorov. Mr. Fyodorov believed that the recent emergence of Russian capital markets created vast opportunities. Fyodorov, former Minister of Finance of Russia, recognized that investing in a post-Soviet era – characterized by inadequate market infrastructure and poor transparency – demanded a unique investment approach amid rising international interest in Russia. Fyodorov set out to start his own brokerage firm, whose two primary functions would be to trade shares and provide market research. He secured $1 MM in funding from Paribas. In 1994, Fyodorov and Charlie Ryan (Harvard '89) founded United Financial Group ("UFG"), an independent Russian investment bank that would offer a broad range of financial services.

In 1995, Sherbovich graduated from Plekhanov Economics Academy and joined UFG as a junior specialist. At the time, the bank was composed of just seven professionals, but quickly gained prominence in the Russian financial sector. UFG subsequently became a research powerhouse, producing comprehensive reports on Russia's major companies, macroeconomy, and political trends.

By 2000, several large international banks such as Goldman Sachs and Morgan Stanley entered the Russian market. The growing presence of foreign banks alarmed UFG, which was convinced that in order to compete, it had to expand from a simple brokerage firm to a full-service domestic investment bank. Ilya Sherbovich played a central role in UFG's transformation process. He was summoned in early 2000 to lead the bank's investment banking team, just five members at its inception. That number quickly grew to eighty-five professionals by 2006, making UFG the largest investment banking group in Russia.

Riding a wave of Russian IPOs from 2003 to 2007, Sherbovich and his team helped UFG rise to the top of the Russian investment banking sector. The team's bandwidth and unparalleled experience from previously advising the securities commission won the bank a significant share of Russian

IPO transactions. The most remarkable sector for these deals was consumer retail, which saw a surge in new small businesses after the Russian economy became privatized. Sherbovich and Victoria Lazareva helped more than thirty fledgling companies to raise additional capital and the entrepreneurs to sell their businesses.

UFG gradually earned its spot as one of the leading investment banks in the country. In fact, UFG ranked first in M&A deal volume from 2003 to mid-2005 in Russia, surpassing Alfa-Bank and Morgan Stanley, with 24 deals totaling $10.7 Bn.[7] Drawn to UFG's strength in sales and trading, equity research, and corporate finance, Deutsche Bank acquired a 40% stake in UFG for an estimated $70 MM in early 2004 with an option to purchase the remaining 60% by 2011.[8] In December 2005, Deutsche Bank exercised its option and raised its stake in UFG from 40% to 100%, valuing the Russian investment bank at around $700 MM according to an independent source – an unprecedentedly high figure for a Russian bank.[9] At the time of the acquisition, Sherbovich was UFG's third largest shareholder.

During his twelve years at UFG, Sherbovich assisted many Russian businesses to reach their next level of growth. Sherbovich's team not only helped mid- and large-cap businesses raise capital and participate in strategic sales, but also played a significant role in institutionalizing these companies, many of which were informally structured and operated similarly to family businesses. Victoria Lazareva explained,

> Whereas Western investment banks typically work on a 6-month horizon for an IPO, Russian companies require two to four years to prepare for an IPO because they often lack the institutional infrastructure. As a result, we have to help them recruit CFOs to bring the companies up to international accounting standards as well as independent directors to improve corporate governance.

Sherbovich and his team were deeply involved in almost every component of Russian businesses from finance to corporate governance. In the process, they learned how to transform family-run businesses with strong strategic fundamentals to well-rounded institutional companies ready for a public market debut. Sherbovich began to wonder whether his team's expertise in advising Russian companies for high levels of growth could be applied from an investor's perspective. He became convinced that the skillset was transferable and thus contemplated a possible transition.

Although Sherbovich's employment contract as part of Deutsche Bank's acquisition of UFG would restrain such a move until the end of 2008, Sherbovich felt that his tasks at the bank were fully carried out earlier than projected. Deutsche Bank agreed, and together they found a replacement to smoothly take over Sherbovich's post. Since Deutsche Bank did not have an asset management or principal investing business in Russia, there was no conflict of interest. Actually, the bank perceived the move as a mutually beneficial relationship, the two parties generating deal flow for each other. Sherbovich received internal compliance from the bank's senior leadership and launched United Capital Partners in late 2006.

United Capital Partners ("UCP") formed as a Moscow-based asset management and financial services company that would specialize in private equity, public markets, and financial advisory services. UCP's private equity business focused on growth equity, middle market, and emerging growth spaces, investing in small and medium-sized enterprises in Russia and the Commonwealth of Independent States.

As of today, UCP has five partners and the firm invests in small and midcap Russian companies (See **Exhibit 1** for partners' biographies). At its inception, the firm aimed to purchase minority stakes in high-growth companies seeking new capital for further expansion. In many cases, UCP hoped to invest in pre-IPO opportunities in which the firm would leverage its partners' strategic, legal, and financial expertise.

Among several notable qualities of the firm, UCP highlighted its partnership approach. While most investors claimed to be a value-added partner to their portfolio companies, many Russian private equity firms, especially those that started in 2006 and 2007, sat idle and collected annual management fees from investments that soured following the financial crisis. On the contrary, UCP demonstrated its partnership mentality and aligned incentives by launching its first fund entirely raised with partners' personal money.

PRIVATE EQUITY IN RUSSIA

Along with the growth of oligarchs, the three major capital markets in Russia – public equity, debt, and private equity – began to emerge. Mass privatization and availability of inexpensive assets on the market led to the rise of private equity in Russia during the 1990's. By 2002, private equity funds in Russia raised about \$3 Bn, much of which came from public sources.[10] The industry continued to quickly grow, reaching \$10.3 Bn in total capital for all Russian private equity funds by the end of 2007 (See **Exhibit 2**). Private equity in Russia soared that year; there were 130 active funds and they raised \$4.3 Bn, tripling the amount raised during the previous year.[11] Backed by larger pools of capital, investors in Russia raised their level of spending across various sectors, especially consumer goods and financial services (See **Exhibit 3**).

Because of its rapid growth, Russia drew many foreign investors including some of the world's largest private equity firms seeking to generate large returns. However, most foreign investors failed to find wildly successful deals, leaving some to question whether the traditional Western private equity approach could be effectively applied in Russia. The Carlyle Group, which twice attempted to enter the Russian private equity market since the late 1990s, was not convinced and shut its Moscow office in 2005. David Rubenstein, a co-founder of Carlyle, once explained, "Russia has not proven to be a place where Western private equity investors can have the returns and realize the profits commensurate with the risks they've had to take."[12]

Michael Calvey, the founder of the Moscow-based private equity firm Baring Vostok Capital Partners, commented, "International firms aren't equipped for Russia... They usually have a lower tolerance threshold for uncertainty and no sense of humor for Russian surprises."[13] [7] In addition to their risk-averse nature, large Western private equity players had an investment focus that was not fit for the Russian market.

Foreign buyout firms typically targeted big, high-profile companies for leveraged buyouts. However, typical going-private deals were uncommon in Russia because there were only a few truly public companies in Russia. Most companies had a controlling shareholder or a small group of shareholders. In addition, Russia's financial markets were less sophisticated than those in Europe or North America and did not allow for easy access to significant amounts of debt needed for leveraged buyouts. In January 2007, 10-year government bond yield was 6.3% (See **Exhibit 4** for Russia's historical interest rates). Alexander Bogdashin, Director of private equity at United Capital Partners, explained that,

> Russia's equity and capital markets are still nascent and therefore, weak... the top ten Russian stocks constitute 90% of the entire value of the key stock market indices MICEX and RTS, while the top four state-owned banks (Sberbank, VTB, Gazprombank, and Russian Agricultural Bank) manage 55% of total assets of Russian banking system. It is very difficult to raise the sort of debt capital needed for leveraged buyouts.

The only group in Russia with the ability to raise large amounts of debt was the oligarchs with their strong relationships with major Russian banks. Many oligarchs built teams of investment professionals that closely paralleled Western private equity firms. This meant that institutional private equity firms in Russia tended to focus on private growth equity capital.

Whether or not it was possible for foreign private equity investors to replicate their prior success in Russia, the following five factors deterred many global players from expanding into Russia: 1) limited investment space; 2) widespread corruption; 3) weak legal system; 4) poor corporate governance; and 5) generally unsophisticated entrepreneurs. First, as mentioned above, leveraged buyout was not a realistic investment space for private equity firms in Russia. Therefore, private equity in Russia was essentially confined to early stage and growth equity investments. Although the typical deal size increased throughout the two decades of private equity in Russia, the average deal size was still only $12 MM in 2007 (See **Exhibit 5** for distribution of investments by portfolio company stages). Therefore, Western investors with multibillion dollar funds were discouraged by the scarcity of deals exceeding $100 MM.

Second, corruption was unmistakably widespread in Russia and impacted the business ecosystem. In 2007, Russia ranked 143rd out of 179 countries in the Corruption Perceptions Index published by Transparency International.[14] In addition, an influential Russian think tank estimated that bribes accounted for 20% of Russia's GDP, amounting to hundreds of billions of dollars.[15] Although the effect of corruption on the dynamics of Russian private equity was not exactly quantifiable, most investors were cognizant of the rampant corruption in the field and considered it a major deterrent.

Similarly, Russia's legal system was in its infancy with a mere two decades of development following the end of the Soviet regime. From Russia's seventy years of state controlled economy, the nascent legal system naturally lacked the foundation of sound market practice and court precedent. Consequently, virtually all M&A and private equity deals involving a Russian target company used British law as the legal framework.

Whereas the Russian legal system historically did not recognize court case precedent when interpreting provisions of the Civil Code, British law was based on legislation as well as on case precedent, hence not set out in a single civil code. Therefore, British law was more adaptable and practical, granting businesses the legal freedom and flexibility to agree to whatever terms desired on their transactions.[16] Similarly, courts in Britain typically upheld the rights of minority shareholders.

There were also weaknesses in the Russian legal system that reinforced foreign investors' hesitation towards executing deals in Russia. Many parties were not confident with the predictability of Russian court rulings and the ability to effectively enforce the decisions. Yuri Kachuro, a partner and the head of legal department at United Capital Partners, explained that,

> As far as the Russian legal framework is concerned, the weakest link is the court system. The law on the books is actually quite advanced,

designed to provide predictable outcomes and protect minority shareholders and investors. However, the court system is still weak because it is only as good as the judges. In order to establish a strong legal system, the profession of a judge needs to be developed with years of private practice, which has been limited in Russia's brief history after the Soviet era.

Even though Russian corporate law constantly improved, its lack of predictability and effective enforcement marred the outlook on Russian private equity.

Similarly, most Russian portfolio companies incorporated as subsidiaries of holding companies registered in offshore jurisdictions governed by English law or other commonly used foreign law. A common approach was to form a holding company, which held all the company's assets, and incorporate in countries where English law applied. There were several reasons responsible for this trend, chief among them being key provisions and Russian courts' enforceability. Leaver provisions, contractual mechanism to cover leaving employees who were also shareholders of the company, were theoretically sound under Russian law. However, Russian court and market practice were limited in this scope. Furthermore, share ratchets, designed to facilitate how much sale proceeds and/or number of shares an employee receives in the event of an IPO or strategic sale, were also not properly tested and proven in the Russian legal system.[17] Therefore, most companies dealing with shareholder agreements preferred to incorporate outside of Russia.

Additionally, corporate governance in Russia was poor by the standards of Western investors. Although the larger companies in Russia began to adhere to sound corporate governance standards by increasing disclosure, bringing in independent directors on boards, and complying with international accounting standards, their efforts were subpar in comparison to those of their Western counterparts (See **Exhibit 6** for Russia's corporate governance scores).

The main theme of the debate on Russian corporate governance was the conflicts of interest between controlling and minority shareholders. As privatization led insiders to attain disproportionately high ownership of companies, myriad disputes arose with little protection for minority shareholders. Many insiders coerced minority shareholders to sell their shares in order to preserve the insider-dominant ownership structures. Controlling shareholders often abused minor shareholder rights by employing cunning methods such as dilution of shares, transfer pricing, and asset stripping.[18] While the federal law on joint stock companies – specifically Articles 31 and 32 – were designed to protect minority shareholder rights, enforcement of those protections was unreliable. Therefore, an alarming concentration of ownership in the hands of insiders led to poor corporate governance, discouraging many foreign investors from committing to Russia.

Last, entrepreneurs in Russia were generally less sophisticated than those in the West, where generations of entrepreneurs established a culture of measured venture growth and institutional investing. They were the first generation of Russian entrepreneurs and many did not follow, let alone understand, the international accounting standards. Therefore, IPOs in Russia took much longer – typically two to four years – because companies required lengthy restructuring and accounting revision procedures.

Moreover, entrepreneurs in Russia were inexperienced with complex financial instruments; most did not know what private equity was – much less how it could help grow their businesses. The idea of private equity was intimidating to many business owners, who had heard too many stories of 'black raiders' forcefully taking over innocent businesses.

While the severity of corporate raiding in Russia varied widely, black raiders were particularly known to use blatant criminal tactics to attack and seize companies. Some of the raiding groups were third party intermediaries. Others were corporate divisions of large investment funds run by oligarchs.

Private equity investors in Russia often found themselves in a catch-22: while investors wanted to show and prove the value-add advantages of private equity for growing a business, high-quality entrepreneurs seeking to grow their businesses were particularly averse to considering external institutional capital. Therefore, investors hoped for exemplary success stories in Russian private equity as proof of concept for skeptical entrepreneurs.

Investors also felt the pressure to validate the sector for limited partners. Convincing limited partners to commit capital to Russia was difficult because the hot emerging markets were Brazil and China, leaving Russia with little or no attention. Even if Russia arguably presented more upside opportunities since it was not as crowded as some of the overhyped markets, many limited partners were unconvinced. There were not enough big success stories in Russian private equity to assure skeptical investors. The challenge was bigger for domestic private equity firms, whose investor base was very limited. Some Russian firms including United Capital Partners raised their first fund entirely from partners' money to both align incentives and establish a track record in Russia.

Despite the generally discouraging perception of Russian private equity, there were a few standout investors that generated attractive returns. For example, Baring Vostok Capital Partners was Russia's largest private equity firm and had enjoyed wide success since 1994. The firm had raised approximately $2 Bn since its inception. Its most famous investment was the Russian search engine Yandex, which generated a whopping 800x return on Baring Vostok's $5 MM investment.[19] Even with such popular examples of wild success, a significant portion of Russian entrepreneurs and limited partners were still not convinced that private equity warranted a valuable role in the Russian economy.

STYLISH WORLD[20]

Stylish World, founded in 2003, was a Moscow-based fashion boutique retail chain that operated under the brand name FLASH. The founding shareholders of one of the leading Russian retailers sought to replicate its business model in the fashion retail space. They teamed up with Alexey Petrov, a fashion retail guru with years of franchise experience with two famous international fashion brands and launched Stylish World.

Built on the founding shareholders' retail expertise and Petrov's experience with the franchise model, Stylish World operated on a unique business model that combined manufacturing of their own designs in Asia coupled with an innovative mix of company-owned and franchised stores (See **Exhibit** 7). Stylish World offered a wide range of women's clothing, spanning from lingerie to casual shirts to formal office wear – all at affordable prices. The retailer highlighted the concept of 'value fashion' and targeted urban women in the 'neotraditional' life stage. The first FLASH store opened in 2005 and by April 2007, the company operated 71 stores throughout more than 40 cities.

Stylish World's rapid success could be attributed to favorable market movements, efficient vertical integration, and strong franchise model. First, the Russian apparel retail market expanded at an 18% compound annual growth rate from 2002 to 2007, reaching a market size of €27 Bn in 2007. Women's wear, the largest component of the market, accounted for €14 Bn. This market in Russia was already the fourth largest in Europe and projected to grow at around 5% per year in the near future.[21]

According to UCP, although Russian fashion retail was a highly competitive market, it was extremely fragmented with no dominant players, allowing Stylish World to consistently capture additional market share. Stylish World's main competitors were H&M, Zara, and Oggi (See **Exhibit 8a** and **Exhibit 8b** for Russian fashion retail's competitive landscape). The retailer differentiated itself by delivering an attractive value proposition to young women with neotraditional lifestyles. FLASH clothing lines were designed for women between the ages 20 and 38 with a median income of $500 to $700 per month, targeting roughly 70% of the total women population in Russia. The clothing lines typically had a wide price range from $10 to $120 with an average check of approximately $20. Stylish World was able to offer quality, modern products at surprisingly low prices largely due to its efficient vertical integration.

Stylish World's key core competency was its integrated business model. The retailer was involved in the entire process segmented into five stages: strategic and financial planning, design, manufacturing, distribution, and marketing and sales. The most noteworthy component was FLASH's in-house design team of over 20 product development specialists who created 12 collections per year based on the latest European fashion trends. Also, Stylish World established long-term relationships with strategic suppliers in Asia.

Furthermore, Stylish World executed a strong franchise model that helped quickly build the FLASH brand with minimal capital expenditure. In 2007, about two-thirds of the FLASH stores were run by franchisees. 95% of the franchisees owned just one or two stores and opened stores in cities with more than 100,000 people. All franchisees operated under 3-year non-exclusive contracts. Stylish World uniformly set and controlled prices and marketing.

Franchisees generally performed well, expecting an average EBITDA margin of 13% for 2007. The distinguishing advantage for FLASH franchisees was that they did not have to pay royalties. Instead, Stylish World collected only the gross margin from the wholesale clothing sales supplied to the franchisees at a 56% discount from the retail price. Franchisees had the right to return their stock twice a year with 20% to 50% discount to the original shipment price. 80% of the franchisees expressed high satisfaction with the model. Stylish World's franchise model allowed for fast store rollouts without heavy capital expenditure during the company's early stage of business development and capital constraint.

Even though Stylish World built and operated on a sound business model, the retail chain was a young company and it was too early to determine its market position going forward. While unaudited EBITDA for 2006 was $1.6 MM, the figure for 1Q2007 was negative $91,000. And despite the rapid growth under the franchise model, there was a tangible risk of exit or bankruptcy by franchisee partners. Moreover, it was difficult to gauge how the large international players in the market such as Inditex, New Look, and H&M – already heightening the level of competition – would work to seize the Russian fashion retail space.

MAKING AN OFFER

Representatives from the aforementioned large Russian retailer – whom Sherbovich and Lazareva met when United Financial Group helped their company to raise financing – approached United Capital Partners in early 2007 to discuss their second project, Stylish World. At that time, Stylish World had no institutional investors. Although existing shareholders could theoretically invest additional capital into the company, they wanted an institutional partner to collaboratively take Stylish World to the next stage of growth and prepare for an IPO. Stylish World's management believed that such a partner would bring tremendous value in facilitating the IPO process as well as in financing for the next expansionary steps.

On one hand, Stylish World seemed to be a promising investment opportunity for several reasons. First, the management team led by CEO Alexey Petrov was a consortium of entrepreneurs that UCP could trust. In contrast, most Russian entrepreneurs did not have enough credible experience in the private sector and thus required a thorough background check. Private equity firms in Russia typically hired investigatory firms to check the background of their potential counterparties. Fortunately, Petrov boasted ten years of relevant industry experience and the other founding shareholders had the unique experience of building a Russian retailer and eventually taking it public.

Next, the market displayed encouraging trends. The Russian clothing market value was estimated by UCP to be between $25 and $40 Bn, 70% of which was represented by low and medium price segments – central to Stylish World's value proposition. Moreover, this market was rapidly growing with a compounded annual growth rate of 18% from 2002 to 2007 (See **Exhibit 9a** and **9b** for an overview of the Russian clothing market).

On the other hand, there were several drawbacks to investing in Stylish World. Since UCP had made only one investment from its first fund thus far, it was pressured to pick a safe investment that would generate returns – albeit modest – in order to build the fledgling firm's track record. The partners also felt pressured to minimize the downside risk given that the fund was entirely raised with their own money. However, Stylish World had generated only a tiny EBITDA, which would most likely show as a loss under International Financial Reporting Standards since it was not calculated under IFRS and not audited. Even if the company's earnings and margins were trending upwards as it rolled out new stores, there was no certainty predicting where the EBITDA figure would be in the near future (See **Exhibit 10** for FLASH's estimated gross and EBITDA margins for 2007).

Another major risk factor was the large competitors. Fashion retail in Russia was an increasingly attractive market, yet no player possessed more than 1% market share.[22] The market trends were promising not only for Stylish World, but also for several fashion retail giants such as H&M and Inditex who then had much stronger brand recognition than FLASH.

Sherbovich and Lazareva, who were also invited to join the investment committee meeting, walked into the conference room. UCP's private equity team gathered on this cold, wintery Monday morning to assess the upside opportunities as well as the risks involved. There were mixed opinions regarding Stylish World's investment prospects. A vice-president at the firm presented his team's 5-year cash flow projections for Stylish World and relevant trading multiple for its competitors (See **Exhibit 11** for projections and **Exhibit 12** for trading multiples).

Stylish World had contacted a number of other private equity firms and it was uncertain which, if any, other private equity firms might make an offer to finance the young fashion retailer. Sherbovich looked at his colleagues and asked, "Should we make an offer to invest in Stylish World and if so, at what valuation?"

NOTES

1 Bernard Black, Reinier Kraakman, and Anna Tarassova, "Russian Privatization and Corporate Governance: What Went Wrong?" *Stanford Law Review* 52 (Fall 1999): 1731-1808.

2 Maxim Boycko, Andrei Shleifer, and Robert Vishny, *Privatizing Russia* (Cambridge: The MIT Press, 1995), p. 89-105.

3 Black, et al. "Russian Privatization and Corporate Governance: What Went Wrong?"

4 Boycko, et al. *Privatizing Russia.*

5 Bernard Black, Reinier Kraakman, and Anna Tarassova, "Russian Privatization and Corporate Governance: What Went Wrong?" *Stanford Law Review* 52 (Fall 1999): 1731-1808.

6 Sergei Guriev and Andrei Rachinsky, "The Role of Oligarchs in Russian Capitalism," *Journal of Economic Perspectives* 19 (Winter 2005): 131-139.

7 "The first ranking of merger and acquisition consultants appeared in Russia. Investment bankers were interesting in the new ranking," *WPS*, August 18, 2005, via ISI Emerging Markets, accessed June 2012.

8 "Deutsche Bank to Acquire 40 Per Cent Stake in United Financial Group," Deutsche Bank IR Releases, November 3, 2003, on Deutsche Bank website, https://www.db.com/ir/en/content/ir_releases_2003_3960.htm, accessed July 2012.

9 "A Farewell to UFG," *Vedomosti*, December 6, 2005, via Factiva, accessed September 2012.

10 Astrid S. Tuminez, "Russian Private Equity: An Opportunity for which the time has not yet come," PONARS Policy Memo No. 72, October 2002, http://www.gwu.edu/~ieresgwu/assets/docs/ponars/pm_0272.pdf, accessed June 2012.

11 "Yearbook: Russian Private Equity and Venture Capital Market Review 2008," Russian Private Equity and Venture Capital Association, p. 30, http://www.rvca.ru/upload/files/lib/RVCA-yearbook-2009.pdf, accessed June 2012.
12 Anne-Sylvaine Chassany and Jason Corcoran, "Russia: Still the Wild West for Private Equity," *Bloomberg Businessweek*, April 28, 2011, accessed June 2012.
13 "A Farewell to UFG," *Vedomosti*, December 6, 2005, via Factiva, accessed September 2012.
14 "Corruption Perceptions Index 2007," Transparency International, http://archive.transparency.org/policy_research/surveys_indices/cpi/2007, accessed June 2012.
15 Chrystia Freeland, "The Next Russian Revolution," *The Atlantic*, October 2011.
16 Ian Ivory and Anton Rogoza, *Use of English Law in Russian Transactions – A Comparative Review* (Moscow: Alpina Publishers, 2011), p. 1-3, http://gblplaw.com/images/LegalUpdates/GBLPEnglishLawinRussianTransactions.pdf, accessed June 2012.
17 Ibid., p. 15
18 Olga Lazareva, Andrei Rachinsky, and Sergery Stepanov, "A Survey of Corporate Governance in Russia," CEFIR /NES Working Paper No. 103, 2007, p. 2-5.
19 Global Private Capital Associates citing *The Moscow Times*, September 11, 2013, "Baring Vostok Funds Pocket US$327 Million from Yandex Stake Sale (CEE and CIS)," https://www.globalprivatecapital.org/newsroom/baring-vostok-funds-pocket-us327-million-from-yandex-stake-sale-cee-and-cis/, accessed July 2023.
20 Unless otherwise stated, this section is taken from United Capital Partners company documents.
21 Stylish World, Management Presentation, p. 10.
22 United Capital Partners company documents.

Ilya Sherbovich	• Founder and Managing Partner of UCP since 2007 • Served as President of United Financial Group (later Deutsche Bank) • Worked at Price Waterhouse, which advised the Russian Federal Commission on Capital Markets • Began his career in 1992 at the International Finance Corporation
Victoria Lazareva	• Co-Managing Partner of UCP's Private Equity unit since 2008 • Worked as a managing director at Deutsche Bank (prior to 2006 – UFG) where she headed the corporate finance practice • Advised UCP on Stylish World transaction • Held various positions at Deutsche Bank's Corporate Finance Group in London from 1997 to 2003
Alexander Shmelev	• Managing Director at UCP since 2006 • Worked at United Financial Group's sales and trading unit from 1995 to 2006 • Began his career at PriceWaterhouse's audit department in Germany
Yuri Kachuro	• Partner and Head of Legal Department of UCP since 2010 • Served as Counsel and Partner in the Russian branch of Clifford Chance focusing on M&A, IPO and private equity transactions • Practiced as a lawyer with Freshfields Bruckhaus Deringer in Moscow and at Sullivan & Cromwell in New York
Mikhail Trofimov	• Partner and Head of Advisory Group of UCP since 2011 • Previously managed the investment banking division of ATON • Served as a managing director at United Financial Group from 2000 to 2009 • Worked at PricewaterhouseCoopers' Corporate Financial Advisory unit

EXHIBIT 1 Biographies of UCP Partners, July 2012
Source: United Capital Partners.

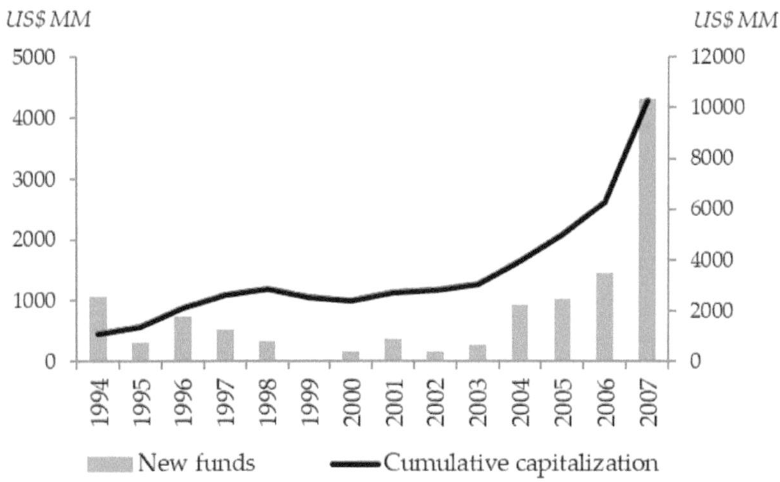

EXHIBIT 2 Capitalization of Private Equity Funds in Russia, 1994 - 2007
Source: Compiled from Russian Private Equity and Venture Capital Association, accessed June 2012.

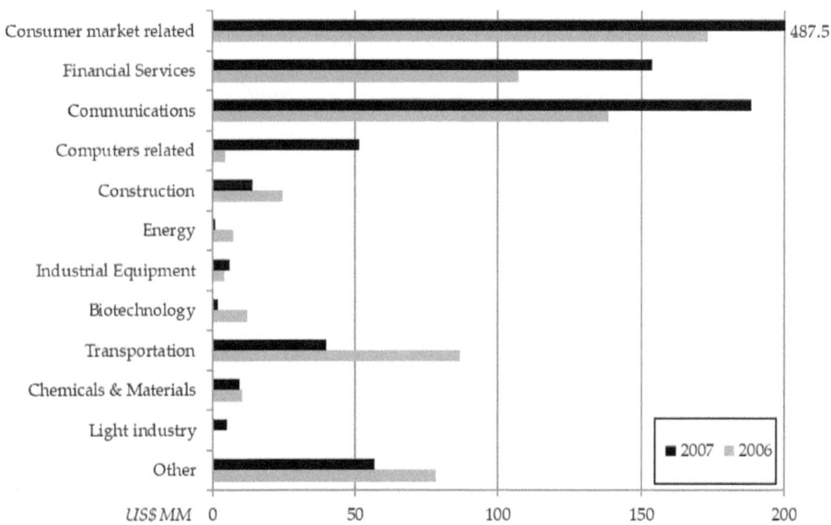

EXHIBIT 3 Russian Private Equity Investments by Industry, 2006 - 2007
Source: Compiled from Russian Private Equity and Venture Capital Association, accessed July 2012.

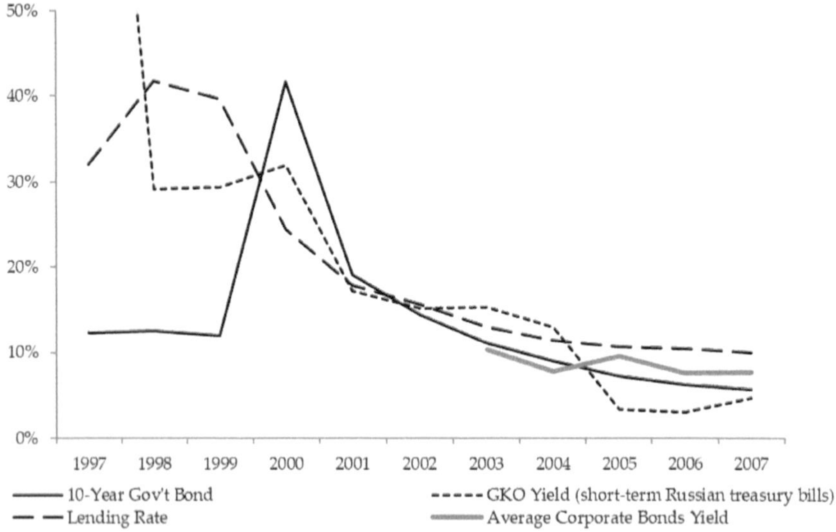

EXHIBIT 4 Historical Interest Rates and Yields in Russia
Source: Global Financial Data and IMF eLibrary, accessed August 2012.

EXHIBIT 5 Distribution of Russian Private Equity Investments by Stages, 2006 & 2007

	2006		2007	
Investment Stage	Amount Invested (US$ MM)	%	Amount Invested (US$ MM)	%
Seed and start-up	38.53	5.9%	42.12	4.1%
Other early stages	36.55	5.6%	66.18	6.5%
Expansion	493.46	75.6%	909.23	89.4%
Restructuring	84.38	12.9%	0	0%
Later stages	0	0%	0	0%
Total	652.92	100%	1017.53	100%

Source: Compiled from Russian Private Equity and Venture Capital Association, accessed June 2012.

EXHIBIT 6 Russian Governance Indicators, 2007

Governance Indicator	1996 Percentile rank (0 - 100)	2002 Percentile rank (0 - 100)	2007 Percentile rank (0 - 100)
Voice and Accountability	39.4	33.9	19.7
Political Stability / Absence of Violence	11.1	22.1	19.2
Government Effectiveness	32.7	42.9	42.2
Regulatory Quality	38.7	42.2	40.3
Rule of Law	23.9	23	16.3
Control of Corruption	15.6	22.4	15.5

*Bottom quartile values highlighted in grey

Source: Compiled from The World Bank Group, accessed July 2012.

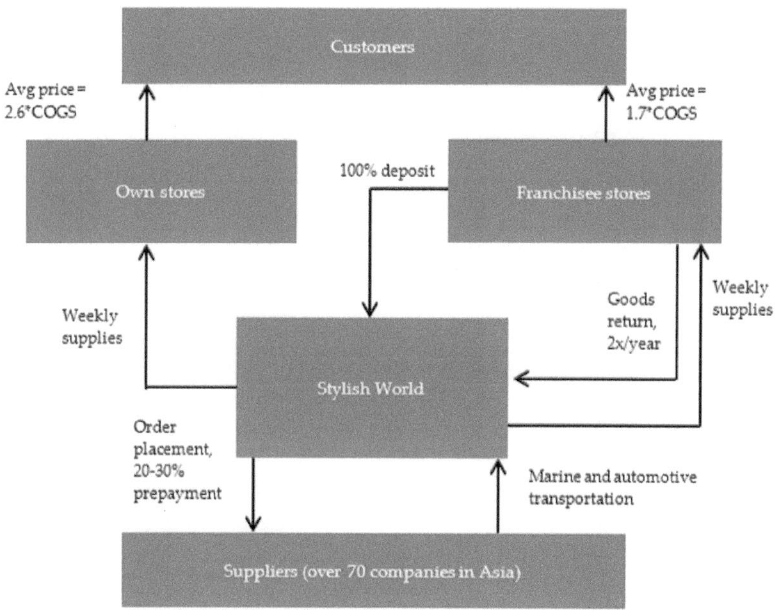

EXHIBIT 7 Stylish World's Business Model
Source: United Capital Partners.

EXHIBIT 8A Store Distribution of Fashion Apparel Retail in Russia

	% sites/outlets		
Brand	**2004**	**2005**	**2006**
Sela	2.9%	3.3%	3.7%
Gloria Jeans & Gee Jay	0.2%	1.0%	1.8%
Econika	0.6%	0.7%	0.7%
Benetton	0.6%	0.7%	0.7%
FLASH	0.0%	0.4%	0.4%
HC	0.4%	0.4%	0.4%
Oggi	0.3%	0.4%	0.4%
Bustie	0.2%	0.3%	0.4%
Dikaya Orkhideya	0.3%	0.3%	0.3%
Ralph Ringer	0.2%	0.3%	0.3%
O'Stin	0.0%	0.1%	0.1%
Zara	0.0%	0.0%	0.0%
H&M	0.0%	0.0%	0.0%
Others	94.4%	92.5%	91.2%
Total	100%	100%	100%

Source: United Capital Partners from Euromonitor data.

EXHIBIT 8B Publicly Traded European Apparel Retail Companies, January 2007

Company Name	Market Cap (US$ MM)	Beta	Price/Earnings	EV/EBITDA	EV/Sales	Total Debt	Debt/Equity
Laura Ashley	$337.46	0.25	41.52	14.83	0.72	0.5	0.01
Alexon	$212.99	0.70	7.48	3.99	0.25	4.46	0.04
French Connection	$393.33	1.65	20.95	7.91	0.59	3.1	0.02
Gant	$505.31	0.78	29.40	18.56	3.78	645	5.31
Gruppo Coin	$799.21	0.85	NA	9.77	0.83	335.78	1.31
H&M	$40,291.13	1.28	30.47	19.09	4.56	0	0.00
INDITEX (Zara)	$32,973.30	1.23	31.52	16.86	3.69	285.29	0.10
KappAhl	$738.26	0.88	17.08	9.24	1.54	1418.4	3.44
Lindex	$858.48	0.97	11.89	8.17	1.16	149.7	0.22
Mulberry	$186.88	0.93	19.67	14.31	2.06	0	0.00
Next	$8,631.45	0.78	14.20	6.91	1.55	432.4	1.69
RNB Retail and Brands	$557.69	0.64	142.12	50.86	4.15	116.82	0.46
Sprider	$157.18	0.27	13.53	10.61	2.07	32.81	0.99
Stefanel	$228.29	0.38	29.25	8.07	1.09	153.1	1.46
Etam	$979.39	0.75	53.99	8.40	0.99	160.47	0.56
Charles Vögele	$690.08	1.15	12.18	6.20	0.74	198.59	0.38

Source: Bloomberg LP, accessed July 2012.

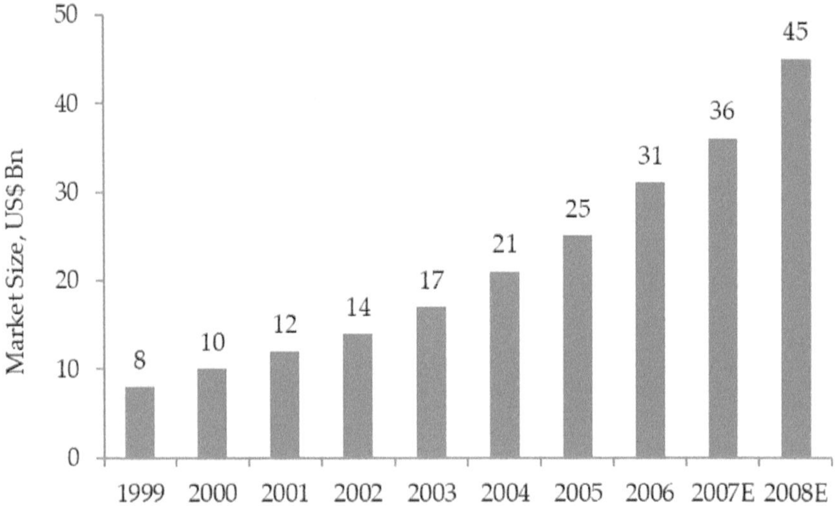

EXHIBIT 9A Russian Clothing Market Size, 1999 – 2008
Source: United Capital Partners.

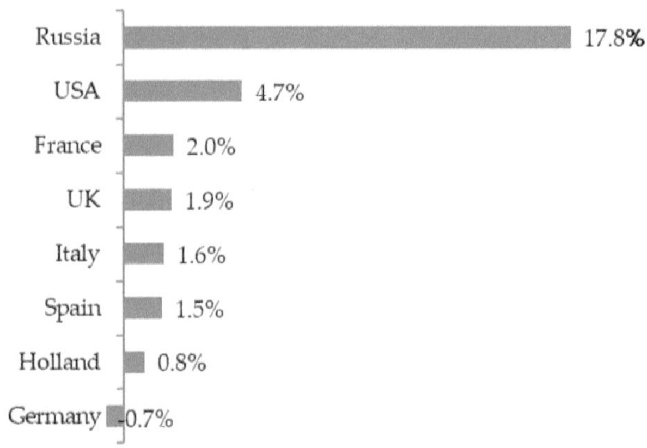

EXHIBIT 9B Clothing Market's Compounded Annual Growth Rates, 2002 – 2007
Source: United Capital Partners.

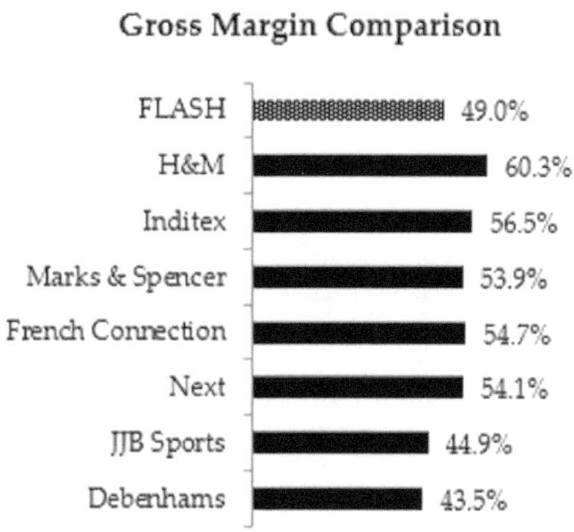

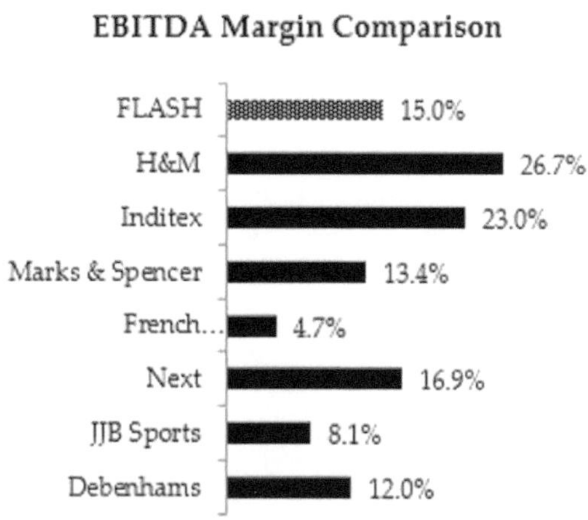

EXHIBIT 10 Gross and EBITDA Margins, 2007E
Source: United Capital Partners.

EXHIBIT 11 Projections for Stylish World

		5-year forecast					CAGR
US$ MM	2006	2007	2008	2009	2010	2011	2007-11
# of shops	55	130	190	240	280	300	23%
Owned stores	19	43	60	77	90	96	
Franchisee stores	36	87	130	163	190	204	
Revenue	11	38	64	96	122	140	38%
EBITDA	1.6	6	12	20	26	29	50%
EBIT x (1-T)		3	8	14	19	22	64%
Depreciation		2	2	1	1	1	-21%
CAPEX		(2)	(2)	(1)	(1)	(1)	-21%
Change in WC		(5)	(7)	(6)	(5)	(3)	-15%
Free Cash Flow		(2)	1	8	14	19	

Source: United Capital Partners.

EXHIBIT 12 Forecasted Trading Multiples for Publicly Traded Retail Companies, 2007 – 2008

	Market Cap	EV/EBITDA		EV/Sales		Price/Earnings	
Company	US$ MM	2007E	2008E	2007E	2008E	2007E	2008E
BJ's	2,176	8.0	7.6	0.3	0.2	21.7	20.2
Dillard's	2,801	7.0	7.1	0.5	0.5	15.4	16.2
Falabella	10,509	15.8	13.1	2.1	1.8	21.6	16.1
Federated Dept. Stores	24,249	9.2	8	1.2	1.2	20.1	15.3
Giordano	694	9.5	9.1	1.1	1.1	17.3	15.7
J. C. Penney	18,763	7.1	7.5	0.8	0.9	13.9	15.3
Kohl's	23,724	11.1	9.5	1.5	1.4	22.5	18.7
Lojas Americanas	4,475	13.1	9.7	1.7	1.3	30.3	23.4
Lojas Renner	1,755	10.3	8.2	1.7	1.3	16.5	13.5
Marks & Spencer	22,668	9.6	8.4	1.5	1.4	17.5	15.1
Matalan	1,544	7.6	7	0.7	0.7	18.1	15.9
PPR	19,911	9.3	8.2	0.9	0.9	19	15.9
La Polar	1,342	15.4	13.3	2.4	2.0	20	16.9
Ripley	2,602	14.3	12.7	1.8	1.5	21.4	18.4
SA SA International	420	9.3	8.5	0.9	0.9	18.2	16.6
Signet Group	4,024	8.2	7.8	1.2	1.1	15.3	14.4
Target	54,364	9.8	8.7	1.1	1.0	19.9	17.4
Woolworths	960	5.6	4.8	0.2	0.2	29.1	21.7
Average		**10.0x**	**8.8x**	**1.2x**	**1.1x**	**19.9x**	**17.0x**
Pure Apparel		**9.3x**	**8.2x**	**1.2x**	**1.1x**	**17.7x**	**15.2x**

Source: United Capital Partners.

CHAPTER 3.4

Valuation in Emerging Markets

Paul A. Gompers

Entrepreneurial activities in emerging markets is growing substantially faster than in North America or Europe. Many global venture capital firms view these markets as the "last frontier" for entrepreneurial activity. Local players are trying to emulate the industry that has developed in the West. Entrepreneurial Finance provides an opportunity to understand how valuation tools need to adapt to emerging markets. Governance rules and legal protections are significantly weaker in most emerging economies. Investors who want to generate attractive returns need to adapt structures and governance accordingly. Similarly, the tools utilized to value and make investment decisions require careful rethinking.

Valuing entrepreneurial firms in emerging markets has several issues that valuing investments in developed markets do not have. This note is designed to highlight the complications specific to emerging market valuations and approaches for addressing these issues.

Specifically, it discusses the following points:

- The additional complexities of investing in emerging markets
- Calculating the appropriate discount rate
- Calculating a domestic currency valuation from foreign currency cash flows

THE ADDITIONAL COMPLEXITIES OF INVESTING IN EMERGING MARKETS

When calculating the valuation of company in emerging markets, one must address issues that do not arise in valuing an investment in a developed market. In particular, one must recognize potentially complex tax treatment of foreign cash flows as well as additional risks that are typically absent

Valuation in Emerging Markets
by PAUL A. GOMPERS, case number 9-221-054 NOVEMBER 24, 2020

when investing in developed markets. The important point to remember is that it is always important to be aware of who is valuing the firm. Is it the entrepreneur? Is it an outside investor? Is that investor globally diversified or do they only hold investments within the specific country in which the entrepreneurial firm operates?

The first significant difference between domestic and emerging market investments (and any foreign investment more generally) is the existence of multiple tax regimes. The relevant tax rate depends on the countries involved, i.e., the country of origin for the investment firm (where it is domiciled) and where the target company is incorporated. Some countries tax worldwide income while others only tax income generated domestically. When the investor is located in a country that taxes worldwide income, the appropriate tax rate is the maximum of the domestic and foreign marginal rate. For the entrepreneur and investors located in the country in which the firm is located, the marginal rate in that country should be used.[1] The complex treatment of international tax laws is beyond the scope of Entrepreneurial Finance. Other courses deal with the complex international tax regime and high paid professionals are typically utilized to structure and account for the differences in tax regimes.

A second difference affecting valuation calculations for emerging market investments is the presence of country-specific risk. In general, emerging market countries are riskier along several dimensions than the United States or other developed markets. These additional risks include an increased risk of government default, risks associated with a different legal environment and uncertain legal enforcement which can lead to management's ability to "steal" value from investors, increased exchange rate risk, added regulatory risk, and the risk of expropriation. In the case where a foreign government defaults on its debt or devalues its currency, which typically occurs in times of macroeconomic crises, the cash flows from investment to domestic investors will be adversely affected. As a result, the valuation needs to account for these additional risks. These additional risks could be diversifiable or they could be systematic.

A variety of Finance academics have argued that it is possible to measure the incremental risk of a company in an emerging market. The country risk premium is sometimes calculated as the ratio of the yield on foreign issued dollar denominated bonds divided by the yield on similar dollar denominated bonds issued by the US and then subtracting one. For instance, suppose that the one-year dollar-denominated Mexican bond has an interest rate of 5.5% while the U.S. one year T-bill rate is 3.5%. Then the country premium for Mexico is calculated as:

$$CP_{Mex} = {}^{1.055}\!\big/_{1.035} - 1 = 1.9\%$$

TABLE 1 Country Risk Premia as of January 2012

	Country Risk Premium
Argentina	9.00%
Brazil	2.63%
China	1.05%
Greece	10.50%
India	3.00%
Italy	1.50%
Mexico	2.25%
Russia	2.25%

Source: Excerpted from Damodran, Aswath, 2012, "Country Default Spreads and Risk Premiums." Web. 16 Aug. 2012, http://pages.stern.nyu.edu/~adamodar/New_Home_Page/datafile/ctryprem.html, accessed February 2021.

This approach to estimating a country risk premium can be useful when dollar denominated bonds trade for the country in question. However, it can often be difficult to accurately calculate the country risk premium because no such bonds exist in these cases. A country risk premium calculated in this way relates to the additional risk that an identical company faces if it were located in an emerging market relative to the U.S. or other developed market. Below we will explore whether this additional equity risk premium gets added to the equity risk premium such that the increment to the discount rate depends upon the company's beta or whether the same country risk premium gets added after beta times the equity risk premium. This note discusses how to appropriately incorporate the risk premiums into the discount rate and what assumptions are implicit with the approach.

Accounting for Diversifiable Firm- and Country-Specific Risks in Valuations

It is important to understand whether the risk that you are measuring is "systematic" in that it is non-diversifiable or whether the risk is a diversifiable risk. This note will first talk about how to account for diversifiable sources of risk and then talk about circumstances in which the risk is systematic. The additional diversifiable risk could be country-specific or it could be firm-specific. There are two common ways of adjusting the calculation of a discounted cash flow valuation when the target is in an emerging market. The first method is to incorporate the additional risks into the discount rate while the second is to adjust the cash flows.

Risk that is diversifiable often affects companies operating in emerging markets. Independent of how global stock markets are doing, it might be possible that the government changes certain ownership laws that affect the value of your equity. There may be the possibility that the management of a company "steals" the assets of the firm or takes away any of your control rights. All of these factors, if diversifiable, should be factored into the cash flows. When assessing a set of projections, one needs to determine whether or not the cash flows are the expected case or whether they represent cash flows from an investment assuming that there is no "stealing". In the latter case, the cash flows would not represent the true expected cash flows to calculate that are required when doing a discounted cash flow analysis. One method to deal with this circumstance would be to create two scenarios that are probability weighted: one that assumes no "stealing" of assets and one that assumes there is. It is always possible, however, to adjust the discount rate in such a way to achieve exactly the same valuation as the one reached by adjusting the cash flows with this weighted scenario. As discussed below, it is sometimes easier to model the additional risk as increasing discount rates and, in other circumstances, by adjusting cash flows may be easier. Practitioners will often add firm-specific or country-specific risk-premia in certain circumstances. This custom implicitly assumes that the cash flows being valued are not the expected cash flows and that there is some additional probability of a significant downside case.

For example, if we assume that there are only two possible cases, one in which you actually achieve the cash flows (CF_1, CF_2, ...) and one in which you get nothing with probability *d*, then we can express the NPV of those cash flows as the following equation assuming that the discount rate for the given firm is r_A:

$$NPV = \frac{(1-d)}{(1+r_A)}CF_1 + \frac{(1-d)^2}{(1+r_A)^2}CF_2 + \ldots$$

Notice that you can express the discount rate as an adjusted discount rate, r_A^{adj}, that captures the cost of default as the following:

$$1 + r_A^{adj} = \frac{(1+r_A)}{(1-d)}$$

Rearranging the adjusted discount rate allows us to see how a constant per period probability of default affects the r_A^{adj} that you use to get the NPV.

$$r_A^{adj} = \frac{(1+r_A)}{(1-d)} - 1$$

$$r_A^{adj} = \frac{(r_A + d)}{(1 - d)}$$

$$r_A^{adj} = r_A + \frac{(d + r_A d)}{(1 - d)}$$

This last expression of the adjusted discount rate has a direct connection to why it might be reasonable to add a country specific risk premium. If there is some per period probability of getting nothing (through expropriation, default, etc.), then adding a country risk premium that is a function of the default rate and the cost of capital can be warranted.

To see this in a specific example, consider a company-specific risk that is common entrepreneurial companies in emerging markets – the risk of the firm going out of business because there is some change in government regulations. Suppose a firm has a constant 5% probability of going out of business every year and projected cash flows (assuming it doesn't go out of business) of $100 in year 1 and $110 in year 2. If one were to account for this risk by adjusting the firm's projected cash flows, the expected cash flows for year 1 would be (100)*(0.95) + (0)*(0.05) = $95 and the expected cash flows for year 2 would be (110)*(0.95)^2 + (0)*(1-0.95^2) = $99.275. With a discount rate of 10%, this yields a net present value of $168.41. However, leaving the cash flow projections unaffected and discounting those cash flows by $[(1+0.10)/(1-0.05)-1]$ also yields a net present value of $168.41. This equivalency naturally extends to country-specific risks such as expropriation that can also result in a complete loss of cash flows.

In thinking about these two approaches, the first approach, which probability weights cash flow scenarios, gets you to the true expected cash flows of the business, i.e., it accounts for the probability of getting nothing. In this case you use the discount rate that reflects only the systematic risk. In the second case (adjusting the discount rate), you are discounting cash flows that are not the "expected" cash flows because they don't include the probability of receiving nothing. Adjusting the discount rate by the probability of failure embeds both the probability weighting and the systematic risk in the discount rate number itself.

Thus, the decision to adjust the discount rate or the cash flows to account for country-specific risk that is not diversifiable is largely up to the individual performing the valuation. If there is a constant per period probability of ending up with nothing (for a variety of reasons this is not uncommon), then it is often easier and intuitive to adjust the discount rate for this per period probability of failure. However, while either can yield an accurate valuation, each method has its own advantages and disadvantages.

Understanding the implicit assumptions in adding a country or firm risk premium, however, is the important lesson.

In particular, adjusting the discount rate is easier when the risks are constant over time. Making adjustments to the discount rate may also be less arbitrary as a country premium (as compared to a firm specific risk premium) often can be calculated using the default spread for sovereign debt. In any case, many analysts will often utilize an additional country risk premium in their discount rates. While most practitioners do not explicitly think about the assumptions they are making, adding a country specific risk premium to the discount rate, say 5%, is identical to assuming that there is a roughly 4.5% per period probability of getting nothing.

Adjusting cash flows, on the other hand, forces one to be more explicit about what exactly the risks are. For instance, the standard method of adjusting the discount rate with the addition of a country risk premium assumes that all investments in the country are affected equally. However, the probability of expropriation, for instance, may be different for an oil firm than for a consumer products firm. Moreover, this approach easily allows for risks to vary over time. For instance, the risk of expropriation of an oil project may decline over time as oil reserves decline. In this case, increasing the discount rate due to the risk of expropriation assumes that the risk is constant over time and will lead to an undervaluation of the investment.

The above example assumed that the risks of failure were diversifiable. Are there circumstances where the systemic risk of emerging markets should be higher? If so, how do we adjust the discount rate for the greater systematic risk? Adjusting the discount rate is always required when the risks are not diversifiable and therefore systematic.

CALCULATING THE APPROPRIATE DISCOUNT RATE WHEN SYSTEMATIC RISK DIFFERS

As in any valuation, when calculating the discount rate, it is important to understand the identity of the ultimate investor. Typically, investors in venture capital and private equity firms are large institutions such as pension funds. Since these investors are generally well diversified and hold portfolios close to the global market portfolio, it is appropriate to use values of the equity risk premium from the global market portfolio. However, there are cases in which the investor is not well diversified. For instance, some countries impose restrictions on the amount on currency conversion. This might make an entrepreneur in that country (or an investor in the entrepreneur's firm) worry about systematic risk in the local market and the local equity risk premium may differ from the global equity risk premium if that country's equity markets are not fully integrated into the global market., The presence of capital controls can limit the ability of these investors to diversify globally. In these cases, one should use values of the equity risk premium from the local market portfolio.

Choosing the Risk Free Rate

The risk free rate should be the government bond rate for the currency in which the projections are denominated. If the projections are in US dollars, the U.S. government bond rate that matches the expected length of the investment should be used. This is true whether or not the projections are for a company in Turkey, Brazil, or Boston.

In the cases where the cash flows are denominated in an alternate currency, the foreign government risk free rate should be used. In these instances, however, it is important to realize that the foreign government bond may not be risk free as it also contains the default spread. To isolate the foreign risk free rate, one needs to calculate the default spread as discussed above and then subtract it from the bond rate.

$$r_{f,EM} = r_{local,EM} - {(1 + r_{\$,EM})}/{(1 + r_{\$,US})}$$

If there are no local government dollar denominated bonds to calculate the country specific risk premium, then it is important to realize that using the yield on local government bonds denominated in the local currency already embeds the country specific risk factor. There is no need to add another country specific risk factor over and above the local currency bond rate because the local government bonds already embed the additional country specific risk premium.

Choosing Equity Risk Premium

Again, under the assumption that the investor is well-diversified, the appropriate β measures the riskiness of the investment relative to the global portfolio. Typically, one can choose the β in one of two ways. For publicly-traded firms, one can calculate the firm's β directly using its return history and the return history of the global market portfolio.[2] Alternatively, services like BARRA, Value-line, and Bloomberg calculate βs for many public companies. Some of these βs use methods that adjust for the noisiness of historical estimation of β. Adjusted βs and BARRA predicted βs make be better estimates of a firm's systematic risk going forward. Additionally, because calculation of βs are estimated imprecisely, one can also identify a number of similar firms that are publicly traded and use the average β of these firms, which can lead to a more accurate estimate. Using adjusted βs, BARRA predicted βs, or averaging across a number of similar firms are all ways to get better estimates of a firm's systematic risk.

The issues of choosing β for investments in developed markets, including that it is backward looking, that it is estimated with error, and that it is dependent on the regression sample, continue to hold for investments in emerging markets. However, there is a further complication for these latter investments. In particular, in cases where the investment is in a private firm, it may be difficult to find similar public firms, particularly in the same country or region as the investment. In these cases, the best solution is often to assume that the firm is equally exposed to market risk as similar firms in developed nations and use the β of developed market firms operating in the same industry to estimate the β of the investment.

For a local investor who holds only (or primarily) local stocks, the estimate of β should be based on the riskiness of the investment relative to the local market portfolio, not the global portfolio. This is because the β estimates the increment to risk relative to the portfolio of the investor. This may be particularly true in markets that restrict foreign ownership of shares.

Choosing the Equity Risk Premium

One source of differential discount rates would be differences in the equity risk premiums in emerging markets. Should the equity risk premium in an emerging market be different from what it is in the US or Europe? How might we adjust the equity risk premium to account for these differences?

The equity risk premium exists because investors are not risk neutral. They require a higher expected return for higher risk. The equity risk premium is just the incremental expected return that is necessary to hold one additional unit of non-diversifiable market risk. In a world where capital moves freely (i.e., where there are not currency convertibility or ownership restrictions), we would expect that the compensation for a given unit of risk should be the same across all countries. If the expected equity risk premium in some country, say Japan, were higher than it was in the US, then we would expect that investors would move money into Japan, increase the value of assets in Japan until the expected return of holding one unit of market risk in Japan was exactly the same as holding one unit of market risk in the US.[3]

Most developed economies have stock markets that are well integrated and have few ownership restrictions and few restrictions on converting currencies. We would expect that the equity risk premiums to be identical in these markets. Emerging markets, however, often have restrictions on ownership/control of domestic companies and/or restrictions on the convertibility of their currencies. Regulation and tax regimes might also hinder capital flows. In these cases, global investors may substantially underweight a given country in their portfolio and may not invest capital to the point where equity risk premiums are the same.

Even absent strong restrictions on equity ownership or currencies, there is reason to believe that global investors may underweight emerging markets in their portfolios. Lack of transparency and information may create asymmetric information hindering capital flows. Home bias has been shown to lead to overweighting stocks in your home country relative to their weight in the global market portfolio. All of this would tend to keep equity risk premiums from converging completely. In general, as capital markets have become more fully integrated, it is likely that equity risk premiums have converged. The important point to remember is that if you assume that the equity risk premium in a given country is higher, you should understand what you are implicitly assuming and why.

The choice of the equity risk premium is guided by where the company is located. Typically, a proxy for the global market portfolio is used and many just use the risk premium for the US because of the quality of the long-run stock return data. However, one should be careful doing so because equity risk premiums calculated from historical data vary widely across countries, even among developed nations. Remember, however, that we want a forward looking equity risk premium and we should if investors have become less risk averse because they understand equity investing, etc., then risk premiums going forward may be lower than historical risk premiums.

When using historical data, one has the choice of the time period over which to calculate the risk premium. Because these data represent a sample, it is important to remember that there is a standard error associated with the estimate of the premium. Thus, using a shorter time period can result in standard errors that are very large relative to the estimate. Longer time periods will lead to an estimate with a much smaller standard error. However, longer time periods may miss a structural break in the premium. For instance, one may believe that the U.S. stock market experience of the 1950s may not accurately reflect expectations of U.S. stock market performance in the 2010s. Thus, choosing a risk premium based on historical data must balance these two issues.

An alternative to using historical data in choosing the risk premium is to estimate a forward-looking premium based on current prices and expected cash flows. For example, consider the S&P 500. It was valued at $1,115.10 as of January 1, 2010.[4] Earnings were projected to grow at 7.2% annually over the next five years. Assuming that dividends and buybacks

TABLE 2 Historical Premia around the World, 1928-2010

	Equity Risk Premium	Standard Error
U.S. Historical Premia		
1928-2010	6.03%	2.38%
1960-2010	4.13%	2.69%
2001-2010	-2.26%	9.00%
International Historical Premia, 1976-2001		
Brazil	9.12%	10.69%
Germany	3.41%	4.08%
Japan	3.91%	4.54%
Mexico	12.55%	12.55%
UK	4.41%	3.93%
US	5.57%	2.95%

Source: Compiled from Damodran, Aswath, 2011, "Equity Risk Premiums: Determinants, Estimation and Implications - The 2011 Edition," https://papers.ssrn.com/sol3/papers.cfm?abstract_id=1769064, accessed February 2021.

grow at the same rate, then cash flows to investors will also grow at 7.2% annually from their starting point of $40.38. The long term bond rate at the time was 3.84%. Assuming that, after five years, payouts also grow at 3.84%, one can calculate the expected return to bonds by solving

$$1{,}115.10 = \sum_{t=1}^{5} \frac{40.38 * (1.072)^t}{(1+r)^t} + \frac{40.38 * (1.072)^5 * (1.0384)}{(1+r)^5 * (r - 0.0384)}$$

This implies that the expected return to the S&P is 8.2% per year. The forward-looking equity risk premium thus is 8.20% - 3.84% = 4.36%.

For an undiversified investor in the emerging market country, the appropriate premium is derived from that country's equity market. In these countries, there is likely a very limited history from which to derive a premium. Many finance academics have argued that the default premium that we calculated above (the ratio of the yield on emerging market US dollars bonds to US issued dollar denominated bonds) should be added to the developed market equity risk premium. For example, Russia, in the table above, has a country risk premium of 2.25%. Some academics argue that you should add that 2.25% to the risk premium (we use 6% in EF) to get the country specific risk premium. For Russia it would be 8.25%. What this implies is that holding a given level of market risk in Russia requires an additional 2.25% return over market risk in the US or developed markets. The cost of capital is then estimated by multiplying this higher risk premium by the β estimate for the country as calculated above.

We are now in a position to compare how we would adjust the discount rate depending upon whether we think the country risk is diversifiable or non-diversifiable. The first approach, when the risk is diversifiable and cash flows do not factor into account the probability of receiving nothing, is to simply add the country premium to the cost of equity. Consider the case of an investment in Mexico-based entrepreneurial company. Further suppose that the risk free rate is 3.5%, beta is 1.2, and the risk premium is 6%. Thus, the cost of equity without accounting for country risk is 10.7%. Including the country premium of 1.9%, the adjusted cost of equity is 12.6%.

The second alternative is to add the country premium to the equity risk premium. In this case, the cost of equity for the investment in Mexico becomes 3.5% + 1.2*(6% + 1.9%) = 12.98%. The first method essentially assumes that all investments in the country are affected equally by this risk while the second method assumes that the investment's exposure to the country risk is the same as its exposure to market risk. In general, adding the country risk premium to your estimate of the equity risk premium should depend upon how integrated the countries markets are with the global markets.

CALCULATING A DOMESTIC CURRENCY VALUATION FROM FOREIGN CURRENCY CASH FLOWS

Cash flows from the investment may be in the home country currency or in the foreign country currency. Since investors typically care about home country currency returns, converting foreign country currency cash flows into a home country currency NPV poses an additional complication. There are two main approaches to this problem. In the first approach, one calculates the valuation in foreign currency and then converts into domestic currency using the spot rate. In the second approach, one converts cash flows into domestic currency and then calculates the valuation.

These approaches will generally yield very similar, if not identical, valuations. As a result, it is largely discretionary as to which is used. However, for investments where exchange rates are potentially volatile, one may prefer the second approach as it better allows for sensitivity analysis.

Approach 1: Calculate foreign currency valuation and then convert into domestic currency

In addition, the domestic discount rate needs to be converted to a foreign discount rate. This is done using the risk free rates in the two countries.

Denote the domestic discount rate as k^d, the domestic risk free rate as r_f^d, and the foreign risk free rate as r_f^f. Then the foreign discount rate, k^f, is given by:

$$1+k^f=\left(1+k^d\right)*\frac{\left(1+r_f^f\right)}{\left(1+r_f^d\right)}$$

With this discount rate, one calculates the present value of the cash flows in foreign currency. The spot exchange rate is then used to generate a valuation in domestic currency.

Approach 2: Convert cash flows into domestic currency and then calculate valuation

In this approach, annual cash flows are first converted into domestic currency before discounting them and calculating the valuation. Thus, one needs estimates of future exchange rates. There are at least three ways to convert the cash flows.

The first method is to exploit uncovered interest rate parity. In this case, one assumes that the change in future exchange rates is tied to the long term risk free rate differential. Thus,

$$\left[e_{d,f}\right]_t=e_{d,f}*\left[\frac{\left(1+r_f^d\right)}{\left(1+r_f^f\right)}\right]^t$$

The second method is to rely on forward exchange rates. However, in many cases, forward rates are not available for many years in the future. In this case, one can calculate forward rates using the zero coupon risk free rate that matches the maturity of the forward rate. This calculation is the same as above but uses the zero coupon rate.

The third method is to rely on expected inflation rates. This calculation is the same as above but uses expected inflation rates as opposed to long term risk free rates.

Once one has converted the cash flows into domestic currency, the domestic discount rate is then used to calculate the valuation.

NOTES

1 Further complicating the situation is the issue of repatriation. For instance, the United States taxes income earned in foreign countries when it is repatriated. As long as the income remains abroad, the income is taxed only at the foreign rate.

2 Typically, a proxy for the global market portfolio is chosen. In particular, for U.S. based investors, it is common to use a measure of returns of the U.S. stock market.

3 In a world of global investing, the equity risk premium should, in theory, be derived from the excess returns of all stocks around the globe, i.e., the excess return of the global market portfolio. Similarly, betas should be calculated relative to global market returns.

4 This example is taken from International Finance Corporation, 2012, *Risk Taking: A Corporate Governance Perspective.*

SECTION 4

Financing the Entrepreneurial Venture

CHAPTER 4.1

Panoramic Power

Paul Gompers and Silpa Kovvali

A perpetual sense of déjà vu is not uncommon among entrepreneurs trying to secure venture capital funding. Making pitch after pitch to partners after partners, often recognizable faces to founders who run in their social spheres, can elicit a feeling of repetitiveness, leading them to question whether they've been here before.

For David Almagor and Adi Shamir, co-founders of Panoramic Power, that feeling was especially pronounced in January 2011, when they met with the venture capital firm Greylock Israel (rebranded in 2014 to 83North). Except in this case, the duo had been in this precise room hoping to woo these precise investors just one year earlier. When Almagor and Shamir met with Erez Ofer and his partners at Greylock Israel in January of 2010, the latter expressed interest in the company's potential but had declined to participate in a funding round. Instead, they constructively explained their reservations and outlined what they thought the company should accomplish next, leaving the door open for a future collaboration.

Twelve months later, Almagor and Shamir returned to the offices of Greylock Israel, boasting product progress, along with more funding and market validation. They hoped to make the most of their second chance, and to get Greylock Israel to commit to an investment, money that Panoramic couldn't do without if the company was to bring its vision to fruition. Would Ofer and his team bite?

BUILDING PANORAMIC

Panoramic Power was founded in 2009 as an energy management company by Shamir and Almagor.[1] (See **Exhibit 1** for the bios of Panoramic Power's core team members.) Almagor, who had a PhD in electrical engineering from the University of California San Diego, was a serial entrepreneur by

Panoramic Power
by PAUL GOMPERS, SILPA KOVVALI, case number 9-818-072 Rev. JANUARY 23, 2019

the time he met Shamir. Having founded six start-ups in the past, he was seeking out an opportunity related to sustainability when he met Shamir. Shamir, who received his M.Sc. in physics from Tel Aviv University,[2] was seventeen years younger than Almagor and hoped to find an experienced entrepreneur to help him run with an idea. After working several years in senior technology roles in a couple of successful startups, Shamir felt the need to become an entrepreneur himself, and realized that an experienced business partner would significantly increase his chances of success. A seemingly perfect match for each other's needs, they spent a little time refining Shamir's proposal before signing a founder agreement and getting down to work.

At the time the duo developed the technology that lay at the core of Panoramic Power, buildings were responsible for 30% of global energy consumption, a proportion they estimated could be reduced by the same percentage through more efficient usage. The team saw this as an opportunity in the burgeoning clean technology space, and engineered a wireless, miniature, self-powered sensor to help buildings effectively and inexpensively track their usage patterns. The unique technology was a revolutionary enabler to cost-effectively collect real time energy data, in unprecedented scale. Beyond the sensor itself, they envisioned a complementary, comprehensive software product that would help clients analyze the collected data and recommend, using artificial intelligence, measures to improve energy efficiency.[3]

Unfortunately for the pair, their timing was not conducive to quick or easy investments. Starting Panoramic Power a year after a global financial crisis posed unique challenges. "In Israel, no VC was making any investments," Almagor said, "Everybody froze." Still, Almagor was able to leverage a personal connection to Ofer to secure a meeting at his firm, Greylock Israel. Though Ofer had never invested in one of Almagor's other ventures, they'd crossed paths over the course of fundraising for his prior companies. Ofer and his team declined to immediately invest, but offered to periodically touch base with Panoramic Power and consider a future investment if Almagor and Shamir continued to make progress. At the time, 83North was deeply exploring the Clean Tech market and hired Noam Gressel, a sustainability expert, as a part-time Venture Partner to evaluate investments, and monitor progress of promising target companies such as Panoramic Power.

Almagor and Shamir had, in fact, made significant progress. After winning a competition organized by Qualcomm, an American wireless technology company,[4] Panoramic Power won $250,000, which it used to fund its operations. They got into the Israel Electric Company's incubator program which paid them $500,000 over the course of nine months, and the Israel-U.S. Binational Industrial Research and Development Foundation

(BIRD)[5] provided another $600,000. Altogether, the funding was enough to further develop their ideas and technology through 2011. Feeling better poised to secure a firm commitment from institutional investors, the team returned to Greylock Israel.

THE EMERGENCE OF "SILICON WADI"

Since Israel declared independence in 1948, it confronted political and economic crises. Within a landmass slightly smaller than New Jersey, there were almost no natural resources. Israel's centralized and protectionist economy plunged into a severe depression during 1973 to 1984 when it experienced hyperinflation,[a] currency volatility, negligible foreign investment, and a major stock market crash.

Despite these challenges, Israel emerged in the 1990s as a high technology powerhouse, becoming known as "Silicon Wadi."[b] Israel had the highest investment in venture capital per capita in the world. From 2005 to 2011, $11.0 billion was invested in high-tech startups.[6] Additionally, Israeli venture capital-backed companies were a major source of IPOs on NASDAQ. In 2011, Israeli firms provided the second largest number of foreign public companies on the NASDAQ in New York (after China) with 60 listings.[7]

Several factors converged to create innovation in Israel leading to the technology boom. The Israeli government invested billions of dollars in military R&D to achieve independent military technological supremacy. Following the economic crises in the 1980s, Israel reduced inflation to low double-digits by moving towards a market-based economy through privatization and deregulation. Government made education a priority, creating one of the most educated countries with a university system closely linked to industry, developing industrial parks adjacent to campuses.

To promote and accelerate Israel's economic shift, the government nurtured innovative companies by engaging in capital risk sharing (funding of up to 85% of R&D costs) and promoting cooperation between military, academia, and industry. International programs encouraged other countries to participate in Israel's technology revolution through contributions of funds and/or research. Multinationals were supplied incentives (e.g., tax and customs benefits) to encourage foreign direct investment

a Hyperinflation reached 300% in 1984 and 400% in 1985.

b "Wadi" refers to a gully or dry riverbed in Arabic and Hebrew.

and knowledge transfer from conglomerates to Israeli nascent industry.[c] National programs supported Israeli ventures from incubation to exit stages of development.

Israel stimulated the birth of professionally managed local private venture capital. In 1992, Yozma Venture Capital was established as a $100 million venture capital fund wholly owned by the Israeli government. Yozma provided investments of $80 million to ten private funds and direct investments to start-up companies of $20 million. Among the conditions required by Yozma was that the fund establish an independent Israeli management company with a majority of Israeli managers. Additionally, the fund needed to engage a reputable foreign financial institution, as well as a reputable Israeli one. A major feature of the Yozma Program was the upside incentive of the program: the Israeli government would purchase a 40% stake, and for up to five years, partners could opt to purchase it back at cost plus interest. Eventually, total capital raised by the program grew to $250 million, which was invested in over 200 start-up companies.

Socio-cultural factors were also important aspects in the growth of a high tech sector. Post-Cold War military cutbacks, along with the influx of 750,000 Russian immigrants, many of which were educated in the sciences, pushed the government to focus on the technology sector to create jobs and harness the talents of this new labor market. Israelis were also fast adopters of new technology. For example, there was a personal computer in nearly one out of every two households, a ratio similar to that of the United States, Canada and a very few European and Far Eastern countries.[8] Compulsory military service for men and women fostered skills in teamwork, risk-taking and creative problem solving. It also provided a way for high tech people to meet and share ideas that they later implemented in the civilian market.

Israel's high tech core was highly concentrated, located in five cities (Haifa, Herzliya, Jerusalem, Rehovot, and Tel Aviv) whose area was not larger than 6,000 square kilometers, half the geographic size of Silicon Valley. Social mobility and advancement within Israel also influenced Israeli opinions towards risk-taking and entrepreneurial ventures. Israel was a young country and almost all of its citizens were immigrants or children of immigrants. This sense of starting anew and coping with change, in both military and civilian ranks, enabled social mobility and advancement through the military and civilian markets. Together, these cultural influences created what some referred to as an Israeli "psyche" described as a mix of entrepreneurial spirit, team work, calculated risk-taking and creative adaptation, that all formed the ingredients necessary to succeed in entrepreneurial environments.

c Companies like Intel (1974), IBM (1972), Microsoft (1991) set up subsidiaries, research centers, invested in Israeli companies, and formed strategic partnerships.

GREYLOCK ISRAEL / 83NORTH

Different venture capital firms blend different approaches to deal flow, often referred to as farmer vs. hunter. In the hunter model partners aggressively pursued deals by identifying investment themes, while in the farmer model they cultivated longstanding relationships with the entrepreneurial community which might eventually lead to deals down the road. Greylock Israel, a Tel Aviv-based global venture capital firm founded in 2006[9] as an affiliate fund of Greylock Partners,[10] used a combination of the two. The firm has found that overtime a majority of their investments were made in referrals that came to them through a trusted network of entrepreneurs.

An exception, one they made for the cleantech industry, was when the firm hoped to develop expertise in a sector generally, rather than simply investing in a firm. This interest, coupled with the domain expertise of Gressel and combined with partner Ofer's personal relationship with Almagor, led to a meeting with Panoramic Power. (See **Exhibit 2** for Ofer's bio.) Though Greylock Israel and, in particular, Ofer, were impressed with Panoramic's product and pitch, and felt market potential was high, they also felt that Panoramic's business model was too underdeveloped and unproven to invest right away. Where the broader funding environment had made it difficult for Panoramic to get off the ground, it worked in Greylock Israel's favor. The fund felt it had time to see how things panned out with Panoramic, and to wait to see early signs of market pull, without having to worry about another investor moving on the deal.

When Panoramic returned to Greylock Israel the next year, company developments, especially their recent Qualcomm competition win and early prototype devices, were enough to convince Ofer there was something there or, as he put it, that there were "signs of oil." Greylock Israel generally liked to make small 'Seed' investments of less than $1 million, which could be done through a quick process and also allowed for a structured follow-on investment decision process if milestones were achieved. Israel Cleantech Ventures (ICV), an Israeli VC company founded five years earlier which focused on, in their words, "innovation for a sustainable future," had already committed to Panoramic. So, Greylock Israel teamed with ICV on the investment, hoping this would give them a chance to better know the company and space before reaching further into their pockets. Because of the nature of Panoramic's technology, they also knew the company would need a more substantial investment in the near future for the deal to be a success. So, they structured an option that would, if they so chose, let them increase their ownership within a year. (See **Exhibit 3** for the proposed capitalization table and **Exhibit 4** for the deal term sheet.)

EVALUATING THE OFFER

Almagor was excited about the prospect of a collaboration with Greylock Israel. He feared that most Israeli VC firms had little understanding of the clean technology space, which also limited their value-add in terms of industry connections. Israel Cleantech and Greylock Israel were rarities in that they had interest in the space at the time. He felt that choosing the right fund to partner with was more important than the amount of money provided initially. Greylock Israel was an established fund with deep pockets, and he felt comfortable moving forward.

Still, the specifics of the deal were not unimportant. As a serial entrepreneur, Almagor had his own approach to evaluating a term sheet. He took a holistic approach to term sheet evaluation, but also considered specific provisions of special interest. He felt liquidation preferences, valuation, and board composition were all hot-button issues, ones that could make or break a deal.

What were the implications to Panoramic Power's founders, employees, and investors of accepting Greylock Israel's funding on the terms the VC firm proposed? How should they go about evaluating the offer?

NOTES

1 Almagor, David. "My (Ad)Ventures." 2017.
2 "Panoramic Power Leadership." *Panoramic Power.* 2017. https://www.panpwr.com/about-us/leadership.
3 Panoramic Power. "Investment Proposal: Seed/A-round." Jan. 2010.
4 Qualcomm. "Panoramic Power Wins Qualcomm Ventures QPrize Business Plan Competition." *Qualcomm.* 11 Nov. 2009. https://www.qualcomm.com/news/releases/2009/11/11/panoramic-power-wins-qualcomm-ventures-qprize-business-plan-competition.
5 "What is BIRD." *BIRD Foundation.* 2017. http://www.birdf.com/?CategoryID=317&ArticleID=374.
6 "Globalizing venture capital: Global venture capital insights and trends report 2011." *Ernst and Young.* 2012.
7 Barak Harif, Tal (6 November 2011). "Nasdaq Loses 'Holy Grail' Status for Offerings: Israel Overnight". Bloomberg Businessweek. Retrieved 13 November 2011. https://www.bloomberg.com/news/articles/2011-11-05/nasdaq-loses-holy-grail-status-for-offerings-israel-overnight.
8 www.israel.org/mf/go.asp?MFAHO1vuO.
9 "83North." *Crunchbase.* 2017. https://www.crunchbase.com/organization/greylock-partners-israel.
10 "83North (formerly Greylock IL)." *83North.* 2017. http://www.83north.com/.

EXHIBIT 1 Panoramic Power Bios

Adi Shamir – Co-Founder

Adi Shamir is a technology leader with an extensive track record of bringing complex multidisciplinary products from ideation to global markets. Prior to Panoramic Power, Mr. Shamir worked at AeroScout, a developer of real-time locations systems (RTLS) for healthcare and industrial consumers, which was sold to Stanley Black & Decker Inc. (NYSE: SWK) for upwards of $250 million. His previous experience includes technical marketing and R&D responsibilities for RFWaves (acquired by VISHAY, NYSE: VSH), a semi-conductor startup that develops short-range wireless communications chipsets.

Mr. Shamir manages an extensive patent portfolio for items ranging from RF antennas to RTLS system design to energy-sensing solutions and machine learning algorithms. He has an M.Sc. and a B.Sc. (cum laude) in Physics from Tel Aviv University with a specialty in electrodynamics.

David Almagor – Co-Founder

David Almagor is a veteran high-tech executive with over 30 years of experience in managing complex R&D as well as business entities, guiding them from startup inception to business success. Before Panoramic, he was involved in a few high-tech ventures. During his first startup experience, he was the founding CEO and Chairman of Mysticom Semiconductor, a network IC provider that he had founded in 1997 that was sold to Transwitch (NASDAQ: TXCC) in 2005. Earlier, David was the DSP Technology Group Director at National Semiconductor. David Almagor is an author of more than 40 publications and a co-author of 4 US patents. He holds a Ph.D. EE and M.S.EE from the University of California, San Diego and a B.S.EE from the Technion, Israel Institute of Technology.

Source: "Panoramic Power Leadership." Panoramic Power. 2017. https://www.panpwr.com/about-us/leadership. "David Almagor." Crunchbase. 2017. https://www.crunchbase.com/person/david-almagor.

EXHIBIT 2 Erez Ofer Bio

Erez Ofer

Erez joined Greylock Partners in 2005 and in 2006 was a founding Partner of Greylock Israel (IL).

Erez formerly served as Executive Vice President in charge of Technology Strategy for EMC Corporation, reporting to the CEO. Prior to this role, Erez served as EMC's Executive Vice President of Open Software, a business that grew from one product line to a multi-hundred million dollar level. During his eleven-year tenure at EMC Erez also held various R&D roles, oversaw development efforts with strategic partners, and established EMC's first R&D presence in California and India.

Erez is a holder of more than 30 patents, and is a graduate of the Technion - Israel Institute of Technology (BSc. and MSc.) and Northeastern University in Boston, Massachusetts (MBA).

Source: "Erez Ofer." *Crunchbase*. 2017. https://www.crunchbase.com/person/erez-ofer.

EXHIBIT 3 Capitalization Table

	Pre-Investment Ownership	Pre-Investment Shares	Investment	Shares Purchased	Post-Investment Shares	Post-Investment Ownership
Almagor	44%	2,750,000				
Shamir	44%	2,750,000				
Option Pool						
Angel Investors	4%	250,000				
Qualcomm	8%	500,000				
Israel Cleantech Ventures			$1M			
Greylock Israel			$1M			
Total	100%	6,250,000	$2M			

Source: Panoramic Power.

EXHIBIT 4 Term Sheet

February 6, 2011

PANORAMIC POWER LTD.

Terms and Conditions of Proposed Investment	
Company	Panoramic Power Ltd., an Israeli company (the "**Company**").
Size of Financing and Capitalization:	An aggregate of up to $4,000,000 (the "**Investment Amount**"), out of which Israel Cleantech Ventures ("**ICV**") will invest at least $2,000,000, Greylock Israel LP ("**Greylock**") shall invest at least $2,000,000, (Greylock and ICV, the "**Investors**"). The Investors shall purchase shares of Series A Preferred Shares (the "**Preferred A Shares**") of the Company at a fully diluted pre-money valuation of $4,000,000, including the Option Pool (as defined below), but excluding the amounts loaned to the Company pursuant to the Loan Agreements with Israel Electric Company Ltd. ("**IEC**"), Qualcomm Inc., and Alexander Schneider Ltd. (each a "**Loan**" and collectively, the "**Loans**"). The price per share of the Preferred A Shares shall be $0.52 (the "**PPS**"). The Company's fully-diluted capitalization pre and post investment shall be as reflected in the Cap Table attached. The pre-money valuation, PPS and the size of the Option Pool (as defined below) are subject to review of the Loan Agreements. As a condition to Closing, the Company and IEC shall amend the Loan Agreement between them so that (i) all interest accrued after the Closing (the "**New Accrued Interest**") is payable, at the option of the Company, in cash upon conversion of the IEC Loan; and (ii) upon a Qualified Financing (as defined in the IEC Loan), IEC must convert the IEC Loan into such Qualified Financing and will no longer have an option to convert into later Qualified Financings. In addition, the definitive agreements shall provide a mechanism whereby, if the New Accrued Interest is not repaid in cash to IEC, then upon the conversion of the IEC Loan the PPS shall be adjusted, so that Investors are not diluted by the conversion of the New Accrued Interest into equity. The Loans granted to the Company by Alexander Schneider Ltd. and IEC will be converted into Series A-1 Preferred Shares and Series A-2 Preferred Shares, respectively each having an original issue price reflecting the discount from the PPS set forth in the Loan Agreement applicable to each such Loan (in each case, a "**Discounted PPS**"), and any rights based on the PPS by their nature, including, but not limited to, 'Liquidation Preference' and 'Anti-Dilution' rights shall be applied based on such Discounted PPS. The Loan granted by Qualcomm Inc. shall convert in to Preferred A Shares. For all intents and purposes, to the maximum extent possible under law, the Series A-1 Preferred Shares and the Series A-2 Preferred Shares shall be deemed a part of the Preferred A Shares and not a separate class. "**Preferred Shares**" shall mean the Preferred A Shares, the Series A-1 Preferred Shares and the Series A-2 Preferred Shares issued upon conversion of the Loans.

(*Continued*)

EXHIBIT 4 (*continued*)

Terms and Conditions of Proposed Investment	
Timing of Investment;	The Investment Amount of ICV and Greylock shall be paid in two installments, such that ICV and Greylock shall each invest $1,000,000 at the Closing (as defined below) and $1,000,000 (the "**Second Installment**") within 12 months after the Closing. Notwithstanding the above, each of ICV and Greylock shall be entitled, at their sole and absolute discretion, to withdraw from the Second Installment. In the event one of ICV or Greylock decides to so withdraw (the "**Withdrawing Party**"), the other shall be entitled to, but in no event under any obligation to, invest the Second Installment of the Withdrawing Party in its stead.
Proceeds:	All proceeds shall be used subject to and in accordance with the budget approved by Greylock and ICV prior to Closing.
Board of Directors:	1) Two directors elected by the holders of the Preferred Shares at the Closing (one nominated by each of ICV and Greylock) (each a "**Preferred Director**"). 2) Two directors elected by the holders of Ordinary Shares as long as the Ordinary Shares constitute at least 25% of the shares of the Company on an issued and outstanding basis and one director as long as the Ordinary Shares constitute at least 10% of the shares of the Company on an issued and outstanding basis, provided, that, notwithstanding the above for as long as David Almagor serves as CEO of the Company and/or Adi Shamir serves as CTO (or some other similar title) of the Company, the Founder(s) in office shall serve as directors, and if the Ordinary Shares may elect one or more directors at such time they shall serve on account of the director(s) that may be elected by the holders of Ordinary Shares. 3) Up to two external directors shall be unanimously nominated by the Preferred Directors and the Ordinary Directors, one of which shall initially be Yuval Shachar. 4) In the event that a new CEO is appointed, then the CEO shall serve as an additional director, provided, however, that if the holders of Ordinary Shares are entitled to appoint two directors, then, in addition, the holders of Preferred Shares shall be entitled to appoint a third director, whom shall be designated by ICV and Greylock. ICV and Greylock shall also be entitled to appoint one observer each.
Dividend Rights:	Holders of Preferred Shares will be entitled to cumulative dividends at a rate of 8% of the respective Original Issue Price (as defined hereinafter), payable ratably if, as and when declared by the Board, in preference to dividends otherwise payable on any other Preferred Shares or Ordinary Shares. Thereafter, any dividend declared and paid shall be distributed ratably to all shareholders on an as converted basis.

(*Continued*)

EXHIBIT 4 *(continued)*

Terms and Conditions of Proposed Investment	
Liquidation Preference:	Upon liquidation, dissolution, or winding up of the Company or a merger, sale or exclusive license of all or substantially all of the assets, or other transaction that triggers the "Drag Along" rights described below ("**Liquidation Event**"), first, the holders of Preferred Shares shall be entitled to receive with respect to each share of Preferred Shares and *pro-rata pari passu* between them an amount equal to the respective PPS (or Discounted PPS) for such shares, plus all accumulated dividends thereon, less any amounts previously distributed to the holders of Preferred Shares as dividends (the "**A Preference Amount**"). Thereafter, the remaining assets available for distribution shall be distributed pro rata on an as-converted basis to the holders of the Preferred Shares and all other shares.
Voting:	Except for the protective provisions described below or as required by law, no series of Preferred Shares or Ordinary Shares shall vote as a separate series or class. (i) The consent of at least a majority of the outstanding Preferred Shares (for actions requiring shareholder consent), or (ii) the consent of at least one Preferred Director (for actions requiring board consent), shall be required to approve (a) the authorization or issuance of any equity security with dividend, liquidation or other preferences senior or pari passu with those of the Preferred Shares, (b) any reclassification, alteration or amendment of any existing equity security that is junior to or on parity with the Preferred Shares, if such reclassification, alteration or amendment would render such other security senior to or on parity with the Preferred Shares; (c) declaration or payment of dividends on any shares or any other distribution; (d) an increase or decrease in the number of authorized Preferred Shares; (e) any amendment to the Articles of Association of the Company that has a material adverse effect on the rights of the Preferred Shares; (f) dissolution, liquidation, or winding up of the Company; (g) pledging or mortgaging (including negative pledge, other than negative pledges in connection with bank credit) of any assets of the company or any subsidiary; (h) incurring any non-budgeted (in the board approved annual budget) contractual obligations that would result in obligations on the part of the Company in excess of $100,000; (i) the appointment and removal of the Company's CEO; (j) increasing the number of directors above 8; (k) acquiring an interest in any other legal entity or establishing subsidiaries (l) the entering into any lines of business that are not substantively related to the business of the Company as proposed to be conducted as of the Closing; (m) any increase of the Option Pool or other employee equity based plans; and (n) any public offering of the Company's share capital other than a Qualified IPO. In addition to the above, the consent of at least 70% of the outstanding Preferred Shares shall be required for a merger or consolidation of the Company or the sale or assignment of all or substantially all of the Company's share or assets. The above shall apply also to actions taken by any subsidiary of the Company.

(*Continued*)

EXHIBIT 4 (*continued*)

Terms and Conditions of Proposed Investment	
Conversion:	Any share of Preferred Shares is convertible at an initial ratio of one-to-one (subject to anti-dilution provisions below) into Ordinary Shares at any time at the option of its holder. Automatic conversion of all Preferred Shares shall occur upon: (a) the closing of a firm commitment underwritten public offering of Ordinary Shares with a Company valuation of at least $100 million and gross proceeds of at least $20 million (a "**Qualified IPO**"), or (b) the consent of 55% of the Preferred Shares.
Anti-Dilution Provision:	Proportional anti-dilution protection for the Preferred Shares, for share splits, consolidation of the Company's share capital, recapitalization, dividends, etc. (*i.e.*, structural anti-dilution protection). In addition, the Preferred Shares shall have anti-dilution on a broad based weighted average formula for issuances at a price less than the then applicable conversion price for such series of Preferred Shares.
Pre-Emptive Rights:	Until a Qualified IPO, the Company shall first offer any new securities it intends to issue to each of the holders of Preferred Shares holding at least 5% of the Company's shares on a fully diluted basis (each a "**Major Holder**") and to each Founder holding at least 5% of the Company's shares on a fully diluted basis (each a "**Major Founder**"), (subject to customary carve outs), on a pro rata basis based on the amount of securities held by all such Major Holders and Major Founders in the aggregate on an as converted basis. The holders of Preferred Shares will have over-allotment rights to purchase any new securities not purchased by other Major Holders and Major Founders.
No-Sale Provisions:	No Founder may sell, transfer, assign, pledge or otherwise dispose of any shares held by him as of the Closing, other than to a permitted transferee (as shall be defined in Company's Articles of Association), until the earlier of (i) a Liquidation Event, or (ii) a Qualified IPO. Notwithstanding the above, but subject to the provisions of the Right of First Refusal and Co-Sale specified below, from and after three years following the Closing, each Founder shall be entitled to sell in any 12-month period up to five percent (5%) of their holdings, but not more than ten percent (10%) of their holdings in the aggregate, of the shares of the Company held by such Founder at the Closing. In addition, upon an IPO, the Founders shall agree to any lockup period imposed by the underwriters.

(*Continued*)

EXHIBIT 4 *(continued)*

Terms and Conditions of Proposed Investment	
Right of First Refusal/Co-Sale:	Until a Qualified IPO or Liquidation Event, no shareholder shall transfer any shares of the Company, except to permitted transferees, without offering a right of first refusal in all such shares to all Major Holders, pro rata to their holdings (based on the total number of Ordinary Shares held by such entitled holders, on an as converted basis) and on the same terms as the proposed transfer. Fully exercising Major Holders shall have over allotment rights. Only with respect to a sale by a holder of Ordinary Shares, if this right of first refusal is not exercised, Major Holders shall have co-sale rights with respect to the offered shares, subject to standard exceptions for transfers to permitted transferees.
Founder Reverse Vesting	David Almagor and Adi Shamir are the Founders of the Company (the "**Founders**"). 65% of the Founders' shares in the Company will be subject to a 3-year, linear reverse vesting mechanism (on a monthly basis) as of the Closing. Notwithstanding the aforesaid, all of the otherwise unvested shares of each Founder shall become fully vested upon (i) disability or death of such Founder; (ii) a Liquidation Event; (iii) or termination of the employment of such Founder by the Company (other than for "Cause" (as such term will be defined in the definitive agreements.
Option Pool: Vesting:	At or prior to the Closing, the Company shall reserve an unallocated option pool for employees, directors and consultants, constituting 12.5% of the Company's share capital after the First installment on a fully diluted basis, not including conversion of the loan granted by IEC to the Company, (the "**Option Pool**") as set out in the capitalization table. Unless otherwise approved by the board, employee share options shall be subject to a four-year quarterly vesting period, with a one-year cliff, based on the Company's share option plan as approved or amended by the Board. The Company shall adopt an option plan on a 102-capital gains track within 90 days of Closing.
Registration Rights:	Commencing from 6 months following an IPO and for five years thereafter, the Holders of the Preferred Shares (the "**Holders**"), shall be entitled to two (2) "demand registration" of their shares, at the Company's expense. A demand registration must have at least $5,000,000 minimum expected proceeds. The "demand registration" shall be subject to initiation by the holders of at least 50% of the Registrable Shares (as shall be defined in the definitive agreements). The Holders will be entitled to unlimited piggyback registrations, initiated by holders of at least 30% of the Preferred Shares, at the Company's expense (subject to the below and subject to standard carve outs). Commencing once the Company is eligible to use Form F-3, the Holders shall have unlimited F-3 registration rights (or the equivalent). In the event of underwriter's cutbacks, the Holders shall be entitled to register a minimum of 30% of the offering in the event of piggyback on the Company's registrations, and shall be entitled to first register their shares prior to the registration of any other shares, on a pro-rata basis.

(Continued)

EXHIBIT 4 *(continued)*

Terms and Conditions of Proposed Investment	
Drag Along:	Subject to the 'Voting Rights' set forth above, prior to an IPO, in the event that shareholders holding more than 60% of the outstanding share capital of the voting power in the Company, determined on an as converted basis, to accept an offer to sell all of their shares to a third party, and such sale is conditioned upon the sale of all remaining shares of the Company to such third party, all other shareholders shall be required to sell their shares, and otherwise cooperate, in such transaction, on the same terms and conditions; provided, however, that the proceeds of the transaction shall be allocated to the shareholders in accordance with the provisions set forth above in the section entitled 'Liquidation Preference'.
Information Rights:	Until an IPO, each of the Major Holders and Major Founders shall be entitled to (i) annual audited financial statements audited by an internationally recognized accounting firm, within 90 days after the end of each fiscal year, and unaudited quarterly financial statements in a form acceptable to ICV and Greylock, within 45 days from the end of each quarter [in $US , US GAAP]. (ii) 12-month forward budget and business plan, operating budget and monthly budgets, no later than December 15th of each year. (iii) Monthly business reports and bank statements within 21 days from the end of each month. (iv) Any other information reasonably requested, subject to customary confidentiality obligations. (v) Customary inspection and visitation rights.
Representations and Warranties of the Company:	Customary representation and warranties for transactions of this type. Founders will give personal representations regarding the capitalization of the Company, due authorization of shares and agreements, IP matters and the lack of indebtedness and liabilities of the Company, subject to customary limitations on personal liability.
Other Conditions:	The Share purchase agreement will contain other general provisions that are customary in a transaction of this type. Customary confidentiality agreements and invention protections with all employees and consultants, including reasonable non-compete and non-solicitation undertakings by employees and consultants.
Management Rights Letter	At the Closing, the Company shall deliver to ICV and Greylock a Management Rights Letter in the form and substance reasonably requested by the Investors.
D&O Insurance	Within 3 months after the Closing, the Company shall purchase a D&O insurance policy in an amount satisfactory to the Investors
Expenses:	The Company will pay from the proceeds at the Closing the legal, due diligence and accounting fees plus expenses for one legal counsel to the Investors up to a maximum of $20,000 plus expenses plus VAT (not including IP counsel or independent IP consultant) and up to a maximum of $10,000 plus expenses plus VAT for IP due diligence.
Anticipated Closing:	The transaction is contemplated to close by March __, 2011 (the "Closing").

(Continued)

EXHIBIT 4 *(continued)*

Terms and Conditions of Proposed Investment	
Conditions of Signing/Closing:	(i) Two key employees designated by the Investors shall enter into employment agreements with the Company; (ii) Due approval of a budget and an operating plan for the 12 month period following Closing, satisfactory to the Investors; (iii) Completion of market/ business (including discussions with pilot customers), legal (including IP issues) and accounting due diligence; (iv) Finalization and execution of definitive agreements satisfactory to the Investors; (v) Investors investment committee approvals have been received, (v) Company shall cause its Articles of Association and any applicable agreements to be amended and restated in accordance with this term sheet and to reflect its content and shall obtain all required waivers and authorizations from shareholders and third parties; and (vi) Company shall enter into Indemnification Agreements with each of the Investor directors. It is expressly understood that the Investors have not completed intellectual property (IP) due diligence of the Company, and that receipt of a "no prior art" and "no infringement" opinion or other independent IP diligence report acceptable to the Investors, constitutes a condition to closing.
No Shop:	For a period of 60 days from the date of this Term Sheet the Company will not discuss any proposals for financing, or seek any financing from, any party, without the explicit approval of ICV and Greylock. Also during said 60-day period the Company shall not issue any securities of the Company without the prior written consent of ICV and Greylock. The Company and the Founders will promptly provide the Investors any documents and information requested by them for their due diligence.
Confidentiality:	The terms and conditions contained in this term sheet and documents and information disclosed during the due diligence procedure are confidential to the parties hereto and shall not be disclosed to any third party (other than the party's advisors) or used for any purpose other than in connection with the transaction proposed herein.

This document is not binding in any way even if signed, except for the No-Shop and Confidentiality sections herein. It is expressly agreed that and the Investors may terminate discussions with the Company and the Founders at any time, provided however, that it is the parties' intent that the definitive agreements drafted between the parties shall be based on the terms set forth herein.

EXHIBIT 4 (*continued*)

Israel Cleantech Ventures	Panoramic Power Ltd., an Israeli company
______________________________	______________________________
Date__________	Date__________
GREYLOCK ISRAEL LIMITED PARTNERSHIP By: Greylock Israel G.P., L.P, its general partner By: Greylock Israel Manager, Ltd., its ultimate general partner By: Greylock Israel Global Management, Ltd.	Founders: Dr. David Almagor: Date___________ ______________________________
By: ______________________________ ______________________________ ______________________________	Adi Shamir: ______________________________
Name: Title: Date__________	Date___________

Source: Erez Ofer.

CHAPTER 4.2

Honest Tea

Paul G. Gompers

Seth Goldman, President and TeaEO of Honest Tea, looked out the window of his office in Bethesda, Maryland. Honest Tea was a three-year-old start-up in the fast growing ready-to-drink tea market with its sights set on increasing brand awareness and distribution. Goldman had been answering e-mails from customers for the past 30 minutes as he waited to call his co-founder and Yale School of Management professor, Barry Nalebuff, so they could discuss their financing strategy. Many of these e-mails stood as testimonials to the vision he had set out to create in his company. Several drinkers even offered to invest in the company if Goldman was seeking to raise new capital.

The December 2000 cold spell had put a chill on the sales of his company's bottled tea product and he now had a bit of time to reflect on his successes of the past three years and what the future might hold for his company, Honest Tea. Honest Tea had received tremendous media attention in the last several months. Goldman, Nalebuff, and the company had been featured in magazines like Fortune, Entrepreneur, and Beverage World and in papers like the Washington Post, the Washington Business Journal, and the New York Times. The media coverage had been critical in raising public awareness of the company.

Looking forward, however, Goldman and Nalebuff knew that 2001 would be an important year for the company. In order to expand distribution, he figured that Honest Tea would have to raise financing. Goldman had recently received an offer from a prominent West Coast venture capital firm to invest $5 million in the company. Goldman was concerned, however, about what the implications of taking that much money from a professional venture capital group would do to the culture and mission of the company. He was particularly concerned that the valuation and control issues that the venture capital group demanded would be difficult for him or his employees to swallow. On the other hand, he could try to raise

Honest Tea
by PAUL G. GOMPERS, case number 9-201-076 Rev. OCTOBER 17, 2001

money from angel investors who shared a common vision for the company and who could add value at the same time. Goldman and Nalebuff had begun to sketch out their plans for raising that money. They had several options and needed to decide soon which one they were going to follow. Goldman reached for the tea kettle to boil some water for a cup of tea and began to work.

THE FOUNDING

In the summer of 1997, Seth Goldman was running in Central Park. The temperature reached the mid-90s and Goldman was parched. On the way back to his friend's apartment, he stopped in a local convenience market to find something to drink. After trying several bottles of iced tea and sports drinks, Goldman found that none of them actually quenched his thirst. This experience led him to call Barry Nalebuff, his Yale School of Management professor. While at Yale, Goldman was intrigued about the beverage industry after reading a case on the cola wars between Coke and Pepsi in Nalebuff's class on competitive strategy. Goldman contacted his former professor, and they soon converged on an untapped opportunity in the beverage market, the space between super-sweet drinks and flavorless waters.

Goldman and Nalebuff both felt that the market for these types of beverages would be quite large. (See **Exhibit 1** for statistics on the ready-to-drink tea market and the bottled water market.) They convened for several marathon tea-brewing sessions in which pots of water were boiled and various teas were mixed and matched. They were certain that others shared their same tastes and that the right beverage would catch on quickly. Several focus groups confirmed their idea. As ideas and investors for the company gathered critical mass, Seth left his marketing and sales post at Calvert Group, the nation's largest family of socially responsible mutual funds, and launched Honest Tea out of the guest room in his house. Using five large thermoses and label mock-ups, he sold the product to the 18 Fresh Fields stores of the Whole Foods Market chain. Four months later, the recipes were set, the teas were sourced, the labels were designed, and the teas were brewed and bottled. (See **Exhibit 2** for management bios and **Exhibit 3** for Honest Tea's mission statement.)

In order to get the tea on the shelves, Goldman actually rented a U-Haul and delivered the tea himself, 50 cases at a time. By the end of the summer of 1998, Honest Tea had become the best-selling tea throughout the Fresh Fields chain and was accepted by several national supermarket chains and distributors.

THE "READY-TO-DRINK" TEA MARKET

The myth of the origins of tea can be trace to 3000 BCE in China where the emperor Shen Nong is said to have ordered that all drinking water should be boiled to avoid disease transmitted by tainted water. According to the myth, one day when the emperor's servants were boiling water for him to drink, leaves from a nearby tree blew into the pot. The boiling water turned brown. Shen Nong is said to have tasted the liquid and was impressed by the drink. The consumption of tea soon spread throughout China.

In 2000, however, tea had become an international drink and was second in overall consumption only to water. The U.S. tea market, however, was considered quite different from the international market. First, overall tea consumption per capita was far lower in the United States than in most other countries. While the ready-to-drink tea market had experienced steady growth prior to 1990s, through most of the decade total tea consumption and per capita tea consumption declined quite dramatically. From 1998 to 1999, however, tea consumption was once again on the rise. Second, 80% of tea consumed in the United States was consumed iced. Nowhere else in the world was such a high fraction of tea drunk cold. (See **Exhibit 4** for statistics on U.S. beverage consumption.)

Goldman and Nalebuff were targeting the "ready-to-drink" tea segment of the U.S. market. In 1999, the ready-to-drink tea market totaled $2.67 billion, up 9% from 1998. The average American consumed nearly two gallons of ready-to-drink tea each year. Many experts predicted that the ready-to-drink tea market would more than double in size over the next decade. Data on tea sales showed that while the majority of the ready-to-drink tea was purchased in supermarkets, other distribution channels were growing more rapidly. (See **Exhibit 5** for a breakdown of beverage sales by channel.)

Several trends were driving the increased interest in tea consumption. First, there was increasing awareness of tea's health benefits versus carbonated soft drinks and alcohol. The growing presence of tea bars around the country was a testament to this trend. As competitors like Arizona Iced Tea and Sobe entered the market and dramatically sought to expand into new markets, ready-to-drink tea moved outside of the exclusive domain of supermarket distribution. By 2000, ready-to-drink teas were available in most warehouse clubs, convenience stores, gas stations, and dining establishments. In 2000 alone, more than $100 million was spent promoting ready-to-drink tea consumption.

The major competitors in the ready-to-drink tea market were all national brands. Snapple was the top brand with 14.6% of the market. Arizona Iced Tea held 10.6% of the market, while Lipton represented 9.5% of the market.

THE PRODUCT AND TARGET AUDIENCE

Somewhere between the pumped-up, sugar-saturated drinks and the tasteless waters, Goldman and Nalebuff saw a need for a healthier beverage, one that provided genuine natural taste without the artificially concocted sweeteners and preservatives designed to compensate for lack of taste. The concept of Honest Tea was to brew pure tea leaves from around the world in spring water and to add just a hint of honey or pure cane sugar.

Unlike most of the bottled teas in the marketplace, Honest Tea was not made with bricks of tea dust, tea concentrate, or artificial sweeteners. The tea had no bitter aftertaste or sugar kick, and did not leave a syrupy film on the tongue. Although taste was the primary benefit of drinking Honest Tea, the product had several attributes that enhanced its acceptance and marketability to four key audiences:

1. Disenchanted bottled tea drinkers who thought existing drinks were too sweet.
2. Bottled water drinkers who longed for taste and variety.
3. Diet soda drinkers who were interested in a low-calorie beverage that did not contain artificial sweeteners such as Nutrasweet.
4. Tea purists who were resigned to brewing tea at home because they had not been able to find "real tea" in a bottle.

The four attributes that made Honest Tea attractive to these consumers were:

1. Low in calories: A 12-ounce serving of Honest Tea had 9 to 17 calories, dramatically less than other bottled teas or comparable beverages.
2. Health benefits of brewed tea: The curative properties of tea had been known for thousands of years. Tea was the richest natural source of antioxidants. (Antioxidants impair the development of free radicals which contribute to cancer and heart disease.) The antioxidants in green tea were believed to be at least 100 times more effective than Vitamin C and 25 times better than Vitamin E at protecting cells and DNA from damage believed to be linked to cancer, heart disease, and other potentially life-threatening illnesses. In September 2000 Honest Tea released a comparative study on the antioxidant levels in bottled green teas performed by Analytical Chemical Services of Columbia. (For results of the study, see **Exhibit 6**.) Honest Tea significantly outperformed other bottled green teas. For example, Honest Tea's Moroccan Mint had six times the amount of EGCG, a key antioxidant, found in Arizona's Green Tea.

3. Organic and all-natural ingredients: With three bottled varieties that were fully organic and organic ingredients included in almost every variety, Honest Tea held a strong position in one of the fastest growing segments of the food industry. As consumers increasingly looked for products produced without chemical pesticides and fertilizers, Honest Tea represented a very approachable way for people to enjoy organic foods.
4. Cultural experience of tea: Each Honest Tea flavor was brewed based on a recipe perfected over generations in a specific region of the world. As a result, drinking Honest Tea became a cultural experience, from the genuine tastes to the distinctive international art and information on the label. While some bottled teas sought to cloak themselves in a cosmopolitan mantle by including exotic-looking drawings on the label, the front of each Honest Tea label featured authentic art from the culture of origin.

WHOLE LEAF TEA BAGS

As their bottled tea gained acceptance, Goldman and Nalebuff began thinking of ways to leverage the brand equity they had established. Ready-to-drink tea sales were highly seasonal, and they hoped introducing new products might dampen the seasonal effects. In March of 2000 the company introduced whole leaf tea bags that were the first fully biodegradable tag-and-bag tea bags. The bags contained whole leaves instead of tea dust, yielding a fuller, fresher taste—the richness of loose tea without the mess and accessories. After some adjustments to the packaging (plastic to paper overwraps), the bags entered natural foods distribution in the fall of 2000, and by December sales were picking up. The bags had been approved for Fresh Fields, Ukrop's, and Giant Eagle. They were made with unbleached paper and came in eight different varieties, five of which were organic. The first shippers, which merchandise the bags in a supermarket setting, were scheduled to enter distribution in December 2000. Food-service merchandisers were scheduled to be completed in March of 2001. (See **Exhibit 7** for data on tea bags and loose leaf tea sales.)

PRODUCTION AND MANUFACTURING

Initially, Goldman rented time in a bottling plant to brew his tea. During this period of time, Honest Tea developed several proprietary brewing tools and techniques that enabled it to manufacture several thousand cases of tea a day on both coasts with the desired consistency. In March 2000, the company consolidated its bottled tea production at Three Rivers Bottling, LLC, a plant Honest Tea had jointly purchased with Vancol Industries, a beverage company based in Denver, and Devine Foods, a food research and development company based in Philadelphia. While Honest Tea received a very attractive deal on its share of the plant, the operations of the plant had put some financial strain on the company, but Goldman felt that it was important to have the ability to control production. Since Honest Tea owned a third of a bottling plant and had a full-time brewmaster on staff, the company retained the knowledge of manufacturing the product, instead of relying on a co-packer for that information. All of the company's bottled tea was produced in the Three Rivers plant and shipped around the country.

The company had invested $300,000 in acquiring the plant and investing in the working capital to get production up and running. Goldman estimated that the plant had capacity to support approximately $30 million in sales. Because the current revenue run rate was far below this level, Honest Tea rented out production time to Arizona Iced Tea and other brands. The agreement with Arizona Iced Tea, however, was structured as a short-term rental and Honest Tea could increase production in short order if necessary.

The company's whole leaf tea bag line was developed through a strong strategic partnership with a tea bag co-packer on the East Coast. The unique bag-and-tag was patented by the co-packer. Honest Tea had manufactured proprietary equipment for the bags and had exclusive rights to those parts and designs.

PACKAGING AND PRICING

Honest Tea's bottled tea line was sold in 16-ounce glass bottles. All of the company's labels featured culturally authentic artwork. (See **Exhibit 8** for sample bottle labels.) All caps had a "pop-button safety seal" and a distinctive black matte finish that complemented the black border on the front of the label. In 2001, Goldman had committed the company to use caps that would have fun and philosophical messages underneath, which would help reinforce Honest Tea's spirited, authentic image. The company's packaging was designed to communicate the attributes of the tea inside in four ways:

- High quality—By using colorful and artistically sophisticated artwork presented with spot labels, (i.e., front and back instead of wrapa-round), the bottles evoked comparisons with a bottle of fine wine and other gourmet food.

- Culturally authentic—By using artwork directly from the culture where the tea came from, Honest Tea presented the tea as it was meant to be, without any "spin" or Westernized interpretation of what an Indian painting might look like.
- Honest—By using the spot labels, there was more space for the consumer to see the tea. Since the company used real tea leaves, it had nothing to hide inside.
- Simplicity—The essence of this millennia-old drink of water and leaves was its simplicity. Honest Tea's packaging had no flashy slogans, advertising callouts, or marketing hype. The package helped condition the consumer for what they were about to experience, an honest taste of tea.

In 2000 the company introduced a variety pack that contained a selection of flavors. This pack, which was first sold to natural food stores, had been approved by Costco for a test in the Southeast and Mid-Atlantic in 2001.

The retail price for a 16-ounce Honest Tea varied between $1.19 and $2.00. In food service accounts, the price range was from $1.29 to $2.50.

COMPETITIVE ADVANTAGE

The results of 2000 clearly indicated that Honest Tea had tapped into a market opportunity. In 1999, Goldman had planned to spend several years building up a strong presence in a local market before expanding nationally. The rapid growth during 2000, however, had changed his mind. (See **Exhibits 9 and 10** for the historical financial performance of Honest Tea and **Exhibit 11** for pro forma projections.) He now saw an opportunity to aggressively expand into new markets.

Market opportunity—Goldman and Nalebuff had created a new beverage category and were currently the only company filling that category. If Honest Tea were to hesitate, other companies would eventually move in.

Compelling brand image and story—The packaging, presentation and profile of the Honest Tea brand fit together extremely well with the product. Although the company might be able to improve on the bottle design in the future, this was a package that came close to selling itself. It was also a brand and a story, which had successfully gained free media coverage.

Management team—Honest Tea had developed a team with the right combination of sales experience and market creativity that was capable of growing the company on a national, and even an international, scale.

Production capability—Even though it was not traditional for a beverage company Honest Tea's size to own a bottling plant, Goldman and Nalebuff made the strategic decision that it was essential to have control over their destiny. In the summer of 1999 several major brands ran into trouble with product shortages. If Honest Tea decided to focus all production at Three Rivers on Honest Tea, it could grow to $30 million in sales before they would need to develop additional production sites.

The excitement that Honest Tea had generated was palpable. In addition to the positive media coverage, the company had received a large number of recognitions in 2000, including:

- Named one of the "100 Most Notable Brands of the Century" by Beverage World
- First prize, National Nutritional Foods Association, best tea
- Socially Responsible Business Award at the Natural Product Expo
- First Recipient of the Specialty Coffee Association of America's Award for Best Sustainable Practices/Product
- Gold Medal for its Web site from Art Directors Club of Metropolitan Washington
- Bronze Medal, Beverage Packaging Awards for First Nation bottled tea
- Seth Goldman selected as one of "20 Rising Stars Under 40" by Gourmet News

EXIT STRATEGIES

Goldman believed that Honest Tea would be capable of financing its own growth through profits within the next 12 to 24 months. Even so, it was likely that the company's success would lead to invitations from strategic partners. Goldman felt that the most likely exit strategy would be either an investment or acquisition by a strategic partner. Sobe, Snapple, and Nantucket Nectars all were either acquired entirely or in part by large, strategic investors at between two and three times sales. In recent years, Coke, Pepsi and Cadbury-Schweppes seemed to be making less effort to build brands internally and more effort to acquire other brands. In addition, other large companies had been interested in the bottled beverage business, including Hain-Celestial, Danone, Unilever (Lipton's parent company), Crystal Geyser, and Suntory.

Although going public was a less traditional form of financing in the beverage industry, if Honest Tea could meet its expectations for growth, the company would consider a public offering to provide liquidity to investors and to raise capital for expansion in the future. Such an exit might eventually provide an opportunity to merge or acquire other beverage brands.

FINANCING OF HONEST TEA

Honest Tea was formally launched in February 1998 with a $300,000 start-up investment by Goldman and Nalebuff. (See **Exhibit 12** for proposed financing structure.) The founders felt that going to a large outside investor at this stage would have been a distraction. The money was used to prove the concept, refine the product, and land distribution agreements. In addition to the common stock that they purchased, the founders were given warrants for creating the company.

Nalebuff came up with the novel financing structure to avoid contentious discussions about what the value of the company should be in the first round. While he and Goldman had put together the projections for Honest Tea right from the start, they were entering uncharted waters. The category of beverage they were targeting did not exist and investors could not be certain that the company would take off. Therefore, Nalebuff thought that by including warrants for the founders with exercise prices staged at multiples of the initial price at which family and friends brought in would avoid such disagreements. If the company did very well, as Goldman and Nalebuff believed, then they would be able to exercise their warrants and they would own a greater fraction of the company. If they did not do as well, then the original investors would own a larger piece of the firm.

Shortly after launching the company, Goldman and Nalebuff approached family and friends to gauge their interest in making rather modest investments in the firm. An additional $217,500 was raised in a relatively short time. The pre-money valuation was assumed to be zero for all of the initial financing.

In late 1998, Goldman realized that the company would need additional capital to continue operations. The goal was to raise a significantly more substantial round to provide the money for expanding the production and distribution. While he felt that family and friends could be counted on for some of the round, Goldman hoped to raise enough money to push distribution into several new channels.

In the process of searching for potential angels, Goldman returned to the pile of e-mails he had received from loyal customers. While the company did not solicit funds over the Internet, Honest Tea, like most start-ups, had a Web page devoted to telling the company's story. Many people who tried the tea loved the product so much that they responded by sending e-mails to Goldman praising the clean and refreshing taste of

Honest Tea. Several satisfied consumers even wrote that they would consider investing in the company should Honest Tea need financing in the future. Goldman decided to send anyone who had expressed an interest in providing capital the investment letter for the company's second round of financing. Goldman was pleasantly surprised and received commitments for $1.2 million. The round placed a pre-money valuation of $4 million on the company. Despite the success in fundraising, however, Nalebuff and Goldman had spent a significant amount of time over the past eight months fundraising during this round. Even when they were not physically raising money, it was always on their mind.

In early 2000, Honest Tea once again needed to raise financing. Nalebuff and Goldman had discussions with a venture group about coming into the round. Before investing, the group wanted to see what commitment would be found from existing investors. Goldman and Nalebuff went to their existing investors and quickly gained a commitment for all the capital they needed. The financing raised a total of $1 million at a $8.5 million pre-money valuation.

WHERE TO GO FOR FINANCING?

Despite all the company's success over the past year, it still needed financing to bring it to breakeven. Goldman had initially estimated that a $2 million round of financing would carry Honest Tea to profitability. The cash was needed to finance operating losses for the next several quarters as well as to invest in new distribution channels. Capital needs included the hiring of a national sales force. With the acquisition of Sobe by Pepsi, Honest Tea had the opportunity to hire several, well-connected sales managers who had helped make Sobe the fastest growing brand in the country. Funds were also needed to purchase marketing and merchandising materials such as coolers and other sales incentives. The company also required capital to support the launch of Honest Tea in several new supermarket chains including Safeway. The launch of Honest Tea in 500 Safeway's required an introductory allowance of one case per SKU per store. Finally, the company needed capital to help get the Three Rivers Bottling plant to profitability.

Goldman and Nalebuff had had several meetings and conversations trying to hammer out details of the financing strategy. Both wanted to diversify the investor base and potentially bring on an investor that could help with the operational aspects of running a start-up. On an early trip to the West Coast, Goldman met with several venture capital groups. One prominent firm had offered to invest $5 million in Honest Tea. While Goldman was excited, he was also concerned. The venture group had proposed a pre-money valuation in the $5 to $7 million range and significant control over the board of directors and future strategic decisions. While the money would help the company grow aggressively and would provide a reputational benefit for the young company, Goldman and Nalebuff were uncertain about whether such a deal made sense at this time. The venture capital firm wanted to push Honest Tea to expand very rapidly and might push Goldman to compromise some of his convictions.

On the same trip, Goldman met with several angel investor groups, including the Investors' Circle (IC), a nonprofit national network of investors. IC was founded in 1992 and had invested more than $70 million in 120 companies. The median investment amount was $225,000, but the group's investments ranged from $10,000 all the way to $6.5 million depending on the company's needs and members' interests. What was unusual about IC was its investment goals. The group invested in socially responsible start-ups. (See **Exhibit 13** for IC's statement of responsibility and **Exhibit 14** for a description of previous investments by IC.) Because Goldman had worked with the IC when he worked at the Calvert Group, he believed that IC's investment philosophy coincided with the mission of Honest Tea. He felt that members of IC might be able to provide as much as $500,000 in the next round of financing.

Even if he could count on the Investors' Circle, however, Goldman had considerably more legwork ahead of him. He had to identify other individuals who would be willing to invest and be able to help Honest Tea. In fact, Goldman was convinced that this round of investment must bring in a new, more value-added set of investors. Goldman hoped to identify a lead investor who would agree to valuation and terms. Then other, smaller investors would fall in line. Negotiating terms with multiple parties was a very real challenge. Each angel investor came to the table with his or her own set of issues.

At the same time, Goldman hoped to establish a real board of directors. If he could attract the right angels, putting them on the board could provide value-added advice and direction. Goldman wondered whether he could find the right investors quickly. While sales were currently at a relatively low point in the year, he didn't feel that he could take a lot of time away from the business. Fundraising was meant to allow the business to operate effectively. It was not supposed to be the business.

DECISION

Now that the kettle was bubbling away, Goldman opened up a pack of Kashmiri Chai tea and began to let it steep. He knew that the market potential for his company was very large. The real questions, however, was what type of investor made sense. On the one hand, taking venture capital funding would save him time and energy and would provide capital to grow Honest Tea quickly. He wondered, however, whether the strings attached to the funding were worth it. On the other hand, Goldman knew that angels could be incredibly high maintenance, needing significant amounts of handholding and information. Most of Honest Tea's investors were relatively unsophisticated, and on more than one occasion, Goldman had had to spend hours just explaining how to interpret an income statement and balance sheet. Communicating information to more than 50 individual investors often demanded a great deal of Goldman's time.

Until now the choices of financing had been driven out of necessity and ease of access. Now, however, Goldman felt that he and Nalebuff needed to craft a plan to bring Honest Tea to the next level. They had proven that a market for their product existed and had begun to craft a strategy to establish it as the market leader in this segment. With money, advice, and a little luck, they just might become the next "must have" brand.

EXHIBIT 1 Tea Consumption vs. Bottled Water Consumption

Tea Consumption			Bottled Water Consumption	
	Gallons	Per capital	Gallons	Per capital
1994	2,682,200	10.4	2,901,900	11.3
1995	2,630,600	10	3,167,500	12
1996	2,590,200	9.7	3,449,300	13
1997	2,528,500	9.4	3,775,800	14
1998	2,548,200	9.4	4,146,000	15.3
1999	2,595,500	9.5	4,646,100	17.0

Source: Compiled from Beverage Marketing Directory 2001.

EXHIBIT 2 Management Biographies

President & TeaEO Seth Goldman launched Honest Tea after leaving the Calvert Group where he was Vice President of Calvert Social Investment Fund, the nation's largest family of mutual funds that invest in socially and environmentally responsible companies. In this role, Seth managed the marketing and sales efforts, including a groundbreaking public awareness campaign that increased Web site traffic eightfold and doubled sales in the company's flagship equity fund. His other work at Calvert Group included active involvement in the company's private equity portfolio and a corporate child labor initiative for the Calvert Foundation. As Calvert's most visible presence within the community of socially responsible businesses, Seth's contacts and connections helped give Honest Tea a mark of credibility. In addition, the target customer for Calvert's equity funds was very much in line with the Cultural Creative profile discussed earlier.

His previous work included directing a nationally recognized demonstration project for Americorps, which gave him experience managing a staff of more than 50 employees, and serving as Senator Lloyd Bentsen's Deputy Press Secretary for two and a half years, which helped him develop strong public relations skills as well as contacts. He had also worked for a year in China (1987–1988) and a year and a half in the former Soviet Union (1989–1990), where he developed, among other things, an appreciation for the role tea plays in many cultures.

Goldman graduated from the Yale School of Management in 1995. While at Yale, he and a classmate were winners of the inaugural Connecticut Future Fund New Enterprise Competition for a business plan they developed based on a diagnostic invented at the Yale School of Medicine. Seth

EXHIBIT 2 (*continued*)

is a graduate of Harvard College, where he was a Class Marshal and a member of the Varsity Track team. He served as Chair of the Yale School of Management Annual Fund and was on the board of the Montgomery Public Schools Educational Foundation. He was a former board member of Students for Responsible Business.

Chairman of the Board Barry Nalebuff was the Milton Steinbach Professor at Yale School of Management. He taught at Harvard and Princeton before coming to Yale where he taught competitive strategy, mergers and acquisition, strategic marketing, and decision-making and game theory. An expert on Game Theory, he was co-author of Thinking Strategically and Co–opetition, which was a Business Week bestseller. He applied the use of game theory in consulting to companies in banking, consumer products, health-care, high-tech manufacturing, insurance, oil, pharmaceuticals software, and telecommunications. He was on the board of Trader.com, Bear Stearns Financial Products, and the Connecticut Citizenship Fund. A graduate of MIT and a Rhodes Scholar, he earned his doctorate in economics at Oxford University.

Chief Financial Officer Christel Bivens, CPA, joined Honest Tea in April of 1999, bringing a wide array of accounting experience, having been involved in all aspects of financial management—from budgeting to collections to cash management and financial analysis. She had worked with Telecorp, a $300 million telecommunications company, managed the IPO of Digene, and oversaw manufacturing plants for Greenstone, a $20 million manufacturing company.

Division Manager (Northeast) Dan Cavanaugh had the beverage business in his blood, having worked as a truck loader as early as the age of 13. He rose from being a route driver to managing Arizona's presence in New Jersey and then Nantucket Nectar's presence in the New York/New Jersey markets. He loved pioneering brands, knows all the players in the Northeast market and has demonstrated tremendous success in DSD and food service channels.

National Sales Manager (Natural/Specialty) Melanie Knitzer came to Honest Tea in October 1998 from her post as Director of Corporate Sales with Gourm-E-Co Imports, a mid-Atlantic specialty food distributor. Melanie also brought 15 years of experience selling artisan products and coordinating promotions with major chains. She was responsible for managing all natural foods and gourmet foods retail accounts.

Brewmaster George Scalf joined Honest Tea in March of 1998 to manage the production of the tea. As the founder of numerous natural beverage enterprises including, Blue Range Natural Foods and New Dawn Natural Foods, George brought more than 20 years of expertise and contacts in beverage manufacturing.

EXHIBIT 2 *(continued)*

Director of Distribution (East) Larry Vinson joined Honest Tea in March of 2000 from Sobe, where he managed the company's rapid expansion in the Southeast. He had more than 25 years of experience pioneering brands and developing DSD distribution networks from scratch, having also worked with Mistic and Snapple.

National Sales Manager (Foodservice) Charlie Woodruff came to Honest Tea from Oregon Chai where he led that fast-growing brand's food service presence on the East Coast. He had pioneered a gourmet beverage into multiple food service channels.

Division Manager (Mountain States) Larry Ziegler joined Honest Tea in April of 2000 after working with Gatorade/Quaker Oats, where he had managed that brand's presence from Idaho through Arizona. He also has worked with Snapple and Sysco, the nation's largest food service distributor. Based in Denver, Larry understands how to manage and develop beverage distribution networks.

Central-South Regional Manager Danny Sky-Eagle. Danny joined the team in early 2001, bringing with him a strong network of distributor relationships he had developed during his tenure as a manager for Sobe in Oklahoma, Arkansas, Louisiana and Missouri. In two years Danny built Sobe's business in that region from 9,000 cases per year to 200,000 cases per year.

Source: Company documents.

EXHIBIT 3 Statement and Aspirations for Social Responsibility

Although a statement of social and environmental responsibility is not usually found in most business plans, these issues are central to Honest Tea's identity and purpose. Not only is the value of our brand based on authenticity, integrity and purity, but our management team is committed to these values as well. We will never claim to be a perfect company, but we will address difficult issues and strive to be honest about our ability or inability to resolve them. For example, we recognize that the labor and environmental conditions on many tea estates are below internationally accepted standards. We will strive to work with our suppliers to promote higher standards while recognizing the limited influence we have as a small company. We value diversity in the workplace and we intend to become a visible presence in the communities where our products are sold. When presented with a purchasing decision between two financially comparable alternatives, we will attempt to choose the option which better addresses the needs of economically disadvantaged communities.

We have taken our first substantive step in that direction with the development of our First Nation Peppermint. After much negotiation with

EXHIBIT 3 *(continued)*

I'tchik, a woman-owned company based on the Crow reservation, we have created a partnership that allows the Crow community to be economically involved in the production and sale of the tea. I'tchik is serving as Honest Tea's buyer for the ingredients, charging a modest administrative fee per kilo of tea with the understanding that over time I'tchik will develop the capacity to harvest the tea on the reservation. In addition I'tchik is licensing the recipe and artwork to Honest Tea in a royalty arrangement. A portion of the royalties are directed to the Pretty Shield Foundation, a non-profit created to address the needs of at-risk Native American youth.

We are in the process of developing partnerships associated with new tea varieties, including City Year, the national urban peace corps program, and tea estates owned by black South Africans.

Source: Company documents.

EXHIBIT 4 Drink Consumption in the United States

	Wholesale Sales		
Drink	1998	1999	Growth
Beer	$28.49	$28.92	1.5%
Bottled water	$4.33	$4.94	14.1%
Fruit beverages	$12.77	$13.41	5.0%
Ready-to-drink teas	$1.34	$1.46	9.0%
Soft drinks	$41.79	$42.20	1.0%
Spirits	$15.55	$15.86	2.0%
Sport drinks	$1.59	$1.75	10.1%
Wine	$10.32	$10.63	3.0%
Total beverages	$116.18	$119.17	

	Retail Sales		
Drink	1998	1999	Growth
Beer	$54.20	$55.05	1.6%
Bottled water	$5.20	$5.92	13.8%
Fruit beverages	$17.50	$18.57	6.1%
Ready-to-drink teas	$2.45	$2.67	9.0%
Soft drinks	$54.30	$54.84	1.0%
Spirits	$34.05	$34.80	2.2%
Sport drinks	$2.65	$2.91	9.8%
Wine	$17.38	$17.91	3.0%
Total beverages	$187.73	$192.67	

Source: Compiled from Beverage World's State of the Industry Report, 2000.

EXHIBIT 5 Sales of Beverage Within Various Channels

DOLLAR SALES

	Supermarkets		Drug Stores		Mass Merchandise		Total FDM	
	Dollar Sales (in Millions)	% Growth	Dollar Sales (in Millions)	% Growth	Dollar Sales (in Millions)	% Growth	Dollar Sales (in Millions)	% Growth
Carbonated soft drinks	$12,525.2	4.0%	$622.7	8.8%	$2,079.2	26.3%	$15,227.1	6.8%
Bottled water	1,432.0	20.9	120.0	20.2	244.0	55.0	1,796.0	24.6
Coffee	2,868.0	-8.2	47.9	-1.5	547.7	5.8	3,463.6	-6.2
Drink mixes	629.6	1.5	5.2	30.2	103.0	37.7	737.8	5.5
Aseptic juice	645.9	8.4	5.5	-4.3	127.1	36.1	778.5	12.0
Bottled juice (shelf-stable)	3,241.8	8.9	142.0	12.2	449.5	18.0	3,833.3	10.0
Canned juice (shelf-stable)	714.2	-0.6	5.2	-14.3	53.1	35.2	772.5	1.2
Instant tea	263.0	-4.6	1.6	-1.6	20.3	32.0	284.9	-2.7
Loose tea & tea bags	638.9	5.7	14.8	13.9	77.0	6.9	730.8	6.0
RTD tea	450.9	7.5	36.5	8.6	42.2	14.6	529.7	8.1
Isotonics	700.6	7.5	49.2	17.0	121.9	29.4	871.7	12.5
Milk	10,179.7	5.5	N/A	N/A	N/A	N/A	N/A	N/A

(*continued*)

EXHIBIT 5 *(continued)*

VOLUME SALES	Supermarkets		Drug Stores		Mass Merchandise		Total FDM	
	Dollar Sales (in Millions)	% Growth	Dollar Sales (in Millions)	% Growth	Dollar Sales (in Millions)	% Growth	Dollar Sales (in Millions)	% Growth
Carbonated soft drinks	$3,341.1	-0.2%	$160.1	10.7%	$626.8	26.5%	$4,128.0	3.5%
Bottled water	1,155.6	14.4	51.7	14.0	205.1	43.6	1,412.4	17.8
Coffee	648.1	-2.2	14.1	17.0	168.0	17.5	830.2	1.6
Drink mixes	6,117.1	-1.2	46.2	19.0	969.6	25.3	7,133.0	1.8
Aseptic juice	1,017.1	5.8	8.6	-5.8	280.0	41.3	1,305.8	11.7
Bottled juice (shelf-stable)	5,615.5	7.4	200.1	9.2	931.3	17.3	6,746.8	8.7
Canned juice (shelf-stable)	1,186.5	-3.2	10.1	-9.3	112.8	33.8	1,309.3	-0.9
Instant tea	2,499.0	-4.8	13.1	-1.2	268.5	34.0	2,780.6	-2.0
Loose tea & tea bags	1,062.4	-0.6	24.4	27.4	171.2	32.5	1,258.0	3.3
RTD tea	952.3	5.6	57.8	7.8	106.9	21.2	1,117.0	7.0
Isotonics	1,141.8	6.6	68.0	13.1	224.6	28.2	1,434.4	9.8
Milk	27,296.2	-1.0	N/A	N/A	N/A	N/A	N/A	N/A

Source: Compiled from Beverage Industry, September 2000.

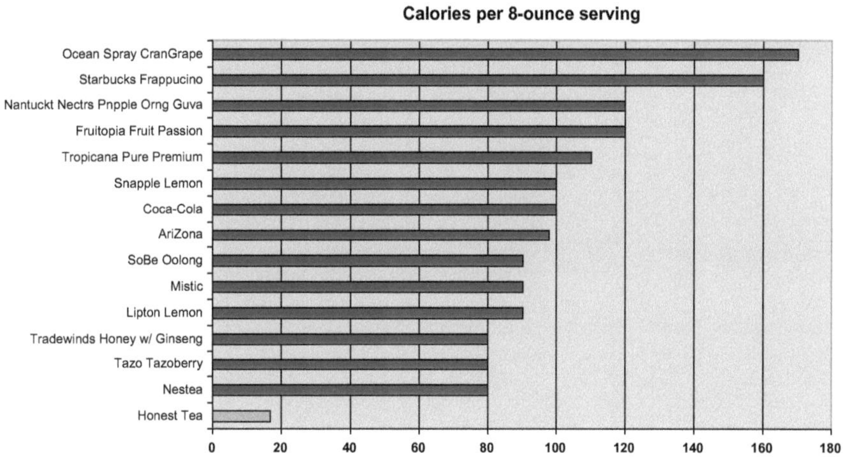

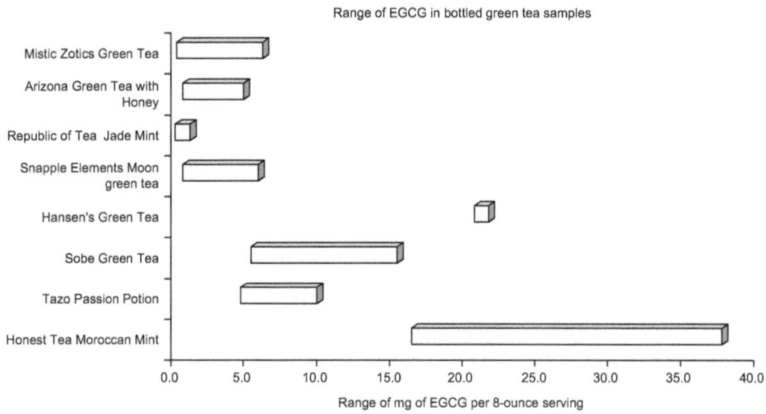

EXHIBIT 6 Honest Tea Characteristics
Source: Company documents.

EXHIBIT 7 Tea and Coffee Consumption (in millions)

	1995	2000
Coffee	$4,023.80	$3,488.80
Ground coffee	$2,447.70	$2,089.20
Instant coffee	$720.00	$596.20
Whole bean coffee	$231.90	$283.80
Cocoa mixes	$347.80	$347.40
Tea bags/loose tea	$636.80	$751.10

Source: Compiled from Beverage Industry, September 2000.

EXHIBIT 8 Honest Tea Bottles
Source: Company documents.

EXHIBIT 9 Historical Financial Performance of Honest Tea

HONEST TEA, INC.
Income Statements, 1998-2000

	Year Ended Dec. 31		Qtr Ended June 30
	1998	1999	2000
REVENUES			
Sales	$273,913	$1,229,882	$630,022
Sales discounts	-$7,807	-$149,027	-$51,756
Other income	$5,862	$15,167	$14,254
Total revenues	$271,968	$1,096,022	$592,520
Cost of goods sold	$222,414	$745,321	$360,459
Gross profit, %	$49,555	$350,702	$232,060
EXPENSES			
Broker commissions	$0	$38,787	$20,649
Consultants	$81,464	$43,659	$27,344
General & administrative	$29,970	$103,242	$56,174
Payroll taxes & benefits	$13,191	$41,559	$17,847
Professional fees	$35,467	$24,307	$675
Research & development	$22,254	$80,957	$8,055
Salaries	$125,976	$390,876	$140,175
Sales & marketing	$87,016	$399,649	$131,278
Travel & entertainment	$15,647	$65,865	$42,519
Total operating expenses	$410,983	$1,188,901	$444,715
Bad debt expense	$0	$31,136	$2,384
Depreciation & amortization	$4,090	$11,916	$13,288
Interest expense	$0	$1,107	$551
Total expenses	$415,073	$1,233,062	$460,939
NET INCOME (LOSS)	-$365,519	-$882,359	-$228,879

EXHIBIT 9 *(continued)*

HONEST TEA, INC.
Balance Sheets, 1998-2000

	Year Ended Dec. 31 1998	1999	June 30 2000
ASSETS			
Current assets			
Cash	$33,578	$450,173	$220,982
Accounts receivable	$61,066	$176,039	$272,028
Inventory	$98,477	$297,571	$433,979
Prepaid expenses & other current assets	$0	$36,131	$49,284
Total current assets	$193,121	$959,915	$976,272
Investment—Three Rivers Bottling	$0	-$38,207	-$38,207
Secured notes receivable—Three Rivers Bottling	$0	$57,742	$82,538
depreciation	$22,644	$69,022	$182,335
of amortization	$1,389	$25,033	$24,737
Deposits	$0	$58,095	$114,336
Total assets	$217,153	$1,131,601	$1,342,011
LIABILITIES			
Current liabilities			
Accts pay & credit card	$1,518	$217,630	$164,945
Total current liabilities	$0	$217,630	$164,945
Long term lease obligation	$0	$1,843	$1,833
Total liabilities	$1,518	$219,472	$166,778
SHAREHOLDER'S EQUITY			
value $.01/share); issued: 125 shares	$1	$0	$0
value $.01/share); issued: 174 shares	$0	$2	$2
Additional paid in capital	$581,153	$2,366,662	$3,161,309
Loss from Investment in Three Rivers Bottling	$0	-$206,657	-$206,657
Retained earnings	-$365,519	-$1,247,879	-$1,779,422
Total shareholder's equity	$215,635	$912,129	$1,175,233
Total liabilities & shareholder's equity	$217,153	$1,131,601	$1,342,011

Source: Company documents. (Data disguised.)

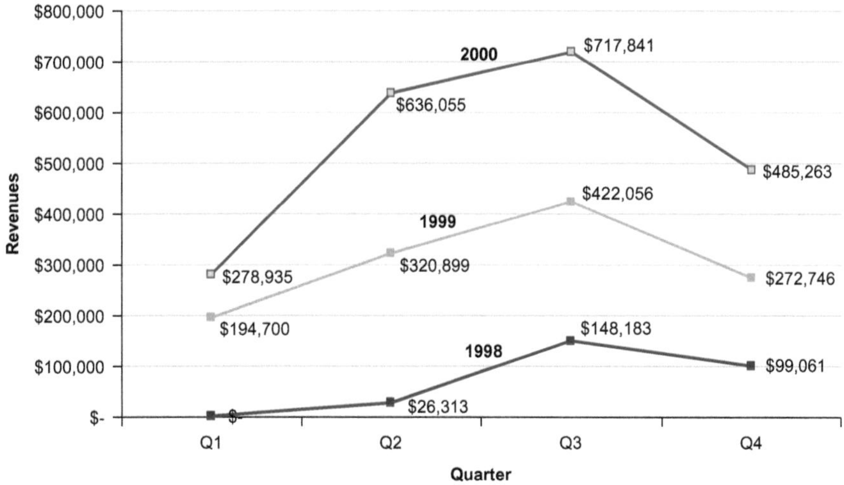

EXHIBIT 10 Quarterly Revenues for Honest Tea
Source: Company documents. (Data disguised.)

EXHIBIT 11 Pro Forma Projections for Honest Tea

2001 Aggressive Growth ($ in thousands)	January	February	March	April	May	June	July	August	September	October	November	December	TOTAL
REVENUE													
Cases sold	38.18	67.38	78.61	87.59	95.46	106.69	101.07	112.30	106.69	89.84	85.35	75.24	1,044.39
RTD sales	$295.9	$522.2	$609.2	$678.9	$739.7	$826.8	$783.3	$870.3	$826.8	$696.3	$661.4	$583.1	$8,094.0
Tea bag/non-RTD sales	$67.4	$61.8	$61.8	$56.2	$56.2	$50.5	$50.5	$89.8	$101.1	$95.5	$106.7	$101.1	$898.4
Gross sales	$261.1	$584.0	$671.0	$735.0	$795.9	$877.3	$833.8	$960.2	$927.8	$791.7	$768.1	$684.1	$8,992.4
Discount/promotion/allowance	5.00%	4.00%	10.00%	4.00%	4.00%	15.00%	5.00%	7.50%	7.50%	4.00%	4.00%	4.00%	
Discount on sales	($18.2)	($23.4)	($67.0)	($29.4)	($31.8)	($131.6)	($41.7)	($72.0)	($69.6)	($31.7)	($30.8)	($27.4)	($574.5)
Damages %	0.5%	0.5%	0.5%	0.5%	0.5%	0.5%	0.5%	0.5%	0.5%	0.5%	0.5%	0.5%	0.5%
Damages on sales	($1.8)	($2.9)	($3.4)	($3.7)	($3.9)	($4.4)	($4.2)	($4.8)	($4.6)	($3.9)	($3.8)	($3.4)	($44.9)
Net sales	$343.3	$557.7	$600.6	$701.9	$760.2	$741.4	$788.0	$883.4	$853.6	$756.1	$733.5	$653.4	$8,373.0
TOTAL COGS	$196.9	$307.4	$351.4	$382.7	$413.5	$453.6	$431.6	$503.1	$489.0	$419.0	$409.2	$365.6	$4,722.9
Gross Profit	$146.4	$250.3	$249.2	$319.3	$346.7	$287.8	$356.4	$380.2	$364.6	$337.1	$324.3	$287.7	$3,650.1
Three Rivers dividend	$0.0	$0.0	$0.0	$0.0	$4.5	$4.5	$4.5	$4.5	$4.5	$0.0	$0.0	$0.0	$22.5
Net revenue	$343.3	$557.7	$600.6	$701.9	$764.7	$745.9	$792.5	$887.8	$891.8	$756.1	$733.5	$653.4	$8,395.4
EXPENSES													
Slotting fees	$89.8	$89.8	$89.8	$89.8	$89.8	$0.0	$0.0	$0.0	$0.0	$0.0	$0.0	$0.0	$449.2
Coolers	$112.3	$112.3	$112.3	$0.0	$0.0	$0.0	$0.0	$0.0	$0.0	$0.0	$0.0	$0.0	$336.9
Marketing & Promotion	$134.8	$134.8	$134.8	$123.5	$112.3	$112.3	$112.3	$112.3	$101.1	$95.5	$95.5	$89.8	$1,358.8
Brokerage/commissions	$5.2	$8.4	$9.0	$10.6	$11.5	$11.1	$11.8	$13.3	$12.8	$11.3	$11.0	$9.8	$125.6
Consultants/Summer interns	$2.8	$2.8	$2.8	$2.8	$16.8	$16.8	$16.8	$20.2	$2.8	$2.8	$2.8	$2.8	$93.2
Legal & Acctg Fees	$2.2	$2.2	$2.2	$2.2	$2.2	$2.2	$2.2	$2.2	$2.2	$2.2	$2.2	$2.2	$27.0
General & Administrative	$6.7	$6.7	$9.0	$9.0	$11.2	$11.2	$11.2	$11.2	$9.0	$9.0	$9.0	$9.0	$112.3
Rent	$3.9	$3.9	$3.9	$6.2	$6.2	$6.2	$6.2	$6.2	$6.2	$6.2	$6.2	$6.2	$67.4
Research & Development	$11.2	$11.2	$11.2	$3.4	$0.0	$0.0	$0.0	$0.0	$0.0	$0.0	$0.0	$0.0	$37.1
Travel/entertainment	$39.3	$39.3	$39.3	$39.3	$50.5	$50.5	$50.5	$50.5	$39.3	$33.7	$33.7	$33.7	$499.7
Bonus & Prof. Development	$7.9	$9.5	$11.2	$11.2	$11.2	$11.2	$11.2	$11.2	$11.2	$11.2	$11.2	$11.2	$129.7
Salaries/wages/benefits	$78.6	$95.5	$112.3	$112.3	$112.3	$112.3	$112.3	$112.3	$112.3	$112.3	$112.3	$112.3	$1,297.1
EXPENSES	$494.8	$516.6	$537.9	$410.3	$424.2	$334.0	$334.7	$339.5	$296.9	$284.2	$283.9	$277.0	$4,533.9
Net income	($348.4)	($266.2)	($288.8)	($91.1)	($73.0)	($41.7)	$26.2	$45.3	$72.2	$52.9	$40.4	$10.7	($861.5)

EXHIBIT 11 *(continued)*

2002 ($ in thousands)	January	February	March	April	May	June	July	August	September	October	November	December	TOTAL
REVENUE													
Cases sold	89.84	101.07	145.99	157.22	168.45	196.53	179.68	224.60	213.37	179.68	168.45	157.22	1,982.10
RTD sales	$696.3	$783.3	$1,131.4	$1,218.5	$1,305.5	$1,523.0	$1,392.5	$1,740.7	$1,653.6	$1,392.5	$1,305.5	$1,218.5	$15,361.2
Tea bag/non RTD sales	$112.3	$101.1	$101.1	$95.5	$95.5	$89.8	$89.8	$112.3	$168.5	$157.2	$224.6	$179.7	$1,527.3
Gross sales	$808.6	$884.4	$1,232.5	$1,313.9	$1,400.9	$1,612.9	$1,482.4	$1,853.0	$1,822.1	$1,549.7	$1,530.1	$1,398.1	$16,888.5
Disc/promo/allow	5.00%	4.00%	10.00%	4.00%	4.00%	15.00%	5.00%	7.50%	7.50%	4.00%	4.00%	4.00%	
Discount on sales	($40.4)	($35.4)	($123.2)	($52.6)	($56.2)	($241.9)	($74.1)	($138.9)	($136.7)	($62.0)	($61.2)	($55.9)	($1,078.4)
Damages %	0.5%	0.5%	0.5%	0.5%	0.5%	0.5%	0.5%	0.5%	0.5%	0.5%	0.5%	0.5%	0.5%
Damages on sales	($4.0)	($4.4)	($6.2)	($6.5)	($7.0)	($8.1)	($7.4)	($9.2)	($9.1)	($7.7)	($7.6)	($7.0)	($84.4)
Net sales	$764.1	$844.5	$1,103.1	$1,254.7	$1,337.8	$1,362.9	$1,400.8	$1,704.7	$1,676.3	$1,480.0	$1,461.2	$1,335.2	$15,725.6
Cost of Goods Sold													
TOTAL COGS	$423.6	$458.9	$631.4	$670.5	$713.7	$817.5	$752.9	$941.1	$937.3	$800.0	$804.1	$729.5	$8,680.3
Gross Profit	$340.5	$385.8	$471.9	$584.2	$624.3	$545.3	$648.0	$763.6	$739.0	$680.0	$657.2	$605.7	$7,045.3
Three Rivers dividend	$0.0	$0.0	$0.0	$0.0	$9.0	$9.0	$9.0	$9.0	$9.0	$0.0	$0.0	$0.0	$44.9
Net revenue	$764.1	$844.6	$1,103.1	$1,254.7	$1,346.9	$1,371.9	$1,409.8	$1,713.7	$1,685.3	$1,480.0	$1,461.2	$1,335.2	$15,770.5
EXPENSES													
Slotting	$89.8	$89.8	$89.8	$89.8	$89.8	$0.0	$0.0	$0.0	$0.0	$0.0	$0.0	$0.0	$449.2
Coolers	$112.3	$112.3	$112.3	$112.3	$0.0	$0.0	$0.0	$0.0	$0.0	$0.0	$0.0	$0.0	$449.2
Mktg & Promo	$179.7	$157.2	$157.2	$157.2	$157.2	$157.2	$157.2	$157.2	$157.2	$157.2	$157.2	$157.2	$1,909.1
Brokerage Comm	$9.5	$10.6	$13.8	$15.7	$16.7	$17.1	$17.5	$21.3	$21.0	$18.5	$18.3	$16.7	$196.5
Consult/SumIntern	$5.6	$5.6	$5.6	$5.6	$22.5	$22.5	$22.5	$24.7	$5.6	$5.6	$5.6	$5.6	$137.0
Legal & Acctg Fees	$2.8	$2.8	$2.8	$2.8	$2.8	$2.8	$2.8	$2.8	$2.8	$2.8	$2.8	$2.8	$33.7
Gen'l & Admin	$10.1	$10.1	$10.1	$10.1	$10.1	$10.1	$10.1	$10.1	$10.1	$10.1	$10.1	$10.1	$121.3
Rent	$6.7	$6.7	$6.7	$6.7	$6.7	$6.7	$6.7	$6.7	$6.7	$6.7	$6.7	$6.7	$80.9
Res & Devel	$11.2	$11.2	$11.2	$3.4	$0.0	$0.0	$0.0	$0.0	$0.0	$0.0	$0.0	$0.0	$37.1
Travel/entertainment	$50.5	$50.5	$50.5	$50.5	$61.8	$61.8	$61.8	$61.8	$61.8	$50.5	$50.5	$50.5	$662.6
Ben/bonus & prof dev	$13.5	$14.0	$14.6	$14.6	$14.6	$14.6	$14.6	$14.6	$14.6	$14.6	$14.6	$14.6	$173.5
Salaries & wages	$134.8	$140.4	$146.0	$146.0	$146.0	$146.0	$146.0	$146.0	$146.0	$146.0	$146.0	$146.0	$1,735.0
EXPENSES	$626.6	$611.4	$620.8	$614.8	$528.3	$438.8	$439.2	$445.3	$425.8	$412.1	$411.9	$410.3	$5,985.0
Net income	($286.1)	($225.6)	($149.0)	($30.5)	$105.0	$115.7	$217.7	$327.4	$322.2	$267.8	$245.3	$195.4	$1,105.1

Source: Company documents. (Data disguised.)

EXHIBIT 12 Proposed Financing Structure

December 15, 2000

OFFERING OF HONEST TEA SHARES

Honest Tea is offering a total of 54 share-and-warrants packages, valued at $37,000 each, at a pre-money valuation of $13,113,000, and a $15,111,000 post-money valuation. The offering therefore represents 2/15, or 13.3% of the company. The shares will be issued on a first-come-first-served basis. In the event the offering is oversubscribed, Honest Tea reserves the right to expand the offering by 10%, or five additional shares.

We have designed a share-plus-warrant package that seeks to protect shareholders against future dilution by offering two half warrants with the shares being offered

Each share-and-warrant package being offered consists of the following:

1.00 share
0.50 warrants at 50k exercise
0.50 warrants at 75k exercise

In any liquidity event, all in-the-money warrants can be called and converted into stock and all out-of-the-money warrants expire worthless. This holds true for all warrants in the company.

EXHIBIT 12 *(continued)*

PRE-FUNDRAISING	Shares	Warrants	Warrants	Warrants	Warrants	Warrants	Warrants
		$5,000	$10,000	$15,000	$25,000	$50,000	$75,000
Founders	80		80	80	80	56	63
Employees/consultants	4	4	3	1	7	1	1
Seed investors	45					22	
First Round investors	48					24	
Second Round investors	38					18.5	18.5
TOTAL	215	4	83	81	87	121.5	82.5

POST-FUNDRAISING	Shares	Warrants	Warrants	Warrants	Warrants	Warrants	Warrants
		$5,000	$10,000	$15,000	$25,000	$50,000	$75,000
Founders	80		80	80	80	56	63
Employees/consultants	4	4	3	1	7	1	1
Seed investors	45					22	
First Round investors	48					24	
Second Round investors	38					18.5	18.5
Third Round investors	**54**					**27**	**27**
TOTAL	**269**	4	83	81	87	**148.5**	**109.5**

The numbers in bold indicate changes to the equity structure

EXHIBIT 12 *(continued)*

December 15, 2000

Performance Guarantee for offering of shares

We have set aggressive sales targets for 2001 and beyond. We are confident we can meet these sales goals; if not, we are prepared to stand by these targets and a post-money valuation of $15,111,000 with a performance guarantee based on 2001 calendar-year sales. The valuation to the investors participating in this round is based on the following formula:

2x tea bottle sales

7x bag sales

$750,000 value of the bottling plant

Two Scenarios:
To see how this works, we provide two scenarios:

1. If bottled sales are $8 million and tea bag sales are $400,000, the company would have the following valuation:

   (2*$8,000,000) + (7*$400,000) + $750,000 = $19,500,000

   Since the resulting valuation exceeds $15.1 million, no adjustment to valuation would be made.

2. If bottled sales are $4 million and tea bag sales are $200,000, the company would have the following valuation:

   (2*$400,000) + (7*200,000) + $750,000 = $10,150,000

   Since the resulting valuation is less than $15.1 million, investors would be issued additional shares. Investors in this round would see their share of the company shift from 13.3% to 19.7% (which is $2 million/$10.15 million).

Source: Company documents.

EXHIBIT 13 Investors' Circle Statement of Responsibility

The Board of Investors' Circle has endorsed the following Statement of Responsibility:

We begin the investment management process recognizing that our responsibility as investors does not end with maximizing return and minimizing risk.

We recognize that economic growth can come at considerable cost to community and environment.

We believe that efforts to mitigate environmental degradation and promote social well-being will be successful to the extent that these concerns are brought from the margins to the center of business and investment decision making.

We recognize that addressing such concerns while pursuing financial objectives is an imperfect process. However, we believe that the development of healthier corporate cultures, and through them a healthier, more sustainable economy, depends upon the recognition of these concerns by management, directors, employees, and investors.

Investors' Circle encourages companies to articulate their own statement of principles relating to corporate responsibility and sustainability.

Source: Company documents.

EXHIBIT 14 Investors' Circle Investments

Earth's Best: Organic baby food.

University Access: Internet-based content in broadband content for higher education.

Mosaic Technologies: Minority-owned biotechnology company.

Energia Global: Renewable power and cogeneration, and energy-efficient products and services in Latin America.

Wild Planet Toys: Maker of nonviolent toys.

Sonic Innovations: Developer of hearing instruments.

Biocorp: Manufacturer of fully biodegradable garbage, grocery, and trash bags.

Brush Dance: Distributor of products that inspire and enlighten, featuring the words and images of leading authors, philosophers, and spiritual teachers.

Latina Magazine: Bilingual magazine by and about Hispanic women.

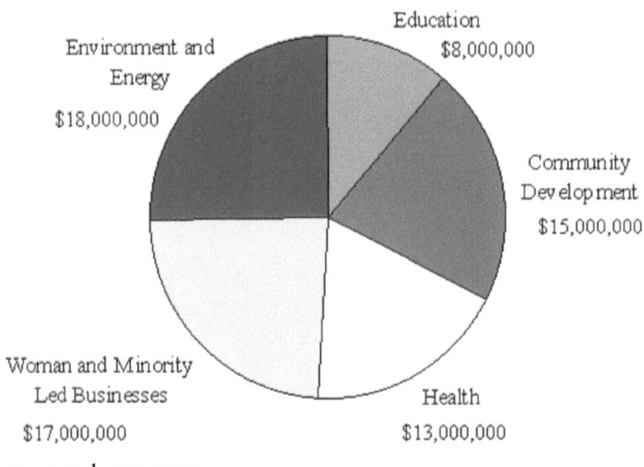

Source: Company documents.

EXHIBIT 15 Comparable Financial Information

TRIARC COS INC	1995	1996	1997	1998	1999
Sales	1184.22	989.25	861.32	815.04	853.97
Net Inc	-36.99	-13.90	-3.62	14.64	10.12
EBITDA	95.19	113.12	105.17	121.35	123.03
Total Assets	1085.97	854.40	1004.87	1019.89	1123.73
Current Assets	412.83	445.66	355.76	409.50	477.64
Current Liabilities	254.56	250.49	225.67	201.14	239.65
Market Value of Equity	329.05	343.67	861.02	465.09	436.88
Total Debt	846.88	594.10	619.01	708.96	893.05
Net Worth	20.65	6.76	43.99	10.91	-166.73
Beta	NA	0.958	0.975	1.138	0.905

SARATOGA BEVERAGE	1995	1996	1997	1998	1999
Sales	3.27	4.38	6.27	8.88	50.74
Net Inc	-0.92	-0.15	0.81	0.87	1.76
EBITDA	-0.72	0.23	1.08	1.53	4.87
Total Assets	2.99	2.63	5.70	7.50	41.35
Current Assets	1.07	1.00	3.80	3.96	13.89
Current Liabilities	0.81	0.61	1.29	1.55	5.40
Market Value of Equity	5.45	2.55	6.31	7.00	26.60
Total Debt	0.15	0.31	1.51	1.57	23.61
Net Worth	2.18	2.01	2.91	4.39	11.99
Beta	NA	NA	0.756	0.886	0.632

NATIONAL BEVERAGE CORP	1995	1996	1997	1998	1999
Sales	350.43	385.43	400.75	402.11	426.27
Net Inc	9.00	10.69	13.10	13.17	13.58
EBITDA	25.50	27.82	30.52	29.52	26.89
Total Assets	177.56	170.90	182.33	180.40	197.75
Current Assets	101.62	96.16	107.34	104.14	113.67
Current Liabilities	58.04	48.54	56.94	46.64	58.77
Market Value of Equity	87.29	184.60	189.56	164.36	151.10
Total Debt	63.50	55.75	41.99	40.27	33.93
Net Worth	47.05	56.70	69.98	82.00	93.69
Beta	0.856	0.831	0.753	1.035	0.887

(*continued*)

EXHIBIT 15 *(continued)*

CLEARLY CANADIAN BEVERAGE, INC	1995	1996	1997	1998	1999
Sales	48.20	50.08	47.27	39.93	36.60
Net Inc	-3.97	0.45	-12.27	0.31	-9.94
EBITDA	-2.00	1.00	-0.88	2.46	-2.99
Total Assets	36.50	52.10	46.66	42.83	33.85
Current Assets	22.71	27.50	18.81	15.73	10.10
Current Liabilities	5.89	7.44	7.05	5.59	5.57
Market Value of Equity	15.11	41.69	31.09	13.64	6.17
Total Debt	2.46	4.10	7.08	6.03	5.69
Net Worth	28.46	43.37	34.68	32.89	23.68
Beta	NA	0.660	0.804	1.076	1.051

Source: Compiled from Compustat.

CHAPTER 4.3

Tutor Time (B)

Paul A. Gompers and Catherine Conneely

Richard Weissman sat in his office at Tutor Time Learning Systems, Inc., a daycare provider based in Boca Raton, Florida. Through the window, the palm trees gently waving in the breeze belied the rush of adrenaline the owner of Tutor Time still felt from reading the day's business news. The headlines of October 14, 1996, announced the acquisition of KinderCare Learning Centers, Inc. (KinderCare) by Kohlberg Kravis Roberts & Co. (KKR), buyout specialists. KinderCare, a giant in the fragmented daycare industry, had been acquired for approximately $600 million. Weissman turned back to John Floegel, Senior Vice President of Corporate Development at Tutor Time. Both men knew that the KinderCare acquisition would focus a lot of attention on the daycare industry. Weissman called the meeting with Floegel and other Tutor Time executives to discuss the company's response to the news of the purchase. A born entrepreneur, Weissman was eager to face the challenges that changing trends would bring to the industry and to Tutor Time.

Set up in 1980 with the first center in Boca Raton, Tutor Time had grown to approximately one-third the size of KinderCare by 1996. Despite several setbacks in the early 1990s, Tutor Time was in a process of rapid expansion. Tutor Time was regarded as one of the industry's most innovative and efficient companies. The main vehicle of growth for Tutor Time had been the franchise market. Franchisees' deposits helped Tutor Time with up-front cash. However, Tutor Time management realized that once-off fees and extended royalty payments from franchisees were not sufficient to finance the development of new centers and product lines. As well as setting up a corporate school (i.e., a Tutor Time wholly-owned center) in each area into which Tutor Time wished to expand, partners for developing sites were sought. The partnership style of ownership provided Tutor Time with initial capital from outside sources and would also produce cash flow once the center was operating.

Tutor Time (B)
by PAUL A. GOMPERS, CATHERINE CONNEELY, case number 9-297-074 Rev. OCTOBER 17, 2001

Weissman knew that with the KinderCare acquisition there would be changes in the daycare industry. Predicting the transformations KKR would make to KinderCare was difficult. No one could tell which way KKR would go with its new acquisition. Notwithstanding the upsurge of interest in the child care industry arising from KKR's newly acquired company, management at Tutor Time was certain that the industry itself had been stagnant for far too long. The future held many changes. Floegel, in charge of Corporate Development at Tutor Time, wondered what was in store for the daycare industry in general and for Tutor Time in particular and the transitions that would have to be made to deal with a revitalized KinderCare. It was his job to set a course for expansion. He also wondered about timing. One thing was certain, however: now was either the best or the worst time in the history of the child-care industry to expand.

IMPLICATIONS OF KKR'S ACQUISITION FOR TUTOR TIME AND THE DAYCARE INDUSTRY

The October 1996 KKR acquisition of KinderCare held a promise of much change in the daycare industry. KKR's involvement brought a stamp of approval to the industry. On the day of the announced acquisition the stock price of KinderCare and other publicly traded daycare companies increased dramatically. The stock of Childtime, the fifth largest daycare provider, increased by 13% over two days following the KKR announcement, while KinderCare stock rose by 23%. The leader in the child care industry, KinderCare had an enrollment of 120,000 children across 38 states and had expanded internationally to the United Kingdom with a total of 1,148 centers.

Ownership of approximately 85% of KinderCare was to be acquired by an entity organized at the direction of KKR. The terms of the deal included the following: Kinder Care would pay $393 million to reacquire stock, warrants, and options; $118 million in debt would be retired; and the acquisition was to be financed by issuing $404 million in new debt and by $148.75 million in equity invested by KKR. The total value of the transaction was $553 million. KinderCare stockholders were to receive $20.25 per share in cash as part of the agreement. In a separate deal in November 1996, KinderCare also increased its revolving credit facility to $200 million from $150 million.

The acquisition of KinderCare had implications for the industry and for Tutor Time as well. It was possible that Tutor Time would be viewed as an acquisition target by buyout companies eager to include profitable firms in their portfolios. The larger national child care chains would also be on the lookout for possible acquisitions to increase their market share and enable them to compete with KinderCare. KKR's management of KinderCare would also have implications for Tutor Time. If KKR decided to squeeze the company for profit, then Tutor Time and other child care providers would benefit. But if KKR decided to expand KinderCare nationally, any expansion plans by Tutor Time would be made all the more difficult. How would Tutor Time grow in the light of the acquisition? Should the company try to grow using the same method? Company management had seen Children's Discovery Centers of California try to expand by taking over smaller, independent daycare providers. The strategy was not appealing to Tutor Time. The success the company had so far was in developing and building centers from the ground up. The company knew that expansion by building more centers was expensive to finance. Management wondered if there were other feasible alternatives.

THE CHILD CARE INDUSTRY IN 1996

In 1996, the child care industry in the United States was large and highly fragmented. The estimates of the size of the industry varied from $14 billion to $40 billion. The 10 largest providers combined represented less than 7% of the market. (See **Exhibits 1** and **2** for Tutor Time competitors.) Small local providers tended to dominate the business. However, as the larger national chains began to consolidate, smaller providers found it difficult to compete against the economies of scale and greater financial and managerial resources of the nationwide chains.

Despite the intense competition between the possible substitute forms of child care, such as bringing the children to relatives, having a private sitter come to the house, or bringing the children to a daycare center, the demographic trends were favorable in the short term for the industry as a whole. (See **Exhibit 3**.) The number of children in the under-five age group had grown to 19.7 million in 1994, from 15.6 million in 1977, a 1.4% average annual increase. But growth in the under-five age group was expected to slow down over the next 15 years. Other favorable demographic trends included the higher percentage of mothers in the workforce. The U.S. Bureau of Labor Statistics estimated that the percentage of married women with children under the age of six participating in the labor force totaled 45% in 1980 and had increased to 60% in 1993. The U.S. economy continued to improve in 1996. Single parents and the nonworking spouse in two-parent families joined the workforce in increasing numbers. The outlook for the child care industry looked good in the short term.

Financially, the child care industry had been underrated. There were many negative perceptions about the industry which were unwarranted for the majority of daycare providers. The involvement of KKR brought an aura of respectability to the industry. Other financial companies would be eager to follow KKR's lead in buying out or acquiring daycare providers. In an industry overripe for consolidation, the opportunities were many.

TUTOR TIME IN 1996

Tutor Time was eager to grow. With over 90 sites open in 1996, not only did management wish to expand geographically, but it sought to develop new products and new structures in which to expand. (See **Exhibit 4** for locations.) Tutor Time's analysis indicated that it should consider developing a new identity as an educator rather than a mere daycare provider.

Tutor Time cherished its reputation for innovation. Licensing the Brigham Young University education format and inclusion of a full-time director of education programs led to new ideas and a constantly evolving learning environment. A testament to their success was the numerous awards that Tutor Time had received. Tutor Time attributed part of its success to tighter management of student-to-teacher ratios than other daycare providers and bigger schools—the typical school size was 10,000 square feet—which allowed the Tutor Time centers to serve more students. But given increasing competition in the industry, Tutor Time knew that it would have to carefully manage other factors in order to remain successful in the future. Geographically, Tutor Time began to choose site locations with greater care. The company examined the demographics of the area for a potential site, the average income of the area, and the number of children under five in the area. Competition studies and the typical rent payments in the area were other factors influencing the decision to acquire a site. Tutor Time would then systematically model whether the proposed expansion made sense.

Tutor Time management knew that the company would need to expand in order to survive among the large publicly traded national chains. Several expansion structure options were available to Tutor Time. Management strategy was to set up a corporate school in an area, and then sell franchise units in the surrounding area. It would also be possible for Tutor Time to grow by acquiring existing daycare centers. Independent operators were finding it hard to compete with the larger companies and to adhere to the strict regulations set by state accreditation agencies. Tutor Time management was not sure if it would take that route, however.

Management wondered how Tutor Time would expand. The typical franchisee paid an up-front fee of $42,000 and a $125,000 site development fee. The associated expense with site development, in an ideal construction scenario, was minimal. Once established, a 5 to 6% royalty fee was paid to Tutor Time out of the franchisee's revenues before profits. A company-owned corporate school provided no up-front fees, and the initial capital financing for construction and start-up of the center had to be found within the company. But Tutor Time was assured of all profits of such wholly owned sites. (See **Exhibits 5–7** for financial statements.)

Beginning in 1996, Tutor Time developed a partnership arrangement, whereby the equity split was 49% to an outside partner and Tutor Time retained a majority holding in the center. The partnership fee was up to $110,000. In forthcoming partnership agreements, Tutor Time attempted to retain a 70% holding in each center in exchange for an up-front partnership fee of about $75,000. Management wanted to develop the optimal mix between the franchisee-owned, partnership sites, and corporate schools to ensure maximum revenues and profits to internally finance company expansion. While the correct mix between the different center structures would be difficult to achieve in the short term, the long-term mix of franchisee-owned sites, partnership-owned centers, and corporate schools would allow the company sufficient cash flow for internal financing of the expansion without having to raise additional outside equity for Tutor Time.

The 1996–1997 estimates for Tutor Time were that about 20,000 children would be served in 97 open sites. Eighty-nine sites would be under construction in 28 states. By the end of 1996, there were approximately 25 corporate schools, 20 partnership schools, and 30 franchise sites in various stages of the design process. Seventy-five sites were planned for construction in 1997 and 110 sites in 1998. (See **Exhibit 8** for 1997–1998 projections.) The primary areas of expansion in the United States were Arizona, Southern California, Colorado, New Jersey, and Florida. These areas had the best demographic characteristics for Tutor Time's expansion. Tutor Time had not intended to expand internationally, but in 1995, the company was approached by a franchisee interested in setting up a center in Jakarta, which proved to be very profitable.

NEW PRODUCTS AT TUTOR TIME

In an effort to more fully utilize the large investment in fixed assets (primarily the centers themselves), Tutor Time continually developed new products. There were several different programs which franchisees could run in the afternoon and on weekends. Tumbling Tots™ was a program designed to offer activities in a fitness-through-play curriculum. The Honors™ was an add-on to after-school activities offering reading and math enhancement in a regimented, proven tutoring system. Insta-Sitta™ was a drop-off babysitting service for children ages two to twelve—parents were issued beepers in case of emergencies. Tutor Time also offered a Summer Program with a more camplike atmosphere than the typical school year curriculum. Franchisees paid additional fees to avail themselves of after-hours programs. Management felt, however, that although the extra programs were successful, the burden on the center's director did not balance the extra revenues. Franchisee-owners needed to take a break from running the centers.

Management was experimenting with add-ons at different locations. Some sites were exploring video vending machines from which parents could rent children's movies and programs on video; others considered having roasted chicken available so parents could pick up their children and have a hot dinner at the same time. The company was eager to further develop curriculum and technology at the centers. Tutor Time considered new programs or revisions to their curriculum as R&D. Tutor Time had been progressive in offering computer labs in the centers in the late 1980s and early 1990s, but more and more daycare centers were beginning to offer computers. Many other child care providers had variations on Tutor Towne™—a specially constructed village that allowed children to use role-play and develop skills in a microcosm of the real world. The company was looking to expand the services it could offer children and parents and was examining tele- and video-conferencing facilities installed in the centers for parents and children.

The company was very aware of security at each center and had developed policies early on which were becoming standard in the industry. All employees had to be carefully screened before they could work at any Tutor Time center, and the physical plant of each center was designed for security with motion detectors, video monitoring cameras in classrooms, and a special lock at the entrance. Tutor Time also used Safe N Sound™, an electronic automated security and business management system created for the child care industry. A magnetic card was issued to all parents, which enabled a computer to monitor the coming and going of students. With other daycare providers catching up to Tutor Time's technological level, the firm was considering outsourcing its technical needs in order to develop a more sophisticated security and technology package. Management began to experiment with hand-print security features at some centers.

In expanding its role as an educator, Tutor Time became involved in a plan to open a private school in September 1997 in Boca Raton, to be known as the Boca Raton Preparatory. Management felt that the timing might not be wholly appropriate for Tutor Time, but it had to take the opportunity presented to it. The U.S. Olympic diving team's practice complex in an upscale neighborhood of Boca Raton was for sale. Tutor Time knew that other child care providers (e.g., Childtime) were also looking to develop their involvement in higher levels of education. The site was in almost perfect condition for a school, consisting of swimming pools, dormitories, and three levels of suitably sized rooms for classes, and would need minimum construction to adapt it to a school format. In order to finance the purchase of the property, Tutor Time negotiated the sale. The financing was off-balance sheet, and Tutor Time had a controlling interest in the school. Situated across the road from a prominent year-round tennis camp, Tutor Time hoped to serve between 80 and 100 students from the tennis center and local area within the first two years of operation in grades K-12. Management thought that if the school was successful, Tutor Time could tap a new growth opportunity. As more states and communities debated charter schools and school vouchers, Tutor Time might be able to expand rapidly.

FINANCING TUTOR TIME'S EXPANSION

An important aspect of Tutor Time's expansion was the company's ability to finance growth. Management believed that the company would continue its planned expansion to 1998–1999 with current funding. Tutor Time had been moving from the traditional in-line sites (i.e., sites located in outdoor malls or office buildings) to free-standing sites. While it took the former 7.9 months from the opening of a school to reach 70% capacity, the latter only took 5.9 months to reach the same point in revenues. The hard costs of starting up each center included $40,000 working capital and training costs of up to $75,000 for the director. This $75,000 included training expenses and salary during the training phase. During site build-out, Tutor Time arranged for landlords to pay for the construction of the center. Approximately $10,000 in fees were spent by Tutor Time in the selections and negotiation of a lease for a site. Lease payments only began when the center opened. These expenses were incurred over six to nine months and were offset by any up-front fees. Tutor Time distinguished itself in the level of support and education that it provided to its franchisees. Similar to the different revenue flows from franchisee, partnership, or wholly owned centers, the financing needs of each ownership style also differed. Tutor Time was careful to ensure that even the franchisee sites had enough funds to reach a profit-making point.

Many exit opportunities had been presented to the company since 1994 when Floegel became Senior Vice President. Two potential buyers had approached Tutor Time. Neither company would set a value for the firm hoping that the owners would reveal a price. There were, however, no results from the negotiations. In 1995 Tutor Time had considered merging with a publicly traded clothing manufacturer. Again the negotiations were not completed. The company had plans to go public itself at the beginning of 1996, but a major investor and board member suggested that Tutor Time should finish constructing planned sites and build its position before issuing stock. Management was understandably reluctant to give up control of the company it had built from scratch. A true entrepreneur, the founder had pulled the company through some tough times, without having to resort to venture capital firms or other forms of outside financing.

TUTOR TIME — PAST PROBLEMS

Tutor Time offered potential franchisees a number of competitive advantages over other methods of setting up a business in the daycare industry. The Tutor Time methodology was tried and tested, and new center directors were trained in the Tutor Time methods of running a child care center. The company helped with site selection and negotiating lease and construction of the center once a site had been chosen. A unique curriculum and state of the art security features made Tutor Time stand out among other daycare centers.

The company's reliance on franchise fees to develop sites, however, meant that a backlog of franchisees who had paid their fees and were waiting for sites had increased considerably by 1992. Construction overruns caused delays in setting up sites. The landlord financed the build-out of the sites. Due to stringent regulations applied to daycare centers and Tutor Time's own unique layout plans, many of the sites ran over the negotiated budgets. Between 1993 and 1994, Tutor Time had a substantial fraction of its capital tied up in site build-outs because it chose to bear any cost overruns. All new site build-outs eliminated this overrun exposure for Tutor Time.

Although his primary focus was on transactions and acquisitions, Floegel played an important role in resolving the problems that plagued Tutor Time in the early 1990s. By 1996, many of the issues had been dealt with satisfactorily. Some of the lasting effects of an unreliable partnership were beginning to die out. Tutor Time had lost opportunities to expand in different directions because of the association with an unstable partner. Notably, the establishment of a production company to make children's programs based on the Tutor Time "Pookie the Panda" character had been shelved. Trying to clean up the problems was one of the biggest cash drains the company faced. Pending litigation had implications for finding outside funds, as companies were understandably wary of financing a company with legal problems. By October 1996, however, Tutor Time was again sailing. Management and Floegel had cleared up legal matters and were focusing on expansion. The issue now was "How quickly could Tutor Time grow?"

"CLOUDS ON THE HORIZON"

The involvement of a buyout firm in the child care industry was not the only foreseeable difficulty in Tutor Time's future. Externally, the Americans with Disabilities Act (ADA) had been used in 1996 against KinderCare to allow a child with diabetes to attend a daycare center in Ohio. Susan Rosario, the head of Tutor Time's development department, changed prototypes and specifications to comply with the ADA.

Proposed welfare reform would also pose potential problems for some daycare providers with a sudden influx of children from low-income families. Some form of federal funding or voucher program would be needed to subsidize the cost of daycare. Some providers might have to raise fees. Because the Tutor Time market was a parent with a typical income of $40,000 to $60,000, however, this was not seen as a big problem for existing Tutor Time centers. Under new legislation, signed by President Clinton in August 1996, additional funding for child care would be available for low-income families as part of welfare reform. It was impossible to tell how much of the funding would be available to the nationwide daycare chains. The company's management felt that Tutor Time should learn how to fill the gap in providing daycare facilities for different income groups.

Internally, Tutor Time needed to examine the management structure at corporate headquarters. Recruiting for management positions had not yet been a problem, but with the proposed rate of expansion, the growing company would soon need to add to the management team. Tutor Time also needed to implement a centralized information technology at the management level. Tutor Time also found it difficult to protect in-house innovations from being adapted and used by other child care companies. Many of the features that had initially brought competitive advantages to the Tutor Time sites gradually became standard for all daycare centers. Tutor Time was continually innovating and creating new features to offer clients.

Another challenge was finding suitable directors for each daycare center. The mandatory training Tutor Time provided for each field director a cost of $75,000 before a center would even open. The stressful nature of the occupation, dealing with the industrywide high employee turnover, children ranging in ages from six months to six years, and parents with changing schedules, made it difficult to attract suitable candidates for the positions. The center director was critical to the success of a unit, combining the skill sets of a caregiver and a businessperson. Labor costs were typically a large percentage of any daycare center's costs. At Tutor Time, however, labor costs constituted a much lower percentage of revenues than industry comparables. During 1996, the U.S. Congress enacted an increase in the minimum hourly wage from $4.25 to $4.75 effective October 1, 1996, with an additional increase to $5.15 to be effective on September 1,

1997. Tutor Time had foreseen the increases in minimum wage and already paid employees above-industry averages to reduce turnover at the centers.

In 1996, all child care providers had to be accredited by the state in order to operate. Strict regulations laid down by each state ensured that parents would be sending their children to safe, clean premises. Most day-care providers considered that state accreditation was adequate testimonial for their centers. But a trend developed among some child care chains and individual centers to gain accreditation from different private organizations such as NACE, the National Association for the Education of Young Children, and the National Corporate Childcare Association. While none of the Tutor Time centers was accredited by any private associations, Tutor Time had begun negotiations with NACE in 1996. The sticking point of the negotiations was the unique curriculum and school layout that Tutor Time had developed and that were integral parts of the Tutor Time system. Tutor Time management considered that the company's centers were superior to many of the other daycare providers despite that lack of accreditation from the private organizations. Having their approval, however, could only work in positive ways for the company.

CONCLUSION

All in all, Tutor Time looked to be in a solid position. Potentially, the sky was the limit for the company's expansion. "You have to think that the industry will consolidate," said a company executive. It was difficult, however, to predict the time frame in which industry consolidation would take place. But over the next 10 years or so, Tutor Time would be able to take advantage of the changes in the fragmented child care industry. With the right mix of corporate schools, franchisee-owned sites, and partnership run centers, Tutor Time would be financially self-sufficient. There would be no urgency to bring the company public. The big decision for Weissman, Floegel, and Tutor Time at the end of 1996 was, how should the company grow and expand?

EXHIBIT 1 Top 10 U.S. Child Care Providers

Company	Total Licensed Capacity[a] (# of children)	Total Number of Centers[a]
KinderCare Learning Centers	140,956	1,147
La Petite Academy	95,000	750
Children's World Learning Centers	62,500	500
Children's Discovery Centers	23,600	239
Childtime Learning Centers	18,285	163
Nobel Education Dynamics Inc	15,000	101
Tutor Time Child Care Learning Centers	13,800	92
Bright Horizons Children's Centers	11,400	118
Corporate Family Solutions	10,132	75
Kids 'R Kids International	9,250	37
Top 10 Providers	399,923	3,222
Top 10 as % of Total Market	6.9	4.0
Total "Paid" Market	5,811,000[b]	80,000[c]

Source: William Blair & Co., Childtime Learning Centers Inc., Company Report, June 20. 1996.

[a] Figures as of January 1, 1996. Source: Child Care Information Exchange Magazine, March/April 1996. Based solely on information supplied by organizations.

[b] Total number of children in paid arrangements. Figure as of 1993. Source: Current Population Reports, U.S. Census Bureau, 1995

[c] Total number of centers. Excludes family day care and in-home paid arrangements. Figure as of 1990. Source: Kisker et al., Mathematical Policy Research, Inc., 1991.

EXHIBIT 2 Financial Data of Publicly Traded Child-Care Companies, Years Ending 1993–1995

	KinderCare Learning Centers, Inc.[a]			Children's Discovery Centers			Childtime Learning Centers, Inc.[b]			Nobel Education Dynamics, Inc.		
	1993	1994	1995	1993	1994	1995	1993	1994	1995	1993	1994	1995
Sales-Net ($millions)	437.20	488.73	506.51	38.56	55.32	77.63	N/A	55.34	65.62	32.59	34.37	44.15
EBIT ($millions)	27.76	50.34	53.42	1.98	4.70	5.42	N/A	5.13	5.48	3.54	3.21	4.48
Net Income (Loss) ($millions)	(10.72)	17.43	22.07	1.11	2.76	2.64	N/A	1.85	2.41	1.71	2.34	3.84
Debt—Total ($millions)	43.64	178.69	160.39	8.21	15.43	19.96	N/A	19.42	1.24	13.94	10.04	22.02
Price/ Earnings	(3.571)	12.887	12.383	25.714	19.956	13.487	N/A	N/A	15.208	8.750	8.654	24.638
Beta	0.641	0.800	0.686	0.617	0.490	0.736	N/A	N/A	N/A	N/A	N/A	0.858

Source: Standard & Poor's Compustat PC Plus CD-Rom, 1996.

[a] KinderCare changed fiscal year end in 1993 from December to May.

[b] Childtime went public in 1994.

EXHIBIT 3 Percentage Change in Population of Children under Six

Time Period	Percentage Change in Population	
	3-5 years old	Under 6 years old
1983–1988	6.2	4.7
1988–1993	7.7	7.6
1993–1998	4.8	0.1
1998–2003	-2.9	-2.1

Source: U.S. Department of Labor, Monthly Labor Review, August 1995.

EXHIBIT 4 Tutor Time ChildCare Center Locations as of November 25, 1996

ALABAMA
Vestavia Hills, AL

ARIZONA
Tempe, AZ
*Chandler, AZ (2)
*Glendale, AZ
*Mesa, AZ (2)
*Phoenix, AZ (4)
*Tempe, AZ

CALIFORNIA
Agoura Hills, CA
Escondido, CA
Fair Oaks, CA
Fontana, CA
Highland, CA
Irvine, CA
Morena Valley, CA
***Rancho Cucamongo, CA**
***San Ramon, CA**
*Santee, CA
*Ventura, CA
*Yorba Linda, CA

COLORADO
Aurora, CO
Colorado Springs, CO
Denver, CO
Littletown, CO
*Aurora, CO
*Highland Ranch, CO
*Lakewood, CO
*Littleton, CO (2)
*Smokey Hill, CO
*Tower, CO

DELAWARE
Bear, CT
***Newark, DE**

FLORIDA
Atlamonte Springs, FL
Boca Raton, FL (2)
Bradenton, FL
Casselberry, FL
Deerfield Beach, FL
Ft. Lauderdale, FL
Jacksonville, FL
Kennedy Space Center, FL
Marketplace, FL
Melbourne, FL
Miami Lakes, FL
Miami, FL
Ocala, FL
Ocoee, FL
Plantation, FL
***Port St. Lucie, FL**
*Sarasota, FL
*Tampa, FL

GEORGIA
Lithia Springs, GA
Marietta, GA
Norcross, GA
***Asworth, GA**
*Marietta, GA
*Norcross, GA
*Smyrna, GA

ILLINOIS
Lombard, IL
Westmont, IL

MASSSACHUSETTS
Pittsfield, MA

MICHIGAN
*Auburn Hills, MI
*Ann Arbor, MI
*Canton, MI
*West Bloomfield, MI

MINNESOTA
Apple Valley, MN
*Andover, MN
*White Bear Lake, MN

MISSOURI
Independence, MO
*St. Johns, MO
***Egg Harbor, NJ**
***Hamilton, NJ**
***Holmdel, NJ**
*Hopewell, NJ
*Kingston, NJ
*McKee City, NJ
*Nutley, NJ
*Old Bridge, NJ
*Parsippany, NJ
*Princeton, NJ

NEW YORK
Armonk, NY
Clay, NY
Clifton Park, NY
Deer Park. NY
East Northport, NY
Holbrook, NY
***N. Amityville, NY**
***Nanuet, NY**
***Oakdale, NY**
*Peekskill, NY
*Rochester, NY
*Smithtown, NY (2)
*Staten Island, NY
*Vestal, NY

NORTH CAROLINA
Cary, NC
Durham, NC
*Mathews, NC
*Charlotte, NC (2)

OHIO
Loveland, OH
*Hubor Heights, OH
***Reading, PA**
*Warrington, PA

TEXAS
Arlington, TX
Carrolton, TX
Cole Fitzhugh, TX
Dallas, TX (2)
Desoto, TX
Houston, TX
Garland, TX
Lake Worth, TX
North Richland Hills, TX
Richardson, TX (3)
San Antonio, TX (2)
*Fort Worth, TX (2)
*San Antonio, TX (1)

Laguna Niguel, CA	*Westminister, CO	Oldsmar, FL	*Hanover Park, IL	**MONTANA**	Islandia, NY	*Cincinnati, OH	**VIRGINIA**
Montebello, CA		Parkland, FL	*Lisle, IL	*Bozeman, MT	Middletown, NY	*Sylvania, OH	*Richmond, VA
Newport Beach, CA	**CONNECTICUT**	Pembroke Pines, FL	*St. Charles, IL		Mineola, NY		
Oceanside, CA	Brookfield, CT	Sunrise, FL		**NEVADA**	Pleasantville, NY	**OREGON**	**WASHINGTON**
San Juan Capistrano, CA	Monroe, CT	Tampa, FL	**INDIANA**	*Las Vegas, NV	Syosset, NY	*Beaverton, OR	Olympic, WA
Santa Clarita, CA	Greenwich, CT	Temple Terrace, FL	Evansville, IN		*Bay Ridge, NY		Kirkland, WA
Thousand Oaks, CA	*Branford, CT	Titusville, FL	Ft. Wayne, IN	**NEW JERSEY**	*Carle Place, NY	**PENNSYLVANIA**	Lacey, WA
West Lancaster, CA	*New London, CT	Wingate, FL	South Bend, IN	Lindenwold, NJ	*Fairport, NY	Allentown, PA	*Richland, WA
*Ceres, CA	*Milford, CT	*Davie, FL	*Schererbille, IN	Succasunna, NJ	*Glen Cove, NY	Erie, PA	*Mt. Vernon, WA
*Glendora, CA	*Newington, CT	*Jupiter, FL		Voorhees, NJ	*Hauppauge, NY	Langhorne, PA	
*Lakewood, CA	*Norwalk, CT	*Melbourne, FL	**KANSAS**	Edison, NJ	*Lebittown, NY	*Exton, PA	**INTERNATIONAL**
*Missiona Viejo, CA	*Woodbridge, CT	*Naple, FL	Shawnee, KS (2)	Runnemede, NJ	*Medford, NY	*Middletown, PA	Jakarta, Indonesia

*Opening Soon—Opening Soon Locations may be modified due to zoning or other contingencies.

EXHIBIT 5 Income Statement for Tutor Time for 1995–1996

	September 30, 1996	September 30, 1995
Revenues:		
Franchise fees	$441,500	$486,100
Site development fees	1,144,388	1,355,640
Other franchise fees	1,264,514	574,748
Real estate commissions	1,240,883	908,404
Royalties	1,033,681	675,905
Architectural fees	471,340	277,681
Other	863,592	521,370
Total Revenue	$6,459,898	$4,799,848
Operating Expenses:		
General and administrative expenses	$2,923,776	$2,193,707
Salaries and benefits	2,458,147	1,618,239
Construction costs	218,607	279,018
Total operating expenses	$5,600,530	$4,090,964
Income from operations	859,368	708,884
Interest expense	266,011	152,197
Income before taxes	$593,357	$556,687
Provision for income taxes	222,509	
Net income	$370,848	$556,687

Source: Company documents.

EXHIBIT 6 Balance Sheet of Tutor Time for 1995–1996

	September 30, 1996	December 31, 1995
Assets		
Current Assets:		
Cash	$1,151,270	$173,627
Accounts receivable, net	7,688,284	4,277,736
Current portion of notes receivable	161,357	280,376
Due from affiliate		95,515
Subscriptions receivable	1,980,769	
Prepaid expenses and other current assets	40,832	211,729
Deferred tax asset	46,000	46,000
Total current assets	$11,068,512	$5,084,983
Property and equipment, net	$107,533	$68,004
Notes and other receivables, net	2,044,699	1,709,535
Due from officers	136,832	139,783
Other assets	1,814,723	835,764
Total assets	$15,172,299	$7,838,069
Liabilities and Stockholders' deficit		
Current liabilities:		
Accounts payable	$2,681,889	$3,262,351
Accrued expenses	881,422	982,259
Income taxes payable	451,509	229,000
Current portion of long-term debt	1,052,167	1,279,973
Deferred fees	4,993,520	4,267,900
Other current liabilities	2,176	49,088
Total current liabilities	$10,062,683	$10,070,571
Deferred fees	$3,662,374	$2,970,450
Long-term debt	1,354,435	835,396
Stockholders' deficit:		
Preferred stock	5,760,307	
Common stock	39,469	39,469
Additional paid-in capital	1,310,931	1,310,931
Accumulated deficit	(7,017,900)	(7,388,748)
Total stockholders' equity	$92,807	($6,038,348)
Total liabilities and stockholders' equity	$15,172,299	$7,838,069

Source: Company documents.

EXHIBIT 7 Statement of Cash Flows for Tutor Time for Nine Months Ended September 30, 1996

Cash flows from operating activities:	
Net income	$370,848
Adjustments to reconcile net income to net cash used in operating activities:	
Depreciation and amortization	103,186
Bad debt expense	200,840
Changes in assets and liabilities:	
Accounts, notes and other receivables	(3,827,533)
Due from officers and affiliate	98,466
Other assets	(350,204)
Prepaid expenses and other current assets	170,897
Accounts payable and accrued expenses	(681,299)
Deferred fees	1,417,544
Income taxes payable	222,509
Other current liabilities	(46,912)
Net cash used in operating activities	($2,321,658)
Cash flows from investing activities:	
Purchase of property and equipment	($63,426)
Purchase of territorial rights	(675,595)
Net cash used in investing activities	($739,021)
Cash flows from financing activities:	
Borrowings under long-term debt	$1,005,624
Repayments of long-term debt	(746,840)
Issuance of preferred stock	3,779,538
Net cash provided by financing activities	$4,038,322
Net increase in cash	$977,643
Cash, beginning of year	173,627
Cash, end of period	$1,151,270
Supplemental disclosure of cash flow information:	
Cash paid for interest	$266,011
Cash paid for taxes	$0

Source: Company documents.

EXHIBIT 8 Projections for Tutor Time for 1997–1998

	1997	1998
Royalty Income	$2,332,500	$3,104,375
Franchise fees	1,328,000	1,660,000
Site development	2,120,000	2,650,000
Real estate commissions	1,296,000	1,728,000
Architectural fees	600,000	800,000
Risk fees	0	425,000
Other	0	
Construction receipts		
School tuition:		
Partnership schools opened–96	1,060,000	1,685,000
Partnership schools opened–97	1,520,000	5,910,000
Partnership schools opened–98		3,420,000
Corporate schools–96	1,130,000	1,770,000
Corporate schools–97	2,280,000	3,940,000
Corporate schools–98		2,280,000
Total revenue	$13,666,500	$29,372,375
Operating expenses	12,084,800	24,720,900
Earnings before interest and taxes	$1,581,700	
Interest expense:	(100,000)	
Interest income ($2,000,000*5%)	100,000	
Earnings before taxes	$1,581,700	$4,651,475
Provision for taxes (37%)	585,229	1,721,046
Net income	$996,471	$2,930,429
Number of shares used to calculate EPS		6,867,911

Source: Company documents.

EXHIBIT 9 Economic Indicators

	Real GDP Bn 1992 $	Inflation	Unemployment (%)	T-Bill 1 month	Treasury Bond 5-Year Note	Treasury Bond 10-Year Note	S&P 500 Index	Hambrecht & Quist Growth Index
Q1Y93	6327.9	2.867	7.0	2.760	5.240	6.030	451.67	1057.61
Q2Y93	6359.9	2.703	7.0	2.820	5.050	5.800	450.53	1184.03
Q3Y93	6393.5	2.327	6.7	2.750	4.790	5.400	458.93	1256.01
Q4Y93	6476.9	2.521	6.5	2.800	5.210	5.830	466.45	1285.02
Q1Y94	6524.5	2.224	6.5	3.350	6.230	6.770	445.77	1216.75
Q2Y94	6600.3	2.351	6.1	3.500	6.970	7.340	444.27	1033.96
Q3Y94	6629.5	2.539	5.9	4.430	7.280	7.620	462.69	1241.49
Q4Y94	6688.6	2.664	5.4	3.660	7.830	7.840	459.27	1337.31
Q1Y95	6703.7	2.716	5.4	5.700	7.080	7.200	500.71	1498.24
Q2Y95	6708.8	2.694	5.6	5.240	5.980	6.210	544.75	1686.6
Q3Y95	6759.2	2.406	5.7	5.280	6.010	6.170	584.41	2112.13
Q4Y95	6796.5	2.324	5.6	3.480	5.380	5.580	615.93	2134.9
Q1Y96	6826.4	2.503	5.5	5.130	6.100	6.340	645.5	2253.43
Q2Y96	6926	2.687	5.3	4.750	6.470	6.730	670.63	2406.72
Q3Y96	6943.8	2.733	5.2	4.930	6.460	6.720	687.31	2538.96

Source: Adapted from Citibase.

EXHIBIT 10 Projections for Model Tutor Time Center

Year 1													
Revenue	1	2	3	4	5	6	7	8	9	10	11	12	Year 1
Total Tuition	$51,708	$56,850	$57,123	$61,452	$63,075	$64,702	$71,203	$73,737	$75,990	$75,990	$76,550	$76,550	$5,96,945
Capacity Utilization	49.8%	*54.7%*	*55.0%*	*59.1%*	60.6%	*62.2%*	*65.9%*	*68.2%*	*70.3%*	*70.3%*	*70.8%*	*70.8%*	47.9%
Operating Costs													
Total Fixed Costs	$27,900	$28,375	$26,651	$29,436	$27,563	$27,470	$27,420	$27,420	$27,420	$27,420	$27,420	$27,420	$2,68,533
Total Variable Costs	$26,028	$27,234	$28,513	$27,943	$26,094	$25,279	$31,482	$28,968	$31,360	$33,450	$30,917	$30,917	$2,69,735
Total Costs	$53,929	$55,610	$55,164	$57,380	$53,657	$52,749	$58,902	$56,389	$58,781	$60,870	$58,337	$58,337	$5,38,269
Profits													
EBIT	-$2,220	$1,240	$1,959	$4,072	$9,418	$11,952	$12,301	$17,348	$17,209	$15,120	$18,213	$18,213	$58,676
Operating Margin	*-4.3%*	*2.2%*	*3.4%*	*6.6%*	*14.9%*	*18.5%*	*17.3%*	*23.5%*	*22.6%*	*19.9%*	*23.8%*	*23.8%*	*9.8%*
Year 2													
Revenue	1	2	3	4	5	6	7	8	9	10	11	12	Year 2
Total Tuition	$80,773	$80,773	$80,773	$88,940	$88,940	$88,940	$88,940	$88,940	$88,940	$88,940	$88,940	$88,940	$10,42,780
Capacity Utilization	*74.7%*	*74.7%*	*74.7%*	*82.3%*	*82.3%*	*82.3%*	*82.3%*	*82.3%*	*82.3%*	*82.3%*	*82.3%*	*82.3%*	80.4%
Operating Costs													
Total Fixed Costs	$27,420	$27,420	$27,420	$27,420	$27,420	$27,420	$27,420	$27,420	$27,420	$27,420	$27,420	$28,321	$3,29,945
Total Variable Costs	$33,450	$30,917	$33,979	$33,232	$30,917	$33,979	$33,232	$33,232	$33,232	$33,232	$33,232	$33,232	$3,95,868
Total Costs	$60,870	$58,337	$61,400	$60,653	$58,337	$61,400	$60,653	$60,653	$60,653	$60,653	$60,653	$61,553	$7,25,812
EBIT	$19,903	$22,436	$19,374	$28,287	$30,603	$27,540	$28,287	$28,287	$28,287	$28,287	$28,287	$27,387	$3,16,968
Operating Margin	*24.6%*	*27.8%*	*24.0%*	*31.8%*	*34.4%*	*31.0%*	*31.8%*	*31.8%*	*31.8%*	*31.8%*	*31.8%*	*30.8%*	*30.4%*

Source: Company documents.

CHAPTER 4.4

A Note on Franchising (Abridged)

Paul A. Gompers

Franchising, according to the U.S. Department of Commerce,[1] is a form of licensing by which the owner (the franchisor) of a product, service, or business method obtains distribution through affiliated dealers (the franchisees). In return for the franchisor's support in starting the business, the franchisee pays the franchisor an initial fee, which may range from $1,000 to $150,000.[2] In addition the franchisee usually pays a certain percentage from his or her gross revenues annually for the continued support of the franchisor and use of brands, trademarks, or business formats. The annual royalty payment can range between 0 and 50%, and the average royalty rate is 7%.[3] Franchising accounts for approximately one-third of total retail sales in North America. **Exhibit 1** shows the total number of franchises in the economy broken down into company- or franchisor-owned and number of outlets held by franchisees for 1969–2007.

HISTORY OF FRANCHISING

Franchising, a term that comes from the French language and means to be free from servitude, developed as a business method in the 1850s in the United States. Some business historians argue that as a method of licensing, franchising developed much earlier in feudal times when the head of the Roman Catholic Church gave his clergy the right to collect tithes or church taxes locally. For this right, the clergy sent a portion of the tithes to Rome.[4] English beer brewers in the eighteenth century also engaged in a form of franchising. Some brewers entered into licensing and financing arrange-ments with tavern owners for exclusive sale of beer and ale brands.

A Note on Franchising (Abridged)
by PAUL A. GOMPERS, case number N9-217-059 FEBRUARY 28, 2017

In the United States, in 1850, Isaac Singer sold licenses to individuals for up to $5,000. These first franchisees established retail outlets for Singer's new invention, the sewing machine, and spread the word of the Singer product line far more quickly than Singer would have been able to if he had sold the machines independently. In 1898, GM established its first independent dealer to sell and service automobiles. In 1899, Coca-Cola sold its first bottling franchise in Chattanooga. Along with the automotive and soft drink industries, the oil industry quickly established itself among the first modern franchisors. Franchising developed in the United States at this time for a variety of reasons; the size of the country meant that there were many logistical problems for producers and manufacturers in distributing goods and establishing national networks. It was also difficult to raise capital for new or expanding businesses. The fees from franchisees helped finance growth.

Two distinct types of franchise systems developed in the United States between the 1850s and 1950s. The first, product franchising, developed in the 1840s when the makers and inventors of new and complex machines used a modification of the agent/licensee system to spread knowledge of their products. The second, business format franchising, first appeared in the 1920s with Howard Johnson's innovation in standardized food preparation techniques. Business format franchising took off in the 1950s as an industry in its own right as fast-food chains such as McDonald's and Kentucky Fried Chicken expanded rapidly throughout the country during the decade. The growth of franchising during the 1950s is attributable to another set of reasons. In the postwar United States the population was growing and increasing mobility meant that it was spreading throughout the country. The country was prosperous, leading to rising disposable incomes and to greater demands for consumer goods and services. The population became familiar with brand names for products and services as technological advances led to television and nationwide advertising and brand recognition.

FRANCHISING FORMATS

Product franchising started in the United States as an independent sales relationship between supplier and dealer. The dealer acquired some of the identity of the supplier as a franchisee concentrating on one company's product line and identifying their business with that company. Examples of product franchises are bottling companies, beer distributorships, petroleum and automotive dealerships, or any single line or primary line brand-name retail outlet. **Exhibit 2** shows the extent of product/trade mark franchising in the economy for 1969–1991.

Business format franchising is the right to license a business or trade style as opposed to selling a particular product. Not only does the franchisee have access to the franchisor's product, but it is also able to utilize the franchisor's business concept, which can include a marketing strategy and plan, operating manuals and standards, quality control, and a continuing process of support and guidance. It has become more difficult to distinguish between product franchising and business format franchising according to Purvin.[5] Most franchisees or dealers of an individual brand look and feel as if they are committed to a common business format. **Exhibit 3** shows the numbers of business format franchise establishments in the economy for 1969–2007E.

Although business format franchises account for approximately 80% of all franchised business in the United States, they only have 31% of the total retail sales from franchising. Product franchisors, on the other hand, represent only 20% of franchising companies in the United States, but account for 69% of retail sales.[6] **Exhibit 4** shows the industry breakdown in business format franchising for 1989–2011E.

In recent years, the concept of multilevel franchising has modified the classical business format model. Multilevel franchising provides the franchisor with more options to grow more quickly and at less cost. The three primary methods employed in multilevel franchising are master (or regional) franchising; subfranchising and area development franchising. A common thread for all three methods is that the franchisor sells development rights in a particular market to one or more franchisees. The differences between the methods involve the depth of the relationship between franchisor, franchisee, and subfranchisees.[7]

The developers in all three models pay an up-front fee to the franchisor who gives them sole responsibility in developing an area.

- The master franchisee must bear the burden of finding individual franchisees for the area. Once the process is complete, the individual franchisees receive ongoing support from the parent franchisor. The master franchisee shares in the fees and royalties of the individual franchisees in that territory.
- The subfranchisor model is similar to the master franchisee; however, the parent franchisor has no involvement with the individual franchisees in the area once the subfranchisor has paid the fee for exclusive development of the area. The individual franchisees are wholly dependent on the subfranchisor for initial training and setup and for ongoing support.
- The area development agreement allows the area developers to either seek independent franchisees or set up individual franchise units of their own. The agreement specifies that a certain number of units must

be developed within a given time period. The area developers do not share in the franchise fees or royalties paid by the individual franchisees not owned by them. The area developers gain only from self-owned franchise units in the area. They profit over time because the up-front fee for the area is usually at a discount to the amount they would have had to pay to develop the self-owned franchise units individually.

REASONS COMPANIES FRANCHISE

The advantages of franchising as opposed to expanding with company-owned outlets are many. The franchisor can establish a presence in the market rapidly and quickly lock in a market position for products or services. Another bonus for the franchisor is the initial fees paid by franchisees to become part of the business. The ongoing royalty payments paid in return for continuous support from the franchisor are also revenue for the franchisor. Franchisees typically need less management and capital than company-owned outlets. Franchisees are working for themselves and are therefore more motivated. They generally set up locally and have knowledge of the area.

The drawbacks of franchising for the franchisor include dealing with complaints from franchisees, failure of the interests of franchisees and the franchisor to coincide (for example, on issues of quality), and a restrictive legal environment. Franchisees need control and monitoring, which is an additional expense for the franchisor. There may be a lack of trust in the relationship between the franchisor and franchisee, particularly if there are communication problems. Given the popularity of franchising, franchisors in some industries might find it difficult to choose a good franchisee from among the many hundreds of applicants.

Those interested in owning a business choose between the alternatives of franchising, in what is generally a proven business system, or setting up an independent business. If the prospective franchisee lacks knowledge or business expertise, then the training provided by the franchisor will help overcome this disadvantage. Franchisees are eager to become business owners, but with the support and assistance from the franchisor. The franchisee also benefits from the brand name, reputation, and image of an experienced franchisor who generally has built up public goodwill. Not only is the capital commitment usually smaller than that needed in setting up independent business, but the franchisor's know-how makes franchising a more efficient use of capital by the franchisee. The franchisee also benefits from the national scale of franchisor's advertising and promotional activities if a larger franchisor is chosen. The franchisee can also avail of the bulk purchasing and negotiating capacity of the franchisor with suppliers. In addition, the franchisee does not have to independently develop new products; any new products, services, or production techniques are usually available to the franchisee from the franchisor's R&D process. As part of a franchising system, the franchisee might have access to information not otherwise available to independent business owners.

The disadvantages of franchising for the franchisee include the imposition of controls on the methods of doing business by the franchisor. Franchise contracts are generally restrictive and might be biased toward the franchisor. The initial fee is usually the first cash outflow for the franchisee and one he or she will not recoup unless the business is successful. In addition, royalty payments must be paid out of gross revenues whether or not the franchisee is breaking even. Sometimes it is difficult for the franchisee to assess a franchisor's quality. The Federal Trade Commission's (FTC) disclosure rule states that the prospective franchisees must be told certain things by the franchisor. However, it is still possible for franchisors to omit material facts that are not covered by the FTC rule.

There is also the possibility that the franchisee might become too dependent on the franchisor through no fault of his or her own. The franchisor can restrict the franchisee from setting up a similar business once the franchise agreement has been terminated. On the other hand, the franchisor might issue policies that affect a franchisee's profitability and the franchisee has no control over the franchisor in this regard. Neither does the franchisee have control over other franchisees who may damage the brand image to his or her detriment.

The most often cited reason for a business organization to embark on licensing its products, services, or business methods to independent operators is availability of capital. However, Rubin[8] in a text on the subject, found that lack of capital was not the most important factor in a company's decision to franchise. He maintains that selling shares in the franchise to franchisees would be less costly. Hence, raising capital by selling franchises would seem to be inefficient. The inefficiency of the capital market is not the main impetus for franchising. Rubin argues that franchising is a response to agency problems.

Factors motivating franchising were found to be monitoring and control within the business organization, risk sharing, and ability of franchisors to exploit economies of scale. Business format franchising is on the rise because of the sharing of financial and managerial risks involved.[9] Lafontaine[10] states that the agency-theoretic explanations for franchising include risk sharing, one-sided moral hazard, and two-sided moral hazard. If the parties to a franchise contract are risk averse, then they both benefit from the "insurance" that arises in the mutually binding agreement.

Moral hazard occurs when one party to a contract tends to alter his or her behavior in such a way that costs to the other party are increased. Moral hazard is one-sided when the franchisor is unable to adequately observe the franchisee's behavior. In this case the contract is a compromise between the need to give the franchisee incentives and the need to provide the franchisee with support. Making the franchisee the residual claimant on the firm's profit provides an incentive to maximize profits. Two-sided moral hazard arises when both parties to the contract need incentives. The franchisee is highly motivated to succeed in the franchisor's system and the franchisor reaps the benefit of franchising the outlet through ongoing royalty payments. The efforts of both the franchisee and franchisor are important to the ultimate success of the business. Franchisees must work hard to maintain quality and service. The franchisor must invest in brand name.

These factors and the franchisor's need for capital explain decisions about the terms of franchise contracts and the setting of royalty rates and up-front franchise fees. These factors may also explain the extent to which companies use franchising. Lafontaine finds that the two-sided moral hazard explanation of franchising is most consistent. This suggests that there are incentive issues on both sides. She also finds that firms use franchising more when they want to grow faster.

Brickley and Dark[11] consider franchising to be a "hybrid" between two methods of controlling agency problems, control devices, such as monitoring, and ownership of residual claims restricted to agents bearing the effects of their actions. They find that opening franchisee-owned outlets instead of company-owned outlets reflects a tradeoff among agency problems. Whereas the agency problem associated with "shirking and perquisite taking by unit managers" is low for franchised outlets and high for company-owned outlets, "inefficient risk-bearing," "free-rider problems," and "quasi-rent appropriation" are considered high-risk agency problems with franchisee-owned outlets and low for company-owned outlets. It is obvious that managers in company-owned outlets would have less incentive to work hard and to ensure that inefficiencies are minimized than the individual owner of a franchised outlet who would bear most if not all, of the consequences of his or her actions. However, the franchisee incurs inefficient risk-bearing by having a substantial proportion of his or her wealth and income tied up in one outlet. The franchisee may be more reluctant to take risks, such as investing in new equipment, and may also expect a higher return from the investment. Both the franchisor and franchisee can be free-riders. The franchisee has the incentive to use low-quality goods when the reputation of the chain is shared with fellow franchisees. The franchisor may also free-ride on the backs of the franchisees by not living up to the franchise agreement by, for example, not protecting the chain's trademark or quality. Quasi-rent is the value of an asset above its salvage value. The franchisee or franchisor may be able to appropriate this value when firm-specific assets exist. An example would be a building specially constructed as part of the franchise agreement. Owned by the franchisee, if the franchise contract ended and was not renewed or the franchisor demanded higher royalty payments, the building would be worth less to the franchisee in an alternative use.

The differences in costs of monitoring store managers and franchisees, as well as the geographic location of the outlet, appear to be important factors in a company's decision to franchise a unit. Outlets close to the franchisor's headquarters are more likely to be company-owned because the costs of monitoring these outlets are less. Brickley and Dark also found that locations where there was a higher frequency of repeat customers were more likely to be franchised than company-owned. For example, a fast food outlet located at a highway rest stop or in a busy area of a city is less likely to have repeat customers. The owner/manager of this unit would have little incentive to keep up the quality of the product or brand name when he or she knew that few customers would come back to the outlet. In this case the company would need to monitor the unit more frequently to ensure that standards were being maintained. Therefore, it is more effective for the company to retain ownership of such a unit. According to Brickley and Dark, factors favoring franchising over owning, when all other factors are held constant, include low investment risk on the part of the franchisee, low incentives for free-riding by both the franchisor and franchisee, and low investment in firm-specific assets.

A reason for the success of franchises is the low variance in output quality between franchise outlets. Consumers expect that wherever they are the quality of the product or service they order at a particular outlet is standard across the franchise system. The returns for franchisors rest heavily on strategies that make it difficult, if not impossible, for a franchisee to operate without their assistance, which can be accomplished through restrictions in the franchise contract or agreement.

TYPICAL FRANCHISING ARRANGEMENTS

A franchise agreement is a contract between two firms, the franchisor and the franchisee. Mathewson and Winter[12] state that the principal ingredient in most franchise contracts is the franchisee's right to use a national brand name in exchange for a share of profits to the franchisor. However, the use of national brand names by local retailers involves a number of potential agency problems discussed in this note.

Rubin states that there are several standard clauses in franchise contracts.[13] The franchisor generally agrees to provide some form of managerial assistance to the franchisee. The support typically consists of start-up assistance and training for the franchisee and ongoing support during the term of the franchise contract. The initial fee provides the franchisor with capital to finance the franchisee's initial training and start-up; the ongoing royalty payments provide for the cost of continuing support.

In the franchise contract, the franchisee agrees to run the business in a manner stipulated by the franchisor. The standard of quality specified by the franchsior in the contract becomes more detailed as the risk of agency problems increases. The remedies for default of quality standards can range from fines to termination of the franchise agreement.

The franchise contract also contains a clause specifying the amount of royalties the franchisee will pay. According to Sen, the initial fees and ongoing royalty payments have several functions.[14] The fee structure is in place to achieve channel control, cover the cost of services, provide a risk-sharing mechanism, and reduce capital market imperfections. Channel control is the ability of channel members to achieve the desired outcome in their relationship with other channel members. The monthly fee usually consists of the royalty and a contribution to the franchisor for advertising on a national level. The franchisee's first cash outflow is initial fee, which is never returned. Therefore, only applicants who are confident they will recoup their investment will apply for a franchise. The number of applications received by the franchisor will be less, which means less work for him or her in choosing a franchisee. The fees also act as a disincentive for franchisee free-riding.

Free-riding can occur vertically, in which case a franchisee may "shirk" his or her obligations in order to reduce revenues and hence the royalty paid to the franchisor. The franchisor, too, can free-ride vertically by not maintaining brand-name strength. The franchisee may also engage in horizontal free-riding on other franchisees. In this case the franchisee will rely on the high quality maintained by the other franchisees to attract customers for the first time to his other store under the same name. However, any diminished quality of service or product on the franchisee's part will reflect on the rest of the franchise chain. The solutions to the free-rider problem include monitoring of franchisees and the initial fee may be considered as a bond or guarantee to the franchisor that the franchisee will not shirk. An additional solution to free-riding is to reduce royalty rates. The imposition of royalty rates prohibits the franchisor's attempts to free-ride by actively involving the franchisor in maintaining the chain's overall quality and because royalties are based on sales, not on profits.

The royalty payments also cover the cost of services. The franchisor provides initial and continuous services to the franchisee, as specified in the contract. The fees enable the franchisor and franchisee to share in the risk of the franchised outlet. One reason a franchisor franchises a location instead of a company-owned outlet is uncertainty. If the location is successful, then the royalty payment enables the franchisor to share in the success. If the franchised outlet fails, then the franchisor will forego the royalty payments. Despite Rubin's assertion that capital market imperfections are not an explanation of franchising, Sen believes that lack of capital for new franchisors influences initial fees.[15] He points to evidence showing that new entrants to franchising charge higher initial fees than more experienced ones.

The typical franchise agreement will also contain a termination clause. This details the specific circumstances in which either the franchisor or franchisee can terminate the franchise agreement. If the contact specifies longer terms, according to Brickley and Dark this reduces the problem of quasi-rent appropriation.[16] A contract with renegotiation provisions (i.e., short contracts with detailed renegotiation provisions) reduces the potential for quasi-rent appropriation. As can be seen in **Exhibit 5**, the duration of franchise relationships varies. A 1988 survey showed that 73% of operating business format franchising companies issued franchise agreements of varying lengths. Many of these franchise agreements, especially in the retail field, were associated with a lease. In all companies, these agreements provided an opportunity for the franchisee to enter into a new agreement at the end of the original term. Although the terms of the agreement vary from one year to a perpetual agreement, 34% of them are for 20 years or longer.[17] According to Sen, legislation reduces franchise terminations.[18] Legislation regulates the manner in which franchise terminations occur. It is no longer the case that a franchisor can terminate an agreement without just cause as laid out in the franchise contract.

Franchise contracts include a number of miscellaneous clauses. These control anything from the supplies the franchisee buys to the amount of local advertising the franchisee is obliged to undertake. Brickley and Dark conclude that franchisors can control certain agency problems associated with franchised units such as shirking and perquisite taking, inefficient risk-bearing, free-rider problems, and quasi-rent appropriation.[19] Multiple ownership, whereby a franchisee is offered a discount to run two or more outlets, can be used to control free-riding. The leasing of assets by franchisor to franchisee reduces problems of rent appropriation. If the contract specifies a standard of quality that the franchisee must uphold, then the free-rider problem is not as much of an issue. By specifying a minimum level of input use, the franchisor can also reduce the free-rider problem.

NOTES

1 U.S. Department of Commerce—Minority Business Development Agency, *Franchise Opportunities Handbook* (Washington DC: U.S. Government Printing Office, October 1994).
2 L.W. Stern and A. I. El-Ansary, *Marketing Channels* (Englewood Cliffs, NJ: Prentice-Hall, 1988).
3 "Data collected for the paper show royalty rates range from 0 to 50%, with 7% as the mean and 4.83% the standard deviation." (Kabir C. Sen, "The Use of Initial Fees and Royalties in Business-format Franchising," *Managerial and Decision Economics* [1993]: 190).
4 See Chapter 3 of *The Franchise Fraud* for a discussion of the history of franchising (Robert L. Purvin, *The Franchise Fraud: How to ProtectYourself Before and After You Invest*, (New York: John Wiley, 1994).
5 Purvin, p. 39.
6 In 1992 there were an estimated 540,000 franchised businesses in the United States which made $757.8 billion in retail sales. (see ibid, pp. 64–65).
7 *Bond's Franchise Guide* (1996 ed.; Oakland, CA: Source Book Publications), p. 15.
8 P.H. Rubin, "The Theory of the Firm and the Structure of the Franchise Contact," *Journal of Law and Economics 21* (1978): 223–233.
9 Frank Cavaliere and Marleen Swerdlow, "The Pros and Cons of Franchising: Two Views—Why Franchise?" *Business Forum* (Summer 1988): 11–13.
10 Francine Lafontaine, "Agency Theory and Franchising: Some Empirical Results," *Rand Journal of Economics* Summer 1992): 263–283.
11 J. A. Brickley and F. Dark, "The Choice of Organization Form: The Case of Franchising," *Journal of Financial Economics* (June 1987): 401–420.
12 G. F. Mathewson and R.A. Winter, "The Economics of Franchise Contracts," *Journal of Law and Economics* 28 (1985): 503–526
13 Rubin, p. 224.
14 Sen, p. 176.
15 Ibid., p. 179.
16 Brickley and Dark, p. 409.
17 Mark P. Friedlander and Gene Gurney, *Handbook of Successful Franchising*, 3rd ed. (Blue Ridge Summit, PA: Liberty Hall, 1990), p. 10.
18 Sen, p. 177.
19 Brickley and Dark, pp. 408–409.

REFERENCES

Bond, Robert E. *The Source Book of Franchise Opportunities.* 1993 ed. Homewood, IL: Dow Jones-Irwin, 1993.

Dicke, Thomas S. *Franchising in America: The Development of a Business Method, 1840–1980.* Chapel Hill: University of North Carolina Press, 1992.

Friedlander, Mark P. and Gene Gurney. *Handbook of Successful Franchising*. 3rd ed. Blue Ridge Summit, PA: Liberty Hall, 1990.

Grant, Clive. *Business Format Franchising: A System for Growth*. London: Economist Intelligence Unit, 1985.

International Franchise Association and Howarth International. *Franchising in the Economy, 1988–1990.*

International Franchise Association and Howarth International. *Franchising in the Economy, 1991.*

International Franchise Association and University of Louisville. *Franchising in the Economy, 1991–1993*. August 1994.

Martin, Robert E. "Franchising and Risk Management." *American Economic Review* (December 1988): 954–968.

Mendelsohn, Martin. *The Guide to Franchising*. 3rd ed. Oxford; New York: Pergamon Press, 1982.

Seltz, David D. *The Complete Handbook of Franchising*. Reading, MA: Addison-Wesley, 1982.

U.S. Department of Commerce. *Franchising in the Economy*. (Various Editions.)

EXHIBIT 1 Franchised Outlets in the United States, 1969–2007

	Number of Establishments			Sales (millions of dollars)		
Year	Total	Company-Owned	Franchisee-Owned	Total	Company-Owned	Franchisee-Owned
1969	383,908	68,863	315,045	119.53	24.82	94.70
1970	396,314	71,934	324,380	111.24	24.83	86.41
1971	431,169	74,721	356,448	128.88	18.65	110.23
1972	445,281	77,539	367,742	143.68	21.00	122.69
1973	453,632	78,850	374,782	161.90	24.35	137.55
1974	440,701	78,680	362,021	165.62	26.16	139.46
1975	434,538	80,561	353,977	182.31	28.72	153.59
1976	443,263	83,229	360,034	217.38	32.80	184.58
1977	450,800	85,941	364,859	253.37	38.14	215.24
1978	451,790	84,867	366,923	287.31	44.18	243.13
1979	452,487	85,280	367,207	312.19	39.55	272.64
1980	442,371	85,475	356,896	336.22	47.16	289.06
1981	442,418	85,905	356,513	364.72	50.60	314.12
1982	439,384	86,827	352,557	376.43	55.08	321.35
1983	441,181	85,789	355,392	422.83	59.16	363.67
1984	444,299	86,964	357,335	492.09	63.64	428.45
1985	455,220	86,443	368,777	542.97	68.30	474.67
1986	462,123	88,500	373,623	569.08	85.37	483.71
1987	479,087	89,483	389,604	599.43	90.61	508.82
1988	480,789	93,945	386,844	648.11	98.28	549.83
1989	492,498	94,574	397,924	677.91	107.45	570.45
1990	521,215	97,008	424,207	713.86	117.07	596.80
1991	542,496	100,496	442,000	757.83	127.21	630.62
2007	828,138	N/A	N/A	802.20	N/A	N/A

Source: Years 1969–1987 are from U.S. Department of Commerce, *Franchising in the Economy, 1986–1988*, February 1988; 1988 is from IFA, *Franchising in the Economy, 1988–1990*; years 1989–1991 are from IFA, *Franchising in the Economy, 1991*. PricewaterhouseCoopers, *The Economic Impact of Franchised Businesses: Volume III*, Results for 2007, February 7, 2011.

Note: Numbers are estimated by U.S. DoC for 1987.

EXHIBIT 2 Product/Trade Name Franchise Outlets in the United States, 1969–1991

Year	Number of Establishments			Sales (millions of dollars)		
	Total	Company-Owned	Franchisee-Owned	Total	Company-Owned	Franchisee-Owned
1969	N/A	N/A	217,822	N/A	N/A	82.10
1970	N/A	N/A	217,028	N/A	N/A	82.49
1971	255,620	44,401	211,219	104.17	5.91	98.25
1972	262,100	45,693	216,407	115.20	7.55	107.65
1973	251,395	43,557	207,838	131.00	8.62	122.39
1974	230,974	39,611	191,363	131.30	9.77	121.53
1975	223,724	38,281	185,443	144.90	10.70	134.20
1976	220,946	37,744	183,202	171.30	11.74	159.56
1977	211,984	35,675	176,309	195.90	5.51	190.39
1978	207,896	33,057	174,839	217.90	13.81	204.09
1979	199,785	31,585	168,200	241.00	15.71	225.29
1980	189,823	28,762	161,061	250.80	19.44	231.36
1981	181,863	27,350	154,513	275.70	19.59	256.11
1982	174,107	26,119	147,988	277.00	19.92	257.08
1983	164,986	24,668	140,318	312.30	19.85	292.46
1984	160,723	23,869	136,854	369.80	19.56	350.25
1985	153,531	22,533	130,998	401.60	19.56	382.04
1986	149,313	22,354	126,959	413.50	32.07	381.43
1987	144,751	N/A	N/A	429.80	N/A	N/A
1988	141,810	20,843	120,967	469.80	373.37	432.46
1989	139,245	20,536	118,709	484.95	402.24	444.73
1990	135,097	19,791	115,306	500.71	450.08	455.70
1991	134,279	19,691	114,588	525.59	491.11	476.48

Source: Years 1969–1987 are from U.S. Department of Commerce, *Franchising in the Economy, 1986–1988*, February 1988; 1988 is from IFA, *Franchising in the Economy, 1988–1990*; years 1989-1991 are from IFA, *Franchising in the Economy, 1991*.
Note: Numbers are estimated by U.S. DoC for 1987. N/A: Data not available.

EXHIBIT 3 Business Format Franchising in the United States 1969–2011

Year	Number of Establishments			Sales (millions of dollars)		
	Total	Company-Owned	Franchisee-Owned	Total	Company-Owned	Franchisee-Owned
1969	N/A	N/A		N/A	N/A	11.63
1970	N/A	N/A	107,352	N/A	N/A	13.44
1971	175,549	30,320	145,229	24.05	12.74	15.97
1972	189,640	33,138	156,502	28.70	13.27	19.43
1973	202,237	35,293	166,944	32.70	15.67	21.63
1974	209,727	39,069	170,658	37.30	16.36	24.54
1975	210,814	42,280	168,534	40.90	19.72	26.88
1976	222,317	45,485	176,832	46.60	34.96	30.84
1977	240,524	50,281	190,243	65.80	24.62	39.68
1978	245,694	51,760	193,934	64.30	29.65	42.75
1979	252,702	53,695	199,007	72.40	35.23	48.27
1980	252,548	56,713	195,835	83.50	34.56	54.55
1981	260,555	58,555	202,000	89.10	40.94	58.06
1982	268,306	60,708	207,598	99.00	46.46	64.04
1983	276,195	61,121	215,074	110.50	51.09	71.21
1984	283,576	63,095	220,481	122.30	63.10	78.21
1985	301,689	63,910	237,779	141.30	62.87	92.63
1986	312,810	66,146	246,664	155.50	67.32	102.28
1987	324,516	N/A	N/A	169.60	N/A	N/A
1988	338,979	73,102	265,877	178.32	60.44	117.37
1989	353,253	74,038	279,215	192.95	67.23	125.73
1990	386,118	77,217	308,901	213.16	72.06	141.10
1991	408,217	80,805	327,412	232.24	78.10	154.14
2007	788,285	108,340	679,495	654.20	505.10	149.10
2008	791,560	N/A	N/A	680.70	N/A	N/A
2009	763,094	N/A	N/A	683.20	N/A	N/A
2010	765,723	N/A	N/A	706.60	N/A	N/A
2011E	784,802	N/A	N/A	739.90	N/A	N/A

Source: Years 1969–1987 are from U.S. Department of Commerce, *Franchising in the Economy, 1986–1988*, February 1988; 1988 is from IFA, *Franchising in the Economy, 1988–1990*; years 1989–1991 are from IFA, *Franchising in the Economy, 1991*. PricewaterhouseCoopers, *The Economic Impact of Franchised Businesses: Volume III*, Results for 2007, February 7, 2011; PricewaterhouseCoopers, Franchised Business Economic Outlook: 2011, January 3, 2011.

Note: Numbers are estimated by U.S. DoC for 1987. N/A: Data not available.

EXHIBIT 4 Industry Breakdown of Business Format Franchising, 2007–2011E

Owned by:	Company		Franchisee		Total	
	2007	2011E	2007	2011E	2007	2011E
Number of Establishments						
Restaurants—All Types	38,954	N/A	141,267	N/A	180,221	186,136
Business Services	15,752	N/A	93,348	N/A	109,100	92,714
Lodging	2,011	N/A	22,597	N/A	24,608	26,011
Personal Services	3,713	N/A	125,630	N/A	129,343	130,895
Retail Food	20,737	N/A	37,663	N/A	58,400	60,841
Real Estate	2,944	N/A	91,375	N/A	94,319	86,825
Retail Products & Services	14,259	N/A	76,637	N/A	90,896	99,592
Commercial & Residential Services	3,875	N/A	66,045	N/A	69,920	70,129
Automotive	6,095	N/A	25,383	N/A	31,478	31,659
Total Establishments	**108,340**	**N/A**	**679,945**	**N/A**	**788,285**	**784,802**
Sales ($ million)						
Restaurants—All Types	54,100	N/A	158,000	N/A	212,100	249,700
Business Services	49,900	N/A	75,100	N/A	125,000	128,700
Lodging	7,000	N/A	57,800	N/A	64,800	70,800
Personal Services	4,500	N/A	66,300	N/A	70,800	86,200
Retail Food	12,400	N/A	18,700	N/A	31,200	38,200
Real Estate	2,200	N/A	57,900	N/A	60,100	51,200
Retail Products & Services	5,500	N/A	18,900	N/A	24,400	29,500
Commercial & Residential Services	5,700	N/A	29,900	N/A	35,500	45,800
Automotive	7,800	N/A	22,600	N/A	30,400	39,700
Total Sales	**149,100**	**N/A**	**505,200**	**N/A**	**654,300**	**739,900**

Source: Results for 2007, February 7, 2011; PricewaterhouseCoopers, Franchised Business Economic Outlook: 2011, January 3, 2011.

EXHIBIT 5 Duration of Franchise Agreements

Number of Years	Percentage
1	1.10%
3	1.50
5	14.8
10	33.1
15	14.6
20	19.6
25	0.90
Perpetual	12.5
Others	1.90

Source: Mark P. Friedlander, Jr. and Gene Gurney, *Handbook of Successful Franchising*, 3rd edition, (Blue Ridge Summit: Liberty Hall Press, 1990), p. 11.

CHAPTER 4.5

Hudson Manufacturing Company

Paul Gompers

It was September 2000 and RockWood Equity Partners LLC, a one year old search fund, was facing its biggest roadblock yet. It had been another grueling day in what had become a very long summer of late nights at the office. Brett Keith and Owen Colligan had spent a lot of time away from their homes in New York City since the equity investment company they had co-founded in 1999 had won the bid for the acquisition of Hudson Manufacturing Company at $12.75 million (leading to a total purchase price of $13.35 million, including transaction fees). The company specialized in the manufacture and sale of diesel engine accessories, and air filtration and heating products for military and commercial markets. Keith and Colligan had waited a long time for RockWood's first investment and with $21 million in sales for fiscal 2000, strong margins, some reasonable growth opportunities, no debt and a seemingly attractive price, Hudson appeared to be the deal for which they had been looking. On July 1, 2000, their bid had taken Hudson off the market and they both knew they had little time to secure financing in order to close the deal. Hoping to give up only a small percentage of ownership to secure the financing of the acquisition, Keith and Colligan had sought to leverage the deal as much as possible. By September, having obtained financing commitments allowing for $1 million from equity investors, $2.50 million in seller financing, and $7.5 million from a local bank (with the remaining $2.35 million of the purchase price to be paid by drawing from the company's existing cash balance of $809,000, marketable securities of some $2.487 million and the cash surrender value on two life insurance policies held by the company of nearly $440,000), Colligan and Keith were celebrating the near completion of RockWood's first acquisition.

Hudson Manufacturing Company
by PAUL GOMPERS, case number 9-203-064 Rev. November 12, 2009

The celebration, however, was short-lived as evidence of the trucking industry's collapse grew and the discovery of toxins in the soil at Hudson's facility in Solon, Ohio reached the two young business school graduates. Colligan and Keith had accumulated a lot of personal debt through school and had also borrowed a significant amount to fund the operations of RockWood and to pay for due diligence and transaction expenses for the Hudson acquisition. Part of the plan had been to pay down some of the $7.5 million bank debt and repay their equity investors (80% of the private capital was in the form of convertible redeemable preferred stock) with the proceeds from the sale of WEBB, a maker of diesel engine components and a subsidiary of Hudson. Even before owning the company, they had secretly signed a letter of intent with a strategic buyer to sell WEBB for $6.5 million. What they had not anticipated was the quick and severe downturn in the trucking industry that summer which scared off the potential strategic buyer. Unable to sell WEBB, Keith and Colligan would have to maintain a higher debt burden in order to acquire Hudson and would have to postpone repaying the equity investors, risking the possibility of losing majority ownership of the company (if the preferred stock was not redeemed within two years, then it would automatically convert to common stock giving the equity investors a majority stake). News of contamination at one of Hudson's facilities only served to exacerbate the predicament in which they found themselves. As part of the due diligence for the bank, Keith and Colligan had been required to hire an environmental consultant to evaluate Hudson's facilities. Their environmental consultant had found that toxins, dumped more than two decades earlier, had contaminated the soil around the Hudson facility in Solon, Ohio. The extent of the contamination and the cost to remediate the problem were unknown, with early cost estimates ranging from $200,000 up to $2 million. What they did know, however, was that if they bought Hudson's stock they would be fully liable for all future legally mandated remediation expenses.

Keith and Colligan weighed their options. Unable to sell WEBB or determine the extent of the contamination with any degree of certainty, Colligan and Keith knew they would be taking on greater risk by proceeding with the acquisition. They believed that waiting for the trucking industry to recover was unrealistic and waiting for additional environmental studies to determine the full extent of the damage would likely take months and potentially cause the deal to fall through. On the other hand, if they backed out of the deal now, they would personally lose close to $450,000 in transaction fees they had accrued thus far and would probably be forced to dissolve RockWood, the company they had worked so hard to build. Colligan and Keith began to outline their choices.

ROCKWOOD COMPANY BACKGROUND

Colligan first got the idea of starting RockWood during his second year at Harvard Business School. Colligan graduated from the University of Buffalo with a B.S. degree in finance and after receiving a J.D. from New York University, he began working in the New York and Hong Kong offices of Kelley Drye & Warren as a corporate attorney specializing in mergers and acquisitions. During his second year at HBS, he began talking to a high net-worth individual who lived in Cleveland, Ohio, about starting something together (see **Exhibit 1** for copies of Keith's and Colligan's resumes). While taking an entrepreneurial finance class at HBS that year, he got the idea of starting a search fund. Keith had received a B.A. degree in both finance and accounting from the University of St. Thomas. He started working as a consultant and CPA for Grant Thornton LLP and Arthur Andersen LLP before becoming Controller of a mid-sized manufacturing company that was owned by a private equity firm. Keith had also worked in the mergers and acquisitions group of Lehman Brothers in New York. At HBS, Keith and Colligan began to explore opportunities to do something together after business school. Soon they began talks with Colligan's contact in Cleveland. After spending the better part of six months discussing their possible roles and the structure of their search fund, they reached agreement and hired a lawyer to draft the documents.

Under the search fund agreement, their Cleveland contact would fund 100% of their operations through quarterly installments and provide 100% of the equity required to fund an acquisition. Keith and Colligan would conduct the acquisition search, negotiate and structure the transaction and help manage the acquired company. In return, Keith and Colligan would receive a 15% to 25% share of the profits (the ultimate "carried interest" was dependent upon the investor's IRR). Keith and Colligan began working in September of 1999 out of a small apartment in New York City. They hoped to buy a small to medium size industrial company with revenues between $10 million and $50 million. Based on their experience, they agreed to focus on low to medium-tech companies in small industries or protected niches. Their goal was to purchase a company and create value through operational improvements while avoiding full-blown financial turnarounds. In addition, they hoped to add value through the acquisition of strategic add-ons and through enhanced organic growth. With this in mind, Colligan and Keith began the quest for their first acquisition.

Their work was quickly interrupted in January 2000 as RockWood faced its first roadblock. Their search fund agreement allowed either the investor or Colligan/Keith to walk away at any point, something their investor opted to do in January of 2000. Obliged to return their financing to date, Keith and Colligan contemplated calling it quits and finding other jobs. They both had accumulated a lot of personal debt through school and were worried about their financial well-being. After much consideration, however, Colligan and Keith decided that they hadn't been given a sufficient chance to make RockWood work and therefore opted to continue and take on more debt in the process. Despite the on-going dot-com euphoria and the high salaries being offered on Wall Street, they were turned off by the idea of joining some of their HBS classmates in investment banks, and they became intent on making RockWood a successful venture.

Their decision to carry forward was followed by a change in strategy. They could no longer rely upon their single investor to pay the bills and provide equity for an acquisition. While simultaneously looking for deals, they would now have to cultivate potential equity investors. They had spent the past months mailing their plan to hundreds of business brokers, lawyers, accountants and anyone who might know of a business for sale. They had also traveled from city to city meeting with anyone who would listen, mainly lawyers, accountants and bankers. They now expanded these meetings to include potential investors. Through this process, they identified several likely investors and they found several businesses of interest, coming close to making an acquisition on more than one occasion, but none of the deals worked out in the end. That changed when they found Hudson Manufacturing Company.

HUDSON MANUFACTURING COMPANY

In April of 2000, a banker for Federal City Bank in Cleveland contacted Colligan and Keith about Hudson's owner's decision to sell. Hudson was a manufacturer of premium heating, air filtration and diesel engine products for the military/government and commercial markets with revenues of $21 million in the fiscal year ended June 30, 2000 (see **Exhibit 2** for Hudson historical financials).

Keith and Colligan made two visits to the city of Cleveland. First, to meet Hudson's president, Gene Strong, and the company's bankers and a second time to meet with the company's 72-year-old owner and CEO, Thomas Grinch. Grinch had acquired Hudson in 1974, nearly four decades following Robert Hudson's founding of the company. At first, both Keith and Colligan had some reservations. Hudson's facilities were run down and outdated and the company relied heavily on its military/government contracts for the majority (65%) of its revenue. Colligan and Keith weren't certain that the defense contracting industry was a good business to enter at the time.

Their initial skepticism quickly began to disappear following subsequent visits. A profitable company with good margins and strong cash generation, Hudson proved to be a dominant player in two small niche markets with some potential for improvement and growth. Although Hudson relied heavily on military contracts for the bulk of its revenue, they felt that this could be offset by the further penetration of the commercial market. They also considered the dozen existing long-term military contracts helpful in diversifying customer concentration risk and providing a secure on-going revenue base to support the proposed acquisition leverage. More importantly, it became apparent to Keith and Colligan that the 72-year-old owner had been pulling back from the business for a number of years and that he had no significant customer contact (often with small privately owned companies, the owner may hold the key relationships with customers and these relationships can be lost after the departure of that owner).

Keith and Colligan considered Hudson a strong niche player with the potential for improvement and growth. They felt that one element crippling Hudson's current growth was its lack of management depth. While Grinch had been able to grow revenue to over $20 million in his 25 years as owner, Keith and Colligan felt he was now holding the business back. They learned that as his career waned Grinch became very secretive and controlling despite spending less and less time at the business. The owner's controlling ways and the company's dysfunctional culture coupled with the fact that the company's management compensation was below market and contained no performance incentive component (such as equity or performance bonuses), led to an inability to retain or attract many talented people. Furthermore, with his engineering background, Grinch favored his product designs and did everything in his power to stop efforts to license technology developed externally or to partner with other companies in the development of products. Hudson's management team was dysfunctional, its employees lacked training, and an adversarial relationship existed between management and union workers. In addition, the company's inventory was in disarray and its facilities were run-down and outdated (the result of a lack of reinvestment for years). While Grinch "ruled with an iron fist," he was simultaneously detached from Hudson's day-to-day activities, its employees, and its customers. Keith and Colligan consequently regarded Grinch's plans to leave Hudson after its acquisition as a blessing and an advantage in realizing Hudson's full potential. They believed they could improve Hudson's operations and increase sales through aggressive management.

Convinced that Hudson was the deal they had been searching for, Keith and Colligan began negotiations with Hudson's investment banker in early June, won the auction in early July--beating out one other company that bid on par with RockWood--and after three weeks of negotiations, signed a letter of intent with Grinch.

HUDSON'S COMPANY BACKGROUND

History of the Company Hudson Manufacturing Company was founded in 1937. Robert Hudson had co-founded the company in Cleveland, Ohio, with the purpose of manufacturing reliable, compact hot-air heaters for military vehicles, tents, and shelters. During WWII, Hudson's heaters proved their reliability and endurance in hostile environments. This success in the military market led to the expansion of products and applications in that market as well as the commercial market. Hudson's expansion, however, became more aggressive with the acquisition of Hudson by Thomas Grinch in 1974. Hudson expanded its customer base to include commercial customers and through a combination of internal development and acquisitions, the company also expanded its product base to include air filtration devices for military applications as well as fuel heaters, fuel/water separators, oil change systems, and fuel monitoring and replenishing systems for the commercial truck market. By June of 2000, the company operated out of four facilities (two in Ohio, one in North Dakota and one in California – see **Exhibit 3**) and employed 147 people, 64 salaried employees and the remaining 83 hourly manufacturing employees. Through the expansion of product offerings and technological innovation, Hudson was able to expand its annual revenues from $1.5 million at the time of Grinch's acquisition in fiscal 1974 to $21 million in fiscal 2000.

Historical Financial Performance Historically, Hudson had enjoyed fully-burdened gross margins (as a defense contractor, Hudson was able to allocate some indirect overhead costs into "cost of goods sold") in excess of 20%. At the time it was acquired by Grinch, Hudson's revenue was $1.5 million with break-even income, sales mainly being derived from small contract military orders. The development of new military heaters and Hudson's expansion into the commercial market in the late 1970s allowed Hudson to enjoy revenues in excess of $10 million per year in the 1980s. The revenue growth was led by the development of a series of auxiliary heaters targeted at the commercial truck market.

By the 1990s, the company's focus turned to developing additional opportunities in the commercial market. For example, in 1992, Hudson introduced its first engine coolant heater. This more powerful heating unit allowed Hudson to expand its heater customer base to include manufacturers of commercial cargo trucks. To further pursue non-military markets, in 1994, Hudson bought WEBB Enterprises, a manufacturer of fuel heating/

water separator devices and other engine components for the truck and off-highway markets. By fiscal 2000, WEBB revenues represented close to 24% of total revenues. The acquisition of WEBB was followed by the acquisition of IDL Defense in 1998. This acquisition served to further penetrate the military air filtration market. Through its two acquisitions and the development of new products, Hudson enjoyed an average pre-tax income of 8.9% during the 1990s and by fiscal 2000 increased its revenue to $21.2 million.

In 1997 and 1998, Hudson experienced a significant drop off in revenue and margins, which were due to the cut in military purchases of heating devices, the expenses associated with the start-up of a new filter operation, the absorption of IDL Defense which Hudson purchased out of bankruptcy, and production problems at the company's Ontario, Ohio, facility. In fiscal 1999, with production problems resolved and better usage of their manufacturing capacities, Hudson's performance improved markedly. Hudson also experienced a major increase in military orders in fiscal 1999 and fiscal 2000. This increased Hudson's net pre-tax income from a loss of $.2 million in fiscal 1998 to $2.4 million in fiscal 2000 and increased its gross profit percentage from 16% in fiscal 1998 to 22% in fiscal 2000. The $3.3 million in cash and short-term marketable securities (along with $440,000 in "cash surrender value" on two life insurance policies owned by the company) represented over 28% of Hudson's net asset value in fiscal 2000. In that same fiscal year, Hudson's retention of profits led to a $1.3 million increase in equity to $11.7 million.

HUDSON'S PRODUCTS

Hudson served military and commercial truck and off-highway markets through the development and production of three main product lines:

Heating Devices Hudson's heating devices, by fiscal year 2000, represented 44% of revenues, of which approximately 75% were composed of military products and approximately 25% were composed of commercial products. This product line included products employing a variety of fuels. Hudson's tent/shelter heaters were typically portable, compact, highly fuel-efficient, and capable of enduring a variety of hostile environments. They were built to operate at temperatures ranging from 160 to negative 50 degrees Fahrenheit and at elevations ranging from sea level to an altitude of 10,000 feet. The line of engine coolant, hot-water, and fuel-fired heaters offered safe, reliable heat to military Humvees, military and commercial trucks, off-highway vehicles, tents and temporary or remote site locations. The fuel-fired heaters relied upon an internal and independent fuel supply to power the heater and were diesel, propane and natural gas compatible. In all, the product line included four basic fuel-fired models and six basic engine-coolant models for both military and commercial applications.

Air Filtration Devices In response to the U.S. military's need to protect against exposure to nuclear, chemical, and biological (NCB) risks, in the late 1980s, Hudson began developing filtered breathing apparatuses for military personnel likely to be exposed to NCB risks. These early air filtration devices were used in airplanes, tanks, military jeeps and other military vehicles. The devices moved and cleansed air as it was taken from the external environment and made it available inside in the form of nontoxic, breathable air. While this product line had been used exclusively to filter the air of transportation equipment, Hudson's acquisition of IDL Defense in 1998 expanded the usage of filtration devices to include government and military shelters, tents, and buildings. By 2000, air filtration device sales constituted 32% of revenues.

Fuel Heaters and Water Separators In response to the truck market's need to improve truck performance in cold weather, Hudson developed a line of engine pre-heaters. This product line provided an economical and energy-efficient solution to the deteriorating effects of cold starts and reduced the use of on-board diesel fuel by pre-heating the engine before ignition. With the acquisition of WEBB, Hudson's offerings broadened to include engine accessories such as stand-alone fuel heaters, heater/water separators, and oil and coolant monitors for the commercial truck market. By fiscal 2000, WEBB's subsidiary revenues represented nearly 24% of total consolidated Hudson revenues. On its $5 million of subsidiary revenues, WEBB generated gross margins of 30%, incurred $500,000 of SG&A expenses but did not contribute any depreciation/amortization charges which resulted in the unit contributing $1 million of EBITDA to the consolidated results of Hudson.

MARKETS FOR HUDSON PRODUCTS

Competitors Historically, the military's focus on the product's nature differed considerably from the focus of commercial markets. The military focused on a product's durability, reliability, and performance. They often would fund the development of products and award long-term contracts, while the commercial market focused more on price and product breadth, and required focused product development and marketing efforts. Hudson's emphasis on product performance and durability and not price enabled the company to compete in the military and government contract markets, but hampered its ability to compete in the commercial markets. Furthermore, Hudson's emphasis on winning development contracts from the military meant that the development of new commercial products was rarely given priority. Within the military market for space heating devices, Hudson competed with Engineered Air Systems Inc., Keco Industries, Stewart Warner Corporation, and Global Thermoelectric and competed in the commercial market with Webasto North America, Espar Products, Inc., and Phillips & Temro Industries Ltd. While Hudson enjoyed a market share of 65% in the military market, its market share was a mere 13% in the commercial market for heating devices.

Hudson's air filtration devices, unlike its heating devices, were sold exclusively to the military market. Within the air filtration market, Keco Industries and Donaldson Company (see **Exhibit 4** for information on Hudson's competitors) were Hudson's two main competitors bidding for military contracts in this narrowly defined niche industry. With a recent contract award, Hudson's product line enjoyed a remarkable 90% market share in the military air filtration market.

While the air filtration devices were sold exclusively in the military market, fuel heaters/water separators were sold exclusively in the commercial market. For this product line, the particular application being addressed determined Hudson's competition. Racor (a division of Parker Hannifin) and DavCo (a division of Penske) were its major competitors in the fuel heater and water separator market where WEBB was a distant third with a market share of no more than 10%. Competitors of other applications included Grote Industries, Truck Lite, ISSPRO Inc., and Kysor/Warren Industrial Corporation. In fiscal 2000, revenues from sales of fuel heaters and water separators constituted 24% of total revenues for that fiscal year.

Customers From Hudson's birth in 1937, the military had formed the greater part of the company's customer base and still represented over 65% of sales in 2000. Historically, Hudson built its success through the development of products that served military applications. Hudson, through time, built a sterling reputation for products and service. It is this reputation that allowed Hudson to win most of its bids on military contracts. The military, beginning in the early 1990's, moved the emphasis of the bidding process away from being based solely upon price to being based upon a company's reputation, financial stability, product and delivery performance and more recently, the ability to design and build products based upon general performance specifications. Hudson's size (with fewer than 500 employees) also qualified the company for "Small Business Set-Aside Contracts", protecting it from competition with larger military producers on certain bids. And each win on a military contract served to give Hudson an advantage in subsequent bids.

Hudson guaranteed its participation in future military bids through the manufacture of products necessary to this customer. Keith and Colligan believed that Hudson manufactured products necessary and vital to the military, products that were unlikely to ever be suspended. The military would always need tent and vehicle heaters and air filters and would probably continue to need them for a long time to come. In addition, by winning contracts to develop prototypes for military products, Hudson often became the sole supplier of many of the products it sold, guaranteeing substantial future sales.

Hudson's performance in the military market facilitated its transition to the commercial market. In fiscal 2000, sales to the trucking and off-highway vehicle commercial market represented the remaining 35% of total revenues. The nature of Hudson's sales to the military, however, varied greatly from those in commercial markets. Sales to the military typically involved the negotiation of long-term contracts, while sales to commercial customers were not long-term in nature. Military contracts were generally one to five years in duration. These long-term contracts with the military allowed Hudson to weather downturns in the commercial market by providing a secure base of future revenues.

Entering the commercial market also forced Hudson into a higher level of competition. Price, product breadth, marketing skill and the ability to lower costs through increased efficiency were the key factors determining a company's success in the commercial market. Hudson's ability to further penetrate the commercial market would require a shift in Hudson's focus to price, marketing, new product development, and gaining operating efficiencies in order to better meet the needs of the commercial market.

PROJECTIONS AND OUTLOOK

Financial projections for the next five years showed steady growth, but it was clear that the qualities that enabled Hudson to grow in the twentieth century would no longer suffice in the long run as the twenty-first century got underway. Hudson's financial projections (see **Exhibit** 5) assumed a 5.5% revenue growth rate for the next five years with revenues reaching nearly $28 million by fiscal 2005. This growth was to be largely driven by sales of air filters and diesel accessories. In addition, Hudson was projected to maintain a gross profit margin of 22% and an EBITDA margin of 14.6% for the next five years. Keith and Colligan believed that these projections were conservative if new management could fulfill Hudson's true potential. Furthermore, these internal projections did not take into account several profitability enhancements planned by Keith/Colligan such as consolidating California's operations into Ohio (estimated to save $500,000 per year). They also understood, however, that there was not much room for error because at current debt levels the interest on the acquisition debt would equal nearly $1 million per year.

Through the years, Hudson had built a reputation for manufacturing quality products to meet market needs, primarily in the military/government market. (See **Exhibit 6** for details on government military expenditures.) The military was a consistent, fairly high margin payer, and historically, not demanding relative to the commercial markets. This, however, was starting to change. The military procurement practices were quickly changing to resemble commercial practices. The military was now starting to demand products that met their specifications ("build to specification"), moving further away from the "build to our print" design demand of the past. This change put a greater premium on engineering and product development skills. The military was also demanding faster and more reliable service of higher quality products. The delivery of product would be expected within seven to 30 days and not Hudson's 90-120 day average. There would also be a demand for shipments to reach customers on time 97% of the time, not 90% of the time. The factors determining Hudson's future ability to grow were dependent upon its ability to continue developing new useful products and adapting to the changing market demands. Hudson would now have to forecast military demand, build to forecast, and ship from stock, closely resembling the practices of the commercial markets. While relying on the protected government/military market to earn most of its revenues had enabled Hudson to prosper in the past, this market's move to resemble the commercial market would force Hudson to shift its focus to better meet commercial needs. Hudson's success in meeting these changing market demands would determine its ability to compete in the long run.

Keith and Colligan believed their purchase of Hudson could bring the company the necessary management insights and allow it to realize its full potential. While neither was suited to be CEO of a manufacturing company based upon their prior experiences, they were willing to roll-up their sleeves and work with the existing President (Gene Strong, currently the number two) until such time as they could recruit new managers for key positions. The two young graduates believed that most flaws with which Hudson was afflicted were "non-fatal" in nature. They were confident that Grinch's exit would allow them to steer Hudson away from its historical practices and to grow the business through new military contracts, new product licenses, teaming arrangements and the acquisition of complimentary product lines. Colligan and Keith would improve Hudson's information systems by upgrading both its hardware and software and by revamping engineers' use of new technology. The facilities would be consolidated (by closing the California facility) and optimized, manufacturing and procurement processes would be modernized, managers would be given incentives through updated compensation packages and stock participation, and relations between management and union employees would be improved through a more progressive approach, including employee education and "pay for skills" programs. Keith and Colligan considered Hudson a company full of potential, unrealized to this date largely because of the entrenched and dysfunctional "old school" management culture

ROCKWOOD'S FIRST ACQUISITION

Financing the Deal On July 1, 2001, Keith and Colligan won the bid for the acquisition of Hudson for $12.75 million (requiring a total of $13.35 million including transaction fees) without having obtained any financing for the deal (other than $2.5 million of seller financing comprised of a $2.25 million note and $250,000 in earn-out payments) (See **Exhibit** 7 for the proposed financing structure.) They knew they had little time to secure financing, otherwise they risked losing all credibility and losing the deal. They decided to set up camp in the basement of Colligan's in-law's home in Cleveland for the summer to keep overhead costs low. The first thing they did was put together a presentation and sit in front of eight banks, both regional and national, with offices in Cleveland. They asked for $7.5 million in debt financing, comprised of a $4 million revolving credit facility (they envisioned drawing only $3.5 million of that at closing) and a $3.5 million term note. The critical aspect in choosing a bank to Keith and Colligan was the aggregate amount of debt offered, with pricing and other terms being secondary. They received term sheets from several of the banks, but did not aggressively play the banks off each other because the offer from Columbus Bank, much to their surprise, gave them exactly what they had requested (See **Exhibit 8** for the Columbus term sheet). Keith and Colligan had apparently caught Columbus at the right time as the bank was looking to get back into the deal market and had a history with Hudson.

The meetings with the banks allowed Keith and Colligan to get a sense of the senior debt financing banks would give them, and armed with the Columbus term sheet, they went ahead and started to arrange the equity financing. With a PowerPoint presentation, they approached the different equity investors with whom they had cultivated a relationship over their first year at RockWood. Keith and Colligan had groomed the investor list not to simply raise capital, but rather, to get "smart money" investors that could offer RockWood advice and credibility. Their initial intentions were to sell $500,000 worth of "units" in RockWood to private investors in exchange for 10% of the venture. After approaching a number of potential investors, Keith and Colligan received greater interest than expected from two investment firms and eight individuals who in aggregate appeared prepared to purchase $1 million worth of these units in RockWood.

In a $1,000,000 equity financing, Keith and Colligan proposed issuing 80,000 shares of common stock in RockWood to themselves as founders of RockWood and then offering a total of 20 units at $50,000 per unit to the equity investors.

Each unit consisted of 10 shares of convertible redeemable preferred stock with a price of $4,000 per share and 1,000 shares of common stock with a price of $10 per share. Each share of preferred stock carried a 15% annual cash dividend based on the share's face value (only payable as permitted by bank loan covenants) and, if it was not redeemed within two years of the closing, was convertible into 500 shares of common stock

Assuming that 20 units were sold to raise the $1 million in equity and that the preferred stock was redeemed within two years of closing, the 20,000 shares of common stock issued to the unit holders would represent 20% ownership of RockWood. Keith and Colligan would hold the remaining 80,000 shares of common stock, representing 80% ownership of RockWood. RockWood, the holding company, in turn, would purchase and then subsequently own 100% of the manufacturing company, Hudson.

With the prospect of a $1 million investor commitment in hand, Keith and Colligan needed to decide whether they should try to close the full $1 million in exchange for 20% of the venture or raise just $500,000 in exchange for 10% of the venture as originally intended.

ACQUISITION'S FIRST SETBACK: WEBB

With both equity and bank financing seemingly secured, Keith and Colligan felt the deal was as good as done. Their joy, however, began to fade after the trucking market began a rapid downturn that summer. While securing their equity and bank financing, Keith and Colligan had been simultaneously negotiating to sell WEBB, Hudson's subsidiary, with the hope of substantially reducing their acquisition debt and redeeming the equity investor's preferred stock thus avoiding a conversion of that stock to common stock. The sale of WEBB, for which they had a letter of intent from a strategic buyer for $6.5 million at the time, would significantly reduce their acquisition debt, assure their ownership stake of the company and give them tremendous credibility with their investors by re-paying them so quickly, but the unexpected and severe downturn in the trucking market during the summer of 2000 caused the potential buyer to eventually rescind its offer. They had accumulated a lot of personal debt through their education, the financing of RockWood since January, and the fees related to Hudson's acquisition. They could call it quits now, but that would not only entail the dissolution of RockWood, but also losing close to $450,000 they had run up in appraisals for banks, environmental consultants, and legal and accounting fees for the acquisition of Hudson so far.

ACQUISITION'S SECOND SETBACK: SOIL CONTAMINATION

Their concern regarding their ability to sell WEBB was followed by news of soil contamination in the soil behind one of Hudson's facilities. In order to secure their bank financing, Keith and Colligan were obliged to hire an environmental consultant to survey Hudson's facilities. The consultants they had hired found contamination in the soil at Hudson's facility in Solon, Ohio. It appeared that someone at Hudson had either knowingly or unknowingly dumped a vapor degreaser decades ago and the extent of the contamination was unknown. It was unknown just how much of the toxin was dumped, in how many locations, and whether the toxin had contaminated the soil water. A bank would be taking higher risk by financing the acquisition of Hudson without further knowledge of the extent of the damage and the likely remediation cost (the environmental consultant initially estimated that remediation could cost anywhere from $200,000 to $2 million). Keith and Colligan felt that if they delayed the close of the deal to find out the extent of the contamination (a process that would likely take months), they would probably never acquire Hudson and they would be forced to dissolve RockWood.

CONCLUSION

Their inability to sell WEBB and the uncertainty surrounding the extent of the contamination caused by the toxins led Keith and Colligan to consider the dissolution of RockWood for the second time that year. Both Keith and Colligan believed Hudson's full potential could be realized under their guidance, but feared that under current circumstances, the company would be highly leveraged with potentially unquantifiable environmental liabilities, and they risked losing majority ownership of the company if they could not refinance their investors' preferred stock. Their inability to sell WEBB presented an enormous setback.

Without the sale of WEBB, Keith and Colligan would have to rely upon the company's earnings to repay Columbus Bank and their private investors, which according to their financial model was doable, but obviously more risky.

The discovery of toxins in the soil at the facility in Solon presented an even greater problem. They had very little knowledge regarding the extent of the contamination and its potential cost. The acquisition of Hudson's stock would make them liable for cleaning the contaminated area once its damage was determined unless they could get the seller to agree to be responsible for the clean-up.

Keith and Colligan felt that postponing the closing until they were certain they could sell WEBB and quantify the exact extent of the contamination caused by the toxins was not really an option. They felt strongly that such a delay would cause the deal to fall through.

They did not want to give up on their dream so soon and they had already spent close to $450,000 in acquisition fees so far, but they were also afraid of becoming too "in love" with the deal such that they proceeded hastily when the prudent thing to do was to wait. While Hudson seemed to be the perfect acquisition candidate, neither Keith nor Colligan knew exactly what they should do to keep the deal on track. The list of potential options looked pretty short. As the evening sun began to set, Keith and Colligan knew it would be another late night.

EXHIBIT 1 Colligan and Keith Resumes

Experience

1999-Present **ROCKWOOD EQUITY PARTNERS LLC** — **NEW YORK, NY/CLEVELAND, OH**

Principal and Founder.

Co-founder and Principal of a private equity firm based in New York and Cleveland that is focused on buyouts of lower middle market industrial companies.

1998 **Schroder & Co. inc.** — **new york, ny**

Associate, Corporate Finance.

Served as associate on corporate finance transactions involving various industries and products. Created financial models and drafted merger, leveraged buyout, and refinancing proposals. Developed valuation analyses, performed due diligence and prepared offering memoranda and rating agency and road show presentations.

- Participated in simultaneous $100mm high-yield offering and acquisition of two retail optical chains.
- Participated in the restructuring of and secondary offering of stock by a railroad company.

1995 -1997 **KELLEY DRYE & WARREN LLP** — **NEW YORK, NY/HONG KONG**

Associate, Corporate Department.

Served as senior associate on corporate transactions, supervising teams of 2-6 lawyers and paralegals. Negotiated and structured mergers and acquisitions, securities, loan, project finance and general corporate transactions. Supervised due diligence and drafted agreements. Transactions included:

- Simultaneous purchase and sale of a controlling interest in a manufacturing joint venture located in Thailand. Also restructured $100mm in joint venture debt.
- Sale of stock of an industrial crane manufacturer for $80mm and assumption of debt.
- Purchase of assets of an elevator manufacturer for $25mm and assumption of debt.
- Refinancing of $18mm revolving credit facility.
- Joint venture between two telecommunications companies for the joint national rollout of telecommunication services.

1991 - 1995 **LANE & MITTENDORF LLP** **NEW YORK, NY**

Associate, Corporate Department.

Served as associate on mergers and acquisitions, securities and general corporate transactions. Negotiated and structured transactions, supervised and performed due diligence, and drafted agreements. Conducted compliance reviews of Proxy Statements and 10-K reports. Transactions included:

- Sale of assets of a wholly-owned subsidiary of a Fortune 500 company in a $25mm LBO.
- Private placement of $30mm in asset-backed securities by a casino gaming company.
- Initial public offering of $5mm of stock by a corporation operating a national franchise chain of bagel stores.

Education

1997-1999 **HARVARD UNIVERSITY GRADUATE SCHOOL OF BUSINESS ADMINISTRATION** **BOSTON, MA**

Received Master in Business Administration degree, 1999. Member of Finance and Venture Capital Clubs.

1988-1991Sep. **NEW YORK UNIVERSITY SCHOOL OF LAW** **NEW YORK, NY**

Received Juris Doctor degree, 1991. Participant in Moot Court Competition.

1984-1988 **STATE UNIVERSITY OF NEW YORK AT BUFFALO SCHOOL OF MANAGEMENT** **BUFFALO, NY**

Received Bachelor of Science degree in finance, *cum laude*, 1988. Dean's List from 1985-1988. Elected to membership of *Beta Gamma Sigma*, the National Management Honor Society.

Personal/ Affiliations Founding member of Associates' Committee of Literacy Partners and member of Committee for the New York Auto Show to benefit East Side House Settlement. Member of Harvard Club of New York, Harvard Business School Clubs of New York and Northeast Ohio, Union Club, and Cleveland Athletic Club.

EXHIBIT 1 *(continued)*

BRETT R. KEITH

Education

1997-1999 **HARVARD BUSINESS SCHOOL** **BOSTON, MA**

Awarded Master in Business Administration, June 1999. Elected Honor Representative. Involved in Principal Investment Club, Small Business & Entrepreneurship Club, Golf Club and Running Club.

1990-1994 **UNIVERSITY OF ST. THOMAS** **ST. PAUL, MN**

Awarded Bachelor of Arts, Business with dual majors in Finance & Accounting. Elected President of Professional Business Fraternity. Recipient of Leadership Scholarship.

Experience

1999-present **ROCKWOOD EQUTY PARTNERS LLC** **NEW YORK, NY AND CLEVELAND, OH**

Principal and Founder – With one partner, formed a private investment firm focused on the acquisition of middle market industrial companies with revenues between $10 million and $50 million.

1998 **LEHMAN BROTHERS, INC.** **NEW YORK, NY**

Associate: Mergers & Acquisitions – As a member of the M&A group, performed quantitative and analytical work in connection with advisory engagements for clients of various sizes. Interacted with management, performed due diligence and developed valuation techniques for companies in different stages of their life cycles.

- Advised in the $3.5 Billion merger between EXCEL Communications and Teleglobe, closed in 1998.
- Used analytical techniques to value a portfolio of patents related to the convergence of the Telecom industry.
- Developed and assessed strategic alternatives for clients in multiple industries.

1996 - 1997 **JACOBSON MACHINE WORKS, INC.** **MINNEAPOLIS, MN**

Corporate Controller - Managed internal and external financial reporting, directed treasury function and served as primary contact for bank relations of a turnaround entity. The company was a portfolio company of a Minneapolis-based leveraged buyout firm.

- Structured complete refinancing of corporate debt for more favorable financing agreement with new lender.
- Implemented downsizing and outsourcing practices which generated 30% reduction in fixed costs. Through the outsourcing of high-volume, low technology items, increased margins on repeat product sales from an average of 0% to 40%, while decreasing selling price to customers 5-10%.
- Developed business plan related to the spin-off of medical waste product line into a stand-alone entity. Created complex and flexible financial model to determine capital requirements for different growth scenarios.
- Advised Senior Management as to the feasibility of various exit strategies including a proposed management-led LBO. The company was ultimately sold to a strategic investor in an asset purchase.

1994 - 1996 **ARTHUR ANDERSEN LLP** **MINNEAPOLIS, MN**

Auditor/Consultant - Audited clients in variety of industries including manufacturing, distribution, airlines, healthcare & insurance. Assumed supervisory position on several audit engagements after one year.

- Participated in audit, due diligence and spin-off transactions and related SEC filings for multi-industry clients. Generated pro-forma Financials for the spin-off of an airline subsidiary into a stand-alone SEC company.
- Consulted to various clients including a $600mm manufacturer of fitness equipment that had experienced an inventory write-down of 35%. Also designed financial/operational model for payroll-processing client to determine capital requirements and time schedule associated with the rollout of their new product offering.

1993 - 1994 **GRANT THORNTON LLP** **MINNEAPOLIS, MN**

Public Finance Analyst

- Performed Agreed Upon Procedures to determine legal feasibility of municipal bond refunding issuances. Designed elaborate spreadsheet models to analyze complex cash flow "waterfall" scenarios.
- Communicated with underwriters, attorneys and bond insurers to facilitate debt offerings to the market.

Personal/ Affiliations Member of Harvard Business School Club of New York, Harvard Club of New York, Harvard Club of Northeastern Ohio, Association of Corporate Growth and the American Institute of Certified Public Accountants. Volunteer for NFTE, the National Foundation for Teaching Entrepreneurship and sponsor in The Student/Sponsor Partnership Organization. Licensed Pilot. Enjoy golfing, running, red wine, travel and theatre.

Source: Company documents.

EXHIBIT 2 Historical Financial Statements

Income Statement as of June 30:

	1995	1996	1997	1998	1999	2000
Net Sales	17,136	17,815	14,711	12,699	17,926	21,200
Cost of Goods Sold	13,217	13,727	11,942	10,617	14,498	16,535
Gross Profit	3,919	4,088	2,769	2,082	3,428	4,665
Gross Margin	*22.90%*	*22.90%*	*18.80%*	*16.40%*	*19.10%*	*22.00%*
S,G & A Cost	2,219	3,106	2,350	2,503	2,398	2,640
EBIT	1,700	982	419	-421	1,030	2,025
EBIT Margin	*9.90%*	*5.50%*	*2.80%*	*-3.30%*	*5.70%*	*9.60%*
Interest Expense	201	146	51	32	82	56
Interest Income	-181	-200	-298	-238	-181	-120
EBT	1,680	1,036	666	-215	1,129	2,089
Tax Expense	665	367	232	-141	386	898
Net Income	1,015	669	434	-74	743	1,191
Cash Flow Analysis:						
EBIT	1,700	982	419	-421	1,030	2,025
Depreciation	175	197	212	211	210	165
Amortization	248	334	343	363	370	412
EBITDA	2,123	1,513	974	153	1,610	2,602
Addback CEO compensation*	700	700	721	664	707	790
Include RockWood Management Fee						-300
Adjusted EBITDA	**2,823**	**2,213**	**1,695**	**817**	**2,317**	**3,092**
Adj EBITDA Margin	*16.5%*	*12.4%*	*11.5%*	*6.4%*	*12.9%*	*14.6%*

* The addback relates to the existing CEO's compensation and is easily traceable by reviewing the company's internal documents, while for fiscal 2000, RockWood's annual management fee of $300,000 was added in as an expense to accurately project what Hudson's EBITDA would be on a pro-forma basis after an acquisition (see projections in Exhibit 3).

EXHIBIT 2 (*continued*)

Balance Sheet as of June 30

ASSETS	1995	1996	1997	1998	1999	2000
Cash	1,255	813	2,344	552	989	809
Accounts Receivable	2,135	2,147	800	1,390	2,621	2,675
Inventory	3,325	3,487	3,113	3,677	4,238	4,198
Marketable Securities	2,143	1,741	1,875	2,143	2,329	2,487
Other Current (prepaid & taxes)	169	243	551	416	238	285
Total Current Assets	9,027	8,431	8,683	8,178	10,415	10,454
PP&E at cost	3,074	3,463	3,680	3,798	3,883	4,046
Accumulated Depreciation	-2,366	-2,878	-2,963	-3,150	-3,358	-3,523
PP&E, net	708	585	717	648	525	523
Goodwill, at cost				513	513	513
Accumulated amortization				-6	-40	-74
Goodwill, net				507	473	439
Patents, at cost				2,816	3,058	3,308
Accumulated amortization				-1,279	-1,611	-1,989
Patents, net	2,376	2,060	1,755	1,537	1,447	1,319
CSV of Life Insurance	629	298	327	357	392	440
Deposits	1	1	1	24	24	24
Total Non-Current Assets	630	299	328	381	416	464
Total Assets	**12,741**	**11,375**	**11,483**	**11,251**	**13,276**	**13,199**

LIABILITIES & EQUITY	1995	1996	1997	1998	1999	2000
Line of Credit					1310	
Accounts Payable	741	396	573	696	762	784
Accrued Expenses	808	372	391	319	361	650
Accrued Income Taxes	91	193	19		285	
Current portion of existing leases	66	79	94	112		
Current portion of existing note	687	220	220	245	9	14
Total Current Liabilities	2,393	1,260	1,297	1,372	2,727	1,448
Deferred Income Tax	90	107	95	118	22	25
Existing leases, net	285	206	112			
Existing note, net of current portion	1,298	495	275	55	14	
Total Non-current Liabilities	1,673	808	482	173	36	25
Common Equity	1	1	1	1	1	1
Unrealized Gain on Securities				76	98	120
Additional Paid-in Capital	80	80	80	80	122	122
Retained Earnings	8,594	9,226	9,623	9,549	10,292	11,483
Total Equity	8,675	9,307	9,704	9,706	10,513	11,726
Total Liabilities & Equity	**12,741**	**11,375**	**11,483**	**11,251**	**13,276**	**13,199**

EXHIBIT 2 (*continued*)

Cash Flow Statement as of June 30:

Cash Flows From Operations	1996	1997	1998	1999	2000
Net Income	669	434	-74	743	1,191
Depreciation	512	85	187	208	165
Amortization					412
Accounts Receivable	-12	1,347	-590	-1,231	-54
Inventory	-162	374	-564	-561	40
Marketable Securities	402	-134	-268	-186	-158
Other (Prepaid & Taxes)	-74	-308	135	178	-47
Accounts Payable	-345	177	123	66	22
Accrued Expenses	-436	19	-72	42	289
Accrued Income Taxes	102	-174	-19	285	-285
Net Cash provided/(used)	656	1,820	-1,142	-456	1,575
Cash Flows From Investing					
Cash Value of Life Insurance	331	-29	-30	-35	-48
Deposits			-23		
P,P&E, at cost	-389	-217	-118	-85	-163
Goodwill, at cost			-507	34	
Patents	316	305	218	90	-250
Net cash flows provided/(used)	258	59	-460	4	-461
Cash Flows From Financing					
Dividends	-37	-37			
Line of Credit				1,310	-1,310
Current portion of existing leases	13	15	18	-112	
Current portion of existing note	-467		25	-236	5
Existing leases, net of current portion	-79	-94	-112		
Existing note, net of current portion	-803	-220	-220	-41	-14
Deferred Income Tax	17	-12	23	-96	3
Unrealized Gain on Securities			76	22	22
Additional paid-in Capital				42	
Net cash flows provided/(used)	-1,356	-348	-190	889	-1,294
Summary					
Net Increase/(decrease) in cash & equivalents	-442	1,531	-1,792	437	-180
Cash & Equivalents at beginning of year	1,255	813	2,344	552	989
Cash & Equivalents at end of year	813	2,344	552	989	809

Source: Company documents.

EXHIBIT 3 Facility Overview

Overview of facilities:

1. The Solon, Ohio facility (located in a suburb of Cleveland) served as the company's headquarters with 50,000 sq ft of manufacturing space and 10,000 sq ft of office space at this owned facility. All administrative functions (excluding those for WEBB) were performed here.
2. The Mansfield, Ohio facility (approx 1.5 hours south of Cleveland) specialized in the assembly of NBC filtration products. This owned facility consisted of 20,000 sq ft of manufacturing space and all administrative work for this facility was done at the company's headquarters in Solon.
3. WEBB, based in Fargo, North Dakota, was a standalone operation which focused exclusively on the manufacture/assembly of diesel engine components in this 20,000 sq ft leased facility. WEBB did not integrate with Solon from either an operational or administrative perspective.
4. The Chula Vista, California facility (just south of San Diego) specialized in the assembly of NBC filtration products. This leased facility consisted of 20,000 sq ft of manufacturing space and all administrative work for this facility was done at the company's headquarters in Solon.

Source: Company documents.

EXHIBIT 4 Comparable Company Financial Information

Engineered Support Systems	1996	1997	1998	1999
Market Value of Equity	30.46	70.62	69.20	80.95
Sales	81.51	88.57	96.97	165.26
SG&A	6.46	7.09	12.39	17.22
Capital Expenditures	1.14	1.99	1.33	1.59
EBITDA	7.81	9.57	13.06	18.98
Net Income	3.31	4.64	5.79	7.31
Total Assets	34.09	37.08	92.16	239.40
Current Liabilities	9.08	8.65	21.83	86.24
LT Debt	2.96	2.07	37.51	80.65
Beta	NA	NA	0.84	0.57
P/E Ratio	9.44	15.89	11.78	9.55
Net Worth	19.25	23.73	30.17	63.42
Volatility	1.86	3.06	3.58	3.87

Engineered Support Systems sells military support equipment such as tank transportation vehicles and loading systems, electronic warfare systems, avionics test equipment, generators, water systems, and plastic faucets manufactured to military specifications. Non-military products include material-handling equipment for the US Post Office and various OEM plastic products. Its largest customer is the US government, representing 82% of sales.

Cummins Inc.	1996	1997	1998	1999
Market Value of Equity	1812.40	2267.98	1487.45	2000.14
Sales	5257.00	5625.00	6266.00	6639.00
SG&A	977.00	1004.00	1042.00	1026.00
Capital Expenditures	304.00	405.00	271.00	215.00
EBITDA	357.00	434.00	498.00	610.00
Net Income	160.00	212.00	-21.00	160.00
Total Assets	3369.00	3765.00	4542.00	4697.00
Current Liabilities	1021.00	1055.00	1071.00	1314.00
LT Debt	283.00	522.00	1137.00	1092.00
Beta	NA	1.17	1.13	1.30
P/E Ratio	11.47	10.64	NM	11.61
Net Worth	1312.00	1422.00	1272.00	1429.00
Volatility	9.83	11.92	11.89	11.55

Cummins manufactures large diesel engines. These engines are used in power school buses, medium-duty trucks, pickup trucks and mining and construction equipment. The company also manufactures power generation

EXHIBIT 4 (*continued*)

products Fleetguard and Nelson, its filtration subsidiaries, manufacture fuel filters and air filters for heavy-duty engines

Donaldson Co. Inc.	1996	1997	1998	1999
Market Value of Equity	623.63	1007.59	908.23	1145.47
Sales	758.65	833.35	940.35	944.14
SG&A	147.23	162.56	176.46	187.29
Capital Expenditures	39.30	47.33	54.71	29.54
EBITDA	97.32	109.21	112.07	116.08
Net Income	43.44	50.62	57.05	62.45
Total Assets	402.85	454.39	499.32	528.36
Current Liabilities	138.58	176.30	167.49	151.14
LT Debt	10.04	4.20	50.35	86.69
Beta	NA	NA	0.58	0.47
P/E Ratio	14.75	20.58	16.00	18.66
Net Worth	228.88	243.87	255.67	262.76
Volatility	4.03	5.23	5.66	6.71

Donaldson manufactures filtration systems and replacement parts to filter air, sound, and liquids. Its engine products (air intake and exhaust systems and liquid-filtration components) serve transportation, construction, and mining industries. Its industrial products (dust, fume, and mist collectors and static and pulse-clean air-filtration systems) are primarily used in industrial gas turbine, computer disk drive filtration, and clean room applications. General Electric is Donaldson's largest customer, accounting for 13% of sales.

In $ millions, except Beta, P/E Ratios and volatility

Source: Compiled from Compustat and Hoovers Online.

EXHIBIT 5 Projected Financial Statements

SUMMARY INCOME STATEMENTS	2001	2002	2003	2004	2005
Revenues	22,366,000	23,596,130	24,893,917	26,263,083	27,707,552
Revenue Growth	*5.5%*	*5.5%*	*5.5%*	*5.5%*	*5.5%*
Gross Profit	4,921,575	5,192,262	5,477,836	5,779,117	6,096,968
Gross Margin	*22.0%*	*22.0%*	*22.0%*	*22.0%*	*22.0%*
Selling, General & Admin. Expense	(2,268,250)	(2,393,004)	(2,524,619)	(2,663,473)	(2,809,964)
Operating Earnings	2,653,325	2,799,258	2,953,217	3,115,644	3,287,004
Operating Margin	*11.9%*	*11.9%*	*11.9%*	*11.9%*	*11.9%*
Interest Expense	954,542	907,118	826,889	766,202	595,258
EBITDA	3,262,060	3,441,473	3,630,754	3,830,446	4,041,120
EBITDA Margin	14.6%	14.6%	14.6%	14.6%	14.6%

SUMMARY BALANCE SHEETS	2001	2002	2003	2004	2005
Net Working Capital	6,797,820	7,129,955	7,480,358	7,850,032	8,240,039
Total Term and Revolving Debt	6,306,150	6,001,587	5,564,490	5,671,335	4,334,097
Seller Note Outstanding	2,250,000	1,750,000	1,250,000	-	-
CAPEX	223,660	235,961	248,939	262,631	277,076
Total Equity	1,060,623	2,057,127	3,198,828	4,478,860	5,971,120
Debt/Equity Ratio	8.1	3.8	2.1	1.3	0.7

SELECT CREDIT RATIOS	2001	2002	2003	2004	2005
EBITDA/Interest	3.42 x	3.79 x	4.39 x	5.00 x	6.79 x
EBITDA less CAPEX/Interest	3.18 x	3.53 x	4.09 x	4.66 x	6.32 x
Sr. Debt/EBITDA	1.93 x	1.74 x	1.53 x	1.48 x	1.07 x
Total Debt/EBITDA	2.62 x	2.25 x	1.88 x	1.48 x	1.07 x

EARN-OUT PAYMENTS	2001	2002	2003	2004	2005
Year 1	83,333				
Year 2		83,333			
Year 3			83,333		
Total	83,333	83,333	83,333	-	-

Source: Company documents.

EXHIBIT 6 Defense Budget Authority – Department of Defense Only (in billions of constant 2003 dollars)

Fiscal Year	Procurement	RDT&E	Operation & Maintenance	Military Personnel	Other	Total
1999	11.6	1.3	4.7	-1.5	-11.1	2.9
1998	3	0.8	1.6	-4.3	-9.2	-0.5
1997	-1.8	2.3	-3.5	-2.2	-8.9	-2.4
1996	-0.7	0.1	-2.9	-4.6	18.3	-1.8
1995	-3.2	-2.2	3.5	-2.2	-12.7	-0.8
1994	-19.9	-10.2	-4.3	-8.4	7.3	-8.7
1993	-15.1	-2.1	-2.7	-10.2	-6.8	-7.7
1992	-15.3	6.1	-15.8	-5.9	11.6	-9.5
1991	-13	-6.4	14.4	1.2	21.2	1.4
1990	-3.1	-7.6	-1.3	-1	-15.4	-2.8
1989	-6.7	-2.9	-0.2	-0.8	-1.8	-2.4
1988	-5.1	-0.7	-0.2	-1.1	2.4	-1.8
1987	-7.7	3.5	1.6	1.2	-7.1	-1.3
1986	-5.9	6.7	-2.5	1.6	-7.7	-1.6
1985	4.8	10.4	7.6	27.6	-3.6	11.4
1984	5	13.4	3.9	0.9	23.9	5.1
1983	14.8	9.4	5.2	1.8	-0.3	7.4
1982	25	14.1	6.9	1.8	18.4	11.3
1981	23.2	13.2	7	2.6	45.6	11
1980	1.3	-0.9	6	0.6	-2.3	1.8

Source: Compiled from Standard & Poor's Industry Survey: Aerospace & Defense, 10/31/02.

EXHIBIT 7 Proposed Sources and Uses of Funds - 2000

Sources and Uses		Amount	%
Sources			
Senior Term Loan	(@ 9.50%)	$3,500,000	26.2%
Revolver	(@ 9.50%)	3,500,000	26.2%
Seller Paper	(@ 9.00%)	2,250,000	16.9%
Preferred Stock	(@ 15.00%)	800,000	6.0%
Common Equity		200,000	1.5%
Other Sources:			
Cash, existing		3,100,000	23.2%
Total Sources		$13,350,000	100.0%
Uses			
Purchase of 100% of Stock		$12,750,000	
Other Assets		0	
Transaction Fees		600,000	
Total Uses		$13,350,000	
		-	

Composition	
Cash	10,500,000
Seller Note	2,250,000
Earn-out	250,000

Borrowing Availability	
Total Revolver:	3,500,000
Availability assuming:	
A/R at 80% and Inventory at 55%	4,693,590
Excess Availability/(shortfall)	1,193,590

Analysis of Fees	
Investment Banking Fee	-
Legal and Accounting	250,000
RockWood M&A Fee	150,000
Other Fees	200,000
Total Fees	$600,000

Source: Company documents.

EXHIBIT 8 Bank Term Sheet

August 21, 2000

Owen M. Colligan
Brett R. Keith
RockWood Equity Partners LLC
141 East 56th Street, Suite 6D
New York, NY 10022

Dear Gentlemen:

Based on the information and representations that have been provided to The Columbus National Bank (the "bank"), we are pleased to deliver to you this revised proposal to provide a package of credit facilities to Newco (the "Borrower"), a company to be formed by RockWood Equity Partners LLC ("RockWood") to acquire 100% of the capital stock of Hudson Manufacturing Company ("Hudson"). The terms and conditions of this proposal are outlined in the following paragraphs and attachment. This proposal replaces our previous proposal dated August 1, 2000 in its entirety.

Please note that this letter and the associated attachment represent only a proposal to be used as the basis for our continued discussions and do not represent a commitment by the Bank. This letter and the associated attachment serve to (a) outline a preliminary financing structure and (b) identify additional information and action needed so that we may complete our due diligence process. Once this due diligence process is completed, the Bank may require alternative terms and conditions or decline to offer financing to Newco.

BORROWER:	Newco
BANK:	The Columbus National Bank
FACILITIES:	A. A two-year Revolving Line of Credit ("Revolver") in the maximum amount of $4,000,000. Advances under the Revolver will be limited to the sum of (i) 80% of Eligible Accounts Receivable plus (ii) 55% of Eligible Inventory as reported on the Borrower's monthly borrowing base certificate. B. A five-year Term Loan in the maximum amount of $3,500,000.
PURPOSE:	A. To support working capital and fund the acquisition of the stock of Hudson. B. To fund the acquisition of the stock of Hudson.

EXHIBIT 8 *(continued)*

SECURITY:	The facilities will be cross-collateralized and secured by a first lien on all of the Borrower's accounts receivable, inventory, machinery and equipment and general intangibles.
GUARANTY:	To the extent that a holding company is formed and remains in place in connection with the contemplated transaction, then the Facilities will be guaranteed by the continuing, unlimited guaranty of such holding company and secured by a pledge of the holding company's ownership interests in the Borrower.
REPAYMENT:	A. The Revolver will mature and be payable-in-full on September 30, 2002. B. The Term Loan will amortize in 59 consecutive, monthly payments of $41,667 plus interest followed by a final payment in the amount of $1,041,647 plus interest (seven-year amortization schedule/five-year maturity).
MANDATORY REPAYMENTS:	A. Not Applicable B. In addition to the repayment schedule outlined above, the Term Loan will incorporate mandatory prepayments in an amount equal to 50% of Excess Cash Flow on an annual basis. Such mandatory prepayments will be applied in the inverse order of maturity and will be payable on September 30, 2002 (for the fiscal year ended June 30, 2002) and each September 30 thereafter.
VOLUNTARY PREYPAYMENTS:	A. At the option of the Borrower, the commitment amount of the Revolver may permanently reduce in minimum amounts of $500,000 and even increments of $100,000 upon prior written notice to the Bank. B. At the option of the Borrower, the principal balance of the Term Loan may be prepaid in minimum amounts of $250,000 and even increments of $50,000 without any type of premium (except for breakage fees associated with any applicable LIBOR contracts) upon prior written notice to the Bank. Such voluntary prepayments will be applied in the inverse order of maturity.

EXHIBIT 8 (*continued*)

INTEREST RATE: The Borrower will have the option of selecting interest rates based on the Bank's Prime Rate or LIBOR (30, 60, 90 and 180 days). In addition, the Bank will provide a "daily" LIBOR option for the Revolver.

The applicable spreads over the Bank's Prime Rate and LIBOR will be performance-driven, based on the Borrower's Leverage as follows:

	REVOLVER		TERM LOAN	
Leverage	LIBOR Spread	Prime Rate Spread	LIBOR Spread	Prime Rate Spread
X > 3.25	2.50%	0.25%	2.75%	0.50%
2.75 < x ≥ 3.25	2.25%	0.00%	2.50%	0.25%
2.25 < x ≥ 2.75	2.00%	(0.25%)	2.25%	0.00%
X ≤ 2.25	1.75%	(0.50%)	2.00%	(0.25%)

Pricing for the Facilities will be determined quarterly based on (i) audited financial statements for one quarter of each fiscal year and (ii) company-prepared financial statements for the remaining quarters and will be adjusted on the first day of the month following each quarter-end.

Notwithstanding the foregoing, the initial interest spreads for the Facilities are highlighted in the above table. These initial interest spreads will remain in effect from closing through December 31, 2000.

Interest on the Facilities will be payable as follows: (i) monthly for Prime Rate and "daily" LIBOR borrowings; (ii) at the end of the term for LIBOR contracts of 30, 60 and 90 days and (iii) at the end of each three-month period for LIBOR contracts of 180 days.

All LIBOR contracts (excluding "daily" LIBOR borrowings) will carry a prepayment fee and will be written in minimum amounts of $500,000 and even increments of $100,000.

FEES: Closing Fee in amount of 0.50% of the commitment amount of the Facilities.

Unused commitment fee in the amount of 0.25% of the unused portion of the Revolver, payable quarterly in arrears.

EXHIBIT 8 *(continued)*

	The Borrower will be responsible for the payment of all of the Bank's legal fees and out-of-pocket expenses in connection with the Facilities.
COVENANTS:	The documentation for the Facilities will incorporate affirmative, negative and financial covenants customary for this type of transaction including, but not limited to, the following: 1. Minimum Cash Flow Coverage Ratio of 1.10:1 2. Maximum Leverage as follows: Closing through 9/29/01 3.50:1 9/30/01 through 6/29/02 3.25:1 6/30/02 through 6/29/03 3.00:1 6/30/03 and thereafter 2.50:1 3. Minimum Net Worth as follows: 6/30/01 through 6/29/02 $750,000 6/30/02 through 6/29/03 $1,500,000 6/30/03 and thereafter $1,500,000 plus 50% of Net Income on an annual basis. 4. Limitation on Annual Capital Expenditures of $250,000 5. Limitation on Annual Management Fees to RockWood of $300,000 6. Prohibition on Dividends
REPORTING REQUIREMENTS:	1. Monthly company-prepared financial statements 2. Monthly borrowing base certificates 3. Quarterly covenant compliance statements 4. Annual audited financial statements
CONDITIONS OF FUNDING:	1. Approval of the Facilities by the appropriate senior management of the Bank. 2. Satisfactory review of the stock purchase agreement and any other related documentation. 3. Receipt by the Borrower of subordinated debt in minimum amount of $2,250,000 from the selling shareholders of Hudson. Such subordinated debt shall, at a minimum, contain the following terms and conditions: (i) all payments of principal and interest shall be subordinated to the prior

EXHIBIT 8 *(continued)*

repayment of the Facilities and (ii) the interest rate and amortization schedule shall be consistent with the letter of intent dated as of July 19, 2000 between the shareholders of Hudson and RockWood.

4. Receipt by the Borrower of preferred stock proceeds in a minimum amount of $475,000 from parties reasonably satisfactory to the Bank. Such preferred stock shall, at a minimum, contain the following terms and conditions: (i) the final maturity date shall extend beyond the final maturity date of the Facilities; (ii) no principal payments shall be required until such time that the Facilities are paid in full and (iii) the cash coupon shall not exceed 15% on an annual basis.
5. Receipt by the Borrower of equity proceeds in a minimum amount of $25,000 on terms and conditions that are reasonably satisfactory to the Bank.
6. Completion and satisfactory review of an initial field examination in connection with Hudson's current assets to be performed by the Bank's auditors.
7. Receipt and satisfactory review of Hudson's audited financial statements for the fiscal year ended June 30, 2000.
8. Receipt and satisfactory review of any other financial information which may be required by the Bank.
9. Execution and satisfactory review of all appropriate legal documentation contemplated herewith or other documentation which may be required by the Bank.

EVENTS OF FAULT: The Facilities will be cross-defaulted and the documentation required for the transaction will incorporate events of default that are standard for this type of transaction.

EXPIRATION: This proposal will expire on August 25, 2000.

EXHIBIT 8 *(continued)*

If the financing proposal outlined above is satisfactory to you, please sign below and return this letter to the undersigned along with your check in the amount of $8,500 (the "Deposit"). This Deposit will serve to underscore your sincere intention to proceed with the financing proposed herein and will be used to offset expenses incurred by the Bank as the result of our review and analysis. Per our previous conversations, this review process will also involve the preparation of initial legal documentation by the Bank's outside counsel. Once received, the Deposit will be accounted as follows:

- If the Facilities are approved and funded, we will apply the Deposit, less any expenses incurred during the course of our review that are not otherwise reimbursed by the Borrower, to the Closing Fee.
- If the Facilities are not approved substantially as outlined herein by the appropriate senior management of the Bank, we will return the Deposit, less any expenses incurred during the course of our review, to you.
- If the Facilities are approved by the appropriate senior management of the Bank and for any reason you decide not to proceed with funding, we will retain the Deposit for time spent, labor and services rendered and all other costs of the review and analysis of the Facilities.

Upon receipt of this letter signed and accepted by you and the Deposit, we will continue our due diligence and credit approval processes. We appreciate the opportunity to structure a financing proposal in connection with the acquisition of the stock of Hudson Manufacturing Company and look forward to working with you.

Sincerely,
Timothy M. Ward
Vice President & Portfolio Manager
Corporate Banking
Newco/RockWood Equity Partners
Accepted on this _______ day of August, 2000
By: ________________________________
Title: ________________________________

Source: Company documents.

EXHIBIT 9 General Macroeconomic Conditions

	March 1998	June 1998	September 1998	December 1998	March 1999	June 1999	September 1999	December 1999	March 2000	June 2000	September 2000
Lehman US Corporate A	6.51	6.46	6.35	5.72	6.04	6.46	7.07	7.42	7.76	7.73	7.82
Lehman US Corporate AA	6.36	6.24	6.12	5.39	5.74	6.17	6.77	7.06	7.46	7.46	7.61
Lehman US Corporate AAA	6.24	6.17	6.01	5.24	5.46	5.98	6.47	6.75	7.22	7.16	7.31
T-Bill-3 Month	5.02	4.97	4.26	4.37	4.37	4.65	4.74	5.17	5.72	5.71	6.05
T-Bill-6 Month	5.07	5.04	4.33	4.39	4.36	4.84	4.79	5.49	5.89	5.96	6.01
Gov Notes-5 Year	5.64	5.47	4.23	4.56	5.12	5.67	5.78	6.36	6.32	6.18	5.85
Gov Notes-10 Year	5.67	5.44	4.44	4.65	5.25	5.81	5.9	6.45	6.03	6.03	5.8
Gov Bonds-30 Year	5.94	5.62	4.98	5.09	5.63	5.98	6.06	6.48	5.84	5.9	5.88
Inflation Rate	1.38	1.62	1.43	1.67	1.79	1.97	2.57	2.68	3.70	3.74	3.52
Unemployment Rate	4.7	4.5	4.5	4.4	4.2	4.3	4.2	4.1	4.0	4.0	4.0
GDP % Annual Growth	3.31	3.43	3.20	3.07	3.08	3.13	3.16	3.02	3.09	3.16	3.33
Gross Domestic Product	8,396	8,442	8,528	8,667	8,733	8,775	8,886	9,040	9,097	9,205	9,218
S&P 500 Comp-LTD	1,101	1,133	1,017	1,229	1,286	1,372	1,282	1,469	1,498	1,454	1,436
Wilshire 5000 Equity	10,494	10,663	9,346	11,317	11,707	12,583	11,713	13,812	14,296	13,618	13,613

Source: Compiled from Compustat and Datastream International.

CHAPTER 4.6

EyeControl: Inspiring Communication

Paul Gompers and Danielle Golan

"Even more important than the freedom of speech is the freedom to speak."
—Stephen Hawking

It was an early afternoon in November 2019 and EyeControl cofounders Or Retzkin, CEO, and Itai Kornberg, CTO, had just wrapped up a visit with their newest client, a housebound Lou Gehrig's disease (ALS) patient for whom speech was becoming increasingly challenging as his disease progressed. The two had spent the morning gathering user feedback on the wearable, light-weight EyeControl unit, a device that would allow the patient to use eye movement to express his basic needs and thoughts to caregivers once his condition robbed him of the ability to communicate verbally. At that advanced state of the disease, he would have a condition known as locked-in syndrome—a neurological disorder associated with motor-neuron diseases, stroke and brain injury. Sufferers were cognitively sound, yet unable to move or speak due to paralysis of all voluntary muscles, with the exception of those that controlled eye movement.

EyeControl was founded in Tel Aviv, Israel in 2016 by Retzkin and Kornberg and a third founder, Shay Rishoni, who suffered from ALS and passed away in May 2018. With a shared personal connection to locked-in syndrome, they were committed to addressing the frustrations that accompanied the loss of communication associated with the condition. Existing solutions were costly (upwards of $10,000), cumbersome, and complex to use. By contrast, EyeControl was reasonably priced ($2,600) and required minimal set-up. Its most appealing feature was that it was screen-free—in fact, it was the first screen-free solution available—and thus easy to use around the clock and in any setting.

EyeControl: Inspiring Communication
by PAUL GOMPERS, DANIELLE GOLAN, case number 9-820-078 Rev. JUNE 21, 2023

EyeControl initially set out to target the home-care segment of permanently locked-in individuals, which the founders estimated was more than 850,000 patients worldwide. As part of their social mission, they had raised $5 million from startup competitions, accelerator awards, grants, and angel and impact investors. Since early 2019, the company had sold around 100 devices in the U.K. and Israel. The cofounders had planned to penetrate the U.S. and EU home-care markets by the end of the year.

However, seeing the efficacy of their device, the cofounders contemplated expanding their early ambitions to include solutions for the hospital facilities segment, a far larger market. EyeControl would allow 24/7 communication for all temporarily locked-in or ventilated patients in intensive care units (ICU) and other medical wards and facilities. EyeControl estimated there were 34,400 such facilities in the world. Yet selling to the facilities segment would require EyeControl to conduct costly clinical trials where they would have to demonstrate that the device would yield cost savings and improved outcomes to the facilities. The sales process to hospital administrators would be far more complex than the straightforward sales for their existing home-care market.

Even though Retzkin and Kornberg had carefully managed the company's expenditures, they had limited time to execute their current home-care business plan with existing funds, and would soon need to raise capital. Yet they also realized that their cash needs would be far greater if they were to now pursue the facilities market opportunity, which they estimated would be very costly. They would have to seek funding outside of grants and impact funds, tapping traditional VC funds who would be interested in the size of the opportunity presented by the facilities market—an estimated $5 billion.

Even as they undertook meetings with VCs in pursuit of the Series A, they wondered whether a strategic corporate partner was a potential alternative solution. Could such a partner lend resources to the sales initiative that would be required to sell to the facilities market? Even if they succeeded in raising VC capital, what would happen if clinical trials for facilities failed to prove reduced costs and improved outcomes for the hospitals? Would they then be relegated to the status of niche player in the home-care market?

While they contemplated the critical decisions before them, the cofounders could not help but also muse about alternative, non-medical applications for their product—for segments such as security, gaming, and driving.

FOUNDING EYECONTROL

Kornberg, a software engineer at Hewlett-Packard and a social entrepreneur, befriended a young man who suffered from Duchenne muscular dystrophy, a rare and often-fatal genetic disease characterized by progressive muscular weakness. Leveraging his expertise in software engineering, Kornberg set out to create a solution to help his friend control a computer with his eyes and launched a hackathon for that purpose in 2014. Shay Rishoni, an ALS sufferer, was the CEO of *Prize4Life*, a non-profit organization dedicated to accelerating the discovery of treatments and a cure for ALS. When Rishoni learned of the hackathon, he secured an invitation to address the participants via video conference. Inspired by the hackathon, Rishoni and Kornberg decided to collaborate and develop an affordable device that would allow users to communicate around the clock.

Solutions in the market were expensive, cumbersome, screen-dependent and required calibration of the system at every use. Using these tools was not intuitive, and the learning curve could take anywhere from several days up to a few weeks. Size and dependency on a screen meant that most existing solutions were not mobile, leaving patients without appropriate means of communication in bed, on the move in a wheelchair or car, or at a hospital. Rishoni envisioned a more affordable, user-friendly solution that could be used anywhere, any time.

A few weeks after the hackathon, Retzkin, who had lost his grandmother to ALS, learned that Rishoni's non-profit was looking for volunteers to help develop an assistive device for ALS patients. Retzkin, who graduated from Physics and Accounting Schools, worked at PwC, decided to volunteer and joined Kornberg and Rishoni's effort, to develop a prototype of their wearable product, which they dubbed EyeControl. (See **Exhibit 1** for the cofounders' bios.) The team, joined by Tal Kellner who also lost her grandfather to ALS, started working on the device.

The EyeControl Device

The EyeControl was a lightweight, screen-free, head-mounted device with an attached camera and a small processing unit with a speaker. (See **Exhibit 2** for photos) The user listened to audio menus, consisting of preset commands and features, via bone conduction, and controlled the audio menus via eye movements. The camera read the movements of the pupil and relayed the designated commands to the processing unit, which converted the selected message to speech and sent it to the output speaker or to a connected Bluetooth device. Built-in prefabricated messages included an alert sound (to call for assistance), predefined sentences such as "I'm hot" or "my hand hurts" and time and weather updates.

Through an intuitive "joystick" interface, users employed eye movements: looking up, down, left, right, and blinking to control the device. If a user lacked the physical capability to make all five gestures, the EyeControl could be programmed to work with fewer gestures, as few as a single one, if necessary. To navigate between menus, the user would look left or right. To enter a menu, the user would look down and then look up to exit it.

To choose an option in a menu, the user would blink. The menus were in English and in Hebrew, but the speaker could broadcast sentences to caregivers in several other languages. The team was working on adding more features, developing such options as listening to audio books and music via bone conduction.

EyeControl's device had several advantages over the competition: its small size enabled easy shipping; it required no calibration to a screen thus could be activated instantly; and its camera used infrared technology so it was operational even in complete darkness. This feature was particularly helpful when a patient woke up in the middle of the night and needed the assistance of a caregiver. The EyeControl could be worn 24/7, therefore providing the ability to communicate in situations that previous solutions had not achieved. The short learning curve enabled users to communicate effectively on first use. (See **Exhibit 3** for user testimonials.)

The Road from Non-Profit to Company Status

The team realized that in order to grow past their early prototype, they needed support from professionals, so they applied for the first cycle of an accelerator program called 8200 IMPACT, which had been launched by the Israeli Defense Force's elite cybersecurity unit to fund ventures that solved social problems through technology.[1] In 2014 they were accepted into the 8200 IMPACT five-month program that offered professional workshops, shared office space, connection to the 8200 alumni network, and exposure to strategic partners as well as access to funding and over 70 mentors. The accelerator was a non-profit program and took no equity in the venture.[2] The team also secured a $150,000 grant from the Israeli government's Chief Scientist Office. Still operating as a non-profit organization, the team started a crowdfunding campaign on the Indiegogo platform, where they raised $43,000.[3] The Indiegogo backers donated money to support future production of the EyeControl and in return received t-shirts as a token of appreciation for their donation.

In early 2016, the team decided to quit their day jobs and shift from the non-profit structure to the creation of a private corporate entity under the name EyeControl. They raised $250,000 from a group of four Israeli angel investors who were inspired by the company's potential social impact. Rishoni donated his shares of the new company to his non-profit.

Keeping the Burn Rate Low

In the early days, the small team worked from Kornberg's apartment. They drew relatively small salaries and used freelancers whenever possible. They relied on cost-effective platforms such Fiverr, an online marketplace for freelance services, and on a variety of third parties for important operations such as marketing. The team also took advantage of government resources available through the Maof Agency, which supported small and medium-sized businesses. Maof subsidized consulting services for legal and regulatory matters, among others.

For the R&D team, instead of hiring software engineers with a computer science degree, the cofounders preferred graduates in other science fields who had coding training. The non-engineering graduates commanded a lower salary, without compromising on their quality of work. Retzkin commented on EyeControl's employee motivation, "Our employees prefer to work for a company they love and relate to its mission. All our employees receive options." For other business related operations, EyeControl relied on interns from top MBA schools in the U.K., the U.S., and Israel.

The team finally left Kornberg's apartment-cum-office when they hired two additional employees. Instead of moving to a trendy, expensive, shared office space in one of Tel Aviv's bustling startup neighborhoods, they opted for a more reasonably priced office space in a less central location. The company had the occasional fun outing, but did not offer the office perks like video games or expensive happy hours so common in other Israeli startups.

EYE CONTROLLED COMMUNICATION DEVICE LANDSCAPE

The Tobii Group was considered the market leader in eye tracking communication devices in terms of market share and its patent portfolio.[4] Founded in 2001, the Tobii Group had over 1,200 employees by 2019, total annual revenue of $143 million, and was listed on the Stockholm Stock Exchange.[5] The company's flagship eye-controlled speech-generating product line featured a 13"–16" screen that weighed approximately 5 lbs. to 6 lbs. Depending on the model, the price ranged from $11,700 to $17,500.[6,7] Revenues from this business line were estimated at $50 million annually.

The eye-tracking assistive device competitive landscape was populated with a number of smaller players. Ohio-based Prentke Romich Company (PRC) was founded in 1966 and had annual revenue of $30 million.[8] It sold various assistive communication tools including head-pointing and eye-gazing devices.[9] PRC's eye-tracking system included two components, an eye-tracking module ($6,900)[10] and a computerized screen ($7,295).[11] Other companies that produced eye-tracking communication devices included Belgium-based Jabbla that specialized in augmentative tools in the field of speech technology and offered communication devices and software;[12] and the U.S.-based Eyegaze[13] that offered eye tracking devices that were not suitable for locked-in patients who had lost the ability to visually dwell on one item.

HOME-CARE MARKET

In 2018, 18,000 units of eye-based speech generating devices were sold globally, with total revenues of $70 million. The majority of sales were in North America, followed by Europe and the rest of the world. Projections for 2025 estimated potential sales of nearly 28,000 units per year, with potential revenues of $100 million.[14] There was also potential in third world countries, where communication technologies were not widely available. The team estimated the total addressable market at $2 billion, based on research that indicated 850,000 home-based locked-in patients and a future lower average unit price of $2,400. After penetrating the Israeli, U.K. and U.S. markets, EyeControl planned to target European markets, primarily Germany and the Scandinavian countries.

Home-Care Clinical Trial

The team had not originally conceptualized the EyeControl as a medical device, but after extensive research, they realized that approval from federal health agencies such as the American Food and Drug Administration (FDA) or the *Conformité Européene*'s CE marking would mean that the device would qualify for reimbursement to users, thus increasing their sales potential tremendously. Reimbursement from healthcare systems and providers would be crucial to reaching more patients

In 2016 and 2017, the team conducted a clinical trial at the Rambam Medical Center in Haifa, Israel, which was required for the FDA and CE certification. The trial's purpose was to demonstrate the safety and feasibility of the EyeControl device in healthy volunteers first, and later in patients with early-stage ALS. Any feedback or safety concerns raised by the healthy volunteers was considered before moving forward to the second group of ALS patients. The device's primary purpose was designated as "supportive care" and the proposed intended use was the facilitation of non-verbal communication by individuals suffering from ALS and other locked-in conditions.[15] After successfully completing the clinical trials, in 2018 the device gained FDA approval, CE marking,[a] ISO 13485[b] and received approval for Medicare/Medicaid reimbursement codes. Medicare could cover 80% of the device's cost, and the remaining 20% could be

a CE marking signifies that products sold in the European Economic Area (EEA) have been assessed to meet high safety, health, and environmental protection requirements.

b ISO 13485 is an internationally agreed standard that sets out the requirements for a quality management system specific to the medical devices industry.

covered by Medicaid or other health plans. Additionally, the device was part of the U.K.'s NHS Supply Chain, and the Israeli Health Basket of the Ministry of Health, meaning it was fully subsidized by the healthcare systems in both the U.K. and Israel.

Sales Cycle and Distribution

Physicians were typically the first to identify the early stages of a degenerative disease such as ALS, even before communication issues arose. As the disease progressed and patients started experiencing speech problems, a speech or occupational therapist would most likely recommend a communication device. In each market, the sales cycle was a bit different, but the principle was similar: a speech therapist would recognize a need for a communication device and submit a request to the respective healthcare agency or provider to subsidize a device. The team attended conferences and workshops dedicated to assistive technology to introduce the EyeControl to speech therapists, and visited rehabilitation centers to train relevant health professionals on the device. Patients might also learn about EyeControl through social media, blogs, and NGOs that assisted locked-in patients.

The EyeControl was more affordable than other solutions. The price of the device in Israel and the U.K. was \$2,600–\$2,800, while the price in the U.S. had not been determined yet. In Israel, communication devices were sold directly to patients, but in the long term, the goal was to team up with relevant medical devices companies and market the product through them. In the U.K., EyeControl had one employee and planned to hire a second one, with a long-term goal of working with a distributor. For each device sold, the team made a home visit to show the patient how to use the EyeControl device and get user feedback, but they planned to conduct these sessions remotely in the future. Even though use of the device was intuitive, remote access would allow EyeControl to support patients anywhere in the world and help personalize their device for their own particular needs.

Consistent with their lean operations and low burn rate strategy, the team planned to approach MBA students in top business schools in London to help with business development as a school project. Sales in the U.S. would require a distributor and possibly a strategic partner.

FINANCING STRATEGY

Competitions and Grants

Part of EyeControl's financing strategy had been to participate in startup competitions that offered cash rewards, a source of non-dilutive capital.

The promised social impact of their product went a long way in generating emotional engagement. As Retzkin commented, "When we pitch EyeControl in competitions, we barely speak about the business model. We discuss the need, the innovation behind EyeControl, our winning previous competitions and our track record of getting approval from federal health agencies and reimbursement options many health care providers." (See **Exhibit 4** for EyeControl's track record.) EyeControl's pitch for competitions evolved over time, Retzkin added, "We received feedback from the judges that the market is not big enough, so we started showing the bigger picture and the vision of where we are going. We want to give all ventilated patients the ability to communicate, and we believe that with advancements in medicine and technology, the number of ventilated patients will grow." The total amount of non-dilutive capital EyeControl received from grants and awards was around $3.5 million.

Impact Angel Investors

EyeControl had a group of four angel investors that had been supporting the team from its early days, when it was still part of Rishoni's non-profit organization. (See **Exhibit 5** for the angel investors' bios.) Itsik Danziger, a veteran executive in the Israeli high-tech sector, had decided about ten years earlier to focus on impact investing and was looking for investment opportunities in double bottom line (financial profit and social return) companies. He had been involved with many impact businesses as an investor, board member and mentor, so it felt very natural to him to be involved in EyeControl. When Danziger met Rishoni, Retzkin and Kornberg, he was intrigued with the potential social value, and as he learned more about the EyeControl project and got to know the team, he and the other angel investors realized the business potential and decided to invest in EyeControl. Danziger commented on their motivation, "The size of the addressable home-care locked-in market seemed smaller than what fits a VC investment, but we saw additional business potential in EyeControl. In addition to the home-care locked-in patients market, there is also a market for hospitalized locked-in patients, which is drastically bigger. And for me, in addition to that, more than 50% of an investment decision depends on the CEO. Even though Or [Retzkin] is a fairly new entrepreneur, he has come a long way and is very capable."

EyeControl's pre-money valuation was $2.7 million, the angels invested $250,000, 60% of which was invested immediately, and the remaining 40% was to be invested after they achieved an agreed-upon milestone, bringing EyeControl's post-money valuation to almost $3 million.

Seed Round

In early 2018, EyeControl raised its seed round, based on a $5 million pre-money valuation. The group of angel investors, along with Zora Ventures, WeWork and Rimonci Capital, invested $1.3 million.

Zora Ventures was a Tel Aviv-based impact investment fund whose mission was to solve global challenges such as climate change, environment, health and hunger. To date, Zora Ventures' portfolio included seven Israeli tech startups and one exit, with plans to invest in ten additional companies. Zora Ventures backed world-class Israeli tech companies with a potential of over $1 billion and game-changing solutions that addressed the United Nations Sustainable Development Goals (UN SDG).[16] The UN SDG included 17 goals representing global challenges related to poverty, inequality, climate change, environmental degradation, peace and justice.[17] Additional investment criteria included good values and commitment to a social or environmental mission; early stage with aggressive growth strategy; short path to monetization and potential exit; raising $1-$3 million with other committed investors; based in Israel.[18]

China-based Rimonci Capital, founded in 2016, had a "Global Visual Science Innovation Fund" that focused on visual science, including ophthalmology, optometry, neuro-ophthalmology and related fields, mainly in the U.S., Israel, European countries and greater China. Rimonci Capital focused on deep technology innovation in a specific field that can improve human life and was looking for long-term partnerships with positive and knowledgeable people.[19] Rimonci's portfolio consisted of eight companies[20] and one exit.[21]

THE FACILITIES MARKET POTENTIAL

Communication problems between medical staff and critically ill ventilated patients could lead to a variety of physical and psychological complications such as anxiety and panic, posttraumatic stress disorder, delirium and delusional experiences, and even violence. Recent studies had shown that eye-controlled communication devices used by ventilated patients in ICUs assisted them with communicating their needs, such as pain, personal hygiene, and anxiety to the medical staff. Caregivers reported perception of improvement in patient care and comfort.[22] The EyeControl could, for example, alert the medical staff when a patient was awake and might need assistance, and it could broadcast to the patient via bone conduction that they were in the hospital and tell them the time of day.

The EyeControl device had the ability to help patients in ICUs who were in a temporary locked-in condition due to mechanical ventilation that prevented them from speaking. It could also help in situations where patients experienced difficulty with or were unable to perform body movements due to fatigue or exhaustion. Communicating with the EyeControl device could improve the well-being of patients, potentially improving clinical outcomes and leading to reduced hospital costs. A patient suffering from delirium, for example, often stayed in the ICU five to ten extra days and was twice as likely to die in the ICU. Delirium was estimated to cost global healthcare systems in the billions of dollars per year. In the U.S. alone, these costs were estimated at $145 billion.[23] Diagnosing delirium and attempting to mitigate its effects could potentially improve clinical results and reduce costs by thousands of dollars per patient.[24]

The Facilities Solution

EyeControl's research indicated that there were 34,400 medical wards worldwide with ventilated patients. EyeControl's potential sales contract for facilities would include a one-time fee for the installation of the system and for connecting several EyeControl devices to the nurses' station. On top of that, EyeControl would charge a recurring fee for disposables including the headset and bone conduction stickers, per system per year, as well as an annual service fee.

The biggest challenge to selling to the facilities market was the lack of reimbursement codes. Hospital executives in charge of procurement were interested in products and services that would either reduce costs or generate revenues. In order to convince them to purchase EyeControl's system, the company would have to prove that their product saved money by improving communication between patients and medical staff. Retzkin commented, "That's the hard sell here, since everybody is focused on the near-term bottom line."

Facilities Clinical Trials

EyeControl planned several clinical trials to demonstrate how its system could assist with communication between ventilated patients and medical staff, reduce the risks of physical and psychological complications in ICUs, and therefore save money for the hospitals. The first was set for a U.S. medical facility.

The trial was expected to begin in Q2 of 2020 and would consist of two phases: The first would establish how the EyeControl would work in a hospital setting and would include 60–100 ventilated patients. The second phase would analyze the effect of EyeControl on 120 new patients, only half of whom would get the device; the other half would serve as a control group. The team hoped the trial would prove that using EyeControl lowers the risk of ICU-related complications. Since ICU-related complications correlated positively with increased expenses for hospitals, proving that EyeControl helped to prevent such complications would convince hospitals of its efficacy and its cost-savings benefits.

The trial at a U.S. medical facility would be critical to determining if EyeControl could become a scalable solution for the billion-dollar market of ventilated and locked-in hospital patients. Retzkin was optimistic: "I feel it's only a matter of resources. The crucial question will be whether we are close enough in the first shot or whether we'll need more adjustments."

Sales Cycle and Distribution

A presence in the facilities market could potentially expose more patients to EyeControl and therefore lead to more sales of the home-care device, as some patients would still need EyeControl during their rehabilitation—or even permanently.

EyeControl had already figured out potential distribution channels for the home-care market, but the facilities market was a different story. The company did not have enough resources, manpower or connections to contact each hospital directly. In order to penetrate the facilities market, it was clear that, pending success in the clinical trials, EyeControl was going to need a strategic partner that was already active in the field to help with sales and distribution.

Strategic Partnerships and Acquisition

The facilities market offered potential strategic partnerships that did not exist in the home-care market. EyeControl was in contact with several medical devices companies, nurses' station management companies, and companies operating in the ICU space, to explore future strategic partnership opportunities. Such strategic partnership could eventually lead to the acquisition of EyeControl by a larger company. EyeControl would be ideal for a medical devices companies like Philips, Medtronic, or even General Electric. Companies like Microsoft, Google and Amazon were also developing their own wearables, and the EyeControl could, for example, speak to Alexa or other virtual assistants. Nurse-station technology companies could also present an interesting opportunity.

PLANNING ROUND A

Because resources were limited, the team debated whether the R&D team should focus on fixing bugs and other issues with the current product for home-care, or if they should start developing new features for the facilities market. Since the home-care device would be the basis for the facilities system, and clinical trials were planned to take place in Q2 of 2020 at the earliest, the team decided to work on improving issues identified by users of the home-care device.

Retzkin expected to finish 2019 with a few hundreds of thousands of dollars in sales of the home-care device. Production and assembly capabilities were limited, but the company was selling all the devices it was able to manufacture. The team was assembling the devices themselves in the office. The team filed for patents in multiple countries. The patents were related to eye tracking and connectivity, some were specific to the hospitals environment, while others had non-medical applications. The upcoming Series A financing would be necessary for funding the clinical trials, moving to mass production, developing additional features for the device, and scaling sales efforts.

Retzkin realized he had to change EyeControl's pitch in order to raise money from traditional VC funds. He already had one pitch for competitions and another pitch for social impact investors. In the new pitch, he had to make sure that EyeControl would not be perceived as a non-profit entity. EyeControl already had a history of receiving grants and awards and being supported by impact funds. Yet the home-care market for locked-in patients was fairly small and might not seem large enough for a traditional venture capital investor.

The founders believed that they could raise capital at a pre-money valuation of $11 million. Existing investors (with the exception of WeWork) would also participate in the round. Retzkin and Kornberg were in the process of negotiating with six traditional VC funds.

LOOKING AHEAD

Retzkin and Kornberg debated their next move. The last few board meetings did not steer them in one direction. Even though they were about to start clinical trials for their facilities product, they still were unsure whether they should start penetrating the facilities market or if they should concentrate all their efforts in the home-care market. Would it be possible to do both?

Danziger outlined what he believed EyeControl needed to do: "Focus. One of the key success factors in a start-up is focus. It is extremely challenging to tackle multiple markets at the same time. Therefore, the initial focus was on the home-care market where the sale is enabled through reimbursement. EyeControl is still learning about the facilities market. It is not yet clear if we can convince hospital management to purchase our solution, and lack of reimbursement options definitely adds another layer of complexity."

The major barriers to entering the home-care market had been lifted. Regulatory approval and reimbursement codes had been accepted, and all that was left was to figure out the proper distribution channels. It might not be a billion dollar business, but annual sales of tens of millions of dollars was a reasonable target. Retzkin knew the importance of the home-care market, "If you ask me who will give us better feedback to make our device perfect, it is the home-care permanent user, not patients in ICU who used the device only for a few days and who we'll never see again." Working on increasing the home-care market was a no-brainer, therefore. The team would still have a great positive social impact on the patients they care about and could still generate modest cash and even be acquired. If the team decided to remain a small, niche player and pursue the home-care market only, raising money from impact investment funds might be sufficient.

The facilities market, on the other hand, had great potential for major financial rewards and for making a much wider social impact, but there were multiple unknowns and risks. The team had a lot to learn before they were able to penetrate this market. First of all, how could EyeControl convince hospitals that the EyeControl system would save them money? Who would the right partners be, and what incentives would be required to entice them to partner with EyeControl? How would they market the devices? How would the organizational structure change? There were also significant risks if the clinical trials failed to demonstrate that the EyeControl system would save hospitals money: EyeControl would be left with the much smaller home-care market, for one. More importantly, EyeControl would be unable to raise another funding round, which meant that they might have to shut down all operations, the home-care market included, thus losing the social impact altogether. If the team decided to pursue the facilities market in addition to the home-care market, they must raise much more money to complete the clinical trials. Was it time for money from traditional VC funds?

NOTES

1 https://www.8200impact.com/. Accessed November 2019.
2 https://www.8200impact.com//#program. Accessed January 2020.
3 https://www.indiegogo.com/projects/communicate-anytime-anywhere#/. Accessed November 2019.
4 https://www.tobii.com/group/about/. Accessed December 2019.
5 https://www.tobii.com/group/about/history-of-tobii/. Accessed December 2019.
6 http://www.inclusive.co.uk/tobii-dynavox-i-series#. Accessed December 2019.
7 http://www.atlclibrary.org/categories.php?id=3&pos=16. Accessed December 2019.
8 https://www.crunchbase.com/organization/prentke-romich-company. Accessed December 2019.
9 https://www.prentrom.com/about-us. Accessed December 2019.
10 https://store.prentrom.com/index.php?route=product/product&product_id=378&search=look. Accessed December 2019.
11 https://store.prentrom.com/accent-1000. Accessed December 2019.
12 https://www.jabbla.com/en/about-us/. Accessed January 2020.
13 https://eyegaze.com/. Accessed December 2019.
14 Eon Market Research, Global Speech Generating Devices (SGD) Market Report, 2018.
15 https://clinicaltrials.gov/ProvidedDocs/29/NCT02891629/Prot_000.pdf. Accessed January 2020.
16 http://www.zora.vc/. Accessed December 2019.
17 https://www.un.org/sustainabledevelopment/sustainable-development-goals/. Accessed December 2019.
18 http://www.zora.vc/. Accessed December 2019.
19 http://www.rimonci.com/index. Accessed December 2019.
20 http://www.rimonci.com/c/default/pageId/58d4ecc39ccde2812bfcefce. Accessed December 2019.
21 https://www.crunchbase.com/organization/rimonci-capital#section-investments. Accessed December 2019.
22 https://www.ncbi.nlm.nih.gov/pmc/articles/PMC6794009/. Accessed February 2020.
23 https://vimeo.com/208820950. Accessed February 2020.
24 https://www.statnews.com/2016/10/14/icu-delirium-hospitals/. Accessed February 2020.

EXHIBIT 1 EyeControl cofounders' bios

OR RETZKIN, FOUNDER & CEO

Or is a Major in the Navy (res). He graduated from Tel Aviv University with B.Sc. in Physics and Accounting and holds a M.Sc. in Finance. Or teaches in the Accounting and Management departments at Tel Aviv University and has worked for PwC in the high-tech and industry audit department. Or also serves as an Alumni Director of the 8200 Impact accelerator program.

ITAI KORNBERG, FOUNDER & CTO

Itai graduated with honors from Ben-Gurion University with a B.Sc. in Software Engineering. Itai has worked for HP (QC/ALM and AGM groups) and NetApp Innovation Lab. Itai also founded a social venture called "Hello World." Hello World's mission is to harness the skills of hi tech companies and academic students, in order to develop technological solutions for the third sector and people with special needs.

SHAY RISHONI (1966-2018), FOUNDER

Shay cofounded EyeControl while he was the CEO of Prize4Life, a non-profit organization dedicated to accelerating the discovery of treatments and a cure for ALS. He was the CEO and founder of Mediterraneo 365, a sports production company that specializes in large cycling races. Previously, he used to work for Flying Cargo Group, where he held various management positions including VP Logistics and VP Marketing. Shay also held an MBA from the University of Hartford.

Shay was an extremely versatile individual. He was a commercial pilot, a tour guide with specialization in the Indian sub-continent and Himalayan treks and a military Colonel (rev.). As a passionate athlete he participated in triathlons, marathons and was an Ironman medalist. Shay also served as a council member at the American Answer ALS foundation and at the Leadership Team of IBT – Israel Brain Technology.

Source: Company Materials, http://www.reboot.org.il/speakers/shay-rishoni/, Accessed December 2019. https://www.eyecontrol.co.il/team-1. Accessed February 2020.

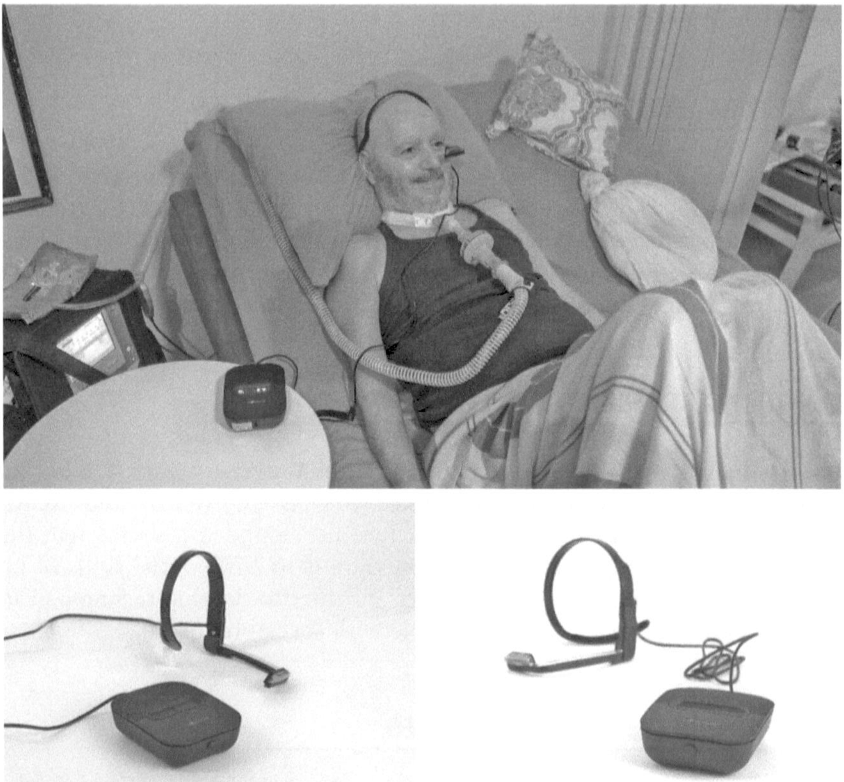

EXHIBIT 2 The EyeControl
Source: Company materials.

EXHIBIT 3 EyeControl User Testimonials

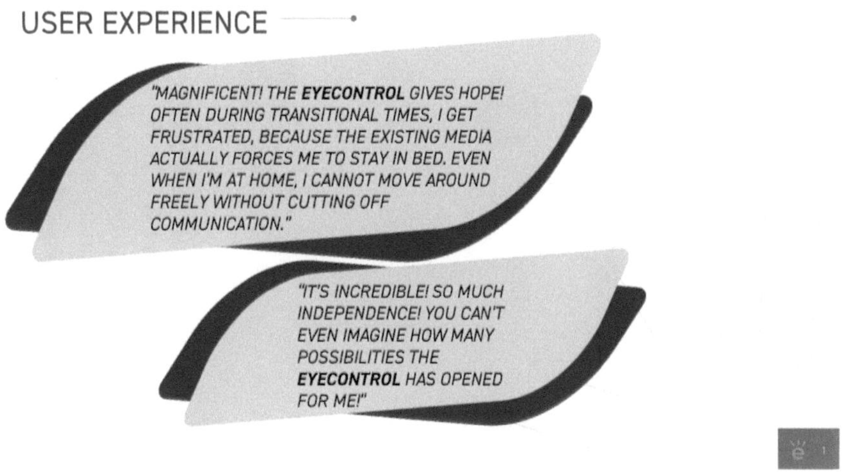

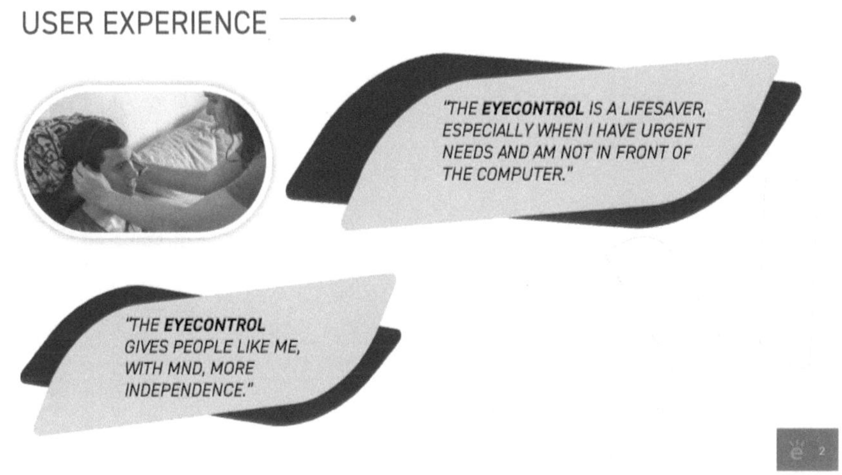

Avichai Kremer, HBS alum, MBA 2007, "What I love about this device is the independence it gives me. Suddenly, I don't have to be bound to a computer to speak. I can sit at the poker table with my friends and 'bluff', or say to my 4 year old daughter I love her at the playground. For an ALS patient it's priceless."

Source: Company materials.

EXHIBIT 4 EyeControl Track Record

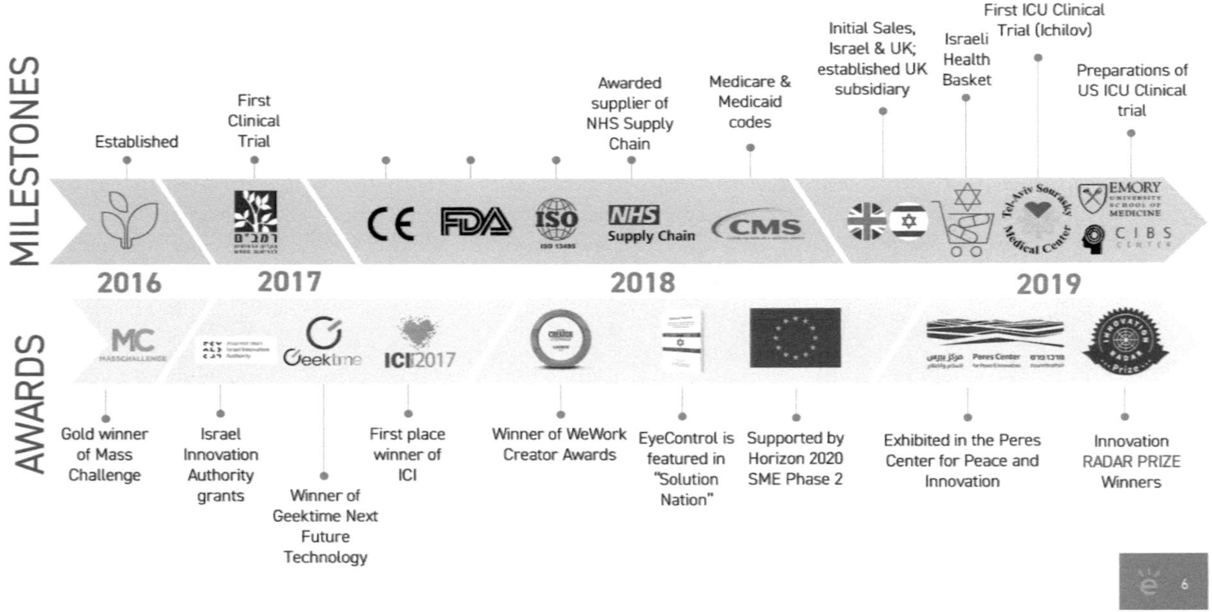

Total awards: July 2016, Winners of Chivas "The Venture" International Competition, $130,000 (https://www.chivas.com/the-venture/alumni/2016/eyecontrol) and another $10,000 from a related pitch. February 2017, Gold Award Winners of MassChallenge Israel Competition, $32,000 and another $10,000 in scholarships. (https://www.eyecontrol.co.il/history). December 2017, Winners of ICI Innovation of the Year award 2017, $2,500. January 2018, 2nd place in the International WeWork Creator Awards (gave equity). February 2018, Silver Prize winners at the Hack Osaka 2018 competition. EC – 2 million EUR.

Source: Company materials.

EXHIBIT 5 EyeControl Angel Investor Bios

BENNY LEVIN

Benny Levin served in the Israel Defense Force (IDF) Intelligence Corps and retired with the rank of Lieutenant Colonel. In 1978 during his army service he was awarded the Chief of Intelligence Decoration for Creative Thinking.

Benny co-founded NICE Systems, a worldwide leader of multimedia digital recording solutions for business interaction management, where he served as NICE's CEO and Director from its inception and as Chairman and CEO from 1998 to 2001. Under Benny's leadership the company achieved impressive growth and raised significant funds, both on NASDAQ and the Tel-Aviv Stock Exchange (TASE).

From 2004 to 2012 Benny served as Chairman of the Board of dbMotion. dbMotion enables forward-looking healthcare organizations to seamlessly connect and coordinate healthcare, linking clinicians within their facilities, beyond their walls and across their networks.

Since retiring from most of his business activities, Benny dedicates himself to a wide array of social and philanthropic activities. He serves as Vice Chairman of the Board of Directors of Israel Venture Network (IVN). IVN is a social investment organization, bridging social gaps and generating systemic change in Israel through high-impact programs and hands-on venture philanthropy for over 10 years.

Benny serves as Active Chairman of the Board of the Ben Yakir youth village and Kedma youth village, assisting youth at risk mostly from the Ethiopian community and he is involved in a variety of other philanthropic activities as a member of the Israeli Board of the Jewish Funders Network (JFN), P2P initiative with the JDC, TEN project with JAFI and the board of the Israeli Public Forum for Youth Villages and Boarding schools for Children at Risk.

Benny serves as a Board member of the Social Groceries Project, a groundbreaking network of social businesses supported by the Jewish Agency for Israel, IVN and other donors, battling Israel's high cost of living and reducing poverty in Israel's socio-economic periphery.

Benny is the Founder of JDOCU, a group of philanthropists and photographers that use the camera as a tool for documenting the activities of Tikkun Olam ('Repair the World') with the partnership of JDC, making it part of a global culture with special emphasis on Israeli and Jewish culture.

Benny has a bachelor's and master's degrees in Electrical Engineering from the Technion – Israel Institute of Technology, Haifa.

EXHIBIT 5 (*continued*)

ITSIK DANZIGER

Itsik brings with him over thirty five years of experience in senior executive positions in the telecommunication technology industry and over thirteen years of experience in board positions of not for profit organizations. Currently, Itsik serves as board member of several technology companies.

From 2009 through 2014 Itsik served as active chairman of Galil Software, a software development outsourcing company located in Nazareth. The company was established with the goal of creating employment opportunities for engineers, mostly from the minorities sector.

From 1985 through 2007, Itsik worked with the Comverse Technology Group in various senior management positions. In his position as President of Comverse Network Systems, he led the company from a startup state to becoming the worldwide market leader of messaging and other value added solutions to telecom carriers with annual revenues exceeding $1B. Later, he served as President of the Comverse Technology Group.

In the NGOs/public sector, Itsik serves as chairman of The Center for Educational Technology (CET), an NGO leading innovation in the education system in Israel. He is also an executive board member of IVN (Israel Venture Network) and chairman of its funds' investment committees, where he is involved in building the innovative social businesses sector in Israel. In addition, Itsik is a board member and Vice President of the New Israel Fund (NIF). In 2004-5 he served as a member of the Israeli government nominated National Task Force for the Advancement of Education (The Dovrat Committee).

Itsik holds BSc cum laude and MSc in electrical engineering from the Technion and M.A cum laude in philosophy and digital culture from Tel Aviv University.

Source: Company materials, https://www.nif.org/people/itzik-danziger/. Accessed February 2020.

CHAPTER 4.7

WeWork - November 2018

Paul A. Gompers, Patrick Sweeney and Alex Gachanja

Shaun Jones, a mutual fund manager at T&R Capital was drinking an iced coffee on the porch of Caffé Medici in Austin, Texas one brisk Sunday afternoon in November 2018. He had been given the task of evaluating a late-stage investment opportunity with SoftBank's Vison Fund. The round, led by SoftBank, would be priced at a staggering $42 billion post-money valuation in the tech start up The We Company ("WeWork" or "the Company"). Since its founding, WeWork had garnered many headlines as it expanded rapidly and raised ever larger sums of capital. Jones reviewed the proposed terms of the financing and was confident that this would be the last round before the company went public. By investing in this round, T&R could obtain a large enough position in WeWork to carry it into the public market for its mutual fund investors. He was expected to make a recommendation to his firm's investment committee the following Wednesday on whether they should proceed with the deal or not. Jones opened PowerPoint and began to collect his thoughts.

TRENDS IN THE VENTURE CAPITAL MARKET

The U.S. venture capital industry in the mid-2010s was characterized by tremendous growth. From 2017 to 2018 aggregate deal activity grew at a breakneck rate from $86.8 billion to $140.2 billion, a 53.4% growth rate (**Exhibit 1**). In the five years leading up to 2019, over $70 billion was deployed into 8,000 plus high-growth startups each year. Roughly 49,000 venture investments attracted an aggregate of $445 billion. By the end of 2018 there were 1,047 venture capital firms managing 1,884 active funds totaling approximately $403 billion in U.S. venture capital assets under management. While capital flows had increased, the dynamics of the industry had changed considerably. The industry tended towards fewer, yet

WeWork - November 2018
by PAUL A. GOMPERS, PATRICK SWEENEY, ALEX GACHANJA, case number 9-220-075
Rev. AUGUST 11, 2020

larger funds with bigger deals and exits. Almost half of the capital invested in 2018 was in mega deals, which were investments over $100 million. Additionally, late-stage financing had grown rapidly since 2014 with an average growth rate of 30.9% for aggregate deal activity. In 2018 alone, the total value of late-stage VC deals grew 79.6%, from $48.8 billion to $87.7 billion. In comparison, early-stage financing had grown at a slightly slower pace of 22.7% since 2014. In 2018 the total value of early-stage VC deals grew 41.6%, from $30.6 billion to $43.4 billion. The majority of the growth for late-stage deals came from larger funds of over $50 million which saw an increase in late-stage deal value activity of 126.8%, from $29.2 billion to $66.3 billion (**Exhibit 2**).[1]

The environment for venture capital backed exits was strong over the five-year period from 2014 to 2019. The average annual IPO and acquisition volume for this time period was $67.2 billion and $51.5 billion, respectively. For comparison, the five years between 2009 and 2013 saw an average annual IPO and acquisition size of $38.2 billion and $25.1 billion, respectively. Additionally, VC backed companies were staying private longer. The median time from first VC investment to an IPO exit between 2014 and 2018 was 6.8 years. This is slightly higher than the median time from first VC investment to an IPO exit between 2009 and 2013, which was 6.7 years. The time period between 2014 and 2018 was dragged down by 2018 which was only 4.77 years. For VC M&A backed exits, the median time from first VC investment to exit between 2014 and 2018 was 4.8 years. Again, this is higher than the median time from first VC investment to an M&A exit between 2009 and 2013, which was 4.3 years (**Exhibit 3**).[2]

Nontraditional investors in VC continued to increase in 2019: 2,746 deals had at least one nontraditional investor and the annual value of these deals was $97 billion. Non-traditional investors included mutual funds and hedge funds. This marked the second year in a row of annual deal value activity near $100 billion (**Exhibit 4**). These investors tended to invest in later stage deals while staying away from angel and seed investments. Participation from both mutual funds and hedge funds in VC deals reached a ten year high of 7.9% in 2019.[3]

SOFTBANK

Early History

SoftBank was founded in 1981 by Masayoshi Son as a wholesale distributor of PC software in Japan, initially under the name "Japan SoftBank." After completing his undergraduate degree in 1980, Son spent 18 months analyzing 40 different industries in which he could begin his career, spanning from developing software to managing hospital systems. He narrowed the list down using 25 self-defined success measures— among them were his "desire to fall in love with a particular business for the next 50 years" and the opportunity to become "number one in that particular business."[4] Son saw particular potential in the nascent personal computer industry, explaining that "the PC was only a toy then" and that it was likely that "personal computers would be a very important product for the entire society in 10 or 20 years."[5]

Without his own hardware or software products to sell directly, Son rented the largest booth at a consumer electronics show in Tokyo and invited twelve software vendors to partner with him— offering a free display and advertising in exchange for their products being placed at his station. Above his booth hung a sign that stated, "Now the revolution has come for software distribution for PCs."[6] Son planned to build a network within the emerging computer industry with him as a matchmaker: software vendors had the product but no one to distribute it, PC dealers had the hardware but no software, and he had the advertising and distribution capacity but no hardware or software.[7] Vendors would come together to establish outlets and consumers would purchase products through SoftBank. This exhibit at the Tokyo electronics show earned him one contract with Joshin Denki Co., the third-largest electronics retailer in Japan at the time. Joshin Denki gave Son exclusive rights to purchase software for the company, after which he began approaching software vendors, including Hudson Software, the largest in Japan at the time.[8] Joshin Denki would purchase software from vendors sourced by Son, and this software would be sold at its PC shops. By having the "biggest software lineup" in Japan, Son predicted that Joshin Denki would be more attractive to consumers than other hardware retailers without software products. This partnership between Joshin Denki and Japan SoftBank was effective— within its first year of operation, Japan SoftBank grew from $10,000 to $2.3 million in monthly sales and the company was serving over 200 dealer outlets by 1983.[9] (See **Exhibit 6** for SoftBank's first ten years of growth).

Six months after jumpstarting this software distribution business, Son began exploring other ventures in the personal computer industry. In 1982, Japan SoftBank entered the publishing industry, releasing two technology-focused magazines titled, *Oh!PC* and *Oh!MZ*. These publications struggled in the initial few months, losing hundreds of thousands of dollars, but grew to 140,000 subscribers by 1990. By this point, Japan SoftBank was the largest publisher of tech magazines in the country, which it used to promote the products it distributed.[10]

Transition

In 1990, Son renamed the company SoftBank Corp. and expanded beyond the Japanese market.[11] He retained the company's strategy as a 'corporate matchmaker'— bringing together software retailers in the United States and Japan-based companies that modified and sold U.S software. In these deals, Softbank served as the distributor of software products from the United States to Japan and earned commission from matching companies.[12]

The first major deal was in 1991 when SoftBank formed a network of technology companies that previously acted as competitors. This venture, called BusinessLand Inc. Japan Co, was valued at $20 million. The lead company, which held 54% ownership, was the U.S.-based computer retailer BusinessLand Inc. SoftBank had a 26% stake in the venture, while Toshiba, Sony, Canon, and Fujitsu each held 5% ownership.[13] Rather than serving the consumer retail market, this venture instead focused on corporate customers in Japan— a strategy that executives hoped would give it an advantage over existing competitors in Japan such as IBM. This venture, however, was unsuccessful and was liquidated that year.[14] Similarly, reports revealed that SoftBank lost $10 million in the same year in another failed venture called Systembank, which sought to provide systems integrations to corporations in Japan.[15]

These initial setbacks were mitigated by the launch of a third venture led by SoftBank in partnership with some of these same companies. This venture— Novell Japan Ltd.— brought together Novell (which held 54% ownership) and hardware manufacturers NEC, Toshiba, Fujitsu, Canon, and Sony (each with a 4% stake).[16] It sold networking systems and hardware products such as cables and boards in Japan, where less than 5% of personal computers were networked at the time. The venture's annual sales had reached $130 million by 1994.[17]

In 1993, SoftBank established its first subsidiary in the United States, named SoftBank Inc. The goal of this subsidiary was to provide software via demo disks, an emerging technology, to consumers. This venture, however, was in direct competition with the parent company's main source of partnerships— software retailers. The subsidiary was dissolved in 1995.[18]

"Mr. Internet"

By the year 2000, SoftBank had a long history of large-scale transactions in the technology sector that portended what the Vision Fund would pursue. The firm went public in 1994 at a valuation of $3 billion— with Masayoshi Son holding 70% interest in the company.[19] From this point, the firm set a pattern of both acquiring established companies and investing at the early stages of what later became top global technology companies.

SoftBank began to concentrate its investments on internet services in 1996. The firm had 5% ownership in Yahoo! Inc. from an earlier purchase in 1995 and expanded this to a 37% stake in 1996[20]— the same year that the internet start-up went public in the United States. During this time, SoftBank and Yahoo! Inc. came together to form Yahoo! Japan Corporation, in which SoftBank held 60% ownership.[21] Yahoo! Japan was the first stock to trade for more than ¥100 million per share in the country when it went public in 2000.[22] The firm made a foray into digital satellite broadcasting when, together with News Corporation Limited, it launched Japan Sky Broadcasting Co., Ltd. Despite these new ventures in internet services, SoftBank did not entirely abandon its previous strategy of investing in retailers. In September 1996, the firm made a purchase for 80% ownership in Kingston Technology Company, a hardware manufacturer of PC memory boards, for $1.51 billion.[23]

In October 1999, SoftBank officially became a holding company.[24] Its most successful investment came in January 2000 when it invested $20 million in the burgeoning China-based e-commerce start-up Alibaba in 2000.[25] This investment surged to over $50 billion when the company went public in September 2014.[26] In July 1998, Softbank paid $400 million for 27.2% of shares in E-Trade, the largest online brokerage during this period.[27] SoftBank's market capitalization had reached $200 billion and its portfolio of internet-based companies showed $15 billion in gains by the end of 1999.[28] By this point, Masayoshi Son had earned the title "Mr. Internet."[29] The firm grew its presence in telecommunications with the acquisition of Vodafone Japan for $15.4 billion in May 2006, giving SoftBank entry into the growing $78 billion mobile phone market in Japan.[30] Vodafone Japan was renamed SoftBank Mobile Corp. in October 2006 and became the dominant player in the Japanese telecommunications sector. It then entered a deal with Apple in June 2008 to bring the iPhone to Japan.[31]

The dot-com bubble burst in the early 2000s, and brought substantial losses for SoftBank. In the second half of 2001, the firm had lost at least $448 million and its market capitalization had fallen below $30 billion after its stakes in Yahoo!, Yahoo! Japan, and E-Trade declined in value by more than 80%.[32] In response, the firm closed 8 of its 11 international offices, let go 75 employees, and sold its private equity stakes in 20 Japan-based companies.[33] SoftBank shares also fell to $21.40, a 95% reduction from its highest point in February 2000.[34] In July 2002, the firm announced that it had lost $62 million after selling its shares in E-Trade. The brokerage company bought back the shares from SoftBank at $3.60 each.[35] Despite all of this, SoftBank's losses during this time were not unusual and were reflective of trends in the venture capital industry at large-- the first quarter of 2001 saw only 13 IPOs compared to the 112 in the first quarter of 2000.

The firm's large investments in over 600 tech firms meant a deeper impact when markets took a turn during this period.[36]

VISION FUND

Development

The venture capital landscape was reshaped dramatically when SoftBank formed its Vision Fund. By its first close in May 2017, the Vision Fund had secured $93 billion in commitments from investors out of a $100 billion goal.[37] Its anchor investor was the Public Investment Fund, the sovereign wealth fund of Saudi Arabia, which pledged to contribute $45 billion over a five-year period. This was followed by SoftBank itself, which had allocated a $25 billion investment to the fund, $8.2 billion of which came from selling 25% of its shares in Arm Holdings.[38] Just a year prior in 2016, SoftBank had acquired Arm Holdings for $32 billion, which at the time was both the largest deal the firm had ever made and the largest purchase of a European technology company ever recorded.[39] Additional investors in the Vision Fund included the UAE's Mubadala Investment Company, Qualcomm, Apple, Oracle, and Foxconn[40] (**Exhibit 5** lists investors in Vision Fund). The Vision Fund, as SoftBank's Chairman & CEO Masayoshi Son noted, would back "the foundational platforms of the next stage of the Information Revolution."[41] With a minimum investment of $100 million per company and targeting a 20-40% ownership stake, the emergence of the Vision Fund stood to make a significant imprint in the venture capital industry and technology sector.

The Vision Fund, however, marked a departure from SoftBank's previous pattern of investing in emerging start-ups at early stages. The fund became the catalyst to a new trend characterized as "mega VC deals"[42]—whereby venture capital firms approached companies at later stages of growth and operated like "kingmakers" by allocating amounts of capital that previously had only been provided in the public markets. With Vision Fund, SoftBank also entered the arena of corporate venture capital (CVC), an industry that reached record levels in 2018. CVC funds are backed by and managed within a larger company, whereby specialized divisions direct the fund's investment activity. Corporate venture capital began to grow significantly in 2009 when it made up 12.7% of all venture capital investment deals— this figure grew to 13.6% in 2010 and 15% in 2011.[43] In 2018, a total of 264 new CVC funds invested for the first time, marking a 35% year-over-year growth rate[44] (See **Exhibit 7** for trends in corporate venture capital). The Vision Fund had reached a size of $98 billion by November 2017. Its investment period is five years from the final closing and its fund period is 12 years from the final closing. Officially classified as private equity, the Vision Fund has a traditional private equity fund structure, whereby managers are compensated via management fees and carried interest.[45] SoftBank Investment Advisors is the fund administrator.

The formation of the Vision Fund can be traced back to a meeting held in central Tokyo at the Geihinkan state guesthouse in May 2017, attended by SoftBank representatives and five hundred Saudi delegates. At this meeting, Masayoshi Son negotiated directly with the Crown Prince of Saudi Arabia and received a $45 billion non-binding five-year commitment from the Saudi delegation.[46] The Vision Fund, with nearly $100 billion available to invest, had the same amount of capital that was raised by all VC-backed companies in 2016.[47] In the press release announcing the first close that month, SoftBank stated that the Vision Fund's investment strategy was to "acquire minority and majority interests in both private and public companies, from emerging technology businesses to established, multi-billion-dollar companies requiring substantial growth funding."[48] The latter focus— "multi-billion dollar companies requiring substantial growth funding"— is the tactic that had the strongest impact on the venture capital industry and in the technology sector.

Early Investments

The Vision Fund portfolio, as the genesis of "mega" transactions, gradually began to alter the relationships between investors and founders and between investors themselves. In November 2017, reports revealed that SoftBank was leading a group of investors that was providing $7.7 billion to Uber for a stake of 17.5% in the company.[49] SoftBank injected an additional $1.25 billion into the ride sharing service and, with a stake of 15%, was its largest shareholder.[50] This was followed by a $538 million Series-D investment in DoorDash in March 2018 alongside Singapore's GIC sovereign wealth fund and Sequoia Capital, a deal that raised DoorDash's post-money valuation to $1.4 billion. DoorDash executives were initially targeting only $200 million in funding, but competition among investors clamoring to get into the deal ballooned the amount that the company took.[51] The business messaging platform Slack raised $250 million from SoftBank in September 2017, bringing the company's valuation to $5.1 billion.[52]

The largest ag-tech deal ever recorded, SoftBank's $200 million Series-B investment in the indoor vertical farming company, Plenty in July 2017 signaled that the firm investments were now expanding beyond information technology-focused companies and into broader technology-related companies.[53] A few months later, in December 2017, SoftBank announced a $450 million investment in Compass, a residential real estate brokerage, alongside the Qatar Investment Authority[54]— the start of SoftBank's investments in real-estate focused technology companies. Likewise, in September 2018, SoftBank announced that the Vision Fund invested $400 million in Opendoor Labs Inc., a marketplace for buying and selling property exclusively online, at a post-money valuation in excess of $2 billion.[55] Opendoor had already raised $325 million in funding from prior investments, but the purpose of the Vision Fund investment, co-founder and chief executive Eric Wu stated, was to catapult its expansion. It intended to go from launching one city per month to two cities per month with additional capital. Other investments in real-estate technology companies included architecture and construction company Kattera Inc. and Indian hotel-booking startup Oyo.[56]

SoftBank was involved in a number of other notable billion-dollar deals with companies such as the Indian e-commerce start-up Flipkart ($2.5 billion), pharmaceutical company Roivant Sciences ($1.1 billion alongside other secondary investors), and online retailer Fanatics ($1 billion).[57] In the venture capital industry at large, supergiant deals (rounds of $100 million or greater) and hypergiants deals (rounds of $250 million or greater) peaked in the third quarter of 2018.[58] SoftBank's investments in WeWork were among the most notable of these mega transaction deals.

WEWORK - BUSINESS MODEL

WeWork was founded in early 2010 by Adam and Rebekah Neumann and Miguel McKelvey in New York, NY. The CEO of the company, Mr. Neumann, had received much attention from the media for his larger than life vision for WeWork and his eccentric lifestyle. Neumann was born in Israel in 1979 and lived in over 13 different homes by the time he was 22. This included some time living on a kibbutz and in Indianapolis, IN. Severely dyslexic, he could not read or write until he was in the third grade.[59] Regardless of this adversity, he gained entrance into an elite Israeli naval officer program where he served for five years and when discharged, held the rank of captain.[60] Upon finishing his service he moved to New York where he enrolled in Baruch College at The City of New York University (CUNY) in 2002.[61] While at CUNY Neumann majored in business and become a serial entrepreneur. He came up with the concept of WeLive for an entrepreneurship competition. He didn't make it past the first round after the professor judging the competition told him that he wouldn't be able to raise enough money to change the way people live. During an interview with TechCrunch, Neumann said "What he said to me influenced me to start WeWork first, and I would not have been able to launch WeLive without the success of WeWork".[62] After his women's shoe lined failed he focused his efforts on a new business endeavor of children's pants with kneepads built in them to protect infants crawling on the floor, simply named Krawler. He struggled with supply chain and logistical issues and was consumed by the business. This ultimately led to him dropping out of college in 2006. Neumann said "for five years, I struggled making payroll each month to my small team of eight employees. It was a constant struggle, and with only four credits left, I dropped out of school, deciding to give every bit of my energy to my business."[63] Soon after this he expanded the product line to make the business a baby clothing company which he named Egg Baby. It was during his time with Egg Baby that he met Miguel McKelvey through a mutual friend. The two quickly bonded over their similar backgrounds and competitive nature. Not long after this they came up with the concept for WeWork[64,65] (**Exhibit 9**).

The mission of the company was to reinvent the way individuals and organizations viewed workspace with their pioneering "space-as-a-service" membership model. Membership provided companies with the ability to scale their workspace needs up or down with relative ease compared to traditional leases. The service reduced the complexity of leasing real estate while offering a premium and bespoke experience to their customers, all while reducing cost on a per employee basis. The community-orientated co-work spaces were designed to enhance the lifestyle and environment of the member companies. In addition, clients could opt for WeWork's premium solution which included "Powered by We." This configuration was a more tailored experience that leveraged WeWork's analysis and technology to improve other workplace experiences for employees, which in turn had the potential to improve productivity and retention.

The leasing model was based off the concept of capitalizing on "rent arbitrage." WeWork would enter into a long-term office space leasing contract with landlords. These long-term leases were, on average, 15 years. WeWork would then renovate the space to fit their co-working community-oriented model.[66] Once the workspace was renovated, WeWork would then enter into membership agreements with members[a]. Membership duration was significantly shorter than the length of the obligations to landlords. In

a WeWork uses the term "members" to refer to the individuals and organizations that enter into membership agreements with them and "memberships" to refer to the cumulative number of memberships they purchase. "Memberships" include both WeWork memberships (which provide access to a workstation) and on-demand memberships (which provide access to shared workstations or private spaces as needed, by the minute, by the hour or by the day).

addition, members could terminate their membership agreement with as little as one month's notice.

Neumann and McKelvey felt they had the opportunity to provide a unique workspace experience to small and medium enterprises which had typically been underserved. By providing more flexibility in leases and modern work environments, WeWork was able to add value to their members in a way that was unprecedented. Not surprisingly, many individuals and organizations seized this opportunity. According to WeWork's internal analysis, the average annualized cost of a "standard lease" with and without build is $21,594 and $17,158, respectively[b]. While the average annualized cost for a WeWork membership and services was $7,304[c],[67] (**Exhibit 10**). In addition, the average square footage per person at WeWork offices is around 50 square feet—compared to an average of 250 square feet in commercial office spaces. In the course of nine years the Company grew memberships at an exponential rate. As of June 30, 2019, WeWork had 527,000 members in over 528 locations in 111 cities across 29 countries.[68] In these 111 cities they estimated a potential market of approximately 149 million members. Additionally, they planned to continue to aggressively expand in the existing cities and launch in up to 169 other cities. Based on WeWork's internal analysis of the Demographia and the Organization for Economic Cooperation and Development data, WeWork believed that market represented a potential member population of 255 million people.[69] Using WeWork's average revenue per member, this would translate to an addressable market opportunity of $945 billion in their current cities and $1.6 trillion including their target cities (**Exhibit 11**).

WeWork monetized its platform primarily by selling memberships and providing ancillary value-added products and services to their members. As of June 30, 2019, approximately 83% of their revenue was derived from recurring monthly membership fees, 5% from business services such as printing and conference room credits, and 12% from additional products

---

b Sources: Building Owners and Managers Association (BOMA); CoStar Office Market Statistics; International Facility Management Association (IFMA); CBRE Office Occupancy Costs; Cushman Global Occupancy Report 2017; and third-party research. Comparison data represents annualized costs based on an average of ten select city centers in the United States, Europe, South America and Asia that are representative of our key markets. "Standard lease" includes the costs associated with food and beverage, events, utilities, insurance, property taxes, facilities management and base rent.

c Represents annualized average membership and service revenue per WeWork membership ("average revenue per WeWork membership") for the six months ended June 30, 2019 across the same ten select city centers as above.

and services offered through the suite of We Company offerings.[70] The profitability profile of locations was driven by the maturity of those sites. It typically took a little over 24 months for a location to become "mature." Once a location became mature and up-front cost had been spent, WeWork typically saw that occupancy stabilized, allowing the location to generate a recurring revenue stream, contribution margin, and cash flow. As of June 1, 2019, due to WeWork's rapid growth, 70% of their locations were "non-mature" and had not reached a point of generating positive cash flow. These non-mature locations had been open less than 24 months.[71] In 2018, 35% of WeWork's new memberships came from existing members and their net membership retention rate was 119%[d].

Top-line revenue was $1.82 billion in 2018 and its revenue growth rate from the prior year of 105%. Over 41% of their revenue came from outside the United States in 2018. WeWork's costs were also growing just as fast. The company lost $1.9 billion in 2018, up 103% from 2017[72] (**Exhibits 12-14**). In addition to revenue and cost, WeWork also tracked a novel metric "community-adjusted EBITDA." Companies often offered adjusted earnings, but in the case of WeWork, their "community-adjusted EBITDA" subtracted not only the typical interest, tax, depreciation and amortization, but also expenses such as SG&A, development, and design costs[73] (**Exhibit 15**). These different financial metrics made it difficult to evaluate exactly how WeWork was doing.

WEWORK – INVESTMENTS

WeWork had received significant amounts of funding even before Vision Fund expressed interest in investing. Its initial financing occurred in July 2012 when Neumann raised $17.5 million in a Series A deal with DAG Ventures at a valuation of $97 million.[74] The company's valuation then reached $318 million in May 2013 when it raised $40 million in a Series B round. WeWork achieved "unicorn" status in the first quarter of 2014 with a valuation of $1.59 billion— four times what it was valued previously— following a $157 million Series C round with investors including Benchmark Capital and J.P. Morgan Chase. Its pre-money valuation had grown to $4.6 billion by October 2014, when it took part in a

d WeWork calculates their net membership retention rate for a given period by dividing (1) the total number of WeWork memberships as of the last day in the period from all members that had at least one WeWork membership as of the first day of the period by (2) the total number of WeWork memberships from those same members as of the first day of the period.

$355 million Series D investment that brought the company's post-money valuation to over $4.96 billion by the end of 2014. In May 2015, Fidelity and other prominent investors committed an additional $433.9 million to WeWork in a Series E deal, doubling its post-money valuation to over $10 billion. Finally, a $690 million Series F round in November 2016 valued the company at $16.9 billion.[75] Within five years of its founding in 2010, WeWork had managed to secure nearly $1 billion in external financing, earning it a reputation as one of the most successful start-ups in New York. Around this time, industry insiders and reports in the press began speculating that the company was planning and preparing for an IPO.[76] (**Exhibits 16-18** show WeWork's rounds of financing, changes in valuation, and types of investors).

The rapid growth that WeWork experienced and its ability to attract top-tier investors did not go unnoticed and without controversy. The company's $5 billion valuation in 2015, just five years after its founding, was met with skepticism by traditional real estate investors. Regus, a public company that had 2,500 locations in 110 countries at the time, had a market capitalization of less than $1.3 billion.[77] Neumann routinely defended the high valuations that his company received, stating that WeWork was "the world's first physical social network."[78]

SoftBank Entrance

The rumored IPO, however, did not occur. The success WeWork had in securing venture financing in its first five years was only a prelude to what it was able to achieve in the next three years. In March 2017, SoftBank revealed that it had invested $300 million in WeWork— what was only a small chunk of a proposed $3 billion deal at the time. Within this $3 billion commitment, the initial $300 million came from SoftBank itself and the remainder would come from the soon-to-be-announced Vision Fund.[79]

Son's strategy for the Vision Fund was to use "mega rounds" of investment to create category winners. At one point, Son told Neumann that his ideas weren't "crazy enough" and that Vision Fund could make WeWork "ten times bigger than [his] original plan."[80] Neumann, when describing what he envisioned WeWork becoming after receiving multiple investments from SoftBank— expressed, "I need to have the biggest valuation I can, because when countries are shooting at each other, I want them [refugees] to come to me."[81] As he saw it, WeWork's future entailed much more than office space provision for entrepreneurs and SMEs. Instead, WeWork would be at the forefront of all real estate-related opportunities, and SoftBank would issue the capital needed to make this happen.

In August 2017, SoftBank officially disclosed its $4.4 billion Series G round investment in WeWork, a marked increase from its initial $3 billion commitment back in March. This $4.4 billion deal consisted of two parts: $3 billion would be invested in the parent company, The We Company, through new shares and the purchase of secondary shares and $1.4 billion would go toward three new ventures— WeWork China, WeWork Japan, and WeWork Pacific. As the largest SoftBank investment in a U.S.-based company, this deal catapulted WeWork's valuation to $17 billion. A month earlier, WeWork had also received $500 million in funding from SoftBank and Hony Capital to bolster its expansion in Southeast Asia and Korea, a plan that seemed promising following the company's acquisition of Singapore-based office space start-up, Spacemob.[82]

WeWork announced in August 2018 that SoftBank had provided the company with $1 billion in convertible debt. Artie Minson, WeWork's chief financial officer, explained that sourcing this supplemental financing from what was already the company's largest investor would allow it to "opportunistically add a billion dollars to the balance sheet."[83] This extra funding would support the company's large-scale expansion plans, domestic and international, on top of the $4 billion in cash and commitments that it held at the time. The debt could be converted to equity under three situations:

(1) If SoftBank were the lead investor in a billion-dollar round, the loan note would convert at the valuation of that round
(2) If a different investor were to lead a billion-dollar round, the debt would convert at a valuation of $42 billion or higher
(3) If the company were to go public, it would convert at the price of the IPO.[84]

NOVEMBER 2018 - T&R CAPITAL

In the fall of 2018, rumors spread that WeWork was organizing a new funding round that would increase its valuation to more than $35 billion. In November 2018, Jones and other managers at T&R Capital were invited to potentially co-invest with SoftBank in a round at an even higher valuation— $42 billion. T&R had a mandate to invest in public technology companies, but had participated in a number of late-stage, pre-public venture capital rounds to deploy capital that was sitting idle. Jones saw the opportunity to invest in the round as a way to get a toehold in WeWork prior to it being public. The strategy had worked very well for several late-round investments over the past several years.

Jones learned that after this round of financing, the Vision Fund would have invested $66.6 billion in 81 portfolio companies. By far, the largest single investment, some $10.4 billion, would have gone into WeWork. Jones tried to understand if that was a good or bad sign for WeWork.

In his due diligence, Jones discovered that certain classes of stock in The We Company (all owned by Neumann) had a voting structure of 20 votes per share, effectively giving Neumann more voting power than all other stockholders of the company combined. This was not an immediate cause for concern as Jones was aware that multi-class voting structures were not uncommon in large technology companies (See **Exhibit 19** for trends in multi-class stocks). Neumann's voting power came from his Class B and Class C shares that had 20 votes to every one vote that regular shareholders had for their Class A shares. Despite this, two aspects of WeWork's corporate structure worried Jones: Neumann's super votes gave him the ability to terminate other stockholders, even the entire board, and company documents noted that, in the case of Neumann's death, his wife (co-founder and co-executive) would have the power to appoint the successor (**Exhibit 9** lists management team).[85] Reports also surfaced that Neumann had borrowed money from the company at little to no interest— two loans of $7 million and $362 million in 2016 at interest rates of 0.64% and 2.89% respectively.[86] Similarly, the company paid Neumann approximately $6 million for the name change to "The We Company," which was a trademark that he owned.[87]

THE DECISION

Shaun reviewed his notes from the presentation to T&R's investment committee which he would give in a few days. Current developments involving WeWork gave him mixed signals. On one hand, WeWork's rapid global expansion and the notable list of investors willing to inject billions into the company suggested that T&R Capital should be willing to place a bet on WeWork. On the other hand, reports of internal mismanagement and a lack of clarity on when cash flow for the company would turn positive provided a warning sign for him. Shaun finished his coffee, packed up his laptop, and left the café around the corner from his office. As he walked back to his office, Shaun thought about his recommendation and what he would say when pressed by his colleague. This certainly was no "slam dunk."

NOTES

1 2019 Yearbook, Mar. 2019. Accessed March 21, 2020 https://nvca.org/research/nvca-yearbook/.
2 Ibid.

3 "Venture Monitor - Q4 2109." Nvca.org. Accessed March 21, 2020. https://nvca.org/wpcontent/uploads/2020/01/Q4_2019_PitchBook_NVCA_Venture_Monitor.pdf.

4 Alan M. Webber, "Japanese-Style Entrepreneurship: An Interview with Softbank'S CEO, Masayoshi Son," *Harvard Business Review*, January 1, 1992, https://hbr.org/1992/01/japanese-style-entrepreneurship-an-interview-with-softbanks-ceo-masayoshi-son.

5 Ibid.

6 Ibid.

7 Ibid.

8 Ibid.

9 Ibid.

10 Ibid.

11 Larry Holyoke, "Japan's Hottest Entrepreneur Hits The U.S.," January 30, 1995, https://www.bloomberg.com/news/articles/1995-01-29/japans-hottest-entrepreneur-hits-the-u-dot-s-dot-intl-edition.

12 James R. Lincoln and Michael L. Gerlach, *Japan's Network Economy: Structure, Persistence, and Change* (Cambridge University Press, 2004), 346.

13 "Businessland in Japan Venture: The Largest U.S....," Los Angeles Times, June 7, 1990, https://www.latimes.com/archives/la-xpm-1990-06-07-fi-1727-story.html.

14 "History of Softbank Corp. – FundingUniverse," accessed March 26, 2020, http://www.fundinguniverse.com/company-histories/softbank-corp-history/.

15 Ibid.

16 Andrew Pollack, "A Japanese Gambler Hits the Jackpot With Softbank," *The New York Times*, February 19, 1995, sec. Business, https://www.nytimes.com/1995/02/19/business/a-japanese-gambler-hits-the-jackpot-with-softbank.html.

17 History of Softbank Corp. – FundingUniverse," accessed March 26, 2020, http://www.fundinguniverse.com/company-histories/softbank-corp-history/.

18 Ibid.

19 Holyoke, "Japan's Hottest Entrepreneur Hits The U.S."

20 Joseph Gallivan, "YAHOO! SOFTBANK CASHES OUT," *New York Post* (blog), June 2, 2000, https://nypost.com/2000/06/02/yahoo-softbank-cashes-out/.

21 History of Softbank Corp. – FundingUniverse," accessed March 26, 2020, http://www.fundinguniverse.com/company-histories/softbank-corp-history/.

22 William Auckerman, "Yahoo Japan Stock Breaks 100 Million Yen Barrier," Internet News: RealTime IT News, January 20, 2000, http://www.internet-news.com/ent-news/print.php/289851.

23 An Interactive Edition News Roundup, "Softbank Buys 80% Stake In Kingston Technology," *Wall Street Journal*, August 15, 1996, sec. Front Section, https://www.wsj.com/articles/SB840097903668072500.

24 "SoftBank Group History," accessed March 26, 2020, https://group.softbank/philosophy/history.

25 Eric Pfanner, "SoftBank's Alibaba Alchemy: How to Turn $20 Million Into $50 Billion - Digits - WSJ," The Wall Street Journal, September 19, 2014, https://blogs.wsj.com/digits/2014/09/19/softbanks-alibaba-alchemy-how-to-turn-20-million-into-50-billion/.

26 Ibid.
27 "Softbank to Buy Stake in E-Trade," Los Angeles Times, July 11, 1998, https://www.latimes.com/archives/la-xpm-1998-jul-11-fi-2613-story.html.
28 "Lessons from Softbank's Hard Knocks," Knowledge@Wharton, April 10, 2002, https://knowledge.wharton.upenn.edu/article/lessons-from-softbanks-hard-knocks/.
29 Neil Weinberg, "Master of the Internet," Forbes, July 4, 1999, https://www.forbes.com/forbes/1999/0705/6401146a.html#328560481e17.
30 Martin Fackler, "Softbank to Buy Vodafone's Japan Cellphone Unit for $15 Billion," *The New York Times*, March 18, 2006, sec. Business, https://www.nytimes.com/2006/03/18/business/worldbusiness/softbank-to-buy-vodafones-japan-cellphone-unit-for.html.
31 SoftBank Group History," accessed March 26, 2020, https://group.softbank/philosophy/history.
32 Ken Belson, "Softbank of Japan Marks Down Portfolio," *The New York Times*, November 21, 2001, sec. Business, https://www.nytimes.com/2001/11/21/business/softbank-of-japan-marks-down-portfolio.html.
33 Ken Belson, "Softbank of Japan Marks Down Portfolio," *The New York Times*, November 21, 2001, sec. Business, https://www.nytimes.com/2001/11/21/business/softbank-of-japan-marks-down-portfolio.html.
34 Ibid.
35 "Softbank Loses $62 Million on E*Trade Stake," CNET, July 26, 2002, https://www.cnet.com/news/softbank-loses-62-million-on-etrade-stake/.
36 "Lessons from Softbank's Hard Knocks," Knowledge@Wharton, April 10, 2002, https://knowledge.wharton.upenn.edu/article/lessons-from-softbanks-hard-knocks/.
37 Zahraa Alkhalisi, "Where the Huge SoftBank-Saudi Tech Fund Is Investing," CNNMoney, September 20, 2017, https://money.cnn.com/2017/09/20/technology/softbank-vision-fund-saudi-investments/index.html.
38 Zahraa Alkhalisi, "Saudi-SoftBank Tech Fund Nears $100 Billion Target," CNNMoney, May 21, 2017, https://money.cnn.com/2017/05/21/technology/saudi-softbank-tech-fund-target/index.html.
39 Mark Scott, "SoftBank Is Said to Be Selling a 25% Stake in ARM Holdings," *The New York Times*, March 8, 2017, sec. Business, https://www.nytimes.com/2017/03/08/business/dealbook/softbank-arm-holdings.html.
40 Ibid.
41 "SoftBank Vision Fund's First Major Closing," accessed March 26, 2020, https://group.softbank/news/press/20170522
42 Jason Rowley, "Inside the Rise and Reign of Supergiant Venture Capital Rounds | TechCrunch," Tech Crunch, July 22, 2018, https://techcrunch.com/2018/07/22/inside-the-rise-and-reign-of-supergiant-venture-capital-rounds/.
43 PWC, "Corporate venture capital activity on Three-year upward trend," press release, February 12, 2012.
44 "The Most Active Corporate VC Firms Globally," CB Insights Research, March 28, 2019, https://www.cbinsights.com/research/corporate-venture-capital-active-2014/.

45 Dana Olsen, "Vision Fund 101: Inside SoftBank's $98B Vehicle I PitchBook," Pitchbook: News & Analysis, August 2, 2017, https://pitchbook.com/news/articles/vision-fund-101-inside-softbanks-93b-vehicle.
46 João Medeiros, "How SoftBank Ate the World," *Wired UK*, February 7, 2019, https://www.wired.co.uk/article/softbank-vision-fund.
47 "What The SoftBank Vision Fund Means For Tech Investing—VCs & Industry Leaders Sound Off," CB Insights Research, July 14, 2017, https://www.cbinsights.com/research/softbank-vision-fund-tech-investing-sound-off/.
48 "SoftBank Vision Fund's First Major Closing," accessed March 26, 2020, https://group.softbank/news/press/20170522
49 Jason D. Rowley, "Uber Finally Seals $9 Billion Deal With SoftBank And Others," Crunchbase News, January 18, 2018, https://news.crunchbase.com/news/uber-finally-seals-9-billion-deal-softbank-others/.
50 Heather Somerville, "SoftBank Is Now Uber's Largest Shareholder as Deal Closes," *Reuters*, January 19, 2018, https://www.reuters.com/article/us-uber-softbank-tender-idUSKBN1F72WL.
51 Theodore Schleifer, "DoorDash Is Raising $535 Million from SoftBank and Others at a $1.4 Billion Valuation," Vox, March 1, 2018, https://www.vox.com/2018/3/1/17065928/doordash-softbank-gic-funding.
52 Ryan Browne, "Slack Is Now Worth over $5 Billion after $250 Million Cash Injection Led by Japan's SoftBank," CNBC, September 18, 2017, https://www.cnbc.com/2017/09/18/slack-worth-over-5-billion-after-250-million-investment-led-by-softbank.html.
53 Emma Cosgrove, "SoftBank Invests in Largest Ever Agtech Deal, a $200m Series B for Indoor Ag Startup Plenty," AgFunderNews, July 19, 2017, https://agfundernews.com/breaking-plenty-raises-200m-series-b-largest-ever-agtech-investment.html.
54 Patrick Clark, "SoftBank-Backed Compass Tells Employees: We're Not WeWork," *Bloomberg.Com*, October 15, 2019, https://www.bloomberg.com/news/articles/2019-10-15/softbank-backed-broker-compass-tells-employees-we-re-not-wework.
55 Eliot Brown and Laura Kusisto, "SoftBank Invests $400 Million in Home-Selling Startup Opendoor," *Wall Street Journal*, September 27, 2018, sec. Tech, https://www.wsj.com/articles/softbank-invests-400-million-in-home-selling-startup-opendoor-1538042400.
56 Ibid.
57 Olsen, "Vision Fund 101."
58 Leonard Sherman, "WeWork's Failure Is SoftBank's Day Of Reckoning," *Wired*, October 19, 2019, https://www.wired.com/story/weworks-failure-is-softbanks-day-of-reckoning/.
59 Leskin, Paige. "The Career Rise and Fall of Adam Neumann, the Controversial WeWork Cofounder Who Is Reportedly Getting $1.7 Billion to Step down from the Company's Board." Business Insider, Business Insider, 22 Oct. 2019. Accessed March 19, 2020. www.businessinsider.com/wework-ceo-adam-neumann-bio-life-career-2019-8#neumann-is-severely-dyslexic-and-couldnt-read-or-write-until-he-was-in-third-grade-3.

60 Nicolaou, Anna. "WeWork Cultivating 'Physical Social Network'." *Financial Times*, 17 Mar. 2016. Accessed March 19, 2020. www.ft.com/content/f2e073a2-d0ef-11e5-831d-09f7778e7377.
61 "WeWork: The Rise and Fall of Co-Founder Adam Neumann." *BBC News*, BBC, 25 Sept. 2019. Accessed March 19, 2020. www.bbc.com/news/business-49817037.
62 Liozos, Connie. "WeWork's Adam Neumann Is Graduating from College Today - 15 Years after He Enrolled." *TechCrunch*, TechCrunch, 5 June 2017. Accessed March 19, 2020. techcrunch.com/2017/06/05/weworks-adam-neumann-is-graduating-from-college-today-15-years-after-he-started/.
63 Liozos, Connie. "WeWork's Adam Neumann Is Graduating from College Today - 15 Years after He Enrolled." *TechCrunch*, TechCrunch, 5 June 2017. Accessed March 19, 2020. techcrunch.com/2017/06/05/weworks-adam-neumann-is-graduating-from-college-today-15-years-after-he-started/.
64 Bertoni, Steven. "WeWork's $20 Billion Office Party: The Crazy Bet That Could Change How The World Does Business." Forbes, Forbes Magazine, 26 Feb. 2018. Accessed March 20, 2020. www.forbes.com/sites/stevenbertoni/2017/10/02/the-way-we-work/#31c85b101b18.
65 Bartlett, Ian. "How Did WeWork's Adam Neumann Build a $47 Billion Company?" Intelligencer, 10 June 2019. Accessed March 20, 2020. nymag.com/intelligencer/2019/06/wework-adam-neumann.html.
66 From the S-1. "The We Company. August 14, 2019. Accessed March 10, 2020
67 From the S-1. "The We Company. August 14, 2019. Accessed March 20, 2020
68 From the S-1. "The We Company. August 14, 2019. Accessed March 10, 2020
69 From the S-1. "The We Company. August 14, 2019. Accessed March 10, 2020
70 From the S-1. "The We Company. August 14, 2019. Accessed March 10, 2020
71 From the S-1. "The We Company. August 14, 2019. Accessed March 10, 2020
72 Primack, Dan. "WeWork Doubled Revenue and Loss in 2018." Axios, March 25, 2019. Accessed March 10 2019. www.axios.com/wework-doubled-revenue-loss-2018-eec75ff5-6466-4f20-9436-2f9a983db21b.html.
73 Brown, Eliot. "A Look at WeWork's Books: Revenue Is Doubling but Losses Are Mounting." The Wall Street Journal, Dow Jones & Company, April 25, 2018. Accessed March 10, 2020. www.wsj.com/articles/a-look-at-weworks-books-revenue-is-doubling-but-losses-are-mounting-1524657600.
74 Taylor Majewski, "A History of WeWork, the Multi-Billion Dollar Company Taking over NYC," Built In NYC, December 22, 2015, https://www.builtinnyc.com/2015/12/21/brief-history-wework.
75 "WeWork Funding Rounds, Valuation and Investors | Craft.Co," accessed March 27, 2020, https://craft.co/wework/funding-rounds.
76 Lauren Clark, "WeWork Snags $400M More, Valuation Doubles to $10B and Boosts Early Investments from JPMorgan Chase, Goldman Sachs and Benchmark Capital (Video)," New York Business Journal, June 25, 2015, https://www.bizjournals.com/newyork/news/2015/06/25/wework-becomes-a-golden-horned-nyc-unicorn-raises.html.
77 Andrew Rice, "Is This the Office of the Future or a $5 Billion Waste of Space?," *Bloomberg.Com*, May 21, 2015, https://www.bloomberg.com/news/features/2015-05-21/wework-real-estate-empire-or-shared-office-space-for-a-new-era-.

78 Reeves Wiedeman, "How Did WeWork's Adam Neumann Build a $47 Billion Company?," Intelligencer, June 10, 2019, https://nymag.com/intelligencer/2019/06/wework-adam-neumann.html.

79 Ellen Huet and Pavel Alpeyev, "SoftBank Invests $300 Million in WeWork," *Bloomberg.Com*, March 21, 2017, https://www.bloomberg.com/news/articles/2017-03-21/softbank-invests-300-million-in-wework.

80 Wiedeman, "How Did WeWork's Adam Neumann Build a $47 Billion Company?"

81 Ibid.

82 Kate Clark, "Timeline: In Seven Years, WeWork Built a $21B Co-Working Empire | PitchBook," Pitchbook: News & Analysis, August 7, 2017, https://pitchbook.com/news/articles/timeline-in-7-years-wework-built-a-21b-co-working-empire.

83 Shona Ghosh, "WeWork Is Raising $1 Billion from SoftBank in a Very Unusual Way, Business Insider - Business Insider Singapore," Business Insider Singapore, August 9, 2018, https://www.businessinsider.sg/wework-raises-1-billion-from-softbank-2018-8.

84 Ibid.

85 Rani Molla and Shirin Ghaffary, "The WeWork Mess, Explained," Vox, September 23, 2019, https://www.vox.com/recode/2019/9/23/20879656/wework-mess-explained-ipo-softbank.

86 Ellen Huet, "WeWork Gave Founder Loans as It Paid Him Rent, IPO Filing Shows," *Bloomberg.Com*, August 14, 2019, https://www.bloomberg.com/news/articles/2019-08-14/wework-gave-founder-loans-as-it-paid-him-rent-ipo-filing-shows.

87 Rani Molla and Shirin Ghaffary, "The WeWork Mess, Explained," Vox, September 23, 2019, https://www.vox.com/recode/2019/9/23/20879656/wework-mess-explained-ipo-softbank.

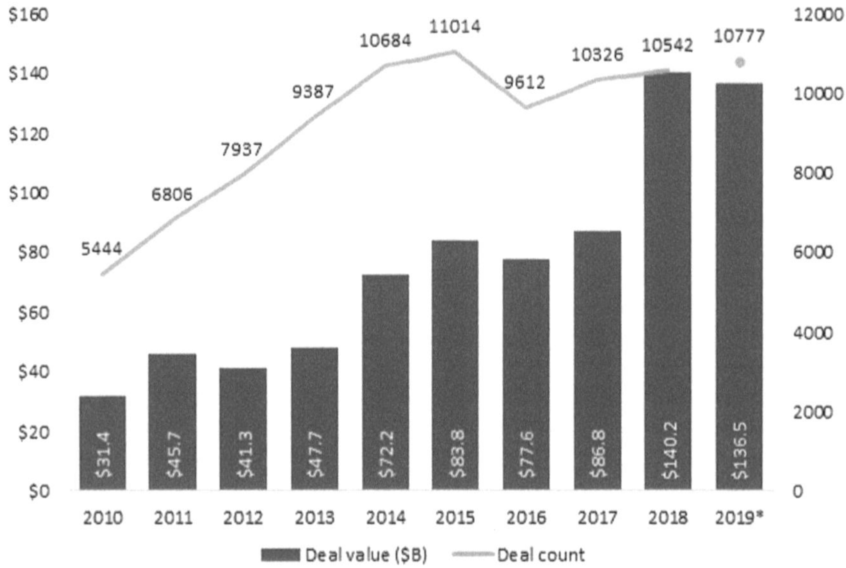

EXHIBIT 1 U.S. Venture Capital Annual Total Value of Deal Activity (2010-2019)
Source: Casewriter; data from 2019 Yearbook , Mar. 2019. Accessed March 21, 2020 https://nvca.org/research/nvca-yearbook/.

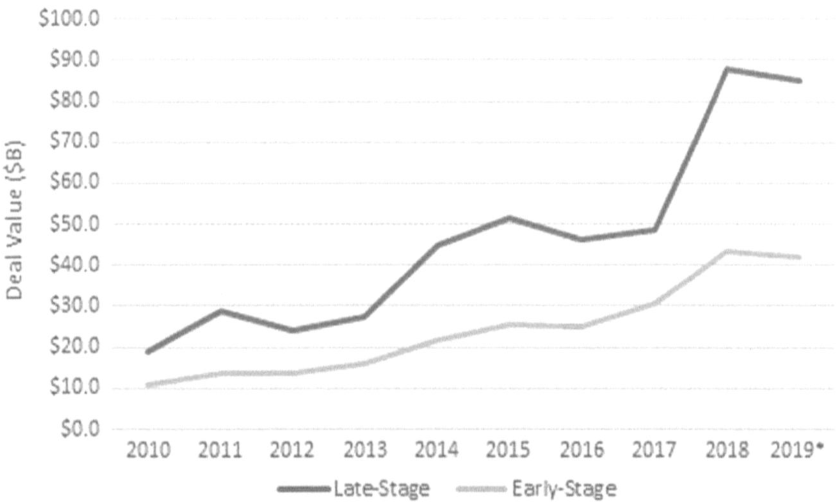

EXHIBIT 2 Venture Capital Late Stage vs. Early Stage Annual Deal Value
Source: Casewriter; data from 2019 Yearbook , Mar. 2019. Accessed March 21, 2020 https://nvca.org/research/nvca-yearbook/.

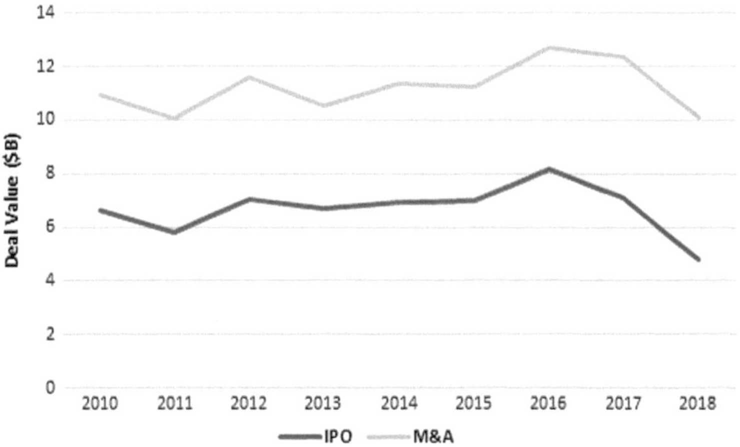

EXHIBIT 3 Median Time from First VC Investment to Exit (2010-2019)
Source: Casewriter; data from 2019 Yearbook , Mar. 2019. Accessed March 21, 2020 https://nvca.org/research/nvca-yearbook/.

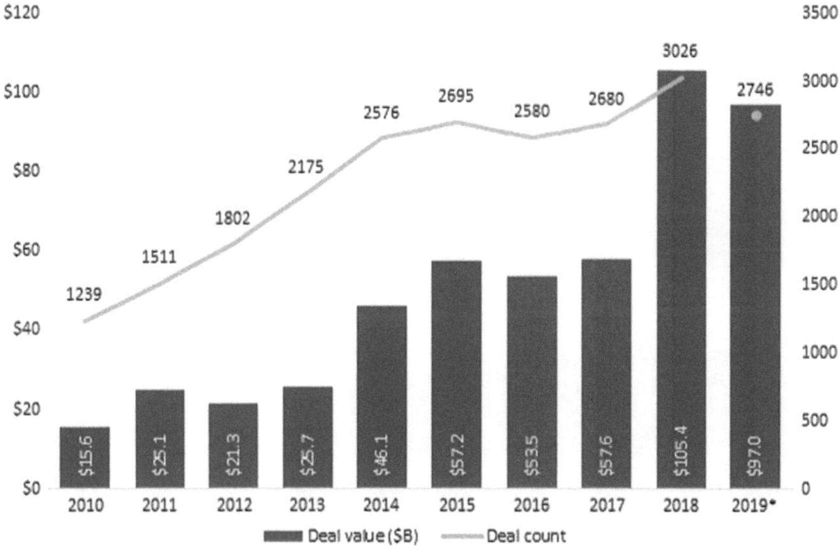

EXHIBIT 4 U.S. VC Deal Activity with Non-Traditional VC Investor Participation
Source: Casewriter; data from 2019 Yearbook , Mar. 2019. Accessed March 21, 2020 https://nvca.org/research/nvca-yearbook.

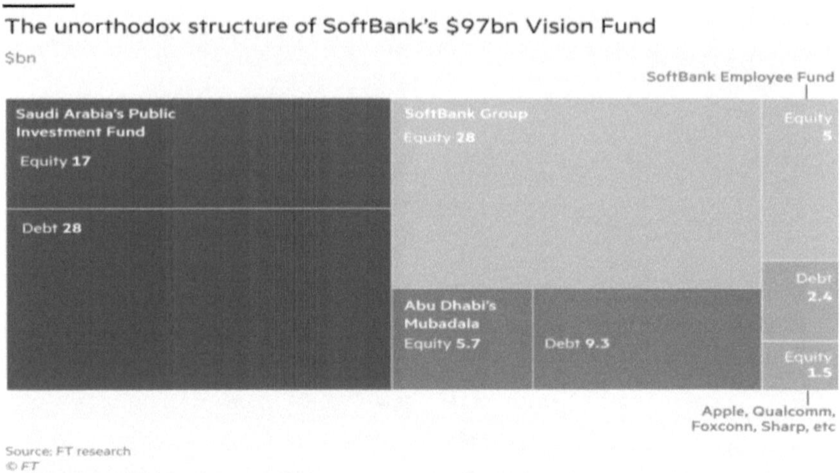

EXHIBIT 5 Vision Fund Investors
Source: © FT Source: Kana Inagaki, Arash Massoudi, and Leo Lewis. 2019. SoftBank: Blind Spots Threaten Masayoshi Son's $100bn Vision. Financial Times / FT.com. 4 November.

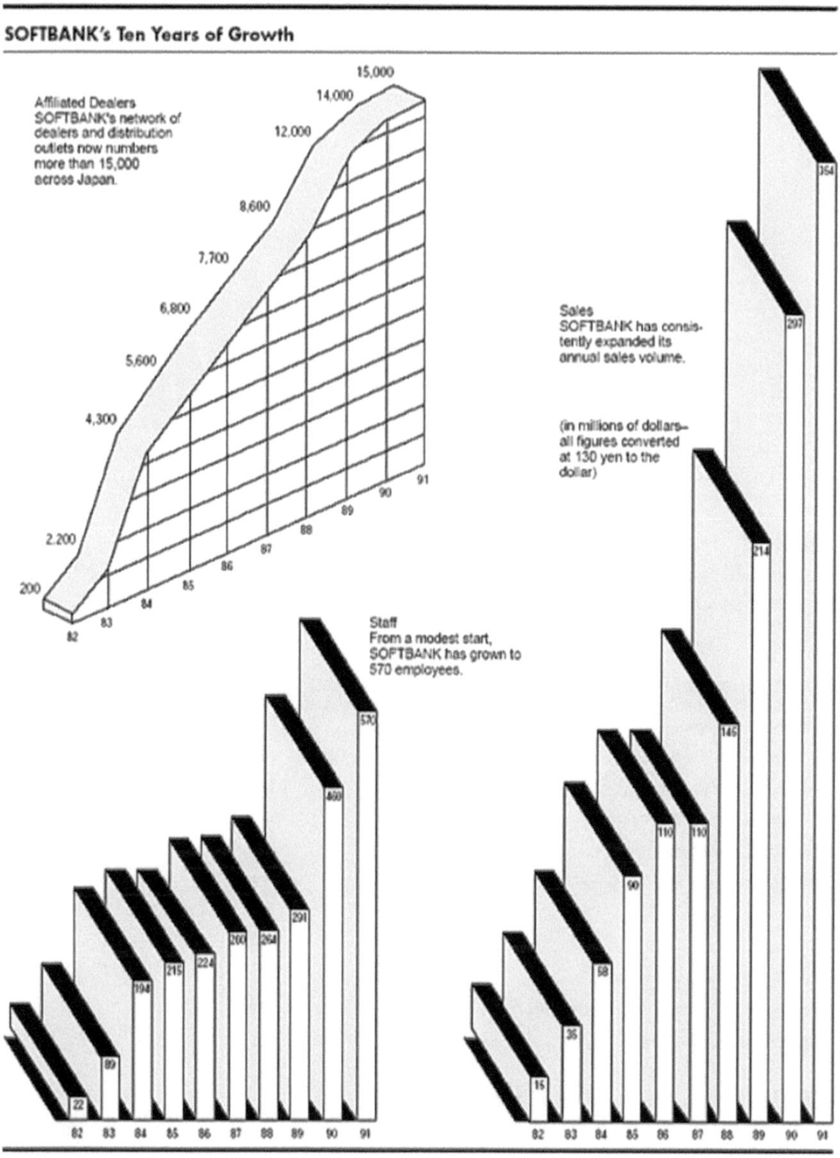

EXHIBIT 6 SoftBank's First Ten Years of Growth
Source: Harvard Business Review, February 1992 Issue, Accessed March 21, 2020.

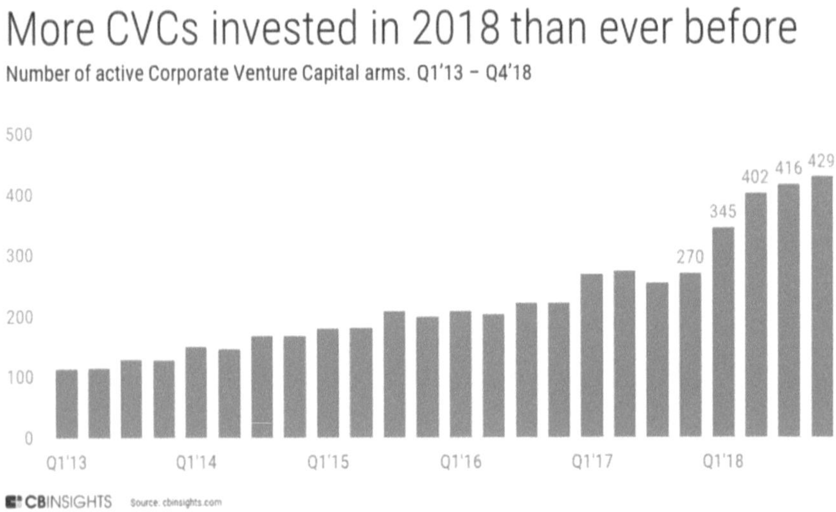

EXHIBIT 7 Trends in Corporate Venture Capital
Source: CBInsights – Research Briefs, March 28, 2019. Accessed March 19, 2020, https://cbinsights.com/resarech/corporate-venture-capital-active-2014/.

Investor Name	Investments	Active Portfolio
Fidelity Investments	309	110
T. Rowe Price (NAS: TROW)	289	94
Tekla Capital Management	205	11
JP Morgan Asset Management	167	68
Wellington Management	165	67
Fidelity Management & Research	135	71
The Vanguard Group	114	79
Caledonia Private Capital (LON: CLDN)	86	21
The Capital Group Companies	77	35
Fidelity Equity Partners (Massachusetts)	71	3
Dimensional Fund Advisors	66	38

EXHIBIT 8 Top Mutual Fund Investors in VC
Source: PitchBook - Investor Type: Mutual Fund , https://my.pitchbook.com/?pcc=308203-30.

Our Leadership Team

The following sets forth certain information relating to our co-founders and global leadership team as of June 30, 2019.

Our Co-founders

Adam Neumann

Co-Founder, Chief Executive Officer and Chairman of the Board

Adam, 40, is one of our co-founders and has served as our Chief Executive Officer and Chairman of the Board since our inception. He serves on our board of directors because of the perspective and experience he brings as our Co-Founder and Chief Executive Officer. We believe his strategic insight, leadership and commitment to the growth of our global team and community will provide us the leadership we need to execute our vision. Adam is married to Rebekah Neumann and is an executive officer.

Rebekah Neumann

Co-Founder, Chief Brand and Impact Officer
Founder and CEO of WeGrow

Rebekah is one of our co-founders and serves as our Chief Brand and Impact Officer. She is also the founder and CEO of WeGrow. Rebekah is married to Adam Neumann.

Miguel McKelvey

Co-Founder and Chief Culture Officer

Miguel is one of our co-founders and serves as our Chief Culture Officer. He previously served as our Chief Creative Officer.

Our Global Leaders

Jennifer Berrent

Co-President and Chief Legal Officer

Jen, 47, has served as one of our Presidents since April 2019 and as Chief Legal Officer since June 2016. From October 2014 to April 2019, she held a variety of positions in the organization, including Chief Operating Officer, Chief Culture Officer and General Counsel. From March 2006 to October 2014, she was a lawyer at Wilmer Cutler Pickering Hale and Dorr LLP, where she served as a partner from January 2011 to October 2014. Jen is an executive officer.

Michael Gross

Vice Chair

Michael has served as a Vice Chair since 2015. Prior to his current role, he served as our Chief Financial Officer from 2013 to 2015. He previously served as Chief Executive Officer of Morgan Hotel Group.

Arthur Minson

Co-President and Chief Financial Officer

Artie, 48, has served as one of our Presidents since June 2015 and as our Chief Financial Officer since June 2016. From June 2015 to June 2016, he also served as our Chief Operating Officer. From May 2013 to June 2015, he served as Executive Vice President and Chief Financial Officer of Time Warner Cable Inc. From 2009 to April 2013, he served in a number of senior management roles at AOL Inc., including Chief Operating Officer and Chief Financial and Administrative Officer. Artie is an executive officer.

EXHIBIT 9 Excerpt from WeWork S-1: Management Team
Source: From the S-1. "The We Company. August 14, 2019. Access March 10, 2020

Technology is at the foundation of our global platform. Our purpose-built technology and operational expertise has allowed us to scale our core WeWork space-as-a-service offering quickly, while improving the quality of our solutions and decreasing the cost to find, build, fill and run our spaces. We have approximately 1,000 engineers, product designers and machine learning scientists that are dedicated to building, integrating and automating the complex systems we use to operate our business. As a result, we are able to deliver a premium experience to our members at a lower price relative to traditional alternatives.

Cost Per Employee: WeWork Versus Standard Lease

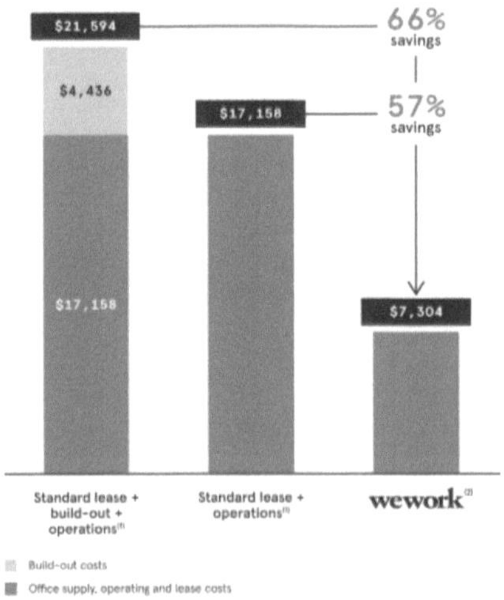

(1) Sources: Building Owners and Managers Association (BOMA); CoStar Office Market Statistics; International Facility Management Association (IFMA); CBRE Office Occupancy Costs; Cushman Global Occupancy Report 2017; and third-party research. Comparison data represents annualized costs based on an average of ten select city centers in the United States, Europe, South America and Asia that are representative of our key markets. "Standard lease" includes the costs associated with food and beverage, events, utilities, insurance, property taxes, facilities management and base rent. "Build-out" includes the costs associated with construction, procurement and design services offset by a tenant improvement allowance amortized over an illustrative five-year lease.

(2) Represents annualized average membership and service revenue per WeWork membership ("average revenue per WeWork membership") for the six months ended June 30, 2019 across the same ten select city centers as above.

We have grown significantly since our inception. Our membership base has grown by over 100% every year since 2014. It took us more than seven years to achieve $1 billion of run-rate revenue, but only one additional year to reach $2 billion of run-rate revenue and just six months to reach $3 billion of run-rate revenue.

EXHIBIT 10 Excerpt from WeWork S-1: Cost per Employee: WeWork versus Standard Lease

Source: From the S-1. "The We Company. August 14, 2019. Access March 10, 202

In the 111 cities in which we had locations as of June 1, 2019, we estimate that there are approximately 149 million potential members. For U.S. cities, we define potential members by the estimated number of desk jobs based on data from the Statistics of U.S. Businesses survey by the U.S. Census Bureau. For non-U.S. cities, we consider anyone in select occupations defined by the International Labor Organization—including managers, professionals, technicians and associate professionals and clerical support workers—to be potential members, because we assume that these individuals need workspace in which they have access to a desk and other services. We view this as our addressable market because of the broad variety of professions and industries among our members, the breadth of our solutions available to individuals and organizations of different types and our track record of developing new solutions in response to our members' needs.

We expect to expand aggressively in our existing cities as well as launch in up to 169 additional cities. We evaluate expansion in new cities based on multiple criteria, primarily our assessment of the potential member demand as well as the strategic value of having that city as part of our location portfolio. Based on data from Demographia and the Organization for Economic Cooperation and Development, we have identified our market opportunity to be 280 target cities with an estimated potential member population of approximately 255 million people in aggregate.

When applying our average revenue per WeWork membership for the six months ended June 30, 2019 to our potential member population of 149 million people in our existing 111 cities, we estimate an addressable market opportunity of $945 billion. Among our total potential member population of approximately 255 million people across our 280 target cities globally, we estimate an addressable market opportunity of $1.6 trillion.

We are able to deliver a premium experience to our members at a lower price relative to traditional alternatives. Data from CBRE Group and Cushman & Wakefield indicates that employers across 155 global cities for which data is available and in which we have existing or planned locations spend a weighted average of approximately $11,700 in occupancy costs per employee each year. By applying the average employee occupancy costs to our potential member population of 149 million people in our existing 111 cities, we estimate a total opportunity of $1.7 trillion. Among the approximately 255 million potential members across our 280 target cities globally, we estimate a total opportunity of $3.0 trillion.

(1) As of June 1, 2019.

(2) Includes existing 111 cities as of June 1, 2019.

We believe these total opportunities reflect the amount employers are willing to spend and present an opportunity for us to capture greater wallet share through additional solutions and product and service offerings. We believe that we will be able to capture a portion of this existing spend per employee given our powerful brand and what we believe is a significant first-mover advantage over our competitors as the pioneer of the space-as-a-service model. We believe that

EXHIBIT 11 Excerpt from WeWork S-1: Addressable Market Size
Source: From the S-1. "The We Company. August 14, 2019. Access March 10, 2020

EXHIBIT 12 Excerpt from WeWork S-1: "Consolidated statement of operations information"

(Amounts in thousands, except percentages and where noted)	Year Ended December 31, 2016	Year Ended December 31, 2017	Year Ended December 31, 2018	Six Months Ended June 30, 2018
Consolidated statement of operations information:				
Revenue:	$ 436,099	$ 886,004	$ 1,821,751	$ 763,711
Expenses:				
Location operating expenses (1)	433,167	814,782	$ 1,521,129	$ 635,968
Other operating expenses (1)	-	1,677	106,788	42,024
Pre-opening location expenses	115,749	131,324	357,831	156,983
Sales and marketing expenses	43,428	143,424	378,729	139,889
Growth and new market development expenses	35,731	109,719	477,273	174,091
General and administrative expenses (2)	115,346	454,020	357,486	155,257
Depreciation and amortization	88,952	162,892	313,514	137,418
Total Expenses	832,373	1,817,838	3,512,750	1,441,630
Loss from operations	(396,274)	(931,834)	(1,690,999)	(677,919)
Interest and other income (expense), net (3)	(33,400)	(7,387)	(237,270)	(46,406)
Pre-tax loss	(429,674)	(939,221)	(1,928,269)	(724,325)
Income tax benefit (provision)	(16)	5,727	850	1,373
Net loss	(429,690)	(933,494)	(1,927,419)	(722,952)
Net loss attributable to noncontrolling interests	-	49,500	316,627	94,762
Net loss attributable to WeWork Companies Inc.	$ (429,690)	$ (883,994)	$ (1,610,792)	$ (628,190)
Net loss per share attributable to Class A and Class B common stockholders: (3)				
Basic	$ (2.66)	$ (5.54)	$ (9.87)	$ (3.87)
Diluted	$ (2.66)	$ (5.54)	$ (9.87)	$ (3.87)
Weighted-average shares used to compute net loss per share attributable to Class A and Class B common stockholders, basic and diluted	161,324,940	159,689,116	163,148,918	162,482,366
Pro forma net loss per share attributable to Class A and Class B common stockholders: (4)				
Basic			$ (4.41)	
Diluted				
Weighted-average shares used to compute pro forma net loss per share attributable to Class A and Class B common stockholders, basic and diluted			338,368,587	
Key performance indicators:				
Workstation capacity (in ones)	107,000	214,000	466,000	301,000
Memberships (in ones)	87,000	186,000	401,000	268,000
Enterprise membership percentage	18%	28%	38%	30%
Run-rate revenue (in billions	$ 0.60	$ 1.10	$ 2.40	$ 1.80
Committed revenue backlog (in billions)	$ 0.10	$ 0.50	$ 2.60	N/R

N/R = Not reported

(1) Exclusive of depreciation and amortization shown separately on the depreciation and amortization line.

(2) Includes stock-based compensation expense of $17.4 million, $260.7 million and $18.0 million for the years ended December 31, 2016, 2017 and 2018, respectively, and includes stock- based compensation expense of $10.5 million for the six months ended June 30, 2018.

(3) Refer to Note 13 to the audited annual consolidated financial statements and Note 15 to the unaudited interim condensed consolidated financial statements, each included elsewhere in this prospectus, for additional information on fair value adjustments included in interest and other income (expense), net.

(4) See Note 22 to the audited annual consolidated financial statements and Note 24 to the unaudited interim condensed consolidated financial statements, each included elsewhere in this prospectus, for a description of how we compute basic and diluted net loss per share attributable to Class A and Class B common stockholders and pro forma basic and diluted net loss per share attributable to Class A and Class B common stockholders. Historical share and per share information does not give effect to the consummation of the stock split to be effected on the closing date of this offering. Pro forma share and per share information gives effect to the consummation of the stock split to be effected on the closing date of this offering pursuant to which each share of our capital stock will be reclassified into shares.

Source: The We Company, August 14, 2019 Form S-1, https://www.sec.gov/, accessed March 2020.

EXHIBIT 13 Excerpt from WeWork S-1: "Consolidated balance sheet information"

(Amounts in thousands)	Year Ended December 31. 2017	2018
Consolidated balance sheet information:		
Cash and cash equivalents	$ 2,020,805	$ 1,744,209
Other current assets	406,291	719,869
Total current assets	2,427,096	2,464,078
Property and equipement, net	2,337,092	4,368,772
Other fixed assets	599,884	1,812,066
Total assets	5,364,072	8,644,916
Total non-current liabilities	1,755,924	4,675,071
Total current liabilities	650,587	1,609,088
Total liabilities	2,406,511	6,284,159
Total convertible preferred stock included as temporary equity	3,405,435	3,498,696
Total redeemable noncontrolling interests included as temporary equ	854,577	1,320,637
Total equity (deficit)	(1,302,451)	(2,458,576)

See pages F-3 to F-4 in the WeWork S-1 for balance sheet

Source: The We Company, August 14, 2019 Form S-1, https://www.sec.gov/, accessed March 2020

EXHIBIT 14 Excerpt from WeWork S-1: "Consolidated cash flows information"

(Amounts in thousands)	Year Ended December 31. 2016	2017	2018	Six Months Ended June 30. 2018
Consolidated cash flow information:				
Net cash provided by (used in) operating activities	$ 176,905	$ 243,992	$ (176,729)	$ (84,363)
Net cash provided by (used in) investing activities	(818,525)	(1,376,767)	(2,475,798)	(888,173)
Net cash provided by (used in) financing activities	727,908	2,724,315	2,658,469	745,794
Effects of exchange rate changes	(2,261)	(763)	(13,119)	2,726
Net increase (decrease) in cash, cash equivalents, and restricted cash	$ 84,027	$ 1,590,777	$ (7,177)	$ (224,016)

See pages F-10 to F-12 in the WeWork S-1 for statement of cash flows

Source: The We Company, August 14, 2019 Form S-1, https://www.sec.gov/, accessed March 2020

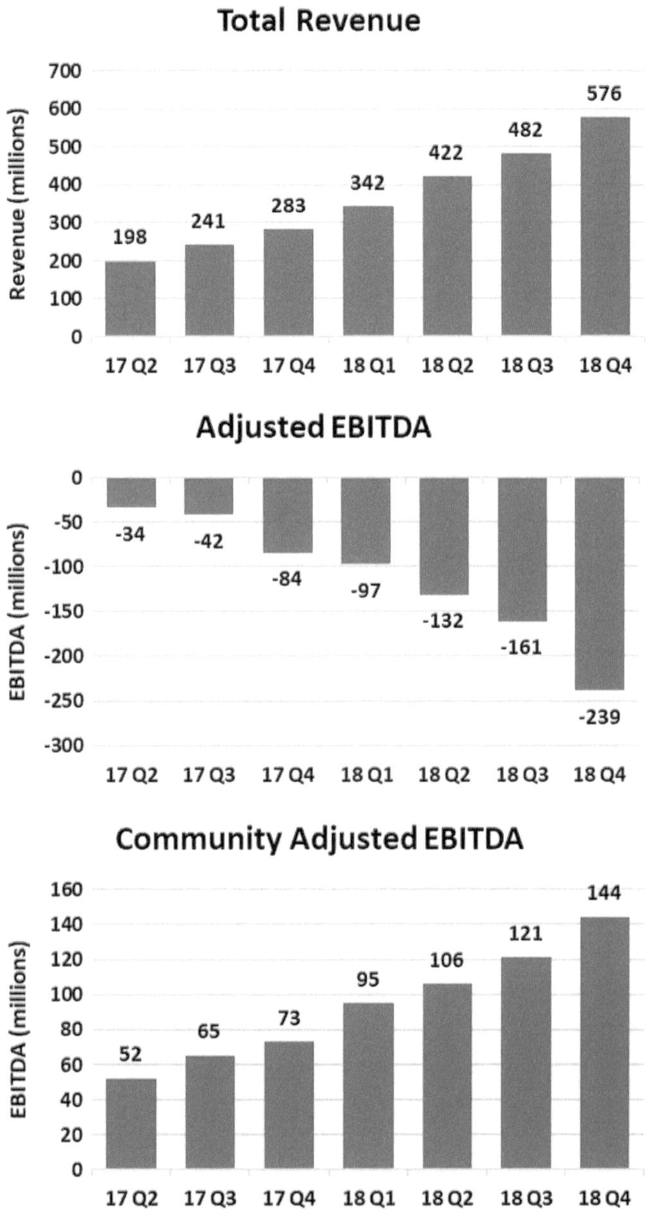

EXHIBIT 15 WeWork Adjusted EBITDA vs. Community Adjusted Beta
Source: Compiled by casewriter based on data from The We Company SEC filings S1 08/14/19, https://www.sec.gov/Archives/edgar/data/1533523/000119312519220499/d781982ds1.htm, accessed June 2020.

EXHIBIT 16 WeWork Capital Raised

WeWork Funding Rounds					
	Date	Amount Raised	Post-money Valuation	Step up	Investors
Series A	Apr-09	$17,500,500	$97,000,000		DAG Ventures
Series B	Nov-10	$41,000,000	$440,000,000	4.54	
Series C	Jul-11	$156,400,000	$1,500,000,000	3.41	Aleph
Series D-1	Jul-11	$198,800,000	$4,800,000,000	3.20	Goldman Sachs, Benchmark, T. Rowe Price, Wellington Management, Harvard Management Company, JP Morgan Chase & Co.
Series D-2	May-12	$156,200,000	$5,000,000,000	1.04	Goldman Sachs, Benchmark, T. Rowe Price, Wellington Management, Harvard Management Company, JP Morgan Chase & Co.
Series E	Jun-15	$433,900,000	$10,200,000,000	2.04	T. Rowe Price, Fidelity Investments, Glade Brook Capital Partners, JP Morgan Chase & Co
Series F	Jul-15	$750,000,000	$15,800,000,000	1.55	Hony Capital, Legend Holdings
Series G	Aug-17	$2,000,000,000	$21,200,000,000	1.34	Primary Venture Partners, SoftBank Group, Alpha JWC Ventures, Syren Capital Advisors, Catalyst Ventures, StraightPath Venture Partners
Series G	Jan-19	$5,000,000,000	$48,700,000,000	2.30	Softbank, Masayoshi Son
Unattributed	Oct-19	$5,000,000,000	$12,000,000,000	0.25	SoftBank Group Corp
		$13,753,800,500			

Source: Compiled by casewriter.

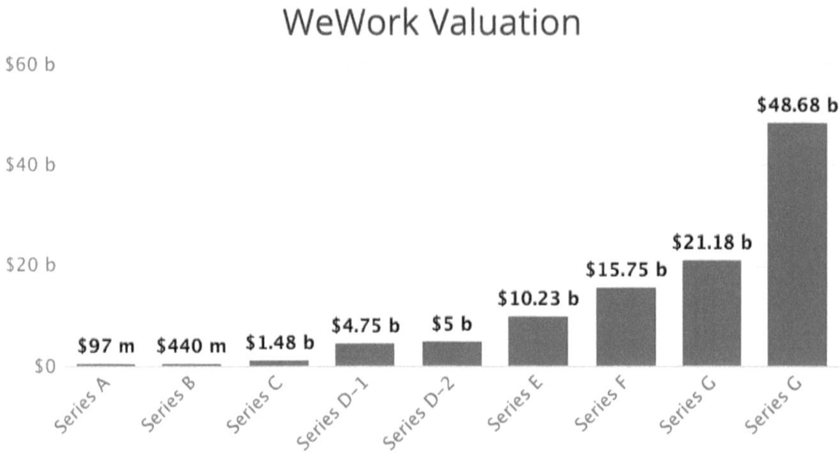

EXHIBIT 17 WeWork Valuation
Source: Craft, "WeWork funding rounds, valuation, and investors." Accessed March 21, 2020, https://craft.co/wework/funding-rounds.

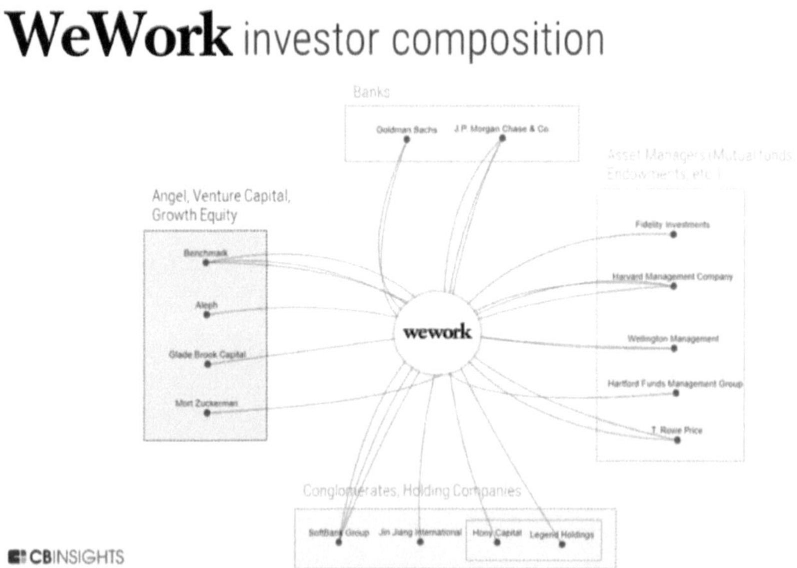

EXHIBIT 18 WeWork Investor Composition
Source: CBInsights – Research Report, "WeWork's $47 Billion Dream: The Lavishly Funded Startup That Could Disrupt Commercial Real Estate." Accessed March 21, 2020, https://cbinsights.com/research/report/wework-strategy-teardown/.

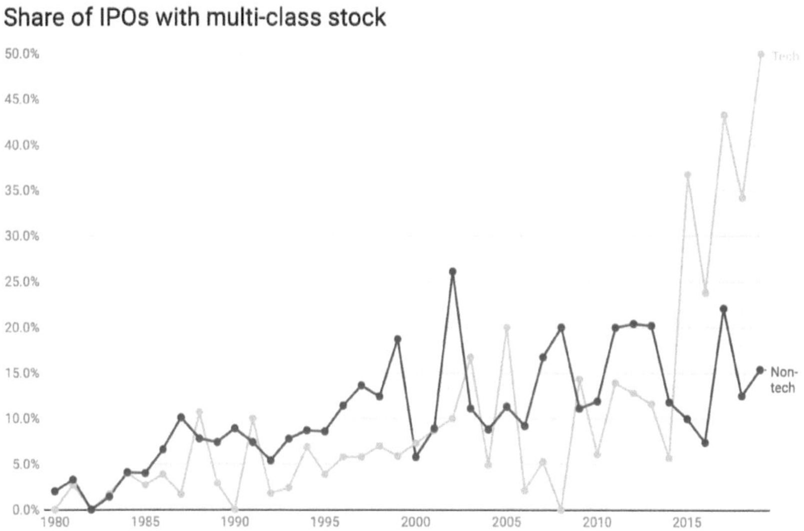

EXHIBIT 19 Trends in Multi-Class Stocks
Source: Rani Molla, "More Tech Companies Are Selling Stock That Keeps Their Founders in Power," Vox, April 11, 2019, https://www.vox.com/2019/4/11/18302102/ipo-voting-multi-dual-stock-lyft-pinterest. Data from Jay Ritter. © Vox.com and Vox Media, LLC.
Note: 2019 data is year-to-date and includes only 17 IPOs, four of which are tech.

SECTION 5

Gender and Diversity in Entrepreneurship

CHAPTER 5.1

Aspect Ventures

Paul Gompers, Danielle Li and Silpa Kovvali

Jennifer Fonstad handed the two resumes of the firm's top two associate candidates across the table to partner and co-founder Theresia Gouw. Sitting in their San Francisco office the two contemplated the decision that faced them. Unlike many of the decisions they had made in the months since founding their venture capital firm, Aspect Ventures, the decision that faced them now may have a lasting impact on team dynamics and culture within the firm. Gouw and Fonstad had left senior partner positions at two of the most prominent venture capital firms in Silicon Valley to build a firm where diversity, collaboration, and a singular focus on early stage investing would deliver strong investment returns. They had achieved an incredible number of successes even sooner than they had envisioned. Deal flow was robust and growing and they had made a number of promising investments. They needed to expand their team to help manage and grow their portfolio, so this was a critical hire.

As they pondered who would be the next investor to join the team, they reflected on what they believed made venture capital firms successful. Both felt that venture capital was a "team sport", i.e., a collaborative venture capital model makes all investors better. Collaboration also enabled their entrepreneurs to have the best chance at success. Gouw and Fonstad had built the firm meticulously and already had hired several investment professionals to join them. With the current team, what were they missing? As they pondered what additional characteristics and experiences they needed to address, they each thought about the relative strengths of each candidate. Both candidates brought a unique perspective, but they were going to make just one offer. Fonstad turned to Gouw and said, "Ok, who is your top choice?"

Aspect Ventures
by PAUL GOMPERS, DANIELLE LI, SILPA KOVVALI, case number 9-217-046 Rev. JANUARY 23, 2019

VENTURE CAPITAL INDUSTRY

Business Model

Venture capital (VC) firms identify, invest, and support start-up companies, typically in high growth industries where innovation happens quickly and bringing the right resources to start-ups can play a key role in the success of a company. (See **Exhibit 1** for diagram.) Different VC firms employ different strategies for how they identify potential investments and where they focus their time and investment dollars to maximize successful outcomes. Based on their strategy, firms develop a pipeline of potential investments, a concept known as a "deal funnel." The vast majority of deals that venture capitalists do come through their networks. The depth and breadth of a firm's networks are therefore important to the "deal funnel." A typical venture capitalist will evaluate 100 opportunities for every deal that they select. Hence, the process of selecting the appropriate deals is also important. VC firms then negotiate with entrepreneurs to structure a mutually agreeable set of investment terms and then take an active role in assisting the company post-investment, often joining the company's board of directors. Deals are generally structured to give the VC firm a return on its investment if a company in its portfolio achieves a successful IPO, merger, or acquisition. If this result is not achieved within a specified time frame, the deal is considered a failure. A sound strategy, steady stream of investment opportunities, or "deal flow", an effective deal selection mechanism, and high post-investment value-add are thus all of vital concern to VC firms.[1]

The internal structure of a VC firm plays a crucial role in achieving these goals. Depending upon the size of the firm, investment professional may consist of analysts who assist with deal support, associates who play a role in deal negotiation and post-investment management, and principals who helm most deal execution and might even source deals for the partners. Partners play a very active role in post-investment company assistance and frequently sit on the boards of portfolio companies. Managing partners, often but not always the founders of the firm, generally have more authority in final investment decisions throughout the firm. Managing partners are typically the public face of the venture capital firm, manage the key aspects of the portfolio and exert a great deal of influence over firm culture.[2]

Of critical importance to deal selection is the investment decision-making process. Depending upon firm culture, firms take different approaches to approving investments. Some venture firms take formal votes and require unanimous consent to approve a deal. Other firms vote but use majority decision rules in the process. Still other firms use a consensus process in which partners hold veto rights over any particular deal. How deals are sourced, vetted, and are approved are often defined as much by the firm's culture as it is by the formal voting process.

Compensation typically has three parts in a venture capital firm. Investment professionals generally receive a base salary with annual bonus similar to many operating companies. The base salary and bonus are usually determined by the managing partners. Beyond this annual compensation, the team members may receive an allocation of the fund's carried interest or synthetic carried meant to reward team members for their role in the firm's success. Should a deal succeed, VC firms typically receive a share of the profits ("carry") from investing (usually between 20 and 30 percent.) Firms adopt a wide variety of sharing rules for carry among team members.[3] (See **Exhibit 2** for compensation overview.) The share of carry allocated to an individual is usually dependent upon one's title as well as tenure and performance in prior funds. At the partner level, firms with a flatter compensation structure might allocate carry equally among all partners, while in other firms managing partners receive a higher share of carry. (See **Exhibit 2** for breakdown.)

As in any organization, compensation structure can have a tremendous impact on a firm's culture and might encourage more individualist thinking or collaborative behavior. It is important for a firm to provide the right incentives for deal sourcing, savvy negotiation of terms, and active management of portfolio companies, but not at the expense of a cooperative firm culture that lends itself to shrewd investment and management decision-making.[4] Appropriate alignment of incentives is especially crucial for venture capital firms that have long time horizons for deals to mature. Balancing between salary, bonus, and carry (long-term profit sharing) are important to team dynamics. (See **Exhibit 3** for industry overview.)

These considerations also bear special relevance in the venture capital industry, as firms' assets primarily take the form of human capital. In other industries, companies control the intellectual property or physical product and, therefore, their revenue stream is not dependent upon a particular employee. For a VC firm, however, the most important assets are generally free to walk out the door. If and when they do, they often boast board seats on portfolio companies or extensive investing track records and networks. A VC firm's careful management of culture fosters a deep sense of vested interest among employees at all levels, whether they remain with the firm or not over the long term.

Deals, Decisions, and Value-Add

While deal flow, deal selection, and post-investment value-add are all crucial to return generation, research shows that deal sourcing and selection play a larger role in driving returns (60%) than post-investment management (40%), with the alignment of deal flow with strategy also having a significant impact. Consensus among VC funds is that deal flow, selection, and value-add all work in tandem to generate returns. A recent survey of venture capitalists asked about the most important contributor to value creation. 23% identified deal flow, 49% identified deal selection, and 27% identified value-add.[5]

Access to deals is an important aspect of the VC business model. While numbers vary significantly from firm to firm, the following are averages across the industry: over 30% are generated through professional networks; 20% are referred by other investors; 8% from a portfolio company; almost 30% are proactively self-generated; and finally, 10% come inbound from company management. Most deal flow comes from VCs' networks in one form or another. Few VC investments come from entrepreneurs who beat a path to the VC's door without any connection. Because young VC firms have neither a vast investment history nor a strong reputation to draw upon as a source of deal flow, they are particularly reliant upon the partners' track record, relationships, and professional networks, as well as the networking done by team members. (See **Exhibit 4** for detailed information on investment sources.)

Given this emphasis on networks for deal flow, diversity of background (education and employment), gender, and race within a particular team might impact access to deals. Research into venture capital and entrepreneurial firms has shown that homophily, the prevalent tendency for individuals to identify, associate, and collaborate with people who share characteristics and experiences, plays a powerful role in the sector. Affinity-based characteristics like gender, ethnicity, having attended a particular school, or having worked for a particular employer predict hiring decisions of venture capital firms, the choice of coinvestment partners for a venture capitalist, and the likelihood of a particular VC investing in a particular startup.[6] While women and underrepresented minorities have dramatically increased their presence in advanced degrees that serve as a precursor to a career in venture capital and startups, their slow progress in both sectors likely represents somewhat of a chicken and an egg phenomenon. It is likely that there are attractive opportunities that remain unexploited because of the homogeneity of the industry.[7] (See **Exhibit 5** for female occupation by year and **Exhibits 6** and 7 for minority occupation.) Leveraging networks to produce deal flow might, then, be suboptimal for many VC firms because they do not contain enough internal diversity in terms of background and identity.

Once a deal is sourced, the decision to invest is also critical to the ultimate success of a venture capital firm. A VC firm might start with hundreds of potential deals to consider, and then whittle those down to a handful of actual investments. However, VCs have different views on how to select investments. VC firms might fall on either side of the horse-jockey divide, with some firms making investment decisions driven by the strength of a company's management team (the jockey), and others investing in a particular product, technology, and business model (the horse.) The former is a more popular metric, with a majority of VCs ranking a potential portfolio company's management team as the number one driver of an investment decision.[8] Overall, VCs rank the management team as the most important factor that drives their selection decisions. This emphasis is a sound one because, to a certain extent, success is persistent in the entrepreneurial sector. Entrepreneurs with a successful track record are far more likely to succeed than first-time entrepreneurs and those who had previously failed.[9]

VC firms employ a variety of processes for deciding how to proceed at this critical juncture. Decisions are generally made via a vote among partners: approximately 50% of funds require a unanimous vote to proceed with an investment, approximately 20% grant some partners veto power, 15% only require a simple majority, and 7% require a unanimous vote minus one. Smaller funds are more likely to require unanimous agreement among partners before proceeding with an investment. Roughly half of funds, particularly smaller funds, required a unanimous vote of partners to make initial investment decisions. Much like compensation structure, these decision mechanisms have broader cultural impact at a firm, establishing power dynamics that can foster a culture of dissent and debate or a culture more prone to deference and groupthink. Given the centrality of the initial investment decision to the VC business model, striking the right balance is key.

Roles played after an investment is made also impact outcomes and success. At this stage of a deal's life, homophily can again be beneficial or detrimental to a deal's success, depending upon how the VC firm's culture promotes or hinders collaboration. Research into venture investing shows that the more similar the venture capitalists who invested in a portfolio company are, the worse its performance. The cost of homogeneity is not driven by selecting inferior startups from the outset, rather, the lower returns are driven primarily by poor decision-making by very similar partners who fall prey to "group think."[10] Furthermore, because many of the emphasized forms of value-add, such as recruiting outside board members and hiring senior managers,[11] draw upon a VC's network, firms with homogenous partners likely draw on a much smaller pool of talent.

JENNIFER FONSTAD & THERESIA GOUW

Twenty-five years before Fonstad and Gouw founded Aspect Ventures, the two met as consultants at Bain and Company.[12] It was Gouw's first post-college job,[13] and Fonstad's second. (She had spent a year teaching math in sub-Saharan Africa.[14])

Both eventually left Bain, and both found their way to the VC industry. Fonstad received her MBA with Distinction from Harvard Business School. In 1997, she joined the VC firm Draper Fisher Jurveston (DFJ), then a $90 million, US-only fund. Fonstad was drawn to the firm because she was attracted to the startup space, and, in particular, early stages of a business. She spent the next seventeen years at DFJ. As a partner and then Managing Director, Fonstad's areas of focus included mobile applications and healthcare IT, with IPOs including NanoString, Netzero (United Online), and Athenahealth as well as acquisitions of Lumenos and Flurry. Fonstad was active in social and political activism, sitting on the boards of Castilleja School, serving on Mitt Romney's Senate campaign staff, and advising Meg Whitmen's gubernatorial run.[15]

After leaving Bain, Gouw, an engineer, joined Silicon Graphics as a product manager.[16] She later received her MBA from Stanford University, and joined Release Software[17] as a founding vice president of Business Development and Sales. Gouw later joined Accel Partners, another prominent Silicon Valley VC firm, where she specialized in the software investments in both Enterprise and Consumer markets with a focus on social commerce and security for fifteen years. As a partner, her successful deals included IPOs for Imperva, PeopleSupport, and Trulia and acquisitions of Kosmix, Xoopit, and Zimbra. Gouw also sat on Brown University's Corporation Board.[18] By 2014, the year Fonstad and Gouw founded Aspect, both had cultivated reputations of excellence: together, they had created over $10 billion in public value and boasted a combined 6 IPOs and over 25 M&A transactions.[19]

At the same time, they felt they had more to offer. In particular, both hoped to start a firm that would help redress what they felt was a limiting view of diversity in the VC industry. Both Fonstad and Gouw were the sole female partners at their firms when they departed to found Aspect,[20] which they considered a business oversight in an industry that ordinarily prized diversification. In an op-ed in Tech Crunch, Fonstad noted that investors aimed for "'diversified' holdings in our portfolios, yet we unconsciously resist diversity in our social and professional communities. As it turns out, this natural tendency toward sameness has become a liability in today's marketplace, costing companies talent, consumer goodwill, and real money."[21]

In 2010, with DFJ's permission, Fonstad co-founded Broadway Angels, an investment group of women in the VC and technology industries.[22] Fonstad found that colleagues would frequently approach her as a potential angel investor or source of information on how to evaluate deals. She decided that putting together a formal angel network would be a more structured way to offer investments or guidance. She also hoped to stay close to early-stage companies being spun out of Silicon Valley. Broadway Angles enjoyed tremendous early success, and Fonstad soon approached Gouw about getting involved. Their conversations reaffirmed the pair's excitement about the early-stage startup space.

Broader structural changes in VC had led Fonstad and Gouw to want to build a firm that brought collaboration, syndication, and early stage back to the forefront. An influx of investor dollars was driving many VC companies to broaden their investments to later-stage companies, which Gouw and Fonstad were less passionate about. "We want to go back to our roots and do the early stage stuff that we love," Gouw said.[23] They also felt this focus presented an opportunity. When, in September of 2013, they realized that both of their firms would soon be raising new funds, they agreed the fortuitous timing presented an ideal opportunity. The two got lunch at Stanford to discuss the idea of founding their own firm, together, and agreed to combine forces right away. They announced their plans in February of 2014. (See **Exhibit 10** for founder bios.)

BUILDING ASPECT

Fonstad and Gouw agreed that they would initially self-fund their investments through Aspect. They publicly shared that they'd make investments in the $500,000 to $2 million range, and that with self-funding this model was sustainable for several years.[24] In response to this announcement, executives at their past portfolio companies offered their public support, praising the pair's strategic skills and vision. Athenahealth CEO Jonathan Bush, for example, noted that Fonstad had the foresight to recognize the company's value. "When the fund opens, I'm in!" he declared.[25]

In keeping with Fonstad and Gouw's passion for early-stage investing, Aspect would focus exclusively on Series A and Seed venture rounds of small companies. In addition to their enthusiasm for building small companies from the ground up, they felt they could fill a void, given that few VC companies made long-term financial and managerial investment in early-stage companies as their funds grew in size over time.[26] It was precisely the kind of work that had drawn both to the VC realm in the mid-90s. "We've launched Aspect to meet the need in the market for a new kind of firm that can provide investment and advice to entrepreneurs over the long arc of their companies' growth," Gouw said. "From the start, Aspect Ventures is built to partner and collaborate - with entrepreneurs and also other players in the startup world from angels to multi-stage venture capital firms."[27]

Building on their combined industry expertise, Aspect would focus on mobile startups, a specialization they felt gave them significant leeway, and was that foundational to the future of the technology sector. "Mobile is a piece of everything we do because if you're a tech company today, mobile falls all the way up and down the tech stack, from security to storage up to apps," Gouw said.[28]

Decision-Making

Fonstad and Gouw's combined decades of experience at various firms had given them a sense of how different structures could elicit different cultures. "The biggest thing for Jennifer and me," Gouw noted, "was to make sure the compensation model was aligned with the investment decision-making model." Both had come from funds where investment processes had varied over time. But Fonstad and Gouw felt that after members of their investment team developed experience, investment, and judgment as they worked their way up the ranks, they'd earned a place at the table.

Just as all members of the investment team were constantly, actively sourcing investments at Aspect, all team members were also involved in the decision-making process to decide whether to invest. The small team gathered every Tuesday for a two to three hour meeting, wherein they reviewed every potential deal, and every deal currently in their portfolio. Each portfolio company and prospective deal would include at least two members of the team. For prospective investments, the team put together a memorandum which summarized their thoughts on the investment to ensure the team fleshed out every possible consideration.

In these meetings, Fonstad and Gouw made sure to consider the positives and negatives of every opportunity, and encouraged everyone to weigh in. If they felt anyone was holding back, they would often call on each team member, from junior to senior, to make sure everyone's perspective was heard. Eventually, the group would make a decision by an informal consensus. Although some team members might be more wary about a deal than others, these concerns could often be addressed by honing in on their skepticism. If, for example, someone was unsure of a company's business model but thought it had a great management team in an interesting space, the group might direct those leading a particular investment to prioritize getting a financial model in order within a set time frame. If a team member's concerns couldn't be assuaged with such a strategy, the firm would pass on the investment.

Both Fonstad and Gouw's experiences had taught them that these decisions not to invest could be as important to a firm's success as its decisions to add a company to its portfolio. "The reality is that our job is saying 'no' 90-95% of the time," Gouw said. "The natural tendency is to find things and then invest, so we go out of our way to make sure that we highlight it as a positive, constructive moment when someone sees a fatal flaw in something." (See **Exhibit 8** for Aspect's investment outcomes.)

Diversity

Much of the response to Aspect's founding focused on gender. As senior partners at highly-regarded VC firms, Fonstad and Gouw were already rarities. But founding Aspect made them historic figures in the world of VC—the company was Silicon Valley's first female-led VC firm.[29] Neither Fonstad nor Gouw tried to deny the relevance of gender to their careers thus far, or downplay that it would likely have an impact on Aspect's future. The two spoke to the media about the importance of diversity and its promotion from a business standpoint, highlighting, for example, research that showed companies with diverse boards boasted superior returns. "We think as women we bring a different perspective to the boardroom and these companies in how they approach problem-solving and strategic thinking," Fonstad said. "It's clearly not an industry that puts a lot of women in it, and we're trying in our own way to illustrate how diversity makes a difference."[30]

However, Fonstad and Gouw never approach potential investments through a gender lens. Their main criterion, following a jockey approach, was to focus on finding the best entrepreneurs. To do so, they tapped into their vast professional networks. Because they were focusing on Series A startups, many repeat entrepreneurs they'd worked with in the past expressed enthusiasm about collaborating again. Though a focus on gender was neither explicit nor deliberate, their own experience as outliers in the world of VC attracted Fonstad and Gouw to non-traditional entrepreneurs, who tackled problems with an approach that might not be served via traditional pipelines. Perhaps as a result, 40% of Aspect's portfolio had at least one female founder, a figure that was 2.5 times the industry average. (See **Exhibit 9.**) The firm had not set any benchmark of sorts. Instead, as Fonstad noted, the figure reflected "the nature of our networks and the deals we are seeing that we think are interesting and groundbreaking."

Gouw elaborated on how the nature of the VC industry, which was only 9% female at the time, impacted Aspect's deal funnel. "We have a wider net, being in that 9% of investors, but it's not something we do specifically. The good news is that it doesn't impact deal processing: we have the same high bar for founders and for management teams. We maintained a proactive focus on specific areas at the time, always adding new and interesting areas of technology. But we weren't looking at anything differently because we had a wider deal flow. We applied the same high standards to any opportunity, which is the way to do it."

HIRING

Both Fonstad and Gouw felt that the years they spent in relatively homogeneous workplaces reinforced the value of different perspectives. Gouw was careful to note that this wasn't limited to gender. "Sometimes that's based on gender, sometimes it's based on having operating executives who have specific knowledge of an area. Too many people with the same background can lead to group think or blind spots, while having a diversity of perspectives around the table is helpful. It's critical to making sure that you're examining investments from multiple aspects." (This multidimensional approach was the source of Aspect's name.)

Both Fonstad and Gouw were also wary of overweighting a particular diversity trait in a way that didn't harness an array of voices most effectively. Said Gouw, "When Accel was bringing in companies that were selling to a female audience, oftentimes the group would look to me for a view on it, which I always found to be dangerous. I was rarely the target customer— often the company had a user base of millennials. You can have different kinds of blind spots when you're the only one in the room."

As such, Fonstad and Gouw tried to build out their team in a parallel manner to how they built their portfolio. They looked for certain proactive themes: a background in cyber-security or digital health, but were also purposeful about building diversity in their team along several dimensions. In hiring, this meant considering who had come from different roles and backgrounds. "You always think about the next hire as being someone you're lacking," Gouw said. "But, just like with deals, if someone's a great athlete sometimes you just make the hire." When Aspect hired Asad Khaliq as an intern, it was precisely because he possessed the qualities of a bright young athlete: he had a background studying technology and was completing a Masters in Computer Science.

Most frequently, however, new candidates were sourced from one of two methods. Candidates had a huge leg up if a team member had worked with them in the past and felt that they would be a good fit if they brought crucial experiences and distinct qualities to the table. Several of the firm's hires-to-date involved someone they had interfaced or worked with in the past.

These connections might extend several degrees. Often, a member of the Aspect team hadn't worked with a candidate before, but a reliable member of their network provided an endorsement. Fonstad and Gouw both took these recommendations seriously when they came from people they'd known for years, who they trusted had a strong sense of the collaboration and cultural fit issues which might eventually arise at Aspect. These relationships also contributed to early hires. (See **Exhibit 11** for team bios.)

Who Next?

In August of 2016, Fonstad and Gouw were considering bringing a fifth person aboard their team. Their final choice came down to two candidates: James Madison and Arjun Agarwal. (See **Exhibits 12** and **13** for resumes.) Though both candidates were promising and qualified, their backgrounds were somewhat varied. (See **Exhibits 11** and **12** for candidate resumes.)

Fonstad and Gouw originally got to know Madison when he was at another good, early-stage venture firm, where he'd risen to the role of Senior Associate. Through their personal and professional interactions with him, they had the chance to see how he interacted with and listened to people. Fonstad and Gouw saw firsthand that he had a team-oriented and collaborative style that would fit in quite nicely at Aspect. The fact that he had firsthand experience at a comparable VC firm was also appealing.

Agarwal came to Aspect through a former portfolio company of one of the founders and had connected with the Aspect portfolio for a possible corporate investment. The start-up experience was appealing, and the Aspect team had enjoyed collaborating with him.

In assessing an interviewee's ability to fit in with the firm culture, Fonstad and Gouw were careful not to confuse collaborative with agreeable. In fact, precisely because the team was fueled by dissent and debate, it was important that team members felt comfortable disagreeing with each other. To test for this trait, they would ask for a candidate's views of a particular company or sector, often purposely talking it up. If a candidate expressed a dissenting view about an investment, and successfully tempered the interviewer's enthusiasm, it was clear they'd be able to hold their own during a weekly investment meeting. Madison had successfully completed this test. Though he was respectful, he asked thoughtful and skeptical questions, a subtlety which elicited a strong cultural fit.

Fonstad and Gouw knew that this hiring decision was a crucial one. Venture capital was very much a team sport, and though two people usually led an investment, a portfolio company was likely to have exposure to all of Aspect's employees over its course. The firm was still relatively young and small, and quick turnover would be frustrating for the company to weather. Furthermore, Aspect's culture was delicately and elaborately crafted, and one team member in a group of five was poised to make a significant contribution to the firm's performance, be it positive or detrimental. Who should they extend an offer to, if anyone?

NOTES

1 Paul Gompers, Will Gornall, Steven N. Kaplan, and Ilya A. Strebulaev, "How Do Venture Capitalists Make Decisions?," August 2016.
2 Glocap Inc., "Glocap Private Equity Compensation Report," 2016.
3 Gompers.
4 Gompers.
5 Gompers.
6 Paul Gompers, Vladimir Mukharlyamov, and Yuhai Xuan, "The Cost of Friendship," June 2012, *NBER Working Paper Series.*
7 Lauren Cohen, Paul A. Gompers, and Sophie Q. Wang, "Diversity in Innovation," December 2016.
8 Gompers.
9 Paul A. Gompers, Josh Lerner, David Scharfstein, and Anna Kovner, "Performance Persistence in Entrepreneurship and Venture Capital, April 2010, *Journal of Financial Economics.*
10 "The Cost of Friendship."
11 Gompers.
12 Miller.
13 Miller.
14 Miller.
15 Aspect Ventures.
16 Aspect Ventures.
17 Willow Bay, "Women to Watch: Theresia Gouw Ranzetta," Huffington Post, November 27, 2012, http://www.huffingtonpost.com/willow-bay/theresia-gouw-ranzetta_b_2018673.html, accessed January 2017.
18 "Theresia Gouw and Jennifer Fonstad Launch Aspect Ventures," Aspect Ventures, February 5, 2014, http://aspectventures.com/theresia-gouw-and-jennifer-fonstad-launch-aspect-ventures/, accessed December 2016.
19 "Theresia Gouw and Jennifer Fonstad Launch Aspect Ventures," Aspect Ventures, February 5, 2014, http://aspectventures.com/theresia-gouw-and-jennifer-fonstad-launch-aspect-ventures/, accessed December 2016.
20 Claire Cain Miller, "Two of Venture Capital's Senior Women Start a New Firm," New York Times, February 5, 2014, https:// http://bits.blogs.nytimes.com/2014/02/05/two-of-venture-capitals-senior-women-start-a-new-firm/?_r=0, accessed December 2016.
21 Jennifer Fonstad, "The competitive advantage of diversity," Tech Crunch, September 16, 2016, https://techcrunch.com/2016/09/16/the-competitive-advantage-of-diversity/, accessed November 2016.
22 Broadway Angels, www.broadway-angels.com, accessed January 2017.
23 Miller.
24 Miller.

25 "Theresia Gouw and Jennifer Fonstand Launch Aspect Ventures," Aspect Ventures press release, in News, Palo Alto, CA, February 5, 2014, http://aspect-ventures.com/theresia-gouw-and-jennifer-fonstad-launch-aspect-ventures/.
26 Aspect Ventures.
27 Aspect Ventures.
28 Miller.
29 Aspect Ventures.
30 Miller.

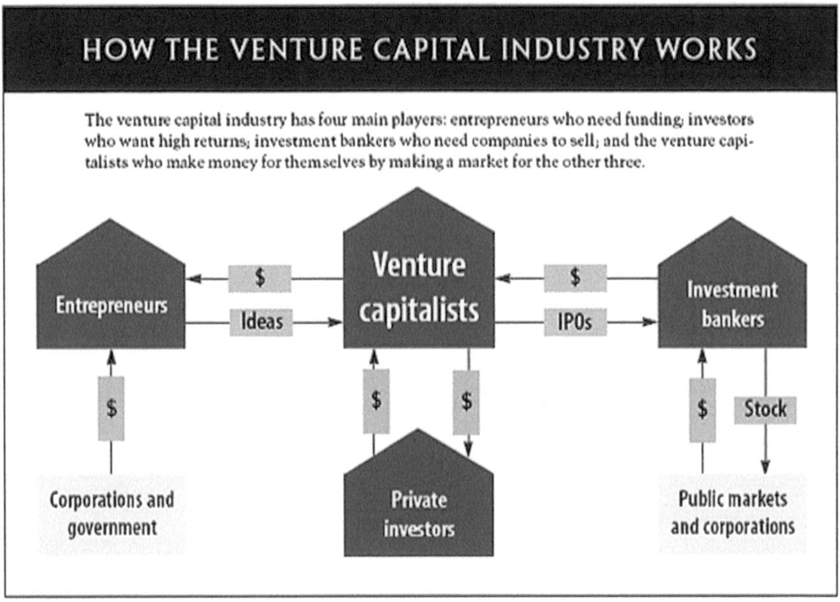

EXHIBIT 1 How the Venture Capital Industry Works
Source: Zider, Bob, "How Venture Capital Works," *Harvard Business Review* (November-December 1998).

EXHIBIT 2 2016/17 Compensation Overview; Venture Capital Funds

	Small ($0-500 Million)		Mid-Sized ($500 MM - 1 Billion)		Large (>$1 Billion)	
	Base	Bonus	Base	Bonus	Base	Bonus
Analyst	60-76k	22-44k	65-87k	23-45k	70-90k	36-63k
Associate	85-102k	31-50k	97-120k	38-60k	102-140k	48-90k
Sr. Assoc	121-152k	37-62k	137-164k	60-95k	140-188k	75-130k
VP	150-182k	50-110k	170-205k	87-148k	183-235k	90-190k
Principal	155-200k	53-113k	180-258k	90-220k	205-325k	112-290k
Partner	263-355k	131-227k	410-560k	295-385k	425-699k	318-505k
CFO	178-230k	89-184k	220-288k	134-263k	252-392k	224-462k
Controller	108-150k	35-77k	135-183k	54-118k	144-285k	75-173k

Source: CompIQ, "Private Equity Compensation Report," 2016.

EXHIBIT 3 Fund Structure

		Stage		Industry		IPO Rate		Fund Size		Location		
	All	Early	Late	IT	Health	High	Low	Large	Small	CA	OthUS	Fgn
Compensation depends on individual success (%)	74%	78%	67%	81%	77%	66%	81%	65%	84%	73%	76%	73%
Number of responses	446	193	74	101	74	118	117	205	244	127	181	154
Partners get equal shares of carry (%)	44%	51%	35%	50%	52%	44%	48%	42%	48%	43%	43%	46%
Number of responses	429	182	71	95	71	113	110	197	234	110	178	152
Partners invest equal shares of fund capital (%)	49%	53%	44%	55%	52%	50%	54%	47%	52%	55%	46%	47%
Number of responses	442	193	71	101	73	118	116	203	242	127	179	152

Source: Paul Gompers, Will Gornall, Steven N. Kaplan, and Ilya A. Strebulaev, "How Do Venture Capitalists Make Decisions?," August 2016.
Note: Figures shown are drawn from a comprehensive survey of 885 institutional venture capitalists at 681 firms. (Survey conducted from November 2015 - March 2016.)

EXHIBIT 4 Sources of Investments

The percentage of deals closed in the past twelve months originating from each source.

	Stage			Industry Size		IPO Rate		Fund Size		Location		
	All	Early	Late	IT	Health	High	Low	Large	Small	CA	OthUS	Fgn
Inbound from management	10%	12%	7%	10%	13%	11%	10%	10%	10%	10%	9%	11%
Referred by portfolio company	8%	9%	4%	10%	6%	6%	8%	7%	8%	7%	7%	10%
Referred by other investors	20%	22%	17%	21%	18%	21%	20%	18%	21%	18%	22%	18%
Professional network	31%	31%	25%	27%	29%	30%	33%	31%	31%	33%	30%	29%
Proactively self-generated	28%	23%	42%	28%	30%	29%	28%	30%	27%	27%	28%	29%
Quantitative sourcing	2%	1%	3%	3%	2%	3%	1%	2%	2%	2%	2%	2%
Number of responses	446	202	72	107	68	114	122	200	246	123	179	160

Source: Paul Gompers, Will Gornall, Steven N. Kaplan, and Ilya A. Strebulaev, "How Do Venture Capitalists Make Decisions?," August 2016.

Note: Figures shown are drawn from a comprehensive survey of 885 institutional venture capitalists at 681 firms. (Survey conducted from November 2015 - March 2016.)

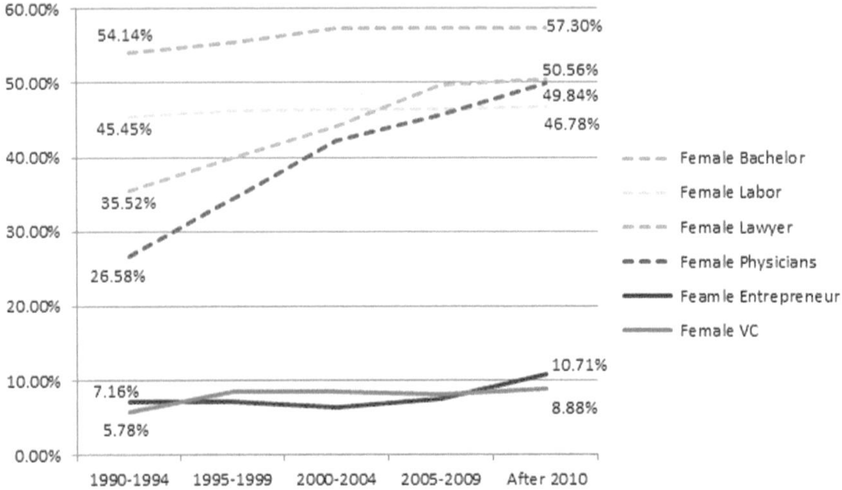

EXHIBIT 5 Female Representation Within Various Professions by Year
Source: Lauren Cohen, Paul A. Gompers, and Sophie Q. Wang, "Diversity in Innovation," December 2016.

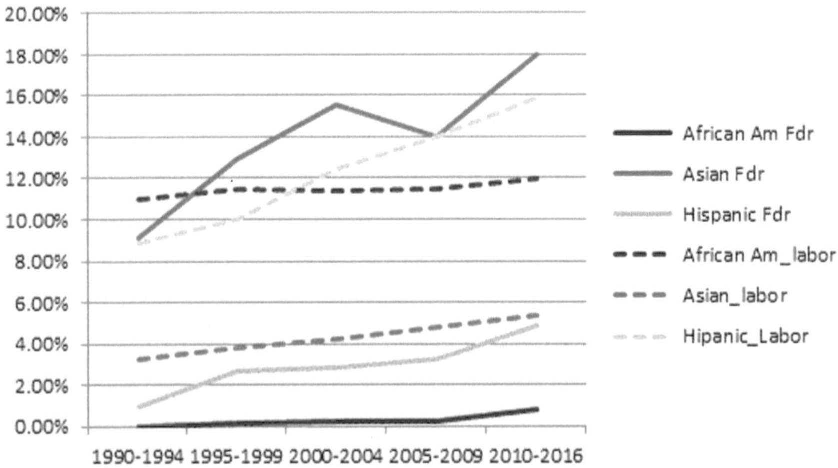

EXHIBIT 6 Percentage of Minority Entrepreneurs Compared to Labor Force
Source: Lauren Cohen, Paul A. Gompers, and Sophie Q. Wang, "Diversity in Innovation," December 2016.

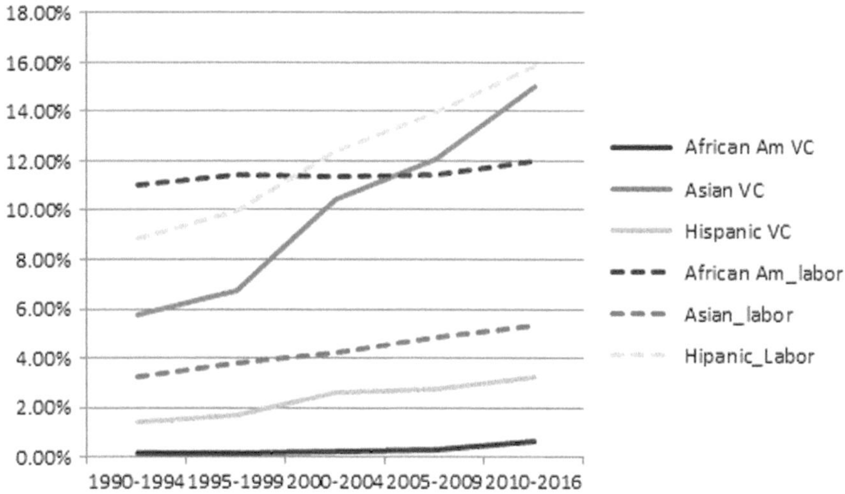

EXHIBIT 7 Percentage of Minority Venture Capitalists Compared to Labor Force
Source: Lauren Cohen, Paul A. Gompers, and Sophie Q. Wang, "Diversity in Innovation," December 2016.

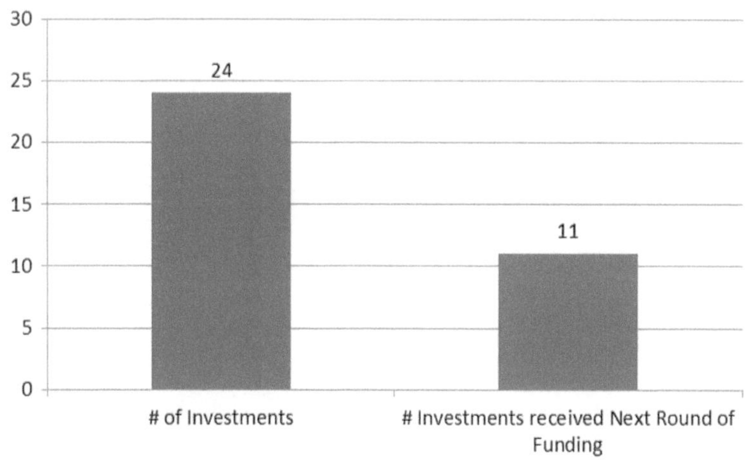

EXHIBIT 8 Success of Aspect Investments
Source: "Aspect Ventures," Crunchbase.com, https://www.crunchbase.com/organization/aspect-ventures, accessed December 2016.

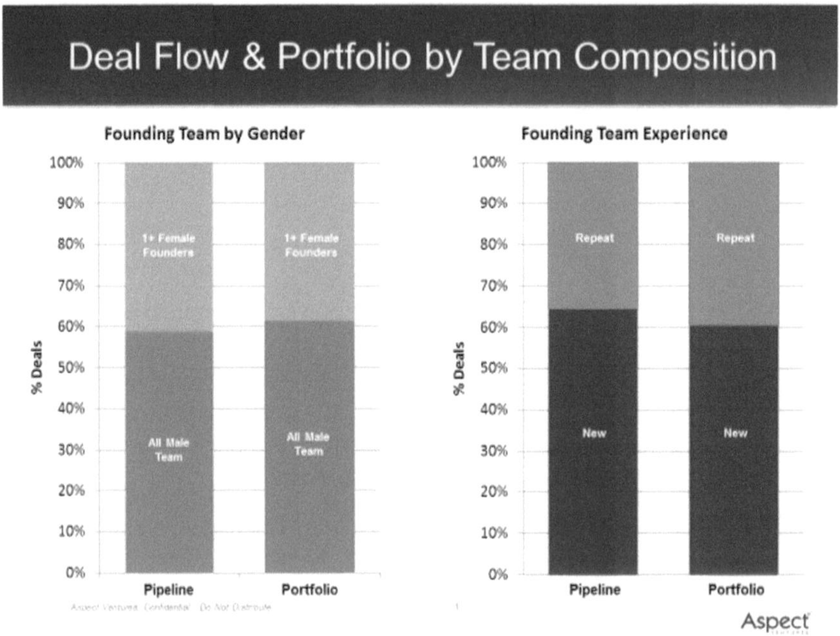

EXHIBIT 9 Aspect Portfolio
Source: Company documents.

EXHIBIT 10 Aspect Founders

	Name: Jennifer Fonstad Position: Co-Founder and Managing Partner	Bio: Jennifer is a graduate of Georgetown University, where she received an ScB in International Economics, and Harvard Business School, where she received her MBA. Before co-founding Aspect Ventures she taught high school math in Africa and worked at Bain and Company. Jennifer chairs the Somely Mam Foundation board, an organization dedication to ending sex slavery, and is the mother of four children.
	Name: Theresia Gouw Position: Co-Founder	Bio: Theresia is a graduate of Brown University, where she received an ScB in Engineering, and Stanford Business School, where she received her MBA. Before co-founding Aspect Ventures she worked at Silicon Graphics, Bain and Company, and was the VP of business development and sales at Release Software. Theresia currently sits on boards at Brown University and Donorschoose.org and is the mother of two children.

Source: Company documents.

EXHIBIT 11 Aspect Junior Investment Professionals

	Name: Lauren Kolodny Position: Member of the investing team	Lauren holds a BA from Brown University in International Relations, an MS in Sustainable Design from Stanford University, and an MBA from Stanford University Business School. Before joining Aspect Ventures Lauren worked under the Clinton Foundation in a clean technology development program for India, at Cowboy Ventures, and in product marketing at Google. Lauren is currently a Trustee Emerita at Brown University and is a member of the President's Leadership Council and the Advisory Committee on Computing and Information Technology. In 2016 Lauren was named in Forbes list of 30 under 30.
	Name: Kamil Saeid Position: Member of the investing team	Kamil holds a degree in Bio-mechanical Engineering from Stanford University. Before working at Aspect Ventures Kamil was an Associate Consultant at Bain and Company.

Source: Company documents.

EXHIBIT 12 Agarwal Resume

Arjun Agarwal

415-900-1234
San Francisco, CA
aagarwal@gmail.com

EXPERIENCE

Dropbox, Inc. San Francisco
Director, Corporate Development May 2015 – Present

- Align with CEO, product teams, and engineering leads to execute on vision and accelerate roadmap inorganically
- Source acquisition opportunities, conduct initial diligence meetings, and manage deal processes internally
- Align various functional groups for successful integrations of acquired businesses

ALTITUDE CAPITAL GROUP ($20bn AUM) Pacific Palisades
Associate, Alternative Assets September 2014 – May 2015

- Worked on transactions across the software, government, healthcare, and business services industries
- Deal responsibilities included modeling, industry and business diligence, and preparing investment materials
- Monitored private and public holdings, attend earnings call and board meetings, and review budgets

TEXAS INVESTMENT PARTNERS ($10bn AUM, 30 software companies) Houston, TX
TIP was named a top performing fund by Bloomberg in 2014
Consultant January 2014 – September 2014

- First junior team member of Vista's new internal general consulting team for our portfolio companies
- Projected product revenue and costs, including build vs. buy modeling
- Implemented sales and pricing best practices and designed compensation plans for a new portfolio company

Analyst, Software Buyouts July 2011 – December 2013
Investment Evaluation and Execution

- Worked start to finish on the $1bn take-private of *Big Software* and on the three-way merger of *Software Solutions*
- Deal responsibilities included modeling, industry diligence, contract reviews, and financial analysis

Portfolio-wide and Internal Initiatives

- Assisted with multiple sourcing projects and the successful fundraising of three new funds
- Presented at portfolio-wide conferences and developed projects for executive development
- Negotiated the purchase of an analytical software tool and managed the roll-out

EDUCATION

THE UNIVERSITY OF CHICAGO Chicago, Illinois
Bachelor of Arts in Economics September 2007 - December 2010

- Cumulative GPA: 3.9 / 4.0, Economics GPA: 3.9 / 4.0, Dean's List, *Phi Beta Kappa*
- GMAT: 750
- SAT: Math 800, Verbal 740

Coursework

- Marketing Strategy (A+), Financial Accounting (A), Economics and Demographics of Marketing (A)

COMMUNITY AND PART-TIME ACTIVITIES

BUSINESS FOR BUSINESS. Houston
Board Member and Interim CEO May 2014 – May 2015

UNIVERSITY OF CHICAGO ALUMNI Various Locations
Volunteer Admissions Interviewer and Alumni Event Organizer January 2012 – Present

Native Hindi speaker.

Source: Company documents.

EXHIBIT 13 Madison Resume

James Madison
1475 Humble St.,. Los Angeles, CA 90001 • jmadison@gmail.com • 925.900.1776

EXPERIENCE

Continental Partners, *Los Angeles, CA*
Senior Associate — *May 2015 – Present*
Associate — *May 2013 – April 2015*
Senior Analyst — *January 2013 – April 2013*

- Key Responsibilities
  - Sourcing investment opportunities, co-leading due diligence, and assisting portfolio companies with business development, strategic and financial analysis, and recruiting
  - Community and brand building for venture capital firm
- Select Investments
  - Blue Kite
    - Sourced opportunity, drove due diligence, and drafted term sheet for $4MM investment into mobile, millennial-focused start-up; advised Series B. Attended all board meetings
  - Analytics-A-Go-Go
    - Performed due diligence for AGG's C, Continental's first later stage investment.. Managed legal process for the investment into the app store analytics provider
  - Hobnob
    - Sourced, championed, and executed investment in text message based custom event invitation platform. Manage relationship for the firm
  - Modelo
    - Championed and co-manage Series B investment into consumer e-commerce company
  - Fasten
    - Sourced opportunity and championed seed investment in marketplace for shared rides

McKinsey and Co, *New York, NY and Los Angeles, CA*
Associate Consultant — *October 2011 – January 2013*
Associate Consultant Intern — *Summer 2010*

- Key Responsibilities: Analytics (e.g., international growth modeling, consumer survey analysis, statistical analysis), Research (e.g., collated analyst consensus on industry growth and supplemented with large-scale primary research), Client Management (e.g., sole responsibility for managing client strategy and planning sessions)
- Sample Casework: Utilities – Organizational Transformation; Media & Entertainment – Reorganization Strategy; Media & Entertainment – Growth Strategy; Medical Devices – International Full Potential Strategy; Business Process Outsourcing – Growth Strategy; Media & Entertainment – Product Strategy

Internships: The Climate Project Spain, Unithrive.org, Recombinant Capital

EDUCATION

Princeton University, *Princeton, NJ* — *September 2007 – May 2011*

- A.B. in Economics, *cum laude*, received May 2011
- SAT Scores: 760M / 760V / 790W; GMAT Score: 740
- Beta Fellows: National Executive Team and Founder of Princeton chapter for a global organization fostering connections among over 500 student entrepreneurs globally
- Peer Advising Fellow; Lead choreographer of multiple cultural productions; seminar leader, CIVICS board member and teacher

SKILLS AND INTERESTS

Languages: Working knowledge of Spanish; **Interests:** Fiction (spy thrillers),, culinary explorer, pick-up basketball; **Favorite Apps:** Headspace, Instagram, Acorns, Delectable, Sonos

Source: Company documents.

CHAPTER 5.2

CashDrop (A)

Rembrand Koning, Paul A. Gompers and Sarah Gulick

In June 2020, CashDrop Founder and CEO Ruben Flores-Martinez sat at his home office in Chicago, Illinois, gazing out of his window at the view of Willis Tower, a luxury corporate office building while taking a break from running CashDrop's Instagram page. For Flores-Martinez, Willis Tower was a reminder of his professional aspirations: "I don't want to have my company offices there," he said. "I want to someday own the whole building." The first step toward this goal was CashDrop, a digital payment and sales platform, which he had launched in September 2019.

Now, four months into the Covid-19 pandemic and working from home, Flores-Martinez had managed to keep CashDrop growing by using word-of-mouth marketing and appealing to businesses that had traditionally only taken cash. After expanding rapidly, CashDrop had attracted a lot of interest from venture capital (VC) companies. "None of these companies were interested when I first approached them, so I made a business plan that didn't need their help, and now they're all interested in CashDrop," said Flores-Martinez. But he had two goals: grow CashDrop into a large company, and create a path for other Latinx entrepreneurs to raise funding for their start-ups. Having decided the time was right to scale, he needed money.

After thinking through his plans for CashDrop, Flores-Martinez had narrowed down his VC choices to a few candidates. He said, "I'm a little worried about the pressure this money will bring because I want to grow CashDrop sustainably. But I'm not just interested in the money—I want to be the person who has all these connections to VC funds." Now he had to decide: what did he need from venture capitalists? Did money alone matter or did reputation and value-add play into the equation? Should other, non-monetary goals of Flores-Martinez factor into his choice of investor? How could he use the funds to grow? And was it worth accepting outside

CashDrop (A)
by REMBRAND KONING, PAUL A. GOMPERS, SARAH GULICK, case number 9-221-051 MARCH 19, 2021

money at all, knowing that doing so would allow a VC fund to influence how CashDrop operated?

FROM CHOPIN TO THE APP STORE

Flores-Martinez knew that he was not a typical tech CEO. He and his family moved from Mexico in 2004, when he was 13, and he grew up undocumented in Milwaukee, Wisconsin. "My original plan was to be the next Chopin.[a] I taught myself to play the piano when I was eight years old, and my dream was to go to Julliard. I would skip class to go to the school auditorium and practice. But then I realized I also wanted to drive a Bentley," he mused, "and being a musician wasn't the best way to do that."

By high school, Flores-Martinez wanted to go to MIT and become an engineer. But his undocumented status precluded him from accessing student loans and most scholarships. Flores-Martinez recalled, "I grew up ashamed of who I was. Growing up with that has always been a self-motivating engine. My dad would always say, 'Hey, these are the cards the universe dealt you. You can feel bad about it, or you can play the game.' I just had to believe that I was the only obstacle in my own way. I wanted to make sure that I lived up to the sacrifices that my parents made."

Instead of taking a traditional route to become an engineer, Flores-Martinez needed a new plan. That came in his senior year of high school: "Apple made this announcement about starting the App Store, where anyone could make an app and release it on Apple's platform. I realized, I just need a laptop and a phone, and then I can teach myself the rest." At the same time, he was unsure what it would look like for him to go from designing an app to running a business, especially without seeing other people take a similar path. He asked himself: "How could I become the Mexican Steve Jobs if I can't see anyone who looks like me doing it? I guess I have to try to become that person for other people. Even if it's not going to be me, it might be the next person who sees me trying."

In his senior year of high school, Flores-Martinez founded the school robotics club and taught himself to use computers from YouTube videos. "Everything I could possibly want to learn was on YouTube. As long as I put in the effort, the sky was the limit," he said.

---

a Frederic Chopin was a 19th Century Polish composer and virtuoso pianist.

Gaining Practical Experience

Working a summer job in high school, Flores-Martinez began to learn the skills he needed to create his apps. He recalled:

> I've always been obsessed with optimization. In Milwaukee, I was offered a summer job doing parking. The guy hiring me said 'Charge $12 per car, park 12 cars, and give me 70%.' I found this so inefficient. He thinks I can fit 12 cars, but I've thought of a way I can fit 25 cars. That was one of my first projects. I thought, 'What if figured out a way to put this on my phone, so I could track how much I'm selling in terms of time?' The guy hiring me doesn't know I'm parking 25 cars—he just wants 70% of 12. He doesn't have to know about the profit I'm making from the other 13.
>
> That was my first project. I started drawing it out, but then I realized, I've done 90% of the work towards an app for this, but I don't know how to code it in. And that's when I went on YouTube and started figuring out how to code: how do you make a button work? How do you display a number? How do you save routines so you don't have to put them in the program again? That's really how I started learning to code.

When Flores-Martinez and his girlfriend married in 2009, he was able to adjust his immigration status and become a permanent resident. "In the year and a half after I graduated high school, I was able to keep studying programming on my own. After I became a permanent resident, I enrolled in college to major in computer science. But once I was there, I realized I already knew all the basics, so I coasted for a while," said Flores-Martinez.

As part of his studies, Flores-Martinez did a co-op internship at an automation company in Milwaukee, working as a firmware test engineer. He recalled, "It wasn't particularly challenging for me, but the pay was great—I had never made that much money before. My parents had never made that much money in their lives. But I'd have month-long projects that would take me a week. I didn't ask for more work, but instead, I'd keep watching YouTube videos and learning more things—I taught myself how to cook, and I started thinking of apps to help home cooks."

Months before he was supposed to graduate from college in May 2015, Flores-Martinez quit his job and dropped out to start his first business. He said "I felt like I was wasting my life not doing something I was passionate about. I was ready to do something for myself."

Sugr

In 2015, Flores-Martinez created his first commercial app, Sugr. "I've always been obsessed with optimizing my time," he recalled. "Like, how do I streamline everything so I can spend more time with the people I love, instead of having to constantly make decisions? Sugr helped with that." Flores-Martinez imagined Sugr as a way for friends to more easily decide on a local restaurant, taking into account the user's food preferences, budget, and location.

Sugr used the user's previous choices, along with machine learning, to make related suggestions. The app only gave a few suggestions at a time and did not include ratings or recommendations, instead relying on the preferences of other users to offer specific matches. Flores-Martinez explained, "[W]e want to validate preferences based on what your peers are doing. What my wife thinks is a lot more important than what a random stranger on the internet thinks. So we weigh recommendations based on what people in your networks are doing."[1]

However, after the initial launch, Sugr folded in June 2019. Flores-Martinez explained, "It never really took off. I realized that I was focused on data when I should have been focused on helping people make money—that's what matters to people. I thought, if I'm interested in optimizing things for people, maybe I should optimize their ability to make money and start a business." However, at the time, he did not know how he was going to pay rent or what to do next. "I sort of bulldozed everything I'd been working on for three years," he recalled. "But I've never been afraid of failure. I know that failure is a piece of the process. Either you die trying or you figure it out."

STARTING CASHDROP

After Sugr folded, Flores-Martinez saw a gap in the market for small, online entrepreneurs, especially young people who would market their products on Twitter or Instagram. "I call them 'DM me' businesses," Flores-Martinez said, referring to the direct messages (DMs) that people would send each other on social media. "People would put up products and say 'DM me if you want to buy this,' and then would complete the transaction via Venmo. Venmo's a subpar solution—it's just a digital wallet, you can't track anything—but it's free and it's very easy."

Flores-Martinez imagined a much simpler, much cheaper business app for entrepreneurs that did not require a big investment in money or time. "People were hiring me to build apps, and to incorporate them into Shopify, or other payment platforms, and they just weren't very good. I knew I could create something better. So I started to build a new platform—just me and a computer."

Flores-Martinez was inspired by a flea market that he saw in his neighborhood growing up in Mexico. "Some vendors there had the same business every week because they found something that worked and kept doing that. But other vendors would sell different things every week—sometimes it would be bicycles and next week, books. They weren't going to build a website or even take credit cards for their business because they needed to be more flexible than that. That kind of place is where commerce is born." Flores-Martinez wondered if there was a way that an app could help small businesses create the same type of flea market flexibility, letting them change products and strategies, which was not encouraged by traditional digital sales tools.

In the American Midwest, Flores-Martinez saw businesses facing similar problems. "Small bodegas and other immigrant businesses don't necessarily have access to major sales platforms, and the high fees that credit card processors charge can cut into their revenue. If people are selling without a traditional storefront, they might just be using their cell phone to run their business. They're not going to set up their own online store. It's not a good investment of their time."

Flores-Martinez imagined a payment platform that was flexible enough to help small businesses and online entrepreneurs. He began to build an app in August 2019, spending a month putting the basic elements together from scratch. "I didn't want to wait for it to be perfect," he said. "Once the bare bones were ready, I wanted to get started."

The Launch

Soon after starting to build the CashDrop app, Flores-Martinez found the first place he could easily try it out. He recalled: "One of my friends in Milwaukee had just opened a food truck park, comprised of six individual food trucks. When we went, each food truck had six or seven customers lined up. My friend said, 'This is great right now, but in the winter it's going to be a big problem. No one will want to wait in the cold for food.' I thought, 'Oh, wow! This is what CashDrop is for, cutting down on the time have to spend waiting.'"

Flores-Martinez and his friend tried the CashDrop interface first on one food truck, and then, when it worked, scaled to all six. "That was my first client," he said. "I started working from there. Milwaukee was a great place to try it because it's not a very tech-savvy town, so if it could work there, it could work anywhere—people don't use Apple Pay, this was their first experience of digital payments. I started explaining the product to people, and I watched them think, 'Wait, this is good enough that I need to learn how to use it.'"

Initial Growth

From the beginning, Flores-Martinez relied on both old-fashioned word-of-mouth communication and social media to tell potential users about CashDrop. The initial CashDrop interface allowed vendors to create an online storefront in 15 minutes, which they could build and operate from their phone. (See **Exhibit 1** for images of the CashDrop interface.) The platform allowed them to easily connect to social media apps, like Twitter or Instagram, creating a way to sell from a social media post.

To build vendor trust, Flores-Martinez added the payment costs to the customer side of the transaction. "I wanted to help vendors, and I knew that there was a massive cost for them to use a website or process credit card fees. But I knew a lot of consumers were willing to pay a bit more to skip a wait, the same way you can pay to skip the line at Disneyworld. At a certain point people value their time more than they value their money," he said. Customers did not have to download the app or create an account and they received a text when their order was ready.

For every transaction, CashDrop charged the customer a 5% fee with a minimum charge of $0.45. The credit card processing was done via the Stripe payment processing platform, and the fee for that was paid by the vendor. Stripe's standard plan charged 2.9% of a card charge, plus $0.30, though the fees could vary for high payment volumes.[2] Stripe payments were often cheaper than or equivalent to other credit card processing fees, so the vendors did not have additional costs from switching credit card processors. Traditional credit card companies charged between 1.9% and 3.30%, plus between $0.05 and $0.10, depending on the company.[3]

Initial Vendors After the first food trucks, many of CashDrop's users came to the app for ease of use. "By putting the fee on the consumer, we were able to remove a big pressure from the merchant, thus making them more willing to use the service and actively advocate for it on social media," said Flores-Martinez.

CashDrop vendors expanded to restaurants offering pickup and delivery, products and services, and people selling tickets to events. The flexibility of the app allowed vendors to use CashDrop within social media apps, so that customers could see a product mentioned on social media and then buy it using a link without ever leaving the social media platform. The first users tended to be mom-and-pop businesses: vendors with small food stalls or takeout restaurants or small-scale grocery or brewing companies.

One deli in Chicago, Illinois saw a 30% increase in its average check size after switching to CashDrop, making approximately $3,600 from 100 sales through CashDrop per month. CashDrop earned an average of $1.45 per transaction.

PAYMENTS INDUSTRY

While the Internet had originally been a non-commercial enterprise, which discouraged sales and advertising, by the 1990s the growth of the Internet, and the ability to access it via personal computers, led to the beginnings of e-commerce. Online payment platforms came next, giving users a way to pay for purchases without sending a check or giving access to their credit card numbers to strangers.

Online Payments

While consumers paid via credit card number starting in the early 1990s, the first major digital payment platform, PayPal, was founded in 1998. In the first three years, PayPal (originally Confinity) had 2.6 million commercial and 10.2 million consumer customers. For many online sales companies, like eBay, PayPal replaced paper checks and money orders, which had to be exchanged after a sale was agreed upon online. PayPal gained an early hold in the market and was purchased by eBay in 2002 for $1.5 billion, although the companies separated in 2014.[4] PayPal charged merchant fees of between 2.7% and 2.9% for most transactions, plus a $0.30 fee.[5]

Founded in 2004, Shopify became a major competitor for online payments. It grew from an online Canadian snowboard retailer into, by 2006, an e-commerce platform, allowing vendors to both sell and process payments through the platform. By 2009 the company had processed $100 million in transactions; its 2015 initial public offering (IPO) valued the company at $1.3 billion.[6] In May 19, 2020, Shopify announced a partnership with Facebook to launch a new Facebook Shops tool that allowed Shopify merchants to set up mobile storefronts on Facebook and Instagram.[7] On Instagram this was known as Instagram Checkout. Customers only needed to enter their information the first time they purchased through Instagram, which then saved their information. However, the merchant fees for Instagram Checkout were $0.40 on sales of $8 of less, or 5% per sale for higher-priced items.[8]

Other companies also served as disruptors for traditional in-person credit card payments, as well as processing payments online. Founded in 2009, Square allowed small merchants to process credit card payments by processing them through the Square website. Before this, vendors were required to undergo an expensive credit card processing registration process. Square instead let vendors use their smartphones or tablets as point-of-sale processors and allowed for some data analysis of those sales.[9] Standard Square merchant fees were 2.6% of a transaction, plus $0.10, although some transactions had fees of 3.5% plus $0.15.[10]

Mobile Transactions

In 2011, Google Wallet was the first major mobile phone payment platform, allowing users to make purchases via an app that held their credit card information. In 2015, other mobile payment apps joined Google Wallet, including Apple Pay, Android, and Samsung Pay.[11] These took the place of a physical credit card.

Other payment apps, including Venmo and Cash App, also launched in 2015. These apps allowed users to exchange money directly via the platform, instead of processing payments via credit card. The apps held money (originally from bank accounts, debit cards, or credit cards) themselves, and allowed free peer-to-peer transfer and for the money to be sent back to bank accounts.[12] As these apps became popular, commercial banks created their own versions of direct money transfer apps, including Bank of America's Zelle app and proprietary apps from JPMorgan Chase and Citibank.[13]

As social media became a popular way for small businesses to market their product, the peer-to-peer platforms also became casual sales platforms for merchants. Flores-Martinez explained, "Now there are a lot of transactions with people selling through Twitter, where someone will say, 'If you want to buy this, send me the money on Venmo.'" This allowed merchants to sell with no official website, and to avoid traditional payment processing fees. "CashDrop is there to let people pay just as easily, but instead of relying on a third-party app, the vendor can link directly to their CashDrop page, without having to leave Twitter to conduct the transaction," he said.

GOING TO MARKET

Flores-Martinez saw CashDrop as having a fundamentally different goal than other payment platforms. "I want to use it to help small businesses grow, and protect them from platforms that would take advantage of them," he said. "I don't need the company to grow super quickly at the expense of customer service. I want to grow because our clients are telling their friends that CashDrop is easy to use." Flores-Martinez wanted to make sure that the product was simple to set up and did not require unnecessary purchases or downloads. (See **Exhibit 2** for sample quotes from app reviews.)

Flores-Martinez also focused on small business needs as he improved the app. "I've used social media to create a frictionless loop backward from our customers to us," he said. "The help button on CashDrop still sends me a text message directly, so I know exactly what problems people are having. That became my obsession—if I get feedback about something, I can change it and deploy it on the app almost instantaneously, sometimes in minutes, and then it's fixed. That's really helpful, although I know I'll have to find another way to do that as we scale." By June 2020, CashDrop was in Chicago, IL, Milwaukee, WI, New York City, Los Angeles, Salt Lake

City, UT, Orange County, CA, Tampa, FL, Des Moines, IA, and Door County, WI.

Flores-Martinez knew other companies could be potential competitors, but was sure that CashDrop had a better understanding of its customers. "I know what it's like to start a small business with almost no overhead," he said. "Before Covid, I've was able to see people using CashDrop every day: in nearby restaurants, in stores near my apartment. I think we have a better grasp on what people need than our competitors. I just need to figure out how to scale." From vendor feedback, Flores-Martinez had already added features to the CashDrop platform, including options for curbside pickup, delivery, and self-checkout. "I have a strong enough technical background that implementing these changes wasn't as challenging as knowing what would most improve the customer experience," he said.

New Competitors

Along with traditional payment platforms, CashDrop was also in competition with food ordering and delivery platforms. When Covid-19 hit in spring 2020, many restaurants changed from full service to takeout- and delivery-only to comply with newly implemented state rules or health guidelines. In doing so, they also needed new payment and order management systems, which CashDrop was able to provide. "As more and more restaurants began using CashDrop, we realized that a lot of places were choosing to use us instead of DoorDash," said Flores-Martinez.

In 2019 and 2020, many of the traditional food delivery ordering platforms, including DoorDash, Grubhub, and UberEats, had faced accusations that they were taking advantage of restaurants through high delivery and service fees. Many restaurants found that they were losing money on online delivery orders, with these fees (paid by the vendors, not the consumers) accounting for up to 30% of the total price.[14] Critics said some restaurants were charged by ordering platforms even when customers ordered directly from the restaurants. Food couriers also accused the platforms of stealing tips that consumers had earmarked for the couriers themselves.[15] Covid-19 exacerbated this, as public health guidelines forced many restaurants to rely on third-party platforms for all business. (See **Exhibit 3** for comparative sample pricing.)

Other Competitors

Along with these payment processors, CashDrop also faced competition from adjacent business models. These included other sellers on social media outlets like TikTok, point-of-sale providers like Square and Toast, online delivery platforms like Grubhub and Postmates, and online storefront management apps like Bentobox, Snackpass, and Olo.

Scaling Up

In early spring 2020, CashDrop had 158 users and $450,000 in monthly transactions. Most of its customers were in a small geographic region, mostly around Chicago and Milwaukee, although many digital sales were also conducted across the U.S. Almost all of the company's growth was still from word-of-mouth. Flores-Martinez planned to grow CashDrop by expanding to more food trucks, restaurants, food halls, events, theaters, and arenas. He estimated that there were approximately 350,000 non-chain restaurants in the U.S. that could be potential customers.

To grow CashDrop, Flores-Martinez knew he needed money, and began to think about how to finance the company's growth right away. "I applied to a few incubators immediately and pitched to a few funds, and they all blew me off immediately," he said. He set aside his plans for outside funding and instead turned to his younger sister, who helped him grow the business. "She became my account executive. With her help, I said fine, I can bootstrap this. I'm making 45 cents to a dollar per transaction right now. I can go door to door to grow the business. A few months later, CashDrop was making $25,000 per month in revenue, and that's when everything switched." (See **Exhibit 4** for financials.)

By May 2020, CashDrop had seven employees, but Flores-Martinez knew that he needed to hire more people for sales and onboarding, product development, and content creation. Nonetheless, he only wanted to hire a few more people. He said, "I know I need help to grow, and it will be good to have more people on our team. But this is never going to need a lot of people—we don't have a lot of overhead. I honestly don't see the CashDrop team going beyond 50 employees. I think 50 would be too many." (See **Exhibit 5** for CashDrop social media posts.)

Growth Business Model

By May 2020, Flores-Martinez had begun to reconsider his plan to self-finance CashDrop's expansion. "I had thought, 'I don't need any help, I can do this on my own,'" he said. But the Covid-19 pandemic changed his plans, as vendors rapidly switched to online sales. He said:

> The market was a complete land grab, so the faster we were able to move, the more revenue we would have coming in. It suddenly made

> sense to take outside money in order to ramp up merchant acquisition. I couldn't do it alone, but at least I would be in control of how much money I took and on what terms. The goal was always to just take enough money to where we could convert it into enough revenue for us to remain in control of the ship without having to keep raising more money.

This growth led to renewed interest from VC. Flores-Martinez remembered: "I started hearing from a bunch of different VC companies that they were interested. At first, I wasn't interested, but then I thought: maybe we should just take $500,000. Then I thought, maybe I should just take a million. And then I started to think about all the ways CashDrop could use that money, and I realized we could seize a lot of opportunities."

Flores-Martinez considered what he could do with that money if he took it: he could use it to fund a faster version of his self-funded plan, or he could come up with a bigger, more expensive plan than he had originally considered, with potentially higher revenue. But he was also wary of the ways that VC could change CashDrop. He said:

> America has this real obsession with growth. [Managing Director of Founder Collective] Eric Paley said to me, 'VC is a drug, you have to be careful with it.' Companies can get put into this fasttrack to keep pushing and spending more money until you lose control of where the company is going and just crash. I don't want to do that. I want to make sure I understand what the customers are looking for and maximize for that, even if it means going slower. I don't want to start taking VC money to increase our revenue in a way that makes it impossible for us to reach a net positive income. The goal is to become one of the most powerful Latinx-controlled companies the world has ever seen, and we can't do that if we have this unsustainable growth.

THE VENTURE CAPITAL LANDSCAPE

The VC industry, the traditional funding route for businesses like Flores-Martinez's that were looking to expand, often proved difficult to approach. This was particularly true for entrepreneurs who did not fit the traditional mold of a white, male CEO.[16] When Flores-Martinez "When I first thought about getting funding, I approached a lot of firms, and they weren't interested. I know people default to giving opportunities to people in whom they see themselves, or with whom they have a connection. I want to know how we find these commonalities across different experiences so that more people get these chances."

At the end of 2018, 1,047 VC firms operated in the U.S.[17] They managed 1,884 individual funds with assets of just over $400 billion.[18] Notable players included Accel, Andreessen Horowitz, Benchmark, Founders Fund, and Sequoia Capital.[19]

VC firms invested in promising young companies in exchange for a share of ownership. Some specialized in a specific industry, while others preferred to build a diversified portfolio.[20] Many took a hands-on approach with their portfolio companies, offering advice and input on major decisions.[21] Because an estimated 60% of startups failed, this type of investing was risky, and VC firms needed to balance the risk with the possibility of huge returns.[22] Firms sought to identify the few successful companies that would exit—meaning they were either acquired or became publicly traded—to make up for the inevitable losses.

In 2019, more VC flowed into the software sector ($44.8 billion) than any other sector.[23] This was followed by the pharmaceutical and biotechnology industry ($16.7 billion), commercial services ($14 billion), health care services and systems ($7.1 billion), consumer goods and recreation ($6.3 billion), and health care devices and supplies ($5.7 billion).[24] The median deal size in 2019 was $12.9 million.[25]

In addition to the financing, founders who secured VC backing gained business expertise, a significant network, and a pathway to fast growth.[26] But there were also disadvantages. Founders not only sacrificed equity but also a degree of autonomy, as most investors expected to be consulted on major strategic and operational decisions.[27]

Increasing Diversity

The VC industry had received criticism for its lack of gender and racial/ethnic diversity. Men comprised 95% of VC partners,[28] and almost 80% of the senior investment teams at VC firms were white.[29] The entrepreneurs in which VCs invested mirrored these demographics, with only 3% of funding going to startups with women and/or minority leaders in 2018.[30] However, entrepreneurship had increased significantly among people of color, especially Black and Latina women.[31]

Some speculated that these mirrored demographics came in part from a bias towards management teams that were similar to those investing, known as homophily. VC firms also often invested in companies where an investor was acquainted with one of the founders or managers. One study found that VCs considered the founding or management team of business as more important than the business idea itself.[32] Even when VCs looked beyond the demographics of the founding team, they often focused on business ideas that served similar groups as themselves, overlooking investments in female-focused inventions like new breast pump technology, businesses operating outside of places like Silicon Valley, and consumer products focused on the needs of non-white Americans.[33,34,35,36]

In recent years, some VC firms had aimed to increase the demographic diversity of their investments. In June 2020, Andreessen Horowitz announced a new VC fund, TxO, aimed at investing in early-stage startups run by non-traditional entrepreneurs. The fund welcomed all backgrounds and genders, but looked for entrepreneurs "from underserved communities." In the blog post announcing the new fund, Andreessen Horowitz cited recent acts of violence towards African Americans, including the murders of George Floyd, Ahmaud Arbery, and Breonna Taylor, as part of the same cultural bias that the firm hoped to combat.[37] At the same time, the post noted that Andreessen Horowitz was run by "venture capitalists, not activists. [. . .] our direct contribution will be doing what we do best: To help entrepreneurs be better entrepreneurs, so they can build great businesses that in turn create jobs and value for others. [. . .] This fund and program aims to fill a gap between the cultural leaders who have made it, and those who haven't had a chance to make it."[38]

Other VC firms took different tacks to increase the diversity of founders they supported. One, Harlem Capital Partners, was founded to support minority groups in entrepreneurship.

Harlem Capital

Harlem Capital was founded in 2015 by two 2019 Harvard Business School (HBS) alumni, Jarrid Tingle and Henri Pierre-Jacques. Tingle and Pierre-Jacques were both African American and had sought to create a fund that focused on supporting startups led by women and minorities. They wanted to create new opportunities for woman- and minority-run startups, but also earn higher-than-average returns.[39] The founders believed that these businesses would outperform the average VC-funded startups,[40] a belief supported by research on diversity and VC profitability.[41]

Focus in 2020 Tingle and Pierre-Jacques were interested in building Harlem Capital into a strong VC brand, which would help to define a new business narrative about what types of companies made successful investments.

After an initial round of investments in 2019, Harlem Capital was looking for new startups to invest in. The firm was industry agnostic, but in 2020 became more focused on deals in the SaaS, E-commerce, and Fintech sectors. These verticals were strong markets that were only being accelerated by COVID-19. Harlem Capital sourced CashDrop through a Managing Director of a Techstars program who knew Flores-Martinez.

Assessing CashDrop For Harlem Capital, CashDrop appeared to be a strong candidate for their support. Harlem Capital had created a rating system for their potential investments, on which Flores-Martinez had scored highly (see **Exhibit 6**). CashDrop also met the fund's investment criteria, including being post-product, having a disruptive business model, a strong, founder-led management team, and a four to seven-year investment horizon.[42] (See **Exhibit 7** for Harlem Capital's rubric assessment of CashDrop.) Tingle recalled "We were instantly impressed by Ruben's story, vision, and strong product developed using minimal resources. CashDrop has a massive long-term market opportunity. In the short-term, however, it has proved to be a platform that empowers restaurants and other merchants to adapt quickly to a new way of doing business during the global public health crisis brought on by the Covid-19 pandemic." (See **Exhibit 8** for Harlem Capital's assessment of CashDrop's commission revenue potential.)

WHAT NEXT?

In May 2020, Flores-Martinez was in a different position than he had been only a few months before. "The same funds that had blown me off earlier are now coming to me," he said. "It's come full circle." Still, his goals were the same: to create an easy way for entrepreneurs to grow their business and make some money, while also creating a business that was successful enough to make growing a business easier for other Latinx entrepreneurs in the future. "I want to inspire people to become entrepreneurs, and to turn a dream into a side hustle and a side hustle into a lifestyle. I want people to have a job they love that they created for themselves. Success is a mindset powered by a purpose, and I want people to find that purpose."

Flores-Martinez was adjusting to the mindset of a VC-funded CEO. "There's about to be more money in my bank account than I've ever had, or than my parents have ever had. In some ways, it's so much money, but in terms of what CashDrop can use, it's not very much at all." He had goals for how to spend the first million dollars, including enhancing CashDrop's integrations with applications including Intuit QuickBooks, Stripe, and WhatsApp, expanding to new businesses, like barbershops. Later he planned to create more robust reporting and analytics tools, a web-based dashboard, and eventual machine learning tools for predictive modeling and consumer behavior insights. (See **Exhibit 9** for CashDrop's revenue build plans.) But, he added, "The money isn't the essential part. The biggest change is that I've been able to talk to a lot of investors and bounce ideas off them, and talk to them about next steps. In a lot of ways, that's more valuable than the funding itself. The opportunity shadows the amount of money. I want to do honor to the opportunity that I have."

As he looked out the window, thinking about what his best options were, Flores-Martinez's email pinged. He had just received a new message from Jarrid Tingle:

Hi Ruben,
Excited to work with you guys. Sending below the terms Harlem Capital has committed to:

- $1 mm investment at $12mm post-money valuation
- Anticipate $1.8mm raise, but minimum of $1.2 mm
- Would prefer priced round
- Expect info rights (quarterly numbers), major investor rights, pro rata rights either in docs or side letter
- Would like board seat
- Don't put this in docs, but think quick monthly updates with rev, key metrics, burn, cash balance are best practice
- Happy to be flexible on most other points. Want to be founder friendly and accommodate your concerns

If open to going to the priced round route, I can turnaround a term sheet quickly (half a day).

-Jarrid[b]

Now Flores-Martinez had to decide: was Harlem Capital the best VC to work with, or would one of the more established funds that he had spoken with be more helpful? Would any VC fund be the right fit for CashDrop? And how could he tell if they were?

NOTES

1 Andreas Rekdal, "Too many dinner options? This app helps you narrow the field," Built In Chicago, August 4, 2017, https://www.builtinchicago.org/2017/08/04/sugr-helps-you-decide-what-do, accessed November 2020.
2 Stripe, "Pricing," https://stripe.com/en-gb-us/pricing#pricing-details, accessed January 2021.
3 Lyle Daly, "Average Credit Card Processing Fees and Costs in 2020," The Motley Fool, July 8, 2020, https://www.fool.com/the-ascent/research/average-credit-card-processing-fees-costs-america/, accessed February 2021.

b The numbers included in this email were disguised.

4 Brian O'Connell, "History of PayPal: Timeline and Facts," TheStreet, updated January 2, 2020, https://www.thestreet.com/technology/history-of-paypal-15062744, accessed November 2020.
5 PayPal, "PayPal Merchant Fees," January 15, 2021, https://www.paypal.com/us/webapps/mpp/merchant-fees#fixed-fees-commercialtrans, accessed February 2021.
6 "A Brief History of Shopify," Digital., September 4, 2015, https://www.born-digital.com/2015/09/04/a-brief-history-of-shopify-2015-09-04, accessed November 2020.
7 Shopify, "Shopify partners with Facebook to help businesses launch branded Facebook Shops," May 19, 2020, https://news.shopify.com/shopify-partners-with-facebook-to-help-businesses-launch-branded-facebook-shops, accessed January 2021.
8 Jillian Warren, "Instagram Checkout: Everything You Need to Know," Later, August 26, 2020, https://later.com/blog/instagram-checkout/, accessed February 2021.
9 Everette Taylor, "Square—How Did Square Grow So Quickly?," GrowthHackers, https://growthhackers.com/growth-studies/square, accessed December 2020.
10 Square, "Fees and Payments FAQ," https://squareup.com/help/us/en/article/6109-fees-and-payments-faqs, accessed February 2021.
11 John Rampton, "The evolution of the mobile payment," *TechCrunch*, June 17, 2016, https://techcrunch.com/2016/06/17/the-evolution-of-the-mobile-payment/, accessed October 2020.
12 Rampton, "The evolution of the mobile payment."
13 Rampton, "The evolution of the mobile payment."
14 Nathaniel Popper, "As Diners Flock to Delivery Apps, Restaurants Fear for Their Future," *The New York Times*, June 9, 2020, updated November 30, 2020, https://www.nytimes.com/2020/06/09/technology/delivery-apps-restaurants-fees-virus.html, accessed November 2020.
15 Amanda Kludt, "Why I'm Deleting Delivery Apps From My Phone," Eater, September 23, 2019, https://www.eater.com/2019/9/23/20879900/from-the-editor-newsletter-delivery-apps-bad; Shira Ovide, "Why Restaurants Are Fed Up With Apps," *The New York Times*, June 10, 2020, https://www.nytimes.com/2020/06/10/technology/food-delivery-apps.html, both accessed November 2020.
16 Bowdeya Tweh, "A New Push for Diversity in Funding Tech Startups," *The Wall Street Journal*, October 21, 2020, https://www.wsj.com/articles/a-new-push-for-diversity-in-funding-tech-startups-11603303872, accessed November 2020.
17 "Latest NVCA Yearbook Highlights Record Levels Reached by the U.S. Venture Ecosystem in 2018," National Venture Capital Association, https://nvca.org/pressreleases/latest-nvca-yearbook-highlights-record-levels-reached-u-s-venture-ecosystem-2018/, accessed November 2020.
18 "Latest NVCA Yearbook Highlights Record Levels Reached by the U.S. Venture Ecosystem in 2018."

19 "The Top 100 Venture Capitalists," Smart Money Venture Capital, March 31, 2019, https://www.cbinsights.com/research/top-venture-capital-partners/, accessed November 2020.
20 Paul Gompers, Anna Kovner, Josh Lerner, and David Scharfstein, "Specialization and Success: Evidence from Venture Capital," MIT Working Paper, February 18, 2006, http://web.mit.edu/iandeseminar/Papers/Spring2006/Lerner.pdf, accessed November 2020.
21 "Advantages vs. Disadvantages of Venture Capital," The Hartford, https://www.thehartford.com/business-insurance/strategy/business-financing/venture-capital, accessed November 2020.
22 William A. Sahlman, "Risk and Reward in Venture Capital," HBS No. 811-036 (Boston: Harvard Business Publishing, 2010), p. 7.
23 "Value of venture capital investment in the United States in 2019, by industry (in billion U.S. dollars)," via Statista, accessed November 2020.
24 "Value of venture capital investment in the United States in 2019, by industry (in billion U.S. dollars)."
25 Nizar Tarhuni, James Gelfer, Alex Frederick, Cameron Stanfill, Kyle Stanford, and Van Le, "Venture Monitor: Q4 2019," Pitchbook and the National Venture Capital Association, January 13, 2020, https://pitchbook.com/news/reports/q4-2019-pitchbook-nvca-venture-monitor, p. 18, accessed November 2020.
26 "Advantages vs. Disadvantages of Venture Capital," The Hartford; Idealogic, "Pros And Cons Of Venture Capital Funding," Medium, October 29, 2020, https://medium.com/@idealogic_company/pros-and-cons-of-venture-capital-funding-122134d40baf; both accessed November 2020.
27 "Advantages vs. Disadvantages of Venture Capital," The Hartford.
28 Leslie Feinzaig, "New data shows the number of women-led VC funds is exploding," Fast Company, October 22, 2020, https://www.fastcompany.com/90567387/women-in-vc-growth, accessed November 2020.
29 "Data Shows Black Entrepreneurship Growing Across the United States: Investors Should Take Note," Founder Institute, February 22, 2020, https://fi.co/insight/black-entrepreneurship-is-growing-in-strength, accessed November 2020.
30 George Serafeim and David Freiberg, "Harlem Capital: Changing the Face of Entrepreneurship (A)," HBS No. 120-040 (Boston: Harvard Business School Publishing, 2019), https://hbsp.harvard.edu/, accessed November 2020.
31 "Data Shows Black Entrepreneurship Growing Across the United States: Investors Should Take Note," Founder Institute, February 22, 2020, https://fi.co/insight/black-entrepreneurship-is-growing-in-strength, accessed November 2020.
32 Paul A. Gompers, Will Gornall, Steven N. Kaplan, and Ilya A. Strebulaev, "How do venture capitalists make decisions?," Journal of Financial Economics 135 (2020), 169-190, June 25, 2019.
33 Emily Chang and Ellen Huet, "A Smart Breast Pump: Mothers Love It. VCs Don't," *Bloomberg*, September 21, 2017, https://www.bloomberg.com/news/articles/2017-09-21/a-smart-breast-pump-mothers-love-it-vcs-don-t?sref=pn6qMxvp, accessed February 2021.

34 Ruiqjng Cao, Rembrand Koning, and Ramana Nanda, "Biased Sampling of Early Users and the Direction of Startup Innovation," HBS Working Paper, No. 21-059, 2020, https://www.hbs.edu/ris/Publication%20Files/21-059_0ec587e4-4b74-4f21-9f8c-3f8920649ab9.pdf, accessed February 2021.
35 Ross Baird, The Innovation Blind Spot; Why We Back the Wrong Ideas—and What to Do About It (Dallas: BenBella Books, Inc., 2017), Google Books.
36 Gabriela Barkho, "'We are over-mentored and under-funded': Minority founders find a cultural disconnect with VCs," ModernRetail, August 18, 2020, https://tinyurl.com/1hi9sjdv, accessed February 2021.
37 "Introducing the Talent x Opportunity Fund," Andreessen Horowitz, June 3, 2020, https://a16z.com/2020/06/03/talent-x-opportunity/, accessed November 2020.
38 "Introducing the Talent x Opportunity Fund."
39 George Serafeim and David Freiberg, "Harlem Capital: Changing the Face of Entrepreneurship (A)," HBS No. 120-040 (Boston: Harvard Business School Publishing, 2019), https://hbsp.harvard.edu/, accessed November 2020.
40 Serafeim and Freiberg, "Harlem Capital: Changing the Face of Entrepreneurship (A)."
41 Paul Gompers and Silpa Kovvali, "The Other Diversity Dividend," *Harvard Business Review*, July-August 2018, https://hbr.org/2018/07/the-other-diversity-dividend, accessed December 2020.
42 Serafeim and Freiberg, "Harlem Capital: Changing the Face of Entrepreneurship (A)."

EXHIBIT 1 CashDrop Interface
Source: Company documents.

★★★★★

SelGaona, 05/09/2020

GAME CHANGER

I'm a small business owner and this app has made transactions so simple! The CashDrop team exceeds expectations of customer service. My clients are able to see the prices of the services I provide and can purchase them with ease. Making any adjustments to prices, names, pictures, etc. is also very simple. That's one of the things that sets this app apart from others. Anytime I'm running specials it's easy to make a new drop and you can just archive the drop whenever you'd like! So happy I decided to use this app for my business

★★★★★

alexjewellalex, 04/30/2020

An app that doesn't take money from restaurants

Most food pickup/delivery apps take large fees from restaurants AND customers, leveraging the power of the middle man to profit enormously. CashDrop doesn't do that: a small fee is charged for the customer, but restaurants are the real stars here and don't pay a dime to be on the platform. Can't wait to see this thing grow.

★☆☆☆☆

daveyjones1, 12/06/2020

Customer perspective

Using this "app" to order (I put that in air quotes because to order food the app just redirects you to a website) I am now unable to select how much I want to tip. You read that right. If you want to tip you HAVE to choose from one of their arbitrary pre-chosen amounts (starts off $2, $5.. are you kidding me?).

Developer Response,

Hello there,

We really appreciate your feedback! Our app is merchant only, we don't believe in customers having to download more apps or having too many accounts and passwords.

The tipping amounts can actually be set up by the merchants, they can either be % based or $ based!

-CASHBOT

EXHIBIT 2 Apple App Store Reviews

Source: App Store, "CASHDROP," Apple website, https://apps.apple.com/us/app/cashdrop/id1478976218, accessed February 2021

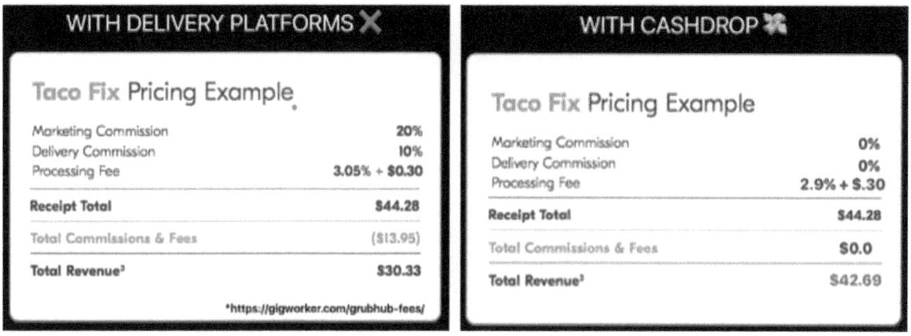

WITH DELIVERY PLATFORMS

Taco Fix Pricing Example

Marketing Commission	20%
Delivery Commission	10%
Processing Fee	3.05% + $0.30
Receipt Total	**$44.28**
Total Commissions & Fees	($13.95)
Total Revenue[3]	**$30.33**

*https://gigworker.com/grubhub-fees/

WITH CASHDROP

Taco Fix Pricing Example

Marketing Commission	0%
Delivery Commission	0%
Processing Fee	2.9% + $.30
Receipt Total	**$44.28**
Total Commissions & Fees	$0.0
Total Revenue[3]	$42.69

EXHIBIT 3 CashDrop vs. Traditional Food Ordering Platforms
Source: Company documents.

EXHIBIT 4 CashDrop Financials

Month	Jan 2020	Feb 2020	Mar 2020	Apr 2020	May 2020	Total	Average
Transactions	255	324	1,459	6,545	17,613	26,196	5,239
Total Merchants	26	33	69	113	158	158	80
Gross Sales	$4,420	$5,858	$40,737	$218,377	$461,615	$731,005	$146,201
Per Customer	$170	$178	$590	$1,933	$2,922	$5,782	$1,158
Revenue	$163	$219	$1,472	$8,583	$17,734	$28,171	$5,634
Per Customer	$6	$7	$21	$76	$112	$222	$44
Transaction Growth (MoM)		27%	350%	349%	169%		
Merchant Growth (MoM)		27%	109%	64%	40%		
Gross Sales Growth (MoM)		33%	595%	436%	111%		
Revenue Growth (MoM)		35%	571%	483%	107%		

Source: Harlem Capital documents.

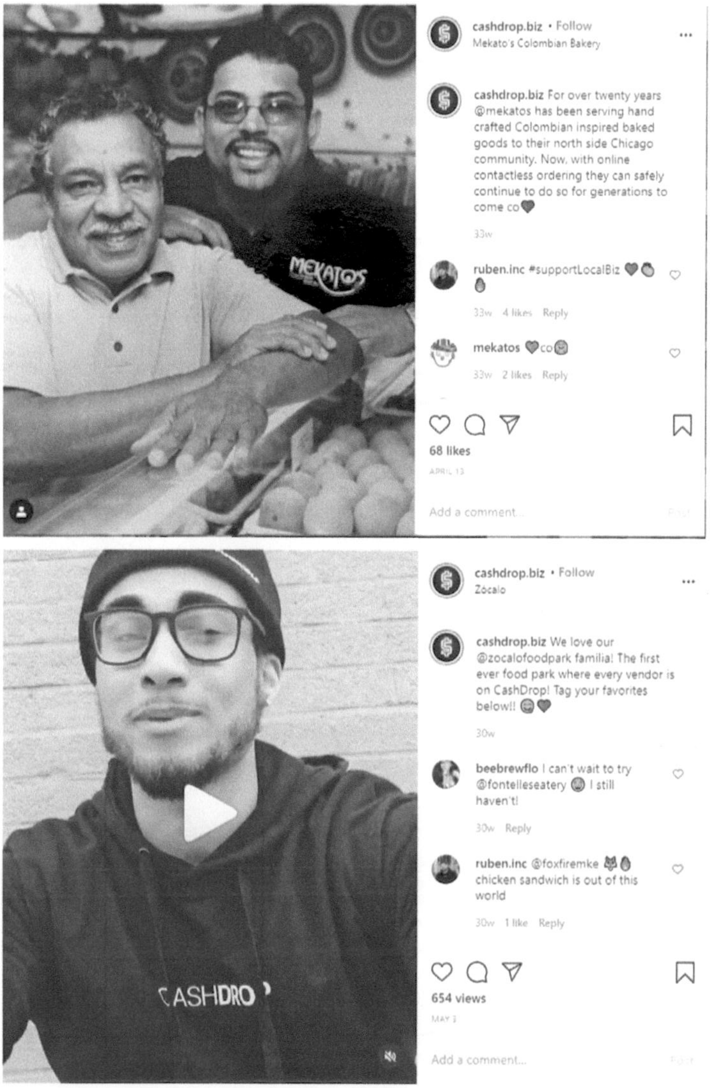

EXHIBIT 5 CashDrop Social Media Post Examples

Source: CashDrop (@cashdrop.biz), "For over twenty years @mekatos has been serving hand- crafted Colombian inspired baked goods to their north side Chicago community. Now, with online contactless ordering they can safely continue to do so for generations to come co♥," Instagram, April 13, 2020, https://www.instagram.com/p/B-7HqmhnwA7/; and CashDrop (@cashdrop.biz), "We love our @zocalofoodpark familia! The first ever food park where every vendor is on CashDrop! Tag your favorites below!! ☺♥▯," Instagram, May 3, 2020, https://www.instagram.com/p/B_vBWZCnz2i/.

Founder Rubric (out of 4)

GRIT	4	• The founder displays confidence and perseverance through their experiences
Passion & Ambition	4	• Display desire to achieve and drive to accomplish
Innovative Thinker	4	• Strongly display the ability to anticipate user needs and ability to capitalize on them through product development and execution
Vision & Team Build	4	• Display ability to inspire a vision and understanding of team needs
Adjustment/Self-awareness/ Coachability	3	• The founder displays EQ and ability to adjust and self-control
People-focus	3	• The founder displays a strong concern for people
Functional knowledge	3	• The founder can learn additional functional groups and have domain over the core elements of the business (product design, sales, vision setting, team building)
Great Reputation /Strong referrals	3	• The founder is highly regarded, has a positive reputation (social media too) and referrals think highly of the founders
Acumen/ Relevant Experience	4	• The founder has full domain of knowledge in the respective area of focus and relevant experience
Nose for the money	4	• The founder understands the need to execute and scale swiftly and efficiently in order to reach necessary revenue growth
Total	**36/40**	

EXHIBIT 6 Harlem Capital Founder Rubric for Ruben Flores-Martinez
Source: Harlem Capital documents.

Investment Thesis (out of 5)

CashDrop's core strength is its merchant first perspective and easy-to-use product with 15-minute onboarding. CashDrop's modern product design and easy link access enables it to standout for mobile-first shoppers and merchants. In order to win, CashDrop must scale and acquire users efficiently, while staying nimble to avoid incumbents like Instagram Shop.

Product	4	• Strong product that has great design, easy onboarding, and thoughtful features for shoppers and merchants
Customers	3	• 158 merchants are on the platform (as of May 2020) • 27K revenue generating transactions
Financials	3	• Apr-20/May-20 Gross Sales: $218k/$461k • Apr-20/May-20 Revenue: $8.6k/$17.7k • Firm is capital efficient and monthly burn is ~$8K. Burn post-raise will be between $50-100K
Management Team	4	• 3 FTE (Founder + 2 sales) • Next hires include a COO, CMO, Sales, and Engineering
Market	4	• Food orders placed via smartphone and mobile apps will become a $38 billion industry by 2020 • Digital ordering and delivery have grown 300% faster than dine-in traffic since 2014 • Delivery sales could rise an annual average of more than 20% to $365 billion worldwide by 2030, from $35 billion. It's estimated that mobile orders will make up close to 11% of all QSR sales by 2020.
Investors	4	• Lot of investor demand MaC VC and Commerce Ventures are potential co-investors
HCP Value Add	4	• HCP can support CashDrop's financial analysis and the development of sales and marketing team; offer ongoing mentorship
Final Thoughts	**26/35**	

EXHIBIT 7 Harlem Capital Rating Rubric for CashDrop
Source: Harlem Capital documents.

We estimate that the 2020 addressable market is $130B in mobile payments volume annually. If CashDrop captured 2% of this volume, they would generate $117M in GMV commissions alone, today.

Mobile Payments is the market for CashDrop

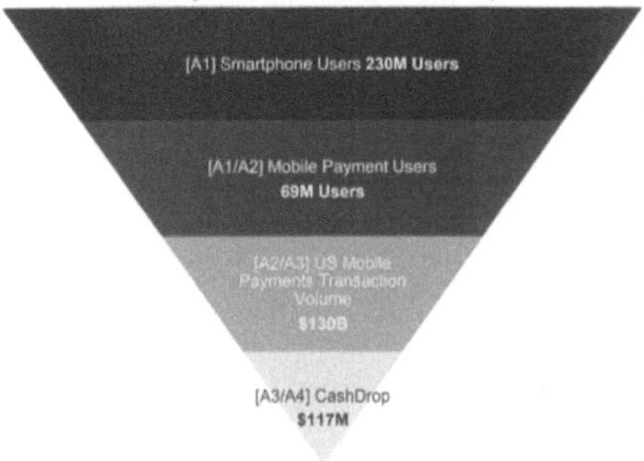

CashDrop Commission Revenue Potential	
Number of US Smarphone Users	230,000,000
Percentage of US Mobile Payments Users*	30%
Total US Mobile Payments Users	69,000,000
Average 2020 US Mobile Payment User GMV	$1,879.11
2020 US Transaction Volume Through Mobile Payments	$129,658,590,000
CashDrop Market Share	1.8%
CashDrop Mobile Payments GMV	$2,333,854,620.0
CashDrop Fee*	5%
CashDrop Annual Revenue	**$116,692,731.0**

(Note: this is a much lower adoption rate than China where 81.1% of all smartphone users utilize mobile payments.)

Confidential Sources: eMarketer

Market Trends *(Mobile Payments)*

Global trends suggest an uptick in the use of mobile wallets and mobile payments offline; however, the US is slow to adopt. There has been steady growth globally in "account-to-account" (A2A) payment methods.

Key Trends in Global Mobile Payments

- *In the US*: 80% of consumers in China used mobile payments in 2018 while the top **US major payment apps were used by less than 10%.**
- *In China*: Emergence of large ecosystem players, like Alipay and WeChat Pay, has boosted the growth of mobile payments: Mobile payments transactions **grew at a 123 percent CAGR in China from 2013 to 2018** and, based on data published by the People's Bank of China, are **estimated to have exceeded 300 billion** (or roughly 210 transactions per capita) in 2018.
- *Globally*: In Africa, for example, **mobile payment users outnumber bank account holders** (M-Pesa is Kenya's most popular payment method) and in Germany, Capita6 reports that **alternative payments account for 66% of e-commerce purchases**
- Overall, there is **growing trust and interest in non-cash, non-card A2A payment methods**. Certain A2A payments methods around the world have successfully gained major footholds in their local payments landscape, often squeezing card's market share in the process. Examples include Swish in Sweden, iDeal in the Netherlands, and Alipay and WeChat in Asia

US Preferred Payment Methods

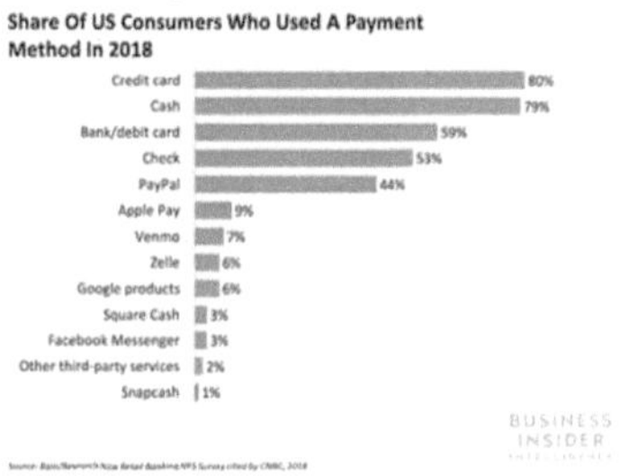

EXHIBIT 8 CashDrop Revenue Potential Slides
Source: Harlem Capital documents.

EXHIBIT 9 CashDrop Revenue Build

CashDrop Revenue Build—Restaurants	
Average Online Order	$33
Order Volume per Day	90
Daily Sales per Restaurant	$2,934
Monthly Sales per Restaurant	$76,284
Annual Sales per Restaurant	$915,408
Merchants on CashDrop	6,250
Total Restaurant Sales	$5,721,300,000
CashDrop Share of Restaurant Sales	35%
CashDrop Gross Sales	$2,002,455,000
CashDrop Fee	5%
CashDrop Annual Restaurant Revenue	**$100,122,750**
Market Penetration	
Total U.S. Non-Chain Restaurants	352,815
CashDrop Restaurants	6,250
CashDrop Market Penetration	1.8%
CashDrop Annual Gross Sales per Restaurant	$320,393
CashDrop Annual Revenue per Restaurant	$16,020
CashDrop Revenue Build—Consumer	
Average Order Value per Merchant	$71
Annual Average Order Volume per Merchant	84
Annual Gross Merchandise Sales per Merchant	$5,964
Total Number of Business on Instagram	25,000,000
Share of Merchants Selling Crafts	4%
Merchants Selling Crafts	1,000,000
Total Merchant Sales	$5,964,000,000
CashDrop Share of Merchant Sales	15%
CashDrop Gross Merchant Sales	$894,600,000
CashDrop Fee	*5%*
CashDrop Annual Consumer Revenue	**$44,730,000**
CashDrop Annual Restaurant Revenue	$100,122,750
CashDrop Annual Consumer Revenue	$44,730,000
Total CashDrop Annual Revenue	**$144,852,750**

Source: Company documents.

CHAPTER 5.3

CashDrop (B1)

Rembrand Koning, Paul A. Gompers and Sarah Gulick

In July 2020, Ruben Flores-Martinez wondered: Who was the best investor for CashDrop? In the past few weeks, he had gotten several term sheets from venture capital (VC) funds. This was a change from only a few months before, when he was unable to get a single investor meeting. "This January, I applied to the Techstars accelerator and didn't get in, although I stayed in touch with one of the Fintech managing directors there," he said. "Then in June, he emailed me saying, 'We want to give you the last slot for this round,' and I had to say, 'No, I'm good.' I didn't need them anymore. Actually, that managing director is leaving Techstars and coming to work for me as CashDrop's COO in October."

By July 2020, Flores-Martinez had already received some funding from the managing director's referral. Earlier that month, he met with an angel investor who had invested $100,000 in CashDrop. "Then somehow, I found myself in this VC bidding war. At one point, I was looking at five separate term sheets," he said.

Flores-Martinez viewed the possibility of VC funding as a privilege, saying, "I wasn't expecting to be in this position, so I want to take advantage of it. I know how rare it is for Latinx immigrants in particular to get VC funding. The opportunity is really overshadowing the amount of money."

At the same time he wanted to be cautious about the attending complications: "I never want to be in a situation where the company is forced into unsustainable growth. What I'm looking for from a VC fund, more than cash, is having a network of people I can call at two in the morning and say, 'I'm not sure what to do about this decision—what do you think?' And I want to be able to call another CEO and have them know who I am because I have VC backing."

Flores-Martinez already had plans for the funds he was raising. "We're growing quickly, so I need to hire some customer service representatives,

CashDrop (B1)
by REMBRAND KONING, PAUL A. GOMPERS, SARAH GULICK, case number 9-221-052 MARCH 19, 2021

as well as other developers. Right now, I'm doing that all by myself, which was fine when this was a small company, but now I don't have enough time to address it all. But I don't need that much cash to do it—I want to make sure that I can fund most of my growth from revenue."

Because of this, Flores-Martinez was wary of VC funds that pushed him to take too much money instead of building a sustainable business plan. Many of the large, traditional VC firms believed that growth for growth's sake was the right strategy. He said:

> I'm not motivated by money in itself. I'm motivated by the chance to uplift immigrants and open up opportunities for other people through my achievements. The prestige of a VC fund is important for that, but I want to work with one that understands my goals and is excited about them. When I said before that I wanted to someday own the Willis Tower, I don't just want to own it to show off. I want to put an immigrant name in it. I want it to be a testament to my community to show what we can achieve.

VENTURE CAPITAL OPTIONS

By July, Flores-Martinez was considering offers from several top tier VC funds, many of which wanted to lead the funding round. "One, when I talked to them, had ideas for growth that were too aggressive, and I decided pretty quickly that I didn't want to work with them," he said. "But the other one, Matheson,[1] seems like it could be really good. I explained that I wanted to be pretty careful with how we grew, but I told them, 'I'll still be making you money.'"

Matheson had offered Flores-Martinez $2 million at a $12 million post-money valuation. The term sheet looked pretty similar to what Harlem Capital sent in their initial e-mail. Matheson had a long track record and almost two decades of experience investing in startups. They had a history of successful exits and building public companies. Flores-Martinez wondered whether Matheson would add similar value to CashDrop.

Flores-Martinez was also waiting to hear back from Harlem Capital Partners (HCP) to see if they would make their offer official. "I've spoken to Jarrid about the email he sent me, and I'm excited about their terms. At the same time, I know Harlem Capital has a reputation for taking a long time to make an offer. They're rushing, but I don't want to wait too long now that I have the momentum."

He also worried that HCP was too new a firm, unable to match a Matheson's gravitas. "I like what Jarrid [Tingle] says whenever I talk to him, but if I'm trying to be a role model for other Latinx entrepreneurs, maybe I should go with the most established option. I want other people to say, 'Wow, Matheson gave him money? I have a better idea than *him*,' so they know they can do it too."

Because of the Covid-19 pandemic, Flores-Martinez was unable to meet potential investors in person: "It's been hard to get a sense of the values of each VC firm over the phone. I want to get the sense that the people I'm working with have an emotional connection to the company, that they share the vision I have—not that they just want to make money."

"To me, it comes down to mission versus prestige," said Flores-Martinez. "HCP might have the most alignment with me in terms of vision, but Matheson can give me the kind of prestige that I'm trying to build. And even then—HCP still hasn't made me an official offer. Should I wait?"

NOTE

1 The name of the VC fund has been disguised.

CHAPTER 5.4

CashDrop (B2)

Rembrand Koning, Paul A. Gompers and Sarah Gulick

In the year since Jarrid Tingle and Henri Pierre-Jacques, the founders of Harlem Capital Partners (HCP), had graduated from Harvard Business School and founded HCP, Tingle and Pierre-Jacques had closed their initial venture fund, with $40.3 million in commitments, in December 2019.[1]

By May 2020, HCP had invested in 18 companies (eight as lead investor). Tingle and Pierre-Jacques had selected the companies carefully. "As a new fund, we need to be aware that every investment sets a precedent," said Pierre-Jacques. "We want to make sure that each company meets our criteria both by being financially viable and by supporting traditionally excluded entrepreneurs. I don't want Harlem Capital to become too focused on making money that we forget about expanding diversity in VC funds, but I also don't want to start funding companies that are too much of a risk." In July 2020, Tingle and Pierre-Jacques were looking for new investment opportunities.

CASHDROP

In early 2020, Tingle and Pierre-Jacques heard about CashDrop through a friend who knew Ruben from his application to the Techstars accelerator program. "Because of the precautions we've had to take for Covid, we've been more focused on doing deals that are referrals, rather than inbound applications directly from startups," Tingle explained.

One of HCP's considerations when assessing a potential investment was the founder's reputation and responsiveness, which traditionally was assessed in part through face-to-face meetings. Tingle recalled: "Even over a video call, it was clear that Ruben was the kind of founder we were looking for. He met our founder criteria, had a clear idea for how his business could scale, and had clear goals for CashDrop. He wants to empower a

CashDrop (B2)
by REMBRAND KONING, PAUL A. GOMPERS, SARAH GULICK, case number 9-221-053 MARCH 19, 2021

lot of other entrepreneurs and become a decacorn[2] in five years, and his growth plans also give Harlem Capital a great exit plan."

"CashDrop is exactly the kind of company that we want to be funding," said Tingle. "It's growing, and it has a sustainable business model, and we're excited about Flores-Martinez's ideas about how the business can expand." There was just one catch, explained Pierre-Jacques: "We usually have significantly more time to review any potential investments, and we're able to get to know the founder a little more in person." CashDrop had had several competing offers from other VC firms, and Flores-Martinez had told Tingle and Pierre-Jacques that he needed to decide in a week and a half.

But Harlem Capital also needed to do its full due diligence. "Our vetting process includes reference checks and industry calls and having a series of touchpoint meetings with entrepreneurs. It's an evolving process, but we still had to ask all our questions, even with the compressed timeline we were working under with CashDrop," said Pierre-Jacques. Conducting many investor feedback phone calls was easier during Covid-19, as many of VCs were more available to speak because they were in their offices instead of traveling. "We were able to speak to everyone we absolutely needed to in just a few days when usually it can take weeks," said Tingle.

Tingle felt that HCP had done enough research to confidently invest in CashDrop. "It's not what we'd do traditionally, but it's too good of an opportunity to pass up," he said. Pierre-Jacques agreed, but was still cautious. He said, "I'm excited about CashDrop, but I'm nervous about moving too quickly." Given the competing offers, HCP did not want to miss out on a deal because of their thorough process. In June 2020, Tingle and Pierre-Jacques sent an outline for preliminary term sheet to Flores-Martinez, while they finished their assessment of the deal.

BUILDING TRUST

For Tingle and Pierre-Jacques, the process of assessing new deals had changed since Covid-19. "Before, we insisted on meeting all founders in person," said Tingle. "Now that's gone, and we're mostly conducting deals on the phone or over video conferencing. Meeting in person was also partially so we could build trust with CEOs, and be able to have them know us as people and know that we're aligned with their goals for the company. Without that, we've had to rely on our virtual touch points and get to know them more informally post-close."

Pierre-Jacques added, "For CashDrop, we needed to make sure that Ruben trusted us as much as we trusted him. Part of that was talking through many of his concerns about VC funding, even when we were all still making a decision. We needed to make sure that he felt comfortable with our vision for the company—if we wind up funding CashDrop, we'd be entering into a partnership."

Tingle and Pierre-Jacques worried that Flores-Martinez would pick a more competitive VC offer while he waited for their final terms. They wondered: should they be more aggressive with the terms they were offering? Which terms should they be flexible on and which should they hold firm? Would HCP actually be overpaying by changing its terms in the hot venture capital market? Had they done all the work necessary to understand the risks involved with CashDrop?

NOTES

1 "Harlem Capital Closes $40mm Inaugural Fund," BusinessWire, December 2, 2019, https://www.businesswire.com/news/home/20191202005849/en/Harlem-Capital-Closes-40mm-Inaugural-Fund, accessed December 2020.
2 A decacorn was a company worth over $10 billion.

CHAPTER 5.5

Ghia and Cleo Capital

Paul A. Gompers and Annelena Lobb

It was July 2020. Melanie Masarin, entrepreneur and creator of Ghia, contemplated the financing choices available to her growing business. Ghia, an alcohol-free *aperitivo*, had launched few months earlier. A traditional *aperitivo* (from the Latin *aperire*, to open) was an alcoholic drink imbibed prior to a meal to awaken the appetite. Ghia had a bitter, citrusy flavor, recalled summery alcoholic drinks such as the Negroni or the Aperol spritz, and could be used to make similar alcohol-free cocktails. Masarin marketed Ghia as a social drink, meant for consumption in groups of friends or family.

Masarin, based in New York, had planned to launch Ghia in restaurants only, branding it as the alcohol-free *aperitivo* approved by chefs and able to perfectly prime the stomach for a good meal. But she had pivoted the business and moved to online direct-to-consumer sales because of the onset of the Covid-19 pandemic, which had coincided with her original launch date of April 2020. Many friends and family members had participated in taste tests and contributed to an early round of financing, as had Cleo Capital, a pre-seed and seed-stage venture capital fund. Word of mouth and stylish online marketing had built buzz around Ghia, and sales had exceeded projections almost every month.

Still, Covid-19 had shut down restaurants and bars across the United States, and many plans for Ghia had shifted as a result. Masarin needed more financing to build the business during and after its pivot. She had to determine whether to raise a second round of funds from friends and family that summer, or to pursue a round of professional venture capital.

Ghia and Cleo Capital
by PAUL A. GOMPERS, ANNELENA LOBB, case number 9-221-067 MARCH 30, 2021

MELANIE MASARIN

Masarin grew up in Lyon, France. A city of 1.7 million people,[1] Lyon featured a vivid gastronomic culture. "It [. . .] remains a place singularly obsessed with dining, even by French standards, a city of charcutiers, cooks, butchers, cheese- and fish-mongers, bakers of bread and pastry alike," wrote an observer.[2] Masarin's family frequently hosted guests for meals, and many of her early memories involved her grandmother preparing food and the *aperitivos* common across the Mediterranean region.

In 2008, Masarin moved to the U.S. to attend Brown University. In 2012, she graduated with a degree in economics. After graduation, jobs remained scarce due to the aftermath of the global financial crisis of 2008 to 2009, but she found an internship and an eventual full-time role in Goldman Sachs' investment banking energy group. In 2014, Masarin moved to the strategy group at a Goldman client company, American Eagle Outfitters.

Masarin and her colleagues ordered lunch one day from Dig Inn, a fast-casual farm-to-table restaurant that advertised a healthy menu. After a poor dining experience, they decided to send an email with constructive criticism to the company. By chance, Dig Inn's CEO was reading email feedback that day, and suggested to Masarin that they meet for coffee. In 2014, the CEO offered Masarin a job as director of strategy; ultimately, she assumed a creative director role for Dig Inn, as well.

In 2016, she left Dig Inn to move to a role at Glossier.com, which sold beauty products and makeup. She was hired to open Glossier's offline channel. During the next two years, she helped open Glossier's retail outlets, including the 2018 launch of its flagship store in New York.

Later in 2018, Masarin left Glossier for freelance work, consulting on the offline brand experience of digitally native, vertically integrated brands (e.g., companies that had originated online, rather than at bricks-and-mortar outposts, and that owned or controlled much of their supply chains), such as Sweetgreen, a fast-casual eatery that sold tossed salads and other healthy foods, and StockX, an online platform to buy and sell high-end sneakers, streetwear, and other products.

Masarin had always struggled with health issues around food, but noticed that they had worsened since moving from France to the U.S. "I was foggy, my cognitive function was worse, and I knew it was because of what I ate," she said. On a 2019 trip to Italy, a delicious pasta lunch with a group of friends at a restaurant in Milan led to a conversation about consuming starches and dealing with subsequent fatigue. Masarin and her friends eventually began to talk about their experiences with drinking alcohol; she had stopped drinking alcohol a few years earlier. "I went on a rant about non-alcoholic drinks, how they are all too sweet. Bitter *aperitivos* prime your stomach better, but I wanted one without alcohol," she said. "I began to see an opportunity."

THE *APERITIVO* TRADITION

Aperitivo culture presumably originated in Milan, Italy, though it was widespread through much of the Mediterranean region.[3] The ritual included not only drinking the *aperitivo* itself, but gathering with others at the end of the day to sit, talk, and spend an hour or two unwinding before dinner. A snack, such as nuts or olives, might be served with the *aperitivo*, which was typically a bitter drink, such as a Negroni, or an aromatized wine, such as Vermouth or Lillet. *Aperitivos* often had low alcohol content.[4]

In 2018 and 2019, spritzes (typically, a drink with a bitter liqueur base, topped with sparkling wine and carbonated water over ice) sparked much public enthusiasm in the U.S., in part due to a marketing campaign by the Campari brand.[5] In the summer of 2018, the Aperol spritz, made with Prosecco, Aperol, soda water, and an orange slice, saw its popularity soar, "in line with rising demand for herbal bitter liqueurs, or *amaro*, more generally."[6] The drink assumed its own hashtag on Instagram (#aperolspritzofficial), and members of the press hotly debated its taste and aesthetics.[7]

THE BEVERAGE INDUSTRY

In 2018, the global market for alcohol was valued at roughly $1.47 trillion, and it was expected to grow by almost 19% by 2024, to $1.75 trillion.[8] Carbonated soft drinks, bottled waters, and juices dominated the non-alcoholic beverage space,[9] which analysts expected to reach $1.25 trillion in value by 2020.[10] Forecasts said that U.S. beverage demand would reach $175 billion by 2023, with demand for alcoholic beverages expected to rise to $93.5 billion by 2023.[11] (See **Exhibit 1**.)

Alcohol-free cocktails filled a niche within the non-alcoholic beverage segment, and as such, estimating market size was challenging. According to one estimate, the U.S. market for low- and no-alcohol beverages would increase by 32% between 2018 and 2022.[12]

Drinking Less Alcohol

Many consumers opted to abstain from alcohol or to curtail consumption for reasons including but not limited to alcoholism. "The world, seemingly all at once, has woken up to the possibilities of not drinking," wrote one journalist.[13] In 2019, a group of friends who stopped drinking alcohol and found themselves happier and better off founded The Zero Proof, a website that tracked news and product launches in the alcohol-free drinks space. They also wanted better non-alcoholic options at bars, and products that provided the same level of pleasure as a good beer, wine, or mixed drink.[14] Sober social clubs and sober bars sprang up to build social connections among those not drinking alcohol.[15]

In the U.K., a 2017 government survey showed that 57% of adults (18 years of age and older) had answered 'yes' when asked if they had consumed an alcoholic drink in the past week, compared with 64.2% of adults in 2005, representing a decrease of about three million people.[16] "Not drinking has become as commonplace as arriving at work in sweaty running Lycra—something that once marked you out as a dangerous fitness freak, but now won't garner a second glance," wrote one observer.[17]

Alcohol-free cocktail makers arose to meet demand. In 2015, then-startup Seedlip debuted a non-alcoholic spirit named Seedlip Spice 94 at the upscale department store Selfridges in London. One thousand bottles sold in the first three weeks. Creator Ben Branson used mixtures of distilled botanical ingredients to create non-alcoholic beverages that did not rely on sweet ingredients for flavor or mouthfeel.[18] Branson was raised on a 300-year-old farm about three hours north of London, and wanted to create a company that drew on his roots as a farmer while creating something new. "We use plants to make adult drinks, but we're always thinking about horticulture and nature," he said.[19]

Other players in the space included Kin, an alcohol-free drink that was branded as a 'euphoric.' Kin worked with individual neurochemistry to restore and balance mood and enhance positive feelings. Creator Jen Batchelor envisioned a space in the market for a product with the purpose of stress relief that wasn't medicinal, alcoholic, or toxic. "This is about opening up flow state[a] and finding a new way to revel," said Batchelor. "We don't want to be in meditation or yoga studios. Find us at the bar."[20] (For a select list of alcohol-free drink makers, see **Exhibit 2**.)

Alcohol makers took notice. In 2016, Diageo, a global corporation with a large portfolio of alcohol brands, bought 20% of Seedlip, and by 2019 held a majority stake.[21] AB InBev, the maker of Budweiser, committed

---

a "Flow state" referred to a condition of complete absorption and focus on a particular task, during which the person in the flow state felt at ease and barely noticed the passage of time. Source: "What is a flow state and what are its benefits?" Headspace.com, https://www.headspace.com/articles/flow-state, accessed February 2021.

to increasing low- and no-alcohol beers to 20% of its beer portfolio by 2025.[22] The category was growing, though it was unclear what direction product development trends would take.

ABOUT GHIA

In 2019, Masarin created the first version of Ghia in New York City. She named it Ghia in honor of the Italian automaker Giacinto Ghia, and as an ode to the flow state one experienced when driving a car along a Mediterranean coast. It was not a thrill one could experience properly if intoxicated.

When developing her recipe, Masarin remembered that her grandmother, a keen hostess, would serve alcoholic drinks to guests at home, but would often lower the alcohol content by offering them blends or spritzes. "If my father brought Champagne, she would add crème de cassis," she said. "She used to make jugs of limoncello, using baskets of fresh citrus grown by her neighbor." When designing her alcohol-free *aperitivo*, Masarin considered what beverages people sought when they ate at restaurants, including the recent spritz mania, as well as the desire to drink something dry or bitter before a meal. She read her grandmother's recipe book, looking for tasting notes and flavors.

In April 2019, Masarin hired a formulator who could help her develop a proprietary mixture for Ghia. She interviewed several candidates and chose the person she felt understood the alcohol-free category best. They created a bitter note using the root of gentian, an Alpine flower. Remembering her family's limoncello, she included notes of citrus. They discovered the right formula after testing many batches with friends and acquaintances. "We had hundreds of people try Ghia before it was Ghia; I cooked brunch for them and took their feedback on Post-It notes, again and again." She also designed many drink recipes, including spritzes, using Ghia as their base ingredient.

One writer, who had conducted a taste test of various alcohol-free cocktails, described Ghia as being "for people who really like bitter drinks. I'm talking more bitter than a Negroni, more bitter than Fernet, more bitter than a bad divorce. It's complex, and comes in punching hard."[23]

Masarin envisioned Ghia as the alcohol-free *aperitivo* that chefs found credible. She had relationships with chefs and restaurants in New York City and Los Angeles, California, because of her previous work experiences, networks of friends, and as a result of spending almost a year freelancing from the dining rooms of her favorite establishments. "We wanted to perfectly prepare your stomach for a meal, and felt this would be a key brand differentiator—the ability to order Ghia confidently at restaurants," she said.

She also wanted Ghia to signal that the person imbibing it was living life to the fullest, without a sense of something being out of the ordinary because the person had opted not to drink alcohol. "While new habits, like choosing not to drink alcohol, are formed at home, the social pressure to drink alcohol is strongest on premise (e.g., in restaurants and bars), so we really wanted to be in those settings," Masarin remarked. In restaurants, consumers also could try Ghia without purchasing a full bottle.

From April to November 2019, Masarin bootstrapped (self-financed) the company. The product was made and bottled in the U.S. and distributed by the Ghia team. At the end of 2019, Masarin decided to premier Ghia on April 1, 2020 in restaurants only. By March 2020, she had three employees across operations and community management roles. She needed to invest in packaging, web development, photography, fulfillment, and production to move Ghia forward.

EARLY-STAGE FINANCING

Pre-seed and seed capital were deployed at a company's nascent stages, often to finance basic expenses such as rent, research and development, salaries, and equipment. Banks and venture capitalists were generally more reluctant to provide funding at such early stages because companies lacked track records. As a result, seed financing traditionally came from family and friends. Angel investors, or high-net-worth investors whom the founder contacted through his or her personal and professional networks, could also provide early funds, either through a loan or in return for future equity.[24] Pre-seed rounds typically had few, if any institutional investors who invested smaller sums. A seed round was usually a company's first institutional round, and was typically up to $2 million, while a Series A round, the first large round of venture capital financing, was often up to $30 million.[25]

Yet since 2015, seed rounds had grown and new groups of pre-seed investors had emerged. In addition, companies were often extending the seed stage. "Already seed-funded companies may opt to raise a 'seed-plus' or 'seed extension' round if they're not quite ready to pursue a proper Series A round," one observer wrote. "Most rounds aren't very big, but they are getting bigger."[26] In a study of early-stage financing, the median funding prior to a Series A round rose from $600,000 in 2010 to $3.0 million in 2018, and again to $3.3 million in 2019. Series A rounds also increased, but their average growth rate was more modest than that of seed rounds (see **Exhibit 3**).[27]

Early-stage financing was traditionally structured as a convertible note, a short-term debt vehicle with an interest rate, maturity date, and the opportunity to convert the debt into an equity stake. Conversion usually occurred when the company secured its next financing round and prior to the maturity date.[28] However, in the 2010s, a new financing vehicle emerged and became popular as an early-stage alternative to convertible debt—the Simple Agreement for Future Equity, or SAFE.[29]

A SAFE offered equity stakes in a future priced round to early-stage investors at a discounted rate. A SAFE set a valuation cap for the company, and sometimes a discount rate on the equity stake; these would determine the potential size of an investor's discount. The valuation cap was a ceiling on the share price a SAFE investor would pay in the Series A. A higher valuation cap generally meant more money upfront for the company.[30] Any discount was set on a percentage basis.

A SAFE functioned similarly to a convertible note, but was not a debt instrument. Thus, the startup did not have to concern itself with the potentially complex legal parameters that came with using debt, including managing terms around possible insolvency, or any need to extend loan maturities.[31] In 2013, a partner at startup accelerator Y Combinator had devised the SAFE as an alternative to convertible debt, dubbing it "a replacement that is essentially convertible debt without the debt."[32]

FOOD AND BEVERAGE INVESTMENTS

During the 2010s, private investment in food and beverage companies had jumped as more venture capitalists bet on new brands focused on health and wellness, as well as on new distribution models for food and beverages as consumers moved away from traditional brick-and-mortar shopping channels. (For growth in investment in the beverage industry, see **Exhibit 4**.)

For example, Drizly, a 13-person Boston, Massachusetts-based company focused on home delivery of beer, wine, and spirits, had raised close to $120 million over nine rounds of venture capital funding. In 2021, Uber bought it for $1.1 billion.[33] "The deal comes amid a massive shift in consumer behavior accelerated by the pandemic, as shoppers increasingly turn to delivery apps to fulfill their everyday needs," wrote one observer.[34] In 2020, Oatly, a Swedish oat milk company with a mission to offer plant-based alternatives to meat and dairy, had raised $200 million from Blackstone and some well-known names from the entertainment world, including Oprah Winfrey and Natalie Portman. The investment represented about 10% of Oatly. "Blackstone is the latest high-profile investor to bet on the growing demand for alternative foods," wrote one observer.[35] (For top 10 beverage deals, see **Exhibit** 5.)

GHIA'S EARLY-STAGE FINANCING

At first, Masarin had kept full ownership and control of the company. But she needed to raise additional funds as salary demands and other business needs arose. Masarin began to contact potential angel investors who could invest their own private funds in exchange for potential upside in the business.[36] "I reached out to people whom I knew were successful at raising money," Masarin said. These included Jen Rubio, co-founder of Away luggage; Nicolas Jammet, Nathaniel Ru, and Jonathan Neman, the founders of Sweetgreen; and Emily Weiss, the founder of Glossier. "All wanted to invest; my friends and family round was very natural, and I had interested contacts from Glossier as well."

In October 2019, Masarin engaged in a SAFE round of financing with friends and family, which she considered a pre-seed round. Masarin set the terms of the SAFE round, including the number of investors, company valuation cap, and minimum and maximum investment levels, all without engaging in much negotiation. "We were very lucky that we got to be picky and practically choose who would be in our round. I had a big community to whom I had shown that I could work hard. I think they were choosing to invest in me as a person," she recalled.

Masarin set a valuation cap of $8.5 million[b], with a minimum friends-and-family investment of $10,000 and a maximum of $100,000. She included more than 25 investors. She deliberately raised money across many people to increase word of mouth about Ghia. "It's a joyful brand, made to be shared," she said. "Raising the SAFE round between a number of investors created incredible buzz." She also did not want to worry that she could not share problems with her investors or seek advice from them because just a few people had large sums at stake, another reason why she spread the investment across more than just a handful of people. Her contacts were very responsive, and Masarin raised a SAFE round of $950,000 over six days during October 2019.

While staying at the home of her best friend in New York (who was another investor in Ghia), Masarin met a scout for Cleo Capital. Venture capital scouts sought out entrepreneurs interested in investing in other

b The actual terms of the SAFE note have been disguised

startups, provided them with capital, and shared in any later returns.[37] She recalled:

> My friend had already introduced me to a lot of people and was an investor himself. I had completed something like 60 fundraising meetings in seven days. And I told him, 'I did it, we have all the commitments from investors,' and he said, 'Great,' and then, he added that some people were coming to his home for drinks. One of them was Lauren, who turned out to be a scout for Cleo Capital. She was very excited to put me in touch with Sarah Kunst, and asked if I would consider just one more meeting.

Ghia had scout funds in the round from Index Ventures, because the ex-CFO and CTO of Glossier, early investors in Ghia, were also scouts for Index. Masarin gladly accepted the meeting with Kunst. In November, they agreed that Kunst would invest another $25,000 in Ghia via the SAFE. Masarin initially planned to raise $650,000 through the SAFE, but the round was oversubscribed, and she increased the targeted total to include more investors, such as Kunst. All of the funds Masarin had raised were meant to last until Ghia's launch in restaurants. After the proposed April 2020 launch, Masarin hoped to raise an institutional-level seed round of approximately $2 million.

SARAH KUNST AND CLEO CAPITAL

Kunst was the managing director of Cleo Capital (Cleo), a San Francisco, California-based pre-seed and seed-stage venture capital fund. In 2008, Kunst graduated from Michigan State University and begun her career in luxury marketing at Chanel. But she moved to startup work and "never looked back," she said. In 2018, Kunst founded Cleo with $3 million. Kunst had worked previously as a scout for Sequoia Capital, a Menlo Park, California-based trillion-dollar venture capital fund, and as a startup executive. She was a senior advisor in the corporate venture capital group of the Bumble Fund.

At Sequoia, most of the scouts were men. Kunst noted that lack of gender and racial diversity among venture capitalists contributed to lack of funding for startups run by founders who were not white and male. "One of the biggest indicators of anyone potentially getting funded is whether or not the investors they're talking to look like them in a literal sense," she said.[38] A 2019 survey showed that women held 9.5% of decision-making roles in venture capital firms, or 105 decision-makers out of a total 1,088.[39] White men invested 63% of venture capital dollars from 2010 to 2020;

white women, 5.5%; Latinx men and women, 4% and 1%; and Black men and women, 0.1% and 0.0%, respectively.

Kunst, a Black woman, described her fund as a response to two systemic issues in venture capital. "One was the lack of diversity—gender, race, all of it—and another was that when you, as an early-stage entrepreneur, went to raise startup capital, it was hard to get a full round. Most funds write you checks of $100,000 to $250,000, which is fine, but you still have to go out and raise another half a million to one million dollars, which takes a long time. I started Cleo to fix those problems," she said.

Kunst hired women as scouts for Cleo. As in other scout programs, their job was to find new companies worthy of early-stage funding. Cleo had six to seven scouts at a time, though this number fluctuated. Kunst hired women as a practical rather than a symbolic move. Female entrepreneurs tended to have large, untouched networks of contacts, a tantalizing untapped market.[40]

CLEO CAPITAL AND GHIA

Kunst knew that Masarin had worked for mutual friends and had a strong professional reputation. She noted, "One of my scouts talked to [Masarin] and said, 'Cleo is interesting, you should look at taking money from them.'" Masarin knew that Kunst was an experienced venture capitalist and potential mentor, and that finding mentors in venture capital who were women or people of color was very challenging. "I had a strong focus on diversity; this was very important to me," Masarin said.

At Cleo, the team used the thesis of the complicated consumer to select companies. Kunst said:

> We invest broadly. Cleo is a generalist fund, and one way we think about the world is through the thesis of the complicated consumer. There are things in your life that are easy to buy. Do you want to buy a new lipstick? That doesn't take much thought. Those areas are overserviced; lots of people invest in 'easy' products. But some areas are harder. Servicing the trend to drink less, or to have a different relationship with alcohol—the obvious answer is just not to drink alcohol, but as anyone who has been to a bar for a birthday and had to drink water or Diet Coke can tell you, it can be a sensitive topic. Ghia is something you can have without providing that explanation for people as to why you are not drinking or drinking less; Ghia fits our complicated consumer thesis.

After Cleo's investment in Ghia, Kunst and Masarin were in touch approximately once a month to discuss the progress of the business. Kunst saw herself as an extension of Masarin's team rather than an overarching figure or manager to whom Masarin was responsible. Kunst said:

> We've stayed hands-on, and we have spent time making strategic introductions for Ghia. But it's less about any specific thing that you do as a venture capital investor. To best help an early-stage founder, you see yourself as a continuation of their team; you help them with whatever they need help with. If you are in a different city, and she calls, and says, 'Hey, I need help moving some Ghia, would you go pick it up?' then you do that, and if she asks for help evaluating a term sheet from another potential investor, then you do that. What isn't helpful is an investor constantly reaching out, thinking they have a great new idea to help, which isn't what the company is focused on at the time.

A DELAY AND A PIVOT

After the first three months of 2020, it became obvious that the Covid-19 pandemic would prompt a massive pivot for Ghia given closures of restaurants, bars, and other establishments. Widespread shutdowns began just as Ghia's April 1 launch date loomed on the horizon. In New York, event cancellations began in early March 2020, and by mid-March, Governor Andrew Cuomo shut indoor dining, though he allowed take-out and delivery of alcoholic cocktails, if sold with food.[41]

Masarin pushed Ghia's launch date to June 2, 2020, and the team focused on orders and direct-to-consumer shipments, posting the phrase "Glass Half Full" on the company's Instagram account and keeping a positive attitude about the business. "We were even unable to go to our warehouse because of the coronavirus, but we took over a closed-down restaurant and built our own warehouse, shipping orders ourselves from there," Masarin recalled.

The company encountered many hurdles as a result of the pandemic, including a delay in a delivery of bottles that were stuck in Italy, an early epicenter of the virus. A factory with which Masarin had contracted shifted its operations to manufacture hand sanitizer, suddenly a high-demand product.

On June 2, Masarin again delayed Ghia's launch as protests occurred throughout the U.S. following the death of George Floyd, a Black man killed by a white police officer in Minneapolis, Minnesota. When she arrived at their restaurant-factory the next day, "the entire street had been burned down," Masarin recalled.

Ghia finally launched on June 16, selling $13,000 of product on its first day and shipping to buyers in 32 different states. Protests had led to widespread calls to address systemic racism, including greater support for

Black business owners. "We lost all of our press. I wasn't a Black founder, and that was the focus, understandably so. But people were still cheering for us. On our Instagram, they had seen us build this thing from nothing," Masarin said. (For sales over time, see **Exhibit 6**.)

Early-stage investors had invested in Ghia as first positioned—e.g., as a brand for launch in restaurants. While the temporary loss of on-premise sales was unfortunate, because they enhanced brand recognition, Ghia's largest expected revenue stream was from retail sales. Kunst reflected:

> You learn about a brand by name on premise, but ultimately, you're not going to order more than three of them at dinner. That's not to downplay the total sum you might sell at restaurants and bars, but ultimately, what will drive sales is then seeing Ghia at a store, where you might buy a bottle to keep at home; or maybe you buy a bottle for a friend, or you even serve some to a friend in your own home, which continues that feedback loop.

Pivoting to direct-to-consumer sales had shifted focus to unexpected areas such as packaging and shipping rates. Thus, Masarin needed more financing in the summer of 2020, much sooner than she had expected. "We definitely got to five digits on the bank account, and that felt really uncomfortable," she recalled. "There was a lot of burn associated with having to delay our launch. That money got us through the formula development, ordering all of the bottles, finding a co-packer, ramping up from small batches to bigger batches, and running taste tests with the small batches." Though the summer of 2020 brought some respite from the pandemic, it was unclear how the winter of 2020-2021 would unfold, how long the pandemic would last, or whether Ghia would need to shift gears again.

FINANCING ALTERNATIVES

One possibility was to raise more money under the terms of the SAFE round (see **Exhibit 7**). Masarin had investors who had wanted to enter the previous round of financing, but could not, and existing investors who were interested in investing more. "You can be better off waiting if you don't absolutely need a round of venture capital," Kunst said. If Masarin chose this path, she would have to raise institutional seed capital later. Kunst added:

> If you wait, you can go out and raise a bit later with a bit more velocity. It could be a better raise, as you start to come out of the

> pandemic. Ghia has all of these relationships, events they were planning, they wanted to get in front of people and have them sample it. For a lot of investors, that can drive the feeling that the company is moving quickly, and that they can invest immediately, or they will miss it. The direct-to-consumer part and store sales are going really well, but the flashy, on-premise part can drive a lot of investor feelings of missing out, get them in a rush to move faster, and that never hurts.

Another option was to formally seek out an institutional seed round. "We are a team of three, and I do all of the marketing, so I would have to take myself out of that role for a month to fundraise," Masarin said. "But we were also getting to the point where we really needed to have more of a cushion and capital to invest in growth, not just day-to-day operations." She began to put an investor deck together for potential pitches to funds (see **Exhibit 8**). Masarin knew that approaching venture capital funds would be time-consuming. Although sales were growing weekly, she was working 18-hour days and was still freelancing for Sweetgreen, because she was taking a very low salary at Ghia.

Masarin had to decide whether to re-open the SAFE round, and raise a smaller sum to keep the business stable as the pandemic progressed and eventually faded; or to showcase her business to venture capital funds in efforts to raise a larger cushion. What was her best option to raise new capital?

NOTES

1 "Lyon, France Metro Area Population 1950-2021," Macrotrends, http://bit.ly/3uvCsGP, accessed January 2021.
2 Brett Martin, "Lyon is the Real Capital of French Food," *GQ*, March 12, 2018, http://bit.ly/2NFUO7d, accessed January 2021.
3 Emma Cooke, "The History and Etiquette of the Italian Aperitivo," *The Telegraph*, August 28, 2019, https://bit.ly/3pU3wMg, accessed February 2021.
4 Michael McNulty, "Unraveling Italian Culture: What is Aperitivo?" *DoTravel Mag*, September 6, 2018, http://bit.ly/3qWz0CG, accessed January 2021.
5 Tariro Mzezewa, "There's a Reason You're Drinking So Much Aperol Spritz," *New York Times*, July 17, 2018, http://nyti.ms/3uFBHLx, accessed January 2021.
6 Mzezewa, "There's a Reason You're Drinking So Much Aperol Spritz."
7 "'The New York Times' Sets Off Debate Over Aperol Spritz," NPR, May 10, 2019, http://n.pr/3dYSGm7, accessed January 2021.
8 "Size of the Alcoholic Beverage Market Worldwide from 2018 to 2024," Statista, December 2019, https://bit.ly/3bDzHdU, accessed January 2021.

9 Jan Conway, "Non-Alcoholic Beverages and Soft Drinks in the United States," Statista, May 2019, https://www.statista.com/topics/1662/non-alcoholic-beverages-and-soft-drinks-in-the-us/, accessed January 2021.
10 Report Overview, "Non-Alcoholic Drinks Market Size," Grandview Research, http://bit.ly/2NXLwn8, accessed January 2021.
11 "Beverages: United States," Freedonia Focus Reports, U.S. Collection, January 2020, accessed January 2021.
12 Julia Bainbridge, "Big Alcohol is Bracing for a More Sober Future," *Bon Appetit*, March 20, 2019, http://bit.ly/37LOVwn, accessed January 2021.
13 Rachel Sugar, "My Intrepid Quest for a Non-Alcoholic Cocktail I Actually Want to Drink," *Bon Appetit*, April 18, 2019, http://bit.ly/37NqBdi, accessed January 2021.
14 The Zero Proof, "About," http://bit.ly/2NwX8O8, accessed January 2021.
15 April Fulton, Allison Aubrey, "Breaking the Booze Habit, Even Briefly, Has its Benefits," NPR, June 23, 2019, http://n.pr/3qTzgCw, accessed January 2021.
16 Harry Wallop, "I'll Have a Nogroni: the rise of the no-alcohol drink," *The Times*, August 6, 2018, via Factiva, accessed January 2021.
17 Wallop, "I'll Have a Nogroni: the rise of the no-alcohol drink."
18 Seedlip Drinks, "Our Story," http://bit.ly/2ZQ81No, accessed January 2021.
19 Esha Chhabra, "Why an Alcohol Giant Funded This Non-Alcoholic Startup Turning Peas into Spirits," *Forbes*, September 28, 2018, http://bit.ly/3aVwcjY, accessed January 2021.
20 Corey Seymour, "I Tried Kin, The New Non-Alcoholic Drink That Promises to Cut Stress and Produce Bliss," *Vogue*, December 5, 2018, http://bit.ly/3bFxH4F, accessed January 2021.
21 Rob Davies, "Diageo Buys Majority Stake in Non-Alcoholic Spirit Seedlip," *The Guardian*, August 7, 2019, http://bit.ly/3qWsWtZ, accessed January 2021.
22 Bainbridge, "Big Alcohol is Bracing for a More Sober Future."
23 M. Carrie Allan, "Zero Proof Can be Good All Year Long," *The Washington Post*, January 13, 2021, via Factiva, accessed January 2021.
24 Carol M. Kopp, "Seed Capital," Investopedia, November 19, 2020, http://bit.ly/2ZSfVWo, accessed February 2021.
25 "Glossary of Funding Types," Crunchbase, http://bit.ly/3pVXpHc, accessed February 2021.
26 Jason D. Rowley, "It's Not Just You, Seed Rounds are Actually Getting Bigger," Crunchbase, February 27, 2020, http://bit.ly/3pWqPVP, accessed February 2021.
27 Peter Wagner, "Seed is the New A—But What's Next?" Wing Venture Capital, April 2, 2020, https://bit.ly/3qYKkyu, accessed February 2021.
28 Michael Nieto, "How to Structure Your Seed Round Financing," Medium, June 4, 2018, http://bit.ly/2O1rlV4, accessed February 2021.
29 Nieto, "How to Structure Your Seed Round Financing."
30 "SAFE Financings Explained Line by Line," PNW Startup Lawyer, September 5, 2017, http://bit.ly/2Msk6Fu, accessed January 2021.
31 "SAFE Primer," FundersClub, http://bit.ly/2NvefzP, accessed January 2021.

32 Paul Graham, "Announcing the SAFE, a Replacement for Convertible Notes," Y Combinator, December 6, 2013, http://bit.ly/3sqNRFZ, accessed January 2021.
33 "Uber," Crunchbase, https://bit.ly/3aTG65p, accessed February 2021.
34 Anissa Gardizy and Janelle Nanos, "Uber buys Boston-based alcohol delivery service Drizly for $1.1 billion," *Boston Globe*, February 2, 2021, http://bit.ly/3qTAuxC, accessed February 2021.
35 Ben Dummett, Miriam Gottfried and Juliet Chung, "Oat-Milk Company Oatly Draws Investment from Blackstone-Led Group Including Oprah," *The Wall Street Journal*, July 14, 2020, http://on.wsj.com/3pVY77k, accessed February 2021.
36 William Kerr, Ramana Nanda, and James McQuade, "Financing Entrepreneurial Ventures," HBS No. 8072, (Boston, MA: Harvard Business Publishing, 2014).
37 Connie Loizos, "A Peek Inside Sequoia Capital's Low-Flying, Wide-Reaching Scout Program," TechCrunch, June 7, 2019, http://tcrn.ch/37JBtsz, accessed February 2021.
38 Ineye Komonibo, "Sarah Kunst's New Venture Capital Fund Invests in Female Entrepreneurship," *Marie Claire*, August 19, 2019, http://bit.ly/2MolMj9, accessed February 2021.
39 Dan Primack, "Venture Capital is Still Very Much a Boys' Club," Axios.com, February 14, 2019, http://bit.ly/37MXxCU, accessed February 2021.
40 Komonibo, "Sarah Kunst's New Venture Capital Fund Invests in Female Entrepreneurship."
41 Tanay Warerkar, "A Timeline of Covid-19's Impact on NYC's Restaurant Industry," Eater, December 30, 2020, https://bit.ly/3bDbmot, accessed January 2021.

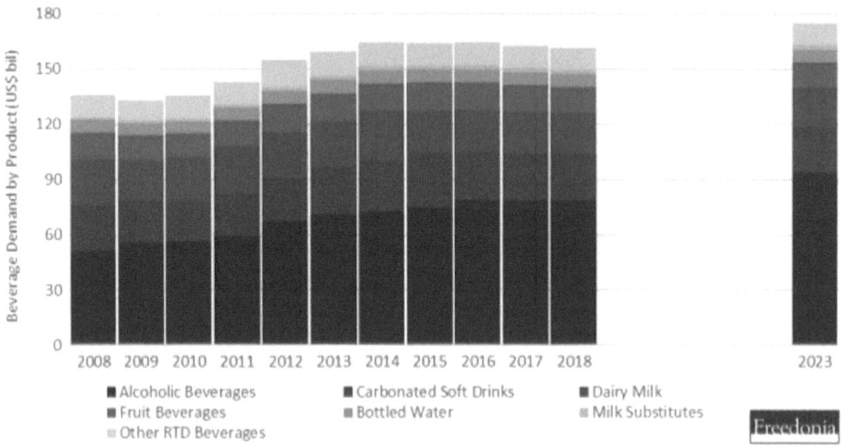

EXHIBIT 1 U.S. Beverage Demand by Product, 2008-2023
Source: "Beverages: United States," The Freedonia Group, January 2020, www.freedoniafocusreports.com, pg. 17, accessed February 2021.

EXHIBIT 2 Select Alcohol-Free Drinks

Name	Description	Launch Date	Created By	Price
Ghia	Alcohol-free bitter spirit with citrus flavors, meant for use in cocktails and social settings	2020	Melanie Masarin	$33 for 535ml
Seedlip	Three alcohol-free spirits, Garden 108, Grove 42, and Spice 94, with herbal and other flavors	2015	Ben Branson	$32 for 700ml
Kin Euphorics	'Euphorics' with mood-elevating effects, including Kin Spritz, High Rhode, and Dream Light	2018	Jen Batchelor	$39 for 500ml
Monday Gin	Alcohol-free gin meant as the base for gin cocktails (G&T, etc.).	2020	Chris Boyd	$39.99 for 750ml
Ritual Zero Proof	Alcohol-free whiskey and gin alternatives	2020	Marcus Sakey, GG Sakey, David Crooch	$26.99 for 750ml

Source: Compiled by casewriter from company websites; Chris Morris, "Just in Time for Dry January: No-Alcohol Whiskey and Gin Alternatives," *Fortune*, January 6, 2020, http://bit.ly/3dShQ5P, accessed January 2021; and Ghia, "Ghia," http://bit.ly/3dLGsNx; Republic.co, "Drink Monday," http://bit.ly/3smtvNW; Drink Monday, "Monday Zero Alcohol Gin," http://bit.ly/3pUkkmj; Seedlip Drinks, "Shop," http://bit.ly/2ZSbPhg; Kin Euphorics, "Products," http://bit.ly/3dIvokd; Ritual Zero Proof, "Products," http://bit.ly/3aTDIvt; all accessed February 2021.

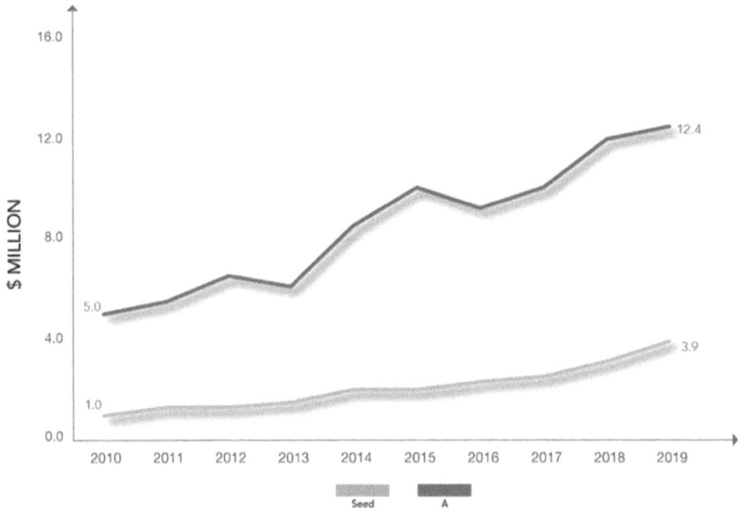

EXHIBIT 3 Early-Stage Financing Sizes, 2010-2019
Source: Peter Wagner, "Seed is the New A—But What's Next?" Wing Venture Capital, April 2, 2020, http://bit.ly/3qYKkyu, accessed February 2021.

EXHIBIT 4 Beverage Private Equity Deals by Announced Year

Announced Year	Number of Deals	Transaction Value (in millions USD)	Announced Year	Number of Deals	Transaction Value (in millions USD)
2000	20	$214.40	2012	213	$1,537.40
2001	17	$70.99	2013	234	$1,153.86
2002	22	$273.37	2014	249	$3,913.53
2003	20	$794.79	2015	268	$4,027.25
2004	33	$175.46	2016	272	$1,261.29
2005	47	$369.79	2017	268	$9,163.88
2006	66	$391.59	2018	319	$4,877.41
2007	79	$718.92	2019	313	$1,598.00
2008	68	$591.47	2020	367	$1,845.85
2009	100	$2,222.76	2021	35 (YTD)	$117.21
2010	157	$1,527.50	**Grand Total**	**3347**	**$41,455.02**
2011	180	$4,608.31			

Source: Capital IQ, a division of Standard & Poor's, accessed February2021.

EXHIBIT 5 Top 10 Deals by Dollar Amount in Beverage Industry, 2000-2021

Year	Target Company	Transaction Type	Total Value	Buyers/Investors
2018	CRH (Beer) Ltd.	Venture Capital	$3,102.35	Heineken N.V.
2017	International Beverage Holdings Ltd.	Growth Capital/ Private Equity	$3,017.81	Thai Beverage Public Company Ltd.
2017	BeerCo Ltd.	Venture Capital	$2,275.33	International Beverage Holdings Ltd.
2011	Anadolu Efes Biracilik ve Malt Sanayii Anonim Sirketi	PIPE	$1,900.00	ABI SAB Group Holding Ltd.
2014	Keurig Dr. Pepper Inc.	PIPE	$1,250.98	Atlantic Industries Ltd.
2009	CEDC Finance Corp. Intl.	Venture Capital	$941.88	-
2015	International Beverage Holdings Ltd.	Growth Capital/ Private Equity	$893.31	Thai Beverage Public Company Ltd.
2017	Coca-Cola Southwest Beverages, LLC	Venture Capital	$800.0	-
2017	International Beverage Holdings (Singapore) Ltd.	Growth Capital/ Private Equity	$720.0	Thai Beverage Public Company Ltd.
2017	International Beverage Holdings Ltd.	Growth Capital/ Private Equity	$717.44	Thai Beverage Public Company Ltd.

Source: Capital IQ, a division of Standard & Poor's, accessed February 2021.

EXHIBIT 6 Sales Snapshot, Ghia, 2020

	June 16-June 30	July	August	September	October	Nov. 1-Nov. 28	Launch to Date
On Premise	$900	$100	$2,400	$1,650	$1,050	$3,750	$9,850
Retail	$550	$2,250	$1,700	$6,500	$2,050	$47,650	$60,700
DTC	$59,000	$54,000	$121,700	$107,300	$86,400	$125,750	$554,150
Gross Sales	$60,450	$56,350	$125,800	$115,450	$89,500	$177,150	$624,700
Net Sales	$54,300	$51,630	$116,400	$107,750	$83,200	$166,300	$579,580
Projected Sales	$52,000	$60,000	$75,000	$75,000	$70,000	$110,000	$442,000
Actual vs. Projected	16%	-6%	68%	54%	29%	61%	41%
On Premise Accounts	7	8	15	24	30	37	37
Retail Accounts	1	6	10	15	39	120	120

Source: Company documents.
Note: Figures through November 28, 2020. Figures have been disguised.

EXHIBIT 7 Pre-Seed SAFE Agreement

THIS INSTRUMENT AND THE SECURITIES ISSUABLE PURSUANT HERETO HAVE NOT BEEN REGISTERED UNDER THE SECURITIES ACT OF 1933, AS AMENDED, OR THE SECURITIES LAWS OF ANY STATE. THEY MAY NOT BE SOLD, OFFERED FOR SALE, PLEDGED OR HYPOTHECATED IN THE ABSENCE OF A REGISTRATION STATEMENT IN EFFECT WITH RESPECT TO THE SECURITIES UNDER SUCH ACT AND/OR APPLICABLE STATE SECURITIES LAWS, OR AN OPINION OF COUNSEL SATISFACTORY TO THE COMPANY THAT SUCH REGISTRATION IS NOT REQUIRED OR UNLESS SOLD PURSUANT TO RULE 144 OF SUCH ACT.

MYMO INC. SIMPLE AGREEMENT FOR FUTURE EQUITY

THIS SIMPLE AGREEMENT FOR FUTURE EQUITY (the "SAFE") CERTIFIES THAT in exchange for the payment by [ ] (the "Investor") of $[ ] (the "Purchase Amount") on [ ], 2019, Mymo Inc., a Delaware corporation (the "Company"), hereby issues to the Investor the right to certain of the Company's capital stock, subject to the terms set forth below. The Investor acknowledges that this SAFE is one of series of simple agreements for future equity of like tenor (collectively, the "SAFEs") being issued by the Company to raise interim financing of up to $1,000,000. The following is a statement of the rights of the Investor and the conditions to which this SAFE is subject, to which the Investor, by the acceptance of this SAFE, agrees:

Section 1. Certain Definitions.

1.1 "Change of Control" means a change in ownership or control of the Company effected through any of the following transactions: (a) a merger, consolidation or other reorganization approved by the Company's Board of Directors (the "Board") and stockholders, unless shares representing more than 50% of the total combined voting power of the voting stock of the successor entity or its direct or indirect parent entity are immediately thereafter beneficially owned, directly or indirectly and in substantially the same proportion, by the persons who beneficially owned the Company's outstanding voting stock immediately prior to such transaction; (b) a stockholder-approved sale, transfer or other disposition of all or substantially all of the Company's assets in liquidation or dissolution of the Company; or (c) the acquisition, directly or indirectly by any person or related group of persons (other than the Company or a person that directly

EXHIBIT 7 *(continued)*

or indirectly controls, is controlled by, or is under common control with, the Company), of beneficial ownership (within the meaning of Rule 13d-3 of the Securities Exchange Act of 1934, as amended) of securities possessing more than 50% of the total combined voting power of the Company's outstanding shares pursuant to a stock purchase transaction or a tender or exchange offer made directly to the Company's stockholders.

1.2 "Conversion Price" equals the quotient resulting from dividing (a) the Valuation Cap by (b) the Fully-Diluted Capitalization immediately prior to the closing of the Qualified Financing.

1.3 "Conversion Shares" means shares with identical rights, privileges, preferences, and restrictions as the Qualified Financing Shares issued to new investors in a Qualified Financing, other than (a) the per share liquidation preference, which will be equal to (i) the Conversion Price at which this SAFE is converted, multiplied by (ii) any liquidation preference multiple granted to the Qualified Financing Shares (i.e., 1X, 2X, etc. of the purchase price), (b) the conversion price for purposes of price-based anti-dilution protection, which will equal the Conversion Price, and (c) the basis for any dividend rights, which will be based on the Conversion Price.

1.4 "Dissolution Event" means (a) a voluntary termination of operations, (b) a general assignment for the benefit of the Company's creditors, or (c) any other liquidation, dissolution or winding up of the Company (excluding a Liquidity Event (as defined below)), whether voluntary or involuntary.

1.5 "Excluded Issuance" means the issuance of (a) debt instruments that are convertible or exercisable for capital stock of the Company to investors in bona fide financing transactions; (b) shares issued upon the conversion or exercise of convertible or exercisable securities or other rights to purchase the Company's capital stock outstanding as of the date of this SAFE; (c) shares issued as a dividend or distribution to stockholders of the Company; (d) securities issued to the Company's or any subsidiary's officers, directors, employees, consultants, advisors, placement agents and other service providers as compensation for services, pursuant to equity grants, agreements, equity option plans, equity purchase plans, or other incentive programs or similar arrangements approved by the Board; (e) securities issued to banks, savings and loan associations, equipment lessors or other similar lending institutions pursuant to commercial credit arrangements, equipment financings, commercial property lease transactions, or similar transactions approved by the Board; (f) securities issued pursuant to bona fide business or technology acquisitions (or licenses) by the Company, whether by merger, consolidation, sale of assets,

EXHIBIT 7 *(continued)*

sale or exchange of equity, reorganization or otherwise, which are approved by the Board; (g) securities issued pursuant to or in connection with sponsored research, collaboration, technology license, development, OEM, supply, marketing or other similar agreements or strategic partnerships approved by the Board; and (h) any right, option or warrant to acquire any security convertible into or exercisable for the securities listed in clauses (a) through (g) above.

1.6 "Fully-Diluted Capitalization" means, as of immediately prior to the conversion of this SAFE, the sum of (i) the outstanding shares of capital stock of the Company (on an as-converted to common stock basis); (ii) the shares of capital stock of the Company directly or indirectly issuable upon conversion or exchange of all outstanding securities directly or indirectly convertible into or exchangeable for capital stock of the Company and the exercise of all outstanding options and warrants; and (iii) the shares of capital stock the Company reserved, but neither issued nor the subject of outstanding awards, under any equity incentive or similar plan of the Company; provided that the Fully-Diluted Capitalization shall not include (x) the SAFEs and the securities directly or indirectly issuable upon conversion or exchange of the SAFEs, and (y) other outstanding convertible promissory notes or other convertible securities issued for capital raising purposes and the securities directly or indirectly issuable upon conversion or exchange of such other outstanding convertible securities.

1.7 "Initial Public Offering" means the closing of the Company's first firm commitment underwritten initial public offering of the Company's common stock, par value $0.0001 per share (the "Common Stock"), pursuant to a registration statement filed under the Securities Act.

1.8 "Investors" means all purchasers of the SAFEs.

1.9 "Liquidity Event" means a Change of Control or an Initial Public Offering.

1.10 "Majority Investors" means the holders of at least 50% of the aggregate purchase amount of all SAFEs.

1.11 "Qualified Financing" means the next transaction (or series of related transactions) after the date of this SAFE in which the Company issues and sells capital stock of the Company in exchange for aggregate gross proceeds of at least $2,500,000 (excluding proceeds received under the SAFEs); provided, however, that any Excluded Issuance shall not be included in nor constitute a Qualified Financing.

1.12 "Qualified Financing Shares" means the stock issued by the Company in a Qualified Financing, together with all associated rights, preferences, privileges, and restrictions, contractual or otherwise.

1.13 "Valuation Cap" means $8,500,000.

EXHIBIT 7 (*continued*)

Section 2. Qualified Financing.

2.1 Closing of Qualified Financing. Upon the closing of a Qualified Financing, the Company will issue to the Investor that number of shares of Conversion Shares calculated by dividing (a) the Purchase Amount by (b) the Conversion Price.

2.2 Qualified Financing Procedure. The Investor acknowledges that it will be required to execute certain agreements relating to the purchase and sale of the Conversion Shares, as well as registration rights, rights of first refusal and co-sale, rights of first offer and voting rights, if any, relating to such Conversion Shares (the "Qualified Financing Documents"), and that such Qualified Financing Documents are anticipated to contain significant restrictions on transfer in respect of the Conversion Shares. The Investor agrees to execute all of the Qualified Financing Documents in connection with the Qualified Financing.

2.3 Fractional Shares; Effect of Issuance. At the Company's election, no fractional share representing a fraction of a share shall be issued to the Investor at the Qualified Financing. With respect to any fraction of a share called for upon the issuance of the Conversion Shares, such fractional share, at the Company's election, shall be rounded down to the nearest whole share, and the Company shall pay to the Investor the amount of such fractional share multiplied by the applicable Conversion Price.

Section 3. Liquidity Event. Notwithstanding any other provision of this SAFE, if a Liquidity Event occurs prior to a Qualified Financing or the expiration or termination of this SAFE, then the Majority Investors may, on behalf of all Investors, elect in writing to the Company either to (a) convert the SAFE into that number of shares of Common Stock determined by dividing the (i) Purchase Amount by (ii) the fair market value of a single share of Common Stock as determined by the Board or (b) be paid the Purchase Amount in cash, and the SAFE shall thereafter be cancelled and be of no further force or effect, whether or not delivered to the Company for cancellation. Any such election must be received by the Company at least 30 days prior to the closing date of the Liquidity Event. If the Majority Investors do not make such timely election, then the company shall elect to treat the SAFE in the method of its sole discretion as between the options set forth in this Section 3.

EXHIBIT 7 *(continued)*

Section 4. Dissolution Event. Notwithstanding any other provision of this SAFE, if a Dissolution Event occurs prior to a Qualified Financing or the expiration or termination of this SAFE, the Company will pay an amount equal to the Purchase Amount, due and payable to the Investor immediately prior to, or concurrent with, the consummation of the Dissolution Event. The Purchase Amount will be paid prior and in preference to any distribution of any of the assets of the Company to holders of outstanding shares by reason of their ownership thereof. If immediately prior to the consummation of the Dissolution Event, the assets of the Company legally available for distribution to the Investors, as determined in good faith by the Board, are insufficient to permit the payment to the Investors of their respective Purchase Amounts, then the entire assets of the Company legally available for distribution will be distributed with equal priority and pro rata among the Investors in proportion to the Purchase Amounts they would otherwise be entitled to receive pursuant to this Section 4.

Section 5. Company Repurchase. Immediately upon the Investor's commission of any act which (a) brings the Investor, the Company or its officers, directors, employees or customers (the "Company Group") into public disrepute, scandal, contempt or ridicule or which shocks, insults or offends a substantial portion or group of the community or reflects unfavorably on the Investor or the Company Group or (b) disparages the business integrity of the Company Group and materially and adversely affects the business reputation of the Company, the Company shall have the option to pay an amount equal to the Purchase Amount to the Investor (a "Repurchase Event").

Section 6. Power of Attorney. By execution and delivery of this SAFE, the Investor hereby irrevocably constitutes, appoints, and confirms the Company or its designee and (if other than the Company) any liquidator as the Investor's true and lawful attorney-in-fact with full power and authority in the Investor's name, place and stead:

(a) To sign, execute, certify, swear to, acknowledge, file and record the Qualified Financing Documents, as applicable, and any other agreement or document that the Boards deem in good faith to be necessary or desirable for the Investor to execute in connection with the Qualified Financing, Liquidity Event or Dissolution Event, as applicable, and any amendments, restatements, supplements or other modifications to any of the foregoing; and any such other documents as may be necessary to complete the transactions described herein; and

EXHIBIT 7 *(continued)*

(b) To sign, execute, certify, swear to, acknowledge, file and record any other certificates, instruments and documents, or amendments thereto, which may be required of the Company or of its stockholders (or the holders of its securities) under any applicable laws or governmental agency or which the Company or such liquidator deems necessary or advisable. The power of attorney granted and confirmed pursuant to this Section 6 shall be deemed to be an irrevocable power coupled with an interest, and such power of attorney shall survive, and not be affected by, the subsequent bankruptcy, death, incapacity, disability, adjudication of incompetence or insanity, liquidation, or dissolution of the Investor (as applicable), or the subsequent transfer of all or any portion of the Investor's investment in the Company.

Section 7. Termination. This SAFE will expire and terminate (without relieving the Company of any obligations arising from a prior breach of or non-compliance with this instrument) upon either (a) the issuance of Company shares to the Investor pursuant to Section 2.1 or (b) the payment, or setting aside for payment, of amounts due to the Investor pursuant to Section 3 or Section 4, provided that Section 6 shall survive the termination of this SAFE.

Section 8. Representations of Investor. The Investor acknowledges, agrees, represents and warrants to the Company as of the date hereof that:

8.1 Organization; Good Standing. If the Investor is an entity, the Investor is duly organized, validly existing and in good standing under the laws of the state of its formation. The Investor has the requisite power and authority (and, if an individual, the capacity) to execute and deliver the SAFE and to perform its obligations thereunder. The SAFE, when executed and delivered by the Investor, shall constitute valid and binding obligations of the Investor, enforceable in accordance with its terms, except (a) as limited by laws of general application relating to bankruptcy, insolvency and the relief of debtors and (b) as limited by rules of law governing specific performance, injunctive relief or other equitable remedies and by general principles of equity.

8.2 Accredited Investor. The Investor is an "accredited investor" within the meaning of Rule 501 of Regulation D prescribed by the U.S. Securities and Exchange Commission (the "SEC") pursuant to the Securities Act of 1933, as amended (the "Securities Act"), as such rule is presently in effect. If an entity, the Investor has not been organized for the specific purpose of entering into this SAFE or acquiring the Conversion Shares.

EXHIBIT 7 *(continued)*

8.3 Purchase Entirely for Own Account. This SAFE is issued in reliance upon the Investor's representation to the Company that the Conversion Shares are acquired for investment for the Investor's own account, not as a nominee or agent, and not with a view to the resale or distribution of any part thereof, and that the Investor has no present intention of selling, granting any participation in, or otherwise distributing the same. The Investor does not have any contract, undertaking, agreement or arrangement with any person to sell, transfer or grant participations to such person or to any third person with respect to the Conversion Shares.

8.4 Investment Experience. The Investor is an investor in securities of companies in the development stage and acknowledges that it is able to fend for itself, can bear the economic risk of its investment and has such knowledge and experience in financial or business matters that it is capable of evaluating the merits and risks of the investment in the Conversion Shares.

8.5 Investment Intent. The Investor is acquiring the Conversion Shares for investment for Investor's own account and not with a view to, or for resale in connection with, any distribution thereof. The Investor understands that the Conversion Shares have not been registered under the Securities Act by reason of a specific exemption from the registration provisions of the Securities Act that depends upon, among other things, the bona fide nature of the investment intent as expressed herein.

8.6 Rule 144. The Investor acknowledges that the Conversion Shares must be held indefinitely unless subsequently registered under the Securities Act or unless an exemption from such registration is available. The Investor is aware of the provisions of Rule 144 promulgated under the Securities Act which permits limited resale of securities purchased in a private placement subject to the satisfaction of certain conditions.

8.7 Information. The Investor has received all the information it considers necessary or appropriate for deciding whether to purchase the Conversion Shares. The Investor has had an opportunity to ask questions and receive answers from the Company regarding the terms and conditions of the offering of the Conversion Shares and the business, prospects and financial condition of the Company. The Investor confirms that the Company has not given any guarantee or representation as to the potential success, return, effect or benefit (either legal, regulatory, tax, financial, accounting or otherwise) of an investment in the Conversion Shares.

EXHIBIT 7 (*continued*)

8.8 Residency. In the case of an Investor who is an individual, the state of the Investor's residency, or, in the case of an Investor that is a corporation, partnership or other entity, the state of the Investor's principal place of business, is correctly set forth on the signature page to this SAFE.

8.9 Tax and Legal Advice. The Investor is not relying on nor has relied on the Company or any of the Company's officers, directors, stockholders, representatives, agents, counsel or advisers, for any advice, including any financial, tax or legal advice in connection with the transactions contemplated by this SAFE and the associated Conversion Shares. The Investor has had an opportunity to consult with its legal counsel and tax and other advisers regarding this SAFE and associated Conversion Shares. The Investor understands no federal or state agency has passed upon the merits or risks of an investment in the Conversion Shares or made any finding or determination concerning the fairness or advisability of this investment. The Investor shall be responsible for any and all taxes, duties and other similar charges payable in connection with the issuance of the Conversion Shares, and hereby agrees to indemnify the Company and its successors and assigns with respect to same. The Investor understands and acknowledges that the Company's counsel has acted solely as legal counsel for the Company with respect to the preparation of this SAFE and the transactions contemplated hereby, and has not acted as legal counsel for the Investor in connection therewith.

8.10 No Disqualification Events. Neither (a) the Investor, (b) any of its directors, executive officers, other officers that may serve as a director or officer of any company in which it invests, general partners or managing members (if Investor is an entity), nor (c) any beneficial owner of the Company's voting stock (in accordance with Rule 506(d) of the Securities Act) held by the Investor, as applicable, is subject to any of the "bad actor" disqualifications described in Securities Act Rule 506(d)(1)(i) to (viii) (each, a "Disqualification Event"), except for Disqualification Events covered by Rule 506(d)(2)(ii) or (iii) or (d)(3) under the Securities Act and disclosed reasonably in advance of the date of this SAFE in writing in reasonable detail to the Company. In furtherance of the foregoing, the Investor represents and warrants that: (1) the Investor has not been subject to a criminal conviction within ten years of the date of this SAFE or to a court injunction or restraining order within five years of the date of this SAFE in connection with the purchase or sale of a security, in connection with making a false filing with the SEC, or arising out of the conduct of

EXHIBIT 7 *(continued)*

any financial intermediaries; (2) the Investor has not been subject to a final order from state securities, insurance, banking, savings association or credit union regulators or federal banking agencies, the Commodity Futures Trading Commission or the National Credit Union Administration (A) that would bar the Investor from associating with a regulated entity; engaging in the business of securities, insurance or banking; or engaging in savings association or credit union activities, or (B) that were based on fraudulent, manipulative or deceptive conduct and were issued within ten years of the date of this SAFE; (3) the Investor is not subject to any SEC disciplinary orders relating to brokers, dealers, municipal securities dealers, investment companies, investment advisers or their associated persons; (4) the Investor is not subject to any SEC cease-and-desist order arising out of any scienter-based anti-fraud violation or violation of Section 5 of the Securities Act; (5) the Investor has not been suspended or expelled from membership in a self-regulatory organization; and (6) the Investor has not been subject to any SEC stop orders or orders suspending a Regulation A exemption issued within five years of the date of this SAFE.

8.11 Foreign Investors. If the Investor is not a United States person (as defined by Section 7701(a)(30) of the Internal Revenue Code of 1986, as amended), the Investor has satisfied itself as to the full observance of the laws of its jurisdiction in connection with any invitation to subscribe for the Conversion Shares, including: (a) the legal requirements within its jurisdiction for the purchase of the Conversion Shares; (b) any foreign exchange restrictions applicable to such purchase; (c) any governmental or other consents that may need to be obtained; and (d) the income tax and other tax consequences, if any, that may be relevant to the purchase, holding, conversion, redemption, sale or transfer of the Conversion Shares. The Investor's subscription and payment for and continued beneficial ownership of the Conversion Shares will not violate any applicable securities or other laws of the Investor's jurisdiction. The Investor acknowledges that the Company has taken no action in foreign jurisdictions with respect to the Conversion Shares.

8.12 Risk Factors. The Investor has read carefully and understands and accepts in their entirety the risk factors and disclaimers set forth on Exhibit A attached hereto and incorporated herein.

Section 9. Representations and Warranties of the Company. The Company represents and warrants to each Investor as of the date hereof that:

EXHIBIT 7 (*continued*)

9.1 Organization, Good Standing and Qualification. The Company is a corporation organized, validly existing, and in good standing under the laws of the State of Delaware. The Company has the requisite company power and authority to own and operate its properties and assets, to carry on its business as presently conducted, to execute and deliver the SAFE, and to perform its obligations thereunder. The Company is presently qualified to do business as a foreign company in each jurisdiction where the failure to be so qualified could reasonably be expected to have a material adverse effect on the Company's financial condition or business as now conducted.

9.2 Authorization; Enforceability. Except for the authorization and issuance of the Conversion Shares, all company action on the part of the Company and its directors, officers and stockholders necessary for the authorization, sale, issuance and delivery of the SAFE, and the performance of all of the Company's obligations thereunder has been taken or will be taken prior to the date hereof. The SAFE, when executed and delivered by the Company, shall constitute valid and binding obligations of the Company, enforceable in accordance with its terms, except (a) as limited by laws of general application relating to bankruptcy, insolvency and the relief of debtors and (b) as limited by rules of law governing specific performance, injunctive relief or other equitable remedies and by general principles of equity.

Section 10. No Rights as a Stockholder. The Investor is not entitled by virtue of holding this SAFE to be deemed a holder of the Company's stock for any purpose, nor will anything contained in this SAFE be construed to confer on the Investor, as such, any of the rights of a stockholder of the Company or any right to vote for the election of the Board or upon any matter submitted to members at any meeting thereof, or to give or withhold consent to any company action or to receive notice of meetings, or to receive subscription rights or otherwise until Conversion Shares have been issued upon the terms described in this SAFE.

Section 11. Charges, Taxes and Expenses. Issuance of certificates for Conversion Shares issued in accordance with this SAFE shall be made without charge to the Investor hereof for any issue or transfer tax or other incidental expense in respect of the issuance of such certificate, all of which taxes and expenses shall be paid by the Company, and such certificates shall be issued in the name of the Investor pursuant to the Company's bylaws.

EXHIBIT 7 (*continued*)

Section 12. Miscellaneous.

12.1 Legends. If the Company certificates its shares, all certificates representing any shares issued by the Company pursuant to this SAFE will bear a legend in substantially the following form (in addition to any legends required under any of the Company's investor agreements): "THESE SECURITIES HAVE NOT BEEN REGISTERED UNDER THE SECURITIES ACT OF 1933, AS AMENDED, OR THE SECURITIES LAWS OF ANY STATE. THEY MAY NOT BE SOLD, OFFERED FOR SALE, PLEDGED OR HYPOTHECATED IN THE ABSENCE OF A REGISTRATION STATEMENT IN EFFECT WITH RESPECT TO THE SECURITIES UNDER SUCH ACT AND/OR APPLICABLE STATE SECURITIES LAWS, OR AN OPINION OF COUNSEL SATISFACTORY TO THE COMPANY THAT SUCH REGISTRATION IS NOT REQUIRED OR UNLESS SOLD PURSUANT TO RULE 144 OF SUCH ACT."

12.2 Waivers and Amendments. This SAFE and the obligations of the Company and the rights of the Investor under this SAFE may be amended, waived, discharged or terminated (either generally or in a particular instance, either retroactively or prospectively and either for a specified period of time or indefinitely) with the written consent of the Company and the Majority Investors; provided, however, that any amendment, waiver or discharge which would disproportionately and adversely affect the Investor relative to the other holders of the SAFEs must be approved in writing by the Investor. Any amendment, waiver, discharge or termination effected in accordance with this Section 12.2 shall be binding upon the Investor and the Company. Without limiting the foregoing, the Investor hereby acknowledges that the Majority Investors have the right and power to diminish or eliminate the rights of the Investor under this SAFE.

12.3 Notices. All notices and other communications hereunder shall be in writing and shall be deemed given if delivered personally or by commercial delivery service, mailed by registered or certified mail (return receipt requested), sent via facsimile (with confirmation of receipt), or by Electronic Notice as provided below to the parties at the address for such party set forth on the signature page hereto (or at such other address for a party as shall be specified). An electronic communication ("Electronic Notice") shall be deemed written notice for purposes of this Section 12.3 if sent with return receipt requested to the electronic mail address specified by the receiving party. Electronic Notice shall be deemed received at the time (during

EXHIBIT 7 (*continued*)

normal business hours) the party sending Electronic Notice receives verification of receipt by the receiving party. Any party receiving Electronic Notice may request and shall be entitled to receive the notice on paper, in a nonelectronic form, which shall be sent to the requesting party within ten days of receipt of the written request therefor. Any party may change any address to which notice is to be given to it by giving notice as provided above of such change of address.

12.4 Severability. If one or more provisions of this SAFE are held to be unenforceable under applicable law, such provision(s) shall be excluded from this SAFE and the balance of this SAFE shall be interpreted as if such provision(s) were so excluded and shall be enforceable in accordance with its terms.

12.5 Successors and Assigns. Neither this SAFE nor any rights hereunder are transferable without the prior written consent of the Company, which the Company may grant or withhold in its sole discretion. Notwithstanding the foregoing, (a) if the Investor is an entity, the Investor shall, upon advance written notice to the Company, be permitted to transfer this SAFE to any affiliate (as that term is defined in Rule 405 of the Securities Act) of the Investor who (i) executes and delivers an acknowledgement that such affiliate agrees to be subject to, and bound by, all the terms and conditions of this SAFE, (ii) makes the representations and warranties to the Company that are set forth in Section 9 and (iii) if requested by the Company, delivers to the Company an opinion of legal counsel, reasonably satisfactory to the Company, that such transfer complies with state and federal securities laws, and (b) if the Investor is an individual, the Investor may, upon advance notice to the Company, transfer this SAFE and/or the Conversion Shares to a trust established for a direct lineal descendant of the Investor or a similar vehicle for estate planning purposes. If a transfer is permitted pursuant to this Section 12.5, the transfer shall be recorded on the books of the Company upon the surrender of this SAFE, properly endorsed, to the Company at its principal offices, and the payment to the Company of all transfer taxes and other governmental charges imposed on such transfer. Subject to the foregoing, the provisions of this SAFE shall inure to the benefit of, and be binding upon, the successors, assigns, heirs, executors and administrators, as applicable, of the Company and the Investor.

12.6 Legal Counsel. The Investor has been advised by the Company to seek the advice of an attorney and an accountant in connection with

EXHIBIT 7 *(continued)*

the execution and delivery of this SAFE. The Company has had the opportunity to seek the advice of any attorney and accountant of the Company's choice in connection with issuance of this SAFE.

12.7 Subsequent Sales of SAFEs; Pari Passu SAFEs. The Investor acknowledges that the Company may sell and issue up to $1,000,000 in SAFEs, which may occur contemporaneously with the closing of the financing represented by this SAFE or at additional closings. The Investor acknowledges and agrees that the payment of all or any portion of the Purchase Amount pursuant to Section 4 shall be pari passu in right of payment and in all other respects to the other SAFEs issued by the Company that are convertible or exercisable for shares of the Company to investors in bona fide financing transactions (the "Other SAFEs"). If the Investor receives payments in excess of its pro rata share of the Company's payments to the holders of Other SAFEs, then the Investor shall hold in trust all such excess payments for the benefit of the holders of the Other SAFEs and shall pay such amounts held in trust to such other holders upon demand by such holders.

12.8 Delays or Omissions. No delay or omission to exercise any right, power, or remedy accruing to the Investor, upon any breach or default of the Company under this SAFE shall impair any such right, power, or remedy of the Investor nor shall it be construed to be a waiver of any such breach or default, or an acquiescence therein, or of or in any similar breach or default thereafter occurring; nor shall any waiver of any single breach or default be deemed a waiver of any other breach or default therefore or thereafter occurring. Any waiver, permit, consent or approval of any kind or character on the part of the Investor of any breach or default under this SAFE or any waiver on the part of the Investor of any provisions or conditions of this SAFE must be made in writing and shall be effective only to the extent specifically set forth in such writing. All remedies, either under this SAFE or by law or otherwise afforded to the Investors, shall be cumulative and not alternative.

12.9 Interpretation. The titles of the paragraphs and subparagraphs of this SAFE are for convenience of reference only and are not to be considered in construing this SAFE. The term "including" or "include" does not denote or imply any limitation, and each gender includes the other gender and the neuter, and the neuter includes each gender. The language used in this SAFE will be deemed to be the language chosen by the parties to express their mutual intent and no rules of strict construction will be applied against any party.

EXHIBIT 7 *(continued)*

References herein to a "party" or the "parties" refers to the parties hereto (and their permitted successors, assigns, heirs, executors and administrators, as applicable). References to a "person" or "persons" includes entities, unless the context otherwise requires.

12.10 Expenses. The Company and the Investor shall each bear its respective expenses and legal fees incurred with respect to this SAFE and the transactions contemplated hereby.

12.11 Finder's Fees. The Investor represents and warrants to the Company that it neither is nor will be obligated to pay any finder's fee, broker's fee or commission in connection with the transactions contemplated by this SAFE. The Investor agrees to indemnify and to hold the Company harmless from any liability for any commission or compensation in the nature of a finder's or broker's fee arising out of the transactions contemplated by this SAFE (and the costs and expenses of defending against such liability or asserted liability) for which the Investor or any of its officers, employees or representatives is responsible.

12.12 Governing Law. THIS SAFE SHALL BE GOVERNED IN ALL RESPECTS BY THE LAWS OF THE STATE OF DELAWARE AS SUCH LAWS ARE APPLIED TO AGREEMENTS BETWEEN NEW YORK RESIDENTS ENTERED INTO AND TO BE PERFORMED ENTIRELY WITHIN NEW YORK. EACH OF THE PARTIES IRREVOCABLY CONSENTS TO THE EXCLUSIVE PERSONAL JURISDICTION OF THE FEDERAL AND STATE COURTS LOCATED IN WILMINGTON COUNTY, DELAWARE FOR ANY MATTER ARISING OUT OF OR RELATING TO THIS SAFE, EXCEPT THAT IN ACTIONS SEEKING TO ENFORCE ANY ORDER OR ANY JUDGMENT OF SUCH FEDERAL OR STATE COURTS LOCATED IN WILMINGTON COUNTY, DELAWARE, SUCH PERSONAL JURISDICTION SHALL BE NONEXCLUSIVE.

12.13 Counterparts; Delivery. This SAFE may be executed in two (2) or more counterparts, each of which shall be deemed an original, but all of which together shall constitute one and the same instrument. Counterparts may be delivered via electronic mail (including pdf or any electronic signature complying with the U.S. federal ESIGN Act of 2000, e.g., www.docusign.com) or other transmission method and any counterpart so delivered shall be deemed to have been duly and validly delivered and be valid and effective for all purposes. Neither party shall be bound until such time as each of the parties have executed this SAFE (or counterparts hereof).

EXHIBIT 7 *(continued)*

[Signature Page Follows]

EXHIBIT A RISK FACTORS AND DISCLAIMERS

1. The Company has a limited operating history upon which to base the evaluation of an investment in the Conversion Shares. The Company will be subject to the risks involved with any speculative new venture. There can be no assurance that the Company's activities and operations will generate any significant revenues or be successful or profitable in the future. If the Company is unable to operate successfully, you may suffer a partial or total loss of your investment.
2. No assurance can be given that you will realize a return on your investment or even that you will receive a return of any portion of your investment.
3. The Company will be highly dependent upon several key personnel and, if any of these individuals resign or become otherwise unavailable, the Company may not realize upon its business strategy and may not become profitable (or remain profitable if it becomes profitable).
4. Your investment in the Company will be extremely illiquid.
5. There is no public market for the SAFEs or any securities issued pursuant to the terms thereof and one will not develop as a result of the transactions contemplated as of the date hereof. You must therefore bear the economic risk of you investment in the Company for an indefinite period of time.
6. A minority holder of shares in the Company will have (a) no right to elect members of the Board or attend Board meetings and (b) no control (affirmative or negative) over any decisions or actions of the Board or management.
7. The Company will require additional capital in the future. There is no guarantee that the Company will be able to obtain sufficient additional capital on acceptable terms, and if additional capital is obtained, any additional shares may dilute the ownership interest, voting rights, liquidation rights and other rights of holders of capital stock in the Company. Additionally, other investors may require the Company to grants rights, preferences and privileges that are senior to or different than your rights. For you to receive capital stock in the Company will require the Company to successfully raise additional capital.

EXHIBIT 7 *(continued)*

9. The Company must comply with a number of state, local and federal regulations as well as industry standards and practices. Should the Company be found non-compliant with any applicable regulation or practice, the Company's operations could be interrupted or terminated until rectified, which could have a material adverse effect on the Company's market position, customer good will, reputation, business or operation.
10. Customers' preferences can change due to a variety of factors, including the age and ethnic demographics of the population, social trends, negative publicity, economic downturn, or Exhibit A other factors. If the Company does not effectively anticipate trends and changing customer preferences, then quickly develop new products in response, the Company's sales could suffer. Developing and launching new products can be risky and expensive. The Company may not be successful in responding to changing markets and customer preferences, and some of its competitors may be better able to respond to these changes, either of which could negatively affect the Company's business and financial performance.
11. Some of the products the Company manufactures may be produced, packaged and distributed by third parties. As independent companies, these co-manufacturers and distributors make their own business decisions. They may have the right to determine whether, and to what extent, they produce and distribute the Company's products, its competitors' products and their own products. They may devote more resources to other products or take other actions detrimental to the Company's brand. They may not comply with regulatory, ingredient, and packaging requirements. Their financial condition could also be adversely affected by conditions beyond the Company's control, and the Company's business could suffer as a result. Deteriorating economic conditions also could negatively impact the financial viability of third party manufacturers. Any of these factors could negatively affect the Company's business and financial performance.
12. The Company's business could suffer or fail if the Company is unable to establish and protect its intellectual property rights, or is liable for infringing the intellectual property rights of others.
13. In addition to the risk factors described herein, the Company's business is generally subject to the risk of adverse changes in general and local economic conditions, adverse changes in local laws and regulations, and unanticipated increases in operating costs. If the U.S.

EXHIBIT 7 (*continued*)

economy falters, the Company's customers may reduce their level of discretionary spending, thereby decreasing the Company's revenues. Adverse economic conditions and any related decrease in discretionary spending by the Company's customers could have an adverse effect on Company revenues and operating results. NOTE: THE ABOVE LIST OF RISK FACTORS IS NOT INTENDED TO BE COMPLETE. AS WITH OTHER INVESTMENTS IN COMPANIES OF THE TYPE CONTEMPLATED HEREIN, THERE ARE OTHER RISKS ASSOCIATED WITH INVESTING IN THE COMPANY, AND THE INVESTOR HEREBY ACKNOWLEDGES ITS RESPONSIBILITY TO ASK QUESTIONS OF AND RECEIVE ANSWERS FROM THE COMPANY, OR OTHERWISE OBTAIN AND/ OR CAREFULLY REVIEW WHATEVER INFORMATION IS RELEVANT OR MATERIAL, WITH RESPECT TO SUCH OTHER RISKS.

Source: Company documents.

Note: Terms have been disguised. For discussion purposes only.

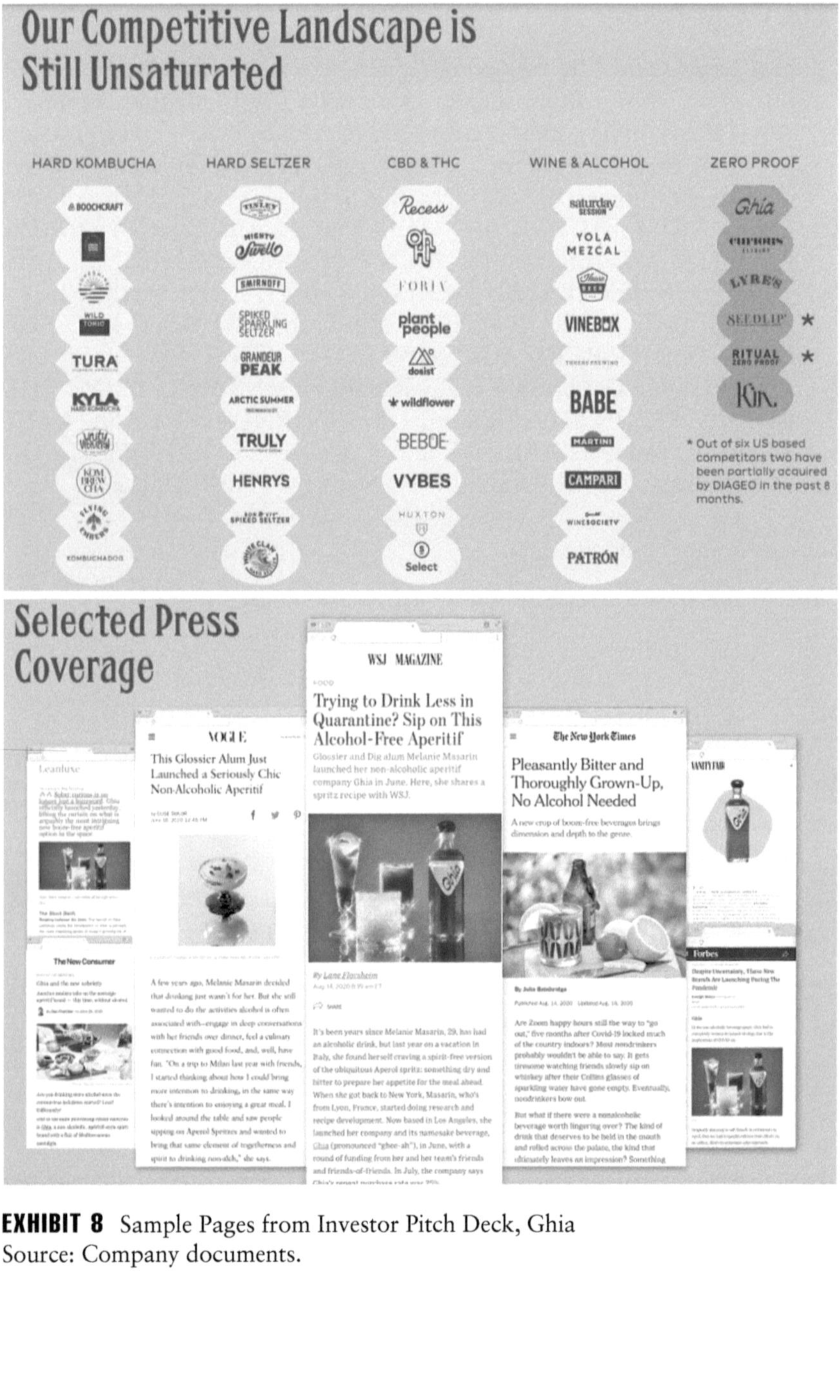

EXHIBIT 8 Sample Pages from Investor Pitch Deck, Ghia
Source: Company documents.

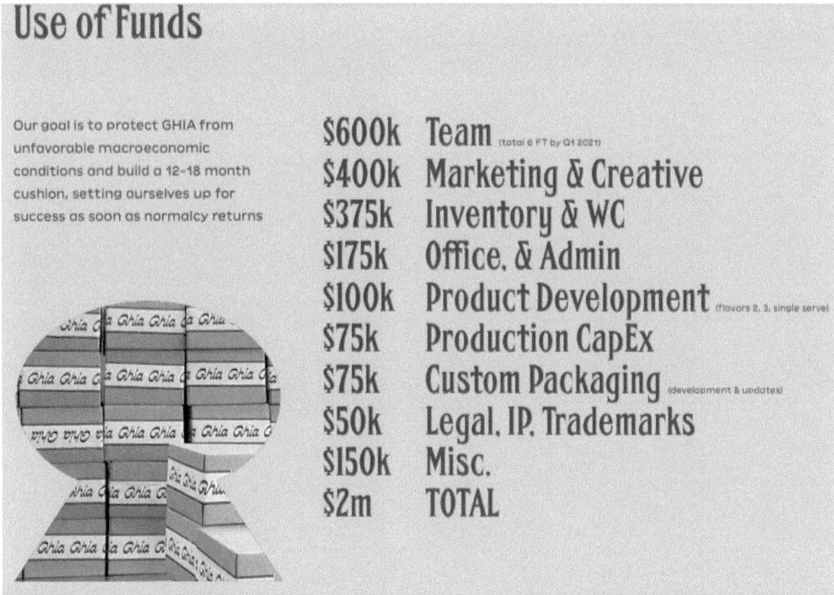

EXHIBIT 8 *(continued)*

CHAPTER 5.6

Convertible Notes in Seed Financings

Ramana Nanda, William R. Kerr and Robert F. White

Unpriced securities, such as Convertible Notes and Y-Combinator's simple agreement for future equity ("SAFE") have taken on growing importance as a funding structure for early startups, particularly among angel investors making seed round investments. In some industry segments such as internet and digital media, over 50% of Seed rounds are raised using unpriced securities.

This note provides an overview of financing using unpriced securities. It begins by outlining the differences between a priced and non-priced round. It then discussed the main differences between two of the most common unpriced securities – Convertible Notes and SAFEs. Finally, the note goes through a specific example of a convertible note, with attention paid to technical details regarding how discounts and valuation caps impact the ownership of all parties involved in the transaction. It closes with some more general observations and references. This note does not discuss the relative benefits of fundraising using unpriced securities compared to the more traditional priced rounds. These issues are discussed in "PunchTab, Inc." (HBS Case No. 812-172), where the founders are evaluating a convertible note financing deal versus a traditional venture capital contract. A broader overview of entrepreneurial finance is provided by "Financing New Ventures" (HBS Note No. 811-093).

UNPRICED VS. PRICED ROUNDS

The fundamental difference between an unpriced security such as convertible notes and a priced round is that there is no valuation assigned to the startup in the former case, while the latter structure assigns a specific

Convertible Notes in Seed Financings
by RAMANA NANDA, WILLIAM R. KERR, ROBERT F. WHITE, case number 9-813-017 Rev.
SEPTEMBER 23, 2016

valuation. That is, in a typical venture capital financing round, \$X will buy Y% of the startup, implying that the startup's post-money valuation is \$X/Y%. On the other hand, a convertible note provides the startup with \$X immediately *without* buying a specific fraction of the startup, instead delaying valuation and pricing until the next round of financing. In this sense, the convertible note is not strictly "priced," since it gives money to the startup without establishing an exact valuation at the time the money is invested. In return for not pricing the round, however, the \$X invested usually converts into equity at a discount to the next round's price (a typical discount is 20%—see the statistic on median discounts on convertible notes in **Exhibit 1**).

For investors, the rationale behind a convertible note stems from two factors. First, the cost of starting firms has fallen substantially over the last decade, particularly in some industry segments, leading the size of Seed rounds to fall considerably as well. Nevertheless, startups at the seed stage still face great uncertainty about the ultimate outcome. The investor has some idea about the capabilities of the founders, but performing due diligence on the market, the opportunity, or the issues related to successful execution can be time-consuming and potentially costly, making it uneconomical to do so for the small sum of money invested in seed rounds. Second, the extremely high failure rates of early-stage startups mean that there is a significant chance the firm will not reach a Series A financing (or that if it does, the investor may choose not to follow on), leading any diligence to be worthwhile only a small percentage of the time.

The convertible note allows investors to make an investment now, while deferring the more complex issues around the pricing and terms till a later date. Relatedly, angel investors who are not as sophisticated can defer the pricing decision till a professional investor such as a VC comes in, and benchmark their valuation to the price taken by the VC by simply contracting on a fixed discount to the next round's price. Unpriced securities can therefore be an attractive investment vehicle for investors making small investments in early-stage startups.

Convertible notes also carry advantages for entrepreneurs. First, they allow an entrepreneur to raise money faster and at a lower price than traditional financing. A convertible note can cost as little as a few thousand dollars in legal fees and the financing can close in a matter of days, compared to the tens of thousands of dollars in legal fees and many weeks necessary to undertake the diligence and documentation associated with priced rounds. Second, by delaying the pricing, the entrepreneur has the ability to increase valuation relative to a priced round. If the venture makes substantial progress between the seed round and the next financing, the entrepreneur can retain a greater ownership share of the venture. Third, the duration of the convertible note, use of discounts and caps allows the entrepreneur to partially tailor the subsequent pricing of the round to the investor in question. For example, a value-added investor can be given a greater discount than friends or family.

While both parties may find convertible notes attractive, one of the issues with a standard convertible note is that the entrepreneur and seed round investor have divergent interests in the period prior to the Series A investment. Since a seed investor with a convertible note will get a discount on the next round's price, the entrepreneur has an incentive to use the money from the seed round to raise the startup's valuation to more than compensate for this difference. Any increase in value greater than 25% (in the case that the discount is 20%) leads directly to lower dilution for the entrepreneur, at the expense of the investor. Ironically, this also means that any advice or help the seed investor provides to the startup can in fact hurt the investor by diluting them more if the advice leads to a higher valuation.

The presence of this conflict of interest, particularly in the context of frothy, entrepreneur-friendly markets, creates a problem for seed investors: if the Series A round of financing gets a very high valuation, the 20% discount they get from the convertible note does not adequately compensate them for the risk they took in the seed round—they are essentially taking downside risk (that the firm fails without a Series A investment), but not being adequately compensated if the firm does well.

Seed investors have therefore begun to use convertible notes with caps. That is, their $X converts at the lower of (1) a discount to the next round's valuation or (2) a valuation cap. The cap therefore works to set a lower bound in terms of the seed investor's ownership upon conversion of the note, and, as we will highlight in the next section, aligns the interests of the seed investor and the entrepreneur to increase firm valuation beyond the point of the cap's binding.

It is worth noting that in general the entrepreneur would like the cap to be as high as possible, while investors would like it to be low; however, there are also arguments to be made for the entrepreneur to incentivize investors by setting the cap low—since the investors then have aligned incentives to grow the value of the company as much as possible before the next round of financing. Angel investors, who typically invest only in early stages of a firm and hence get more and more diluted across future rounds, are the most sensitive to the cap. On the other hand, VC investors with several hundred million dollars under management care much less about the cap at the seed round, as the seed investment is tiny compared to the rest of the investments they are likely to make in the firm.

This is important to bear in mind as the entrepreneur approaches different investors to finance their venture. An example that nicely illustrates this is the case of PunchTab, where founder Ranjith Kumaran reflected on the use of convertible notes for his seed round financing: "I want to use a convertible note because it is faster, costs less and angels are comfortable with them... VCs don't really care about the cap, but some of the angels wonder how they will make money with such a high cap and think it is too rich for an early stage company."

CONVERTIBLE NOTES VS. SAFE

Exhibit 2 provides an example of a convertible note and **Exhibit 3** provides an example of a SAFE. One primary difference between convertible notes and a SAFE is that the former is debt instrument while the latter is equity. This has several practical implications: First, convertible notes have a maturity date – the point at which the loan comes due. This causes a particular problem if the loan comes due before a qualified round of financing has occurred, by creating the potential for insolvency if the founders cannot repay the loan. In addition it often requires potential extensions to the loan, which can lead to time consuming and costly negotiations between the entrepreneur and Seed investors. Second, debt instruments typically have an interest component to them, which the SAFE does not.

A second major difference lies in the way liquidation preference is calculated when the unpriced security converts into preferred stock in the next round of financing. In the case of convertible notes, the convention is to issue the same security to the Seed investors as that received by the Series A. This has the unintended consequence that of the liquidation preference equalling the value of the investment at the time of the Series A rather than the face value of the investment. That is, since the holders of the convertible note convert at a discount to the Series A investor's price or a capped price, they hold a "stepped up" value of their investment. This leads Seed investors to receive a liquidation preference that is more than 1X (e.g. in the case of a 20% discount, the step-up and hence the liquidation preference is 1.25X; with a cap the step-ups can be much higher). The SAFE accounts for this by creating a new security at the time of Series A financing with all other rights of the Series A, but where the liquidation preference is equal to the face value of the investment as opposed to the stepped-up value. While the difference is insignificant for small investments, it can get more meaningful for larger investments where there cap binds well below the price of the Series A financing.

IMPLICATIONS OF VALUATION CAPS AND DISCOUNTS ON OWNERSHIP SHARES

We now use the example in **Exhibit 2** to highlight how the mechanics of a discount and a cap work in the context of a Series A financing. The mechanics of this calculation are identical for the SAFE, although the nomenclature used is slightly different.

It can be seen from **Exhibit 2** that the seed investors are considering a $750,000 investment in the form of a convertible note, which will convert at the lower of (1) 80% of the price per share in the next equity financing or (2) a pre-money valuation of $5 million. The next equity financing is defined as a round of financing where at least $2 million is raised, including the conversion of the $750,000 convertible note. We now look at two situations, one where the Series A investor takes 40% for a $4 million investment (a $10 million post money valuation) and the second where the Series A investor takes 20% for a $4 million investment (a $20 million post money valuation). In the calculations below, we assume there are 900,000 founder shares and a 10% issued and unallocated option pool of 100,000 shares. Collectively we will refer to these as 1 million shares for founders and management.

Scenario 1: Series A investor takes 40% for $4 million investment

Note first that the cap has been set at a $5 million pre-money valuation. As is often the case with convertible notes, there is some ambiguity about whether the $5 million pre-money refers to the Series A round of investment or the Seed round of investment. The convention is usually to treat a pre-money cap as being prior to the Seed investment, thereby including the founder and management shares and any shares allocated to the option pool. In our example, we have assumed founder and management to have 1,000,000 shares, so following the convention we have that the $5 million pre-money cap implies a price-per-share cap of $5 million /1,000,000 million shares = $5/share.[a] Hence the cap implies that the maximum price the Seed investors will need to pay (i.e. the cap) is $5/share.

---

a If the pre-money cap referred to the pre-money valuation of the Series A instead, then this would mean that the *post money* valuation of the Seed Round was no greater than $5 million. This would mean that sum of founder & management shares AND the Seed investor shares would be worth $5 million. The $750,000 invested by the Seed investor would thus own 750,000/5,000,000= 15%. Given that 1 million founder and management shares are now equal to 100%-15%=85%, the Seed investors under this interpretation would get 15%/85%*1,000,000 shares= 176,471 shares, implying a share price of $750,000/176,471=$4.25. Note therefore that the convention of using the pre-money valuation of the Seed round is always more entrepreneur friendly since it implies a higher price-per-share cap. This logic (and convention) also applies to valuation caps for SAFEs, which explicitly note that the cap is on the pre-money of the Seed Round.

Since the Seed investor has the option to convert their $ 750,000 at the lower of the capped price per share, or 80% of the price per share implied by the Series A financing, our task is to figure out the whether 80% of the price per share implied by the $10 million post money valuation (40% for a $4 million investment) is more or less than the $5 cap.

To do this, note, however, that since the Seed investors buy in at a 20% discount to the Series A price, they get more shares than they would have gotten if they simply bought in at the Series A price per share. These extra shares will dilute the ownership of the Series A investors, who will now get less than their 40% ownership if they stick to the original price per share. Since the Series A investors will not be willing to settle for less than their required ownership stake, they will need to be compensated with more shares, implying a slightly lower Series A share price. Now, however, the Seed investors' 20% discount needs to be applied to this lower price, further diluting Series A investors and requiring them to take an even lower price. This circularity resolves itself at a fixed point that can most easily be calculated using the following logic (but note that a more detailed step-by-step guide is included in **Exhibit 4**):

- Suppose the Series A price is $X. The Seed investors' share price will then be $0.8*X.
- The Series A investors put in $4,000,000, so they are allocated $4,000,000/$X shares
- The Seed investors put in $750,000, so they are allocated $750,000/$0.8X shares
- The total number of shares are equal to the post money valuation divided by the share price, implying that the total number of shares are $10,000,000/$X

Since founders and management have 1 million shares, this allows us to set up the following simple equation: 1 million (F&M shares) + $750,000/$0.8X (Seed investor shares) + $4,000,000/$X (Series A investor shares) = $10,000,000/$X (total shares).

It is now trivial to solve for X, leading to a Series A price per share of $ 5.0625. The Seed investors get to buy in at 0.8* $ 5.0625 = $4.05.

Since the Seed investors can choose the lower of the valuation cap ($5/share) or 80% of the implied price per share in the Series A financing ($4.05), it is easy to see they will choose to convert using the discount rather than the cap. They will therefore receive $750,000/$4.05 shares = 185,185 shares which imply an ownership of 9.4% of the fully diluted shares following the Series A round of funding. The Series A investors will receive $4,000,000/$5.0625 = 790,123 shares, implying the full 40% ownership they needed, and founders and management's 1,000,000 shares now account for 50.6%.

Scenario 2: Series A investor takes 20% for $4 million investment

We can follow the same logic as above in Scenario 2. The valuation cap remains at $5/share. Our task is therefore to determine whether 80% of the price-per-share implied by the $20 million post money valuation ($4 million for 20%) is higher or lower than the cap. We do so following the same steps as above:

- Let the Series A price again be $X. The Seed investors' share price will then be $0.8*X.
- The Series A investors put in $4,000,000, so they are allocated $4,000,000/$X shares
- The Seed investors put in $750,000, so they are allocated $750,000/$0.8X shares
- The total number of shares are equal to the post money valuation divided by the share price, implying that the total number of shares are $20,000,000/$X

Since founders and management have 1 million shares, we get that: 1 million (F&M shares) + $750,000/$0.8X (Seed investor shares) + $4,000,000/$X (Series A investor shares) = $20,000,000/$X (total shares). Solving for $X leads to a Series A price per share of $ 15.0625. The Seed investors get to buy in at 0.8* $ 15.0625 = $12.05.

Since the Seed investors can choose the lower of the valuation cap ($5/share) or 80% of the implied price per share in the Series A financing ($12.05), it is easy to see they will choose to convert using the cap rather than the discount. They will therefore receive $750,000/$5 shares = 150,000 shares. Note now that since the Seed investors bought in at a much lower price per share ($5 vs. $12.05), the Series A investors need to also get a somewhat lower share price to compensate them for this extra dilution. To calculate the Series A investors' ownership, note that since they need 20% of the fully diluted shares for their $4 million investment, F&M and the Seed Investors will account for the balance 80% of the ownership. Since F&M have 1,000,000 shares and Seed investors have 150,000 shares, we know that 1,150,000 shares account for 80% of the capitalization and hence the balance 20% must be 287,500 shares. The Series A investors therefore needed to buy in at $4,000,000/287,500= $13.913 as opposed to the original $ 15.0625 because the Seed investors converted at the cap. Note that since the Series A investors are protected from dilution, the full extent of dilution due to the discount / cap is borne by the founders and management.

In this example, F&M end up with 69.6% and Seed investors with 10.4%, but if there was no valuation cap and the Seed investors had converted at the $12.05 share price, F&M would have ended up with 75.3% and Seed investors with only 4.7%.

The chart below highlights the distinction between what a seed investor obtains with and without the $5 million pre-money valuation cap, depending on the Series A post money valuation. As can be seen from the chart, this difference (and hence the value of the cap) increases with the post-money valuation of the Series A investment. Note also that the seed investor's ownership percentage actually goes up once the cap binds. The reason for this is that once the cap binds, the seed investor is much like an "insider" and hence shares in the benefits of increased valuation. That is, once the cap binds, the seed round is in effect "priced" at a value that is less than the next round of funding. Any increase in valuation beyond that point is shared between the founder and the seed investor (at the expense of

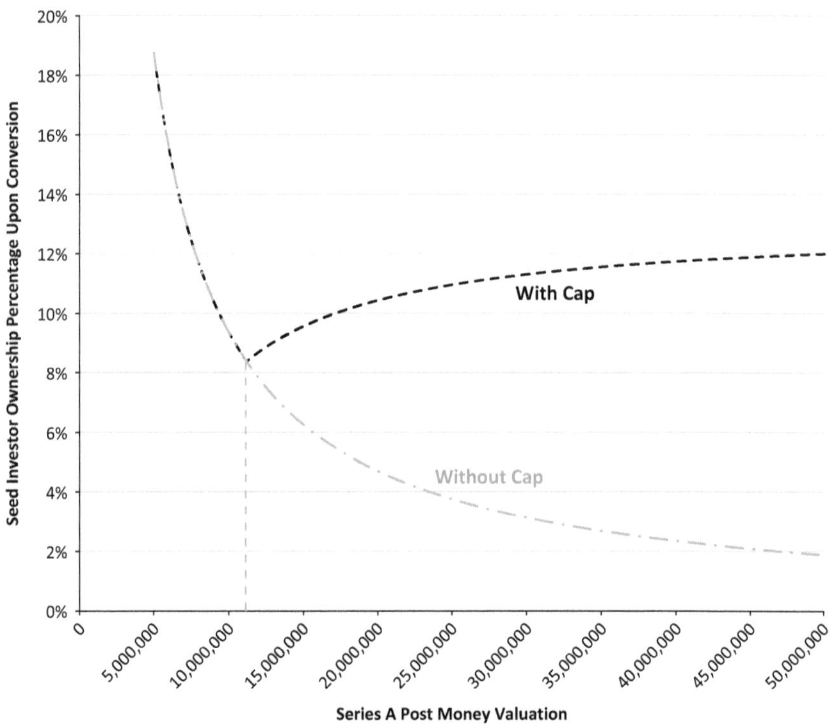

FIGURE 1 Seed Investor's Ownership Percentage with and without Valuation Cap
Source: Casewriters.

the Series A investor)—even though the number of shares the seed investor gets is the same, the Series A investor gets fewer shares and hence the seed investor gets a larger share.

ADDITIONAL TERMS FOR CONVERTIBLE NOTES

We now highlight some of the main terms that are associated with a convertible note. Our focus in this note is mostly about the mechanics of a convertible note's discounts and valuation caps, as this is where confusion is greatest, but the broader landscape is also important as negotiations regarding discounts and valuation caps are undertaken alongside these other features. Not all these terms are included in term sheets, but it is important for the entrepreneur to remember that several of the contingencies outlined below do take place, and it is helpful to have a clear understanding of what will happen to the seed investor's shares in the event of these contingencies. Also note that the SAFE is a standardized document

	Conventional	Entrepreneur-Friendly	Investor-Friendly
Duration of the note	18 months	24-36 months	12-18 months
Interest rate paid on the note	6-8%	As low as 0.5%; simple interest	As much as 14%; compounded interest
Discount when converting?	Yes, 20%	No (or low discount)	Yes, up to 50% discount
Valuation cap?	Yes	No	Yes, capped at low valuation
Board seats?	No	No	Yes
What happens in the event of an acquisition?	Return investment plus 2X premium	Return principal plus interest; no (or low) premium	2-4X premium over and above principal or conversion right
What happens in the event that no financing takes place in the stipulated duration of the note?	Loan extension	Automatic conversion	Right to redeem or force company into bankruptcy

FIGURE 2 Typical Seed Investment Terms for Negotiation
Source: Compiled from Fenwick & West 2011 Seed Financing Survey,[1] Scott Walker's posts on TechCrunch[2,3,4] and WilmerHale's 2016 Venture Capital Report.[5]

so does not vary as much as a convertible note. Due to the fact that the SAFE is an equity investment, it does not have a duration, an interest rate and does not require a stipulation of what happens when no financing event takes place within the duration of the note.

ADDITIONAL RESOURCES AND STATISTICS

- Three-part series in TechCrunch on convertible note financings by Scott Walker, which includes a discussion of securities law and accredited investor status:
  - http://techcrunch.com/2012/04/07/convertible-note-seed-financings/
  - http://techcrunch.com/2012/04/21/convertible-note-seed-financings-econ-101/
  - http://techcrunch.com/2012/05/13/convertible-note-seed-financings-part-3/.
- Another convertible note example: http://www.scribd.com/doc/51681290/Convertible-Note-Financing-Term-Sheet.
- https://www.ycombinator.com/documents/.
- Fenwick and West's 2011 Seed Financing Survey of Internet/Digital Media and Software Industries: http://www.fenwick.com/FenwickDocuments/2011_Seed_Survey _Report.pdf.
- WilmerHale 2016 Venture Capital Report: Available for download at https://www.wilmerhale.com/uploadedFiles/Shared_Content/Editorial/Publications/Documents/2016-WilmerHale-VC-Report.pdf.
- Silicon Legal Seed Financing Report: http://www.siliconlegal.com/reports/seed-financing-report-2015.

NOTES

1 Kramer, Barry J. and Steven S. Levine, *2011 Seed Financing Survey – Internet/Digital Media and Software Industries*, Fenwick & West LLP, March 21, 2012, http://www.fenwick.com/publications/Pages/Seed-Finance-Survey-2011.aspx.
2 Walker, Scott E., "Everything You Ever Wanted To Know About Convertible Note Seed Financings (But Were Afraid To Ask)," April 7, 2012, post on blog "TechCrunch," http://techcrunch.com/2012/04/07/ convertible-note-seed-financings/.
3 Walker, Scott E., "Convertible Note Seed Financings: Econ 101 for Founders," April 21, 2012, post on blog "TechCrunch," http://techcrunch.com/2012/04/21/convertible-note-seed-financings-econ-101/.

4 Walker, Scott E., "Convertible Note Seed Financings: Founders Beware!," May 13, 2012, post on blog "TechCrunch," http://techcrunch.com/2012/05/13/convertible-note-seed-financings-part-3/.

5 WilmerHale, "2016 Venture Capital Report" Downloaded September 12, 2016 from: https://www.wilmerhale.com/uploadedFiles/Shared_Content/Editorial/Publications/Documents/2016-WilmerHale-VC-Report.pdf.

EXHIBIT 1 Trends in Convertible Note Financing

Convertible Note Seed Financings	2011	2015
Median amount raised	$1,000,000	$1,000,000
Median interest rate	5.5%	5%
Median term	18 months	18 months
Percentage of deals in which valuation on conversion is capped	82%	55%
Median valuation cap	$7.5 million	$7.5 million
Percentage of deals that convert at a discount to the next equity round valuation	83%	89%
Median initial discount	20%	20%
Treatment of note if company is acquired prior to an equity financing:		
Receive return of investment plus a premium	61%	53%
Median premium	1.0x	2.0x
Percentage in which investors receive a board seat	4%	6%

Source: Compiled from Fenwick & West 2011 Seed Financing Survey,[1] WilmerHale's 2016 Venture Capital Report and Silicon Legal 2015 Seed Financing Report.

EXHIBIT 2 Convertible note example

MEMORANDUM OF TERMS FOR THE PRIVATE PLACEMENT OF SECURITIES OF ____________________

THIS TERM SHEET SUMMARIZES THE PRINCIPAL TERMS OF THE PROPOSED FINANCING OF __________ (THE "COMPANY"). THIS TERM SHEET IS FOR DISCUSSION PURPOSES ONLY; THERE IS NO OBLIGATION ON THE PART OF ANY NEGOTIATING PARTY UNTIL A DEFINITIVE NOTE PURCHASE AGREEMENT IS SIGNED BY ALL PARTIES. THIS TERM SHEET IS SUBJECT TO THE SATISFACTORY COMPLETION OF DUE DILIGENCE. THIS TERM SHEET DOES NOT CONSTITUTE EITHER AN OFFER TO SELL OR AN OFFER TO PURCHASE SECURITIES.

Type of Security:	Convertible promissory notes (the "Notes").
Amount to be Raised:	$750,000.
Investors:	Investor 1: $475,000. Other Investors: $275,000, subject to the mutual agreement of the Company and Investor 1.
Interest Rate:	6% per annum.
Maturity Date:	Twelve months from the date of issuance.
Prepayment:	The Notes may not be prepaid.
Conversion:	Principal and accrued and unpaid interest shall be automatically converted into Series A Preferred Stock on the closing of the Company's next equity financing in an aggregate amount of at least $2,000,000 (including conversion of the Notes) (the "Next Equity Financing"). The principal and accrued and unpaid interest shall convert at the lesser of (i) 80% of the price per share in the Next Equity Financing and (ii) the price per share at which the Company's shares would be valued at a pre-money, fully diluted valuation of $5,000,000 (assuming an authorized, unissued option pool of 10 % of the Company's equity). Investor 1 shall have the right to purchase in the Next Equity Financing 40% of the securities issued in such Next Equity Financing.
Next Equity Financing:	The Next Equity Financing shall be in the aggregate amount of at least $2,000,000 (including conversion of the Notes).
Acquisition:	If the Company is acquired prior to the conversion as provided above, Investor 1 shall be entitled to receive 150% of the outstanding principal of the Note as of the closing of the acquisition.
Board of Directors:	Until the Next Equity Financing, the Board of Directors shall consist of two members. The two members shall be _______ and _______.

EXHIBIT 2 *(continued)*

Exclusivity:	From the signing date hereof until the earlier of i) 5:00 pm Pacific Time on January 31, 2011, (ii) the Closing, or (iii) written notification by Investor 1 that it does not intend to proceed with the financing of Company. Company agrees that it shall not solicit, encourage others to solicit, encourage or accept any offers with respect to the acquisition or financing of the Company, and it shall not negotiate with or enter into any agreement or understanding with any other person with respect to any such transaction.
No Obligation:	This memorandum of terms represents the basis upon which the parties intend to negotiate toward a definitive agreement. This memorandum shall not, however, be binding on any party, nor shall any party be obligated to consummate a transaction on the terms proposed herein or otherwise (and no obligation on the part of either party shall arise by virtue of such things as parol evidence, extended negotiations, "handshakes," oral understandings or course of conduct) until such time as a definitive agreement shall have been negotiated, prepared and executed by the parties.

If you are in agreement with the terms and conditions set forth above and desire to proceed on
that basis, please sign this letter in the space provided below and return an executed copy to the
undersigned.

ACKNOWLEDGED AND AGREED:

By ____________________	By ____________________
Date ____________________	Date ____________________

Source: Casewriters.

EXHIBIT 3 Sample of a SAFE

THIS INSTRUMENT AND ANY SECURITIES ISSUABLE PURSUANT HERETO HAVE NOT BEEN REGISTERED UNDER THE SECURITIES ACT OF 1933, AS AMENDED (THE "**SECURITIES ACT**"), OR UNDER THE SECURITIES LAWS OF CERTAIN STATES. THESE SECURITIES MAY NOT BE OFFERED, SOLD OR OTHERWISE TRANSFERRED, PLEDGED OR HYPOTHECATED EXCEPT AS PERMITTED UNDER THE ACT AND APPLICABLE STATE SECURITIES LAWS PURSUANT TO AN EFFECTIVE REGISTRATION STATEMENT OR AN EXEMPTION THEREFROM.

[COMPANY NAME]

SAFE

(Simple Agreement for Future Equity)

THIS CERTIFIES THAT in exchange for the payment by [Investor Name] (the "Investor") of $[_______] (the "Purchase Amount") on or about [Date of Safe], [Company Name], a [State of Incorporation] corporation (the "Company"), hereby issues to the Investor the right to certain shares of the Company's capital stock, subject to the terms set forth below.

The "**Valuation Cap**" is $[__________].
The "**Discount Rate**" is [ ]%.
See **Section 2** for certain additional defined terms.

1. ***Events***
   (a) Equity Financing. If there is an Equity Financing before the expiration or termination of this instrument, the Company will automatically issue to the Investor a number of shares of Safe Preferred Stock equal to the Purchase Amount divided by the Conversion Price.

   In connection with the issuance of Safe Preferred Stock by the Company to the Investor pursuant to this Section 1(a):

   (i) The Investor will execute and deliver to the Company all transaction documents related to the Equity Financing; *provided,* that such documents are the same documents to be entered

EXHIBIT 3 (*continued*)

into with the purchasers of Standard Preferred Stock, with appropriate variations for the Safe Preferred Stock if applicable, and *provided further,* that such documents have customary exceptions to any drag-along applicable to the Investor, including, without limitation, limited representations and warranties and limited liability and indemnification obligations on the part of the Investor; and

(ii) The Investor and the Company will execute a Pro Rata Rights Agreement, unless the Investor is already included in such rights in the transaction documents related to the Equity Financing.

(b) Liquidity Event. If there is a Liquidity Event before the expiration or termination of this instrument, the Investor will, at its option, either (i) receive a cash payment equal to the Purchase Amount (subject to the following paragraph) or (ii) automatically receive from the Company a number of shares of Common Stock equal to the Purchase Amount divided by the Liquidity Price, if the Investor fails to select the cash option.

In connection with Section (b)(i), the Purchase Amount will be due and payable by the Company to the Investor immediately prior to, or concurrent with, the consummation of the Liquidity Event. If there are not enough funds to pay the Investor and holders of other Safes (collectively, the "**Cash-Out Investors**") in full, then all of the Company's available funds will be distributed with equal priority and *pro rata* among the Cash-Out Investors in proportion to their Purchase Amounts, and the Cash-Out Investors will automatically receive the number of shares of Common Stock equal to the remaining unpaid Purchase Amount divided by the Liquidity Price. In connection with a Change of Control intended to qualify as a tax-free reorganization, the Company may reduce, *pro rata*, the Purchase Amounts payable to the Cash-Out Investors by the amount determined by its board of directors in good faith to be advisable for such Change of Control to qualify as a tax-free reorganization for U.S. federal income tax purposes, and in such case, the Cash-Out Investors will automatically receive the number of shares of Common Stock equal to the remaining unpaid Purchase Amount divided by the Liquidity Price.

(c) Dissolution Event. If there is a Dissolution Event before this instrument expires or terminates, the Company will pay an amount equal to the Purchase Amount, due and payable to the Investor immediately prior to, or concurrent with, the consummation of

EXHIBIT 3 (*continued*)

the Dissolution Event. The Purchase Amount will be paid prior and in preference to any Distribution of any of the assets of the Company to holders of outstanding Capital Stock by reason of their ownership thereof. If immediately prior to the consummation of the Dissolution Event, the assets of the Company legally available for distribution to the Investor and all holders of all other Safes (the "**Dissolving Investors**"), as determined in good faith by the Company's board of directors, are insufficient to permit the payment to the Dissolving Investors of their respective Purchase Amounts, then the entire assets of the Company legally available for distribution will be distributed with equal priority and *pro rata* among the Dissolving Investors in proportion to the Purchase Amounts they would otherwise be entitled to receive pursuant to this Section 1(c).

(d) Termination. This instrument will expire and terminate (without relieving the Company of any obligations arising from a prior breach of or non-compliance with this instrument) upon either (i) the issuance of stock to the Investor pursuant to Section 1(a) or Section 1(b)(ii); or (ii) the payment, or setting aside for payment, of amounts due the Investor pursuant to Section 1(b)(i) or Section 1(c).

2. *Definitions*

"**Capital Stock**" means the capital stock of the Company, including, without limitation, the "**Common Stock**" and the "**Preferred Stock.**"

"**Change of Control**" means (i) a transaction or series of related transactions in which any "person" or "group" (within the meaning of Section 13(d) and 14(d) of the Securities Exchange Act of 1934, as amended), becomes the "beneficial owner" (as defined in Rule 13d-3 under the Securities Exchange Act of 1934, as amended), directly or indirectly, of more than 50% of the outstanding voting securities of the Company having the right to vote for the election of members of the Company's board of directors, (ii) any reorganization, merger or consolidation of the Company, other than a transaction or series of related transactions in which the holders of the voting securities of the Company outstanding immediately prior to such transaction or series of related transactions retain, immediately after such transaction or series of related transactions, at least a majority of the total voting power represented by the outstanding voting securities of the Company or such other surviving or resulting entity or (iii) a sale, lease or other disposition of all or substantially all of the assets of the Company.

EXHIBIT 3 *(continued)*

"**Company Capitalization**" means the sum, as of immediately prior to the Equity Financing, of: (**1**) all shares of Capital Stock (on an as-converted basis) issued and outstanding, assuming exercise or conversion of all outstanding vested and unvested options, warrants and other convertible securities, but excluding (A) this instrument, (B) all other Safes, and (C) convertible promissory notes; and (2) all shares of Common Stock reserved and available for future grant under any equity incentive or similar plan of the Company, and/or any equity incentive or similar plan to be created or increased in connection with the Equity Financing.

"**Conversion Price**" means the either: (1) the Safe Price or (2) the Discount Price, whichever calculation results in a greater number of shares of Safe Preferred Stock.

"**Discount Price**" means the price per share of the Standard Preferred Stock sold in the Equity Financing multiplied by the Discount Rate.

"**Distribution**" means the transfer to holders of Capital Stock by reason of their ownership thereof of cash or other property without consideration whether by way of dividend or otherwise, other than dividends on Common Stock payable in Common Stock, or the purchase or redemption of Capital Stock by the Company or its subsidiaries for cash or property other than: (i) repurchases of Common Stock held by employees, officers, directors or consultants of the Company or its subsidiaries pursuant to an agreement providing, as applicable, a right of first refusal or a right to repurchase shares upon termination of such service provider's employment or services; or (ii) repurchases of Capital Stock in connection with the settlement of disputes with any stockholder.

"**Dissolution Event**" means (i) a voluntary termination of operations, (ii) a general assignment for the benefit of the Company's creditors or (iii) any other liquidation, dissolution or winding up of the Company (excluding a Liquidity Event), whether voluntary or involuntary.

"**Equity Financing**" means a bona fide transaction or series of transactions with the principal purpose of raising capital, pursuant to which the Company issues and sells Preferred Stock at a fixed pre-money valuation.

"**Initial Public Offering**" means the closing of the Company's first firm commitment underwritten initial public offering of Common Stock pursuant to a registration statement filed under the Securities Act.

EXHIBIT 3 (*continued*)

"**Liquidity Capitalization**" means the number, as of immediately prior to the Liquidity Event, of shares of Capital Stock (on an as-converted basis) outstanding, assuming exercise or conversion of all outstanding vested and unvested options, warrants and other convertible securities, but excluding: (i) shares of Common Stock reserved and available for future grant under any equity incentive or similar plan; (ii) this instrument; (iii) other Safes; and (iv) convertible promissory notes.

"**Liquidity Event**" means a Change of Control or an Initial Public Offering.

"**Liquidity Price**" means the price per share equal to the Valuation Cap divided by the Liquidity Capitalization.

"**Pro Rata Rights Agreement**" means a written agreement between the Company and the Investor (and holders of other Safes, as appropriate) giving the Investor a right to purchase its *pro rata* share of private placements of securities by the Company occurring after the Equity Financing, subject to customary exceptions. *Pro rata* for purposes of the Pro Rata Rights Agreement will be calculated based on the ratio of (1) the number of shares of Capital Stock owned by the Investor immediately prior to the issuance of the securities to (2) the total number of shares of outstanding Capital Stock on a fully diluted basis, calculated as of immediately prior to the issuance of the securities.

"**Safe**" means an instrument containing a future right to shares of Capital Stock, similar in form and content to this instrument, purchased by investors for the purpose of funding the Company's business operations.

"**Safe Preferred Stock**" means the shares of a series of Preferred Stock issued to the Investor in an Equity Financing, having the identical rights, privileges, preferences and restrictions as the shares of Standard Preferred Stock, other than with respect to: (i) the per share liquidation preference and the conversion price for purposes of price-based anti-dilution protection, which will equal the Conversion Price; and (ii) the basis for any dividend rights, which will be based on the Conversion Price.

"**Safe Price**" means the price per share equal to the Valuation Cap divided by the Company Capitalization.

"**Standard Preferred Stock**" means the shares of a series of Preferred Stock issued to the investors investing new money in the Company in connection with the initial closing of the Equity Financing.

EXHIBIT 3 *(continued)*

3. *Company Representations*
   (a) The Company is a corporation duly organized, validly existing and in good standing under the laws of the state of its incorporation, and has the power and authority to own, lease and operate its properties and carry on its business as now conducted.
   (b) The execution, delivery and performance by the Company of this instrument is within the power of the Company and, other than with respect to the actions to be taken when equity is to be issued to the Investor, has been duly authorized by all necessary actions on the part of the Company. This instrument constitutes a legal, valid and binding obligation of the Company, enforceable against the Company in accordance with its terms, except as limited by bankruptcy, insolvency or other laws of general application relating to or affecting the enforcement of creditors' rights generally and general principles of equity. To the knowledge of the Company, it is not in violation of (i) its current certificate of incorporation or bylaws, (ii) any material statute, rule or regulation applicable to the Company or (iii) any material indenture or contract to which the Company is a party or by which it is bound, where, in each case, such violation or default, individually, or together with all such violations or defaults, could reasonably be expected to have a material adverse effect on the Company.
   (c) The performance and consummation of the transactions contemplated by this instrument do not and will not: (i) violate any material judgment, statute, rule or regulation applicable to the Company; (ii) result in the acceleration of any material indenture or contract to which the Company is a party or by which it is bound; or (iii) result in the creation or imposition of any lien upon any property, asset or revenue of the Company or the suspension, forfeiture, or nonrenewal of any material permit, license or authorization applicable to the Company, its business or operations.
   (d) No consents or approvals are required in connection with the performance of this instrument, other than: (i) the Company's corporate approvals; (ii) any qualifications or filings under applicable securities laws; and (iii) necessary corporate approvals for the authorization of Capital Stock issuable pursuant to Section 1.
   (e) To its knowledge, the Company owns or possesses (or can obtain on commercially reasonable terms) sufficient legal rights to all patents, trademarks, service marks, trade names, copyrights, trade secrets, licenses, information, processes and other intellectual property rights necessary for its business as now conducted and as

EXHIBIT 3 (*continued*)

currently proposed to be conducted, without any conflict with, or infringement of the rights of, others.

4. ***Investor Representations***
   (a) The Investor has full legal capacity, power and authority to execute and deliver this instrument and to perform its obligations hereunder. This instrument constitutes valid and binding obligation of the Investor, enforceable in accordance with its terms, except as limited by bankruptcy, insolvency or other laws of general application relating to or affecting the enforcement of creditors' rights generally and general principles of equity.
   (b) The Investor is an accredited investor as such term is defined in Rule 501 of Regulation D under the Securities Act. The Investor has been advised that this instrument and the underlying securities have not been registered under the Securities Act, or any state securities laws and, therefore, cannot be resold unless they are registered under the Securities Act and applicable state securities laws or unless an exemption from such registration requirements is available. The Investor is purchasing this instrument and the securities to be acquired by the Investor hereunder for its own account for investment, not as a nominee or agent, and not with a view to, or for resale in connection with, the distribution thereof, and the Investor has no present intention of selling, granting any participation in, or otherwise distributing the same. The Investor has such knowledge and experience in financial and business matters that the Investor is capable of evaluating the merits and risks of such investment, is able to incur a complete loss of such investment without impairing the Investor's financial condition and is able to bear the economic risk of such investment for an indefinite period of time.
5. ***Miscellaneous***
   (a) Any provision of this instrument may be amended, waived or modified only upon the written consent of the Company and the Investor.
   (b) Any notice required or permitted by this instrument will be deemed sufficient when delivered personally or by overnight courier or sent by email to the relevant address listed on the signature page, or 48 hours after being deposited in the U.S. mail as certified or registered mail with postage prepaid, addressed to the party to be notified at such party's address listed on the signature page, as subsequently modified by written notice.

EXHIBIT 3 (*continued*)

(c) The Investor is not entitled, as a holder of this instrument, to vote or receive dividends or be deemed the holder of Capital Stock for any purpose, nor will anything contained herein be construed to confer on the Investor, as such, any of the rights of a stockholder of the Company or any right to vote for the election of directors or upon any matter submitted to stockholders at any meeting thereof, or to give or withhold consent to any corporate action or to receive notice of meetings, or to receive subscription rights or otherwise until shares have been issued upon the terms described herein.

(d) Neither this instrument nor the rights contained herein may be assigned, by operation of law or otherwise, by either party without the prior written consent of the other; *provided, however*, that this instrument and/or the rights contained herein may be assigned without the Company's consent by the Investor to any other entity who directly or indirectly, controls, is controlled by or is under common control with the Investor, including, without limitation, any general partner, managing member, officer or director of the Investor, or any venture capital fund now or hereafter existing which is controlled by one or more general partners or managing members of, or shares the same management company with, the Investor; and *provided, further*, that the Company may assign this instrument in whole, without the consent of the Investor, in connection with a reincorporation to change the Company's domicile.

(e) In the event any one or more of the provisions of this instrument is for any reason held to be invalid, illegal or unenforceable, in whole or in part or in any respect, or in the event that any one or more of the provisions of this instrument operate or would prospectively operate to invalidate this instrument, then and in any such event, such provision(s) only will be deemed null and void and will not affect any other provision of this instrument and the remaining provisions of this instrument will remain operative and in full force and effect and will not be affected, prejudiced, or disturbed thereby.

(f) All rights and obligations hereunder will be governed by the laws of the State of [Governing Law Jurisdiction], without regard to the conflicts of law provisions of such jurisdiction.

(*Signature page follows*)

Source: Ycombinator.com (Safe: Cap and Discount).

EXHIBIT 4 Step-by-Step solution to Example

SCENARIO 1: SERIES A INVESTOR TAKES 40% FOR $4 MILLION INVESTMENT

- First, we calculate the pre money valuation implied in the Series A investment. Since $4,000,000 buys 40%, the post-money valuation is $10,000,000 ($4,000,000/.4). Thus the pre-money valuation is $6,000,000 (Post valuation of $10,000,000 less Investment of $4,000,000).
- We then calculate the 20% discounted valuation at which the Notes would convert as $4,800,000 ($6,000,000 *0.8). This is the post money valuation of the Seed Investment and therefore the pre-money valuation is $4,050,000 ($4,800,000 - $750,000). Since the pre-money valuation of the Seed Round using the discount is lower than the pre-money valuation cap, Seed investors will use the discounted valuation for their investment and calculate their ownership and conversion price as follows:
    - Ownership attributable to the converted notes is 15.625% ($750,000/$4,800,000).
    - Number shares allocated to the Seed Investors is 185,185 (New Shares = 1/(1 – new ownership) * old shares * new ownership. So (1/(1 – 15.625%) * 1,000,000 * 15.625%).
    - Price per share of $4.05 ($750,000/185,185). Note also that the price per share equals the pre-money valuation ($4,050,000) divided by the pre-money shares (1,000,000)
- We can now calculate the price paid and number of share issued to the Series A investors as follows:
    - Ownership purchased by series A is 40% for $4,000,000.
    - Number shares for the Series A investors is 790,123 (New Shares = 1/(1 – new ownership) * old shares * new ownership. So (1/(1 – 40%) * 1,185,185 * 40%).
    - Price per share is $5.06 ($4,000,000/790,123).
- The total number of shares will be 1,975,699 after the Notes convert and shares are issued to the new Series A investors (1,000,000 Founders + 185,185 Converted Notes + 790,123 Series A Investors) and ownership percentages as follows:
    - The Founder Retains 1,000,000 / 1,975,699 = 50.6%
    - The Converted Note Holders 185,185/1975,699 = 9.4%
    - The Series A Investors 790,514 / 1,975,699 = 40%

SCENARIO 2: SERIES A INVESTOR TAKES 20% FOR $4 MILLION INVESTMENT

- First, we calculate the pre money valuation implied in the Series A investment. Since $4,000,000 buys 20%, the post-money valuation is $20,000,000 ($4,000,000/.2). Thus the pre-money valuation is $16,000,000 (Post valuation of $20,000,000 less Investment of $4,000,000).
- We then calculate the 20% discounted valuation at which the Notes would convert as $12,800,000 ($16,000,000 * 80%). Since this discounted market valuation is greater than the capped valuation, the price per share and the number of shares for the converted Notes are calculated at the cap valuation of $5,000,000.
  - The implied price per share is $5 since there are 1,000,000 shares outstanding prior to the investment and these are valued at $5,000,000.
  - Number shares = $750,000/$5 = 150,000
- We can now calculate the price paid and number of share issued to the Series A investors as follows:
  - Ownership purchased by series A is 20% for $4,000,000.
  - Number shares for the Series A converted notes as 287,500 (New Shares = 1/(1 – new ownership) * old shares * new ownership. So (1/(1 -20%) * 1,150,000 *20%)).
  - Price per share of $13.91 ($4,000,000 / 287,500).
- The total number of shares will be 1,437,500 after the Notes convert and shares are issued to the new Series A investors (1,000,000 Founders + 150,000 Converted Notes + 287,500 Series A Investors) and ownership percentages as follows:
  - The Founder Retains 1,000,000 / 1,437,500 = 69.6%
  - The Converted Note Holders 150,000 / 1,437,500 = 10.4%
  - The Series A Investors 287,500 / 1,437,500 = 20%

Source: Casewriters.

SECTION 6

Entrepreneurial Finance in Emerging Markets

CHAPTER 6.1

Pakistan Rising: Bazaar's Growth Story (A)

Paul Gompers and Gamze Yucaoglu

The impact we want to have is not limited by the problem we are trying to solve: We are creating an inspirational story out of Pakistan that brings together the country's best talent and will breed the next generation of entrepreneurs for the country.

—Hamza Jawaid and Saad Jangda,
Co-founders, Bazaar

In June 2021, Hamza Jawaid and Saad Jangda, the co-founders of Bazaar Technologies (Bazaar), a high-growth B2B e-commerce marketplace in Pakistan, were proudly looking over the company's metrics. (See **Exhibit 1** for an overview of the core team.) Just over a year after its launch, Bazaar was flourishing, and the company was already working with some of the largest global FMCG[a] companies to serve 75,000 grocery merchants across five cities, generating close to $7 million in monthly revenues. (See **Exhibit 2** for a snapshot of Bazaar.) A leader in the country's nascent e-commerce ecosystem, Bazaar was educating its customers on how to order via the Bazaar app, which would save them precious time used up traveling long distances do their weekly procurement. In April 2021, the company launched Easy Khata, its digital ledger vertical, and saw more than 100,000 merchants sign up in under two months. Now, feeling confident about how far their e-commerce and digital ledger arms had come, the co-founders were contemplating whether, in order to assure their company's success and sustainability, they needed to venture into providing financing for its mostly-unbanked customers.

a FMCG stands for fast-moving consumer goods and refers to products such as non-durable household goods that are sold quickly and at a relatively low cost.

Pakistan Rising: Bazaar's Growth Story (A)
by PAUL GOMPERS, GAMZE YUCAOGLU, case number 9-822-098 Rev. FEBRUARY 28, 2023

When Bazaar was founded in mid-2020, its main product was an e-commerce app that facilitated inventory procurement for offline grocery retailers and mom-and-pop stores across the country. The company was disrupting a very manual $125 billion-a-year retail market, $48 billion of which was attributed to groceries.[1] Just months after its founding, the company made headlines for having raised $1.3 million in a pre-seed round. Both co-founders had global experience. Jawaid had worked at McKinsey, and Jangda had worked at Snapchat and later at the ride-hailing company, Careem. They had ambitious plans to build an operating system for traditional retail in Pakistan that would empower merchants, simplify their procurement, and encourage growth, but more importantly, they were also on a mission "to build an awesome company in and from Pakistan."

Jangda and Jawaid were proud of the progress they had made. They realized, however, that they had merely scratched the surface. With many more cities to cover and thousands of merchants yet to be tapped, the company had great potential. Bazaar had solidified its foothold with its main e-commerce app, and it had cracked the complex logistics issue by partnering with several third-party service providers. The digital ledger had also taken off beyond the team's expectations, but would these successes create a foundation that would ensure Bazaar's sustainability and profitability in the long term? Most of its customers were unbanked; if they had access to financing, they would be able to grow much faster—so should Bazaar consider launching a financing product? Or would the introduction of a Fintech service spread the young company's focus and resources too thin at a time when there were still many new markets to penetrate with their first two services? As the competitive environment heated up, members of the Pakistani diaspora—lured by prospects of claiming a piece of the e-commerce market—had started returning home, bringing with them solid experience in tech hubs abroad. Jawaid and Jangda found themselves in the position of having to decide quickly what direction they would take moving forward.

PAKISTAN AND THE GROCERY RETAIL MARKET

Located in South Asia, Pakistan was bounded by Iran to the west, Afghanistan to the north and northwest, China to the northeast, and India to the east and southeast.[2] In the south, the multi-ethnic country bordered the Arabian Sea.[3] (See **Exhibit 3** for a map of Pakistan.) Pakistan was the world's 33rd largest country by area, and with its population of almost 227 million (2020), it was the fifth most populous.[4] (See **Exhibit 4** for economic and demographic indicators.) With over 64% of the population below the age of 30, it had one of the largest young populations in the world[5]— 41.6% of its total labor force was between the ages of 15 and 29.[6] Thanks to these demographics, combined with a growing middle class, the country had the seventh largest retail market in the world.

In Pakistan, grocery retail was largely traditional and offline. *Kiryana*s, the country's ubiquitous mom-and-pop stores, were found in virtually every neighborhood. They sold everything from fresh foods to durable household goods, cleaning supplies, beverages, and tobacco. Some of these local stores grew into regional enterprises.[7] Of an estimated two million neighborhood stores in Pakistan, 800,000 were kiryanas,[8] which accounted for 70% of all grocery purchases in the country.[9] Even when international chains like Metro and Carrefour entered Pakistan, kiryanas continued to dominate the market. The latest data, from 2012, showed that kiryana stores had an annual turnover of approximately $3 billion, while domestic convenience stores had only $200 million. The more modern supermarkets came in at $176 million.[10] (See **Exhibit 5** for an overview of players and market shares.) Other important players in the Pakistani grocery retail value chain included manufacturers, distributors, and wholesalers. Manufacturers (such as P&G and Nestlé) supplied to major retailers and distributors. To procure their inventory, kiryanas usually relied on distributors that came around the neighborhoods for curbside delivery every few days.[11] In more remote areas, store owners periodically closed their stores to travel to a more central location to procure their weekly assortment. With an estimated population of 100 million, Pakistan was home to the world's third largest unbanked population after China and India.[12] Small and medium-sized enterprises (SMEs), which included kiryanas, made up around 40% of Pakistan's GDP. Most of these were unbanked,[b] so they operated manually, dealt in cash,[13] and had virtually no access to loans.[14,c] Those that did have financing used it to meet their working capital needs, leaving no resources to finance growth.[15] (See **Exhibit 6** for overview of unbanked population in Pakistan.)

---

b Unbanked adults tend to have low educational attainment. In Pakistan, 75% (global average was 65%) percent of the unbanked had a primary education or less, compared with about half of adults overall in developing economies. Global Findex Database, "The Unbanked", The World Bank, 2017, https://globalfindex.worldbank.org/sites/globalfindex/files/chapters/2017%20Findex%20full%20report_chapter2.pdf, accessed January 2022.

c Between 6-13% percent of adults without an account at a financial institution cited religious concerns as a reason, and many complained about the lengthy documentation process and multiple branch visits needed to open an account. Global Findex Database, "The Unbanked", The World Bank, 2017, https://globalfindex.worldbank.org/sites/globalfindex/files/chapters/2017%20Findex%20full%20report_chapter2.pdf, accessed January 2022.

In 2020, the COVID-19 pandemic prompted precautionary buying—people stocked up on staples in case there might be shortages, and lockdowns led to a rise in home cooking, marking a shift away from foodservice outlets like restaurants and cafeterias. The result was that the food and groceries market grew by 11.3%.[16] The highly fragmented and inefficient retail market was ripe for disruption and starting 2015, several e-commerce players entered the market. MandiExpress, a fresh produce delivery service in Karachi, launched its operations both in B2C and B2B; it catered to prominent restaurants and other e-commerce platforms and also traded in the wholesale market.[17] The same year, Daraz a big fashion e-commerce player backed by Rocket Internet, launched Dfresh, which offered B2B and B2C fruit and vegetable delivery.[18] Such enterprises helped educate both retailers and end customers while creating an awareness around technology startups, various business models, and fundraising and financing. In 2018, Alibaba acquired Daraz for an undisclosed amount.[19]

THE STARTUP ECOSYSTEM

In the past decades, ongoing struggles with Afghanistan had posed a security threat and created political instability in the country. As such, Pakistan remained underinvested by foreign venture capital. It was also one of the least digitized economies in the world: in 2021, it ranked 76th out of 100 countries.[20] Starting in 2015, as the political and economic climate stabilized and confidence in the security in the country and the region was restored, startups that addressed local challenges with a globally competitive angle began to appear on the scene, and investment started to flow in. This trend was amplified by increasing Internet and smartphone penetration. As of 2020, with 76.4 million users, Internet penetration was estimated to be around 35%,[21] and smartphone penetration stood at 51%, having grown fivefold since 2014.[22] (See **Exhibit** 7 for digital penetration and e-commerce metrics.) The infrastructure improved with the arrival of broadband Internet coverage, which in 2104 included 4G. To help cultivate the ecosystem, incubators and training programs for startups such as NIC Peshawar (established in 2018) and the Durshal network of incubators[23] launched over the years.[24]

With increased confidence in the economy and regional stability, local angel and seed investors entered the scene, universities began to host startup competitions, and every year more than 20,000 students graduated with degrees in IT and engineering.[25] (See **Exhibit 8** for Pakistani startup ecosystem snapshot.) The diaspora had carved itself a niche in IT—Silicon Valley alone was home to 12,500 Pakistanis. Pakistani entrepreneurs were inspired by the success of startups elsewhere in the region like Careem, the ride hailing app that Uber purchased for $3.1 billion in late 2019.[26] Many from the diaspora were returning to Pakistan to start their own business, taking advantage of opportunities offered by the burgeoning startup culture.[27] In 2020, the pandemic magnified the need for digitizing and modernizing the economy, thereby accelerating the tech boom.[28] The same year, Pakistan had an estimated 97% increase in venture capital (VC) funding, and the number of startups grew from 32 to 41, with the value of investment surging from $47.5 million to $65.7 million.[29] In 2020, Pakistan was the world's 46th largest market for e-commerce,[d] ahead of Peru and behind Greece, and the revenues were on the rise.[30] (See **Exhibit 9** for an overview of e-commerce growth.) Fashion, which accounted for 68% of the revenues, was the largest segment, followed by electronics and media (13%), then food and personal care (10%), and toys, hobby and DIY (5%).[31] As of the third quarter of 2020, it was estimated that there were 2,980 startups in Pakistan.[32] Nonetheless, the country lagged behind its neighbor, India, and the Middle East in the number of startups and funding received.

COMPETITIVE ENVIRONMENT

It was against this backdrop that e-commerce players first emerged in Pakistan. As of 2021, Bazaar's most serious competitors— Dastgyr, Jugnu, Tajir, and Retalio—all served kiryana stores, and each provided similar offerings in the online inventory procurement segment.[33] Founded in 2019, Jugnu had onboarded 12,000 retailers. In 2020, the Lahore-based Tajir raised $1.8 million.[34] Retailo Technologies, founded in 2020 in Riyadh, Saudi Arabia by former Careem executives, entered the B2B supply chain industry and had been growing its GMV[e] at 35% month-over-month since closing its pre-seed round in October 2020.[35] It was serving over 30,000 retailers in Karachi and Riyadh as of year-end 2020.[36] Dastgyr, also founded in 2020 by ex-Careem executives, was a Karachi-based B2B mobile e-commerce marketplace that had raised an undisclosed six-figure

---

d The e-commerce market included online sales of physical goods to a private end user (B2C), via computer as well as mobile purchases via smartphones and tablets. The definition excluded digitally distributed services (e.g., travel tickets), online stores dedicated to digital media downloads or streams, online stores dedicated to B2B markets, and sales between private individuals (C2C) within the e-commerce market. "The Ecommerce Market in Pakistan", EcommerceDB, https://ecommercedb.com/en/markets/pk/all, accessed January 2022.

e GMV referred to gross merchandise value, which denoted the volume of goods sold on an e-commerce platform.

(USD) investment from angel investors in the United States, the Middle East, and Pakistan;[37] by September 2020, it too was serving 30,000 kiryanas.[38] The same year, Blink (by Eat Mubarak) entered the market with a B2B2C model that provided an online ordering solution to restaurants and hotels.[39] During the pandemic lockdowns, these startups grew significantly, and in 2021, 17% of the total investments raised in Pakistan (five out of 26 deals) were channeled to B2B grocery startups. These included Tajir, Bazaar, MandiExpress, and Dastgyr.[40] (See **Exhibit 10** for a grocery retail industry map.) Over the years, the multi-national chains had launched their online channels, and new pure-online players and platform players were forming partnerships with grocery. The Pakistan grocery retail remained fragmented, however, and most retail was still offline.

BAZAAR'S FOUNDING STORY

In 2020, Jawaid received a call from Jangda that led to his decision to leave his comfortable, lucrative job at McKinsey in Dubai. He recalled, "Following Uber's acquisition of Careem that made Careem the region's first unicorn Saad was convinced that the startup ecosystem in Pakistan would be the next one to take off and that this was the time to come back home to start our own venture. Compared to India, Indonesia, Vietnam, and Egypt, Pakistan was getting very little venture funding, but experienced Pakistani talent was already coming back from abroad." Jangda chimed in: "Careem was a Middle Eastern story, Foodpanda was a Rocket-Internet story... I found myself asking why no one had built a story out of Pakistan yet. Here we have this incredible talent that ends up leaving the country because the opportunities just aren't there. With Hamza's experience and mine combined, I felt we were in the best position to create that story." For Jawaid, the conversation was a "call to action" that made him feel compelled to become a catalyst of change in his home country.

As soon as Jawaid arrived in Karachi, he and Jangda got together for a brainstorming session. The duo had a grand vision: they wanted "to create an awesome company in Pakistan where everyone would want to work." Searching for the business idea, they were looking for a "very Pakistan-focused" opportunity, where technology could play an enabler or discovery-role. They were looking for a "very large dollar opportunity to be able to attract wide and deeply talented pool of local people." Drawing on their experience in consulting, they conducted a benchmarking analysis to see where Pakistan stood vis-à-vis markets in other developing countries. Meanwhile, Pakistan had become the fifth biggest revenue generator for TikTok, the video-focused social networking company, according to the co-founders. Jawaid commented, "This just showed us how eager Pakistani consumers were for digital products, and it also provided us an active user-base who we could build products for." Jangda and Jawaid found themselves shortlisting B2B and B2C opportunities. Shortlisting ideas, they finally decided to build a B2B platform to help the millions of merchants procure their inventory. Jawaid said, "Both our fathers were merchants, and Saad and I grew up observing the many problems our fathers had to deal with. We were certain B2C e-commerce would also take off in time, and we felt that the best way to enter the market would be through digitizing the B2B supply chain and addressing merchants' problems."

Jawaid and Jangda did their field research and personally met with 300-400 merchants to get a grip on what their lives and challenges looked like. While suppliers like Unilever and P&G had exclusive distributors who served the tier 1[f] merchants, estimates suggested that these reached only 200,000 of the one million merchants. Most merchants had to travel weekly to buy supplies from wholesalers. Distributors and wholesalers operated with thin margins—on average, 4% net after deducting the cost to serve (3%). By building a B2B platform, Jawaid and Jangda could connect underserved merchants with brands and leave out the middlemen. They figured that manufacturers, who were unable to reach 80% of the market, would be willing to sell directly to Jawaid and Jangda to get a better market penetration. The two friends knew the margins would not be very attractive, but the volume itself—one million kiryanas—was enormous, and they could use technology to create efficiencies and the scale to minimize last mile costs.

Next, using channels like LinkedIn and their own network, Jawaid and Jangda reached out to entrepreneurs who had experience launching successful B2B platforms in other developing markets. They managed to arrange meetings with the founders of Ula in Indonesia and MaxAB in Egypt. Jawaid explained, "We asked these founders about the challenges they had faced, which problems they managed to solve, and what to expect. We wanted to learn from their journeys where we could, instead of making all of their mistakes ourselves." In April 2020, they conceived Bazaar and rolled up their sleeves to create a minimum viable product. The plan was to start in Karachi, the biggest city in Pakistan, to test and refine the model and then replicate it in other cities. Jawaid recalled, "We went to an actual retailer and asked him what he buys and where he buys it from. Then we went to the supplier and arranged for us to procure on the retailer's behalf and deliver it to him. It was an offline pilot, one we built on Google Sheets and monitored using our mobile phones, but it helped us understand

f Bazaar defined Tier 1 kiryanas as those that generated more than $8,000 in monthly revenues.

how the supply chain worked." While the pilot ran, the two friends each reached out to their own networks to connect with founders who had raised money, aiming to get a better understanding of the process before creating an investor deck. Jawaid recalled, "We put together a couple of slides showing what we thought the market size was, how we planned to address pain points in the supply chain, and who we are. We then asked literally everybody in our network to connect us with VC funds and lined up some meetings." They were soon reviewing term sheets, and in June 2020, they closed a seed round of $1.3 million. Bazaar officially launched in June 2020. Aatif Awan, founder of Indus Valley Capital, was a lead investor. He recalled, "Hamza and Saad approached the problem with a learn-it-all mindset, not with a know-it-all attitude, to borrow a phrase from Satya Nadella. They wanted to learn from other founders solving similar problems in Indonesia, Egypt and elsewhere. This is something great founders do; they really wanted to create a success story, and it was inspiring."

Culture and Recruitment

Jawaid and Jangda had been best friends since the age of nine and were very much aligned in terms of values and vision. Their individual skill sets were complementary, which made it easy to divide up the work and responsibilities. Jangda took on the CTO role, overseeing products, and Jawaid agreed to lead the talks with investors and commercial partners as CEO. Jangda said:

> We respected each other's experience and expertise and decided to abide by a simple rule in case we couldn't come an agreement on a particular issue: to agree to disagree. So if Hamza thinks something is right in terms of finance, strategy, or operations, and I am convinced it's wrong, we simply agree to disagree—and then I defer to his position and commit to it 100%. We're able to do this because we've known each other since we were children and have full trust in each other, so we are able to express our views openly. This is a huge advantage.

The co-founders worked on a values framework for the company. Jangda explained their thinking: "We would be tapping into a young workforce to lead hypergrowth and we knew that company culture would be the glue to keep everyone aligned. Hamza and I each wrote down four values that define us—values we would build our culture and strategy on." On their final list was dreaming big, getting things done, looking out for each other, and having fun. Jangda commented, "Our vision was a bold one. We wanted to create an awesome company that brings together and cultivates

Pakistani talent, and in the process, we wanted to have fun as the company scaled, making sure that we looked after each other's wellbeing at the same time."

Next, the co-founders narrowed down the core competencies Bazaar would need—e-commerce, logistics, and technology—and set out to hire their core team. To build the tech team, Jawaid and Jangda tapped into their own local networks to find their head of engineering and software engineers, whom they hired from local software houses. Jangda said, "The best entrepreneurs are the best talent recruiters, and that's where we spend most of our time, with a very simple thesis: 'Hire the best people and then get out of their way and leave them to do their job.'" Jawaid added:

> The existing talent pool of people with global experience is limited in Pakistan. We are also constrained by the fact that investors want to see the big names, the corporate logos, on the CVs of our executive team. So, if we fall in love with someone, we bend over backwards to get them to join the team, even if we don't know exactly what this person will be doing. We knew if we got the right talent, we could repurpose them along the way.

The co-founders agreed that with a combination of a strong, values-driven culture, an exciting mission, and a well-defined framework, the right hires could do wonders. They also knew that unless they themselves exhibited the values and lived the mission, these would not stick. Jangda said, "If you have to put the mission up on a wall, it is not engrained. We live these and talk about them in each meeting and every townhall. We also make sure that, in interviewing every potential hire, we share our mission with them personally." From his experience at Snapchat and Careem, Jangda also knew how big a role the art of product design played in a company's success: not just for external communication with the customer, but also internally, to drive momentum. He would need to get the product right.

The E-Commerce Product

Bazaar wanted to make a meaningful improvement in merchants' lives and help them grow their businesses. The co-founders knew that if they built the right product, focused on low prices and convenience, and offered a customer-friendly, easy-to-use interface, they could get customer engagement. Jangda said, "We placed product at the core of our strategy." He continued, "We could only solve merchants' problems if we created a product they would actually use, so we focused on simplicity and ease of use and positioned the product close to the customer." The initial ordering platform was very basic, with the backend completely offline on Excel and Google Sheets. They tested it extensively. The ordering app had a simple interface where the merchants could select the products and indicate the order date. Once an order came in, the app directed it to the nearest warehouse, where the order was prepared, loaded onto the next outgoing truck, and delivered to the customer the next day.[g] A typical order was around $45, and merchants typically ordered five times a month. Payment was cash on delivery. Bazaar surveyed merchants to learn their top 10–20 stock keeping units (SKUs) and at first offered a limited assortment of the most sought-after low-margin bulky items such as pulses, sugar, and flour. Once they had enough traction, the company widened its SKU portfolio to include high-margin branded products from Unilever, P&G, and Nestlé. Ahmed Siyadat, head of B2B business, said, "Pakistan has a well-developed distribution network, so it wasn't easy for us to persuade the suppliers that they should bypass the distributors and sell directly to us so that we could reach merchants the distributors were not able to serve. Distributors were not even trying to reach beyond tier 2; those merchants were too small to be worth their time."

One value proposition Bazaar offered to suppliers and manufacturers was its ability to help them serve these merchants. It could also provide actionable insights on purchase patterns and trends. Bazaar therefore planned to cast a wide net to capture merchants in tiers 2 to 4 areas and then focus on increasing inventory share with the active users. Merchants could use the app to order as often as they wanted, and as the volume of orders increased, Bazaar's last mile cost and cost to serve decreased. At the beginning, manufacturers were wary about alienating their long-time distributors, but over time, they got more comfortable selling directly to Bazaar. The company absorbed negative margins in favor of building a relationship with the suppliers, and then when it got more volume and therefore more negotiation power, it focused on driving the margins up. Adnan Siddiqui, the company's head of finance, commented, "In our business, the elasticity of discount to revenue is significant. Even half a percent can take you a long way in terms of growth. But is it sustainable? We need to be careful about that balance." Thus, from the get-go, the operations team kept a close eye on metrics such as average order value and monthly order per user[h] and made frequent corrections at every level.

g Bazaar delivered all orders that the company received by 10 pm on day one, the next day.

h Bazaar focused on both increasing the number of SKUs sold and order frequency, both of which helped the company increase its wallet share per merchant.

Customer Acquisition For Bazaar, acquiring customers would mean breaking merchant habits and behaviors that had been cemented over many years. Marketing would need to be from the bottom-up and would have to focus on developing relationships and building trust. As attractive as it might have seemed, the co-founders decided against hiring an experienced executive from the FMCG world. Jawaid explained that they wanted a completely fresh perspective to disrupt the market. "If we hired an experienced person," he said, "we knew they would carry on with the old ways of doing business, and with their assumptions and prejudices." Overall, the co-founders looked for: young people who were driven problem solvers who would bring a fresh mind and work hard, and for senior people with experience in a global startup or a local supply chain who were passionate about Bazaar's mission.

One piece of advice the co-founders had gotten from founders in the region was "not to be shy about leveraging the cheap human capital in the region." Jawaid explained: "Capital is expensive. We were encouraged to 'throw people at the problem,' so we contracted 40–50 people to set up kiosks around Karachi to recruit drivers and acquire customers (merchants). At $8 an hour, this was much cheaper than ads on Facebook or Google!" Jandga added, "We realize that people are the key to our success; we personally interview everyone. We have low-paid, under-educated guys driving vehicles from the 1980s and '90s. They are our point of contact with the customer. We have invested a lot in training." On average, it took a team member about three visits to convince a merchant—so that comes to about $1.2 per customer." The team focused on acquiring a critical mass of merchants in one neighborhood before moving on to the next, letting word-of-mouth entice other merchants. Before long, 90% of the orders were coming in from the app—an uptake rate much higher than what had been observed in the region—and 10% of the orders were taken when team members visited the merchants.

Technology The co-founders set up a decentralized organization and created squads of 12–15 people, complete with a product manager, a product designer, an engineering manager, and analysts to attack issues at hand. The operations squad worked closely with the warehouses, and the business squad collaborated with customer acquisition. Jangda said, "We have an insane organizational culture where we optimize for speed over anything else." He continued, "Both Hamza and I are very involved in everything that's happening, including in the different functions and verticals. We join huddles and product meetings as observers—but the decision-making power lies with the person who is leading a particular effort." (See **Exhibit 11** for the organizational chart.) To develop new features for Bazaar's products, the tech team closely examined exactly how TikTok had captured its audience. "We wanted to create features that would draw the user into using the app," Jangda said. "We throw a lot of darts to see what sticks; we don't waste time on designing the perfect architecture or the best solution. Instead, we build something quick in the simplest way and then flesh it out if it's successful." The team visited customers every week to sit down with them to show new features and to do user testing on those features. If something was not enthusiastically received, it was scrapped. Jangda estimated that one in every five ideas was a hit. One of these was Payya, the Urdu word for wheel of fortune. Jangda explained, "Early on, to increase the merchants' order value, we got the idea to gamify the ordering experience on the app. One of our interns suggested a 'wheel of fortune' on the app, with prizes like bicycles, washing machines, and coins. The probability of winning was pretty low, but people went crazy over it, and we were the talk of the town. It is all about finding things your users care about." Some months later, the sales team realized that, while the merchants were in fact businessmen, they had no business cards. Giving them business cards seemed like an easy way to make them feel good about themselves. The product team therefore added a "business card" button on the app that helped merchants design business cards for themselves that they could then download and have printed. The team on the ground, seeing that most merchants were observant Muslims, suggested a "prayer time" function for the app. This too was very popular, and it boosted engagement on the app. The customer experience-driven approach was paying off, and Bazaar's customer retention rate[i] was above 90%. (See **Exhibit 12** for app interfaces.)

Meanwhile, Bazaar integrated a few off-the-shelf solutions, such as the one they used to optimize routes. For products that ran on the backend, however, they developed products in-house. For example, the team built a custom-designed app for the riders, the first mobile warehouse management software that allowed every warehouse operation to be done through an Android app, and another one for the sales team to use for acquiring and retaining customers. For the headquarters, the team built "control towers," tools to help management monitor processes and transactions across the cities where they operated so that the finance team could automate the reconciliation process.

---

i Bazaar calculated retention as the percentage of previous month's customers who transacted in the current month using the following formula: {(Previous month active users who are active this month/Previous month active users)*100}. For purposes of comparison: Twiga Foods, a B2B platform in Africa, tracked revenue retention rates, which grew by 140% in six months.

Last Mile and Fulfillment

Last mile delivery and warehousing were the backbone of any supply chain business, and e-commerce was no exception. Jawaid and Jangda sought out an experienced operations person and hired Zarak Khan, who previously led the performance team for Careem's ride-hailing business in Karachi and eventually went on to set up Careem's delivery business across the several countries where it operated. (See **Exhibit 1**.) Khan had gone abroad to pursue his career after graduating from college. "It was the dream and purpose of building something in Pakistan that got me back." His mandate at Bazaar was to build the first layer of logistics for the company. He first broke down all the tasks. Everything that happened inside a warehouse was fulfillment, starting from receiving inbounds, to placing them, and then getting the orders ready to hand off to the last mile team. And then there was last mile, which looked into the entire delivery operations. Khan immediately immersed himself into the day-to-day workings of the supply chain and logistics. He spent his first few months in the warehouse, setting up the workflow, hiring a team, and identifying the key performance indicators (KPIs), including cost per delivery and rider utilization—just to get the team thinking about these metrics. He said, "At Careem I saw what a performance-based mindset can do. Data can drive operations, especially in startups where the quantum of transactions is so large. Data needs to be the guiding light in our decision-making." Khan's team digitized all the data points on the demand side (the sales touchpoints). Khan said, "It's important to digitize manual processes, because unless you get the data to talk to each other, things go unnoticed." For the next couple of months, Khan focused on performance planning. The team focused on figuring out how the city worked and mapping it. They also spent time to figure out how to drive agent performance and how to get customers to order particular food categories. During this time, Khan also set up the data pipeline and the reporting structure, all of which would serve as the blueprint for when the company expanded beyond Karachi.

Warehousing To ensure reliability and minimize stock-outs, the co-founders had decided that Bazaar should own its inventory (versus doing just-in-time delivery). Initially, Bazaar was running its operations from a 20-foot by 20-foot section of Jawaid's grandfather's warehouse, where they had access to wholesalers and a place where vehicles could dock and undock. When they outgrew that, they acquired part of Jangda's father's electronics warehouse and moved the operations there. Clearly, a more professional and sustainable warehousing strategy was needed. Jawaid and Jangda first tried to partner with a third party but quickly gave up, deciding instead that they needed to build or lease their own warehouses for Bazaar. Jangda commented, "The ecosystem was totally barren. We could either wait for other startups to emerge and address warehousing and last mile logistics—or we could build the warehouses ourselves. Building your own adds to the operational complexity in the short term, but it creates a scalable foundation that connects everything. When we have the entire tech stack, we can customize as we need along the way." In October 2020, Hashim Khan joined Bazaar as its head of operations, bringing with him valuable supply chain experience from P&G, Unilever, and Daraz. (See **Exhibit 1**.) At that point, the company was growing 35% month-on-month, so Hashim[j] was tasked with scaling the infrastructure in line with the company's growth and with streamlining the processes. He recalled, "Usually, you can use a two-by-two matrix— urgent versus important—to prioritize tasks, but this filtering didn't work at Bazaar when I joined. There were simply too many important things that needed to be done at the same time. The work was around the clock, so our first order of business was to buy ourselves mattresses to sleep on in the warehouse." He quickly realized that his top priority should be building a team and empowering them to tackle the tasks. He said, "You find one solution to an issue, but when the volumes start growing exponentially, you need a different solution for the same problem. For example, as the number of SKUs increased, we needed bigger warehouses, and then we needed to define new processes to manage the bigger warehouses."

Logistics On the logistics side, rather than building from scratch, the company decided to partner with national players that had their own fleet and drivers and the ability to scale as Bazaar scaled up. The operations team specified the number and type of (non-branded) vehicles it needed (types ranged from motorbikes to eight-ton pick-ups, depending on the size of the delivery) and also contracted local, smaller logistics companies to meet spikes in demand when needed. The national partners were paid either a weekly or a monthly fixed rate, and the local partners were paid a daily rental fee when used. Operations also contracted with recruitment agencies to interview, select, and train logistics partners and riders,[k] Bazaar riders who delivered the goods to merchants and collected the cash payments.[l] Riders, who wore Bazaar-branded jackets, were compensated with a fixed monthly salary plus a bonus that depended on on-time in-full delivery and on gross to net conversion.[m] The operations team trained the rid-

j The case will refer to Hashim Khan as Hashim to avoid confusion with Zarak Khan, whom the case refers to as Khan.

k In some cases, the riders were also the drivers themselves.

l Close to 100% of the business was conducted in cash.

m Gross to net conversion referred to how much of the gross order value the rider was able to convert into cash.

ers, aiming to promote them to team leaders who could then onboard and train the next 10–15 riders in the Bazaar culture.

GROWING BAZAAR

Having started with 100 products, Bazaar built a catalogue of thousands of SKUs over time, and by early 2021, the Karachi market was behaving like a mature market. The company had signed on nearly 80% of the city's retailers, and they were giving repeat orders, many of which included higher margin, branded goods. Awan commented, "Bazaar ended up having to build the operations itself due to the lack of an existing 3PL[n] ecosystem. This is a logistics-heavy business, so transportation and warehousing costs matter. By doing this in-house, we preserved margins, built a world-class operations system that gives the company control over all aspects of the business, helps it scale faster and widens its moat." Bazaar was thus ready to focus on increasing its margins in Karachi and was looking to grow elsewhere as well.

Vertical Expansion: Easy Khata

In January 2021, the company raised $6.5 million in the largest seed round in the country to date.[41] Christopher Schroeder, founder of Next Billion Ventures, who had joined the round said:

> This was our first deal in Pakistan, and as soon as I met the co-founders, I decided to go for it. I have in invested in B2B marketplaces from East Africa to Latin America, so I had some sense of the real challenges setting up logistics and other services, but I also knew that each market has its own unique challenges. Hamza and Saad know the market realities inside out. The solutions needed here are very different—the problem all but unheard of—in Silicon Valley and is enormous as over 70% of all retail sales go through small markets like this. Pakistan is where Egypt was five to ten years ago, but from those lessons and the acceleration of tech adoption everywhere, it will catch up very quickly.

The money came in around the time the core team was discussing a new vertical. Jawaid explained the impetus: "When our sales team visited

---

n 3PL referred to an organization's using a third-party logistics company to outsource its elements of its distribution, warehousing, and fulfillment services.

stores, they would see piles of physical registers that the merchants used for keeping track of their accounting and the credit lines they had given out to their customers." He continued, "The customers, just like the merchants themselves, are unbanked, so all the business is in cash, and merchants build on these credit lines. On top of that, it's culturally awkward for merchants to ask their customers to pay the money they owe, so many of them struggle to get payment and end up with a working capital problem." This seemed like a rather easy problem to solve with technology. The core team decided to address this pain point by building a bookkeeping app that was modeled on examples they had seen in India, Mexico, and Egypt. The co-founders turned to those global startups to understand how best to monetize such an app—but then they decided to offer it for free. Jawaid explained, "Monetizing this stand-alone app looked very challenging, so we decided to view it as a customer acquisition channel for our B2B app. That way, it would also help us gather more data on our merchants." To run a pilot, Jangda assembled a small team with a couple of engineers and a product manager. After a successful pilot, this digital vertical, called Easy Khata, was launched in March 2021. It was run by a business head supported by product managers and engineers. Awan commented, "There are successful digital ledger companies and successful B2B platforms globally, but no one had combined the two before. They have the same userbase, but their use cases are different. Bazaar used the ledger to grow its B2B business, acquire customers cheaply, convert them efficiently, and gather data to decide where the company should go next. It's a remarkable strategy that's given them a competitive advantage."

Geographic Expansion

By early 2021, margins in Karachi had improved and were moving into positive territory. (See **Exhibit 13** for financials from Karachi operations.) The company was now ready to establish itself in other metro cities to create a larger footprint. The operations team dissected the country into three broad regions—south, center, and north. They set up a local team (to take care of operations and admin) for each region and agreed to target urban cities with more than 3,000 retailers. Khan explained how they decided which ones would come first: "We first look at macro factors like the number of retailers, the total market size, and availability of infrastructure. We also study consumption factors and the availability of supplies and suppliers. We then assign scores to prospective cities, rank them, and create an expansion roadmap." Lahore, having ranked at the top, would be the next city. Khan took with him a number of "launchers," experienced operations people who understand the workings of Bazaar and its culture and set up a base in Lahore. He recalled, "The second city to launch is usually the trickiest. You have the operational know-how and the tech stack but expanding requires a new team and a new physical infrastructure. You have to rent warehouses, contract and onboard logistics ..." The launch team did the high-level hiring, trained the staff, and remained in the city a month or two for an incubation period before moving to the next launch city. The launch team periodically checked in with the local teams, visited these markets regularly to transfer learnings across cities, and checked that culture, ownership, and values were being integrated. Last mile was done through Bazaar's existing logistics partners and the ad hoc local partners.

In the summer of 2021, the operations team rolled out a customer satisfaction survey. Retailers could select a happy or a sad face to indicate how they felt about their experience. Fortunately, 90% of the feedback was positive, so Bazaar planned to introduce NPS[o] scoring in the upcoming months. Hashim commented, "I'm confident about the way we plan operations. Our challenges in this expansion phase will be maintaining our amazing work culture, finding good infrastructure in the new cities, and keeping the data and the processes standardized."

LOOKING AHEAD

The operations team was working full force to launch Bazaar in Faisalabad and Multan by the end of the year and was aiming to reach 15 cities in the following six months. Financially, Karachi was close to breaking even, and the co-founders were confident they had found a good balance between growth and profitability for their B2B business. On its e-commerce app, the company had close to 30,000 active users monthly, and Easy Khata had reached one million active users since its launch. With its 70-strong engineering team, the company had already built a very advanced stack of technology for operations and last mile, and it was considering spinning out its logistics vertical to make it a revenue-generating business. On the collection side, Bazaar was contemplating ways to offer digital payments via the retail app. The team had grown to 181; the average age was 27.

The co-founders were confident about the future of the company and were eager to fuel the growth story ahead of a new fundraising round. At the moment, growth was coming from geographical expansion and customer acquisition, but both seemed to have capped. Without access to loans, merchants could only buy as much as they had available cash for; they had no

o NPS stands for net promoter score, which measured a customer's likelihood of recommending a product or company to a friend.

other way to grow order volumes. One potential solution was for Bazaar to lend its customers money to grow their businesses. Traditionally, banks and microfinance institutions had avoided lending to these SMEs because the cost to acquire and serve and the cost of risk were too high. Since Bazaar already had a relationship with the merchants, might the company be better positioned to provide financing to this unbanked population? Jangda said, "For years, the merchants have been ignored. If and when they were offered any financing, it was always very expensive; interest rates were usually over 50%. But at Bazaar, we won't have a customer acquisition cost because we already know our merchants—we deliver their goods. We also have a digital relationship with them via our apps, where we collect data on their purchases and payments." Jawaid added, "Our risk to serve is also low. We already have data on the customers from their purchasing and payment patterns, so we can easily assign credit scores. And what's more, their livelihood depends on buying from us, so they won't want to default on us. Our cost to serve should be relatively low, too. The B2B business is cash-based and we already have a system to collect cash from our customers. We also have capital."

While all these factors looked positive, the co-founders also knew that a lending business would require a totally different skill base. It would also be subject to different set-up regulations, and given its complexity, it might divert the focus of the executive team as the company was aggressively expanding into new cities. They also wondered if expanding into financing was the best use of their capital. Jawaid said, "We raised this round with blood, sweat, and tears, and we live in a part of the world where the tide can turn any day and disrupt capital inflows. Is a financing vertical the best use of our capital?" Siddiqui commented, "It's very important for the business to become cashflow positive; it isn't okay to burn money just because we have it. We have to identify our real market and move toward profitability. A new vertical could also potentially alarm our investors." And would a lending vertical be spreading a hyper-growth company too thin? Would it take away from the company's sharp focus on the B2B business and the culture the co-founders had so carefully nurtured? On the other hand, lending might be the key to sustainable growth for the company. The pros and cons seemed equally compelling, so a rather tough decision awaited Jawaid and Jangda.

NOTES

1 Invest2Innovate, "Dare To Disrupt – The Rise of Grocery Startups in Pakistan", https://invest2innovate.com/the-evolution-of-b2c-online-grocery-shopping-in-pakistan/, accessed January 2022.

2 Britannica, "Pakistan" https://www.britannica.com/place/Pakistan, accessed January 2022.
3 Britannica, "Pakistan" https://www.britannica.com/place/Pakistan, accessed January 2022.
4 Britannica, "Pakistan" https://www.britannica.com/place/Pakistan, accessed January 2022.
5 Ali Rehmat Shimshali, "Youth as national dividend", *International The News*, May 27, 2021 https://www.thenews.com.pk/print/840454-youth-as-national-dividend, accessed January 2022.
6 Asma Kundi, "Pakistan currently has largest percentage of young people in its history: report", *Dawn*, May 3, 2018, https://www.dawn.com/news/1405197, accessed January 2022.
7 Invest2Innovate, "Dare to Disrupt – The Rise of Grocery Startups in Pakistan", https://invest2innovate.com/dare-to-disrupt-the-rise-of-grocery-startups-in-pakistan-part-1/, accessed January 2022.
8 Muhammad Mohkum Awaisi, "Retail channels in Pakistan — changing trends and future outlook", *Daily Times Pakistan*, April 22, 2020, https://dailytimes.com.pk/600117/retail-channels-in-pakistan-changing-trends-and-future-outlook/, accessed January 2022.
9 Invest2Innovate, "Dare to Disrupt – The Rise of Grocery Startups in Pakistan"(PDF file), November 18, 2020, https://invest2innovate.com/wp-content/uploads/2020/12/Dare-to-Disrupt-The-Rise-of-Grocery-Startups-in-Pakistan.pdf, accessed January 2022.
10 Invest2Innovate, "Dare to Disrupt – The Rise of Grocery Startups in Pakistan"(PDF file), November 18, 2020, https://invest2innovate.com/wp-content/uploads/2020/12/Dare-to-Disrupt-The-Rise-of-Grocery-Startups-in-Pakistan.pdf, accessed January 2022.
11 Invest2Innovate, "Dare to Disrupt – The Rise of Grocery Startups in Pakistan"(PDF file), November 18, 2020, https://invest2innovate.com/wp-content/uploads/2020/12/Dare-to-Disrupt-The-Rise-of-Grocery-Startups-in-Pakistan.pdf, accessed January 2022.
12 Global Findex Database, "The Unbanked", The World Bank, 2017, https://globalfindex.worldbank.org/sites/globalfindex/files/chapters/2017%20Findex%20full%20report_chapter2.pdf, accessed January 2022.
13 "Cashflow management services provider raises funds to digitise Pakistani mom-and-pop stores", *Arab News Pakistan*, April 27, 2018, https://www.arabnews.pk/node/1963686/pakistan, accessed January 2022.
14 Mettis News, "Where does SME financing stand in Pakistan? Here are the numbers", Dawn, May 19, 2021, https://www.dawn.com/news/1624501, accessed January 2022.
15 Mettis News, "Where does SME financing stand in Pakistan? Here are the numbers", Dawn, May 19, 2021, https://www.dawn.com/news/1624501, accessed January 2022.
16 MarketLine, "Food and Grocery Retail in Pakistan - Market Summary, Competitive Analysis and Forecast to 2025", July 2021, https://www.marketresearch.com/MarketLine-v3883/Food-Grocery-Retail-Pakistan-Summary-30131649/, accessed January 2022.

17 Invest2Innovate, "Dare to Disrupt – The Rise of Grocery Startups in Pakistan"(PDF file), November 18, 2020, https://invest2innovate.com/wp-content/uploads/2020/12/Dare-to-Disrupt-The-Rise-of-Grocery-Startups-in-Pakistan.pdf, accessed January 2022.
18 Invest2Innovate, "Dare to Disrupt – The Rise of Grocery Startups in Pakistan"(PDF file), November 18, 2020, https://invest2innovate.com/wp-content/uploads/2020/12/Dare-to-Disrupt-The-Rise-of-Grocery-Startups-in-Pakistan.pdf, accessed January 2022.
19 Jon Russell, "Alibaba buys Rocket Internet's Daraz to expand its e-commerce empire into South Asia", *TechCrunch*, May 8, 2018, https://techcrunch.com/2018/05/08/alibaba-buys-rocket-internets-daraz/, accessed January 2022.
20 Invest2Innovate, "Khyber Pakhtunkhwa Startup Ecosystem Report 2021," https://invest2innovate.com/kp-entrepreneurship-ecosystem-report-2021/, accessed January 2021.
21 Kemp, Simon. "Digital 2020: Pakistan", DataReportal, February 18, 2020, https://datareportal.com/reports/digital-2020-pakistan, accessed January 2022.
22 Smartphone penetration rate as share of connections in Pakistan from 2014 to 2020, via Statista, https://www.statista.com/statistics/671542/smartphone-penetration-as-share-of-connections-in-pakistan/, accessed January 2022.
23 Invest2Innovate, "Khyber Pakhtunkhwa Startup Ecosystem Report 2021," https://invest2innovate.com/kp-entrepreneurship-ecosystem-report-2021/, accessed January 2021.
24 Tim Hinchliffe, "The Pakistani entrepreneurial ecosystem, an inside glimpse", *The Sociable, February 18, 2022* https://sociable.co/technology/pakistani-entrepreneurial-ecosystem/, accessed January 2022.
25 Invest2Innovate, "Dare to Disrupt – The Rise of Grocery Startups in Pakistan"(PDF file), November 18, 2020, https://invest2innovate.com/wp-content/uploads/2020/12/Dare-to-Disrupt-The-Rise-of-Grocery-Startups-in-Pakistan.pdf, accessed January 2022.
26 Michelle Evans, "Uber Acquires Careem For $3.1 Billion As The Middle East Startup Pushes To Become A Super App", *Forbes*, Mar 26, 2019 https://www.forbes.com/sites/michelleevans1/2019/03/26/meet-careem-ubers-3-1-billion-new-acquisition-in-the-middle-east/, accessed January 2022.
27 "EcoSystem of Pakistan related to startup", Oak Business Consultants *(blog)*, n.d. https://oakbusinessconsultant.com/the-ecosystem-of-pakistan-related-to-startup/, accessed January 2022.
28 Haseeb Ahmed Khawaja, "What are the problems faced by the retail sector in Pakistan?", Macro Pakistani, May 22, 2021, https://macropakistani.com/retail-sector-in-pakistan/, accessed January 2022.i
29 StartupBlink, "Global Startup Ecosystem Index 2021" (PDF file), https://www.startupblink.com/startupecosystemreport.pdf, accessed January 2022.
30 Ecommerce Pakistan, via Statista, https://www.statista.com/outlook/dmo/ecommerce/pakistan#revenue, accessed January 2022.
31 Ecommerce Pakistan, via Statista, https://www.statista.com/outlook/dmo/ecommerce/pakistan#revenue, accessed January 2022.

32 "Startups in Pakistan", Tracxn, https://tracxn.com/explore/Startups-in-Pakistan, accessed January 2022.
33 Invest2Innovate, "Dare to Disrupt – The Rise of Grocery Startups in Pakistan"(PDF file), November 18, 2020, https://invest2innovate.com/wp-content/uploads/2020/12/Dare-to-Disrupt-The-Rise-of-Grocery-Startups-in-Pakistan.pdf, accessed January 2022.
34 Zubair Naeem Paracha, "Bazaar, Pakistan-based B2B ecommerce marketplace raises $6.5 million in one of region's largest seed rounds", Menabytes, January 19, 2021, https://www.menabytes.com/bazaar-seed/, accessed January 2022.
35 Zubair Naeem Paracha, "Riyadh-based Retailo raises $6.7 million seed to grow its B2B marketplace in MENAP", Menabytes, May 6, 2021, https://www.menabytes.com/retailo-seed/, accessed January 2022.
36 Haseeb Ahmed Khawaja, "What are the problems faced by the retail sector in Pakistan?", Macro Pakistani, May 22, 2021, https://macropakistani.com/retail-sector-in-pakistan/, accessed January 2022.
37 Invest2Innovate, "Dare to Disrupt – The Rise of Grocery Startups in Pakistan"(PDF file), November 18, 2020, https://invest2innovate.com/wp-content/uploads/2020/12/Dare-to-Disrupt-The-Rise-of-Grocery-Startups-in-Pakistan.pdf, accessed January 2022.
38 Zubair Naeem Paracha, "Pakistan's Dastgyr raises $3.5 million seed for its B2B ecommerce marketplace", Menabytes, July 25, 2021, https://www.menabytes.com/dastgyr-seed/, accessed January 2022.
39 Invest2Innovate, "Dare to Disrupt – The Rise of Grocery Startups in Pakistan"(PDF file), November 18, 2020, https://invest2innovate.com/wp-content/uploads/2020/12/Dare-to-Disrupt-The-Rise-of-Grocery-Startups-in-Pakistan.pdf, accessed January 2022.
40 Invest2Innovate, "Dare to Disrupt – The Rise of Grocery Startups in Pakistan"(PDF file), November 18, 2020, https://invest2innovate.com/wp-content/uploads/2020/12/Dare-to-Disrupt-The-Rise-of-Grocery-Startups-in-Pakistan.pdf, accessed January 2022.
41 "Bazaar launches digital ledger app Easy Khata, 100,000 merchants sign on in less than two months", KrAsia, April 15, 2021, https://kr-asia.com/bazaar-launches-digital-ledger-app-easy-khata-100000-merchants-sign-on-in-less-than-two-months , accessed January 2022.

EXHIBIT 1 Bazaar Core Team Bios

Team Member	Title	Bio
Hamza Jawaid	**Co-Founder**	Hamza Jawaid is a co-founder of Bazaar Technologies, a B2B e-commerce platform that connects medium-sized retailers and small businesses through an app. Prior to founding Bazaar Technologies, he started his career as a consultant and held various positions at McKinsey & Company that included business analyst, senior associate, and manager for new ventures. After over four years at McKinsey, he and Saad Jangda founded Bazaar Technologies in 2020 and raised more than $37million in total funding. Both founders were honored in the 2021 Forbes 30 under 30 Asia list. Jawaid graduated from the London School of Economics and Political Science in 2015 with a bachelor's degree in government and economics. During his university education, he worked at Counseling Pakistan and the Oliver Wyman Forum.
Saad Jangda,	**Co-Founder**	Saad Jangda is the Co-Founder of Bazaar Technologies. Prior to founding Bazaar Technologies, he served as a product manager at Snapchat in New York. After a year, he moved to Dubai and joined Careem. At Careem, he held different roles including associate product manager for web platform, product manager for Careem for Business, and senior product manager for Careem NOW before taking the decision of founding Bazaar Technologies with Hamza Jawaid. Saad Jangda hold a bachelor's degree in Economics from the University of Michigan, class of 2016. Before his graduation he held roles as business operations & strategy intern at Quixety and as product development intern at Rapt.fm, in Silicon Walley.
Ahmed Siyadat	**Head of B2B Business**	Ahmet Siyadat leads the strategy and business operations at Bazaar Technologies. He began his professional career at Unilever as a management trainee and served in various positions that included territory sales manager, assistant brand manager, and sales operation manager. He was then promoted to channel development manager and was responsible for maximizing highest contributing channels and managing the traditional trade portfolio and supporting e-commerce team. In 2019, he joined Swvl as operations manager and became assistant general manager in Kenya. Ahmed Siyadat holds a bachelor's degree in economics from the Lahore University of Management Science (class of 2016).

Adnan Siddiqui	**Head of Finance & Strategy**	Adnan Ahmed Siddiqui is head of finance and strategy at Bazaar Technologies. Siddiqui started his career in finance and worked as a financial analyst at the Insitor Impact Asia Fund before moving to Acumen, where he held various positions, including portfolio analyst and portfolio associate. He also took roles as finance associate at AKD Securities Ltd. and performance manager at Careem. Before joining Bazaar Technologies, he worked in Swvl in Dubai in the global marketplace and supply management departments. Siddiqui graduated from the Lahore University of Management Science in 2016 and holds bachelor's degree in economics and political sciences. His expertise is in finance and forecasting.
Zarak Khan	**Head of Business Operations**	Zarak Khan leads Founding Team/Operations & Performance at Bazaar Technologies since 2020. He started his career as Equity Analyst in Elixir Securities, focusing on steel and automobile sectors. Next, Khan worked as an Associate in Product, Strategy & Innovation in TPS Worldwide before moving to Dubai to join Careem. At Careem, he held the following positions: Supply Lead on Performance & Strategy for Ride-Hailing, Senior Supply Lead for Performance & Strategy for Deliveries across UAE, KSA, Pakistan and Jordan. After Careem, Zarak Khan joined Kitopi as a Manager of Strategic Projects, taking roles on customer conversion, alternate revenue channels, and logistics. Zarak Khan graduated from Lahore University of Management Sciences in 2016 and hold bachelor's degree in Science, Management Science. During his university education, he held a number of internships positions at the departments of risk management in National Bank of Pakistan, supply chain in Daraz.pk, and sales in RB. He also worked as director of operations in Counseling Pakistan, the first free online college counseling service in Pakistan, for over two years.
Hashim Khan	**Head of Operations**	Mohammad Hashim Khan is the head of Operations department at Bazaar since late 2020. He started his career at Procter & Gamble as a process engineer. After seven months, he joined Nestle and held various positions including Supply Chain Team Leader, Supply Chain Development Specialist, and Demand-Supply Planning Manager. He also worked as Global Campaign Manager – Operations and Global 3PL Operations Manager at Daraz. Hashim Khan holds his bachelor's degree in Material Engineering from National University of Science and Technology.

Source: Company documents.

EXHIBIT 2 Snapshot of Bazaar (September 2021)

Number of employees	181
Number of cities	3
Number of merchants served	75,000
Number of suppliers	~50-70
Monthly GMV (USD Million)	~ 4-6
Number of SKUs	~1,200

Source: Company documents.

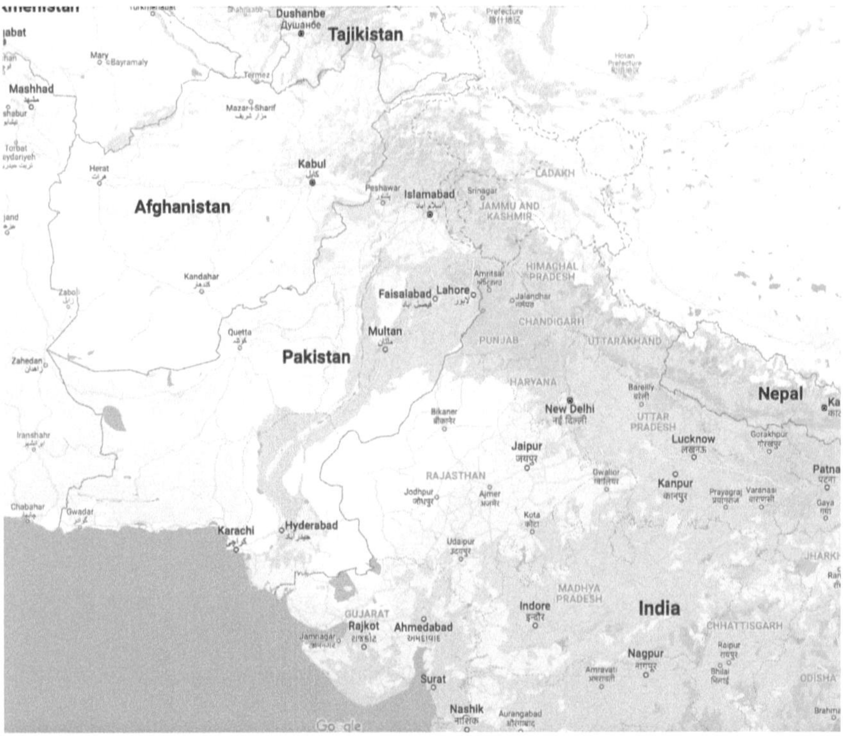

EXHIBIT 3 Map of Pakistan
Source: Compiled by the casewriters using data from Google Maps, Google, https:// www.google.com/maps/ , accessed February 2022.

EXHIBIT 4 Economic and Demographic Indicators

	2010	2011	2012	2013	2014	2015	2016	2017	2018	2019	2020
GDP (billion $)	177.17	213.59	224.38	231.22	244.36	270.56	278.65	304.57	314.57	279.06	262.61
GDP per capita (current $)	987.4	1,165.0	1,198.1	1,208.9	1,251.2	1,356.7	1,368.4	1,464.9	1,482.2	1,288.6	1,188.9
GDP growth rate (%)	1.61	2.75	3.51	4.40	4.68	4.73	5.53	5.55	5.84	1.14	-0.93
Gross domestic saving (% of GDP)	9.97	9.11	7.06	8.18	8.22	9.26	8.67	6.81	6.24	5.46	7.91
Inflation rate (%)	12.94	11.92	9.68	7.69	7.19	2.53	3.77	4.09	5.08	10.58	9.74
Current Account Balance Account (BoP, current $ billion)	-1,.35	-2.21	-2.34	-4.42	-3.66	-2.80	-7.19	-16.18	-18.86	-8.56	-0.65
Population growth (annual %)	2.2	2.2	2.1	2.1	2.1	2.1	2.1	2.1	2.1	2.0	2.0
Total population (in million)	179.4	183.3	187.3	191.3	195.3	199.4	203.6	207.9	212.2	216.6	220.9
0-14 years (%)	37.7	37.3	36.9	36.6	36.2	35.9	35.7	35.5	35.3	35.1	34.8
15-64 years (%)	58.1	58.4	58.8	59.1	59.4	59.8	60.0	60.2	60.4	60.6	60.8
Over 65 years (%)	4.2	4.3	4.3	4.3	4.3	4.3	4.3	4.3	4.3	4.3	4.3
Male (%)	51.5	51.5	51.5	51.5	51.5	51.5	51.5	51.5	51.5	51.5	51.5
Female (%)	48.5	48.5	48.5	48.5	48.5	48.5	48.5	48.5	48.5	48.5	48.5
Unemployment (%)	6.0	6.1	6.5	6.3	5.8	6.0	5.8	5.7	5.5	4.1	4.4

Source: World Bank Databank, The World Bank Group, accessed January 2022. Trading Economics, "Pakistan Unemployment Rate", https://tradingeconomics.com/pakistan/unemployment-rate, accessed January 2022.

EXHIBIT 5 Overview of B2B Retail Players

B2B Ecommerce Grocery Retailers	Number of Merchants Served	Traditional Grocery Retailers	Number of Outlets/Stores		Modern Grocery Retailers	Number of Outlets/Stores	
			2019	2020		2019	2020
Tajir	15,000	Utility Store	5940	5267	PSO Outlets	194	200
Retailo	30,000	Gourmet Foods	130	132	Total SA	84	87
Bazaar	75,000	K&N's	124	126	Shell (Royal Dutch Shell)	78	80
Dastagyr	40,000	Rahat Bakers	30	32	Al Fatah Supermarket	16	17
Sabzi.Pk	-	Pie in the sky	18	22	Madina Supermarket	11	11
Jugnu	5,000	Rehmat e Shireen	18	20	Carrefour	8	9

Source: Compiled by casewriters using data from Jugnu, “Home”, https://jugnu.pk, accessed January 2022. Bazaar Technologies, “Home”, https://www.bazaar-tech.com, Babar Khan, “Empowering mom-and-pop stores to grow their business”, Tajir (Blog), June 05, 2020, https://www.tajir.app/blog/empowering-mom-and-pop-stores-to-grow-their-business, Retailo Technologies, “Home”, https://retailo.co, Dastgyr, “Home”, https://www.dastgyr.com, Euromonitor International, “Modern Grocery Retailers in Pakistan, March 2021, Euromonitor International, “Traditional Grocery Retailers in Pakistan”, March 2021, accessed January 2022.

EXHIBIT 6 Overview of Unbanked Population in Pakistan (2021)

Country	Unbanked Population (%)
Nigeria	60
Mexico	63
Philippines	66
Egypt	67
Vietnam	69
Morocco	71
Pakistan	71

Source: Created by casewriters using data from Bloomberg, "Pakistan Startup to Offer Financial Services Post Fund Raise" June 3, 2021. https://www.bloomberg.com/news/articles/2021-06-03/world-s-fifth-largest-nation-gets-its-first-digital-bank-in-june, accessed December 2021.

EXHIBIT 7 Digital Penetration and E-Commerce Metrics

	2019	2020	2021
Internet Penetration (% of population)	17.1	20.4	24.0
Smartphone Penetration (% of population)	15.9	18.4	18.0
E-commerce Penetration (% of population)	-	19	22.8
E-commerce Revenue (billion $)	2.1	4	7.3

Source: Compiled from Statista, Ecommerce Pakistan, https://www.statista.com/outlook/dmo/ecommerce/pakistan, State Bank of Pakistan, Annual Report 2021, https://www.sbp.org.pk/reports/annual/arFY21/Vol-1/Chapter-2.pdf, Statista, "The eCommerce market in Pakistan", https://ecommercedb.com/en/markets/pk/all, Newzoo, "The Global Mobile Market 2019 -Light Version, https://newzoo.com/insights/trend-reports/newzoo-global-mobile-market-report-2019-light-version/, Newzoo, "Top Countries by Smartphone Users", https://newzoo.com/insights/rankings/top-countries-by-smartphone-penetration-and-users/, Euromonitor International, "Internet Penetration In Pakistan" (Excel File), downloaded from Euromonitor International database, https://www.portal.euromonitor.com/portal/StatisticsEvolution/index, accessed December 2021.

EXHIBIT 8 Pakistani Startup Ecosystem Snapshot

	2019	2020	2021
Start Up Ecosystem Ranking	61	82	75
Number of Deals	32	41	51*
Investment value (million US dollar)	45.7	65.7	278*

Source: Created by casewriters using data from StartupBlink, Global Startup Ecosystem Index 2021, https://www.startupblink.com/startupecosystemreport.pdf, accessed December 2021.

EXHIBIT 9 Overview of E-Commerce in Pakistan

Country	Average Annual Growth Forecast in 2016-2021 %)
Algeria	4.6
Vietnam	4.8
Saudi Arabia	4.9
UAE	4.9
Kenya	4.9
Guatemala	5.2
India	5.3
South Korea	5.8
Cameroon	7.4
Pakistan	8.2

Source: Created by casewriters from Bloomberg, "135 Million Millennials Drive World's Fastest Retail Market", September 27, 2017. https://www.bloomberg.com/news/articles/2017-09-28/135-million-millennials-drive-world-s-fastest-retail-market, accessed January 2022.

EXHIBIT 10 Grocery Retail Industry Map
Source: Invest2Innovate, "Dare To Distrupt - The Rise of Grocery Start Ups In Pakistan," https://invest2innovate.com/wp-content/uploads/2020/12/Dare-to-Disrupt-The-Rise-of-Grocery-Startups-in-Pakistan.pdf, accessed December 2021.

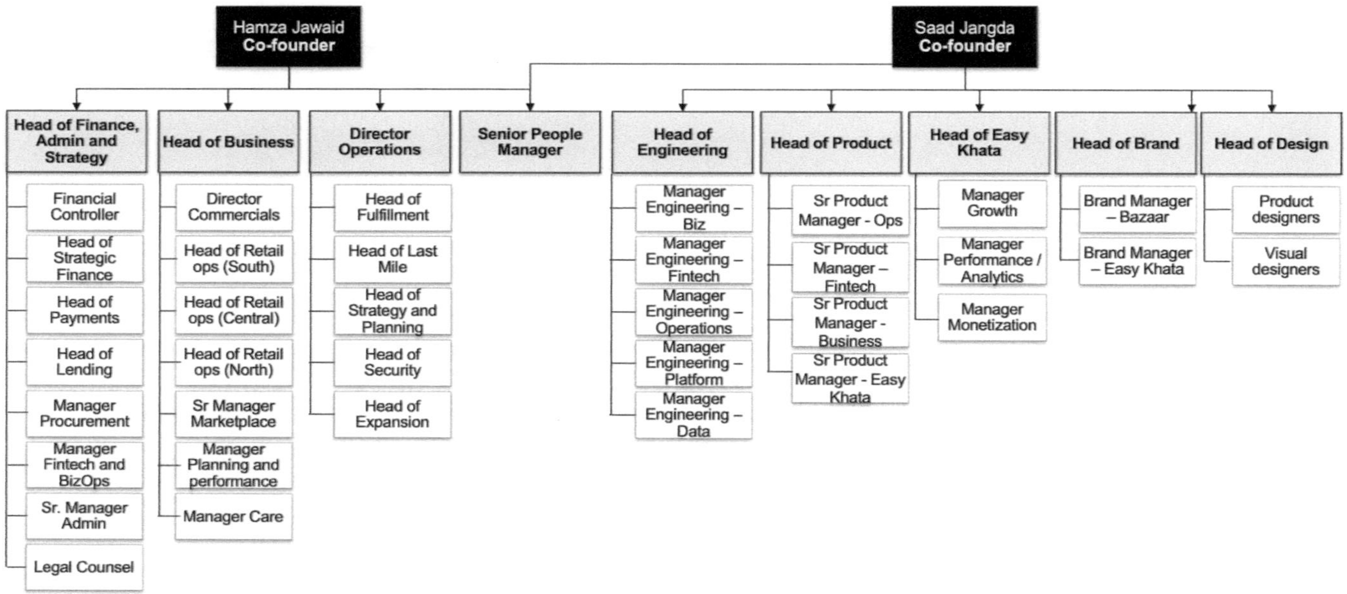

EXHIBIT 11 Organization Chart
Source: Company documents.

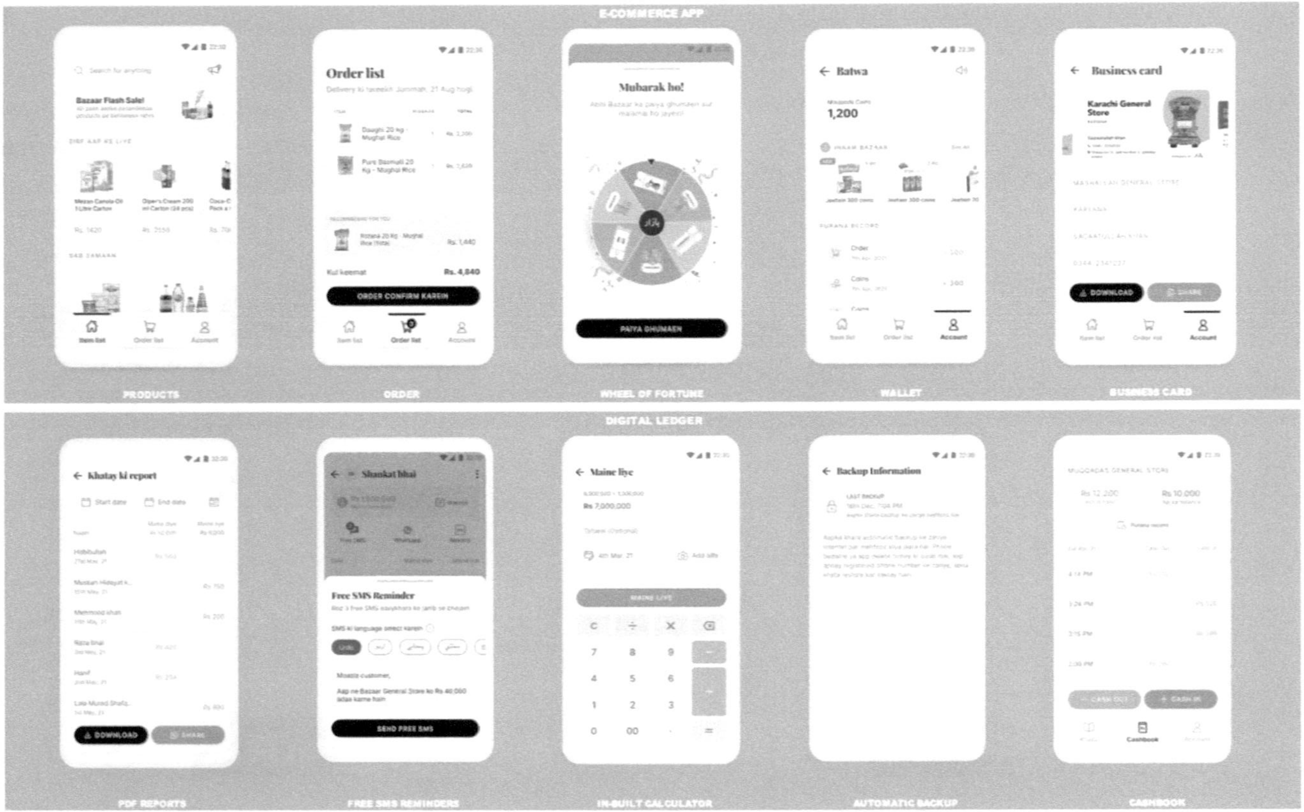

EXHIBIT 12 Bazaar App Interfaces
Source: Company documents.

EXHIBIT 13 Karachi Financials

Total Users	~30-40K
Active User	~15-20K
GMV/month	~USD 3-7 million
Average order value	~USD 40-45
Orders per user	~4-6/month
Retention Rate	~85-90%
% Order received on App	~80-85%

Source: Company documents.

CHAPTER 6.2

Nykaa.com: A Passion for Beauty

Paul Gompers, Anjali Raina and Rachna Chalwa

Laying your own path, being bold and doing things that have not been done before is important. It's equally important to know what not to do.[1]

—Falguni Nayar, CEO, Nykaa

INTRODUCTION

Falguni Nayar, CEO *Nykaa*, and her daughter Adwaita (HBS MBA 2017) were discussing how they should restructure *Nykaa*. It was June 2017; Adwaita had just returned to India, post HBS.

Falguni founded *Nykaa* in April 2012, saying, "We want to be the best beauty destination"[2]. In five short years, *Nykaa* seemed to be well on the way to reaching that goal. The first order placed on *Nykaa* was on October 24th, 2012, on the festival of Dussehra[a], for a lipstick and a nail color. The startup team had five members. By June 2017, *Nykaa* was hitting 297,900 orders a month, and represented over 733 brands, both mass and luxury. It had launched a private label, opened five *Nykaa* Luxe stores, and the *Nykaa* app had been downloaded 5.5 million times. It stocked 75,000 SKUs,[b] served 29,000 zip codes, and had 2.5 million social media followers. *Nykaa*.com had 21.9 million monthly visits, and 7.1 million monthly visitors, of which 60% were repeat consumers. It had a team of 500 plus employees. (See **Exhibit 1a** for Consolidated Financials and **Exhibit 1b** for Key Statistics.)

a Dussehra is a Hindu festival that celebrates the victory of good over evil.
b SKU—(Stock Keeping Unit) is a product identification code, (often machine-readable barcode) that tracks inventory.

It hadn't all been smooth sailing. After a promising start, Falguni had run into some headwinds, and in August 2013, Adwaita had given up her role as an Associate Consultant at Bain and Company to join *Nykaa*—nominally as the Chief Operating Officer, but actually as 'Chief Troubleshooter' as she described it. *Rakhi*, a festival when brothers and sisters traditionally celebrated their bonds, was on August 20th of that year, and customers were leveraging the flexibility and variety offered by *Nykaa* to buy gifts for each other. Operations had not kept pace. Having Adwaita as a trusted partner had brought peace to Falguni, but when Adwaita left for HBS in 2015, Falguni hadn't been sure she would return. Now Adwaita was back, but to a Nykaa which had grown from a team of 120 to a team of 550, from 4,000 orders a day to 25,000 orders a day and from one warehouse to four warehouses. Structuring Adwaita's role and planning the next phase together was proving to be both fun and challenging. How should they organize and structure the team and organization to deliver?

FALGUNI NAYAR

Falguni graduated from the Indian Institute of Management Ahmedabad, (IIMA), India's premier business school, in 1985, and then spent the next 26 years in the finance world, first with A.F. Ferguson & Co.[c], and then from 1993 with Kotak Mahindra Capital. Her choice of ethnic outfits and calm demeanor masked a fierce energy and global outlook. Falguni set up international operations for Kotak Mahindra Capital in London and New York, ran their mergers and acquisition business, advising major deals such as Hutchison's sale to Vodafone Plc., and finally left as head of Investment Banking and the institutional equities business. The business world recognized her acumen, requesting her to serve on corporate boards as diverse as Tata Motors Ltd, Dabur India Ltd, and ACC Ltd. She was recognized as the top woman achiever in the field of banking in 2008 and the top businesswoman in 2009 and 2011[d]. Along the way, Falguni married Sanjay, a classmate from IIMA, and became the mother of twins—Adwaita and Anchit. (See **Exhibit 2** Falguni Nayar.)

Falguni's choice to be a salaried employee initially "disappointed" her father. She explained, "My father and mother owned and ran a small bearings company and our family conversations centered around investments,

c A.F. Ferguson & Co. was a leading accounting, advisory and corporate services firm that merged with Deloitte Haskins & Sells

d By FICCI FLO and Business Today

the stock market and trade. Given that I'm a *Gujarati*[e] and a *Mumbaikar*—by birth and context, entrepreneurship runs in my veins."

In January 2012, as Falguni was turning 50, she decided to fulfill her lifelong dream of being an entrepreneur. She said, "Adwaita and Anchit had left to study in the U.S. I wanted to experience entrepreneurship before I was too old. All was going well at Kotak, but I'm an adventurer, the first to jump into a pool even if I can't swim well." Adwaita understood her mother's longing to explore uncharted waters, despite the risk to reputation, income and security. She shared a poem—*Ithaka*—with her. The idea of life being a journey not a destination, resonated with Falguni, and inspired her to take the plunge.

THE FIRST STEPS

Falguni had considered three business possibilities. She said, "I was a consultant and a banker. I had a framework for evaluating business. As a professional turned entrepreneur, I didn't have deep pockets. I wanted an early-stage industry, so I could make a place for myself before the entry of bigger players." The first business she explored was to brand small nursing homes and hospitals and market their services. The potential downside of being sued by disgruntled patients or their relatives dissuaded her from moving ahead. The second was to set up a high-end vacation platform, akin to a luxury Airbnb, but the vagaries of the Indian weather put her off that idea.

She finally narrowed it down to her third choice. She said, "With India's growing population, the rise of tier 2 and tier 3 cities and online shopping, and the emergence of the Indian woman, with her ambition to access and experience the best, I decided a woman-centered business with a multi-brand retail format in the area of beauty and wellness was the right choice." There were detractors, but Falguni knew women from smaller cities often visited urban centers to shop, or requested friends from overseas to bring select brands to India for them. (See **Appendix 1** for Indian Personal Care and Beauty Industry—Size, Opportunity, and Segments.) In April 2012, she set up her company, FSN Ecommerce Ventures Pvt. Ltd., with a three-member Board consisting of her father-in-law, her mother, and herself.

e Gujarati: those who ethnically identify with the state of Gujarat; traditionally considered to be very entrepreneurial.

Crafting a Brand: Nykaa

Falguni was inspired by a visit to *Sephora*, the French multi-brand cosmetics retailer, and impressed by the artistically displayed products and variety of brands. She noticed that customers consulted the beauty specialists for advice. In India, beauty products were primarily sold through single-brand outlets or through Mom and Pop stores which offered a limited range, often had expired products, and could not guarantee genuine products. Beauty advice was not available. Some retailers like 'NewU' and 'Health and Glow' stocked mass brands, and sales agents pushed specific brands. Falguni decided her company would hold the position of a trusted advisor on health and wellness, and enable women to discover and uncover different aspects of their persona.

She enlisted the help of her classmate from IIMA, Alpana Parida, to craft a memorable brand identity. Parida recommended the name *Nykaa*, which, being a coined word, was copyright protected. Falguni explained, "*Nykaa* is derived from the Sanskrit *Nayaka,* which means Actress. I believe every woman deserves to have the spotlight on her and to be the main actress in her life." *Nykaa*.com claimed to be "all about celebrating women, celebrating the star in you."

Hiring the Startup Team

Falguni's decision to found a startup was met with disbelief in most quarters. The headhunter fraternity assumed that Falguni and her boss had fallen out and approached her with job offers. Falguni laughed, "One savvy head hunter believed me; instead of circulating my resume to prospective employers, he started sending me resumes of folks and delivered four of my first five recruits." Since the headhunter was not a specialist e-commerce recruiter, the initial team had generic skills rather than specific e-commerce experience.

The first person to join was Madhavi Irani, Chief Officer–Content. Falguni said, "Madhavi came to me through this recruiter, but we've built a strong bond." Irani shared:

> I was intrigued by Falguni's dream. Beauty for Falguni is holistic; it's not about using makeup to look good—it's inside-out beauty. She said we were going to replicate online the experience that a beauty advisor provides in a face-to-face interaction. I'd been a health and wellness counselor, a journalist, and worked in an e-commerce start up, and this seemed to marry my interest and skills. I joined as I believed I'd add value. Initially, I committed to work 3 days a week, as I wanted to continue being a health coach. . . . As work became more intense I came on full time.

The second recruit was Baiju Ajmera (Site Curator and Cataloguing Associate). Ajmera had limited work experience. Falguni shared, "She approached me as her grandmother is a friend of my mother's, and shared her interest in working for *Nykaa*. If people are passionate about beauty I often take them on board; passion achieves a lot. Baiju brings a skill set of caring for beauty." Falguni shared that Ajmera's current role was to onboard new brands—"as she has the knack to be able to figure out which one of 80 products will do well."

Falguni described her third recruit, who joined as the Chief Business Officer, as "a self-made person from a small town in Andhra Pradesh—with an aggressive and entrepreneurial streak, who was able to get things done. He was an engineering graduate, but not from an IIT[f] and was an MBA drop out; however, he had worked at Microsoft for three years and at Infosys for six years, which in my eyes added credibility." Falguni shared, "I initially applied a very India centric view of talent assessment thinking a combination of IIT Mumbai or IIT Delhi with IIMA was the best, as I was aware that in India these institutions attract high quality talent. Both the Chief Technology Officer (CTO), and the Chief Operating Officer (COO) held an engineering degree from IIT Mumbai, and were alumni of IIMA.

Falguni reflected, "Of my first five recruits, three had started their own company and one had worked in a start-up. . . . They must have all had a higher risk appetite than average. I was good at finance, I was good at sales, I was good at managing people, but I didn't know retail, I didn't know beauty, I didn't know technology. Yet so many people were ready to come on board with my vision. I thought I was lucky to have attracted such senior talent within a month of starting *Nykaa*."

Adwaita Nayar

Adwaita happened to be in Mumbai for the initial months, between her graduation from Yale University and analyst role with Bain Consulting in New York in August 2012. In the crucial first three months, Adwaita worked alongside Falguni figuring out the site's wire frame and basic structure. Adwaita remained informally in touch with the business even when she went away to New York, speaking regularly on the phone to Falguni and engaging with every little decision. Falguni explained, "While Adwaita didn't have a formal role at *Nykaa*, she was always involved; she

f IIT- colloquially used to refer to 'Indian Institute of Technology', India's premier brand of engineering colleges, distinguished from each other by the city they were situated in- hence IIT Mumbai, IIT Delhi, IIT Kanpur etc.

was like my advisor, and always had a view. She adds value to whatever I am thinking."

BUILDING THE BUSINESS: PHASE 1

Irani described the excitement of the first months- working out of Falguni's home, using A4 sheets of paper to conceptualize the webpage, and crafting the business model. Falguni decided that *Nykaa*.com would be the largest, most reliable provider of authentic beauty and wellness products across India, predominantly via e-commerce with a handful of strategic physical stores. She was focused on sustainability, profitability, and margins, and decided she needed to include a private label. Customer retention and employee stickiness were both important to her, as were deep knowledge and innovative thinking.

Falguni recruited fresh graduates for marketing, brand management, and customer service. She said, "I didn't want to create a heavy structure. While the senior most team member was a specialist, I put the others into any role that was required."

Building the Brand

Falguni was committed to providing a comprehensive selection of genuine brands ranging from mass products to luxury products across makeup, skin care, bath and body, herbal fragrances, and wellness, including products for men and mothers.

To overcome the mental barrier of buying a lipstick or a nail polish without physically testing it out, and to breach widespread reluctance to buy online, *Nykaa* had to sell products and brands that were well known, but lower priced. Falguni did think that bringing well-known brands on board would be a challenge, but was pleasantly surprised to find respected brands such as HUL, P&G and L'Oréal, Paris signing up, with a total of 20 brands on board in the initial months. She reflected, "The goodwill that I had built over the years came in to play. When I went to L'Oréal and HUL to convince them to do e-commerce, they got comfort because I was a seasoned management person, even though I was not a seasoned entrepreneur." Irani said they built trust with brands by a focus on controlling quality and created micro strategies that focused on the growth of each individual brand. (See **Exhibit 3** for Brand Portfolio 2012–2017.)

Irani and Falguni both agreed that content was critical to educate the customer and provide a differentiated experience by walking customers through a range of ideas and solutions.

Irani commented, "I spent an entire month while Falguni was away at her kids' graduation cold calling every expert in skin care, make up, etc. that I could think of. This became the base for our expert portal." *Nykaa* launched the *Nykaa* 'Beauty Book', an online magazine with advice on what to buy, how to buy, and how to use products, and introduced the concepts of a virtual makeover and guided selling through on-page advice. Content spanned a variety of channels—ranging from blogs and vlogs[g] to product reviews (occasionally sponsored).[3] Irani proudly shared, "When Falguni goes to meet with big brands they are impressed by the content we create." (See **Exhibit 4** for Nykaa webpage.)

By October 2012, *Nykaa*.com was receiving 10 orders a day, moved into an office, and rented a 5000 sq. ft. warehouse. The beta site was launched in Nov 2012. (See **Exhibit 5** for Nykaa's journey.)

Nykaa sold only what it had in stock and used no third-party sellers. Falguni clarified, "I believe in an inventory-led model of e-commerce, for beauty in particular. As many beauty products have a long shelf life, expiry dates are critical." She explained that Amazon and Flipkart in India started with inventory-led models, but since they had foreign investors they had to switch to a marketplace model to comply with Indian regulatory requirements.

Marketing Platform

In February 2013, *Nykaa* tried out an agency for marketing. Falguni said, "They just kept disappointing us. Then we took in a hire who was recruited for customer service and asked him to work with Google to build our own marketing. We got some success." In March 2013, *Nykaa's* Facebook page had 50,000 fans, and by July 2013 they had started substantial Google advertising. By August 2013, *Nykaa*.com was getting 60 orders a day.

Adwaita recalled

> I moved back on August 20th, 2013. The business felt very young. It was a tiny team, maybe 15 people to 20 people, in a small office. We had an idea, a website that was running and ties with a few brands. Beyond that, we didn't have any ops in place. We didn't really have a tech team or any marketing structure. We were building everything from scratch. My mother did have a team of 4 senior people heading content, tech, ops and business, but I could see that this was a very weak team (except for Madhavi, who has been a rock-solid support).

g video-blogs.

A Setback

Problems surfaced in the area of operations, with delayed and missed deliveries, and a slew of customer complaints. Falguni said, "The first COO I hired was an intelligent, sincere person with a blue-chip resume that I was enamored with. I didn't catch while interviewing him that he was just not dynamic enough." As the business grew, the COO, who had a long commute and was stressed, resigned. Falguni recalled,

> That period in 2013 from *Rakhi* to *Ganapati*[h] was the worst.[i] The COO said he wanted to work from home for *Rakhi* and didn't even pick up the phone. We struggled for a fortnight without him. He quit during *Ganapati*, again a busy festival! There were only three people with him in the Ops team. He had unilaterally sanctioned one's leave, and the other team members just stopped coming. We had nobody. I call Adwaita my just-in-time resource. She had just moved back.

Adwaita remembered,

> My mom threw me into ops when the whole team disappeared. I remember thinking, '*What am I doing? What does the warehouse look like?*' I started going to the warehouse, 3 hours away. We were completely dependent on the Ops head to get the orders out, as no one else was involved. I had no clue how to ship the packages, what products to put in them, or which couriers to use. People asked, "Do you have an ERP?" I said, "Uh, an ERP, I don't think so," and then started googling "what is an ERP."

Adwaita enlisted the help of a fledgling startup to source an ERP. Adwaita said, "As orders come in, the ERP is the system that communicates with the backend so you know what you need to pick, to pack and to ship. It keeps your inventory in control, in real time. As orders ship, inventory depletes and that reflects on the front end." The CBO wasn't supportive of the ERP decision, but Falguni insisted on implementation over a long weekend in September. Falguni recalled, "Adwaita and I rolled up our sleeves; the CBO helped a bit, but Adwaita was the main trouble shooter because she could handle complex tasks. I had a macro perspective. We put the firm back on track." The ERP took 3 weeks to implement, which meant every

---

h Ganeshotsav, aka Ganapati or Ganesh Chaturthi, is a 10-day Hindu festival in honor of Ganesha..

i Rakhi was on 20th August 2013, and Ganeshotsav was from 9th to 19th September 2013.

day at the warehouse, mapping bar codes to SKU codes, managing the FIFO (first in first out) method and looking at expiry dates. Adwaita said, "We're still using that ERP; it's very weak. I don't know if it was the right choice."

The lack of experience in operations continued to surface. Falguni said, "We made every mistake that we could. We didn't know that there was something called 'connect' in the courier system. Once you hand over the packages you need to 'connect' through paperwork, which we didn't do. We learnt in a really, really hard way." Adwaita noted in her diary that sometimes Falguni and she would be packing boxes till 3am.

As they were trying to figure things out, orders kept coming in. Adwaita said, "Even though it was only 60 orders per day, we were not able to clear them. When you don't send people orders for 2 weeks, your customer complaints can grow to the thousands. We had only one person looking at customer service. In the day, I would be working on the ERP and at night I would be answering customers." Irani said, "There was complete chaos and Falguni was ready to cry by the end of it. Adwaita gave her number to customers who began calling her. Apparently, she sobbed the whole night because people were so angry."

Nykaa ceased marketing until they could bring in an Operations Head. Falguni recalled, "We allowed orders to shrink to 20 a day."

Manoj Jaiswal was referred to Falguni by one of her informal advisors. Jaiswal had started working when he was 17 years old, had managed courier services, ecommerce ops and warehouses across different companies, and had deep experience with B2C businesses. Jaiswal was incredibly driven, and had risen rapidly in whichever company he was in. He had grown from delivering packages on a bicycle to a shift executive in Blue Dart[j], to Regional Head for Western India at Aramex[k] at 24 years, leading a team of 4,000 people and 278 branches. He was part of the start-up team at I3PL (a logistic company) where he learned warehouse management from the ground up. He had also worked with 70MM[l] and Future Group[m]. Adwaita said, "He had a range of experience which no one else on the team had." (See **Exhibit 6** for current org structure). Jaiswal said, "I had a competing offer from a large Indian conglomerate. I thought that if I joined them, I would be working for their processes. I was excited at the thought that at *Nykaa* I would be able to create my own processes." He joined in November 2013.

---

j Blue Dart Express is a premier courier and integrated express package-distribution company.

k Aramex is an international express, mail delivery and logistics services company.

l 70MM Entertainments is a film production house.

m Future Group is an Indian conglomerate focused on retail.

Jaiswal was resourceful. He recruited two members into the operations team who joined before he did, as he had to serve notice. Jaiswal laughed, "I was not used to being micro managed. One day I told Falguni in private, "Please leave things to me, give me three months and I shall do a good job." Since then, Falguni has not come into this office or the warehouse. Falguni's trust is empowering."

Jaiswal revamped the processes, reduced the order fulfillment time, and introduced weekly reporting. By December 2013, *Nykaa* touched 100 orders/day." Jaiswal persuaded Falguni to let him manage the warehouses and rented 15,000 sq. ft. of warehouse space in Mumbai and Delhi.

BUILDING THE BUSINESS: PHASE 2

Falguni realized that to scale the business they needed very high-quality tech capability. Falguni recalled, "It was hard to build the tech team; I was well networked in the financial arena, had some connections with marketing teams in companies such as Levers and L'Oréal, but I had no network to speak of in the technology world."

The Search for a CTO

The first CTO left in less than a year. Falguni reflected, "I didn't choose wrong—he was bright, hardworking and selfless, a very nice individual who wanted to contribute to the business. However, he was also a management graduate and hence had broad interests which distracted him from tech development." Falguni then recruited a second CTO, a graduate from IIT Mumbai who didn't have an MBA thinking that, "For tech, I should have a pure tech person; a business school degree is unnecessary." He also left after a year. Falguni reflected that there was a mismatch of expectations. The second CTO had a long commute, and wanted to reserve Saturdays to stay abreast of new technology, whereas *Nykaa* worked six days a week. At first there was an agreement that he could work from home on Saturday, but as the team grew, Falguni felt that the CTO needed to be available for the team. The third CTO *Nykaa* recruited took some time to join, and then left after three months.

Building the Tech Team

Adwaita shared that initially the primary responsibility of the tech team was to "get a website that could handle scale as the current website would buckle with a couple of thousand visitors. Tech is at the heart of the business and is a very high-pressure job; if the website goes down all eyes are on you." Third party vendors were used to launch the new website in 2014 and later the *Nykaa* apps on iPhone and Android in 2015. Adwaita recalled, "Those three platforms were built by a very scrappy team of people all under the age of 24." Falguni continued, "I had a hard time recruiting not just the top tech talent, but also the next level. We couldn't get good people from IIT Bombay and IIT Delhi because we were one of the last companies on day 13 for interviews. "Adwaita complained,

> You do 80 interviews with people who can't put a sentence together and it's demoralizing. When a company is young and has nothing to show for itself, tables are turned, it's almost like you're begging someone to join. For a lot of our early recruits, the conversations were about using the first 20 minutes to figure out if they could add value, and using the next 40 minutes convincing people to join. In those early days, we had a hard time retaining people; sometimes we had three resignations a week. Maybe we were not able to engage with them in the way that they required.

Falguni remembered, "Everybody said *in Mumbai you don't get tech talent*, so we built the team by recruiting from the smaller IITs where we were day 1 or day 2. While it took effort and travel, we did get better talent. We took 7–8 people from the same IIT, as we felt that if there were a large team from the same place, they'd feel more comfortable." They used headhunters to identify and recruit three product managers, (two engineering graduates from IIT Delhi who had three years of e-commerce experience, and a person who had worked with Apple). *Nykaa* also recruited an engineering/infra person. Falguni felt that with this tech team in place, she did not need to hire a CTO.

Building the Marketing Team

Adwaita reflected, "In the early days, the people I could easily convince to join were friends of friends and acquaintances through school; they were people like me who studied in Bombay, and then studied abroad. There were probably 10 such people. I filled a lot of teams with them."

Riah Daswani was one of them. Daswani described herself as a nerd who excelled at science and had studied biochemistry in the UK. She shared, "I found I hated working in a lab. In London, I got hooked onto beauty; I spent all my money on make-up and watching YouTube videos. I was much happier in shops, talking to people, and engaging with social media." Daswani returned to India to work in PR and joined *Nykaa* as its 37th employee in May 2014.

Daswani joined at a time when "everyone did everything." She joined in marketing and PR but answered customer calls and worked in the catalog section, and her first project was to make the Wikipedia page for *Nykaa*. She described her early days, "Back then the team was super close. We were all sitting in one office. The designers were to my left, the tech team to my right, and Falguni's cabin was in front of me, while behind me was the then Chief Marketing Officer." Daswani and the tech team worked closely together. She said,

> Uploading a banner onto the website is about coding and inserting the image in the right brackets. All four members of the tech team worked tirelessly on the website. They taught us how to code. We are creative and know which products fit with each other. They taught us the language; we used our brains to fit the pieces together.

Finding the correct CMO was not easy. Adwaita shared, "In my first two years, we went through three CMOs. For a while I was handling marketing. I could understand digital, I could give clear direction. *We need to have Google ads. We need to have Facebook ads. We need to have re-marketing, re-targeting.* Our partners at Google and Facebook supported us a lot." Marketing channels expanded to include search marketing, search engine optimization, display marketing, and remarketing through Google, Facebook, Yahoo, and AdRoll. They had ties with banks and corporates, great relationships with beauty bloggers, and engaged with social media through Twitter, Facebook, Pinterest, and Google Plus. The marketing team forged strong external partnerships with various parties to promote the brands housed within *Nykaa*. They established the Nykaa Femina Beauty Awards with beauty magazine Femina, and Bollywood celebrity engagement, starting March 2015. At the event, *Nykaa* recognized the 35 best-selling beauty brands and products across its platform, thus strengthening its relationship with these partners. The pre-event advertising in print, on radio, and on billboards coupled with post-event coverage in print, social media, and blogs built for *Nykaa*.com.

Raising Funds

At first, Falguni funded the company from her own and family resources, mentally limiting herself to a budget of ₹50 million. Two years later when she did go to the market to raise funds, she had committed almost ₹120 million—the majority her own funds, and some as a working capital loan from banks. She then leveraged the strong relationships she had forged with industry leaders during her investment banking days to raise funds from individuals. She explained her approach:

> I have never sold castles in the air. Having been a broker and head of investment banking, I have an innate sense of what is fair valuation. I talk often to advisors who reminds me that you have to give a return to the investor. If you raise money at very high valuation how will you give a return? There have been cases such as Zivame or Grofers where the valuation seems insane.

The "good, clean reputations," as Falguni described it, that she and her husband had built over years of working in high profile companies such as Citibank, KKR, and Kotak, helped while raising funds. Falguni was clear that she wanted to follow the letter and spirit of the law, and her informal advisors endorsed that view. Indian regulations prohibited companies with foreign investors from having an e-commerce business model that is inventory-led. Falguni said, "To be able to legally, legitimately do the inventory model, we stayed away from foreign money and raised only domestic funding". (Some e-commerce companies in India have raised funds from foreign investors, and operate e-marketplaces, but also operate partially on their own inventory).[4]

In July 2014, *Nykaa* raised ₹200 million ($3.07 million) at a pre-money valuation of ₹800 million ($12.30 million/). Nykaa raised money again in 2015 and 2016. (See **Exhibit** 7 for details of funds raised.) Falguni issued pure equity, though convertible issues were more accepted for startups.

BUILDING THE BUSINESS: PHASE 3

Falguni wanted to build a long-term sustainable business model, which she attributed to her background as a broker. She said, "From the beginning I knew which lever to press. First, I managed labor cost; then digital marketing costs. Now I manage overheads." She managed expenses by synchronizing growth in office space and head count with fund raising. She said, "Once we are sure the fund raise is going through we start growing. We have a view on how many new customers we should acquire, based on what we can afford. It is a tricky equation." (See **Exhibit** 8a for Balance Sheet and **Exhibit 8b** for Profit and Loss Statement.)

By June 2015, *Nykaa* had 100 employees, hitting 45,000 orders a month, and represented over 320 select, well-priced brands, both mass and luxury. It had developed deep marketing partnerships with a number of brands, was the exclusive online partner for several brands such as Inglot,

Sleek Cosmetics, Makeup Academy, Real Technique, L'occitane and L'oreal Luxury fragrances, had launched a private label for bath and body products, opened the first *Nykaa* Luxe store at New Delhi airport and introduced an Android based mobile app which had been downloaded 75,000 times in five months and accounted for 15 to 20% of total revenue.[n] 35% of *Nykaa's* customers came from India's smaller cities.

Adwaita's impending departure (she had been admitted into the HBS MBA 2plus2 program in 2012, her final year at Yale) had created a dilemma. After checking with ~20 informal influencers and advisors Adwaita had first deferred her admission to HBS for a year, and then decided to join the MBA class of 2017. Falguni valued education, and had ambitious dreams for her daughter. However, in the next month, she needed to launch the *Nykaa* app for the iPhone. In the next six months, she planned to onboard 150 more brands including Truefitt and Hill, Sleek Makeup, Lord & Berry, Makeup Academy (MUA), MAC, Estee Lauder, Clinique, and Bobbi Brown. Exclusive product launches for brands L'Oréal Paris, Maybelline, and Lux were in the offing. She also planned to import and distribute brands Shavedoctor, Mades Cosmetics, and Sleek Cosmetics to add exclusivity, and add makeup and skin care to the *Nykaa* private label. She needed to add a warehouse in Delhi, bring on additional couriers, tighten delivery dates and launch two more stores in Delhi and Mumbai. It was clear the team needed to expand.

Expanding the Team

In March 2015, Hitesh Malhotra was recruited as the new CMO, and in May 2015 Nihir Parikh joined to support strategy (see **Exhibit 6**).

Adwaita reflected,

> I decided to go to business school because I felt overwhelmed by the business. My mom and I are different. She is relaxed, a natural entrepreneur. I'm a reluctant entrepreneur. I get stressed out. When people quit, we'll come home and she'll just put the TV on, watch TV, talk on the phone, talk about the food, and I'll be sitting in my room crying. We're opposites. When investors say no to her, they'd pretty much say *your business sucks*. She would walk out and think *who cares? I don't want their money anyway* and I would walk out saying *how can they say that? Don't they see what we built?* I'm more emotional and so sensitive; every setback was triply hard on me and the early days with setback after setback, I just didn't know if I could do it. I left when I thought,

n First Luxe store in June 2014.

okay, at least the business will not fail. There are people in place. Orders have picked up. But there was no guarantee that I would come back.

Both Malhotra and Parikh moved from well-paid jobs lured by the promise of stock options. Falguni said, "In many ways, the equity at which they came was indicative of my strength, their belief in my vision, and the future value of the company." In India, regulations required that stock options vest after only one year. Falguni shared that, "Funnily enough both the first CTO and first COO left before they completed one year. The first CBO stayed for 2 years and left with an equity upside." The first CTO resigned only a day before his stock options would have vested.

At first, *Nykaa* didn't have a CFO. Falguni said, "I used to say I couldn't afford a CFO. My friend told me that *the CFO is the second most important position in a company after the CEO*! But I managed with an accountant, and I had to get involved with the first couple of balance sheet closings." In Sep 2015, after the second fund raise, the current CFO, Sachin Parikh was recruited from Deloitte. (See **Exhibit 6**.)

To control costs, Falguni personally managed HR for the first few years, with the help of a young aide. Falguni said, "She did her HR role superbly and was always available despite doing her MBA alongside. You get great talent if you are willing to take a risk on folks who lack experience."

As word spread about *Nykaa* it became easier to recruit. Falguni shared that she regularly received emails from people who worked with brands associated with *Nykaa* saying that they were keen to join as a consultant or a full-time employee.

Falguni had no patience with people who lacked commitment but was happy to support folks who lacked relevant experience. Adwaita shared, "Most of the time, you can't find people who meet all your expectations. My mom helped me realize that's okay. You take the person for the part of the job they can do." Falguni added, "I don't like to lose people for interpersonal issues and will transfer people to another department if they don't get along. However, I am ok to lose people who don't show commitment, argue too much, and can't get into detail."

Referrals from current employees, brand partners, and family friends were a good source. However, Adwaita shared that she believed recruiters were needed. She said, "At the pace we were losing and hiring, there is only so much you can find within your own circle."

Board Constitution

In 2015, post the second fund raise, the board was strengthened with the induction of two new members, and more were added in 2016. Board members who had been her advisors, (such as Alpana Parida), were selected.

Others had relevant experience or were promoters. One suggested *Nykaa* experiment with warehouse outsourcing. (See **Exhibit 9** for the profile of *Nykaa* Board Members).

CRAFTING THE CULTURE

Over the course of *Nykaa's* journey, the culture evolved.

Adwaita reflected,

> I don't know how you build the right culture when things are not good. In the first 2 years, we held weekly town halls, we spoke constantly of the importance of teamwork, and we planned social events and retreats. But if the business is fundamentally weak and people don't see job security, I don't know how far that can take you. There were silos, distrust amongst teams, commitment and accountability was questionable. Today, business is thriving and culture has never been better. We're having conversations about what values are important to us. People are creative, highly committed, hang out before work, after work, have deep friendships and help each other. You will find people at 7 AM, at midnight. It's evolved into something beautiful.

Adwaita reflected on the improvement in quality. She said, "People always knew that they can't come to a meeting without data, but they used to come with terrible data. Now they come with good data. Nihir and Sachin have put in place a lot of reporting and MIS and budgeting and data structures from their prior experience at GE and Deloitte."

Zero Error Focus

Nykaa never showed a product that was out of stock, and though it handled many orders daily, it was able to fulfill all orders without any delay. Falguni attributed much of *Nykaa's* success to a strong technology platform, saying, "Our technology enables execution of thousands of complex tasks simultaneously and effortlessly. The scope for system error is close to zero. If there is an error it is because a person made a mistake. Often customer complaints are the best place to identify these process and people issues—so I make it a point to read complaints every day." The goal was to build trust through impeccable delivery and consistent experience so that customers would be comfortable buying expensive products online.

Adwaita described e-commerce as a coordinated dance between many different people, where departments such as sourcing, marketing, tech, backend, operations and customer service had to come together. She explained, "If even one team drops the ball, the ramifications are felt through to all teams. Adhering meticulously to strong processes and timelines is at the heart of this business."

But some things remained out of the firm's control. Jaiswal grumbled that last mile delivery was still dependent on third party couriers. These partners tended to face high attrition and were sometimes unreliable. Delivery to certain zip codes was challenging.

Brand Partnerships

The partnerships that *Nykaa* forged with brands were also an asset. Falguni acknowledged that, for customers who wanted standard personal care products, *Nykaa* didn't have much of an edge. She said, "However, *Nykaa* is uniquely positioned for customers who want to discover more on beauty and are ready to try new products."

Irani shared that social media had helped to build a community. Sometimes there were 80 comments on a single image with people advising each other. She said, "*Nykaa* posts are very informative and we do it in the *Nykaa* way, as we know what the Indian customer likes. We attract many eyeballs and are a powerful beauty influence." By 2017, *Nykaa* was present across multiple channels including Instagram, Pinterest and Snapchat, in addition to Facebook, Twitter and Google+.

Experimentation and Decision-Making

Falguni was influenced by her experience of working at Kotak Investment Bank where business heads were expected to think through their business even if the final decision required ratification. Nihir shared, "Culturally everybody has a voice in the company. 25-year-olds have built a lot of the departments with a free hand. We have always tried every idea. We try, may fail, learn from our mistakes and move ahead. Falguni has always learnt from mistakes." Adwaita reflected that Falguni's management style was to throw people in the deep end. For example, she tasked the Head of private label to deliver business of ₹60 million and then left her to it. She said, "It's an interesting management style where she will hire someone with no experience, no background in something, and then just expect them to deliver. I think most people can come around and do it. Since she doesn't micromanage people, it leaves her brain free for other things." Falguni added, "While I do empower my direct reports, they know exactly when and what they need to check with me."

MOVING FORWARD

Falguni and Adwaita sat in *Nykaa's* offices shortly after Adwaita's graduation from HBS in the summer of 2017 and charted the next chapter of *Nykaa's* expansion. *Nykaa* would seek to expand its physical retail footprint and Adwaita would lead that effort as the Chief Executive Officer of the Retail Business. Falguni had been clear from day one that *Nykaa* was a beauty business, and that e-commerce was just the first leg with both private label and offline retail being important building blocks. She was dreaming about launching services, selling overseas and more. Adwaita said, "Even when current businesses are struggling, Falguni is thinking *if I need to build a defensible business two years from now, what are the sort of the things I need to put into motion today?* She gets a lot of pushback from the team internally, who often consider new initiatives as distractions. But to her, it's not about not lack of focus, it's about setting us up for the future. She could have just stayed at an e-com business, but she set the private label into motion and she is setting the physical retail into motion. She is far sighted "

Falguni and Adwaita knew that they wanted to build 14 new physical retail stores, taking the total to 17 by March 2018 and 55 by March 2019. Building out the online business had taken time, and Falguni now felt that despite many early recruiting mistakes, the online team was motivated, talented, and firing on all cylinders. Building out the physical retail team would take a set of people with different background and skills. Adwaita felt that *Nykaa* would be an attractive place to join given its growing profile. Both Falguni and Adwaita, however, wondered how they should go about building out the team. Should they rely on their own networks? Should they once again use recruiters? Should they look for the most talented candidates or should they look for specific domain expertise? Similarly, how independent should the retail business be? How could *Nykaa* realize the tremendous synergy that their online and physical presence represents? Now that they were a 550-person organization how could they make sure that they were still one team and were not congealing into silos?

The opportunity to build her own company was a dream that Falguni had had since she was a child. That fact that she was doing it with her daughter made it much more exciting and meaningful. Still, she was the founder and with that came control over the most important decisions. While she sought advice from many people, *Nykaa*, like Adwaita, was her baby.

NOTES

1 ET Bureau "ET Startup Awards 2017: ET-Facebook women ahead award goes to Falguni Nayar of Nykaa" Economic Times, July 24, 2017, https://economictimes.indiatimes.com/small-biz/startups/et-startup-awards-2017-et-facebook

-woman-ahead-award-goes-to-falguni-nayar-of-Nykaa/articleshow/59729236 .cms, accessed November 2017
2 Gupta, Soumya, "Nykaa: Selling Beauty Online", Live Mint, September 27, 2017, http://www.livemint.com/Companies/yNqDkYCT4LSuuuKIzQPcmK/ Nykaa-Selling-beauty-online.html, accessed November 2017.
3 Venkatrama, Aarti, "Nykaa And The Art Of Retailing: Revolutionising The Online Beauty Industry With 10K Orders A Day," Inc42, May 29, 2017,https:// inc42.com/startups/nykaa-growth-story/, accessed January 2018.
4 Gupta, Soumya, "Nykaa: Selling Beauty Online", Live Mint, September 27, 2017, http://www.livemint.com/Companies/yNqDkYCT4LSuuuKIzQPcmK/ Nykaa-Selling-beauty-online.html, accessed November 2017.
5 Assocham India , "Grooming, Cosmetic Products set for Exponential Growth in India," July 07, 2016, http://www.assocham.org/newsdetail.php?id=5792, accessed January 2018
6 Roy, Shobha, "French Cosmetics Retailer Sephora to Dec Up India in Premium Products," The Hindu-Business Line, January 08, 2018, http://www.thehind ubusinessline.com/companies/french-cosmetics-retailer-sephora-to-deck-up -india-in-premium-products/article10020409.ece, accessed January 2018
7 Anand, Shubham, " Indian Cosmetics Industry," RedSeer Consulting (July 2017), http://redseer.com/wp-content/uploads/2017/10/118-Cosmetics -Industry-Report_Final_July2017.pdf, accessed February 2018
8 Anand, Shubham, " Indian Cosmetics Industry," RedSeer Consulting (July 2017), http://redseer.com/wp-content/uploads/2017/10/118-Cosmetics -Industry-Report_Final_July2017.pdf, accessed February 2018
9 Hanne, Elise, L'Oreal, "Strategy: Five Facts on Indian Beauty Market," January 02, 2016, http://www.loreal.com/media/news/2016/jan/five-facts-on -indian-beauty-market, accessed January 2018
10 Gulati, Payal, "Rural Contributes 30 of India's Cosmetics Industry," Rural Marketing, November 19, 2018, https://www.ruralmarketing.in/interview /advertising-marketing/rural-contributes-30-of-india-s-cosmetics-industry, accessed January 2018
11 Arsha Consulting, "Doing Business in India: The Rise of Tier II and III Cities" October 10, 2017, https://www.arshaconsulting.com/en/blog/posts/2017/ october/doing-business-in-india-the-rise-of-tier-ii-and-tier-iii-cities/, accessed January 2018
12 Ibid.
13 Ibid.
14 Nair, Athira A," How Purplle Won the Online Cosmetics Industry and Grew Sales from ₹45,000 to ₹15cr a Month," Yourstory, July 28, 2017, https:// yourstory.com/2017/07/purplle-startup-online-cosmetics-beauty-products/, accessed January 2018
15 Anand, Shubham, " Indian Cosmetics Industry," RedSeer Consulting (July 2017), http://redseer.com/wp-content/uploads/2017/10/118-Cosmetics -Industry-Report_Final_July2017.pdf, accessed February 2018
16 RH, Raghavendra,, "An Overview of Unorganized Retail Sector in India," https://www.elkjournals.com/MasterAdmin/UploadFolder/6. %20AN%20OVERVIEW%20OF%20UNORGANIZED%20RETAIL

%20SECTOR%20IN%20INDIA/6.%20AN%20OVERVIEW%20OF %20UNORGANIZED%20RETAIL%20SECTOR%20IN%20INDIA.pdf, accessed January 2018

17 "Beauty And Personal Care in India May 2017," Euromonitor International, accessed January 2018

EXHIBIT 1A Consolidated Financials

Particulars	FY13A	FY14A	FY15A	FY16A	FY17A
Net Revenue	0.9	27.1	169.5	584.4	2140.1
Growth (x)	-	31.7x	6.3x	3.4x	3.7x
Gross Margin	0.1	3.2	35.9	129.5	604.0
Gross Margin (%)	10.2	11.8	21.2	22.2	28.2
EBITDA	(9.2)	(49.1)	(147.2)	(333.1)	(450.8)
EBITDA Margin (%)	(1074.4)	(181.4)	(86.8)	(57.0)	(21.1)
PAT	(7.3)	(53.7)	(92.8)	(256.9)	(363.6)
PAT Margin (%)	(855.5)	(198.5)	(54.7)	(44.0)	(17.0)

Source: Company documents.

EXHIBIT 1B Key Statistics

Particulars	Aug-13	Jun-14	Jun-15	Jun-16	Jun-17
Monthly orders	1,430	10,932	34,542	93,720	
Orders by new customers/month	1,217	8,145	20,733	43,658	
% of customer retained***	49	57	54	53	
Women : Men	83.6 : 16.4	83.9 : 16.1	89.3 : 10.7	87.7 : 12.3	
Prepaid COD **	52.8 : 47.2	58 : 42	48.6 : 51.4	37.7 : 62.3	
Desktop : Mobile : App **	100:00:00	86:14:00	57.7:26.3:16.0	28.8:27.9:43.3	
Avg monthly visits	NA	NA	NA	4,237,968	
Time spent on site (mins)	NA	NA	NA	10	
Conversion Rate%	NA	NA	NA	2.21	
Database Size *	164,907	214,066	440,362	1,123,591	
Number of warehouses	0	1	3	4	4
Warehouse capacity (sq-ft)		5,000	35,000	50,000	50,000
Number of employees	NA	NA	110	303	
Number of offices	2	2	6	8	12
Number of items/order	2.69	4.13	3.77	4.15	
Average Order value	NA	NA	1,200	1,454	

Numbers are for the month mentioned - Not average of any time period
MRP is present in DB from July 2015 onwards (so AOV is present till Jun-14)
* Database size includes :- customers, guest buyers, newsletter subscribers, oos subscribers
** Based on Orders
***Based on cohort data updated as of Sep-17

Source: Company documents.

Falguni Nayar, Founder and Promoter CEO for FSN E-Commerce Ventures Pvt. Ltd, (known as Nykaa.com), has over 25 years of experience in the financial services industry, serves on the board of a number of companies including Tata Motors, Kotak Securities and Dabur India, and is a founding member of the Asia Society in India. Earlier Falguni was part of the top management at Kotak Mahindra Bank, where she set up the firm's international operations in London & New York, led the institutional equities business, and was managing director of the firm's investment banking arm.

After graduating from the Indian Institute of Management, Ahmedabad, Falguni worked as a consultant with A. F. Ferguson & Co. Her undergraduate degree in commerce is from Mumbai University. She was given the FICCI Ladies Organization (FLO) award for top woman achiever in banking, and the Business Today award for being one of the top 25 women in business.

Source: Company documents and Dabur - Board of Directors (http://www.dabur.com/in/en-us/about/leadership/board-of-directors/mr-falguni-nayar), Tata Motors – Leadership (http://www.tatamotors.com/about-us/leadership/); Bloomberg (https://www.bloomberg.com/research/stocks/people/person.asp?personId=241115705&privcapId=874652),accessed February 2018.

EXHIBIT 2 Falguni Nayar

EXHIBIT 3 Brand Portfolio (2012–2017)

Year	Luxury	Prestige	Masstige
Aug-13	1	12	91
Jun-14	5	22	134
Jun-15	25	28	235
Jun-16	32	38	382
Dec-17	51	70	668

Source: Company documents.

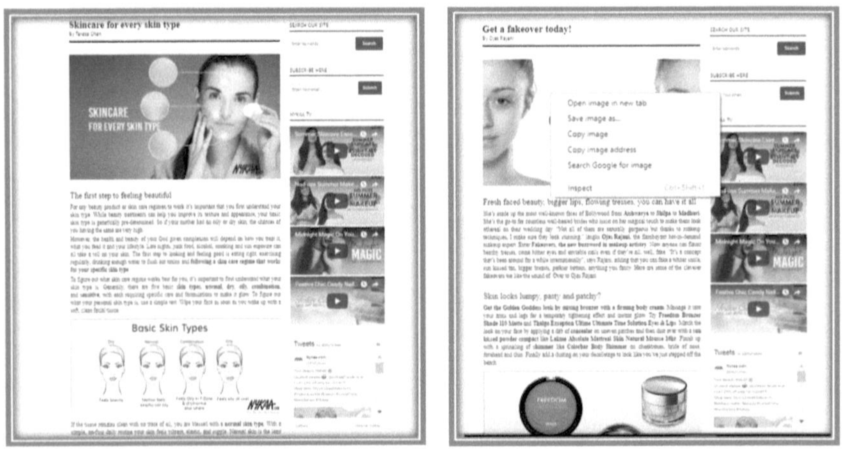

Examples of articles in the Expert Portal

EXHIBIT 4 *Nykaa* Webpage

Expert portal homepage

EXHIBIT 4 *(continued)*

Examples of the home page of the Beauty Book till 2015

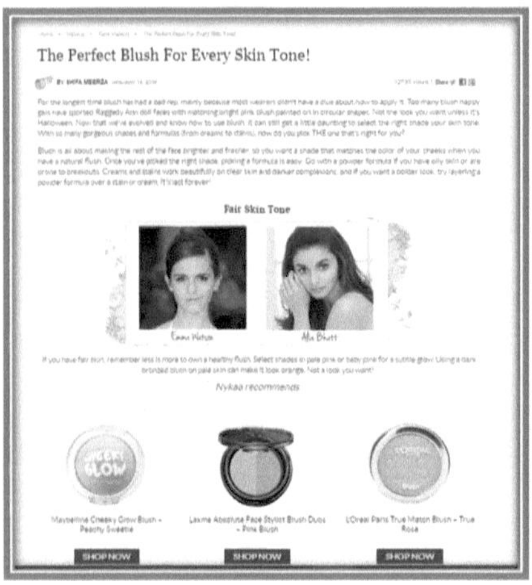

Example of articles in the Beauty Book

EXHIBIT 4 (*continued*)
Source: Company documents.

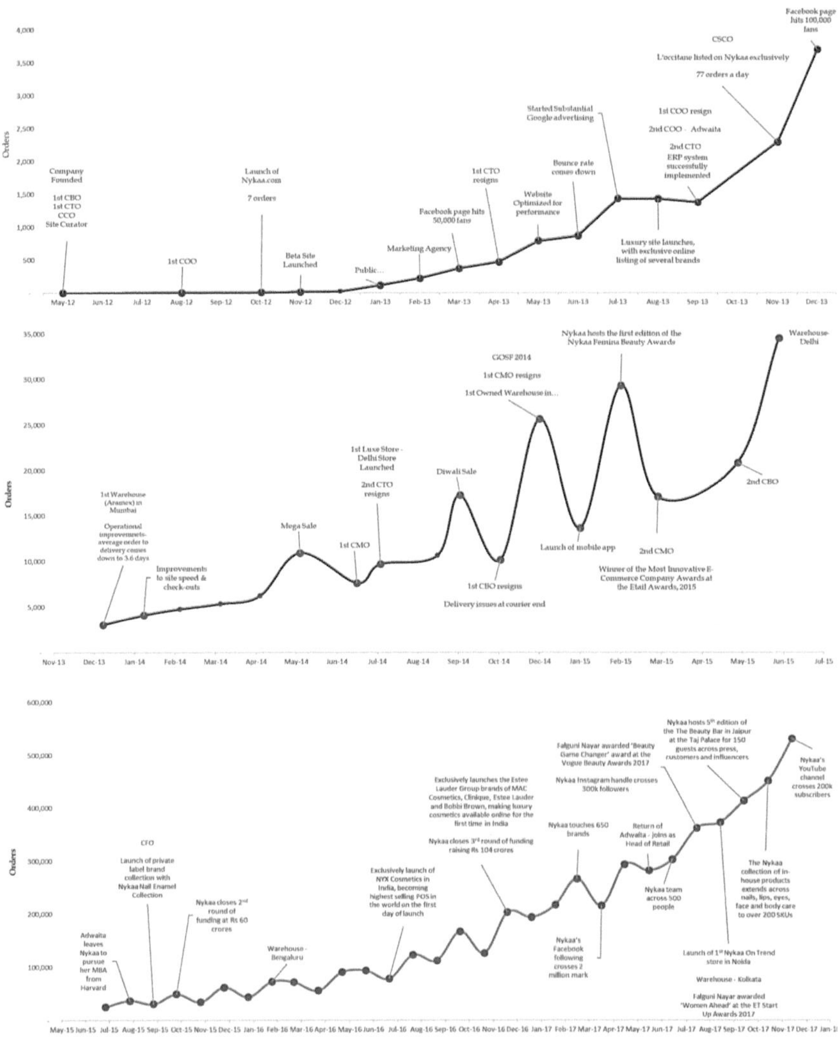

EXHIBIT 5 Nykaa's Journey 2012 to December 2017
Source: Company documents.

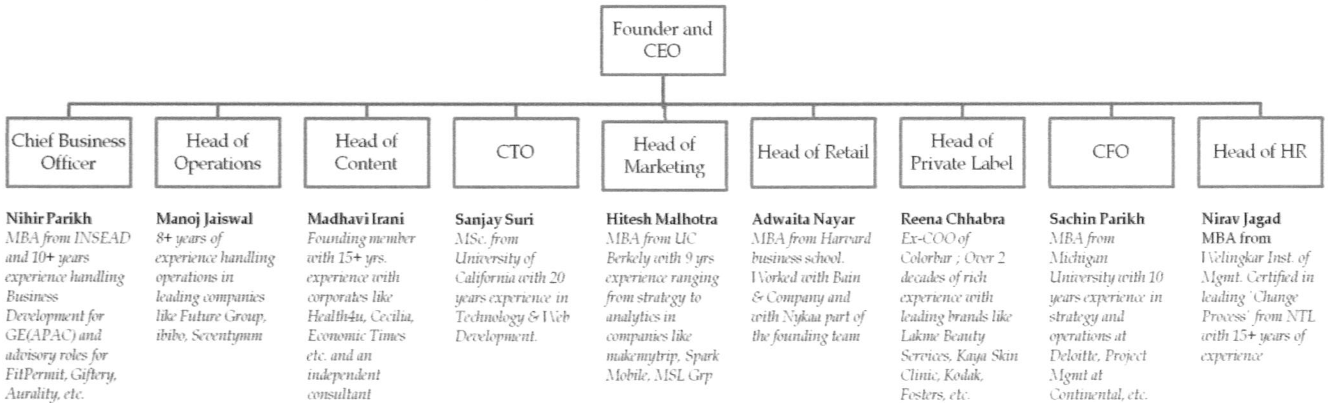

EXHIBIT 6 Organization Structure
Source: Company document.

EXHIBIT 7 Funds Raised

	Previous fundraise		
Year	July-14	July-15	November-16
Amount invested	₹ 200 million	₹ 600 million	₹ 1040 million
Post money Equity Valuation	₹ 1000 million	₹ 4270 million	₹ 8790 million
Lead investors	Family Offices & HNI	1. TVS Capital 2. Mariwala Family Office 3. Atul Nishar Family Office 4. Dalip Pathak 5. Michael Carlos 6. Other Family Offices & HNI	1. Munjal Family Office 2. Max I. Ltd 3. Mariwala Family Office 4. Other Family Offices & HNI

Note: Sequence of investors does not signify their quantum of investment in the respective round

Source: Company documents.

EXHIBIT 8A Balance Sheet (2013–2017)

(₹ in millions)

Balance Sheet	March 31, 2013	March 31, 2014	March 31, 2015	March 31, 2016	March 31, 2017
EQUITY AND LIABILITIES					
Shareholders Funds					
Share Capital	4.20	74.00	102.67	119.34	135.51
Reserves and surplus	(7.30)	(61.05)	25.62	348.60	1013.89
Non-current liabilities					
Long-term borrowings	19.00	9.70	-	-	-
Long-term provisions	0.28	0.58	0.89	-	5.00
Current liabilities					
Short term borrowings	-	-	50.02	123.11	292.42
Trade payables	0.18	2.90	12.67	80.61	345.45
Other current liabilities	2.66	7.95	21.20	103.79	237.62
Short term provisions	-	0.05	7.49	12.60	40.67
TOTAL	**19.02**	**34.13**	**220.56**	**788.06**	**2070.57**
ASSETS					
Non-current assets					
Fixed assets					
Tangible assets	2.50	4.45	14.47	44.43	82.99
Intangible assets	9.32	5.89	7.62	37.93	71.02
Non current investments	-	-	-	-	-
Deferred Tax asset (net)	3.25	3.01	63.31	166.84	309.80
Current assets					
Current Investments	-	-	36.32	201.30	642.83
Inventories	1.89	11.88	59.18	167.10	577.89
Trade receivables	0.23	2.07	21.67	62.54	218.56
Cash and bank balances	1.08	1.82	1.93	41.73	37.15
Short-term loans and advanc	0.44	3.85	15.01	63.85	111.54
Other current assets	0.31	1.17	1.04	2.34	18.79
TOTAL	**19.02**	**34.13**	**220.56**	**788.06**	**2070.57**

Source: Company documents.

EXHIBIT 8B Profit and Loss Statement (2013–2017)

(₹ in millions)

	March 31, 2013	March 31, 2014	March 31, 2015	March 31, 2016	March 31, 2017
Revenue from operations	0.83	25.16	143.44	470.16	1699.86
Other Income	0.03	1.91	26.05	114.24	440.21
Total Revenue	**0.85**	**27.07**	**169.49**	**584.40**	**2140.07**
Cost of goods sold	0.77	23.88	133.62	454.94	1536.05
Gross Margin	**0.09**	**3.19**	**35.87**	**129.46**	**604.02**
Expenses					
Direct Variable expenses	0.18	3.73	20.14	71.48	186.27
Marketing expenses	0.97	16.50	81.61	221.40	376.96
Employee benefits Expense	5.53	21.94	50.02	105.88	268.40
Tech expenses	0.23	2.33	6.56	18.54	80.47
Other expenses	2.36	7.79	24.69	45.30	142.68
Total expenses	**9.26**	**52.29**	**183.02**	**462.60**	**1054.79**
EBITDA	**(9.17)**	**(49.11)**	**(147.16)**	**(333.14)**	**(450.77)**
Depreciation and amortization expenses	1.33	4.36	4.17	11.96	29.75
EBIT	**(10.50)**	**(53.47)**	**(151.32)**	**(345.10)**	**(480.52)**
Finance Costs	0.05	0.03	1.77	10.39	26.08
Profit/(Loss) before tax	**(10.56)**	**(53.50)**	**(153.09)**	**(355.49)**	**(506.60)**
Tax expenses					
Current Tax	-	-	-	-	-
Deferred Tax	(3.25)	0.25	(60.30)	(103.53)	(142.96)
Profit/(Loss) for the year before exceptional items	**(7.30)**	**(53.75)**	**(92.79)**	**(251.95)**	**(363.64)**
Prior Period Items	-	-	-	4.94	-
Net Profit/(Loss) for the year	**(7.30)**	**(53.75)**	**(92.79)**	**(256.90)**	**(363.64)**

Source: Company documents.

Nykaa Board Members

Falguni Nayar	Narayan Ramachandran	Alpana Parida	Milan Khakhar	Anita Ramachandran	Vikram Sud	Sanjay Maliah	Yogesh Mahansaria
See Exhibit 2	*Investor Director September 28, 2015* Operating Partner at Gaja Capital; Led portfolio management at Morgan Stanley's Global Asset; B.Tech, IIT; MBA, University of Michigan; Chartered Financial Analyst	*Independent Director September 28, 2015* President of DY Works; Served as Head of Marketing with Tanishq; MBA IIM Ahmedabad	*Promoter Director (Non-Executive Director) September 28, 2015* Managing Director and Chairman at Solid Stone Company since 1994; B.Com.; B.Law	*Independent Director October 12, 2015* Founder & CEO of Cerabrus Consultants Pvt Ltd.; Consultant with A.F. Ferguson & Co (1976 to 1996); Writer; MBA from Jamnalal Bajaj Institute of Management Studies, Mumbai	*Promoter Director (Non – Executive Director) July 6, 2016;* Head of Operations and Technology for Asia Pacific Citigroup Inc. (2011 to 2015); COO of Kotak Mahindra Bank Ltd (2006 to 2008); Managing Director of Citigroup at New York; MBA XLRI Jamshedpur; B.Com	*Promoter Director (Non Executive Director) September 9, 2016* Managing Director and & CEO at M/s Empee Syndichem Pvt. Ltd.; B.Com	*Promoter Director (Non-Executive Director) since November 9, 2016* CEO & Director of ATC Tires Pvt Ltd (2015); Founder, CEO & Director of Alliance Tire Group (ATG) (2007 – 2015)

EXHIBIT 9 Nykaa Board Members
Source: Company documents.

APPENDIX 1: THE INDIAN PERSONAL CARE AND BEAUTY INDUSTRY—SIZE, OPPORTUNITY, AND SEGMENTS

In 2017, the Indian beauty industry was worth $6.5 billion. Hair care, driven by hair oil sales, was the biggest category (43% share), followed by oral care (25%), skin care (23%), fragrances (7%), and color cosmetics (2%). Women accounted for 60% of product revenues but men between the ages of 18-25 spent more on beauty products than women.[5] The premium segment (products priced above $16) accounted for approximately one-fourth of the market, and was growing at a faster rate than the mass-market segment.[6]

By 2025, analysts expected the Indian beauty sector to reach $20 billion, account for 5% of global sales, and be one of the top five global markets by revenue. These forecasts were driven by expectations of strong growth in the Indian economy and the ensuing rise in disposable income of a predominantly young population. Other growth drivers included urbanization, a more image-conscious working class, a greater willingness to spend on personal care and grooming, and the increasing influence of social media.[o7]

The Indian market was segmented. In metropolitan centers (cities with populations of above 1 million), consumers had high brand and product awareness and there was high demand for luxury and foreign products. In semi-urban centers, consumers were increasingly interested in personal care, and were willing to experiment with higher price-point brands and products.[8] Finally, in rural areas, consumers were just starting to use basic personal care products like soap and shampoo. (In 2017, only half of Indian households bought shampoo and just under a quarter bought skin care products.[9]) These extremely price-sensitive customers preferred affordable products and smaller sachet sizes.[10]

Analysts emphasized the importance of semi-urban areas in India's beauty industry growth story. The concentration of household income in Tier II-III cities[p] was 30 times that in India's 8 biggest cities. Many consumers from these towns visited metros for luxury purchases.[11] By 2025, these towns were expected to account for 45% of India's consumption.[12] A senior Amazon India executive noted that 70% of Amazon's new customers came from Tier II and III cities.[13] Sephora India's COO noted that 40%

o In a recent survey, 68% of young adults said that the use of grooming products boosted their confidence.

p The RBI classified Indian cities according to population size. Tier 1, 2, 3, 4, 5 were cities with populations above 100000, 50000, 20000, 10000 and 5000 respectively.

of the company's revenues came from outside the metros and Tier 1 cities. Purplle, an online marketplace for cosmetics, got 60% of its orders from non-metro cities.[14]

Distribution Channels

There were broadly three modes of retail distribution in India—unorganized retail (small mom-and-pop general goods, grocery, and drug stores), organized retail (exclusive brand outlets, multi-brand outlets, department stores, supermarkets, hypermarkets, beauty salons, and direct sales), and online retail.

Unorganized retail, primarily used by mass-market brands, accounted for 75% of total cosmetic sales.[15] In India, the unorganized sector consisted of millions of family-run corner mom-and-pop shops. Capital investment in these shops was low and infrastructure was rudimentary. Only 4% of such shops had a size greater than 500 square feet. Consumers found shopping at their local corner shop convenient, given the significant gaps in physical infrastructure. Shop owners offered credit, phone service, and free home delivery.[16] It was not unusual for deliverymen to fulfil, at no cost, home delivery orders worth $1 within half an hour of receiving them. However, this distribution channel presented a few drawbacks for beauty product buyers, including the lack of a wide product range, the lack of any specific guidance during the buying process, and a proliferation of counterfeit and grey market products. In recent years, the market share of unorganized retail in the beauty industry had decreased, giving way to organized and online retail.[17]

CHAPTER 6.3

ICSGroup

Paul A. Gompers, Christopher Stanton and Silpa Kovvali

Medina Jett had a vision that her firm, ICSGroup, would eventually be a multinational compliance firm with enough business to support regional directors across the country and around the world. Based in Hartford, Connecticut, she had just ended a call discussing terms for the potential acquisition of a competitor in Atlanta that would give her access to new clients and new talent. As she pondered the firm's future, she also wondered whether to go through with organic expansion into Africa and whether she could handle the management challenges associated with simultaneous domestic and international expansion.

Jett started ICSGroup in 2009 and worked as an independent compliance consultant for several years before making her first external hire. Slowly ceding control hadn't come easily, and Jett was especially measured in doing so because of the unique reputational consequences of bad hires in compliance consulting. Although Jett's extremely thorough and lengthy hiring process had meant slowly growing the size of her company over the decade since ICSGroup's inception, her restraint had paid off. ICSGroup got rave reviews from its clients, and its reputation was not only intact, but thriving.

Entering the last quarter of 2018, the new opportunities for expansion—an acquisition and entry into an exciting international market—now left Jett wondering whether a more aggressive pursuit of rapid growth would best suit her and her company's needs.

MEDINA JETT

Although Jett hadn't set out with the explicit goal of founding her own compliance firm, her background left her uniquely suited for the task. As an undergraduate at Wesleyan University, Jett had majored in American

ICSGroup
by PAUL A. GOMPERS, CHRISTOPHER STANTON, SILPA KOVVALI, case number 9-819-097

Politics and Government. A member of the Pre-Law Society, she was focused on a career as a lawyer, and began law school at Georgetown University immediately following her 1987 graduation. At Georgetown, Jett participated in Moot Court and wrote for the Immigration Law Journal, and also served as a student law clerk to the Honorable T.S. Ellis III in the U.S. District Court for the Northern District of Virginia. She received her JD in 1990 with a focus on Corporate Law.[1]

As a law student, Jett had interned at Murtha Cullina Richter & Pinney, LLC[2] as a summer associate, and upon graduation she accepted a full-time position in their Hartford, Connecticut office. Jett later looked back at the experience as foundational. Working in the firm's corporate law division, she developed a deep understanding of financial markets. Jett's role was primarily research-based, with a focus on "blue sky" research, the founding of investment firms, and annual reports for the firm's Fortune 500 clients. Still, the role was wanting in some respects. The corporate law department was composed almost entirely of white men over the age of fifty, and as a young African-American woman, Jett felt it wasn't a place where she could fully be herself. Two years after beginning at Murtha, Jett decided to move on.

Jett next went to Updike Kelly & Spellacy, a firm that focused on litigation, and she specialized in employment law, counseling and defense for several years. Eventually, in 1997,[3] Jett took a position running group insurance claims at Aetna, a move she described as "coming home." A common theme throughout her career, her prior experience proved valuable in unexpected ways. The claims management division at Aetna was fundamentally broken, and the company needed someone with a background in litigation to repair it. Skills like knowing how to depose physicians or set up disability plans were crucial, and because of her stint as a litigator she understood that process well. Running the 600-person division was a new and interesting challenge, and it was then that she first became acquainted with compliance work. Strong compliance practices were vital; there was simply no way to manage a claims organization of Aetna's size and complexity without vigorous and standardized practices in place.

Jett remained at Aetna for five years, and developed a mentorship-mentee relationship with its head of financial services due to her strong legal foundation, a valuable asset in the financial services sector. This mentor, now the president of Cigna Retirement & Investment Services ("CRIS") encouraged her to apply for the chief compliance officer role at CRIS. He was impressed with Jett's work at Aetna, taking note of her ability to manage large groups of people, manage risks and turn a division around. In 2004,[4] the acquisition of CRIS by Prudential was announced and Jett was offered the role of chief compliance officer for Prudential Retirement. The integration of the two companies was a 2-year task and required significant travel between Hartford, New Jersey and Prudential Retirement's other offices throughout the country. Though Jett remained passionate about compliance, she now had three children under ten, and couldn't keep up with the travel demands of her new position.

She decided to transition to the chief compliance officer position in the group benefits division of The Hartford, an insurance and financial services company headquartered in Simsbury, CT.[5] Though the position provided some of the stability she'd been hoping for, Jett—always with an eye toward her next steps—felt it fell short in some ways. She had a knack for sales, confirmed by a number of her colleagues on the sales team, and considered herself a people person. However, her role as CCO was less oriented toward interpersonal interactions than she would have preferred. Additionally, she wanted to learn more about how businesses ran and gain P&L responsibility. She shared these desires with her boss, the president of the group insurance division, who suggested she enroll in business school to hone her financial and business acumen.

In September of 2006, Jett began the Executive MBA program at the University of Connecticut, and was sponsored by The Hartford. In the program, she took a class on how to create and run a business, an independent course, which required that students develop a business plan, complete with a marketing strategy and sales projections. Naturally, she focused on the creation of a compliance business. Jett not only received an A on the project, but also encouragement from her professor, who recommended that she pursue the business for real. She agreed that the opportunity would provide her with everything she hoped for in a career, including and especially an emphasis on sales.

When she ran the idea by her boss at The Hartford, however, she received a very different reaction. It was 2008, the year of the financial crisis, and a recession was imminent. Her boss warned her against starting a business at such a volatile time. Still, her broader professional network encouraged her to give it a shot and reassured her that a career in the corporate world was waiting for her if her plans fell through. In July of 2008, Jett resigned from The Hartford and got to work building what would become ICSGroup.

STARTING ICSGROUP

Jett's first step was to reach out to a group of advisers she knew personally and professionally, primarily those who were running hedge or private equity funds. They were supportive and generous, and readily opened their rolodexes to her. Jett found one of her most valuable connections in JoAnn Price, co-founder and managing partner of Fairview Capital,[6] one of the largest black-owned private equity companies in the United States. Jett and Price served on a non-profit board together several years prior and had established such a close relationship that Jett often referred to Price as her "corporate mom." Fairview was located right in West Hartford, and Price happily met her for lunch to discuss her new business idea. They had an intensive and granular discussion about what exactly Jett wanted to do, what market and clients to pursue, and even what to name the company. Jett left the lunch with a name—ICSGroup, short for Integrated Compliance Solutions Group.[7] By the time ICSGroup was ready to launch, Jett had earned her first client in Fairview.

Though she was off to a promising start, having snagged Fairview and a handful of other clients, Jett soon began to wonder whether she'd made a mistake. The market was still tanking, especially on Wall Street. She would obtain a promising new client only to have them shut their doors because of the recession. Jett found herself asking whether her former boss at The Hartford was right. Should she have waited for a better time?

Then, in December of 2008, a prominent Manhattan financier was arrested and charged with criminal securities fraud for executing what was revealed to be an enormous Ponzi scheme in the guise of an investment firm. The high-profile Bernie Madoff case,[8] along with renewed scrutiny of Wall Street reform and passage of the Dodd-Frank regulations in the wake of the financial crisis, proved a boon to Jett. She reflected, "Reform was alive and real. New regulations were emerging, as was the notion that private funds shouldn't just be able to operate without regulation. For the first time, advisors to private funds were required to register with the SEC and comply with the Investment Advisors Act." Many of her contacts were in that private space, and began to seek her out in search of compliance advice and support with registering with the SEC and navigating the new regulatory environment that they were now subjected to.

Jett marketed ICSGroup's initial core offering as SEC registration and compliance program development. She described the company as a hands-on provider of quality compliance services to help investment advisors get and stay compliant. "We can help you understand these regulations and help you avoid regulatory violations." However, Jett knew that there was a limit to how far this offering would take the company. "Firms aren't going to want to spend money just to avoid something," she observed. "Their primary focus is growing their business." Jett wanted to leverage this short-term value proposition into a broader story, mission, and vision that would help keep and add clients in the long term, one that was geared toward helping them achieve success, not just avoid failure.

Jett found that vision in the emerging managers space: firms that were either minority- or women-owned or managed \$1 billion or less. She found that this niche group of companies was most interested in the services offered by ICSGroup; they didn't have the resources needed to hire full-time compliance officers, so an external consulting firm perfectly met their needs. Jett was also able to relate to each of these business owners on a deeper level, such that they became mutually vested in each other's success. "Many of these managers were struggling to grow while they watched their counterparts, friends, or family members grow very quickly. They didn't have the same resources to help them get started," Jett said. "I realized that if we were going to serve this market, we'd have to help those businesses survive and grow, and in doing so we could do the same."

When targeting these firms, Jett was able to readily distinguish herself among predominantly white male competitors, but it was important to her that ICSGroup's distinguishing value was the quality and nature of its services. Often, she found that emerging managers wanted compliance services that weren't about tackling regulatory issues, but impressing institutional investors. These established investors require firms to complete due diligence questionnaires and closely evaluate their operational and compliance infrastructure. Jett set out to hire a team of consultants who came from the institutional side as she had, where they themselves had developed high-quality, deep, and broad compliance experience. "We really touched on something," Jett later said. "We positioned ourselves to help firms grow by developing operational infrastructures that would be attractive to institutional investors vetting them for capital. Who better to do that than a compliance team with significant experience working for institutional investors? We were quite successful."

In late 2011/early 2012, ICSGroup responded to a request for proposal (RFP) from the Connecticut Pension Plan. At the time, the coveted contract belonged to the largest compliance firm in the state. Still, Jett was confident that ICSGroup could provide a superior service. She went in for a panel of interviews and was eventually awarded a 5-year contract with the State of Connecticut. As a result of that contract and several others, ICSGroup now had the consistency of cash flow needed to scale.

GROWING ICSGROUP

From ICSGroup's inception, Jett had been thoughtful about process. "Given my history, I understood the benefit of having a consistent and repeatable approach," Jett said. "It had served me well. Because I'd spent so much time as a compliance executive, I'd interviewed countless people. I understood soft skills and also knew that I needed strong partners." In going about selecting and recruiting those partners, Jett would draw on the skills she'd learned throughout her career.

While hiring practices were crucial to any business's success, they had enhanced primacy in a compliance business, particularly a small one that couldn't necessarily withstand the reputational risks of a single bad hiring decision. Jett instituted an unusually long interview process to gauge how interviewees would perform and react in different environments. She would fly out to where they were and assign them a case, then have them go through it step-by-step in person. "I didn't just want to grow," Jett said, "I wanted to grow with the right people."

In selecting employees, Jett found that that her personal network was her most valuable resource. She'd developed a strong presence on LinkedIn and maintained close contact with her connections there. She realized early on that this could be a venue to not only market her business but also to identify talent. She spent a great deal of time on the social network, constantly culling through her contacts and making new connections. Similarly, Jett frequented compliance conferences and regularly reached out to their organizers. Often, they invited her to speak on panels. Like her online presence, her physical presence at these conferences validated and raised the profile of ICSGroup. Equally important, it allowed her to meet other people who were in the compliance space or working at small asset management firms.

Consequently, Jett's very first full-time hire was the result of a referral. Rather than hiring a client-facing compliance consultant, Jett hired an employee to help her with business operations. This included everything from establishing onboarding procedures and billing to buying office furniture and setting up IT.

After internal SOPs had been developed to support a larger team, Jett began recruiting the larger consultant workforce she eventually onboarded. "In a way, ICSGroup didn't *really* start until 2014. That is when we really started to scale." While I ultimately had faith in my business, I recognized that not everyone would share that faith. It was hard to convince a quality person to leave their job and join a small firm."

Jett recounted the story of an early interviewee with whom she went through a lengthy evaluation process. She'd always felt that there needed to be a chemistry between employees at a small firm, so she had gotten to know him personally. Just as he had wanted to ensure that she was going to be a good manager, and mentor, she had wanted to ensure that he had an entrepreneur's mindset and fit with the culture she was developing for ICSGroup. After fully vetting each other, she extended an offer, which he readily accepted. He had spent three months unemployed while going through this lengthy vetting process, and was eager to get started, but then he received an offer from a larger, more established firm. "He had two daughters in college," Jett relayed, "and needed to be able to come to work every day without wondering if the firm was going to fold. He had no choice but to think about his family and take the other job."

Jett found that hiring at a small firm was a persistent challenge. She knew that, one day, employees would be glad to have joined the company at its early stages. She had a vision of ICSGroup as a multinational company with regional directors across the country. But she still had to sell that vision and get potential employees to buy into it enough to take a major risk. "I had to sell them on ICSGroup," Jett said, "as much as they needed to sell me on themselves."

MANAGING ICSGROUP

Remote Management

Many independent compliance consultants serviced local clients. When she started ICSGroup, Jett realized that her initial target clients, emerging asset managers, were scattered around the country. In fact, one of her very early clients was in Baltimore. Despite anticipating a great working relationship, at first the client was skeptical that Jett would be able to service the account from Hartford. She explained the firm's hybrid approach, "We don't need to be on site on a daily basis. Our role is to develop a compliance program, implement it, provide training and leave your employees to comply with it. Our goal is to get policies and procedures in place that comply with regulatory expectations. We will be available for questions and issue resolution remotely through e-mail or conference calls, supplemented with periodic site visits depending on the level of service the client has elected." As Jett started to hire new consultants, she realized that not only would her clients be dispersed around the country but so too would her employees. This structure arose partly from necessity due to the sparsity of compliance talent in Hartford. While Jett felt she had to go where the talent is, she also believed this broad reach could help with client perceptions. When trying to sign new accounts, mentioning that ICSGroup had consultants in Austin, Chicago, and Atlanta and also had clients in various states across the country helped to demonstrate the national scope of the firm. This arrangement allowed ICSGroup to access talent without any geographic limitations and without having to relocate people to Hartford.

The remote model helped ICSGroup in the war for talent that is any professional services business. The consultant contract set forth ICSGroup's expectations for consultants in delivering the service model and also protected the firm through the use of non-solicitation restrictions. Consultants were also offered additional incentives for bringing in new business. (See **Exhibit 1**.) Jett conveyed the benefits of this model to consultants. "ICSGroup consultants get the added benefit of being able to work in their PJs unless they're flying to a client location. Consultants love getting to meet with a client when needed while having the flexibility of working from home. It's a win-win for them." Moreover, ICSGroup consultants' status as contractors allowed them to choose their own level of engagement, appealing to those tired of 50-hour weeks with rigid schedules; this enabled consultants to have a flexible work schedule that fit their desired work-life balance.

Research from randomized job ads suggested this type of contract would be especially appealing to some candidates. A recent field experiment by Alexandre Mas of Princeton and Amanda Pallais of Harvard showed job applicants different position amenities, like flexible hours or the ability to work from home. The researchers then looked at patterns of how workers chose between jobs with different combinations of wages and these amenities, allowing them to estimate applicants' willingness to pay for workplace benefits, or what economists call compensating differentials.[9] Applicants had a wide distribution of willingness to pay for these amenities. **Exhibit 2** displays estimates of the willingness to pay for amenities relative to a base hourly wage rate of $17.50. Although many workers would accept lower wages to land a job with stable hours and face-to-face interactions with co-workers, the reverse was true for a substantial fraction of the workforce. These applicants were willing to accept lower wages for amenities like working from home. ICSGroup attracted talent to the firm by offering similar benefits.

Despite the benefits, running ICSGroup as a virtual firm carried the increased potential for reputational and business risks and Jett was aware of these challenges. Many studies concluded that telephone or video conversations are less effective for transmitting information than in-person communication, and practically all remote businesses contend with how this affects onboarding employees and monitoring distant workers. To combat these risks, Jett formalized practices for recruiting, onboarding, training, monitoring, and general people management. A substantial portion of her time was spent not only attracting new recruits, but also vetting them. Jett never hired anyone that wasn't within two degrees of separation. She looked to hire people she had worked with before or who came highly recommended from a trusted source. Every new hire went through formal background checks and extensive reference checks as, in Jett's words, "The compliance industry is actually quite small; nobody is an island. I can learn a lot with a few calls to my network."

Further screening and vetting then occurred. Jett required writing samples and case analyses to assess whether consultant candidates were comprehensive in identifying issues; she would screen by giving out actual pitch books, seeking candidates' comments and recommendations for changes. The same few pitch books were used across candidates, providing a comparable measure. Finally, Jett looked for consultants who fit the ICSGroup mold, those with soft skills supporting a high touch, consultative approach, which is part of ICSGroup's value proposition as opposed to a "harsh 'no, you can't do that' approach, which is common among some compliance professionals." The process might take three to five months.

Upon finding a good match, Jett tailored onboarding and training based on the consultants' prior experience. All consultants shadowed Jett, but for experienced consultants, the shadowing and onboarding period focused mainly on aligning with the ICSGroup style of service delivery and becoming familiar with ICSGroup's many compliance tools and resources. Less experienced recruits received substantial coaching and real time feedback during client engagements, with Jett often listening in on calls and monitoring behavior.

To this point, Jett believes this conscientious approach had been successful. Still, she was quick to cut off problems as they arose, with controls in place to mitigate potential disaster. On one occasion, a junior consultant provided inaccurate guidance to a client without reviewing her proposed guidance with a senior consultant as required. The issue later came up in an SEC exam. Jett said,

> The consultant gave a simple answer to what she assumed was a simple question, but she wasn't experienced enough to understand the downstream impacts and exceptions. The actions the client took as a result of the consultant's advice later posed an issue for an SEC examiner, which I had to deflect. While they appreciated that I stepped in and was able to resolve the issue to the examiner's satisfaction, it isn't something I'd want to have happen again. Because of the highly technical nature of asset management, that type of situation could potentially happen often if operational controls falter or review procedures are not followed. I eventually had to let the consultant go because she wasn't responding to coaching, and I couldn't bear the risk of these problems recurring.

Jett worried about how new consultants would fit with these practices and whether adding new consultants and new markets would detract from her hands-on recruiting, onboarding, and coaching. Jett also recognized that letting go of some control, even gradually, had been extremely hard due to the potential risk to the firm's reputation that she had worked so hard to build. In order to grow she would have to trust her senior consultants to perform at a high level with less hands-on supervision. A consultant who wasn't paying attention to all the issues and facts could jeopardize the firm's reputation.

Economics

ICSGroup separated clients into three tiers based on their needs and budget, each of which was billed at a separate, standardized rate. Companies paid either $40,000, $60,000, or $80,000 annually for a broad range of core compliance functions. Many clients originated because they needed to become registered with the SEC. When firms began to manage assets of a significant size—defined as $150 million or more—they were required to become a Registered Investment Adviser (RIA) under SEC guidelines. This essentially meant a firm would then be subject to SEC oversight. ICSGroup would assist firms with the registration process while helping to develop a compliance manual and code of ethics commensurate with their new standing. This service carried a $20,000 fee, in addition to the $40,000/$60,000/$80,000 annual pricing plan for ongoing support throughout the year.

Additionally, ICSGroup provided ad-hoc services. Clients often approached the company while preparing for an SEC exam, for example. In such a case, a company anticipating an upcoming SEC investigation might hire ICSGroup to perform a mock exam that allowed them to uncover and address any issues before a visit from a potential regulator. For such a service, ICSGroup might charge $20,000 to $25,000 depending on the complexity of the fund, the number of employees, and the amount of data they might have to gather. ICSGroup was also called upon to perform in-person or web-based compliance training, for which they might charge $5,000 to $10,000 depending on how in-depth and lengthy the training. For less standard services, clients would be billed by the hour because of the difficulty in anticipating costs. One client, for example, reached out before going out of business. The company needed advice and counsel surrounding how to wind down from a tactical standpoint, including what notifications and withdrawal forms were required.

The cost structure to provide these services was largely in payments to the consultants employed by ICSGroup. Consultants are paid on an hourly basis, generally in the range of $75 to $125 depending on their level of expertise. A consultant with experience in mutual funds or broker-dealer compliance might command a hire hourly fee, while a junior consultant whose experience was limited to investment advisory compliance might get paid on the lower end of the range. While Jett would put together billing guidelines based on client service levels in order to meet margins, she does not share client billing information with the consultants servicing them.

A tier one client, generating revenues of $40,000 annually, generally required 100 hours of consultant time per year. The typical consultant handled five to six clients in addition to several ad hoc assignments. Jett attributed ICSGroup's margins to the efficiency of ICSGroup's infrastructure she had rigorously constructed from the moment of the firm's inception. First and foremost, Jett's thorough vetting process ensured that consultants were both highly experienced and highly efficient. But additionally, Jett had developed a collection of compliance toolkits and templates that could be tailored for each client. (See **Exhibit 3** for the Table of Contents of ICSGroup's compliance manual.)

When a consultant conducted a mock exam, for example, they started with a Document Request List from the firm's mock exam folder and a checklist of everything an investigator might test based on a client's investment strategy, including the questions that would arise in a standard review. The step-by-step tools require customization based on each specific client, but they create tremendous efficiency for the consultants. No resulting compliance review report, the eventual output provided to a client, was ever the same, but the format and template language was consistent across the board.

Jett relayed some concerns about her compensation structure, noting that consultants who were paid by the hour were incentivized to have a "law firm mentality," where their primary concern was billing many hours. While some competitors eliminated this risk through a flat fee payment system, Jett instead mitigated it via her toolkit, which implicitly laid out billing guidelines for the types of tasks that were required for each client including resolving ad hoc issues. Of course, the guidelines were estimates and anticipated deviations were to be raised and discussed in advance.

Medina supplemented the billing guidelines with close and careful observation of consultant billing hours and, of course, her own experience and judgment. As expected, consultants getting paid $75/hour weren't yet going to be as efficient as her higher-paid consultants. Similarly, a new consultant who was still getting up to speed might face a steep learning curve and bill more hours during a break-in period. So, Jett monitored trends in each consultant's billing. She aimed for each consultant to hit an 80% profit margin, using a small portion of overhead for in-house staff, tools, and operating procedures.

By 2018, ICSGroup had grown to a size of six consultants, in addition to Jett, when she was faced with the opportunity to acquire a similarly-sized compliance firm based in Atlanta. (See **Exhibit 4** for pre-acquisition organization chart.) Jett led ICSGroup into the acquisition with the long-term goal of establishing a dominant presence in the Southern region. Because Jett hoped to helm ICSGroup's transition to a larger firm servicing a wider set of regions, she hired a compliance executive who had served most recently as the Chief Compliance Officer of a major investment firm in Atlanta, to manage the expansion in the Southern market.

Jett viewed the expansion as "acquiring the Atlanta firm's clients, but not its business." In explaining her process to integrate the Atlanta firm, Jett relayed:

> The firm had not developed internal processes and tools to support its business model so I anticipate leveraging internal tools to drive an increase in profits. I also plan to interview the acquisition target's consultants through the same rigorous process I have always applied. I will have the benefit of actual work product and client feedback to fully assess consultant performance and will then extend offers only to those I decide are a good fit.

AFRICA EXPANSION

Fresh off the heels of a proposed acquisition that would double the size of her firm, Jett was also considering yet another major expansion, one that would make her international vision of ICSGroup a reality. Jett described how she first arrived at the idea to offer ICSGroup's compliance services to companies in Africa:

> Quite a few public pension plans have emerging manager programs where they are looking to get capital to minority and women-owned firms who've been excluded from this space. Managers of these plans know me: Prior to ICSGroup I was the CCO at three major investment advisors and have developed relationships with the staff at quite a few plans. Since starting ICSGroup, I interact with staff from the major pension plans often in meetings with ICSGroup's clients, at conferences, etc. We've discussed the challenges associated with investing in the African market, but they feel there are so many risks. They're worried about corruption and the lack of strong compliance programs at these firms; they don't want to damage their name and reputation by investing with the wrong African fund.

With this issue, and a potential resolution provided by ICSGroup in mind, Jett attended the Africa Venture Capital and Private Equity Conference in Morocco in 2018, and met with private equity firms in Africa to do a needs and appetite assessment. She found that many private equity funds were investing in African infrastructure projects, but there was not a lot of capital available to support its high potential for growth. American companies wanted to know that the firms they were funding had strong compliance controls on par with US regulatory standards. Jett realized that providing compliance guidance to these companies abroad could be a win-win: it would allow ICSGroup to provide a valuable service to a new array of international clients and would enable African private equity firms to have better access to US capital.

Jett began laying the groundwork for a potential expansion by joining the African Private Equity and Venture Capital Association, where she was appointed to the Compliance and Best Practices Committee, raising her level of exposure. Though she was still at the early stages of determining whether Africa was a feasible market for ICSGroup, joining AVCA was a substantial move in that direction because of its non-trivial membership dues. "We were dipping more than a toe," Jett said. "We were up to our knees!" Of course, the membership brought perks beyond publicity. "It gave us valuable intel in assessing how firms in Africa were managing compliance and whether they recognized the need to focus on compliance more going forward. As I suspected, either no one was responsible for compliance or the people handling compliance often weren't compliance experts, which means they were a perfect prospect for ICSGroup's services."

The Risks

As with any form of expansion, entering a new geographic market carried risks. One of them was opportunity cost. There was the possibility that ICSGroup might be leaving domestic business on the table by pursuing clients abroad. However, Jett wasn't especially concerned. "I didn't see a tradeoff," she said, "but a benefit. International companies are generally more highly regarded. My appointment to the Compliance and Best Practices Committee got a lot of attention on LinkedIn and generated new calls from US-based firms in need of compliance support. If you're good enough that firms in other countries want to hire you, the thinking goes, you become a hot commodity for the domestic market." Jett also pointed to a number of firms in the US with African branches who were trying to get more involved with infrastructure and private equity investment in Africa, enticed by high returns but afraid of the risks.

There were other risks, more pressing on Jett's mind. One was the Foreign Corrupt Practices Act (FCPA), and other regulations designed to prevent bribery or other corrupt practices. While corruption was a risk in any market, US investor's lack of familiarity with business norms abroad might leave them vulnerable to reputation-damaging scandals. US investors would rest easier knowing that certain private equity firms in Africa had been fully vetted and had effective compliance programs in place. This benefit would be an incentive for Africa private equity firms to work with ICSGroup.

Primarily, Jett hoped to focus, at least initially, on companies that had already raised capital overseas, particularly in the US, as they are more familiar with regulatory standards. She believed these companies would benefit from the services ICSGroup provided. While the regulatory requirements were slightly different, Jett was comfortable that her team could learn what they needed to implement proper policies and procedures. Most importantly, because the African firms were seeking to raise capital from US investors, they were expected to meet US regulatory standards, which were more rigorous than the standards on their country.

Concerns regarding bribery and corruption, in particular, were much more of an issue for African firms. The corrupt reputation that African firms have to deal with, make a strong FCPA policy, procedures and controls extremely critical. The ICSGroup team would have to be especially thorough in surveilling communications between employees and outside parties, scrutinizing travel and expense reports and keeping detailed records on who employees were having dinners with or sending gifts to. When internal controls were effectively designed, Jett's experience had been that policies were relatively hard to circumnavigate or, more likely, unintentionally violate.

The issue of Chief Compliance Officer liability is a concern for outsourced compliance consultants. When an employee was intent on committing a crime (as, again, was as much the case domestically as abroad), Jett's experience had been that it was virtually impossible to stop them. For this reason, when effective suspenders were put in place, the SEC rarely held a compliance officer accountable for violations that happened within a firm. If Jett were to go forward with the expansion, she planned to revisit ICSGroup's contractual language around liability and indemnification to be sure that internal chief compliance officers, and not ICSGroup or its consultant, were ultimately responsible for any wrongdoing that might occur. However, while these careful considerations could protect ICSGroup from legal scrutiny, Jett noted that they could never control the impact of a reputational injury, a risk any compliance company had to accept as part of doing business, no matter the market.

The Approach

Jett considered several options if ICSGroup chose to pursue the Africa expansion. One was to outsource hiring altogether. Jett learned of overseas staffing firms that specialized in hiring oversees for US-based firms. She intended to begin with a potential launch in Nigeria, based largely on the density of the population and the number of investment firms there. If she were to provide a region, set of job descriptions, and a skill set analysis to the staffing firm, they would be able to recruit and hire a set of appropriate individuals there. The staffing firm would then become the official employer—Jett would, of course, have input in the hiring process and get to interview and vet candidates, but once they were hired they would become an employee of another company that paid their salary and benefits. Jett would then pay the staffing firm the amount of the employee's salary and benefits, plus a premium for its services. She considered this as one option that might allow her to hire overseas without having to get entangled in foreign regulations and taxes, particularly those surrounding employment.

There was also the possibility of essentially maintaining her current model of a remote workforce while expanding the geography of serviced clients. In her discussions with management at African firms that she met with, Jett learned that, like their American counterparts, many didn't see the need for a full-time compliance employee. While she didn't expect her consultants to relocate to Africa or engage in frequent travel there, several consultants on hearing of the opportunity have expressed a desire to do so, if needed.

Just as a consultant based in New York City might service clients in Chicago, a consultant based in the US could also maintain a roster of six clients, or even more, in Cape Town, South Africa. The role would, of course, require slightly more flexibility than ICSGroup currently expected, but the difference was marginal, particularly as Jett envisioned a measured growth path in the new market. She imagined a headcount of two or three consultants focused exclusively on the Africa market over the next several years. Not a massive number of new hires objectively, or relative to the size of her firm, this tempered growth could ensure that ICSGroup had sufficient opportunity to test the staffing model, with her ability to monitor the engagement and address any issues early on. In the event that Jett underwent this model of expansion, she also anticipated travelling to Africa frequently along with her consultants so she could better understand the culture, the nuances particular to African firms and provide the level of assistance the African firms would anticipate. She expected consultants to be committed to a similar level of immersion in the market, with respect to frequent travel but also in developing regional expertise.

Finally, Jett toyed with the idea of taking a more hands-on approach, even moving to Africa for a year or two herself to get ICSGroup's initial expansion off the ground. The timing was perfect from a personal perspective; with Jett's youngest daughter leaving for college in the coming year she would soon be an empty-nester. She had personal social ties to Nigeria, with close friends who were from or currently residing in the nation. Jett reflected, "In many ways, it seemed like a perfect opportunity was waiting for me to figure out how to put it all together and make it work."

Jett pondered her potential next steps. ICSGroup's evolution was ongoing whether she chose to enter a new market at this juncture or not. Should she take time to more thoroughly integrate her recent acquisition before taking another great leap? Or was, as her intuition told her, an opportunity waiting to be seized? If Jett did decided to enter this exciting new market, where and how should she begin?

NOTES

1 "Medina Jett," *LinkedIn*, accessed in January 2019, https://www.linkedin.com/in/medinajett/.
2 *LinkedIn.*
3 *LinkedIn.*
4 *LinkedIn.*
5 "The Hartford," *Fortune*, accessed in January 2019, http://fortune.com/fortune500/hartford-financial-services/.
6 "JoAnn H. Price," *Fairview Capital*, accessed in January 2019, http://www.fairviewcapital.com/our-team/joann-h-price.
7 "Integrated Compliance Solutions," *ICSGroup*, accessed in December 2018, https://www.i-c-solutions.net/.
8 "The Madoff Case: A Timeline," *The Wall Street Journal*, accessed in December 2018, https://www.wsj.com/articles/SB112966954231272304.
9 Mas, Alexandre, and Amanda Pallais. 2017. "Valuing Alternative Work Arrangements." American Economic Review, 107 (12): 3722-59.

EXHIBIT 1 Selected Components of ICSGroup Consulting Agreement

AGREEMENT

1. SCOPE OF SERVICES

A. Compliance Services. Consultant will provide the following professional compliance consulting services ("Compliance Services"):
- Provide compliance support to ICSGroup clients, as assigned by ICSGroup, consistent with the Compliance Program Rules, common industry practices, and regulatory guidance;
- Conduct compliance reviews of clients' marketing materials to ensure compliance with SEC rules, no-action letters, and other relevant industry guidance;
- Attend meetings with ICSGroup management, as requested by ICSGroup, for the purpose of discussing Consultant's background and experience and selling ICSGroup's services
- Assist the firm with internal practice development (such as developing annual review procedures) and general business development (such as penning a white paper) activities

Subject to the supervision and direction of ICSGroup, Consultant will provide the Compliance Services consistent with the provisions of the Investment Advisers Act of 1940 and other regulations applicable to investment advisors.

B. Business Development Services. If he desires, Consultant may also solicit prospective clients on ICSGroup's behalf ("Business Development Services"). Business Development Services are separate and distinct from the Compliance Services and will be compensated separately as detailed in the Fee for Services section below. In order to be compensated for Business Development Services, the prospective client must be an entity with which ICSGroup had no interaction for the prior 6 months and Consultant must have played a significant role in securing the client engagement. "Significant role" is defined as making the initial introduction and/or persuading a client to retain ICSGroup. Any clients acquired through the Business Development Services shall remain clients of ICSGroup after termination of this Agreement.

2. DISCRETION AND JUDGEMENT

A. There will be no exact work hours or required work location. However, Consultant will be available to ICSGroup as necessary and as dictated by each assignment.

EXHIBIT 1 *(continued)*

B. Consultant will have the right to exercise reasonable discretion and judgment to determine the allocation of time and efforts that will be required to perform the services contemplated by this Agreement.

3. FEE FOR SERVICES

A. In consideration of the Compliance Services rendered pursuant to this Agreement, the Company will compensate Consultant at a rate of $115/ hour. In the event that the parties agree that due to the complexity of the assignment, a higher hourly rate is appropriate, such rate will be discussed and approved prior to the commencement of the assignment. Consultant shall complete detailed weekly timesheets. ICSGroup will issue payment to Consultant every two weeks within 3 business days after the completion of time entry for the prior 2 week period.
B. ICSGroup will reimburse Consultant for business-related travel expenses (such as lodging, meals and mileage) deemed necessary to perform the Compliance Services so long as

ICSGroup has pre-approved the expenditure in writing.

C. Consultant shall be compensated for Business Development Services at the following rates:

- Year 1— 20% of the revenue generated and paid by the client in the first 12-month period starting on the date the client retains ICSGroup
- Year 2 — 10% of the revenue generated and paid by the client in the second rolling 12-month period

There shall be no compensation paid for Business Development Services beyond 24 months after a client retains ICSGroup.

4. TERM OF AGREEMENT

A. The term of this Agreement shall commence on June 13, 2015 and shall continue indefinitely until terminated in writing by either party. This Agreement may be terminated for any reason or no reason by either ICSGroup or Consultant at any time, upon the giving of not less than 30 days' prior written notice to the other party.
B. Upon termination, ICSGroup will pay for all services rendered on ICSGroup's behalf before the date of such termination or which are reasonably necessary thereafter.

EXHIBIT 1 *(continued)*

5. RELATIONSHIP OF THE PARTIES

A. Consultant agrees to become a consultant for ICSGroup; his official title will be "Senior Consultant".
B. The parties intend that an independent contractor relationship will be created upon commencement of the engagement. Consultant is not to be considered an employee or agent of ICSGroup generally and also as defined under federal, state and local securities laws, SEC rules and regulations and SEC forms, and shall not have the power or authority to contract in the name of or bind the Firm, except as may be designated by the managing members of the Firm.
C. As an independent contractor, Consultant is not entitled to participate in employee programs, or any of the benefits that ICSGroup provides for its employees.
D. ICSGroup will file and provide Consultant with a 1099 after the end of each calendar year. Consultant will have sole responsibility for the withholding and payment of all taxes, fees and assessments due to federal, state, local or other authorities with regard to any payments it receives from ICSGroup under this Agreement.

6. CONTRACTUAL RESTRICTIONS

By entering into this Agreement Consultant represents that he has not entered into any agreement or covenant against competition or similar restrictions which would affect the performance of his obligations under this Agreement. Consultant also agrees that he will not enter into any agreement that conflicts with the provisions of this Agreement.

This Agreement in no way limits or restricts Consultant from entering into or performing any other compliance consultant engagement for any other firm or company so long as Consultant makes ICSGroup aware of such engagement and ICSGroup agrees that no conflict of interest is created as a result of the respective clients' overlapping business relationships.

7. CONFIDENTIALITY AND NON-DISCLOSURE

"Confidential Information" shall constitute all data relating specifically to any party's business and any other information, which reasonably should be understood to be confidential information of such party. Each party's proprietary software, tools, methodologies, templates, techniques, ideas, and know-how are Confidential Information. In connection with Consultant's performance within this Agreement, the parties may become aware of or have access to confidential information related to the other or its employees.

EXHIBIT 1 (*continued*)

Each party shall use Confidential Information of another party only in furtherance of the purposes of this Agreement and shall not disclose such Confidential Information to any third party without that other party's prior written consent. Each party agrees to take reasonable measures to protect the confidentiality of another party's Confidential Information and to advise its employees of the confidential nature of the Confidential Information and of the confidentiality provisions and use prohibitions herein.

The terms and conditions of the Agreement shall be considered Confidential Information and no party may disclose the terms and conditions of the Agreement without the other parties' prior written consent.

8. <u>INDEMNIFICATION</u>

ICSGroup agrees to hold harmless and indemnify Consultant against all claims, damages, liabilities, expenses and costs (including reasonable attorney's fees and disbursements) arising in any manner out of or in connection with the Compliance Services, except for such claims, damages and costs resulting from any actions by Consultant constituting gross negligence, reckless or intentional acts or omissions, or unlawful conduct.

Consultant shall defend, indemnify and hold ICSGroup, its managing members, officers, agents, employees, representatives and affiliates harmless from and against any and all liability, loss, expense (including reasonable attorneys' fees) or claims for injury or damages arising out of the performance of this Agreement but only in proportion to and to the extent such liability, loss, expense, attorneys' fees, or claims for injury or damages are caused by or result of Consultant's gross negligence, reckless or intentional acts or omissions.

9. <u>NON-SOLICITATION</u>

Consultant agrees that he will not directly or indirectly solicit, counsel, induce, or attempt to induce any ICSGroup employee or consultant to leave his or her employment or relationship with ICSGroup, for any reason whatsoever while this Agreement is in effect and for a period of one year following termination of this Agreement.

Consultant also agrees that he will not solicit any ICSGroup client, whether retained as a result of the Business Development Services or not, while this Agreement is in effect and for a period of two years following termination of this Agreement.

IN WITNESS WHEREOF, each of the parties hereto has executed this Agreement in multiple counterparts as of the day and year first above written.

Source: Medina Jett.

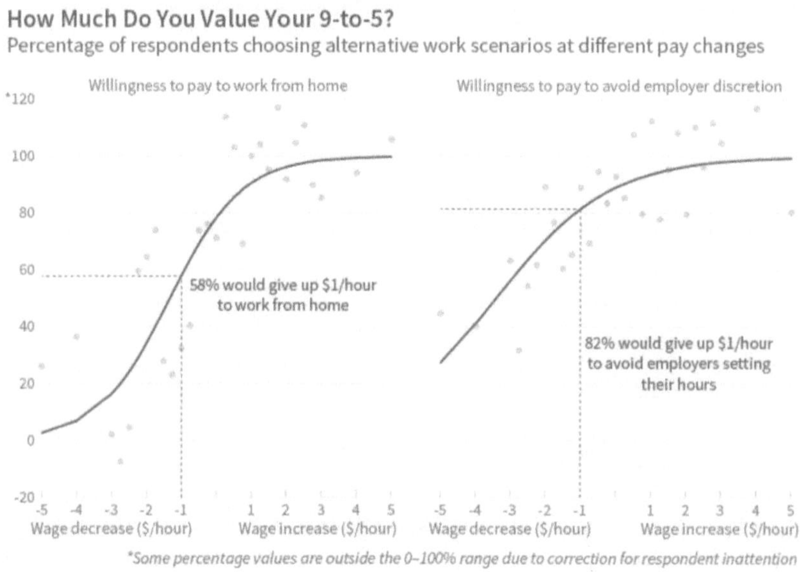

EXHIBIT 2 Estimates of Willingness to Pay for Job Amenities Relative to an Average Hourly Wage of $17.50

Source: NBER Digest Report on "Valuing Alternative Work Arrangements" by Alexandre Mas and Amanda Pallais, available at https://scholar.harvard.edu/files/pallais/files/december_2016_nber_digest.pdf.

EXHIBIT 3 Table of Contents—ICSGroup Compliance Manual

TABLE OF CONTENTS

Attachments

Source: Medina Jett.

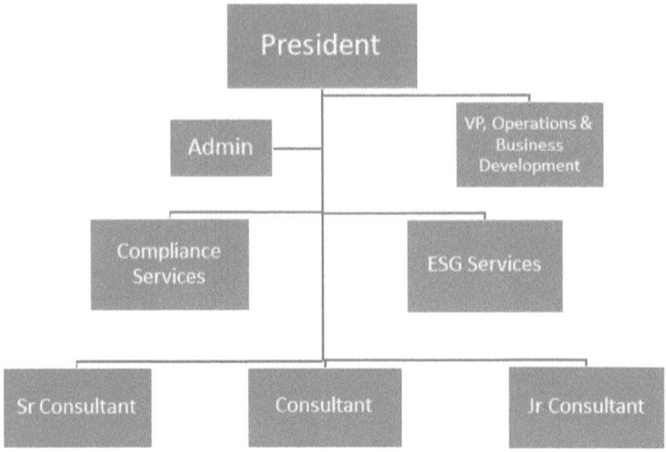

EXHIBIT 4 Organizational Chart
Source: Medina Jett.

CHAPTER 6.4

New York Bagel: Hungary, April 1994

Paul A. Gompers and Catherine M. Conneely

Gathered in the vaulted cellar office of New York Bagel (NYB) shop in Budapest, Robert Brooker and his staff were jubilant, having posted another day of record revenue. His partner, Adam Weiss, was meanwhile meeting with contractors at the site of NYB's upcoming 3,000 square foot shop. Brooker, Co-founder and Co-CEO of NYB, stepped over to his fax machine and read line by line the incoming term sheet. This was the last round of a long-negotiated deal with Euroventures-Hungary (EVH), that Brooker and Weiss hoped would finally help them realize their dream of a multi-unit chain of bagel shops. The terms from the venture capital fund were much worse than he had expected.

Brooker had to once again remind himself where the business stood. Their first shop, despite its out of the way location, experienced a growing base of regular customers, not to mention a flurry of local and international press intrigued by the reintroduction of bagels to Hungary after centuries of absence. He and his partner realized that the fixed costs of pioneering the market could not be recouped in a single store, so they prepared for expansion, which included installing multi-unit retail systems, building a real estate development team, and securing a lease on a prime urban location. These measures were complete; all the partners needed was capital to finance the expansion.

However, cash was a serious problem. Until the new store opened, the business would continue to post operating losses. Brooker had not paid himself a salary for the past three months, and funds trickling in from the US, thanks to the fund raising efforts of their third partner, Andrew Bednar, would not last long. Other potential large investors had recently dropped out, yet Brooker worried about the valuation of the EVH term sheet, and the feelings of investors who invested at a higher valuation a short time ago.

Later that day, Brooker and Weiss prepared to call Mark Sandler, a former venture capitalist and an NYB investor, to ask his advice.

New York Bagel: Hungary, April 1994
by PAUL A. GOMPERS, CATHERINE M. CONNEELY, case number 9-297-078 JUNE 20, 1997

"PROJECT BAGEL"

Robert Brooker and Adam Weiss became friends as students in the Class of 1989 at Harvard College. Brooker, with a degree in Economics, joined Lehman Brother's recently spun off economics department, where he was initially an analyst, then moved to head up its marketing and operations function. Weiss, after a year at a boutique M&A firm, decided to go to Columbia University Law School, where he met Andrew Bednar, a second generation Hungarian-American who had worked for an investment bank in Budapest. (see **Exhibit 1**)

When the allure of corporate life lost its glow in 1992, the three decided to explore opportunities in newly opened Eastern Europe. Brooker had experienced Eastern Europe during his work writing for Let's Go Travel Guides; Weiss had recently returned from a honeymoon in Hungary. All three were aware of the historic nature of Hungary's imminent transition and eager to be part of it. Fortunately for them, there was a groundswell of support for emerging markets in the early 1990s among investors. The pace of economic reform was good and although it was a low-income country, the per capita GNP was a lot higher than that of other economies in the region.[1] The partners brainstormed how they might bring value to Hungary as young outsiders.

Their first idea was to make use of obsolete telecommunications equipment that AT&T was eager to get rid of at bargain prices. After consulting with technical experts, though, the partners could not identify any category of equipment that would be compatible with Eastern European standards.

Another idea considered was a T-shirt production and distribution business. The partners hoped to license the rights to certain cartoon characters that they hoped would be popularized by the influx of Western media. However, the partners were wary of their ability to protect their franchise given the difficulty of enforcing Hungarian intellectual property laws.

A third idea was starting and operating a Tex-Mex restaurant, which would serve as a promotional platform for Jose Cuervo Tequila and other liquor brands. The real money would be made, the partners speculated, by securing exclusive country-wide distribution rights for a portfolio of liquor brands popularized by the restaurant. This idea collapsed when the liquor manufacturers encountered difficulty wriggling out of their existing contracts with Eastern European distributors.

The bagel business was chosen for several reasons. McDonalds and Burger King had already entered Hungary and were experiencing phenomenal customer flows. The partners figured that the bagel's reputation for healthiness and freshness would set it apart from the burger concepts and traditional Hungarian cuisine, which often called for fat-laden goose lard. Already there was a growing sense that trends toward healthy eating, largely responsible for the bagel business's stellar growth in the US, were catching on in Hungary and would accelerate as Western influence continued. They also had a sense of bringing the bagel "home". Folklore suggests that the bagel was developed in the Austro-Hungarian Empire in 1683 to celebrate the banishment of the despised Turks. The round-shaped bread with the hole in the middle was named after the stirrups of the victorious cavalry; the German word for stirrup is "bugel". Fortunately, the word had dropped out of the Hungarian language, enabling the partners to trademark the word "bagel" in Hungary. The large captive market of American expatriates in the Hungarian capital, longing for the tastes of home, would also provide an initial customer base.

Thinking farther ahead, Brooker and Weiss imagined that a successful track record in Hungary would enable them to expand the bagel concept into other European countries, where bagels still had yet to arrive. Besides, conversations with the large US bagel chains revealed no interest in Europe until the U.S. became saturated, an event that was likely to be years away. Pioneering the European market meant not only the opportunity to become a major player, but also an attractive acquisition target for U.S. bagel chains once they decide to expand abroad.

The decision to open a bagel store in Budapest - "Project Bagel" - had come about quickly. Brooker, Weiss, and Bednar had already collected some money into a fund to search for opportunities in Hungary. In order to reach the initial starting capital of $200,000 projected for opening a bagel shop, the partners raised capital from individuals in the United States, mostly family and friends. Recognizing the comfort for investors of investing in a U.S. company, the partners set up a Delaware-based holding company, Hungarian Ventures, Inc., which would own 100% of New York Bagel Corp. in Hungary. This way, investors would be protected by U.S. laws.

Driven to acquire hands-on experience of the bagel business, Brooker took several part-time jobs at bagel stores in the Boston area while still at Lehman Brothers. His new employers were suspicious, noticing that Brooker showed up to work in a suit and tie before changing to perform the nightly cleanup. On weekends, his responsibilities alternated between tending the bagel boiler, cleaning, and serving customers. "When a senior colleague from Lehman walked in with his family one Saturday, there I am with my little hat and apron, and he's trying to recall whether I got stiffed at bonus time." Once Brooker announced his departure plans, though, his boss was supportive and even invested personally in the bagel venture.

All three partners prepared for the move to Hungary in 1993, with Bednar planning to return after the heady startup period to finish his last year at law school. Brooker and his wife had just moved their belongings into storage when a letter arrived at their empty apartment. It was an acceptance to Harvard Business School. Weiss had just received an offer at a prestigious investment bank. Both wondered if it was worth giving these up for the uncertain road that lay ahead.

DOING BUSINESS IN HUNGARY[2]

Hungary was considered one of the more economically progressive countries of the Soviet Bloc during the Cold War. Starting in 1980, reforms were introduced which allowed private shops to open, industries were decentralized, and restrictions on direct foreign trade were lessened for domestic companies. The government of the time also introduced price and tax reforms, set up commercial banks, established a legal structure for firms and corporations, and generally lifted restrictions on economic activity. By the end of the decade, political parties were established and the first free elections were held in 1990 from which a coalition government was formed.

As a result, investors flocked to the country. The influx of foreign direct investment (FDI) was beneficial, aiding economic reform. From the early 1990s, Hungary received the most foreign investment of all eastern Europe countries, obtaining over 50% of all FDI in the region. In 1993, foreign investors had brought $2.3 billion to the country. Many factors played into investors decision to go to Hungary, namely the relatively low rate of inflation[3], political and social stability, low asset prices, low wages and a relatively well-developed institutional infrastructure. (see **Exhibit 2**) Hungarians had also kept their ties outside the Soviet Bloc. Many had been educated outside the country and could speak English and other foreign languages.

Another attraction of doing business in Hungary was that operating costs were low. Hungarian salaries in the early 1990s were only about one-tenth of German or American levels. The standard of living was high compared to other eastern European countries. About 90% of all households possessed televisions, washing machines, and refrigerators in the mid-1990s.

Everything, however, was not easy. There were uncertainties of doing business in another country. The risk that investors would suddenly lose interest in a particular market always existed. While Hungary itself had a peaceful transition from Communist rule, other countries in the region were experiencing general unrest. Investors were understandably nervous about providing funds in a risky environment. It also made it difficult to take funds out of the country to repay investors or purchase foreign supplies. Although Hungarian law allowed conversion of the local currency to dollars, its frequently changing legal institutions gave no comfort that the law would not change.

Broad economic reforms had occurred, but once past the planning stages of the business foreign entrepreneurs found themselves caught up in a weighty bureaucracy. The problems of finding a location in a country where most commercial property was government-owned were compounded by the "web of planning and health authorities" including the chimney committee, the refrigerator officials, the toilets authority, the egg committee, and the music authority, encountered by the bagel makers. The entrepreneurs argued that playing Van Morrison should exempt them from paying into the Hungarian Musicians' Fund, but such arguments were of no concern to the gray-suited regulators. In another instance, the bagel shop's purchasing manager was nabbed by officials for "illegal transport of turkeys". By this time, however, the bagel enterprise mobilized its own web of bureaucrats, referring the officials to the store manager, who referred them to the architect's secretary, who then sent them to a lawyer with a broken telephone. Confounded, the officials gave up their pursuit of payment.

Usually, shortages of good and services which arose during socialist times could usually be alleviated by a small payment to the right person; Hungary's new money only exacerbated the situation. The partners avoided such practices, since they wanted to eventually return to the United States and were wary of the Foreign Corrupt Practices Act.[4] The existence of dual accounting software also came to NYB's attention. Some domestic firms had installed a program on their computers in order to avoid paying taxes. Press a single button and your income miraculously disappeared! Other, more violent options to solve problems were similarly abhorrent to the partners. Once, when an equipment supplier absconded with a deposit, the company's lawyer was quick to recommend someone to break his legs, considering it more practicable than a two-year long restitution through the court system.

They also felt that foreign entrants underestimated the amount of capital and management energy needed due to lack of business and institutional infrastructure. From his experience working in U.S. bagel shops, Brooker was used to suppliers who delivered whatever was needed on demand. In Hungary, Brooker spent endless hours "crawling up the supply chain." The absence of cream cheese in Hungary required that Brooker contact an expert from Cornell University to send over a recipe; even then, none of Hungary's dairy product manufacturers owned the requisite equipment, so Brooker worked with them to come as close as possible to producing true "Philly" cream cheese. Similar problems existed for most of NYB's staple ingredients. There were no trained servicepeople for NYB's imported equipment, including a sensitive bagel forming machine. Fortunately, the partners found an engineer who formerly specialized in reverse-engineering U.S. military equipment; he figured out how to service the bagel former simply by staring at it for a while. Usually, though, the skills NYB needed were simply absent in Hungary, so the partners had to spend much of their time explaining what they wanted. Brooker even had to train his accountant in the basics of accrual accounting. At first, a translator had to be present, further slowing the process, but after a year of intensive tutoring in Hungarian, the partners fared adequately on their own.

The entrepreneurs forged close relationships with their Hungarian colleagues, who were often able to pull off "miracles". For example, often when a problem seemed insurmountable, their purchasing manager would say "my father, he has a friend . . . ", and this friend would often be the sole person in Hungary who could solve the problem.

Brooker and Weiss also found it extremely difficult to raise money at reasonable rates from Hungarian institutions. Hungary's erratic inflation rate and low savings rate made lending risky and capital scarce. Banks were even reluctant to loan against real estate assets, since municipal governments had the power to arbitrarily block foreclosures. For the most part, the partners had to rely on capital from abroad.

"WHAT'S A BAGEL?"

Because municipal governments still owned most commercial property, finding a location in the inner city required a lengthy period of developing relationships with city officials. There were 24 districts in Budapest, so every new location NYB sought required starting over in forming relationship with a new district. Even though the municipality owned a property, its current occupant had to be persuaded to leave. Most occupants leased property from the municipality under "rental rights", or perpetual leases that never expired. Since these leases were often granted decades earlier and contained no inflation adjustment, current occupants were reluctant to leave unless bought out. Subleasing was generally illegal and therefore could not be enforced.

Fortunately, the partners found a loophole that avoided the need to plunk down their scarce capital to buy out a tenant. NYB could enter into a "partnership" with the leaseholder in which it paid 5% of profits every month. However, according to the contract the monthly payment had a minimum threshold which far exceeded any reasonable "profit share", making the contract perform very much like a standard lease. Finding a willing "partner" was tough, since occupants of prime locations were receiving lump sum payments from willing buyers, many of whom were large foreign firms. So NYB settled for a location in a somewhat downtrodden neighborhood, though its proximity to major subway and tram stops made the site readily accessible by potential customers.

The first store was launched in June 1993. Brooker and Weiss considered this first store their "beta-test!" Everything was brand new to the Hungarian employees, customers, and the American owners. "To create a concept we had to jump through eighteen regulatory hoops and spent extensive time training staff to adopt a 'customer first' attitude." Even with Brooker's bagel experience, the partners felt that they needed an expert at the helm, at least in the start-up stage of the store. Stan Goldfarb, whose family had been making bagels in New Jersey for three generations, went to Hungary to help start the company. His services entitled him to buy shares in NYB at a discounted price.

In an effort to expand awareness, NYB launched a marketing campaign to the Hungarian public. Unique billboard advertisements proclaimed "Where's the Bagel?" and "What's a Bagel?". A bagel-starved disk jockey and former New Yorker sparked excitement with the theme of "Sex, Bagels and Rock N' Roll" on his Saturday night radio shows – performed in exchange for a gratis bagel or two. NYB took frequent customer surveys and reacted quickly to the data to adjust the marketing mix or introduce new menu items. By 1994, the bagel shop had expanded its menu from bagels, sandwiches, and beverages to include salads, muffins, cakes, and cookies. The chocolate chip cookies, created by Brooker's wife, were so successful that they often outsold the bagels.

Revenues for the first store were between $13,000 and $20,000 per month. (see **Exhibits 3-5**) Despite the enthusiasm which greeted the bagel enterprise, operational losses for the first six months were approximately $10-20,000 per month. A number of factors contributed to the losses. For one, NYB employed a full-time purchasing manager and two people responsible for new store development. The partners figured that they needed a core group of employees willing to work long hours to get the business off the ground. McDonalds had spent three years and millions of dollars actively developing their supply sources and real estate before they started building their first store. Fortunately, the NYB team coalesced well, resulting in a store opening in less than six months, but the partners were well aware of the cash drain of the core team, not to mention the partners' salaries, plus the expense of installing retail management systems. If financing would not be forthcoming, Brooker and Weiss considered a "no expansion" scenario whereby the core team would be dismantled and Brooker and Weiss would return to the U.S.; even then the shop would have a hard time making money due to the large fixed costs of producing bagels.

On the other end of the spectrum, the partners felt they had the capability and could generate sizeable returns for investors by developing a bagel production commissary serving up to 20 stores. This would lower costs by spreading the fixed costs out among as many stores as possible.

NYB'S SECOND STORE

NYB started to look for second store within three months of opening the first. In September 1993 they found a location in the city's prime office district and right across the street from a subway station packed full with commuters. The Belvarosi Vendeglato Vallalat (Inner City Restaurant Company), which owned all city restaurants, had a charter to auction off their rental rights, and NYB submitted a bid of $200,000 in December 1993. The rental right was a perpetual lease which the store would have to pay to the city. Although rents had not been raised for years, there was no body of law which governed how or even whether municipalities could raise rents. Recently, districts which attempted to raise rents were met with angry tenants who refused to pay the hiked bills. The districts eventually backed down. The partners hoped that such precedents would deter other districts from attempting the same or expected that they could partake in the same disobedient recourse, but were nonetheless cognizant of the risks of this legal uncertainty.

Although they did not have enough capital at the time of the auction, they felt that they could not forgo the opportunity of the location. They only had $150,000 of the $400,000 they estimated was needed to pay for the rental right and refurbish the store. They also wanted to have adequate funds available to set up more stores after the second store was up and running. (see **Exhibits 6-8** for store projections) The location in the city center on Bajcsy-Zsilinszky Avenue would also be perfect for the construction of NYB's flagship store.

The NYB bid won the auction on December 17, 1993, but the partners still did not have adequate funds to refurbish the store. Even with possession of the rental right, they could not use it as collateral for a bank loan. They had a tough decision to make. They wondered if they should risk investors' money on a second store. The location of the store was critical to the success of the future chain and it would take another three to six months to find a similarly situated property, by which time the business would probably run out of cash. They did not want any further delay in opening the second store.

FINANCING DECISIONS

Brooker and Weiss looked at their options for raising more capital. They could continue to get funds from individual investors, go to institutional investors, or approach venture capital firms. They had raised $200,000 between December 2, 1993 and mid-January 1994 from several individual investors. A wealthy venture capitalist, who dropped by one day in his limousine to try the bagels, suggested that the entrepreneurs use his bank. Along with opening an account came a $20,000 credit line which bolstered the entrepreneurs' credibility in Hungarian business circles.

The partners knew that they had some critical financing decisions to make. Until now they had used equity financing and debt placement to successfully collect funds from investors. How should the capital structure of the business be set up? Who did they want for investors? How would they deal with unexpected capital needs? They also needed to start securing assets. Until now investors had been paid in company stock - payment in kind (PIK) bonds. 10% of principal per year had to be repaid, a relatively long repayment period. Interest payments, 12%, were payable in equity. This meant there was no cash outlay for interest. Another portion of NYB's debt did pay cash interest, but payments were under moratorium. Borrowing via a secured note would allow investors to take control of business. The business was valued at $1 million or $100 per share down from a previous valuation of $300 per share.

Most of the individual investors in NYB were family and friends, many of them in the United States. Although most investors were highly supportive of the partners, and some even provided valuable advice and referrals to other investors, there were also disadvantages to having so many investors. Brooker estimated that they spoke with about 200 potential investors and had a yield of approximately 25%. The individual investors each had different needs. One investor wanted to give NYB 100,000 bottles of wine for a $50,000 share in the chain. Another potential investor, a wealthy lumber magnet from Canada, liked Hungary and the bagels, but NYB did not have the open fires he required for baking the bagels to his preferred taste. Some investors wanted the partners to set up a seed venture capital fund, dividing the partners' attention among several different businesses. Satisfying all investors would be impossible. Brooker and Weiss also felt they were always raising money, which proved a distraction from operations, marketing, and new store development which really brought the results.

Another prospective investor, a prominent local businessman, seemed interested from the outset but would not return phone calls when he was expected to take or pass on the deal. Then, Brooker opened a newspaper and discovered that the businessman was embroiled in a scandal. Apparently the wife of a major regulatory agency chief appeared on his payroll, but seemed to have no office.

NYB also approached institutional investors such as the European Bank for Reconstruction and Development (EBRD) among others. The EBRD was very encouraging, referring the partners to several agency banks which extended and administered EBRD loans. As the partners met with the various loan officers, it quickly became apparent that the banks were in the habit of loaning to large projects with substantial assets, typically sponsored by multinational corporations. Plus, the EBRD application was an inch thick, peppered with conditions, including the deployment of environmental engineers to take samples in and around the bagel shop for environmental analysis. The partners had to be careful to allocate their fund raising efforts in an efficient manner, and thus ruled out the EBRD and similar quasi-governmental investors by early 1994.

The advantages of obtaining funds from venture capital firms were obvious. The partners of NYB would no longer have to raise funds from individual investors, allowing them to spend more time running the company. The venture capital firms also knew the business environment in Hungary. The partners had long-term plans of either exiting from the business or bringing the company public. The venture capital firm purported to have knowledge of going public in Europe and would eventually support NYB for a profitable sale or to recoup their investment. However, since Hungary was such a new market, no venture capital firms had taken an investment public to date. There were only two venture capital firms in Hungary in the early 1990s, Venture Capital Hungary and Euroventures - Hungary (EVH). Venture Capital Hungary declined to pursue discussions with NYB after speaking with EVH.

EUROVENTURES - HUNGARY B.V.

In December 1993, NYB approached EVH which was the subsidiary of a venture capital firm, Euroventures B.V., based in the Netherlands. EVH was founded in July 1990 and had committed capital of approximately $20 million. The investment advisor to the fund was Antra kft. and the managing director in Budapest was Andras Geszti. EVH only invested in Hungary. Brooker and Weiss had inquired about the reputation of EVH. Budapest was a "small" city socially and in terms of business relationships. It did not take long before Brooker and Weiss discovered that friends or friends of friends had had business contact with EVH. These people reported EVH acting in bad faith on more than one deal. EVH had funded two firms in Hungary that NYB knew about: Semilab Semiconductor Physics Laboratory Co., a Budapest firm engaged in research, development, and manufacturing of electronic testing equipment; and Alfa Trading Co., the largest wholesale food distributor in Hungary.

Ed Sandborn, formerly a stock broker in California, had recently joined EVH as a Senior Investment Manager. Although rumor had it that Sandborn was under tremendous pressure to close a deal, Brooker and Weiss were concerned that neither Sandborn nor his partners had a firm understanding of the retail business and that this would slow down the process. Their going "up the learning curve", at the expense of Brooker's and Weiss's time, was a major concern. Most of NYB's current "angel" investors had done retail deals before; their advice proved of great value to the business. EVH would be much different.

Even so, on February 4, as a preliminary step to doing a deal, EVH sent NYB a letter asking for the right to invest approximately $500,000 in the company for 60 days from the date of the letter.

In March, EVH brought Gabor Kalman into the picture. Kalman, a native Hungarian, had many business interests in Hungary - he had the John Bull pub franchise in Hungary, ran an accounting firm, a trading company, a pharmaceutical company, and three or four other businesses. He would contribute some real estate in Budapest to the company in return for stock. Funds were still coming in to NYB from the cash call that Brooker and Weiss had made. The partners were becoming impatient with EVH's lack of progress on the deal. On April 6, they sent a letter of impatience to EVH stating that the company would have to withdraw from the deal if it were not completed soon.

The initial term sheet arrived at NYB's office on April 10. EVH valued the company at $1.3 million (post money valuation). Based upon that valuation, EVH agreed to provide $560,000 in capital. Both Brooker and Weiss liked the terms and it was accepted by NYB, contingent on the approval of the boards of both companies and Kalman's involvement in NYB. NYB also inserted a term stating that the more cash NYB raised from private investors, the less EVH would be able to put into the deal. Brooker wanted to show EVH that NYB did not need to rely on the venture capital fund. It also allowed NYB to keep any promises that had been made to investors for a share in the company. (see **Exhibit 9**)

On April 11, Kalman pulled out of the deal. He sent a fax to Brooker and Weiss citing "certain unforeseen events" in his private live for his decision.

Brooker tried to get in contact with Kalman and EVH. Kalman did not reply to any messages by fax or telephone. Brooker was concerned about the changes that Kalman's withdrawal from the deal would have on the term sheet. Brooker felt, however, that the original terms were still workable.

EVH'S SECOND TERM SHEET

EVH sent the second term sheet by fax on April 15. It was much worse than NYB had expected. The new valuation of the company was only $660,000 and the venture capital firm would invest only $100,000 initially, with the remaining $460,000 staged in only if NYB meets its revenues targets. This clause was extremely risky as the projections were subject to the very uncertain business environment in Hungary. There were so many things that could go wrong or spin out of control. Brooker surmised that it would not be difficult for EVH to get control of NYB based on second term sheet. He felt that accepting such an agreement would be unhealthy for the business and investors. (see **Exhibit 10**)

NYB management had estimated that $400,000 was needed to complete plans for a central store and expand to other locations. $270,000 had already been collected from approximately 45 individual investors by the time EVH delivered the bombshell to the company. Brooker and Weiss saw that several options were open to NYB. It could accept the terms of the second term sheet from EVH and run the risk of losing the company if a tentative business schedule was not met. They could try to renegotiate the term sheet with EVH. To that end he sent a fax to EVH giving them five days to get back to NYB with another deal. Naturally, the company hoped that EVH would offer the original deal. The third option would be to complete the cash call. Brooker and Weiss estimated that the minimum amount the company could get by on was $320,000, of which they needed $50,000. If NYB decided to take this route, then there would be no flexibility in spending, essentially postponing the vision of quickly expanding across the city.

A fourth option occurred to Brooker and Weiss. EVH asked only to invest in NYB, not NYB's holding company, Hungarian Ventures, Inc (HVI). Perhaps Brooker and Weiss could negotiate loose management contracts, and parlay the track record of a successful bagel chain in Hungary to build bagel businesses in other countries under the HVI umbrella. This way, even if investors had to partly "write off" their investments in Hungary, they could still benefit from the partners' experience in building bagel businesses. The partners had been recently approached by a prospective partner in Vienna who had an inner city retail space to offer them.

The telephone line crackled as the partners explained the predicament to Mark Sandler. Sandler emphasized that taking on an investor was like entering a marriage; you want to choose someone who shares your basic values. Recalling the history of the relationship with EVH: the unexplained departure of Gabor Kalman from the deal and the warnings of others who had been "burned" by EVH, the partners' sense of uneasiness suddenly grew deeper. Sandler worried that EVH could easily take control of the business and oust the partners. NYB's investors, far away in America, would have little recourse.

On the other hand, all three partners were haggard from the constant search for funding. For the hours spent paying visits to prospective investors and pulling together materials for them, the partners were conscious of delayed opportunities to introduce new products, train employees, and look for new sites. Having an assured flow of funds, even if tied to performance targets, meant freeing them from this burden. Moreover, the vision of building a multi-unit food business was instrumental in securing the enthusiasm of employees, faith of investors, and special efforts of suppliers and real estate partners. Should NYB be forced to continue to grow in fits and spurts, this momentum would likely wane. “It was like a bicycle,” remarked Brooker, “we had to keep pedaling or else we would fall.”

Brooker and Weiss ordered up a few cappuccinos and thought hard.

NOTES

1 Per capita GNP in 1992 was US$3,210. World Tables 1995, The World Bank.

2 Information in this section is from the Economist Intelligence Unit, 1995-96 Country Profile of Hungary.

3 The inflation rate was 35% in 1991, 23% in 1992, 22.5% in 1993, 18.8% in 1994, 28% in 1995.

4 The Foreign Corrupt Practices Act was passed by the U.S. Congress in 1977. It addresses the corruption of foreign governments by U.S. companies doing business internationally. It is illegal for U.S. companies to bribe foreign government officials in order to obtain or maintain business. All publicly traded companies are required to keep detailed records under the Act even though they do not engage in international trade. An exception to the Act is “grease payments”, so-called because such payments secure or expedite required government action.

EXHIBIT 1 Biographical Information

Robert Brooker grew up in Texas and was first introduced to bagels in 1985 when he came to the Northeast to attend Harvard College. As a student, he spent his summers as a writer/researcher for the Let's Go Travel Guides in Eastern Europe and the Middle East. Upon graduating in Economics he joined The Boston Company Economic Advisors, Inc., a newly-formed economic advisory and publications house, where he served as Research Assistant, Associate, and then Director of Marketing. The firm was subsequently acquired by Lehman Brothers. His responsibilities included sales & marketing, planning, and systems development.

Adam Weiss graduated Phi Beta Kappa from Harvard College in 1989 with a major in fine arts. After working for one year at a middle-market M&A boutique in Boston (Joseph Anton, Inc.), he attended Columbia Law School, where he was a Kent Scholar. Internships while in law school included: the Honorable Miriam Goldman Cedarbaum (Federal District Judge, S.D.N.Y.) and the criminal division of the United States Attorney (S.D.N.Y.). Weiss worked as a Summer Associate at Wachtell, Lipton, Rosen & Katz.

Andrew Bednar graduated from Cornell University's 5-year BA/MBA program, where he was a Gannett Fellow. Afterwards he spent six months working in Budapest for Innofinance, a merchant bank then owned by the Hungarian government. Bednar's work at Innofinance included helping with the creation of the Budapest stock market and the privatization of Innofinance itself. Bednar attended Cornell Law School for one year, where he was selected to be a member of the Law Review, before transferring to Columbia Law School, where he achieved honors as a Stone Scholar. Bednar also worked as a Summer Associate at Sullivan & Cromwell.

Mark Sandler was a partner at Donaldson, Lufkin & Jenrette and then at Bear Stearns. He is currently an investor and board member of several growth companies.

EXHIBIT 2 Hungary: Domestic Economy 1987-1993

	1987	1988	1989	1990	1991	1992	1993
Nominal GDP (Billions of Froints)	1,226.4	1,440.4	1,722.8	2,089.3	2,491.7	2,935.1	3,537.8
GDP Growth Rate (%)	12.64	17.45	19.61	21.27	19.26	17.80	20.53
GDP per capita (Froints)	116,877.9	137,837.3	165,542.4	201,572.6	241,560.8	285,960.6	346,503.4
Population (thousands)	10,493	10,450	10,407	10,365	10,315	10,264	10,210
Inflation (% change)	8.68	15.79	16.94	28.97	34.24	22.95	22.50
Average Exchange Rate (Froints per US$)	46.971	50.413	59.066	63.206	74.735	78.988	91.933
Enterprises with FDI in Hungary							
Number of organizations					9,117	17,182	20,999
Capital paid in (Millions of Froints)					475,589	713,035	1,113,158
Foreign capital paid in (Millions of Froints)					214,697	401,792	662,872

Source: World Bank and International Monetary Fund Tables, Central Statistics Office of Hungary

EXHIBIT 3 Cash Statement for New York Bagel, as of December 21, 1993 (Thousands of US Dollars)

Cash flows from operations	
Pre-first store startup expenses	29
First store	318
Overhead expenses for 1993	69
Second store	23
Interest expense	9
First store initial operating losses	40
Net Cash used by operations	488
Cash flows from investment activities	
Initial Funding from Hungarian Ventures, Inc.	603
Expenses paid by Hungarian Ventures on behalf of NYB	147
Net cash used in investing activities	750
Ending Cash Balance	262

Source : Company Documents

EXHIBIT 4 Cash Flow Statement for NYB, 1993-94 (Thousands of US dollars)

	93Q1	93Q2	93Q3	93Q4	94Q1
Revenues	$389	$2,169	$55,628	$53,494	$61,135
Costs					
Overhead					
Management	0	5,050	6,750	31,351	25,106
Travel, Setup, & Benefits	4,429	7,794	37,226	20,628	7,235
Office & Related	2,285	5,681	12,358	11,715	6,799
Marketing	0	15,446	18,927	9,556	1,531
Professional Services	4,671	1,975	4,697	28,452	2,925
Total Overhead	$11,385	$35,946	$79,958	$101,702	$43,596
Ferenc Korut Store					
Labor	$0	$851	$31,109	$28,252	$16,249
Food Costs	0	5,740	21,376	19,382	14,912
Supply Costs	0	5,201	23,488	10,446	6,850
Rent	0	10,130	9,721	9,280	6,000
Leasehold Improvements	0	86,251	15,235	1,221	0
Equipment	0	73,726	25,897	108,477	14,455
Maintenance, Utilities, Insurance	0	254	3,586	3,980	3,639
Taxes and Fees	0	43,833	47,667	7,504	6,815
Total Costs - Ferenc Korut	$0	$225,986	$178,079	$188,542	$68,920

(*continued*)

EXHIBIT 4 *(continued)*

	93Q1	93Q2	93Q3	93Q4	94Q1
Bajcsy-Zsilinszky Store					
Labor	$0	$0	$0	$0	$0
Food Costs	0	0	0	0	0
Supply Costs	0	0	0	0	0
Property (Purchase & Rent)	0	0	0	178,704	1,531
Leasehold Improvements	0	0	0	1,547	176,786
Equipment	0	0	8,900	11,155	65,168
Maintenance, Utilities, Insurance	0	0	0	0	2,633
Taxes and Fees	0	0	0	2,725	35,980
Total Costs - Bajcsy-Zsilinszky	$0	$0	$8,900	$194,131	$282,098
Operating Cash Flow	$(10,996)	$(259,763)	$(211,309)	$(430,881)	$(333,479)
Interest Payments	1,000	100	0	10,675	5,403
Total Cash Flow	$(11,996)	$(259,863)	$(211,309)	$(441,556)	$(338,882)

Source: Company Documents

EXHIBIT 5 Detailed Income Statement for New York Bagel, first quarter, 1994 (US Dollars)

	January	February	March
Revenues	$20,228	$20,025	$20,882
Costs			
Overhead			
Management	9,563	9,257	6,285
Travel, Setup, & Benefits	2,944	2,351	1940.67
Office & Related	2,892	1,761	2,146
Marketing	749	773	8
Professional Services	1,112	937	877
Total Overhead	$17,260	$15,079	$11,257
Ferenc Korut Store			
Labor	$5,798	$5,159	$5,293
Food Costs	5,243	4,874	4,795
Supply Costs	2,636	2,001	2,213
Rent	2,000	2,000	2,000
Leasehold Improvements	0	0	0
Equipment	4,915	4,500	5,039
Maintenance, Utilities, Insurance	1,264	1,271	1,104
Taxes and Fees	2,242	2,222	2,350
Total Costs - Ferenc Korut	$24,098	$22,027	$22,794
Bajcsy-Zsilinszky Store			
Labor	$0	$0	$0
Food Costs	0	0	0
Supply Costs	0	0	0
Property (Purchase & Rent)	510	510	510
Leasehold Improvements	0	65,919	110,867
Equipment	0	2,679	62,489
Maintenance, Utilities, Insurance	0	18	2,615
Taxes and Fees	0	10,103	25,877
Total Costs - Bajcsy-Zsilinszky Store	$510	$79,229	$202,358
Operating Cash Flow	$(21,641)	$(96,311)	$(215,527)
Interest Payments	0	5,403	0
Total Cash Flow	$(21,641)	$(101,714)	$(215,527)

Source: Company Documents

EXHIBIT 6 Projections for Profit and Loss (excluding startup and capital expense) and Cash Flow Statements for New York Bagel, 1993-1998 (Thousands of US Dollars)

		1993	1994	1995	1996	1997	1998
Budapest							
Store 1	Sales	$113	$165	$353	$353	$353	$353
	EBIT	(40)	(40)	87	87	87	87
Core Store 2	Sales		329	1044	1063	1370	1446
	EBIT		118	375	382	492	520
Store 3	Sales		59	353	353	353	353
	EBIT		15	87	87	87	87
Store 4	Sales			176	353	353	353
	EBIT			41	87	87	87
Store 5	Sales			88	353	353	353
	EBIT			22	87	87	87
Pecs							
Core Store	Sales			44	353	353	353
	EBIT			11	87	87	87
Store 2	Sales				264	353	353
	EBIT				65	87	87
Store 3	Sales				176	353	353
	EBIT				44	87	87
Debrecen							
Core Store	Sales				44	353	353
	EBIT				11	87	87
Store 2	Sales					323	353
	EBIT					80	87

Szeged							
Core Store	Sales					264	353
	EBIT					65	87
Store 2	Sales					176	353
	EBIT					44	87
Gyor							
Core Store	Sales						264
	EBIT						65
Store 2	Sales						44
	EBIT						11
Franchise	Sales			57	162	247	332
	EBIT			47	152	237	322
Total Sales		$113	$553	$2,114	$3,471	$5,200	$5,963
Total EBIT Contributed by Stores		(40)	93	670	1,089	1,614	1,875
Overhead		69	102	192	244	254	291
Commissary		19	34	24	32	40	40
Non-capital Startup Expense		303	137	163	146	108	70
Depreciation		10	61	137	227	317	397
EBIT		$(421)	$(241)	$153	$440	$896	$1077
Interest - Investors		8	26	21	21	21	21
Interest - Bank		0	0	22	0	0	0
Pretax Profit		(449)	(267)	111	419	875	1,057
Income Tax		0	0	0	0	(241)	(370)
Profit After Tax		(449)	(267)	111	419	634	687

Source: Company Documents

EXHIBIT 7 Projected Expenses for New York Bagel for 1993 - 1998 (Thousands of US dollars)

	1993	1994	1995	1996	1997	1998
Salaries & Benefits						
Operations MD	$9	Equity	$50	$50	$50	$50
Development/ Investor MD	9	21	50	50	50	50
Development Manager	8	9	20	20	25	30
Chief Financial Officer	5	11	12	13	14	15
Field Manager	0	0	0	10	10	10
Accounting	0	0	0	7	7	14
Secretary	0	0	5	5	5	10
Office Rent & Utilities	5	5	0	28	28	35
Office Equipment & Supplies	12	16	14	18	20	25
Professional Services	18	20	18	20	22	22
Travel & Entertainment	0	5	8	8	8	12
Marketing (non-startup)	3	15	15	15	15	18
Total	$69	$102	$192	$244	$254	$291
as % of revenues	61%	18%	9%	7%	5%	5%
Capital expenses						
Budapest - Store 1	$100	$0	$0	$0	$0	$0
Core Store 2	0	372	0	0	0	0
Store 3	0	150	0	0	0	0
Store 4	0	0	150	0	0	0
Store 5	0	0	150	0	0	0
Pecs - Core Store	0	0	150	0	0	0
Store 2	0	0	0	150	0	0
Store 3	0	0	0	150	0	0
Debrecen - Core Store	0	0	0	150	0	0
Store 2	0	0	0	0	150	0
Szeged - Core Store	0	0	0	0	150	0
Store 2	0	0	0	0	150	0
Gyor - Core Store	0	0	0	0	0	150
Store 2	0	0	0	0	0	150
Total - Capital	$100	$522	$450	$450	$450	$300
Other Startup Expenses						
Pre-Store 1	62	0	0	0	0	0
Budapest - Store 1	241	41	38	27		0
Core Store 2	0	61	20	14	3	0
Store 3	0	35	0	0	0	0
Store 4	0	0	35	0	0	0
Store 5	0	0	35	0	0	0

(continued)

EXHIBIT 7 *(continued)*

	1993	1994	1995	1996	1997	1998
Pecs - Core Store	0	0	35	0	0	0
Store 2	0	0	0	35	0	0
Store 3	0	0	0	35	0	0
Debrecen - Core Store	0	0	0	35	0	0
Store 2	0	0	0	0	35	0
Szeged - Core Store	0	0	0	0	35	0
Store 2	0	0	0	0	35	0
Gyor - Core Store	0	0	0	0	0	35
Store 2	0	0	0	0	0	35
Total-Other Startup Expenses	$303	$137	$163	$146	$108	$70
Commissary Expense						
Salaries & Benefits						
Baker	9	9	9	9	9	9
Assistant Baker	0	0	5	5	5	5
Purchasing	9	9	9	9	16	16
Driver	0	0	0	7	7	7
Other Expenses						
Vehicle	0	15	0	0	0	0
Gasoline, Maintenance, Supplies	0	2	2	3	3	5
Total	$19	$34	$24	$32	$40	$40
as % of revenues	17%	6%	1%	1%	1%	1%

Source: Company Documents

EXHIBIT 8 Cash Flow Projections for New York Bagel - 1993-1998 (Thousands of US dollars)

	1993	1994	1995	1996	1997	1998
Operations						
Profit after Tax	$(449)	$(267)	$128	$419	$628	$687
Depreciation	10	61	137	227	317	397
Capital	(100)	(522)	(450)	(450)	(450)	(300)
Total	$(539)	$(727)	$(185)	$196	$495	$784
Financing						
Equity	$603	$560	$0	$0	$0	$0
Debt						
Hungarian Ventures, Inc.	147	0	0	0	0	(147)
Secured Financing	0	200	0	0	0	0
Bank	0	0	40	(40)	0	0
Total	$750	$760	$40	$(40)	$0	$(147)
Net Cash Flow	211	33	(145)	156	495	637
Cumulative Cash	211	244	99	255	750	1,387

Source: Company Documents

EXHIBIT 9 Major terms of first term sheet from EVH

1. Parties to the agreement - NYB, EVH, Gabor Kalman.
2. The initial investment of $560,000 would be made in cash ($472,000) and in kind contribution from Kalman in the form of the right to a prime retail property with an agreed-upon value of $88,000.
3. EVH and Kalman would receive 43% of NYB shares.
4. Anti-dilution: If NYB falls behind targets and requires additional *equity* capital, EVH/Kalman would not experience dilution.
5. Clawback: Upon successful exit, HVI would be entitled to a "claw-back" in the amount of half of any return in excess of 30% ARR received by EVH/Kalman.
6. Conversion: EVH/Kalman would have the right to convert their NYB shares into HVI shares at a conversion ratio proportional to the level of HVI and NYB sales.
7. Compensation for Brooker and Weiss: based on market level for top managers in similar startup ventures in Budapest.
8. Board of Directors: Brooker, Weiss, an EVH nominee, Kalman, and a fifth board member mutually agreed upon by all members.
9. EVH/Kalman would have the right to take a controlling interest in NYB for $100 if one of the following events occurs:
   a. aNYB does not operate or franchise a minimum of five stores by yearend 1995.
   b. NYB is not profitable pretax for the second half of 1995.
   c. NYB becomes bankrupt or insolvent.
10. Legal fees will be paid by NYB is the deal closes, split half-half between EVH and NYB if it does not close.

Source: Company documents

EXHIBIT 10 Major terms of second term sheet form EVH

1. Parties to the agreement - EVH, NYB.
2. EVH agrees to invest $560,000 in cash, minus money raised in the current "cash call", staged in according to the following plan:
    - $100,000 immediately at a valuation of $660,000.
    - The remaining $460,000 would be invested in stages according to an agreed-upon schedule and only if NYB attains proposed revenue targets.
    - If the entire $560,000 is invested, the weighted average valuation of NYB would be $1.3 million.
3. EVH would obtain a new class of NYB equity which would be senior to HVI's class in the event of sale or liquidation of NYB.
4. EVH would have veto rights over major corporate decisions.
5. Once EVH has invested a minimum of $200,000, EVH would have the right to take a controlling interest in NYB for $100 if one of the following events occurs:
    a. NYB does not operate or franchise a minimum of five stores by yearend 1995.
    b. NYB is not profitable pretax for the second half of 1995.
    c. NYB becomes bankrupt or insolvent.
6. Items 4, 5, 6, 7, 10 remain according to Exhibit 9.

Source: Company Documents

SECTION 7

Harvesting

CHAPTER 7.1

Celtel International B.V.

Felda Hardymon and Ann Leamon

In Celtel, my heart, my head, and my wallet are aligned.

—Mo Ibrahim, Chairman of the Board

On June 21, 2004, Mohamed (Mo) Ibrahim, chairman of the board of Celtel B.V., the largest pan-African wireless service provider, had a lot on his mind. Not only was this the date of the annual strategy meeting in London, to be followed by a board dinner, but it coincided with Euro 2004, the European football (soccer) championships, when England would be playing Croatia in an attempt to avenge its loss to France at the start of the tournament and stay in contention for the championship. To his delight, a television was brought into the dining room and periodically throughout the evening, the clink of cutlery against china and the murmur of conversation would be drowned in cheers or groans.

Celtel's history thus far had given rise to similar responses. Over the six years since its founding, the firm had flirted with going public once and almost been acquired twice. It had steadily increased its holdings in Africa and by June 2004 it operated 15 properties in 13 countries (see **Exhibit 1** for map). It had a remarkable board, consisting of U.S. and European venture capitalists, development finance institutions (DFIs), one English peer, one knight, and a number of politicians, including the former prime minister of Tanzania (see **Exhibit 2** for board membership). The political and natural environments posed constant challenges; civil war was always a threat, as were floods and famine. Yet Celtel forecast revenues approaching $1 billion in 2005, and had succeeded in closing seven rounds of financing at steadily increasing valuations (see **Exhibit 3** for Celtel's financials).

Celtel's most recent success was winning the hotly contested acquisition of Kenya's second wireless operator in May 2004. This had vaulted the company into the realm of hundred-million-dollar deals. Ibrahim and his team knew, though, that they needed to continue acquiring properties even

Celtel International B.V.
by FELDA HARDYMON, ANN LEAMON, case number 9-805-061 Rev. JULY 18, 2006

as they operated their existing franchises. Now that the worldwide telecommunications industry had stabilized and the initial public offerings (IPO) window had reopened after the crash of the technology market in 2001, Celtel was considering an IPO on the London market to provide liquidity to its shareholders and to increase its capital base for further acquisitions.

This would pose an entirely new set of challenges. While the company had instituted transparent governance procedures and a strict code of ethics, moving from an identity as a private entrepreneurial firm with a strong focus on doing deals to a public operating company would be difficult enough. Revising the debt/equity levels on the balance sheet, particularly at the group level, would certainly be more challenging. But the biggest challenge would likely be alleviating the industrialized world's "Africa fright," and explaining how Celtel had succeeded despite (or because of) operating in the poorest continent on earth.

"Everyone thinks Africa is full of starving people and pretty lions," Ibrahim mused. "They don't realize that it's also full of normal people who want to do normal things, like make a telephone call. Our customers buy our service. Our investors, some of the most hard-nosed and pragmatic people around, buy our proposition. But will the markets?" As his dinner companions cheered England's win, propelled by two goals from the 18-year-old phenomenon Wayne Rooney, he hoped that next year, they would be cheering another young phenomenon's rising share price on the London Stock Exchange. But could they make the world understand Celtel?

BACKGROUND: AFRICA AND TELECOMMUNICATIONS

When someone said "Africa" in a developed country in 2004, most listeners thought of lions, uprisings, dictators, deserts, or AIDS, rather than cell phones. Certainly, the continent contained all of these. But the story was far more complex. The African continent included 52 countries, with a total population exceeding 800 million spread over 11.7 million square miles (30.3 million square kilometers),[1] ranging from the bazaars of Morocco and the pyramids of Egypt to the steel and glass towers of Johannesburg, South Africa and the spice markets of Zanzibar.

Celtel's operations concentrated in sub-Saharan Africa (SSA), a region with a 2003 population of 702.6 million in an area of 24.3 million square km.[2] In general, the eastern part of the continent had been colonized by English speakers and the west by French speakers. This was reflected in patterns of trade and in the inflows of foreign aid. Drivers of economic activity included subsistence agriculture, fishing, mining, and (in a few lucky countries) oil and gas extraction. Exports included rice, cocoa, coffee, cotton, tea, and sugar, along with various minerals, and oil. With commodity prices highly variable, the tax base small, and tax collection uncertain, many governments depended on foreign aid for a significant portion of their budgets. One ongoing challenge for tax collection and development was the uncertain system of land ownership. Many families had no formal title to land that they had farmed for generations, which precluded its use as collateral for loans and dissuaded foreign operators from establishing commercial operations. [3]

Total gross domestic product (GDP) of the region in 2003 was estimated at $400.3 billion, with the annual per capita figure at $595, or less than $2 per day. Like all averages, however, this masked huge variations, from the low of $110 in countries such as Burundi and Ethiopia to a high of $3,850 for Mauritius and $2,600 in South Africa.[4] Official figures, however, were misleading. Africa had an extensive informal economy consisting of people who worked for unreported cash. In Tanzania, with an average annual per capita income of $280, the government had exempted businesses with annual revenues less than $40,000 from paying taxes, to focus on more lucrative tax evaders. Even people on official payrolls usually had a second source of income, whether a minibus or car for rent, a printing service, or hairdressing. Part of this was the custom of supporting one's tribe: the brightest member of a village family would come to the city or overseas for education and to get a job, supporting the family back in the village.

Politically, most SSA countries had adopted a degree of democracy, even though, in the words of one development expert, "One African nation or another will always be in turmoil." In 2004, the Cote d'Ivoire unrest was still a problem, along with issues in Sudan and the eastern edge of the Democratic Republic of Congo (DRC). In almost every SSA country, some refugee camps housed people displaced by unrest in nearby nations.

In the mid-1990s, many SSA nations began liberalizing their economies. Much of the impetus for market reforms stemmed from the end of the Cold War. With the U.S. and the former Soviet Union no longer pouring money into African nations as proxy battlegrounds, development finance institutions (DFIs) had become the primary source of the aid on which most governments depended. Pressure from the International Monetary Fund (IMF) and the World Bank persuaded many governments to open formerly closed portions of their economies. Telecommunications, especially wireless, became the focus of this effort.

The informal economy and scarce banking services led to a widespread cash culture. Credit was rare, as the infrastructure for checking references and credit histories was in its infancy. Celtel, like most other wireless operators, provided its services on a prepaid basis, with post-paid arrangements only for large commercial customers. A customer would purchase a handset with a SIM card that held the person's phone number, then buy "scratch card vouchers" with a number hidden under a silver coating. The user would scratch off the coating, and enter the number on the phone, which would add the card's value to the account. Most fixed-line operations, on the other hand, charged on a post-pay basis and faced rampant fraud.

African infrastructure, whether roads, trains, airstrips, or telecommunications, was extremely under-developed. By the end of 2003, Africa overall (not just SSA) had 25.1 million fixed-line telephone subscribers, half the number of mobile phone subscribers (51.8 million).[5] The mobile phones were not a luxury—fixed-line phones were frequently inoperable. Overall, mobile phones had reached 6% penetration (2.8% in SSA) by end 2003,[6] as opposed to a world average of 22%, but Africa's compound average penetration growth of 76% between 1998 and 2003 led the world.[7]

Africa had huge unfilled demand for communication and African customers eagerly adopted additional services. The paucity of communication alternatives to wireless (unreliable and slow postal service, non-existent fax, and little Internet) meant that second-generation services, such as texting and mobile banking, had been adopted more quickly in Africa than in the developed world.[8] By 2010, Africa was forecasted to have between 100 million and 200 million mobile phone subscribers, a penetration rate between 10.2% and 20.4%.[9]

Unlike the U.S., which had a hodge-podge of cellular standards, African countries used the European GSM, which already had more than 1 billion users worldwide.[10] This technology offered a number of benefits, including its range and clarity, and the low cost and technical simplicity of its components. By 2004, the major players in African mobile phone service included two South Africa-based companies—Vodacom (a subsidiary of the quoted South African Telkom and partly owned by Vodafone) and MTN (listed on the Johannesburg stock exchange)—in addition to Egypt-based Orascom, and Celtel.

CELTEL AND AFRICA: "IT'S NOT A COUNTRY!"

Celtel initially was "something no one quite knew what to do with," in the words of Terry Rhodes, chief strategy officer—three minority equity positions in emerging market mobile phone systems that Ibrahim's earlier company, a consulting firm specializing in the design of mobile phone systems, had obtained, both through direct investment and as payment for work it had done on license bids. Ibrahim, who described himself as "a reluctant entrepreneur," had founded the consulting firm Mobile Systems International (MSI) after earning a Ph.D. in pre-cellular telecommunications in England and designing the first mobile system for British Telecom (BT). While working for BT, he had encountered the first hand-portable mobile phone and been entranced. He founded MSI in 1989 as the mobile telephone industry took off, and "lots of firms found themselves with licenses and no idea how to design the system." Joined by most of his staff from BT, Ibrahim made MSI into an extremely profitable worldwide consulting operation and, by 1995, software house.

In 1996, MSI received venture investment from General Atlantic. Ibrahim said, "We had become a software house and we didn't know a thing about being a software house. This also allowed the shareholders—including staff members, who had purchased MSI stock, even though the U.K. did not have a strong shareholding culture—to achieve some liquidity. It changed the dynamic, though, because suddenly we had financial people in the board room." The new investors pointed out the possible conflicts of interest inherent in MSI's ownership of minority stakes in mobile operations in Hong Kong, India, and Uganda. As a result, the $11 million value of these positions was dividended out to the shareholders and, in 1998, the three holdings were placed in an Amsterdam holding company and named MSI-Cellular Investments (since renamed Celtel International).

"At this point," said Ibrahim:

> . . . nations in Africa started opening up their telecoms markets. Licenses were affordable there, unlike in the developed world. If there ever was a place on earth that needed telecommunications, it was Africa. And the big operators were afraid to go there; they thought that business in Africa meant dealing with corruption, wars, and famines. I am African and the other senior executives of the company either have extensive backgrounds in emerging markets or come from Africa too. This gives us a unique insight into the continent. In particular, we were keenly aware that Africa is not a country.

Said Rhodes, one of the founding members of the company, "Yes, Africa posed a unique set of challenges. But it also offered unparalleled opportunities."

In March 1998, operating a cellular business in Africa meant that Ibrahim and his team simultaneously had to build a company and a culture, raise money, and bid on licenses. If successful, they would then have to design, build, and operate mobile phone systems, in countries that were roughly an eight-hour flight away from the Amsterdam headquarters.

Building the Organization

As he sought financing, Ibrahim knew he wanted more than money from his investors. "I wanted our investors to be active and involved with the company," he said. "I didn't want them to write a check and go home." Celtel's investors had to possess two characteristics: the highest levels of business ethics, and the willingness to invest in African telecommunications, a field with high perceived risk (see **Exhibit 4** for Celtel's shareholders). Happily, explained Adrian Robinson, an investor with CDC Capital Partners[11] when it funded Celtel and now Celtel's corporate finance director:

> We say there is a "Wall of Money" trying to get into Africa. Lots of groups want to help Africa, but there are not enough good deals to take all the money raised. That means you have the situation of an African-focused infrastructure fund investing in mining operations. Infrastructure means many things—ports, roads, concrete plants even—but hardly mines. The issue is the scarcity of real business investment opportunities.

A number of development groups, including Actis Capital (then CDC Capital Partners, an arm of the U.K.'s international aid agency), the German group DEG, the Dutch FMO, and the IFC branch of the World Bank, funded Celtel on the premise, as Robinson said, "that there are lots of development opportunities but not many that are both developmental and have the prospect of a good financial return."

Other funding came from pure financial players, such as Bessemer Venture Partners (BVP), Zephyr Asset Management, and Citigroup Venture Capital International (CVC International). Said Mark Jacobson, the representative of CVC International:

> We are returns-oriented investors. We invested in Celtel because it was a good business deal that happened to be based in Africa. I'm from South Africa, so I could understand the added benefit of telecoms there. What was extremely helpful was the fact that one of our Investment Committee members is originally from the DRC. He still has family there and he knows what they have to go through to make a phone call—you can walk an hour or more to a pay phone and then find it doesn't work because someone has stolen the copper. There is simply huge demand for telecoms in Africa but it's hard for outsiders to believe.

Ibrahim built a large, inclusive board. Even investors with relatively small ownership could attend meetings as observers. Board members brought not only financial resources, but also telecommunications knowledge and political contacts. Outside board members included Lord James Prior, a member of Britain's House of Lords and former U.K. secretary of state for Northern Ireland and chairman of GEC; Sir Gerald Whent, the first CEO of Vodafone, who joined the Celtel board after his retirement; and Salim K. Salim, the former prime minister of Tanzania and past secretary general of the Organization of African Unity. This membership gave the company not only capital and domain expertise, but also entrée to the highest ranks of government throughout much of the continent. Likewise, the presence of quasi-governmental organizations as investors also burnished Celtel's image. As Ibrahim said, "Should we be asked for a bribe, we can always say we have to clear it with our shareholders. And no one asks the World Bank for a bribe."

From the outset, Ibrahim determined that Celtel would be run to the highest ethical standards. Africa, he knew, was viewed as "rife with corruption." He saw the situation in that continent somewhat differently:

> Bribery is a crime committed by two consenting adults—and yet the onus has traditionally been placed on the African participant. I am convinced that much of the bribery that occurs is the idea less of the African than of the westerner, who gets frustrated at the slow pace of negotiations and hotels he isn't used to and unusual foods and smells, and decides to speed things along with a bribe. We at Celtel never take or offer bribes. We may have lost some deals because of that, or had some delays, but bribery is like blackmail; once you start you can never stop. And there are a large number of people in Africa who are honest and want to do the right thing. Our ethics are up front, and if we're ever in an uncertain situation, we can call on our board members to help out—or we can walk. And we have walked in the past. Oddly enough, some of the opportunities that we have left have come back to us when it transpired that the group that won the license could not perform.

Celtel's management discovered that the nature of bidding for telecoms licenses tended to reduce unethical behavior. "These governments saw the license deal as a means of proving to the DFIs that they were opening their economies," said Ibrahim. "Often they'd even invite observers to certify that the process was conducted fairly. This encouraged transparency."

Fund Raising

In March 1998, Celtel began with three properties and five key employees: Ibrahim, Rhodes, the CFO Kamiel Koot, a business developer, and Heather White, Ibrahim's long-time assistant. It had $11 million in assets and, as these had been funded through the parent organization's balance sheet, $11 million in preferred stock that MSI owned. Rhodes observed, "We were lucky in our timing. In 1998, the financial community would fund a concept, and apart from our industry experience, that's all we had." (See **Exhibit 5** for telecoms indices over time.)

In its first year, Celtel raised $16 million through three different debt and equity rounds to acquire GSM licenses in Malawi, Zambia, Sierra Leone and Congo (Brazzaville), along with a minority stake in Egypt. Participants included two VC firms that had explored investing in Ibrahim's earlier venture, MSI. BVP, a U.S.-based early-stage VC firm, had done extensive due diligence before declining to participate in MSI's 1996 round, on price concerns.[12] Jay Metcalfe, whose Palio fund also invested in an early Celtel funding round, had recently left Millicom International Cellular, an emerging markets telecoms operator where he was President and CEO, which had made the first attempt to buy MSI. Metcalfe explained his reasons for investing in the new venture [Celtel], saying, "I knew and liked Mo. At Millicom, I'd seen the uptake in cellular services when we entered Latin America, and I knew that there was a huge opportunity in emerging markets."

The next year, 1999, saw Celtel acquire licenses in Gabon, Chad, the Democratic Republic of Congo (DRC), and Guinea, raising $35.2 million in equity and debt to do so. In the following year, the company raised $63.1 million to purchase interests in Burkina Faso, Niger, and Sudan, with an additional $153.7 million raised in 2001 to build out these properties and to acquire 35% of Tanzania's fixed-line network, TTCL, along with a cellular license. This was the last major acquisition until the 2004 purchase of Vivendi's 60% share of Kencell, a Kenya operator, at a cost of nearly $250 million (including fees), but the financing issues did not cease (see **Exhibit 6** for financing rounds and prices and **Exhibit 7** for Celtel's properties and market position).

Celtel sometimes bid for licenses with the stipulation that it would find local financing. In some countries, this proved difficult, as potential partners might not have sufficient funds to invest in the deal. Sometimes the partners would want an exit for their own corporate needs, requiring Celtel to buy back the shares. In other cases, the company might find additional financing through various funds set up to invest in certain countries. "We look to local banks for loans, not equity," said David Wilson, CFO. "We like to have local entities with some 'skin in the game.' It can be very helpful to have local partners whose interests are aligned with ours."

Kamiel Koot, Celtel's first CFO and now the head of Celpay, the mobile commerce company that Celtel founded, recalled the continuing effort to find financing for the company:

> We were forever missing our funding budgets because we underestimated demand. The market dynamics were scary; there was so much latent demand and the market leader got the lion's share; if we didn't

> grow, we'd lose the market. Early on, we vowed that we would truly run a network; we had an obligation to serve that came with the license. And this meant building and operating a network on the ground, which is an expensive proposition. Hence we were always short on capital and had to be creative with technology and sweat the assets.

Rhodes elaborated:

> When we entered Gabon, the doors to our office were literally knocked off the hinges on the day we opened. That's how badly people want to make a phone call. In the DRC, a cellular operator had entered in 1987. It had never institutionalized or built out the network, just charged dollar pricing and pocketed the money. We entered DRC in 2001, 14 years later, and became market leader in 14 days. We operate a real network with real service and real coverage.

Another reason for the continuous financing was the short-term nature of most of Celtel's loans. This had both benefits and drawbacks. The benefits included the speed with which commercial banks would grant short-term loans, and the flexibility these conferred, as Koot described:

> Central bank provisioning requirements [capital adequacy ratios] made commercial money only available on a short-term basis, but that was a blessing in disguise. It addressed the needs of a rapidly growing enterprise and benefited from Africa's steep yield curve—the rapid up-take of our services. We needed to attract new money on a regular basis in any event as we grew. We would refinance the old loan and raise new money in a single transaction each year—and nothing focuses the mind like a default deadline! It was exhausting but rewarding.

The speed with which commercial banks could work also helped, as Celtel would have six or eight months to concentrate on raising equity. Robinson added another reason for short-term financing. "Long-term money takes a long time to close. If it comes from DFIs, it may take a year to get through the approval process. Short-term money is quick."

In late 2000, Celtel explored an IPO but shelved the plan when it acquired the Tanzanian property in early 2001. Any IPO would have to wait until the issue of audited accounts was sorted out, especially as the final payment on the two-tranche purchase was predicated on retrospective audits. NASDAQ had also started its swoon, accompanied by problems in the telecoms sector, which would likely have prevented an IPO in any event.

Also in 2001, a merger fell through at the last minute. This posed significant problems, as Celtel had expected a $250 million cash injection and been advanced $45 million by the prospective acquirer. The deal's collapse left the company with severe illiquidity—not only did it not receive the anticipated injection, but it had to repay the $45 million loan to its erstwhile suitor. In mid-2001, Ibrahim's first company, MSI, was sold to Marconi and Ibrahim asked Sir Alan Rudge, who had been chairman of the MSI board, to take over as CEO of Celtel. Rudge was not enthusiastic. "I had just retired from BT. I was looking forward to doing some sailing and serving on the boards of several non-profits. I didn't want to be CEO of anything. But one of Mo's strengths is persuading people to do things they don't necessarily want to do. I agreed to two years."

Growing Celtel

Rudge's tenure as CEO of Celtel, during which he commuted between the U.K. and Amsterdam, coincided with a dramatic slowdown on the license acquisition front. Described by one investment bank in 2000 as "a very sophisticated investment bank with telecom assets," Celtel found that the financial world's antipathy to telecoms and the stock market slump had a profound effect on its business. Rudge said, "The company had to move on from doing a lot of exciting deals to actually running and developing a group of operational mobile networks."

Celtel had relied upon vendor financing, with terms of 180 to 360 days, to build new networks. As properties usually became EBITDA positive within a year of starting operations, the company would be able to pay for the equipment from cash flow. Between 2000 and 2002, though, the vendors struggled through their own cash constraints and required cash up front. "Celtel had much to learn about running and growing operational businesses with very tight cash constraints," said Rudge:

> The transition from entrepreneurial to operational had begun in earnest. This involved putting all the processes in place—regulatory relations, accounting controls, government liaisons—everything to manage a complex web of political, cultural, tribal, and religious interests. We learned that it's not impossible to do business in Africa, it's just different. The attitude of government is critical, just as it is here. It's often an issue of understanding the local politics. We want to run a good telco. The other guy may want to be president. It's a different orientation.

The company's diverse board membership and management team proved helpful as it built relationships (see **Exhibit 2** for board membership and **Exhibit 8** for management team). Explained Rhodes, "We have an advantage, because we can be many things. We can be European, U.K., or African, English- or French-speaking, Christian or Muslim. Holland doesn't have a strong colonial past in the SSA countries, which can be useful."

Rudge emphasized the importance of relationships. "We are gaining confidence and trust. If we're in a country at war, for instance, we stay strictly neutral. And, sadly, our revenues go up in warring regions. Rebels and government need to talk. And it's all prepaid. No one sabotages our equipment because it hurts both sides equally if a tower goes down." Celtel had won a license in war-torn Sierra Leone. The company installed the network as long as workers were safe; when Freetown fell to rebels, Celtel pulled its people out of the country. The teams returned with the United Nations peace-keeping troops, whom they provided with phones and service. Celtel became the market leader in the country. "The immediate aftermath of hostilities," said Wilson, the CFO, "is a good time to be on the ground. We're not government nor rebels, just the builders and operators of much-needed communications systems. And there tend to be fewer competitors."

Another example of the importance of relationships occurred in the two Congos. The capitals of DRC and Congo-Brazzaville faced each other across the Congo River, the two closest capitals in the world. A wireless call from one country to the other, however, followed the old colonial trade routes and went via satellite to Europe, through two exchanges in two different countries and back to a satellite and to the local network, at a cost of $1 per minute on Celtel's network, or $1.50 on the competitors'. People would ride a ferry across the river rather than incur that cost. Although Celtel had licenses in both countries, it could not carry calls internationally. Said Rudge, "We don't want an international license, we just want to cross borders—in your best interest as well as ours!" In 2002, after a year of negotiating with both governments, the company received permission to establish a microwave link across the border. The price of a call fell to 28¢ per minute and traffic soared 700% in the first week. "Crossing borders" became a Celtel theme as its pan-African strategy developed.

There were ongoing challenges. Rudge recalled one license that the company had forgone. He had left his office to go to that country and just missed receiving a fax with a list of people who should receive bribes to facilitate the meeting. As Rudge related:

> I met with the minister of communications anyway and, unbeknownst to me, his name had been at the top of the list. I had seven issues that needed confirmation—license documentation, the fact that we did own it, the fact that fees wouldn't change, the regulatory structure and the

> like. He was noncommittal, and later I met with some of his people, who were clearly waiting for something. I had no idea what at the time. But when I returned to headquarters and got the full picture, I recommended that we should not pursue the license. Celtel is not involved in bribery and if we cannot do business which is aboveboard then we will not do it at all. We have stuck firmly to this policy and although the going seems hard at times, I am sure our reputation in Africa is all the better for it. Our goal is to build a highly successful pan-African company which is well respected and here to stay.

In the case of wars, natural catastrophes, and unethical situations, Celtel felt that its portfolio approach to Africa, in which it had a presence in many countries, provided an advantage. "Thirteen countries are not going to go *kaflooey* at once," said one board member. There were, however, particular risks that no one had expected. Said Ibrahim, "We had a call once that people in rural areas were breaking their arms falling out of trees and it was our fault. I said, 'How can it be our fault?' It turns out that they were climbing trees to get better reception. I hope that we're curing that one as we expand the network."

To that end, and to reduce connection costs and provide enhanced voice and data services, Celtel purchased LinkAfrica, a satellite communications provider, in 2002. At the end of the year, the company was once again left at the merger altar. "The potential partner would have been nearly perfect in terms of strategic fit," said Wilson. "At the last minute, we were told that their board had to revisit the agreement, despite the fact that three of the board members had negotiated it. This was difficult for our company. Merger and acquisition efforts make significant demands on the time and attention of key management."

By mid-2003, the telecommunications and emerging markets sectors were starting to recover. Rudge reached the end of his two-year tenure as CEO, but retained the title of president and a seat on the board. Marten Pieters, who had led the international activities in emerging markets for the Dutch telecommunications firm KPN, joined as CEO. "What's fun about Celtel," said Pieters, "is that it's growing. Most telcos are these days like utilities, very flat, and all you do is worry about cutting costs."

Costs, especially taxes, were a significant challenge, though. "In Africa," said Pieters:

> . . . many countries have small tax bases and we normally are one of the biggest taxpayers. We are also very transparent. Governments love transparent companies because they make it easy to collect taxes. We are not praised for being good taxpayers; we are often asked to pay more. It becomes especially difficult near the end of the tax year,

> when budgets are running out. We import our equipment because you can't buy it locally, and because it's infrastructure investment, we pay reduced duty. But sometimes we'll be asked to pay duty—we protest up to the minister. We have to do lots of lobbying. Laws are not as developed as one would like so we run into many uncertainties about telco regulation, interconnect fees, license fees and the like. Governments in Africa are still learning about regulation and legal structure.

A Pan-African Brand

In January 2004, Celtel changed its branding. "We had gone in with a very conservative, cold identity," said Tito Alai, chief marketing officer who had joined Celtel in 2002 from leading the emerging market groups for Kodak and Unilever:

> Part of this was an effort to counteract our youth as a company. It was also because we were a company of engineers. Telco is unusual in that it's technology driven, not consumer driven. The engineers think up something and convince the consumers they need it. But there has been a shift from marketing the functional to the aspirational benefits. Once the market for basic services was developed, once we had proven we were here for the long term and operating good networks, we could rebrand as something more aspirational.

The brand rollout occurred in all but three of Celtel's countries in early 2004 and would extend across every country except minority-owned Sudan by the end of the year. From blue and white, the brand colors changed to brilliant red and yellow. The slogan changed from "Let's talk/Parlons nous" to the more aspirational "Making life better/La vie en mieux," and the marketing message changed to a "brandspeak" of a verb, a dot, and a qualifier. Thus, an ad campaign ran "Communicate. More./Communiquer. Plus." and "Roam. Far & Wide./Voyager. Sans limite." While the earlier brand message had used various regional dialects and expressions, the new brand appeared initially only in English and French. The only country to deviate from this dictum was Tanzania, where English literacy fell off rapidly outside the major cities. The Tanzanian advertisements appeared in English and Swahili but not in regional dialects.

"It is important that we're seen the same way in all of our countries," said Alai. "Look at Coke—Coke's brand image doesn't change from country to country. We want Celtel to be the same whether you are in Kenya or Sierra Leone." In June 2004, Alai was cautious about declaring the brand relaunch a success. "It's early days still. But it appears to be successful." The brandspeak and slogan had been widely adopted, to the point where the head of the Tanzanian operations said, "When I drive around the country and tell people I'm from Celtel, they often smile and reply, 'Celtel. Making Life Better.'" On a more prosaic note, users of a ladies' room in the Celtel-Tanzania offices were urged to "Make our lives better" by keeping it tidy.

CELTEL ON THE GROUND: TANZANIA

To understand the complexity of the Celtel operation, one must examine it on the ground. While each country faced unique challenges, Celtel Tanzania (hereafter, Celtel-TZ) provided a good example of the challenges encountered in running an African cellular operation.

Celtel acquired the Tanzanian operation in early 2001 after much internal debate. The government was privatizing the fixed-line service, TTCL, and only by purchasing a minority share in that operation could Celtel receive a wireless license. By November 2001, the wireless service was operating.

Celtel-TZ entered the market as the fifth of five wireless networks. Said Steve Torode, managing director (CEO) of the operation and formerly head of both Celtel's Zambia and Malawi operations, "We entered a hotly contested market, which was more challenging yet because one of the players was going out of business. This made customers wary of doing business with an upstart like us. So we had to be innovative and deliver what we promised. We had to ensure we understood this market well. And even at number two in the market now, we have the benefit of a big, well-capitalized, serious competitor to keep us on our toes ensuring we do not sit back and miss opportunities. Tough competition has actually contributed to our growth and that of the market."

To differentiate itself, Celtel-TZ first decided to charge in the local currency, Tanzanian shillings (Tsh), rather than U.S. dollars as the competition did. "Tanzania is essentially a dual-currency country," explained Torode:

> But the government and the people like to see companies use the local currency, and tariffing in shillings said that we were local, we were here to stay. It's a challenge for us, as our income is in shillings and our major bills and debt in dollars. We were taking currency risk. Over our first year, the value of the shilling fell. In people's minds, the value is \$1 to 1,000 Tsh, but it fell to \$1 to 1,100 Tsh. It meant that our vouchers, at 1,000 Tsh, gave less time than a competitor's at \$1. We developed a reputation for being expensive, the network of rich people.

> Once our competitors were charging in Tsh, people could see that we actually gave better value. We then rolled out the widest geographic network coverage. And now we're building a strong distribution network to get vouchers to our customers. Customers want to recharge their account whenever they need to, wherever they are. Coverage is based on two issues—if we lose a transmission tower [service], that's a problem—but it can be an equally significant problem if vouchers or handsets aren't available.

Celtel-TZ also introduced billing for calls on a per-second basis, rather than rounding and charging to the nearest minute. "People didn't like paying for time they didn't use, and at the low end of the market, they can't afford it," said Torode. "Pricing on a per-second basis allows customers to control their spending. People in Africa want the same things as people in the rest of the world, but because they have less money—only money for that day, perhaps—they buy it in smaller quantities but more regularly." To this same end it was important to sell recharge vouchers in affordable denominations. As Torode pointed out, "Here in Africa even gin is sold in shampoo-like sachets, as people may not have the cash to buy a bottle!"

Celtel-TZ also set up the country's first 24-hour-a-day free phone help line for customer care. It was a great success, although Torode mentioned a problem: "If people don't have money but they do have a phone, they'll call customer care just to make a call. And they do so repeatedly. This either forces genuine callers to endure long waits in the queue, or means we have to increase staff."

Customers

Celtel-TZ worked with its commercial customers, visiting them frequently and understanding their needs. Having switched to Celtel-TZ from Vodacom, the market leader, these customers looked to Celtel-TZ for help in managing their phone bills. Said the manager of a major Dar es Salaam hotel:

> Celtel has helped us save money. They installed Premicell with their service [a switch that ensures wireless calls use the least expensive routing option], which has cut our monthly bills. And Dar is a small place. They do business with me, I like to do business with them. But we all have to polish our silverware—when we first give a phone to a new manager, he'll run up a 40,000 Tsh bill. We need something that cuts him off at 10,000 Tsh and then he has to pay for the rest himself.

The director of a mining operation had witnessed the growth of wireless firsthand:

> Two years ago, we had two cell phones in the company. Now we have 48. People do more on wireless here than they do in Australia. Landlines are impossible here. People tap into them; you'll get a bill for $6,000 worth of calls to Russia. We used to have conference calls with North America and Australia via land-line and the connection would drop constantly; now we use wireless and it's perfect.

Like the hotel manager, the mining firm's director wanted Celtel-TZ to develop a method that would bill an individual directly after a certain value of calls had been made. In addition, he said, "We make our money in the back of beyond and our guys don't get to town except once a month. If we had data service, they could submit their billings more frequently. Sometimes a monthly bill is too much for a client to handle; it would be easier if we billed biweekly."

The large commercial customers were billed on a post-pay basis and received free handsets when they signed a two-year contract. "They expect it," said Torode. "And some of the guys can lose phones like you wouldn't believe."

Individual customers had to buy their own phones, which started at 60,000 Tsh. In a country with an average income of 2,000 Tsh per day, this could be prohibitive, but phone ownership worked in intriguing ways. Sometimes a family or a group of friends would purchase a phone together, allocating its use to each owner on a different day. In other cases, a family member working in the city would send a phone home to the village. The informal economy also increased the population's true income, making phone ownership more widespread than official numbers would imply. "When we extend our coverage to another village," commented Torode, "we find that traffic increases from the cities, as more people can call home. You can't underestimate the difficulty of travel here. People here take four-week vacations because they need six days for a round trip to their village."

One safari guide had switched from Vodacom to Celtel-TZ and had contacted his sister for the first time in years:

> My sister lives in the northwest, near Lake Victoria. I haven't seen her for 20 years. Now when I was with Voda, the signal would always drop. Always! You'd talk for a minute, ask a question, and bam, the signal drops. But with Celtel, it's fantastic. My sister and I talked for an hour. And Celtel has other services—I can transfer money from my Celtel account to someone else's, if their account is low. And I can

> subscribe to magazines. Instead of paying for a monthly subscription, I can get the headlines for much less.

Coverage

Part of Celtel-TZ's growth was due to its coverage. Observed Andrew Edmondson, director of operations and formerly the director of Uganda's operations, "Coverage is king. We are building networks where there are no roads. But people have money. Some Maasai herdsmen are very rich, likewise the fishermen in the western lakes. And they want to make a phone call."

Providing the means to make a phone call was difficult. Before he could put up a tower, Edmondson had to determine who owned the land. Land rarely had clear titles in Tanzania, but was "owned" by families who had farmed it for generations. After the harvest, though, the land became community grazing property. If a plot was unfarmed for more than three years, it could be claimed by a different family.[13] Edmondson explained:

> I have a team dedicated to land rights. We triangulate to determine ownership—first we talk to the guy who says he has the rights, then we talk with the tribal leaders and also the village council. That way, we know we are renting from the person who has title to the land in the eyes of the community. Some companies don't bother with that and end up with extremely contentious situations. We are completely aboveboard on this. We drive branded trucks, we tell them we're building a tower and not using it for farming, even though that means we pay more. And we pay the same amount to everyone. People talk, and if they learn that you paid someone else more for his land, they feel ill-used. And that can lead to vandalism. Given the value we get from carrying calls, you can easily lose more than you save if you cut corners.

Another problem was getting the towers to the site:

> Some of these areas have roads that are part creek bed, part cattle path. We bring the towers, which sometimes cost $250,000, in by sea to Dar es Salaam, then use four-wheel-drive tractor trailers to bring them as close to the site as we can. We hire a team of 25 men who carry the sections the rest of the way. Then a group of six trained riggers constructs the thing. They'll be standing up there on an eight-inch-wide girder, bolting another section above them. And a tower sways . . . they're amazing.

A new tower gave an area a shot of economic adrenalin. "I've gone back to these places a month or two later," said Edmondson, "and haven't recognized them. A little town springs up. Partly it's because the people who live there can now call their relatives in the city and have them send money. But we as a company also have a developmental role."

In addition to paying rent for the land, Celtel-TZ hired locals to serve as "askaris" or watchmen. "Some companies come in and bring their own people," explained Edmondson:

> And I'm sure they have their reasons, but it brands them as outsiders. We will hire three men from the village, two 12-hour shifts and one to fill in. They keep an eye on the place and ensure that the diesel for the generator [that powers the air conditioning unit keeping the equipment cool] doesn't disappear. We encourage them to plant a garden on the grounds. It adds to a sense of ownership. We find that we rarely lose diesel.

Distribution

The same road conditions that complicated tower construction also complicated the delivery of scratch cards. To solve it, Torode's sales team, led by Mike Dabaly, who had come from the tobacco industry because he wanted to sell something good for people, developed a cascading distribution system. National dealers in Dar es Salaam appointed distributors in the regions. The Celtel headquarters delivered SIM cards and scratch vouchers to the regional offices and the distributors took them into the countryside. One of the dealers distributed batteries and cooking oil nationwide, and adding the cards to the deliveries was simple.

Limited literacy complicated Celtel-TZ's ability to provide new services. To introduce new products to the frontline salesperson, often the proprietor of a village shop, the company needed personal contact, in Torode's words, "feet on the street." As labor in Africa was affordable, Celtel-TZ supported its sales activities with face-to-face contact. During school vacations, the company would train 10 college students on a new phone function and send them out to train shop owners in Swahili.

Torode recalled a similar situation:

> When we rolled out roaming [the ability to call using a Celtel network in a different country] in Zambia, we realized that a GSM phone remembers whether roaming was available in a certain place and on what network. Roaming hadn't been available there and phones had to be manually switched. We had to tell travelers how to access a roaming

network. So we got special permission to have a team of attractive, articulate young women (we tried men too but people wouldn't talk with them) to meet travelers in baggage claim at the national airport and tell them how to switch their phones to roam on Celtel.

Celtel-TZ's service reached 11 million people, roughly 30% of the population, but only 1.3 million had phones. Barriers included the price of the handset and the availability of scratch cards. The reward for obtaining a customer, though, was substantial, as Tanzanians tended to be very brand loyal. To ensure that their first telephone experience was with Celtel-TZ, the company had developed Personal Call Offices (PCOs), a briefcase with a metered phone. Operators would purchase a PCO and contract with someone to manage it in the countryside, setting prices to make a margin. "Communication is addictive," said Sales Director Mike Dabaly:

> The person with the PCO will sit in the café or the shop, and someone will come in to make his first call. He always brings a friend for moral support. He has a number written on a scrap of paper. The person operating the PCO will show him how to use the phone—you have to understand, many people will pick up the phone and hold it in front of their mouths, not beside their heads, because they think it works as if they were actually speaking to a person there in the room. So the person makes the call, pays for the time, and leaves. Next week, he's back, alone, with two numbers. Then with eight numbers and he's familiar with telephones and aware of the value of a phone call. And about that time, purchasing a phone becomes something he's willing to save for. If he's seen Celtel-Celtel-Celtel on the PCO he's been using, he'll think Celtel when he has his own phone and needs service.

Phone stores, which sold both the handsets and the SIM cards, served as another link in the distribution system. Although Celtel-TZ did not own the stores, it wanted to make a major statement with them. The company would offer to paint them Celtel's bright red and yellow colors or to put up large Celtel banners, relegating competitors to less desirable placement in the shop. One dealer not only had his shop painted in Celtel colors but had (at his own expense) dressed his clerks in a similar color scheme, bright red suits with yellow blouses.

While the handset was a capital purchase, the scratch vouchers were fast-moving consumer goods (FMCG) and the company aimed for ubiquitous availability. Celtel-TZ not only wanted its scratch cards at neighborhood shops but also in high-end retail outlets, such as grocery stores, shopping malls, airports, and 24-hour gas stations, as 8% to 10% of the subscriber base generated 45% of the cellular expenditure, and voucher availability was the key to capturing that revenue.

Strategy

The focus on the customer reflected a general shift within the operation from being project-driven to being customer-driven. The finance operation, led by Ted Sauti-Phiri, the finance director, balanced the two and ensured that every project made business sense, which was defined as achieving a 25% IRR.

The company's success presented a number of challenges. The network and service offerings had to expand rapidly to maintain momentum, yet growth could easily outstrip available financing. Industry risk and fraud were other concerns, ameliorated by intensive training about integrity and ownership behavior and supported by internal controls, an audit staff, and regular reports to headquarters in Amsterdam. Another challenge lay in cultural differences. The executives were expatriates, the rules were European, yet the people who implemented them were enthusiastic but part of the Tanzanian culture, which was still adapting to the requirements of international business. As the company grew, however, banks had started to approach it to offer their services, which was interpreted as a vote of confidence.

Sauti-Phiri, who had left the Malawi operations to help start Celtel-TZ, and Georgia Mutagahywa, external affairs director, worked closely with the government in explaining Celtel-TZ's strategy and getting regulatory support for it. Two of their biggest successes included influencing the reduction in the excise duty on airtime from 10% to 5%, and the reduction in interconnect charges (the charges paid by each operator for carrying calls to other operators or the fixed-line system) from 17.5¢ to 10¢.

Said Mutagahywa, "We continue to work with the government to get them thinking of cellular as basic infrastructure, a necessity and not a luxury. People will receive calls even if they don't make them. It helps the country and it means we make money. We also work with various business groups to create awareness in government that if the tax base is small, we need to expand it rather than tax the existing businesses more. "

Along with government relations, Mutagahywa also managed Celtel-TZ's social responsibility program. She said:

> If you give money, you have to manage it and we're not in that business. Instead, we work with increasing AIDS awareness and prevention, organizing medical camps, and road safety. Our biggest program, though, is kids and schooling. We've done a big "Build. Our Nation."

campaign through which we gave books to under-privileged schools all over Tanzania. We derive our profits from the community and therefore need to support the community in which we do business. We are, after all, part of the nation, not just a fly-by-night operation here to make a quick buck off Africa.

Development

"It is amazing how developmental a phone call is," said Torode. "Fishermen can call to find out which restaurant will give them the best price for their catch, you can call your hairdresser to come by your house and cut your hair, I can call the water truck driver when I need a delivery of house water—a real need in Tanzania where water mains may not exist."

The operation was expanding its coverage, moving into the rapidly developing southern part of the country. "It's exponential," said Torode. "When we expand to another region, we see more traffic in our existing regions as people can reach relatives who were previously cut off."

CELTEL INTERNATIONAL: GOING FORWARD

Ibrahim and his team knew that while the past had been a wild ride, the future had its own challenges. Celtel's customers produced average revenue per user (ARPU) of $22.50 per month, compared to 90 South African rand ($13.30) for Vodacom (see **Exhibit 9** for Vodacom's financials).[14] The cost structure was encouraging: adding an incremental customer cost $180, compared to £1,000[15] in the United Kingdom when it was at a similar early stage of network development in the 1990s. But even with Kenya, Celtel only had a presence in the SSA countries. To get into the big leagues, it would have to expand into the Middle East or North Africa. But how would it pay for such acquisitions? Should it look to an IPO? Or a merger? Stay independent and revise its financing to permit larger acquisitions?

Merger?

"Celtel would be a great bolt-on acquisition right now," said Rhodes. "We have great growth—Vodafone Germany, Europe's largest wireless operator, added 430,000 customers in the second quarter of 2004; we added 650,000 in the same period. The telcos are starting to realize that the last frontier is Africa. They are generating a lot of cash now and their shareholders want them to do something useful with it, rather than just throw it at another big merger. "

Unlike European telcos buying one another, buying an African operator would be accretive to earnings. In addition, a merger would give the company a clear view of its purchaser, unlike the uncertain mélange of the public market. A merger would likely be more financially lucrative to the existing shareholders. The Kencell acquisition had been priced at 4.8x 2004's estimated EBITDA. This would provide a nice return to the patient shareholders, and liquidity to those employees who also owned stock.

Yet a merger would likely displace the existing management team, or at least require those who stayed to integrate into a new operation with new values and standards. A major concern for those who had been through the two aborted merger processes was whether the company would be jilted yet again. "If there was to be a next time, I'd want to see their money on the table before I 'opened the kimono,'" said Wilson, the CFO. "A merger process is extremely distracting to management and I, for one, would need to know the suitors were completely serious."

IPO?

An IPO would certainly keep the management team and the company's internal culture in place, but it had its own challenges. "We would have to manage the 'Africa Fright Factor,'" said Wilson.

CEO Marten Pieters agreed, "The environments we're in are very tough. They aren't predictable. A coup in one nation may close down the network for two or three weeks and affect our quarterly revenues. Yet the governments have never revoked a license, so it would only be a short-term problem. Would the markets understand that? We can't set our targets too low, but if we're over-optimistic, we risk falling short. Will the markets understand Africa?"

Rhodes and Ibrahim agreed that an IPO, if it occurred, would have to be viewed as one more step in the company's history, not the end. Being able to use its shares as currency for acquisitions would be a huge advantage, though. Pieters commented, "It would be great to better balance the base between East and West by adding a few more West African assets. With public stock, we would have access to bigger opportunities."

Licenses were coming available, he knew, but often with high price tags. Morocco and Algeria had minimum entry costs of more than $1 billion. Others, such as Ethiopia, Libya, and Ghana, would be difficult to enter for other reasons.

Staying Independent

Another option was continuing as an independent group for a few years. "If we could do three more acquisitions," mused Rhodes, "with appropriate financing and a stronger balance sheet, and continued 40% annual growth and margins, we might be even more attractive than we are now." By then, he reasoned, the telco industry would have run out of growth options, leaving only Africa. Of the four significant African plays, only Celtel was private.

The Color of Money

Regardless of the path the company took, the executive team knew that the balance sheet needed to be revised. The company's low debt level subjected the shareholders to unnecessary dilution, but it stemmed from a number of reasons, one of which was timing. Wilson explained, "We funded the Kencell purchase partly with equity because we only had 28 days to raise the money and debt finance cannot be arranged as quickly as funds from friendly shareholders. It was a pragmatic practicality."

Ibrahim pointed out the wariness of banks. "First we are in Africa and second we are a telco. They are afraid of the first and were burned by the second. We have a good business model, but the analyst has to be willing to spend the time to understand it."

The company's structure further complicated the issue, with a Dutch holding company and African operating companies. Said Wilson, "The countries that see who we are and what we do don't have strong banking systems and we have no customers in Holland, where we're headquartered." In addition, if a bank lent to a holding company with remote operations, it needed to be sure that the holding company could service the loan, and that the cash flows to the parent were predictable. The holding company's only cash was that which the operating companies returned. Wilson noted:

> Banks want to be sure that we will get management fees, interest, and other payments. Ostensibly we have charged a management fee of 3% of revenue to the operating companies. We are moving to cost-plus pricing because it's more demonstrably arms length per Dutch tax authorities. But some operating companies can't pay the management fee because they're not cash-flow positive yet. If we add it to the shareholder loan they already have, some governments charge withholding tax at invoicing rather than at payment. Sometimes, therefore, we've forgiven management fees in the early life of an operation, because charging them would have cost us money.

Wilson had considered several options to increase the company's debt. One was to work harder with the banks. "We need visibility, desirability, and negotiation. That means we need relationships with the banks, we need to look good to them, and we need to convince them they'll get good returns. But we don't want to borrow money we don't need or need money we can't borrow."

Another option was to increase debt at the operating-company level. This was tax efficient, because shareholder loans were often seen as a form of equity with the interest on such loans subject to withholding tax as if they were dividends. It was also more equitable, as Celtel's shareholder loans on top of its equity ownership meant that any local partners received a free ride. It gave the company more local support, which was important. Wilson explained, "We're in difficult markets. Loans from local banks would align interests and add to the people we had in our corner if something went wrong."

Yet operating-company debt posed the problems of exchange rate risk management and the complexity of managing 13 deals in 13 countries. The ideal might involve working within the fledgling regional institutions to arrange borrowing facilities that covered a number of countries, but with the limited banking services in those countries, the process would be extremely time-consuming.

Increasing holding-company debt would allow "dry powder" for times when a business development opportunity was suddenly available. Rhodes still grimly remembered when the Nigeria license came up for auction: "It went for $285 million. We had a limit of $250 million and not a penny more." Wilson knew he could work to renew, refresh, and increase the existing loan facilities from the syndicate of Standard Bank, Development Bank of South Africa, ING, and others. The first principal repayment was due at the end of the year. "We could pursue refinancing it with something that differs slightly, because we are a bigger, less risky company," he said. But then he would have to balance the security with terms, rates, fees, flexibility, complexity, and the amount of time that the negotiation would take.

"We'd like to increase our banking resources," said Wilson. "We love our current banks, believe me. But they're not the biggest in the business." A possible vehicle might be a combination of a revolver and a term loan, acting like acquisition financing and a bridge. "I'm trying hard to replace our current complex securities with plain vanilla equity and plain vanilla debt," he observed. "People get 'instrument envy'—they see one wild and crazy vehicle and want something wilder and crazier. With revenues growing towards $1 billion and more than 4 million managed customers, we're big enough that we don't need to do that anymore. I hope." (See **Exhibit 10** for Celtel's subscriber growth.)

THE NEXT FRONTIER

Ibrahim lit his pipe and looked around the now-quiet room as servers cleared the table. He thought about his company, the second business success founded by a reluctant entrepreneur. He knew the company was wrestling with the issues attending growth toward $1 billion in seven years—he had seen the headquarters staff at leadership training classes; he knew that the commercial directors were having a major get-together and learning session in Tanzania soon and the managing directors had just done the same. "We have a good business idea and a proven track record. If you deal with people with integrity and honor, it comes back around," he mused. "We have demonstrated that we can do good business. In 10 years of designing networks with MSI, I never had a complaint. It's a small world in the end."

NOTES

1 Data from www.africaonline.com and www.fact.index.com, accessed October 19, 2004.
2 World Bank data, from http://www.worldbank.org/data/databytopic/reg_wdi.pdf, accessed October 18, 2004.
3 Economist Intelligence Unit, *Sub-Saharan Africa: Country Forecast* (London, UK: Economist Intelligence Unit, August 2004), p. 18.
4 World Bank data from http://www.worldbank.org/cgi-bin/ ICT at a Glance for countries mentioned, accessed November 24, 2004. Figures are best estimates for most recent year available (2002 or 2003) and are not adjusted for purchasing power parity.
5 Press release, "Africa: The World's Fastest Growing Mobile Market," *International Telecommunication Union*, April 25, 2004, www.itu.int/newsroom/press_releases/2004/04.html, accessed September 28, 2004.
6 *International Telecommunication Union*, www.itu.int/ITU-D/ict/statistics/at_glance/cellular03.pdf, accessed November 16, 2004.
7 Celtel International, Corporate Presentation June 2004, and press release, "Africa: The World's Fastest Growing Mobile Market," *International Telecommunication Union*, April 25, 2004, www.itu.int/newsroom/press_releases/2004/04.html, accessed September 28, 2004.
8 Press release, "Africa: The World's Fastest Growing Mobile Market," *International Telecommunication Union*, April 25, 2004, www.itu.int/newsroom/press_releases/2004/04.html, accessed September 28, 2004.
9 Ibid.
10 Press release, "GSM: the business of a billion people," *GSM Association,* February 2004, www.gsmworld.com/news /press_2004/press04_10.shtml, accessed November 24, 2004.
11 CDC Capital Partners' investing function has been spun off and renamed Actis.
12 At the time of Celtel's 1998 spin-out from MSI, BVP invested in both entities.
13 Economist Intelligence Unit, *Sub-Saharan Africa: Country Forecast* (London, UK: Economist Intelligence Unit, August 2004), p. 18.
14 Vodacom information from Cellular Online, http://www.cellular.co.za/vodacom.htm, accessed November 10, 2004.
15 Or $1,839 at the June 2004 conversion of £1 = $1.839 per www.oanda.com, accessed November 15, 2004.

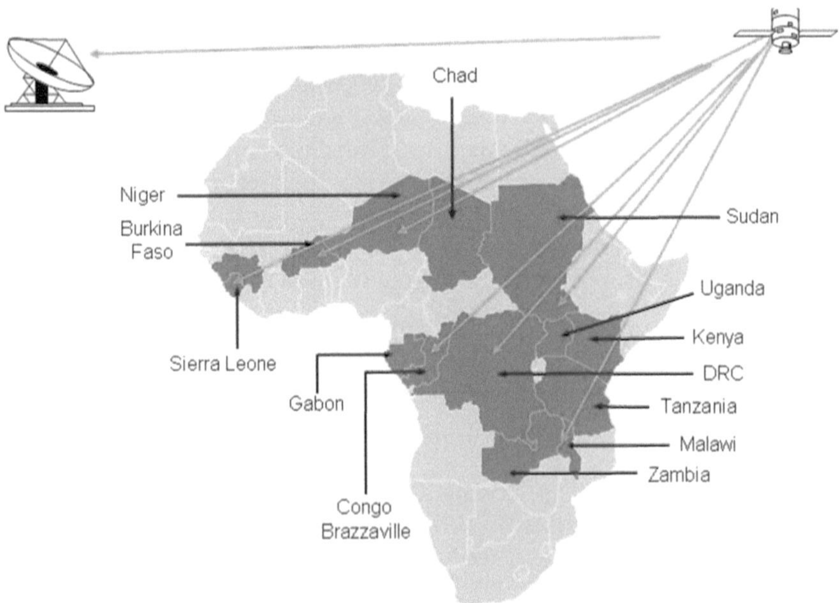

EXHIBIT 1 Map of Celtel's Service Territory in Africa
Source: Celtel International.

EXHIBIT 2 Celtel International's Board of Directors, as of June 2004

Name	Organization	Since
Dr. Mo Ibrahim	Exec. Chairman and Founder, Celtel and MSI	03/98
Joseph Solan	International Finance Corp.	10/02
Lord James Prior	Former Chairman of GEC, UK Cabinet Minister during Thatcher	03/00
His Excel. Salim K. Salim	Former Secretary General of the OAU, former Prime Minster of Tanzania	01/02
Tom Barry	Zephyr Asset Management	12/00
Jonathon Bond	Actis (fka CDC Capital Partners)	10/02
Ashley Dunster	Capital International Investments	03/04
Thomas Gibbian	Emerging Markets Partnership	04/04
Felda Hardymon	Bessemer Venture Partners	03/98
Mark Jacobson	CVC International	01/01
Jay Metcalfe	Palio Fund, formerly with Del Sol Fund, former CEO of Millicom	03/98
Marten Pieters	CEO, Celtel, formerly with KPN	12/04
Sir Alan Rudge	President of Celtel, former Deputy CEO of BT	03/98

Source: Celtel International.

EXHIBIT 3A Celtel's Income Statement

In thousands $	Dec. '03	Dec. '02
Revenues	$380,073	$265,610
-- Total direct cost	$(84,241)	$(69,267)
Contribution margin	**$295,832**	**$196,343**
-- Network operating expenses	$(41,306)	$(21,301)
-- Employee expenses	$(45,393)	$(36,313)
-- Sales and Marketing expenses	$(23,531)	$(12,233)
-- General and administrative	$(59,128)	$(60,523)
EBITDA	**$126,474**	**$ 65,973**
-- Depreciation & amortization	$(47,755)	$(52,927)
EBIT	**$ 78,719**	**$ 13,046**
-- Net interest income/(expense)	$(25,586)	$(28,686)
-- Capital gain on sale of investment	$ 23,935	$ -
-- Income from associates	$ 18,069	$ 3,098
-- Exchange gain/(loss)		
Profit/loss before tax	**$ 95,137**	**$(12,542)**
-- Income tax	$(13,495)	$ (9,401)
-- Minority interests in subsidiaries (net of tax)	$ (7,766)	$ (1,957)
Profit/loss after tax	**$ 73,876**	**$(23,900)**

Source: Celtel International annual reports.

EXHIBIT 3B Celtel's Balance Sheet

Balance Sheet (*in thousands $*)	Dec. '03	Dec. '02
Fixed Assets		
-- Intangible assets	$ 57,256	$ 42,056
-- Tangible assets	$267,570	$203,152
-- Long-term loans	$ 313	$ 1,535
-- Other	$194,127	$179,908
Total Fixed Assets	**$519,266**	**$426,651**
Current Assets		
-- Cash	$132,444	$ 19,041
-- Inventory	$ 7,275	$ 3,810
-- Other	$ 56,150	$ 38,926
Total Current Assets	**$195,869**	**$ 61,777**
Total Assets	**$715,135**	**$488,428**
Group equity & liabilities		
Equity		
-- Shareholders' Equity	$308,470	$213,443
-- Paid-in capital		
-- Retained earnings	($111,081)	$ (87,181)
-- Results for the year	$ 73,876	$ (23,900)
-- Reserve and unrealized results of investments	$ 45,807	$ 23,969
Total Equity	$317,072	$126,331
Minority interests	$ 12,869	$ 15,678
Total provisions		
Long-term liabilities		
-- Redeemable preference shares	$ 10,000	$ 49,314
-- Interest bearing loans	$127,992	$ 81,462
-- Deferred proceeds and tax liabilities	$ 2,744	$ 23,030
Total Long-term Liabilities	**$140,736**	**$153,806**
Current liabilities		
-- Short-term loans	$ 99,847	$101,126
-- Loans due within a year		
-- Accounts payable	$ 33,178	$ 26,754
-- Income tax & other taxes payable	$ 22,899	$ 9,055
-- Other liabilities[a]	$ 40,905	$ 8,161
-- Accrued liabilities	$ 47,629	$ 47,517
Total Current Liabilities	**$244,458**	**$192,613**
Total Equity & Liabilities	**$715,135**	**$488,428**

Source: Celtel International annual reports.

[a]In 2003, these were both deferred revenue and deferred proceeds on divestments; in 2002, this was deferred revenue only.

EXHIBIT 4 Celtel's Shareholders

Name	Description
Actis	Formerly part of CDC, the British government's development finance agency; now an independent fund investing in emerging markets.
AIG Infrastructure Fund	Managed by EMP, the largest private equity infrastructure manager in emerging markets.
African Merchant Bank	South Africa's premier merchant bank supporting the development and serving the growth of the emerging African economies.
Blakeney Management	Fund management in emerging markets.
Bessemer Venture Partners	The investment arm of one of the oldest funds in the USA.
Capital International	Part of the Capital Group, a leading investment group with over US$700 billion under management.
Celtel staff	
Citigroup	The global financial services group.
Communication Venture Partners	Specialist mobile telecoms venture capital firm.
Corporation Financiers Alba	A Spanish holding company forming part of the Grupo March, one of Spain's leading business and financial groups.
DEG	The German development finance agency.
FMO	The Dutch development finance agency.
Fonditel	A Spanish fund, part of Telefonica.
IFC (International Finance Corporation)	The private sector arm of the World Bank and the largest source of private equity for developing countries.
Ibrahim Family Trusts	Representative of the interests of Celtel's chairman, Mohamed Ibrahim, Ph.D., founding shareholder of Celtel International.
Old Mutual	The leading fund management company in South Africa.
Palio	The Swiss technology investment company.
Standard Bank of London	The head office of the international banking activities of the Standard Bank Group, Ltd.
Zephyr Management, L.P. Fund	An American venture capital firm focused on B2B applications that use the Internet and related technologies.

Source: Celtel International Annual Report 2003, p. 33.

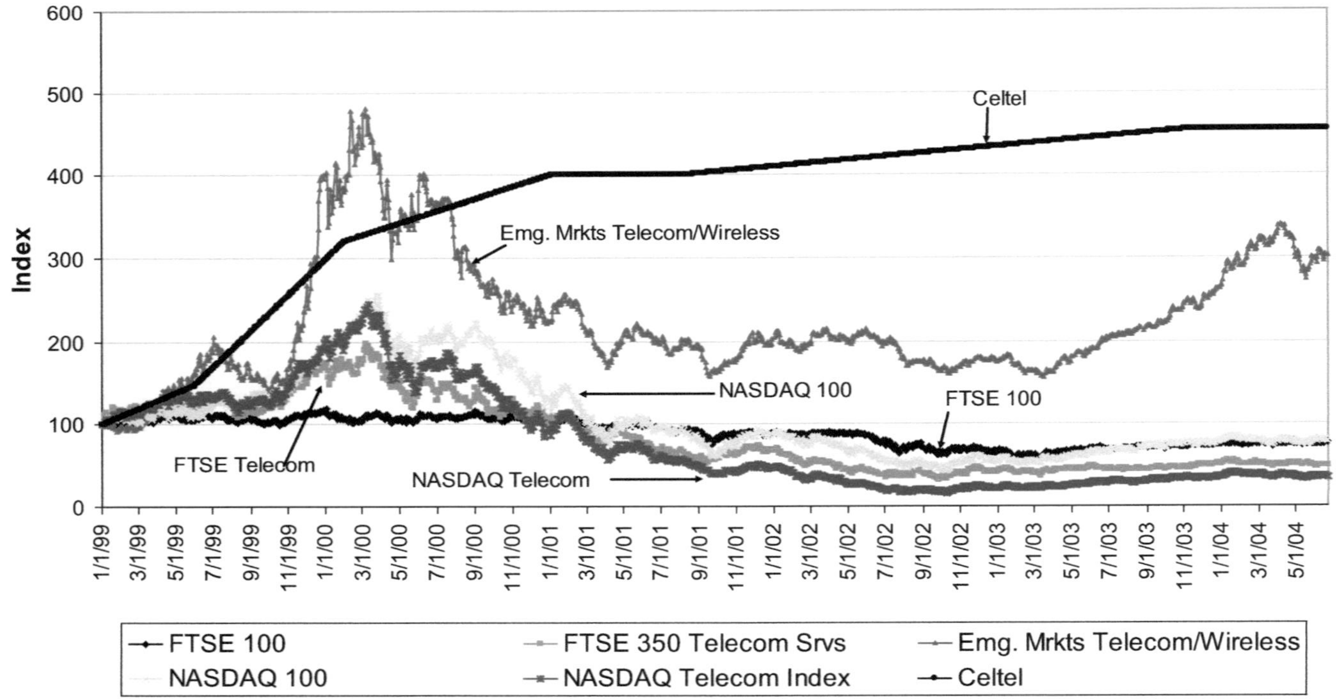

EXHIBIT 5 Index of Celtel Share Price Compared with Major Indices to June 21, 2004
Source: Data from Thomson Financial Datastream. Note: Indices based on January 1, 1999.

EXHIBIT 6A Celtel's Financings: Equity

Date	Share Price ($)	Amount ($MM)	Total Paid in Capital ($MM)	Lead Investors
Mar-98	2.06	11.1	11.1	Ibrahim, Bessemer, Staff
Jun-98	3.75	5.0	16.1	Ibrahim, Staff, Del Sol
Jun-99	5.50	35.2	51.3	Worldtel, Zephyr, IFC
Feb-00	12.00	63.0	114.3	Citigroup, EMP, Palio, Alba
Jan-01	15.00	56.2	170.5	Various, including Staff
Aug-01	15.00	72.5	243.0	CDC, IFC, Old Mutual, DEG
Aug-03	17.00	15.0	258.0	FMO
Dec-03	17.00	62.0	320.0	Capital Group
Jan-04	17.00	93.5	413.5	Existing shareholders

Source: Company information.

EXHIBIT 6B Celtel's Financings: Debt

Date	Prime Lender	Amount ($MM)	Cumulative Amount Raised ($MM)
Jun-98	ING	15.0	15.0
Sep-98	CDC	22.5	37.5
Jun-00	CDC	25.0	62.5
Aug-00	ING et. al	50.0	112.5
Feb-01	ING	25.0	137.5
Feb-01	SBL	20.0	157.5
May-01	CAI	20.0	177.5
Jun-01	VTI	45.0	222.5
Dec-01	SBL	20.0	242.5
Aug-01	Moponi	18.4	260.9
Aug-01	FMO	10.0	270.9
Mar-02	Belgolaise	10.0	280.9
Jan-03	ING	10.0	290.9
Feb-03	ING et. al	109.0	399.9
Feb-03	EAIF	8.0	407.9
Apr-04	ING (acquisition finance)	70.0	477.9

Source: Company information.

EXHIBIT 7 Celtel's Countries, Ownership, and Market Position as of June 2004

Country	Launch	Celtel Ownership	Local Partner	Market Position
Burkina Faso	Jan-01	96%	Cauris Private Equity	1
Chad	Oct-00	100%	-	1
Congo (B)	Dec-99	100%	-	1
DRC	Dec-00	100%	-	1
Gabon	Jul-01	84%	General Business Machines	1
Kenya	acquired, May-04	60%	Sameer Group	2
Malawi	Oct-99	100%	-	1
Niger	Nov-01	70%	SONI	1
Sierra Leone	Sep-00	100%	-	1
Sudan	acquired, Mar-01	39%	Sudatel (local fixed-line operator)	1
Tanzania (Fixed-TTCL)	privatization, Feb-01	35%	Tanzanian Government	NA[a]
Tanzania (GSM)	Nov-01	35%	TTCL	2
Uganda	Jul-95	100%	-	3
Zambia	Dec-98	89%	IFC	1

Source: Celtel International.

[a]NA is Not Applicable; TTCL is the only fixed-line operator in the country.

EXHIBIT 8 Celtel's Executive Team

Mohamed Ibrahim, PhD. Chairman.
Dr. Ibrahim was Technical Director of the U.K. mobile operator BT Cellnet (now known as O2) before founding MSI plc (Celtel's parent company) in 1989.

Marten Pieters, LLM. Chief Executive Officer.
Marten joined Celtel from KPN Royal Dutch Telecom, where he held senior positions, including membership of the executive management board.

Tito Alai, MBA. Chief Marketing Officer.
Tito held senior management positions at Kodak Eastman and Unilever before joining Celtel.

(continued)

EXHIBIT 8 *(continued)*

Frans Bruinzeel. Chief Human Resources Officer.
Frans held senior positions at Royal Dutch Shell before joining Celtel.

Moez Daya, BSc. Chief Technical Officer.
Moez was Head of Cellular Planning at BT Cellnet (now known as O2) before joining MSI plc. He now leads Celtel's technical and engineering functions.

Tsega Gebreyes, MBA. Chief Business Development Officer.
Tsega joined Celtel as a board member representing Zephyr Asset Management. She is now responsible for business development.

Omari Issa, MBA. Chief Operating Officer.
Before joining Celtel, Omari worked with the World Bank, funding telecoms projects in Africa, Asia and South America.

(continued)

EXHIBIT 8 *(continued)*

Terry Rhodes, MSc, MBA. Co-founder and Chief Strategy Officer.
Terry was a Director of BT Cellnet (now known as O2) and later a Director of Cable and Wireless in the U.K. responsible for strategy, pricing and regulatory economics. He joined MSI plc in 1995 and helped set up Celtel in 1998.

David Wilson, MBA. Chief Finance Officer.
David has held senior financial positions in British Telecom, ADT, Mars, Hewlett-Packard and Hoover.

Source: Celtel information, www.celtel.com/leadership, accessed November 12, 2004.

EXHIBIT 9 Comparison to Peers

Income Statement	Celtel			MTN Group			Vodacom		
Year ending December ($ millions)	2001	2002	2003	2001	2002	2003	2001	2002	2003
Revenue	152	266	380	1,441	1,845	3,159	1,872	1,880	3,107
Growth	-	75.0%	43.1%	-	28.0%	71.2%	-	0.4%	65.2%
EBITDA	26	66	126	420	628	1,220	653	637	1,028
Margin	16.9%	24.8%	33.3%	29.2%	34.0%	38.6%	34.9%	33.9%	33.1%
Growth	-	157.1%	91.7%	-	49.3%	94.3%	-	(2.4%)	61.3%
EBIT (adj.)	(9)	13	79	206	392	826	413	412	693
Margin	(6.2%)	4.9%	20.7%	14.3%	21.3%	26.2%	22.1%	21.9%	22.3%
Income from associates	(0)	3	18	(1)	0	1	0	0	0
Net income (adj.)	(34)	(14)	54	138	304	600	280	220	414
Margin	(22.7%)	(5.3%)	14.3%	9.6%	16.5%	19.0%	15.0%	11.7%	13.3%
Capex	78	72	105	389	373	668	511	292	372
As a % of revenue	51.5%	27.2%	27.7%	27.0%	20.2%	21.1%	27.3%	15.5%	12.0%
Current assets	52	62	196	348	618	1,290	345	546	1,030
Of which cash and cash equivalents	12	19	132	131	249	796	60	141	354
Non-current assets	406	427	519	1,937	2,662	3,486	952	1,430	1,969
Total assets	458	488	715	2,284	3,280	4,776	1,298	1,976	3,000

Current liabilities	89	193	244	373	718	949	684	834	1,468
Of which debt	24	101	100	40	186	66	234	116	241
Long-term liabilities	181	154	141	517	472	653	158	336	383
Of which debt	120	81	128	442	378	554	65	202	182
Total liabilities	270	346	385	890	1,190	1,602	842	1,170	1,851
Shareholders' equity	166	126	317	1,326	1,987	2,962	455	796	1,135
Minority interest	22	16	13	68	103	212	1	10	14
Total equity and liabilities	458	488	715	2,284	3,280	4,776	1,298	1,976	3,000
Net debt/(cash)	132	164	95	351	316	(177)	239	177	68
Gearing[a]	70.3%	115.2%	28.9%	25.1%	15.1%	(5.6%)	52.4%	22.0%	6.0%
Net debt / EBITDA	5.1x	2.5x	0.8x	0.8x	0.5x	(0.1x)	0.4x	0.3x	0.1x

Source: Adapted from Rothschild, Peer Comparisons, private document.

Notes: MTN Group and Vodacom have financial years ending March—figures shown are as of year ending March of the following year, e.g., December 2001 reflects results of the year to March 2002.

MTN Group and Vodacom projections based on forecast S. African Rand: US$ exchange rates from EIU.

EBIT adjusted for exceptional items, net income adjusted for exceptional items and goodwill amortization.

[a]Gearing defined as net debt/book value of shareholders' equity (including minority interest).

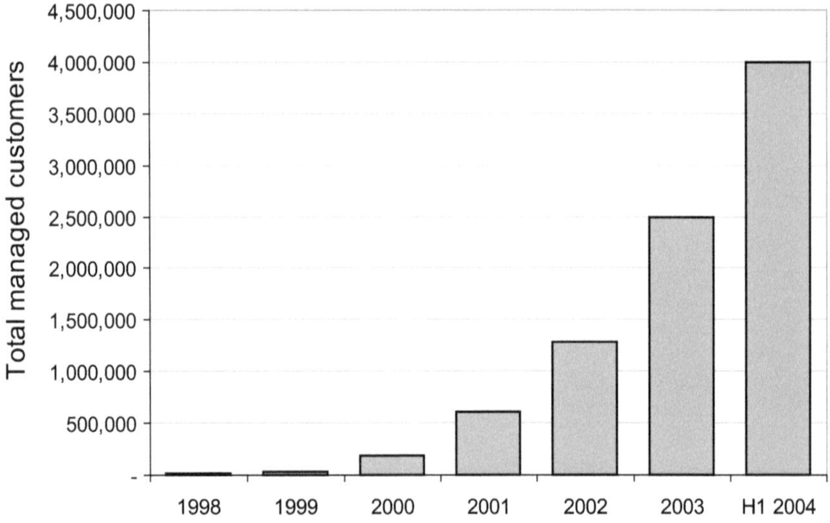

EXHIBIT 10 Subscriber Growth 1998–H1 2004
Source: Celtel International Annual Report 2003. Note: H1 2004 includes Kencell subscribers.

CHAPTER 7.2

Entrepreneurial Exits

Paul Gompers

Every entrepreneur or investor in an entrepreneurial company needs to consider harvesting at some point. Harvesting can take many forms. Successfully planning for harvesting of the entrepreneurial venture is critical to maximizing the value of your input. This note will explore various modes of harvesting like initial public offerings (IPOs) as well as strategic and financial acquisitions. The emphasis is on assessing whether the entrepreneurial firm is "ready" for harvesting. In addition, we will emphasize the structural, legal, and dynamic issues of various modes of harvest.

The public markets are a significant source of capital for emerging companies. For many firms, accessing the public market is just the next phase of their operating and financial strategies. For others, it represents the beginning of the ability to receive the fruits of their labors. This note explores the various motivations for "going public" and the advantages and disadvantages of being a public company. Structural and legal issues will be discussed. In addition, this note explores the impact that the cyclical nature of the initial public offering market has on firms access to capital. The role of various intermediaries will be examined and the motivations of various parties discussed.

The note then covers acquisitions, both strategic and financial. Most firms will never be large enough for the public market and will therefore need to find a specific buyer. The ability to find the best buyer and negotiate the best deal terms for the entrepreneur are critical. We emphasize the role of bargaining and auctions in the context of acquisitions. The motivations of buyers and sellers must be understood to ensure the conclusion of a successful deal.[1]

Entrepreneurial Exits
by PAUL GOMPERS, case number 9-224-036 OCTOBER 3, 2023

EXIT ROUTES: PROS AND CONS

This section discusses the relative advantages and disadvantages of the three most frequent forms of exit: IPOs, strategic sales, and financial sales.

Initial Public Offering

IPOs tend to have several advantages over other forms of exit. The most important is that IPOs typically result in higher valuations than either strategic or financial sales. However, this increased valuation does come with some costs. IPOs are also time consuming, often taking up to six months to complete. Management teams may also bristle at the disclosure requirements of becoming a public company.

Moreover, management and investors (including venture capitalists, angels, and private equity firms) sell only a small portion of their stake in the IPO. One can imagine the negative signal that would be sent to the market if insiders were selling large percentages of their ownership at the time the firm went public. These pre-public shareholders continue to hold the majority of their equity holdings for an extended period of time. As a result, IPOs leave insiders (founders, managers, and investors) exposed to the risk of a significant decline in firm value as well as decrease the ability to time exits to coincide with peaks in valuation.

The Role of Lockups

The risk of price movements is exacerbated by the fact that management, venture capital investors, and private equity firms are generally not permitted to divest any of their equity holdings in the first 180 days following the IPO. This period of time is referred to as the IPO lockup. When the issuing firm and the investment bank enter into an agreement to offer securities in an IPO, they sign an underwriter agreement. As Bartlett explains, these agreements typically include a covenant such as:

> "The Selling Securityholders agree that, without your (the investment bank's) prior written consent, the Selling Securityholders will not, directly or indirectly, sell, offer, contract to sell, make any short sale, pledge or otherwise dispose of any shares of Common Stock or any securities convertible into or exercisable for or any rights to purchase or acquire Common Stock for a period of 180 days following the commencement of the public offering of the Stock by the Underwriters."

Bartlett argues that the lockup, which is "typically" 180 days in length, "prevents a surplus of stock hitting the market all at once." The agreement to not sell or sell-short their equity holdings is governed only by this underwriter agreement. It is not mandated by any SEC or state securities laws that regulate insider trading.[2] Typically, when a firm's equity comes off of lockup, the stock price experiences a significant stock price decline, even though the date is fully known and the expiration is fully anticipated.

In addition, insider trading is likely to be regulated by the firm itself. A large proportion of firms have a policy in place restricting insider trading by employees as well as pre-specified blackout periods in which the company prohibits trading by insiders. Insiders who are governed by these self-imposed company restrictions are sometimes granted permission to trade during the blackout periods for liquidity or diversification reasons.

Distribution of Proceeds[3]

Even after the lockup expires, venture capitalists and private equity managers will often continue to hold the shares in the company for months or even years. Once they decide to liquidate their positions, there are two alternatives. First, venture capitalists and private equity mangers can sell the shares they hold on the open market and distribute cash to limited partners. More often, these managers distribute shares to each limited partner and (frequently) themselves. Distribution of equity on a pro rata basis to limited partners is, by far, the predominant form of exit for venture capital funds and private equity firms after an IPO. There are several factors that influence this decision.

A number of reasons are responsible for the preponderance of distributions in kind. First, SEC rules restrict sales by corporate insiders. The sale of restricted securities, that is, stock purchased in a private placement directly from an issuer before the company is public, is governed by SEC Rule 144. Rule 144 allows for the sale of restricted securities in limited quantities in the aftermarket. Specifically, a person who has beneficially owned shares of common stock for at least six months (one year if the firm is not subject to reporting requirements) is entitled to sell, within any three-month period, a number of shares that does not exceed the greater of 1% of the number of shares of common stock then outstanding or the average weekly trading volume during the four calendar weeks preceding the filing of a notice on Form 144 with respect to the sale.

Because venture capital and private equity funds may hold large fractions of a company's equity, selling the entire stake may take a long period of time. It is not uncommon for a venture capitalist to own twenty percent (or more) of a company when it goes public. Private equity firms often own substantially more, perhaps up to eighty percent of the equity. We the venture capitalists or private equity managers to sell all of that equity, the share price would plummet. By distributing shares to limited partners, who are usually not considered insiders, the venture capital and private equity fund can dispose of a large block of shares more quickly.

Second, tax motivations may also provide an incentive for the venture capital and private equity managers to distribute shares. If they sell shares and distribute cash, taxable limited partners (e.g., individuals and corporations) and the venture capital and private equity managers themselves are subject to immediate capital gains taxes. These investors might prefer to postpone these taxes by receiving distributions in kind and selling the shares at a later date. These considerations will be unimportant to tax-exempt limited partners (e.g., pension funds and endowments). By distributing stock, venture capital and private equity funds provide limited partners with the flexibility to make their own decisions about selling the stock.

Third, if selling the shares has a large negative effect on prices, venture capital and private equity funds may want to distribute shares. The method of computing returns employed by venture capital and private equity funds and outside fund trackers (e.g., Cambridge Associates, the Burgiss Group, etc.) typically uses the closing price of the distributed stock on the day the distribution is declared. The actual price received when the limited partners sell their shares may be lower.[4] If prices decline after the distribution, actual returns to limited partners could be substantially less than calculated returns. Research has actually shown this to be the case. Venture capital and private equity investors appear to be able to time the market quite well. Centering returns around the distribution date reveals an interesting pattern. Stock prices generally tend to go up prior to the decision to distribute, then drift down over the days after the distribution. Venture capital and private equity managers care about stated returns on their funds because they use this information when they raise new funds. Thus, the potential price from selling the shares will typically lower than the price that they can quote if they distribute the shares directly.[5]

Finally, the venture capital and private equity managers' compensation can be affected by distribution policy. If the fund has not returned committed capital to its limited partners, most funds distribute shares of portfolio companies in proportion to the partners' actual capital commitments (usually 99 percent to limited partners and 1 percent to general partners). By distributing overvalued shares prior to the return of committed capital (or a return that meets the hurdle rate if there is one), the venture capitalist moves closer to the point where general partners collect a larger share of the profits. Once committed capital has been returned, venture capital and private equity managers still have an incentive to distribute overvalued shares. They may be able to sell their portions at a high valuation before limited partners receive their shares and the market discerns that a distribution has occurred.

Venture capital and private equity investors' reputational concerns may not overcome the incentive to distribute overvalued shares. In fact, as **Figure 1** shows, this appears to be the case; IPOs of high reputation and low reputation PE firms have similar post-distribution performance.

There are several explanations for this result. First, many institutional investors and advisors also care about stated returns. They may be compensated based on how well the funds that they select do relative to a benchmark (calculated using the distribution price). This is particularly true if the shares are transferred immediately on receipt of the distribution to its public equity managers. Any price decline may be attributed to the public equity group. Second, certain investors may be unaware of the problem. Investors may not track stock price performance against an appropriate benchmark. Similarly, record keeping of the price at which the shares were sold is often incomplete.

Few SEC regulations cover distributions by venture capital and private equity investors. Rule 16(a) states that individuals who are affiliates of a firm, such as directors, officers, and holders of 10 percent of the company's shares, must disclose any transactions in the firm's stock on a monthly basis. Provision 16(a)-7, however, explicitly exempts distributions

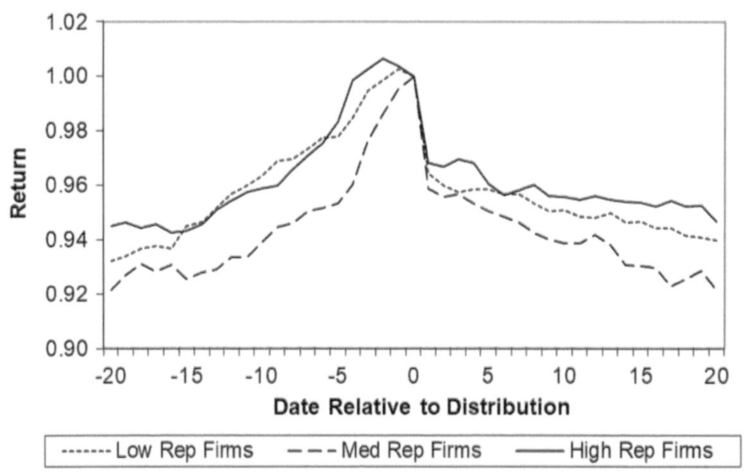

FIGURE 1 Return around Distribution Date, by PE Firm Reputation
Source: Timothy Dore, Paul Gompers, and Andrew Metrick, "Reputation and Contractual Flexibility: Evidence from Venture Capital Distribution Pricing Policies," (HBS Working Paper, unpublished work, 2012).

of securities that (i) were originally obtained from issuers and (ii) are being distributed "in good faith, in the ordinary course of business." An interpretation widely accepted within the industry is that venture capital and private equity managers distribute investments in the normal course of business, and that they do not convey any information unless the venture capital and private equity manager makes an explicit recommendation to hold or sell the shares at the time. Venture capital and private equity lawyers have applied the same principles when considering the applicability of Rule 10(b)-5, the most general prohibition against fraudulent activity in the purchase or sale of any security.

When one examines the price reaction around the distribution date, i.e., the date that the venture capital or private equity manager distributes shares to their limited partners, the evidence is consistent with the market reacting to the inside information of the private equity fund: there is a systematic two to three percent drop around the distribution is akin to the reaction to public announcements of secondary stock sales even though venture capital and private equity distributions are not publicly disclosed.

Strategic Sale

There are several advantages to a strategic sale relative to other common exits. First, a strategic buyer will often realize synergies from the deal. As a result, it typically can offer a higher price than a financial buyer. Second, such a sale offers a complete exit from the investment, which is not the case with an IPO.

Offsetting these advantages are a few disadvantages. Strategic sales can face resistance from management, who are often significant (albeit minority) shareholders. In these sales, the acquirer commonly either replaces firm management with their own managers or eliminates the positions in an attempt to eliminate redundancies.

Another downside to strategic sales is that they carry a degree of competitive risk. Potential acquirers need access to the firm's accounting information and other confidential records in order to formulate a bid. While some firms may show genuine interest, others may simply be feigning interest in order to understand any competitive advantages the firm has. Nondisclosure agreements can mitigate this concern but cannot eliminate it entirely.

A final important disadvantage is that strategic sales can be slow and/or risky to consummate. When one competitor seeks to acquire another, there can be antitrust concerns. In the case where these concerns are important, review of the proposed acquisition by the federal government can slow the closing of the deal or kill it entirely.

Financial Sale

Like a strategic sale, a financial sale has the benefit of providing a complete exit of the investment. In the past decade, the role of financial sales for both venture capital and private equity firms has increased. With the increasing amount of private capital available, private equity firms often look to source deals from other private investors. Unlike a strategic sale, however, antitrust concerns are not an issue so, assuming the purchasing private equity firm has lined up the financing, financial sales can be relatively quick. This can be particularly important for a venture capital or private equity fund that is reaching the end of its contractual life. Financial sales also eliminate the issue of competitive risk while often permitting the firm's current managers to retain their jobs.

The main downside of a financial sale is that of price. Because a financial buyer is unlikely to realize any potential synergies, it will be unable to offer as high of a price as a strategic buyer, holding all else equal. Additionally, because financial buyers typically rely on significant levels of debt, there is a possibility that their financing falls through and scuttles the deal.

NOTES

1 Gompers, Paul A., and Timothy Dore, "Private Equity Exits." HBS No. 213-112, (Boston: Harvard Business School Publishing, May 2013. (Revised July 2014)).

2 It is important to note that the underwriter can release any of the securities subject to the lock-up agreements at any time without notice. Brav and Gompers (2003) find that early release was used in approximately 16% of the IPOs in their sample.

3 This section based in part on: Paul Gompers, Josh Lerner, "Venture Capital Distributions: Short-Run and Long-Run Reactions," The Journal of Finance, Volume 53, Issue 6, December 1998, Pages 2161-2183.

4 Distributions are typically declared after the market closes. The recording distribution price is typically the closing price on the distribution day. Actual receipt of certificates and the ability to sell the shares may take several days.

5 The price quoted in cases where the PE firm transfers the shares is dictated by the agreement between the general partners and limited partners of the fund. It is often the closing price on the day that the shares are transferred, although an average closing price of the previous one or two weeks is also common. See Dore, Gompers, and Metrick (2012).

REFERENCES

Bartlett, Joseph, 1995, Equity Finance: Venture capital, buyout, restructurings, and reorganizations, (John Wiley: New York).

Brav, Alon, and Paul Gompers, 2003, The Role of Lock-ups in Initial Public Offerings Provisions," Review of Financial Studies 16, 1-29.

CHAPTER 7.3

Knoll Furniture: Going Public

Paul A. Gompers

John Lynch, president and chief executive officer of Knoll Inc., sat in his black leather office chair gazing out the window at the gently falling snow. It was March 1997, and he had just gotten off the phone with Warburg Pincus Ventures, the investment firm that had taken Knoll private in a leveraged buyout in February 1996. Lynch had just had another conversation with Warburg about the possibility of taking Knoll public. Warburg had first approached Lynch in the fall of 1996 about the possibility of taking Knoll public sometime during the first half of 1997.

In early 1994 when Lynch had joined Knoll, it would have seemed improbable to suggest a public offering for the struggling furniture company. But Lynch had completely revitalized the firm in the past two years, and Knoll now stood out as a strong IPO candidate. Lynch had been considering the implications of going public for some time, but he remained unsure whether to go through with the process just yet. He still had numerous questions regarding the process and implications. While the IPO market in 1996 had been quite active, the market had begun to cool off in the first quarter of 1997 after the Federal Reserve Chairman Alan Greenspan warned of "irrational exuberance" driving stock prices above their fundamental values. Was this the right time to take Knoll public, or would the company benefit by waiting until it had a longer track record of improving sales and earnings? Furthermore, what would Knoll gain from an offering? The company did not need the cash that would be generated from the IPO. In addition, the company already had a strong reputation in the furniture industry and did not need to go public to improve its image and visibility. Was he prepared to deal with the additional responsibilities of being a public company? The significant costs from the offering process and future registration procedures also had to be taken into account. Lynch was also concern that the "road show" process and meetings with investors during the offering process would distract senior management at a time when the

Knoll Furniture: Going Public
by PAUL A. GOMPERS, case number 9-202-114 APRIL 1, 2002

company was still trying to prove itself? He leaned back in his chair and closed his eyes. It was going to be a long month.

BACKGROUND

History of Knoll, Inc.[1]

Knoll Inc. was founded in 1938 by the German immigrant Hans Knoll. The company was considered a widely recognized leader in the design and production of office systems and business furniture, a growing segment of the overall furniture industry. (**Exhibit 1** shows the recent growth in office furniture shipments in the United States. **Exhibit 2** shows Knoll's position in the office furniture market.)

Knoll was purchased in 1990 by the Westinghouse Electric Corporation in a series of office furniture acquisitions that included the Shaw-Walker Company and Reff Inc. These companies were combined into Westinghouse's existing office furniture business, Westinghouse Furniture Systems, as The Knoll Group. By combining these four companies under the Knoll title, Westinghouse created a business with a complete line of office furnishings, a reputation for high quality and superior design, and an internationally recognized brand name.

For a variety of reasons, the combined business proved to be a poorly integrated and inefficient entity whose performance declined in the years immediately following the acquisition. Sales and net income deteriorated from 1991-1993, and revenues fell from $671 million in 1991 to $508 million in 1993; over the same period, U.S. office furniture shipments rose at a 5.7% annual rate. Westinghouse's announcement that it planned to sell Knoll in 1991 created a great deal of uncertainty among Knoll's employees and customers which exacerbated the company's problems.

After receiving several inadequate offers, Westinghouse management took Knoll off the market in December 1993 and focused instead on trying to improve the company's performance. Burton Staniar, then head of the highly successful Westinghouse broadcasting unit, and John Lynch were hired to head the turnaround. (See **Exhibit 3** for management biographies.) In 1994, the two initiated a major restructuring program that led to significantly improved financial performance. Sales increased from $508 million in 1993 to $652 million in 1996; gross margins increased from 25.9% in 1994 to 35.6% in 1996; and operating income improved by $114 million. (See **Exhibit 4** for Knoll's financial information from 1992-1996; **Exhibit 5** shows information on comparable firms over the same period. **Exhibit 6** shows Knoll's share of the furniture market in 1996.)

A change in management at Westinghouse led to Knoll being placed on the market again in 1995. The new administration felt that the future of Westinghouse lay in broadcasting. Faced with a weakened balance sheet and a $2 billion bridge loan due in early 1996, Westinghouse focused on eliminating all non-core businesses. Knoll's strong recent performance made it an excellent asset to sell. The firm was eventually purchased by Warburg Pincus Ventures in February 1996 for $565 million in a leveraged buyout, $160 million in equity and $405 million in debt.

Since the acquisition, Knoll continued to build on the success of the turnaround program and maintained its rapid growth. With the U.S. economy performing well and sales in the office industry remaining strong, Knoll's operating and net profits continued to rise significantly. (**Exhibits 7–9** show financial forecasts for Knoll from 1997-2001.)

HISTORY OF WARBURG PINCUS VENTURES[2]

Warburg Pincus could trace its history to E.M. Warburg & Co., which was founded by the German immigrant Eric Warburg in New York in 1938 to provide investment services to German-Americans. After World War II, Warburg became increasingly involved in the management of his family's banking interests in Hamburg. Unable to devote sufficient attention to his American firm, Warburg sold a half-interest of the company to an experienced investment banker named Lionel Pincus in 1966. Pincus redirected the company's activities to emphasize private equity investing, believing that the firm could reap greater returns if their investments were undertaken in a more systematic way. The result was a unique approach to private equity investing, which was termed "venture banking." (See **Exhibit 10** for information on Warburg Pincus' management.)

After initially investing only its own money, the firm raised its first formal private equity fund in 1971. This and subsequent private equity funds were organized as limited partnerships with life spans of roughly ten years. Around the same time as its first fund was raised, the company assumed its current name. The fund that had invested in Knoll, Warburg Pincus Ventures, raised $2.8 billion in 1994 and represented a record for private equity funds at the time. Despite its size, however, Warburg Pincus Ventures was largely invested by early 1997.

The Warburg Pincus approach to private equity investing was distinctive for several reasons. The first was a willingness to go against industry trends. While many private equity groups invested with a herd mentality, following the latest hot sector, Warburg Pincus focused on companies with real business plans and real opportunities to create value. As such, the Warburg Pincus portfolio covered a very broad range of industries and a broad range of stages of development. Second, the firm had been willing to build a large core group of managers in contrast to the small staffs of many other venture and buyout funds. While the typical private equity fund may have eight to ten employees, Warburg Pincus employed more than 100 people globally in 1997. The firm was entirely owned by its partners, all of whom were directly involved in the company's private equity business. Third, Warburg Pincus had been extremely aggressive in raising capital; the 1980 and 1989 funds were also the largest funds ever raised to that date by private equity organizations at those dates. Indeed, the Warburg approach had proved to be extremely successful: the average annual return from 1971-1990 was over 25% for the first five Warburg funds. (**Exhibit 11** is a complete list of Warburg Pincus funds with the amount invested in each.) The funds had generated impressive returns from a diverse array of investments, including buyouts, investments to finance industry consolidations, and start-ups. (**Exhibit 12** shows the historical investments of the company.)

THE INITIAL PUBLIC OFFERING CONSIDERED

Warburg's phone call suggesting that Lynch should consider taking the company public was hardly surprising. With its proven track record, strong management, desirable products, and good earnings potential Knoll stood out as an excellent IPO candidate within Warburg Pincus's current portfolio. In addition, the timing seemed right for an offering. The private markets were continuing to build on the success of the early 1990's. (**Exhibits 13 and 14** show private equity returns and the private equity fundraising for this period.) After a downturn in the late 1980s and early 1990s, returns on venture capital investing as well as new commitments to venture capital funds dramatically increased. Similarly, investments in other private equity asset classes also took off.

The IPO market, on the other hand, was beginning to soften following a "hot" period at the end of 1996, but it seemed as if another small window might be opening up at the start of 1997. (**Exhibit 15** shows IPO market activity from 1994-1997.) The overall market had become cautious in December 1996 following Federal Reserve Chairman Alan Greenspan's comment on "irrational exuberance" which had created considerable uncertainty as to how much longer the bull market could continue its unprecedented run. (**Exhibit 16** shows general macroeconomic conditions from 1993-1997Q1.) While these patterns in IPO markets were well-known phenomena, it was not known what caused them. Some researchers believed that the pace of technological innovation created the opportunity for major new investments which ultimately led to new IPO waves. Others believed that investor sentiment in the overall market about new technologies often led investors to overestimate future prospects for IPO firms. This could potentially lead to a rash of new equity offerings as managers attempted to take advantage of this overpricing.

Whatever the cause, these waves of IPO activity often came and went without warning. For example, in 1986, 610 companies went public in the United States. Two years later, only 219 firms could manage to issue equity for the first time. In addition, those firms that were able to issue equity could only do so at lower valuations and raising substantial smaller sums of capital. The rapid opening and closing of the IPO window placed pressure on firms to consider issuing shares when the market was hot.

Advantages to Going Public

Knoll did not appear to need a public offering. Unlike many other firms issuing equity for the first time to the public, Knoll did not need to raise additional capital. The firm had performed spectacularly well since going private in 1996. Revenues and earnings had increased steadily. And while the firm was still highly levered, Knoll had substantial cash flow to pay interest and principal and did not appear to be in any danger of violating covenants on any of its outstanding debt issues.

Warburg Pincus, however, had its own motivations for wanting Knoll to go public. The investment firm had committed nearly all of the $2.8 billion in capital that it had raised in its 1994 fund. With the fund fully invested, there was increasing pressure on the company to raise additional capital. A peculiar feature of private equity fund accounting, however, potentially played into the decision. Private equity funds typically carried their investments at cost until the particular investment was either written off, had a subsequent investment by a new private equity group (at which point the private equity firm would write up the value of their investment to the new investment price), or the investment exited via an IPO or acquisition (when the investment would be written up to the exit valuation). Keeping investments at cost, while conservative from an accounting perspective, made it difficult to accurately portray the profitability of underlying companies. Firms which needed to demonstrate the value of their underlying investments, often would take firms public in order to write up the investment. By writing up the investment to the value at the IPO, the private equity funds internal rate of return would increase markedly.[3]

Going Public and Venture Capital Investors

Venture capitalists typically exited successful investments by taking them public.[4] They usually did not sell shares at the time of the IPO, but rather undertook a "lock-up" agreement with the investment banker underwriting the offering in which they promised to refrain from selling their shares for several months. Even after the lock-up expired, venture capitalists often continued to hold the shares in the company for months or even years. Once they decided to liquidate their positions, there were two alternatives. First, venture capitalists could sell the shares they held on the open market and distribute cash to limited partners. More often, venture capitalists distributed shares to each limited partner and (frequently) themselves.

A number of reasons were responsible for the preponderance of distributions in kind. First, SEC rules restricted sales by corporate insiders. Insiders, including the venture capitalist, were only allowed to sell shares each quarter up to the greater of one percent of the outstanding equity or the average weekly trading volume. The venture capital fund might typically hold a large fraction of the company's equity and selling the entire stake might take a long period of time. By distributing shares to limited partners, who were usually not considered insiders, the venture capitalist could dispose of a large block of shares more quickly.

Second, tax motivations also provided an incentive for the venture capitalist to distribute shares. If venture capitalists sold shares and distribute cash, taxable limited partners (e.g., individuals and corporations) and the venture capitalists themselves were subject to immediate capital gains taxes. These investors might prefer to postpone these taxes by receiving distributions in kind and selling the shares at a later date. These considerations would be unimportant to tax-exempt limited partners (e.g., pension funds and endowments). By distributing stock, venture capitalists provided limited partners with the flexibility to make their own decisions about selling the stock.

Third, if selling the shares had a large negative effect on prices, venture capitalists might want to distribute shares. The method of computing returns employed by limited partners and outside fund trackers (e.g., Venture Economics) used the closing price of the distributed stock on the day the distribution was declared. The actual price received when the limited partners sold their shares might be substantially lower. If prices declined after the distribution, actual returns to limited partners could be substantially less than calculated returns. Venture capitalists cared about stated returns on their funds because they used this information when they raised new funds.

Finally, the venture capitalist's compensation could be affected by distribution policy. If the venture capital fund had not returned committed capital to its limited partners, most funds distributed shares of portfolio companies in proportion to the partners' actual capital commitments (usually 99 percent to limited partners and 1 percent to general partners). By distributing overvalued shares prior to the return of committed capital, the venture capitalist moved closer to the point where general partners collect a larger share of the profits. Once committed capital had been returned, venture capitalists still had an incentive to distribute overvalued shares. They might be able to sell their portions at a high valuation before limited partners received their shares and the market discerned that a distribution had occurred.

A venture capitalist's reputational concerns might not overcome the incentive to distribute overvalued shares. First, many institutional investors and advisors also cared about stated return. They might be compensated based on how well the venture funds that they select do relative to a benchmark (calculated using the distribution price). This was particularly true if the shares were transferred immediately on receipt of the distribution to its public equity managers. Any price decline might be attributed to the public equity group. Second, certain investors might be unaware of the problem. Investors might not track stock price performance against an appropriate benchmark. Similarly, record keeping of the price at which the shares were sold was often incomplete.

Few SEC regulations covered distributions by private equity investors. Rule 16(a) stated that individuals who are affiliates of a firm, such as directors, officers, and holders of 10 percent of the company's shares, must disclose any transactions in the firm's stock on a monthly basis. Provision 16(a)-7, however, explicitly exempted distributions of securities that (i) were originally obtained from issuers and (ii) are being distributed "in good faith, in the ordinary course of business." An interpretation widely accepted within the industry was that venture capitalists distribute investments in the normal course of business, and that they did not convey any information unless the venture capitalist made an explicit recommendation to hold or sell the shares at the time. Venture capital lawyers applied the same principles when considering the applicability of Rule 10(b)-5, the most general prohibition against fraudulent activity in the purchase or sale of any security.

In the case of Knoll, it was unclear what Warburg Pincus would do after the offering. If the stock market performance was good, Warburg would likely want to return capital to their investors. If the performance was flat, then Warburg might continue to hold their shares in Knoll for sometime after the offering. Lynch wondered whether Warburg Pincus would continue to be involved in Knoll and whether that would affect the company in the long run.

Going Public and Investment Banks

In addition to the role of Warburg Pincus, Lynch began to consider which investment bank might lead the offering of Knoll shares if he decided to take the firm public. Investment bankers served an important function in the process of issuing equity to the public in an IPO. They led "road shows" where the company management and the investment bankers met with potential investors. These road shows provided an opportunity for the company to provide critical information to investors prior to the offering. During the road show, investment bankers also collected stated interest that investors might have for the firm's offering and created a book of those demands. Once the investment banker had collected potential investor demand, they priced the offering and issued securities to investors on the first day of trading. Similarly, investment bankers often provided price stabilization for several weeks following the IPO and made a market in the company's stock for after-market trading.

In addition, the investment bank usually required that the firm's management and pre-public investors agreed to refrain from selling their stock in the aftermarket for a period of time after the IPO. This agreement is usually referred to as a "lock-up". When the issuing firm and the investment bank entered into an agreement to offer securities in an IPO, they signed an underwriter agreement. These agreements typically include a covenant such as:

"The Selling Securityholders agree that, without your (the investment bank's) prior written consent, the Selling Securityholders will not, directly or indirectly, sell, offer, contract to sell, make any short sale, pledge or otherwise dispose of any shares of Common Stock or any securities convertible into or exercisable for or any rights to purchase or acquire Common Stock for a period of 180 days following the commencement of the public offering of the Stock by the Underwriters."[5]

The lock-up, which is "typically" 180 days in length, "prevents a surplus of stock hitting the market all at once." The agreement to not sell or sell-short their equity holdings was governed only by this underwriter agreement. It was not mandated by any SEC or state securities laws that regulated insider trading. Underwriter could, at their discretion, release any of the securities subject to the lock-up agreements at any time without notice.[6]

Lynch realized that an IPO also held certain advantages for Knoll. When Warburg Pincus had bought Knoll, they wanted to retain several of the top management at the company. The result was a lucrative incentive program for nearly 50 of the top officials at Knoll who received stock in the company. This stock held little value as long as Knoll remained a private company, but these members expected a large payout if the company were to be taken public. These stock options were a strong reason for senior management at Knoll to go forward with an IPO. (See **Exhibit 17** for the beneficial ownership of Knoll stock prior to the offering.)

Disadvantages to Going Public

Despite these obvious benefits, Lynch still had several reservations about the offering. In his mind, there was no immediate need for Knoll to go public. Offerings were typically seen by firms as a way to raise funds when they were unable to raise enough financing from other sources. After the restructuring, however, Knoll was performing extremely well and growing at a fast rate; raising capital was thus not a strong concern at the moment for Lynch. Another reason for firms to go public was a desire to improve the company's image and visibility. Again, this did not worry Lynch since Knoll had already built a solid reputation throughout the furniture industry.

Lynch also had reservations about the whole ordeal of taking the company public at the moment. The IPO process alone would be extremely costly and time-consuming. As he sipped coffee from his University of New Hampshire mug, Lynch considered the numerous steps that would be involved in the offering.

Knoll would first have to file an S-1 registration statement with the Securities and Exchange Commission (SEC). This document would provide facts regarding Knoll's operations, properties owned, transactions between the company and its officers/directors, management backgrounds and compensation, and risk factors for the company. Lynch was unconcerned about divulging such information to competitors; unlike other industries, such as biotech, it was unlikely to be of much use.

While the firm was undergoing regulatory review from the SEC, Lynch and other company officials would have to begin marketing the offering. This meant that they would have to distribute a preliminary prospectus known as a "red herring" to prospective investors.[7] Lynch and other top management would also have to undertake a "road show" to discuss the company's business operations and prospects with potential investors. This entailed further expenses for training and maintaining a good personal relations team to manage the flow of public information. He knew from experience that the total process could range anywhere from $150,000 to over $300,000 for an offering. On top of this, the company would have to hire an underwriter to help guide the company through the whole process and sell its securities; the usual commission for these investment banks was around 7.5-10%. There would also be expenses for annual accounting and continuous filing with the SEC.

In addition to the significant costs of the IPO, Lynch was even more worried about the amount of time that would be lost as a result of taking the company public. He figured that the IPO process alone would take nearly six months and would divert his attention away from running the company at this critical juncture when the company was just beginning to build momentum. Lynch knew that being a public company would present a significant time and financial cost in the future as well. Lynch figured that investor relations alone might take up nearly 35% of his time. This would leave less time for him to focus on the important day-to-day management of the company.

All of these concerns were heightened by Lynch's belief that there was a considerable amount of work to do improving Knoll for the future. Centralization and integration of MIS, purchasing, manufacturing, and customer service were not yet completed. Similarly, there was currently no Vice President of Manufacturing and as such, Lynch had fifteen or twenty managers reporting directly to him.

Lynch was also concerned about the fundamental transformation of his company that would come as a result of taking Knoll public. For the last year, Lynch knew who his shareholders were and those shareholders were, he thought, investing for the long run. In the public market, individuals and institutions might buy and sell his stock on a whim. Similarly, if he and his management team made a wrong move or said something that was misconstrued, he and his company might end up on the receiving end of a shareholder class action lawsuit. Finally, Lynch was concerned about the perception going public might have on his hourly employees. Many of them had seen the company go through tough times at Westinghouse and Lynch was just beginning to rebuild trust and morale.

The Decision

The choice was not easy of whether to begin the IPO process was not easy. Once begun, the process would gain momentum and become difficult to reverse. In fact, canceling the offering would reduce the chances of a successful offering in the future. As he weighed the pros and cons, Lynch thought about the strategic, financial, and fiduciary issues that an initial public offering raised. As Lynch leaned back in his office chair and pondered the future, he realized that it would be another late night.

NOTES

1 This section is based largely on Dressen, HBS No. 200-041 written by Thomas R. Piper and Jeremy Cott.

2 This section is largely based on Acme Investment Trust, HBS No. 296-042, written by Josh Lerner.

3 This phenomenon, known as "grandstanding", was documented by Paul A. Gompers, 1996, "Grandstanding in the Venture Capital Industry," *Journal of Financial Economics* 42, pp. 133-156.

4 For a discussion of venture capital distributions, see Paul A. Gompers and Josh Lerner, 1998, "Venture Capital Distributions: Short-Run and Long-Run Reactions," *Journal of Finance* 53, pp. 2161-2184.

5 Joseph Bartlett, 1995, Equity Finance: Venture Capital, Buyout, Restructurings, and Reorganizations, John Wiley, New York.

6 Ibid.

7 It is called a "red herring" since the disclaimers on the document's cover are typically printed in red ink.

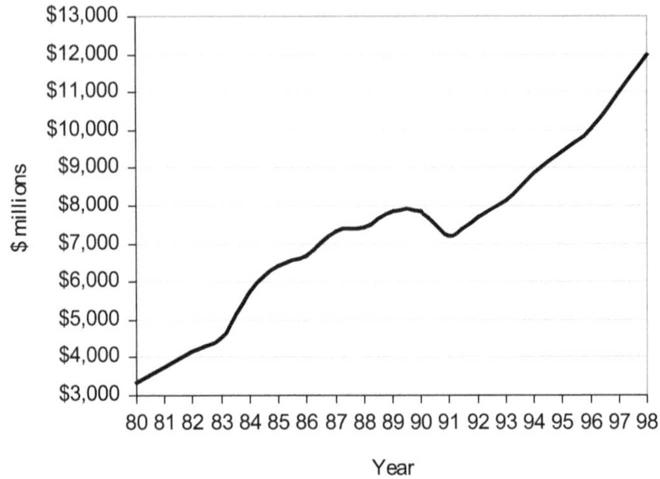

EXHIBIT 1 Office Furniture Shipments
Source: Compiled by casewriter from Merrill Lynch Analyst Reports.

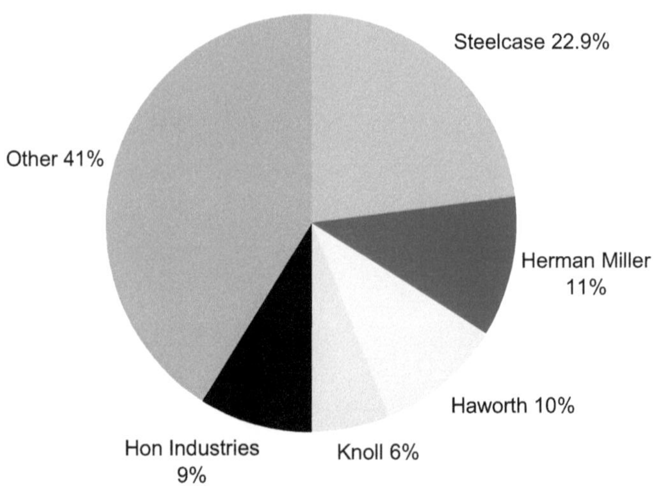

EXHIBIT 2 Market Share Breakdown
Source: Public company documents.

EXHIBIT 3 Knoll Management

Burton B. Staniar was appointed Chairman of the Board of the Company in December 1993 to effect the restructuring of the Company and restore it to profitability. Mr. Staniar served as Chief Executive Officer of the Company from December 1993 to January 1997. Prior to that time, Mr. Staniar had held a number of assignments at Westinghouse, including President of Group W Cable and Chairman and Chief Executive Officer of Westinghouse Broadcasting. Prior to joining Westinghouse in 1980, he held a number of marketing and general management positions at Colgate Palmolive and Church and Dwight Co., Inc.

John H. Lynch joined the Company as President and Vice Chairman of the Board in April 1994 and was elected Chief Executive Officer in January 1997. Prior to joining the Company, Mr. Lynch was a partner in BGI, a consulting company, and an associate dean at the Harvard Business School. Mr. Lynch is a director of Renaissance Cosmetics, Inc.

Wolfgang Billstein was recruited in November 1994 to lead the restructuring of the Company's European operations as Managing Director--Knoll Europe. A German citizen, Mr. Billstein previously worked in Europe for The Procter & Gamble Company and Benckiser GmbH, a consumer products company.

Kathleen G. Bradley was named Senior Vice President--Sales, Distribution and Customer Service in January 1996, after serving as Divisional Vice President for Knoll's southeast region since 1988. Prior to that time, Ms. Bradley was regional manager for the Company's Atlanta territory, a position to which she was promoted in 1983. She began her career with Knoll in 1979.

Andrew B. Cogan has been a director of the Company since February 1996. He has held the position of Senior Vice President--Marketing and Product Development since May 1994. Mr. Cogan has held several positions in the design and marketing group since joining the Company in 1989.

Source: Public company documents.

EXHIBIT 4 Knoll Historical Financial Performance

Knoll Income Statement	1992	1993	1994	1995	1996
Total sales	$577	$508	$563	$621	$652
Cost of goods sold	417	377	410	418	420
Gross profit	160	132	153	203	232
Selling, general & admin. exp.	166	163	167	138	153
EBIT	(6)	(31)	(14)	65	79
Corporate exp. allocated from Westinghouse	5	5	6	10	—
Interest expense	4	3	3	1	40
Other income (expense)	1	2	1	(2)	0
Pretax income (loss)	42	(44)	(52)	52	39
Net income (loss)	49	(41)	(60)	29	17

Knoll Balance Sheet Items	1992	1993	1994	1995	1996
Total assets	$726	$691	$705	$657	$675
Total interest-bearing debt	20	15	12	4	354
Preferred stock	0	0	0	0	160
Common stock	540	486	458	480	18

Knoll Cash Flow Statement	1994	1995	1996
Net income	$(60)	$29	$17
Depreciation & amortization	28	26	—
Other	(2)	0	—
Changes in working capital	18	(3)	—
Subtotal: operating cash flow	(26)	52	—
Capital expenditures	(20)	(19)	(17)
Acquisition of company from Westinghouse	0	0	(580)
Subtotal: investing cash flow	(20)	(19)	(597)
Proceeds from (repayment of) debt	(6)	(30)	348
Proceeds from (redemption of) preferred stock	0	0	160
Proceeds from (repurchase of) common stock	0	0	0
Receipts from (payments to) Westinghouse	34	(7)	61
Other	0	0	0
Subtotal: financing cash flow	28	(37)	569

EXHIBIT 4 (*continued*)

Knoll Operating Performance Percent of sales	1992	1993	1994	1995	1996
Cost of goods	73.9%	76.0%	72.8%	67.3%	64.4%
Selling, general & administrative	27.2	30.4	29.7	22.2	23.5
EBIT	(1.1)	(6.4)	(2.5)	10.5	12.1

Source: Public company documents.

EXHIBIT 5 Comparable Furniture Manufacturers (all $ in millions) (Years ended December 31)

Mity Enterprises Inc. Selected Financial Data 1993-1996

	1993	1994	1995	1996
Sales	$9.9	$13.0	$15.4	$18.7
Net income	1.8	1.9	1.9	2.5
EBITDA	2.1	2.7	3.2	3.9
Total assets	4.1	9.1	11.3	14.3
Current assets	3.2	7.8	10.0	10.8
Current liabilities	2.0	0.9	1.1	1.3
Market value of equity	NA	24.6	24.8	45.8
Total debt	0.0	0.0	0.0	0.0
Net worth	2.1	8.2	10.2	12.9
Beta	NA	NA	NA	0.78
Interest expense	0.0	0.0	0.0	0.0

(*continued*)

EXHIBIT 5 *(continued)*

Hon Industries Selected Financial Data, 1992-1996

	1992	1993	1994	1995	1996
Sales	$706.5	$780.3	$846.0	$893.1	$998.1
Net income	38.7	45.1	54.2	41.1	68.1
EBITDA	76.8	87.3	106.2	95.7	128.2
Total assets	322.7	352.4	372.6	409.5	513.5
Current assets	171.3	188.4	188.8	194.2	205.5
Current liabilities	91.8	110.8	111.1	128.9	152.6
Market value of equity	760.7	886.9	820.6	706.7	980.5
Total debt	61.4	57.7	61.0	48.9	99.7
Net worth	163.0	179.6	194.6	216.2	252.4
Beta	NA	NA	NA	NA	0.67
Interest expense	3.4	3.1	3.2	3.8	4.3

Kimball International Selected Financial Data, 1992-1996

	1992	1993	1994	1995	1996
Sales	$617.3	$722.4	$822.5	$895.9	$923.6
Net income	38.6	30.6	36.2	41.4	45.1
EBITDA	74.4	76.8	85.9	91.9	96.7
Total assets	422.0	452.7	471.4	497.1	538.2
Current assets	275.5	295.5	288.2	306.8	342.3
Current liabilities	80.8	100.1	102.2	105.0	122.0
Market value of equity	504.3	619.3	492.0	572.2	574.9
Total debt	10.8	7.3	3.6	3.1	5.8
Net worth	321.1	333.3	351.0	371.3	391.0
Beta	NA	NA	NA	NA	.61
Interest expense	1.1	1.3	0.5	0.3	0.4

(continued)

EXHIBIT 5 (*continued*)

Miller (Herman) Inc. Selected Financial Data 1992-1996

	1992	1993	1994	1995	1996
Sales	$855.7	$953.2	$1,083.1	$1,283.9	$1,495.9
Net income	22.1	40.4	4.3	45.9	74.4
EBITDA	74.8	93.3	92.7	136.5	193.2
Total assets	484.3	533.7	659.0	694.9	755.6
Current assets	207.6	228.7	297.1	334.9	385.9
Current liabilities	144.9	177.7	257.5	219.0	285.6
Market value of equity	640.7	602.5	537.1	762.6	1,645.6
Total debt	39.9	70.0	144.2	134.6	153.1
Net worth	283.9	296.3	286.9	308.1	287.1
Beta	NA	NA	NA	NA	0.49
Interest expense	2.1	1.8	6.3	7.9	8.8

Steelcase Inc. Selected Financial Data 1995-1996

	1995	1996
Sales	$2,155.9	$2,408.4
Net income	123.5	27.7
EBITDA	262.7	324.9
Total assets	1,884.5	1,922.1
Current assets	791.3	824.6
Current liabilities	315.7	350.0
Market value of equity	NA	NA
Total debt	0.0	0.0
Net worth	1,393.6	1,380.0
Beta	NA	0.65
Interest expense	1.5	2.1

(*continued*)

EXHIBIT 5 *(continued)*

Tab Products Selected Financial Data, 1992-1996

	1992	1993	1994	1995	1996
Sales	$127.0	$140.1	$150.0	$152.70	$154.45
Net income	1.057	2.176	1.219	2.761	3.761
EBITDA	8.220	9.583	7.821	10.046	11.632
Total assets	73.04	86.16	81.65	79.127	80.699
Current assets	49.08	56.13	51.33	48.715	51.405
Current liabilities	17.03	22.70	21.25	21.291	22.942
Market value of equity	53.24	47.07	30.93	36.39	46.562
Total debt	16.74	24.40	22.05	17.954	14.141
Net worth	37.62	38.65	39.83	41.462	44.527
Beta	NA	NA	NA	NA	0.385

Source: Compiled by casewriter from Compustat.

EXHIBIT 6 Knoll Market Share (by Product Category)

Product Type	U.S. Market Size	% of U.S. Market	% of Knoll Sales	Knoll Share of U.S. Market
Office systems	$3.4	34.1%	66.6%	11.2%
Seating	2.6	25.4	8.9	2.0
Storage	1.4	14.1	5.3	2.1
Desks/Casegoods	1.6	16.4	3.8	1.2
Tables	0.7	6.6	1.4	1.8

Knoll 1996 Market Share 5.8%

Source: Public company documents.

EXHIBIT 7 Knoll Pro Forma Earnings ($ millions except EPS)

	1997E	1998E	1999E	2000E	2001E
Net sales	$742	$804	$884	$973	$1,070
Cost of goods sold	(465)	(505)	(555)	(611)	(672)
Gross profit	277	299	329	362	398
Margin %	37.3%	37.2%	37.2%	37.2%	37.2%
Operating expenses	(167)	(181)	(197)	(215)	(234)
As % of sales	22.6%	22.6%	22.3%	22.1%	21.9%
EBIT	109	118	132	147	164
Margin %	14.7%	14.6%	14.9%	15.1%	15.3%
Interest expense	(25)	(21)	(18)	(16)	(15)
Other, net	(0)	0	0	1	2
Pretax income	84	96	114	131	151
Margin %	11.3%	12.0%	12.9%	13.5%	14.1%
Taxes	(35)	(41)	(48)	(55)	(63)
Tax rate	42.0%	42.0%	42.0%	42.0%	42.0%
Net income	48.8	55.9	66.0	76.1	87.4
EPS	1.113	1.30	1.53	1.77	2.03
% Change:					
Sales	14%	8%	10%	10%	10%
EBIT	39	8	12	11	11
Pretax income	61	15	18	15	15
Net income	61	15	18	15	15
EPS	61	15	18	15	15

Source: Compiled by casewriter from Morgan Stanley Dean Witter Equity Research Estimates.

EXHIBIT 8 Knoll Cash Flow Pro Formas ($ in millions)

	1997E	1998E	1999E	2000E	2001E
Sources :					
Net income	$48	$56	$66	$76	$87
Depreciation & amortization	36	39	42	44	44
Noncash restructuring charges	0	0	0	0	0
Amortization of goodwill & financing fees	0	0	0	0	0
Asset sales proceeds	0	0	0	0	0
Other, net	1	0	0	0	0
Total sources	85	95	108	120	131
Uses:					
Capital expenditures	(30)	(30)	(30)	(30)	(30)
Total uses	(30)	(30)	(30)	(30)	(30)
Sources – uses	55	65	78	90	101
Total change in working capital	(12)	(8)	(10)	(10)	(10)
Changes in Financing:					
Borrowing of long-term debt	0	0	0	0	0
Borrowing (repayment) of short-term debt	18	0	0	0	0
Repayment of long-term debt	(43)	(55)	(55)	(55)	(55)
Net receipts from (payments to) parent company	0	0	0	0	0
Effect of foreign exchange	0	0	0	0	0
Equity offering	136	0	0	0	0
Redemption of preferred stock	(80)				
Senior subordinated note paydown	(58)				
Premium on note paydown	(6)				
Fees & expenses (@ 6% gross spread)	(11)				
Total change in financing	(43)	(55)	(55)	(55)	(55)
Change in cash	0	2	13	25	36
Beginning cash	9	9	11	24	49
Ending cash	9	11	24	49	85

Source: Compiled by casewriter from Morgan Stanley Dean Witter Equity Research Estimates.

EXHIBIT 9 Knoll Balance Sheet Item Pro Formas ($ in millions)

	1997E	1998E	1999E	2000E	2001E
Selected Balance Sheet Items					
Debt	$253	$198	$143	$88	$33
Equity	265	321	387	463	551
Total capitalization	519	520	531	552	584
Debt / equity	95%	62%	37%	19%	6%
Net debt / equity	92	58	31	8	(9)
Debt / capital	49	38	27	16	6
Return on equity	18	17	17	16	16
Return on capital	9	11	13	14	16

Source: Compiled by casewriter from Morgan Stanley Dean Witter Equity Research Estimates.

EXHIBIT 10 Warburg Pincus Management on Knoll Board of Directors

Jeffrey A. Harris, a director of the Company since February 1996, has been a General Partner of Warburg, Pincus & Co., a private investment firm ("Warburg, Pincus"), and a Member and Managing Director of E.M. Warburg, Pincus & Co., LLC ("E.M. Warburg") and its predecessors since 1988, where he has been employed since 1983. Mr. Harris is a director of Newfield Exploration Company, Comcast UK Cable Partners Limited, Industri-Matematik International Corp., ECsoft Group plc and several privately held companies.

Sidney Lapidus, a director of the Company since February 1996, has been a General Partner of Warburg, Pincus and a Member and Managing Director of E.M. Warburg and its predecessors since January 1982, where he has been employed since 1967. Mr. Lapidus is currently a director of Pacific Greystone Corporation, Caribiner International, Inc., Grubb and Ellis Company, Journal Register Company and Panavision Inc., as well as several privately held companies.

Kewsong Lee, a director of the Company since February 1996, has been a General Partner of Warburg, Pincus and a Member and Managing Director of E.M. Warburg and its predecessors since January 1997. From January 1995 to January 1997, Mr. Lee was Vice President of Warburg,

EXHIBIT 10 (*continued*)

Pincus Ventures, Inc. From 1992 to 1995, Mr. Lee was an associate at E.M. Warburg and prior to that had been a consultant at McKinsey & Company, Inc. since 1990. Mr. Lee is currently a director of RenaissanceRe Holdings Ltd. and several privately held companies.

John L. Vogelstein, a director of the Company since February 1996, is a General Partner of Warburg, Pincus, and has served since 1982 as Vice Chairman, and since 1994 as President, of E. M. Warburg and its predecessors, where he has been employed since 1967. Mr. Vogelstein is currently a director of ADVO Inc., Aegis Group plc., Golden Books Family Entertainment, Inc., Journal Register Company, LCI International, Inc., Mattel, Inc., Value Health, Inc., Vanstar Corporation and several privately held companies.

Source: Company Documents.

EXHIBIT 11 Warburg Pincus Funds

Fund Name	Amount (MM)	Date Closed
EMW Venture Inc.	US $ 41.50	1/1/71
WP Assoc.	US $ 101.00	1/1/80
WP Cap. Part.	US $ 341.00	1/1/83
WP Cap. Co.	US $ 1,175.00	1/1/86
WP Investors	US $ 1,775.00	1/1/89
WP Ventures	US $ 2,800.00	1/1/94

Source: Compiled by casewriter from VentureOne.

EXHIBIT 12 Warburg Pincus Investment History

	# of Companies	% of Total
Business Statuses		
Private	59	40%
Public	48	32%
Acquired	20	13%
Chapter 11	2	1%
Out of business	17	11%
Undetermined	3	2%
	149	100%
Industries		
Information technology		
Communication	13	9%
Electronics	4	3%
Semiconductors	5	3%
Software	28	19%
Information services	12	8%
Healthcare		
Healthcare services	11	7%
Medical IS	6	4%
Biopharmaceuticals	13	9%
Medical devices	15	10%
Retail & Cons/Bus Prod/Serv		
Retailers	3	2%
Cons/Bus products	3	2%
Cons/Bus products	29	19%
Other		
Energy	3	2%
Adv spec mat & chem	1	1%
Other companies	3	2%
	149	100%
Round Classes:		
Seed round	7	3%
First round	74	33%
Second round	51	23%
Later stage	59	26%
Restart	5	2%
Buyout	4	2%
Public investment	5	2%
Secondary transaction	1	0%
Debt / non-equity	4	2%
Non-VC	13	6%
Private equity	3	1%
	226	100%

Source: Compiled by casewriter from VentureOne.

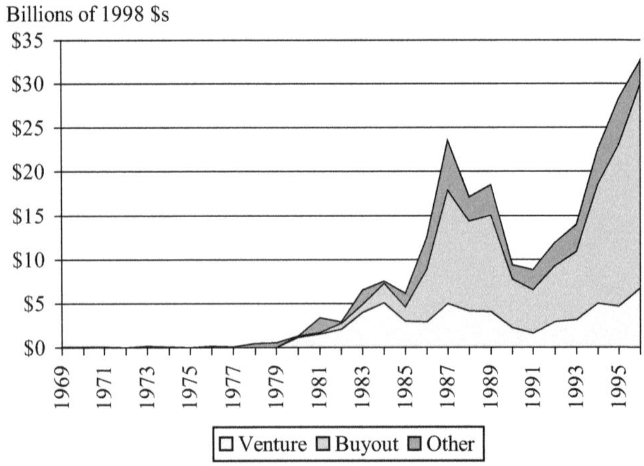

EXHIBIT 13 Venture Capital Fundraising
Source: Compiled by casewriter from Venture Economics and Asset Alternatives.

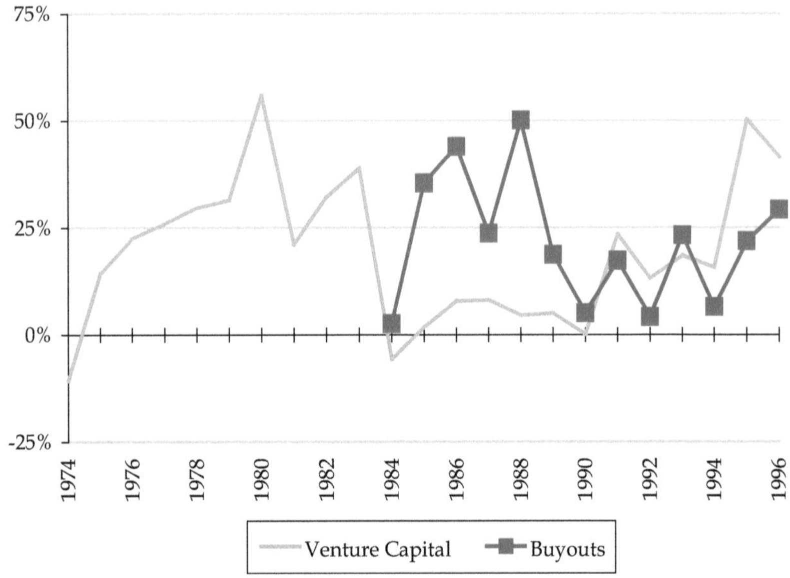

EXHIBIT 14 Venture Capital and Buyout Returns
Source: Compiled by casewriter from Venture Economics.

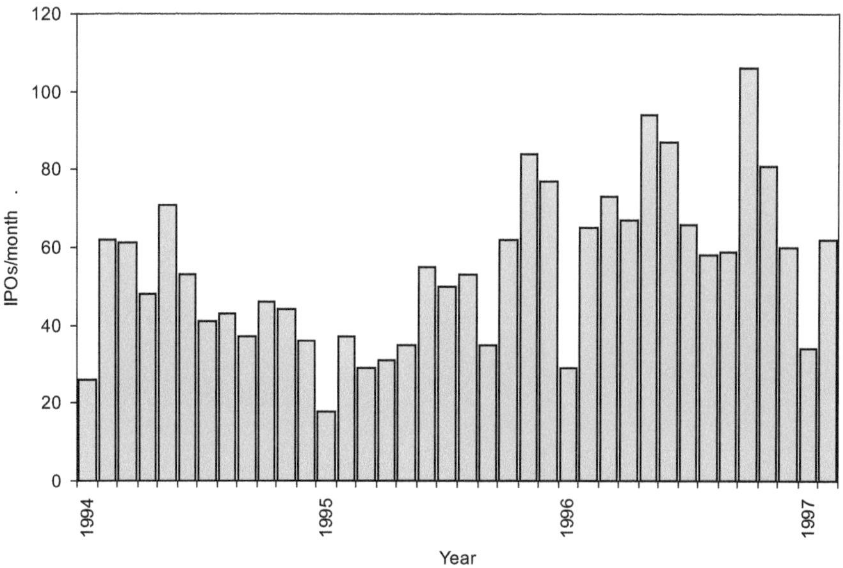

EXHIBIT 15 IPO Market Activity, 1994-1997
Source: Compiled by casewriter from http://bear.cba.ufl.edu/ritter/ipoall.htm

EXHIBIT 16 Macroeconomic Conditions

	Q3 Y94	Q4 Y94	Q1 Y95	Q2 Y95	Q3 Y95	Q4 Y95	Q1 Y96	Q2 Y96	Q3 Y96	Q4 Y96	Q1 Y97
Moody's corporate yields (A rated)	8.73	8.76	8.32	7.59	7.52	7.03	7.74	7.86	7.83	7.59	7.96
Moody's corporate yields (AA rated)	8.61	8.65	8.23	7.47	7.41	6.89	7.59	7.71	7.71	7.47	7.91
Moody's corporate yields (AAA rated)	8.5	8.49	8.13	7.35	7.27	6.71	7.42	7.54	7.54	7.27	7.71
Moody's corporate yields (BAA rated)	9.12	9.14	8.69	7.95	7.88	7.38	8.12	8.24	8.22	7.97	8.32
Moody's corporate yields (Composite)	8.74	8.76	8.34	7.59	7.52	7.00	7.72	7.84	7.83	7.58	7.98
Inflation (%)	2.539	2.664	2.716	2.694	2.406	2.324	2.503	2.687	2.733	2.909	2.434
Consumer price index	1.494	1.503	1.513	1.525	1.532	1.541	1.556	1.567	1.579	1.592	1.599
Unemployment rate	5.9	5.4	5.4	5.6	5.7	5.6	5.5	5.3	5.2	5.3	5.2
T-Bill (1 Month)	4.430	3.660	5.700	5.240	5.280	3.480	5.130	4.750	4.930	4.830	5.140
T-Bill (2 Month)	4.590	4.930	5.720	5.410	5.270	4.680	5.050	4.960	4.950	4.950	5.210
T-Bill (3 Month)	4.660	5.540	5.700	5.440	5.240	4.940	5.010	5.040	4.910	5.040	5.200
T-Bill (6 Month)	5.220	6.220	5.850	5.380	5.330	4.950	5.000	5.170	5.060	5.100	5.330
T-Bill (12 Month)	5.620	6.750	6.050	5.330	5.330	4.880	5.130	5.390	5.390	5.260	5.680

Prime rate	7.750	8.500	9.000	9.000	8.750	8.650	8.250	8.250	8.250	8.250	8.300
Gov't Bond (5 Year)	7.280	7.830	7.080	5.980	6.010	5.380	6.100	6.470	6.460	6.210	6.770
Gov't Bond (10 Year)	7.620	7.840	7.200	6.210	6.170	5.580	6.340	6.730	6.720	6.430	6.920
Gov't Bond (30 Year)	7.820	7.890	7.440	6.630	6.490	5.960	6.670	6.900	6.930	6.650	7.100
Current GDP ($ Bil)	6629.5	6688.6	6703.7	6708.8	6759.2	6796.50	6826.4	6926.0	6943.8	7017.4	7101.6
Real GDP ($ Bil)	6629.5	6688.6	6703.7	6708.8	6759.2	6796.5	6826.4	6926.0	6943.8	7017.4	7101.6
Wilshire 5000	4605.8	4540.6	4920.4	5348.8	5806.6	6057.2	6365.9	6612.8	6765.7	7198.3	7213.5
S&P 500	462.7	459.3	500.7	544.8	584.4	615.9	645.5	670.6	687.3	740.7	757.1
Hambrecht & Quist	1241.5	1337.3	1498.2	1686.6	2112.1	2134.9	2253.4	2406.7	2539.0	2376.3	2056.7

Source: Compiled by casewriter from Citibase.

EXHIBIT 17 Knoll Ownership

Name	Shares of Series A Preferred	Percent	Shares of Stock	Percent
Warburg, Pincus Ventures, L.P.	1,469,081	91.6%	2,884,351	66.0%
NationsBanc Investment Corp.	79,950	5.0%	156,972	3.6%
Burton B. Stanier [a]	20,507	1.3%	416,995	9.5%
John H. Lynch[a]	20,507	1.3%	416,995	9.5%
Wofgang Billstein [a b]	320	*	628	*
Kathleen G. Bradley [a b]	640	*	38,929	*
Andrew B. Cogan [a]	3,998	*	158,541	3.6%
All current directors & executive officers as a group (14 persons)	1,520,969	94.9%	3,607,829	82.5%

* Less than 1%

Source: Public company documents.

[a] Excludes 565,098, 565,098, 0, 226,039, 150,692 and 2,015,514 restricted shares of Common Stock for Messrs. Staniar, Lynch, Billstein and Cogan, Ms. Bradley and all current directors and executive officers as a group, respectively, which have not yet vested.

[b] Does not include options to purchase 376,731 and 188,365 shares of Common Stock held by Mr. Billstein and Ms. Bradley, respectively, which vest at a rate of 20% per year beginning March 1998.

CHAPTER 7.4

Globant: Going Public

Paul Gompers and Natee Amornsiripanitch

"Happy new year" said Francisco Alvarez-Demalde, founding partner of Riverwood Capital, as he lowered his desk phone's handset onto its resting place. It was the first day of 2013 and the end of another conference call with the other founding partners of Riverwood. The main discussion was about the firm's investment in Globant. Riverwood first invested in Globant, an offshore IT services company in Argentina, in 2007. From there, Riverwood made two follow-on investments in 2008 and 2011. The investment had done very well over its 5-year life span and, despite the recent sale of a minority stake to WPP, it was time to find a more substantial exit opportunity. One of the main questions Riverwood was contemplating was whether to take Globant public or to pursue a sale of Riverwood's holdings to another investor.

Back in 2007, Riverwood had high hopes for Globant. The firm aimed to grow Globant from a leading IT service and outsourcing company in Latin America into a global leader in software creation with a focus on emerging technologies. After almost 6 years, Riverwood was very fortunate that the company had been able to achieve this goal and was now considering taking Globant public. In addition to providing an avenue for Riverwood to exit its investment, an IPO would increase Globant's visibility to existing and potential customers and partners, serve as a large marketing opportunity, and give the company access to capital to fund both organic and inorganic expansion initiatives. However, the IPO process and execution were daunting tasks and required a long-term commitment from both Riverwood and Globant to ensure a successful outcome. Alvarez-Demalde rubbed his forehead as he considered the things that needed to be done in order to prepare Globant to become a public company. Perhaps even more worrisome, were the risks that Riverwood would be taking on as it continued to hold on to Globant's stock after the IPO. Given the recent strong performance of financial assets, the world could very well

Globant: Going Public
by PAUL GOMPERS, NATEE AMORNSIRIPANITCH, case number 9-215-021 Rev. APRIL 13, 2015

be heading for another market downturn. On the other hand, a sale to another financial or strategic investor would be much easier. Riverwood would exit the investment completely and would potentially get a higher price per share than from an IPO. Despite these risks, Riverwood was still extremely confident in Globant's founders, management team, and future growth prospects as a standalone business. If Globant continued to perform well, Riverwood would be giving up significant upside by not taking part in Globant's IPO. As the pros and cons of each choice circled in his mind, Alvarez-Demalde swiveled his leather chair around and peered over the New York City skyline, in search for some clear thinking.

RIVERWOOD CAPITAL

Riverwood Capital was a private equity firm that was founded in 2007 by six partners with backgrounds in private equity investment, investment banking, operations, and financial management. Each founder was experienced in the technology sector in North America and Latin America (See **Exhibit 1** for Riverwood's founding partners' experience.) The firm had offices in Menlo Park, New York, and Sao Paulo. Riverwood mainly invested in middle market technology companies in the United States and Latin America. A smaller percentage of Riverwood's investments were in other emerging markets. Within the technology sector, Riverwood invested in semiconductors, hardware, consumer electronics, consumer internet, software, and IT services companies. More generally, Riverwood aimed to invest in technology companies with high growth potential and a need to scale.

Riverwood's strategy was to add value by scaling these businesses through customer base growth, geographical and product expansion, and business process improvement. The firm leveraged the founding partners' backgrounds in finance and operations to accelerate growth of middle market firms into global leaders in their respective businesses. Riverwood did not typically use leverage in its investments. A typical investment ranged from US$25 million to US$100 million and had a time horizon between three and seven years.

GLOBANT

Globant was founded in Buenos Aires in 2003 with only US$5,000 contributed by four founders. The founders had backgrounds and experience in IT work at leading technology companies in Latin America, the United States, and the United Kingdom (See **Exhibit 2** for Globant's founders' experience). The founders' goal was to create a leading offshore IT services company based in Latin America that would also provide world-class career opportunities for IT professionals in the region. They saw an opportunity to make Latin America into a key player in offshore IT services along with India. With regards to clients in the United States, Latin America had several advantages over India. These advantages included cultural affinity, similar time zone, high quality human capital, and large numbers of emerging technologies experts. Given Argentina's currency devaluation in 2002 and the country's reputation for programming talent, an Argentinian offshore IT services company could offer higher quality services for certain projects at a comparable, or even better price, than its competitors in India could.

Globant primarily provided innovative software solutions for large companies that relied on software to connect with their customers. In the beginning, Globant grew its client base through referrals from former colleagues and past clients. Just one year after opening its doors, Globant's sales reached US$3 million and the company managed to acquire a high-profile client, Lastminute.com. It was a travel website based in the United Kingdom. After this first break, Globant was able to build its brand and attract more high-profile clients and IT talent. It was not long until other blue-chip clients came knocking on Globant's doors. By 2006, Globant was serving Coca-Cola, Banco Santander, Accenture, and EMC. With each big client that it acquired, Globant developed expertise in particular areas of software solutions such as open source software and IT infrastructure. These accumulated experiences allowed Globant to further differentiate itself from its competitors. In that same year, to accommodate growing demands from its clients, Globant opened a software development office in Tandil, Argentina.

Another key moment in Globant's history was when Google hired the company to be its first ever external provider of software product development services. With Google, Globant worked on large projects such as the AdWords online-advertising system, Google Checkout, and YouTube. This engagement attracted significant attention, new clients, and new hires. In addition, Globant became familiar with Google's various technologies, which were considered to be innovative and cutting-edge.

From the end of 2006 to the end of 2012, Globant experienced strong growth in sales and profitability. Net sales increased from US$11.4 million to US$128.8 million, which was an average compounded annual growth rate of 49.7%. Throughout this period, Globant maintained a healthy gross profit margin of approximately 40%. With constant margin and growing sales, EBITDA grew from US$1.8 million to US$17.0 million, which was an average compounded annual growth rate of 45.4% (See **Exhibit 3** for Globant's past performance). Globant owed its success to its unique expertise and services. With time, Globant evolved from a leading Latin American offshore IT services company into a global leader in software creation and emerging technologies. In the U.S. market, there were only several comparable public companies (See **Exhibits** 4 and 5).

OFFSHORE IT SERVICES INDUSTRY

Offshore IT services began in the year 2000 during the internet business boom in the United States. American companies felt the need to establish their business presence on the World Wide Web. Most companies did not have internal capabilities to undertake this task and so they began outsourcing this work to domestic companies that specialized in this area. With help from the Indian government, India became a hub for offshore IT services by having a strong telecom infrastructure, a large pool of technology professionals, and low-cost labor. Other emerging hubs were Ireland and Israel, which also grew to meet the ever-growing demand from the United States.

"Outsourcing 1.0" was purely a competition on price and quality. Clients remained satisfied as long as their outsourcing firm could complete the assigned tasks at a reasonable price. However, the offshore IT services industry began to develop a new model. "Outsourcing 2.0" turned to the outsourcing firm's scalability to improve profit margin and business impact. Firms like Globant accomplished this by using open source solutions, learning from users, adapting the product frequently, and recycling code and know-how from one client to the next. These methods allowed outsourcing firms to add more value by improving its product quality, cutting turnaround time, and developing expertise in niche areas.

In 2006, the global offshore IT services industry was a US$18.9 billion business. The United States alone contributed US$13.8 billion or approximately 73% of the global industry. Through 2012, the industry continued to experience a robust growth rate, with the exception of 2009. By the end of 2012, the industry grew to be US$46.3 billion. The United States remained a significant portion of the pie. The main driver behind this growth was spending in application outsourcing. IDC forecasted that the industry would continue to experience strong growth rates throughout 2016 (See **Exhibit 6** for offshore IT services spending data).

RIVERWOOD INVESTS IN GLOBANT

Riverwood had been acquainted with the founders of Globant for several years. After Globant opened its doors for business, Riverwood tracked the company's performance and was impressed by Globant's high growth rate and profitability. Globant was an attractive investment target because, by 2007, it had already acquired many blue-chip clients and the company was emerging as a leader in offshore IT services in Latin America. Riverwood believed Globant had some meaningful advantages over the competition and saw an opportunity to invest fairly early into Globant and grow it into a global leader in offshore IT services and software development. From a macro perspective, the outlook for the global offshore IT services industry, especially software development services, was very robust. Furthermore, by 2007, several private equity firms already expressed interest in making an investment in Globant and strategic acquirers were already looking to buy a major stake.

In the middle of 2007, Riverwood purchased ~26% of Globant for US$7.8 million. The shares had a 1.0x liquidation preference, various standard minority protections, and a strong set of veto rights over major corporate decisions. Globant's pre-money valuation was US$28 million. Riverwood purchased shares from the founders and angel investors who had provided some of Globant's early funding and also capitalized the company. The prior relationship between Riverwood's founding partners and Globant's founders helped Riverwood win the deal. Riverwood was also an attractive partner for Globant because they proposed a minority investment instead of a control transaction. Riverwood's investment thesis was for Globant to scale into a global leader in offshore IT services by improving business processes, scaling human capital, growing the customer base, developing a more professional management team, establishing professional governance and a strong board of directors, and developing specific expertise to increase competitive advantage.

FOLLOW-ON INVESTMENTS IN GLOBANT

After the initial investment, Globant continued to experience strong top-line and bottom-line growth. Between 2006 and 2007, Globant's net sales grew from US$11.4 million to US$22.8 million and EBITDA grew from US$1.8 million to US$3.4 million. Globant's net sales reached $128.8 million by 2012. One of the most important factors that contributed to Globant's high growth rate was the development of specific and differentiated expertise. A major trend in the IT services industry was that clients, mostly large companies, needed to rely more and more on software to interact with customers and specific expertise in consumer software design and emerging technologies was highly sought after in offshore IT services companies. Over time, Globant developed "studios" or areas of expertise to capitalize on these emerging technology trends. Some of these trends included the digitalization of the global economy across every industry vertical, the consumerization of enterprise software, the need for constant improvement in design and user interface, the growth in digital and mobile applications, the use of big data to understand consumers, the development of cloud computing and the internet of things, the rise of gamification, and more.

In late 2008, Riverwood made a follow-on investment of US$3 million and increased its stake to ~29% and also invited FTV Capital to invest in Globant. FTV Capital purchased ~19% of Globant for US$10 million. In addition to providing some capital into the business, both Riverwood and FTV Capital also acquired shares from the founders and the remaining angel investors who were not bought out completely in the first round. The funds that went into the company were intended to finance acquisitions and fund working capital as the business scaled.

Riverwood's choice to invite FTV Capital to invest was a strategic one. FTV Capital was a private equity firm that has strategic relationships with various financial institutions, e.g. banks and insurance companies. With FTV Capital as a major shareholder, Globant was able to increase its footprint in the finance vertical through FTV's network and guidance.

At this point, Globant was not only growing organically, but also through acquisitions. In 2008, Globant acquired Accendra to deepen its expertise in Microsoft Technologies as well as Openware to deepen its expertise in infrastructure services. The Riverwood team helped Globant develop and execute M&A strategies and processes. Globant continued to acquire smaller technology firms either for their specific technical expertise, geographic footprint, or strategic customer base.

Finally, early in 2011, Riverwood and FTV Capital made their last round of investment in Globant. Riverwood invested US$10 million to increase its holdings to ~39% and FTV invested US$5 million to increase its stake to ~24%.

WPP'S INVESTMENT

WPP plc was a British multinational advertising and public relations company. It was headquartered in London, England. By revenue, it was the largest advertising company in the world. It owned some of the most prominent advertising agencies, public relations firms, and market research firms. As the advertising business shifted towards digital marketing and Globant rose to prominence, some of WPP's subsidiaries became Globant's clients.

In December 2012, in an effort for Riverwood and FTV Capital to exit part of their investments and in order to bring a strategic partner to the company, WPP was offered the opportunity to invest in Globant. As a strategic buyer, WPP acquired ~20% of Globant's stock, purchasing the stake dividedly from every shareholder. The total investment amount was US$73.2 million and Globant's equity was valued at US$360 million. This transaction decreased Rivewood's and FTV Capital's stakes to ~31% and ~19% respectively (See **Exhibit** 7 for Globant'sownership structure.)

As an advertising giant, WPP acquired a minority stake in Globant to start developing a more strategic relationship with the company. WPP, together with its subsidiaries, lacked some of the development capabilities that Globant specialized in, and the WPP team saw the investment as an opportunity to improve its value proposition to customers. WPP saw that it could combine Globant's expertise in consumer software development with its marketing capabilities to effectively execute digital campaigns and develop a comprehensive marketing strategy for its clients. This investment and partnership also helped Globant. Globant was able to grow its customer base through WPP's subsidiaries and the clients of those subsidiaries.

THE EXIT CHOICE

With the arrival of 2013, Riverwood's investment in Globant seemed to be ripe for an exit. Riverwood had been invested in the company for more than 5 years. Globant was among the first and most successful of Riverwood's initial investments in Latin America. Exiting at an attractive return would help develop Riverwood's franchise as a major player in the Latin American private equity landscape. Globant grew from a fledgling offshore IT services company into a world leader in the industry. In that time, many financial and strategic buyers had expressed interest in acquiring stakes in the company. Furthermore, the world M&A market and IPO activity had started to recover from the trough in 2008 (See **Exhibits 8** and **9** for world M&A and IPO trends). With respect to Globant, there were several comparable M&A transactions in 2012 (See **Exhibits 10** and **11**). The U.S. IPO market seemed ripe for a stock like Globant because Investors' appetite for emerging technology stocks, such as cloud computing and social media, and foreign stocks was on the rise. Lastly, the U.S. government bond yield curve was upward-sloping, which indicated future economic growth (See **Exhibit 12**), and underwriting fees were on a downward trend (See **Exhibits 13, 14,** and **15** for U.S. IPO data).

An initial public offering would necessitate Riverwood to monetize its investment over time, thereby subjecting itself to Globant's future performance, either to the benefit or to the detriment. The firm had confidence in Globant's founders and management team and believed that Globant could continue to grow as a standalone business. If Riverwood's forecasts were correct, the firm stood to gain even better return on its investment (See **Exhibit 16** for Globant's financial forecasts from J.P. Morgan research as of August 2014). Furthermore, an IPO would help Globant increase its visibility to existing and potential customers and partners, would serve as a large marketing opportunity both internally and externally, and would give the company access to capital to fund both organic and inorganic expansion initiatives. These factors, in isolation, summed to a brighter future for Globant and even greater profits for Riverwood.

However, an IPO had many disadvantages. First, an IPO would typically be discounted from the price that the underwriters believed was the fully distributed valuation of the company. Underwriters typically priced the shares so that there would be a price increase of approximately 10%-20% during the first few days of trading. This represented real capital that the company was leaving on the table. Second, Riverwood would be subject to a 180-day lock-up period imposed by the underwriters that would be extended by 45 more days if there was an earnings announcement close to the end of that 180-day window. Riverwood would be less concerned about the offer price and more concerned about the direction that the stock price would move over this period of time. Third, given Riverwood's large stake, it would take even more time for Riverwood to sell all of its holdings to the public market. An insider such as Riverwood would be subject to black-out periods and, even in normal times, could not sell a large portion of its holdings at once in the open market. Exiting its ownership after an IPO would take significant time and potentially important strategic choices. For example, should Riverwood sell its stake on the open market, or should it "slice up" its equity stake and distribute shares back to its investors for them to sell on their own respective timetables? Furthermore, as Riverwood would try to sell its shares over the following few years, it would be faced with risks that come with holding a publicly-traded stock. These risks would include market risk and macroeconomic risk. Finally, an IPO was a long and costly process. It would take a lot of work before Globant was ready to become a publicly-traded company and Riverwood would need to contribute significant resources to help Globant through the process.

On the other hand, a sale to a financial or a strategic buyer would give Riverwood a higher short-run return and a return that was locked in once the transaction closed. Riverwood would need to decide whether Globant should pursue financial buyers, strategic buyers, or both. A strategic buyer tended to offer a higher price because it could benefit from the synergies created between Globant and its existing businesses. At the same time, a strategic buyer would likely turn Globant into a department in its business and potentially limit management from enjoying any significant upside that might accrue in the future. Theoretically speaking, if management wanted to preserve such upside, it would likely have a strong preference for selling to another private equity firm. In addition, from Riverwood's perspective, pursuing a financial buyer might allow them to roll-over a portion of their equity into the new firm and allow them to participate in the future value creation at Globant if desired.

EXECUTING AN EXIT

Among the first decisions Riverwood and Globant would have to make was to choose bankers. Given the success of Globant, there would be many options from which to choose. Bankers would guide Globant through the IPO process, develop interest for research coverage, and contribute to market-making activity for the stock. The fees, however, were generally virtually identical across banks. Alvarez-Demalde wondered what criteria he should use to narrow the choice.

If Riverwood decided to go ahead with the IPO, then it had to choose which stock exchange on which to list. There was the possibility of a local listing in Latin America, or a dual listing including the United States. Most of Globant's clients were in the United States and the United Kingdom. Additionally, given that Globant was a software company, having sophisticated sell-side analysts covering its stock and institutional investors interested in holding its stock would help the offering succeed. Few analysts in Latin America understood the software sector. Investors in the U.S. were also more comfortable holding technology stocks for a longer period of time.

THE DECISION

The choice was a difficult one. Once Globant committed to an IPO, it would be costly to reverse the process. Initiating the process would generate an expectation from every constituency in the company. Furthermore, as the IPO date drew closer, the more difficult it would be to cancel the offering without damaging the public's perception of Globant. If Riverwood decided to take Globant public, which stock exchange was the ideal exchange for Globant's stocks? Furthermore, should Globant also list its stocks in Latin America? The city was waking up. Dark windows flickered as offices came back to life. Alvarez-Demalde realized that time waited for no one and that he best figure out this dilemma soon.

EXHIBIT 1 Riverwood's Founding Partners' Biographies

Michael Marks was an experienced private equity professional and corporate manager. Before founding Riverwood, he was a Partner at Kohlberg Kravis Roberts & Co. Prior to his role at KKR, he served as CEO of Flextronics International Ltd. for 13 years. Mr. Marks received an M.B.A. from Harvard Business School and a B.A. and M.A. from Oberlin College.

Chris Varelas had background in investment banking. Before founding Riverwood, he was the Global Head of Technology, Media, and Telecom Investment Banking at Citigroup Global Markets. In addition, he was also Head of Citi's National Investment Banking. Mr. Varelas earned an M.B.A. from the Wharton School of Business and a B.A. from Occidental College in Los Angeles.

Francisco Alvarez-Demalde was an experienced investment professional. Before starting Riverwood, he was an investment executive at Eton Park Capital Management, where he focused on private equity investments in Latin America. Prior to Eton Partk, he served as an investment executive at KKR, where he focused on LBOs in the Technology industry. Before KKR, he was an investment banker at Goldman, Sachs & Co. Mr. Alvarez-Demalde earned a Licentiate in Economics from San Andres University.

Tom Smach was an experienced CFO. Prior to Riverwood, he served as the CFO of Flextronics International Ltd. He oversaw acquisitions, spinoffs, and capital raising activities at the company. Mr. Smach received his B.Sc. in Accounting from State University of New York.

Nicholas Brathwaite had deep experience in operations of technology companies. From 1996 to 2007, he served as the CTO at Flextronics International Ltd. Prior to Flextronics, he was a founding member of nChip, where he was mainly responsible for development of the industry-leading advanced multi-chip module assembly process. Mr. Brathwaite received a M.Sc. Degree in Polymer Science Engineering from the University of Water and a B.Sc. Degree in Applied Chemistry from McMaster University.

Jeff Parks had background in private equity investment. He was an investment executive at KKR, where he focused on private equity investments in the technology sector. Prior to KKR, he was an investment professional in the Principal Opportunities Fund at Oaktree Capital Management. He started his career as an investment banker at UBS. He received his B.A. in Economics and Mathematics from Pomona College.

Source: Riverwood Capital LLC's Website www.riverwoodcapital.com, accessed October 2014.

EXHIBIT 2 Globant Founders' Biographies

Martin Migoya, CEO, was a serial entrepreneur and had deep experience in the technology sector. He worked in the technology industry for more than 18 years. Roles included Business Manager at Origin HV in Holland and Project Manager at Repsol-YPF. He earned his B.A. in Electronic Engineering from La Plata University and his M.B.A. from CEMA University.

Martin Umaran, head of M&A and Chief of Staff, was responsible for the company's strategic planning, business management, process improvement, and M&A activities. Before Globant, Mr. Umaran completed IT projects for Santander Bank, Caja de Ahorro y Seguros, YPF Ecuador, and various Latin American governments. He earned a B.A. in Mechanical Engineering from La Plata University and a M.B.A. from IDEA University.

Guibert Englebienne, CTO, led the Premier League, which was a group of technology gurus within Globant that was responsible for developing new disruptive technology for customers and Globant Labs. He was the main driver behind Globant's transformation into an expert in cutting edge practices such as social network, videogames, and mobile.

Nestor Nocetti, EVP of Corporate Affairs, was in charge of Globant's relationship with governments and chambers around the world. Prior to Globant, he worked on several projects related to Geographic Information Systems for Light Rio de Janeiro and UTE. He also worked as a consultant on issues related to IT development, strategy, and operations in the oil-and-gas market for ENAP Chile and YPF Argentina. He received his B.A. in Electronic Engineering from La Plata University and a degree in Business Direction from IAE University.

Source: Globant's Website www.globant.com, accessed October 2014.

EXHIBIT 3 Globant's Past Performance

Income Statement	FY 2006	FY 2007	FY 2008	FY 2009	FY 2010	FY 2011	FY 2012
Net Sales	**11.4**	**22.8**	**38.1**	**38.5**	**57.1**	**90.1**	**128.8**
% Growth	114.9%	100.2%	66.8%	1.1%	48.1%	57.8%	43.0%
Gross Profit	**4.6**	**9.8**	**15.4**	**14.3**	**22.5**	**38.0**	**54.8**
Gross Margin	40.6%	42.9%	40.4%	37.1%	39.3%	42.2%	42.6%
EBITDA	**1.8**	**3.4**	**6.0**	**4.5**	**8.9**	**12.4**	**17.0**
Margin	15.8%	15.1%	15.7%	11.7%	15.6%	13.8%	13.2%
EBIT	**1.6**	**3.2**	**5.5**	**3.5**	**7.5**	**9.9**	**12.3**
Margin	14.5%	13.8%	14.4%	9.0%	13.1%	11.0%	9.5%
Net Income	-	-	**1.7**	**2.3**	**5.4**	**7.1**	**10.4**
Margin	-	-	4.4%	6.0%	9.4%	7.9%	8.1%

Balance Sheet	FY 2010	FY 2011	FY 2012
Assets			
Cash & Near Cash Items	2.7	7.0	7.7
Short-Term Investments	2.3	2.2	0.9
Accounts & Notes Receivable	12.4	19.9	27.8
Other Current Assets	8.1	5.8	7.3
Total Current Assets	**25.5**	**34.9**	**43.7**
Net Fixed Assets	4.0	8.5	10.9
Other Long-Term Assets	3.7	15.9	26.7
Total Long-Term Assets	**7.6**	**24.5**	**37.6**
Total Assets	**33.1**	**59.4**	**81.3**
Liabilities & Shareholders' Equity			
Accounts Payable	1.6	2.8	4.0
Short-Term Borrowing	0.0	2.3	11.7
Other Short-Term Borrowing	7.2	11.9	19.2
Total Current Liabilities	**8.8**	**17.0**	**34.9**
Long-Term Borrowings	3.8	6.7	0.1
Other Long-Term Liabilities	0.4	2.9	3.4
Total Long-Term Liabilities	**4.2**	**9.6**	**3.5**
Total Liabilities	**13.0**	**26.6**	**38.4**
Minority Interest	0.0	0.0	0.0
Share Capital & APIC	18.1	23.5	44.5
Retained Earnings & Other Equity	2.2	9.2	-1.5
Total Equity	**20.3**	**32.7**	**43.0**
Total Liabilities & Equity	**33.3**	**59.3**	**81.4**

Source: Compiled from Riverwood Capital LLC's company documents and Bloomberg database, accessed October 2014.

EXHIBIT 4 Comparable Companies Selected Financials as of FY2012 ($ in million except Beta)

	GLOB	VRTU	CTSH	SAPE	EPAM
Revenue	128.8	277.8	7,346.5	1,161.5	433.8
EBITDA	17.0	32.2	1,518.1	130.6	76.9
Short-term debt	11.7	0.0	0.0	0.0	0.0
Long-term debt	0.0	0.0	0.0	0.0	0.0
Total liabilities	38.4	56.6	1,667.2	314.8	64.5
Total equity	42.9	218.2	4,854.4	496.4	286.3
Market capitalization	-	428.2	22,288.8	1,457.5	804.4
Beta	-	1.038	1.189	1.263	1.047

Source: Bloomberg database, accessed October 2014.

EXHIBIT 5 Description of Comparable Companies

Virtusa Corporation (VRTU) was a global information technology services company. The company's services included a broad range of information technology services, including IT consulting, technology implementation and application outsourcing.

Cognizant Technology Solutions Corporations (CTSH) provided custom IT consulting and technology services as well as outsourcing services. The company's core competencies included technology strategy consulting, complex systems development, enterprise software package implementation and maintenance, data warehousing, and business intelligence.

Sapient Corporation (SAPE) provided integrated management consulting services, internet commerce solutions, and systems implementation services. The company's services included design and development of internet commerce solution, implantation and integration of packaged software solutions, design and development of custom software solutions, and production support.

EPAM Systems, Inc. (EPAM) provided software development, outsourcing services, e-business, enterprise relationship management, and content management solutions.

Source: Bloomberg database, accessed October 2014.

EXHIBIT 6 Offshore IT Services Spending ($ in million)

Worldwide	**2006**	**2007**	**2008**	**2009**	**2010**	**2011**	**2012**	**2013E**	**2014E**	**2015E**	**2016E**	**2017E**
Application outsourcing	2,601	3,759	4,828	5,017	6,059	7,397	8,343	9,633	11,038	12,596	14,359	16,312
Custom application development	5,070	6,237	7,092	6,819	7,929	9,408	10,418	11,621	12,869	14,164	15,487	16,858
IT consulting	958	1,163	1,334	1,275	1,456	1,745	1,972	2,215	2,465	2,717	2,972	3,239
Infrastructure outsourcing	1,208	1,692	2,252	2,450	2,993	3,853	4,805	6,092	7,581	9,318	11,333	13,668
Systems integration	4,138	5,404	6,524	6,336	7,492	9,236	10,359	11,702	13,148	14,687	16,372	18,195
Other	4,883	6,138	7,150	7,380	8,219	9,369	10,384	11,235	12,148	12,995	13,809	14,638
Total	**18,858**	**24,392**	**29,179**	**29,275**	**34,148**	**41,009**	**46,282**	**52,497**	**59,248**	**66,476**	**74,331**	**82,911**
Growth rate	-	29.35%	19.63%	0.33%	16.65%	20.09%	12.86%	13.43%	12.86%	12.20%	11.82%	11.54%

United States	**2006**	**2007**	**2008**	**2009**	**2010**	**2011**	**2012**	**2013E**	**2014E**	**2015E**	**2016E**	**2017E**
Application outsourcing	1,456	1,891	2,340	2,421	2,916	3,627	4,173	4,763	5,377	5,983	6,577	7,179
Custom application development	3,466	4,072	4,518	4,253	4,993	5,988	6,641	7,324	8,021	8,712	9,375	10,038
IT consulting	767	880	985	941	1,067	1,262	1,424	1,589	1,755	1,914	2,067	2,223
Infrastructure outsourcing	607	850	1,265	1,357	1,716	2,189	2,672	3,218	3,823	4,470	5,160	5,910
Systems integration	2,912	3,668	4,380	4,190	4,967	6,069	6,825	7,597	8,354	9,067	9,756	10,436
Other	4,586	5,713	6,637	6,731	7,540	8,582	9,457	10,298	11,062	11,733	12,366	12,991
Total	**13,794**	**17,074**	**20,125**	**19,893**	**23,198**	**27,718**	**31,192**	**34,789**	**38,391**	**41,878**	**45,301**	**48,776**
Growth rate	-	23.78%	17.87%	-1.15%	16.61%	19.48%	12.53%	11.53%	10.35%	9.08%	8.17%	7.67%

Source: IDC, Worldwide Offshore IT Services 2013 Forecast, doc #248062, April 2014.

EXHIBIT 7 Globant's Ownership Structure as of June 2013

Common Shares Ownership Structure	Number	Percent
Directors and members of Senior Management:		
Francisco Alvarez-Demalde	0	*
Michael E. Marks	0	*
Bradford Eric Bernstein	0	*
Martin Migoya	19,098,656	5.72%
Guibert Andres Englebienne	19,098,656	5.72%
Nestor Nocetti	19,098,656	5.72%
Martin Gonzalo Umaran	18,061,238	5.41%
Gustavo Barreiro	1,085,945	*
Mark Gauger	1,330,216	*
Guillermo Mariscovetere	1,596,258	*
Alejandro Scannapieco	1,809,092	*
Wanda Weigert	127,701	*
Guillermo Willi	319,252	*
Andres Angelani	1,399,295	*
Patricio Pablo Rojo	0	*
Natalia Kanefsck	23,944	*
All executive officers and directors as a group	83,048,909	24.32%
5% or More Shareholders:		
Riverwood Capital LLC	69,196,118	20.73%
FTV Partnerships	62,543,252	18.74%
Riverwood Partnerships	32,743,771	9.81%
WPP Luxembourg Gamma Three S.a.r.l.	71,829,458	21.52%
Paldwick S.A.	19,421,760	
Other:		
Endeavor Global Inc.	3,601,691	5.82%
Total	342,384,959	

Source: Globant's F-1 form filed with the SEC on 8/27/2013.

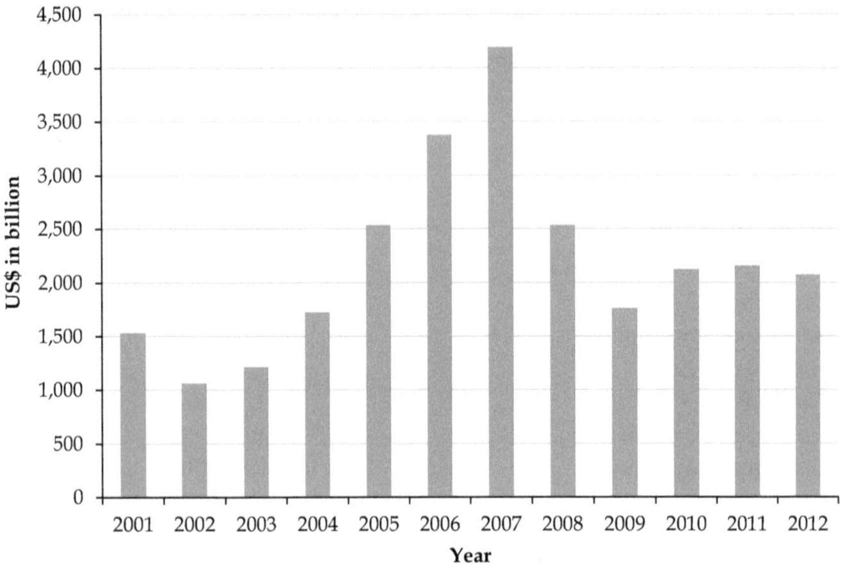

EXHIBIT 8 Global M&A Volume by Deal Value ($ in billion)
Source: Casewriters compiled from Ernst & Young Dealogic.

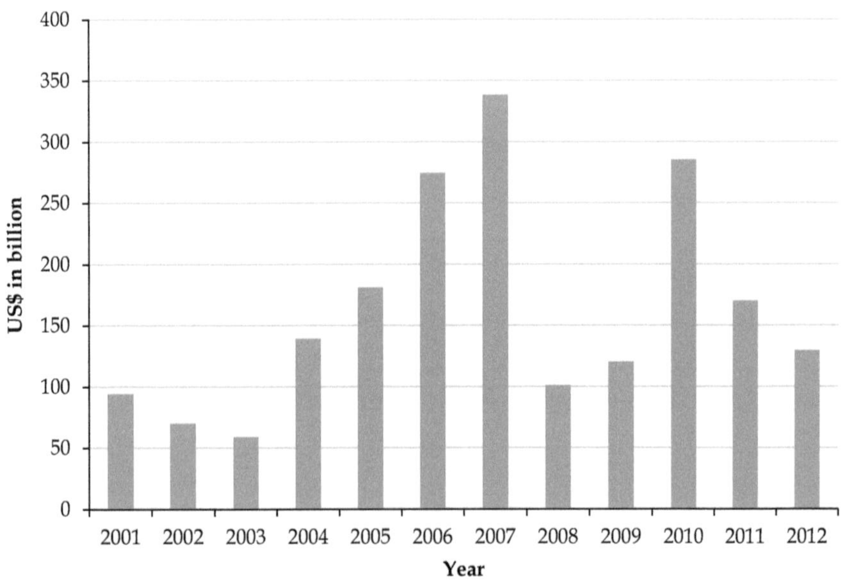

EXHIBIT 9 Global IPO Volume by Capital Raised ($ in billion)
Source: Casewriters compiled from Ernst & Young Dealogic.

EXHIBIT 10 Comparable M&A Transactions in Offshore IT Services

Closed Date	Geographic Region	Target	Buyer	Sellers	Transaction Value ($US mm)	EV/Revenue (x)	EV/EBITDA (x)
01/27/2012	Africa / Middle East	Sapiens International Corporation N.V.	Formula Systems (1985) Ltd.	Kardan Technologies Ltd.; Formula Vision Technologies (F.V.T) Ltd.	6.4	1.97	14.1
12/28/2012	Asia / Pacific	Yucheng Technologies Limited	-	Shah Capital Management, Inc; C2 Capital Limited	81.07	0.9	7.94
11/20/2012	Asia / Pacific	Nippon Office Systems Ltd.	Kanematsu Electronics Ltd.	NTT Communications Corporation; IBM Japan, Ltd.	8.61	0.21	8.14
08/22/2012	Asia / Pacific	Nihon Unisys, Ltd.	Dai Nippon Printing Co. Ltd.	Mitsui & Co. Ltd.	144.63	0.34	4.33
07/09/2012	Asia / Pacific	SinoCom Software Group Limited	SJI (Hong Kong) Limited	-	57.99	0.74	6.13
05/22/2012	Asia / Pacific	Hitachi eBworx Sdn. Bhd	Hitachi Ltd.	CSE Global Limited (SGX:544); OSK Capital Partners Sdn. Bhd.	58.03	2.68	12.09
03/30/2012	Asia / Pacific	iGATE Computer Systems Limited	Pan-Asia iGATE Solutions Limited	-	265.8	1.44	9.05
10/01/2012	Europe	Planet Soft Spólka Akcyjna	-	JW Investments Sp. z o.o.	0.04	1.08	8.87
08/20/2012	Europe	Logica PLC	CGI Group Holdings Europe Limited	Artemis Investment Management Ltd.; Schroder Investment Management Limited; FIL Limited	3,441.21	0.57	18.71
07/17/2012	Europe	Info AG	QSC AG	-	19.64	0.82	8.49
03/19/2012	Europe	InfoVista S.A.	Thoma Bravo, LLC	BRED Banque Populaire S.A.; CDC Investment Management Corporation	35.11	1.24	9.1
03/02/2012	Europe	WorkPlace Systems International plc	LDC (Managers) Limited	Hargreave Hale Limited; Schroder Investment Management Limited; Liontrust Investment Services Ltd.	62.57	3.95	84.87
09/27/2012	United States and Canada	Quest Software Inc.	Dell Inc.	Paulson & Co. Inc.	2,670.73	2.72	13.7
03/30/2012	United States and Canada	ATS Corporation	Salient Federal Solutions, Inc.	CM Equity Partners; Lampe, Conway & Co. LLC; Athena Capital Management, Inc.; Revelation Capital Management Ltd	76.54	0.84	7.63

Source: Capital IQ database, accessed October 2014.

EXHIBIT 11 Description of Target Companies from Exhibit 10

Sapiens International Corporation provided software solutions for the insurance industry in North America, the United Kingdom and rest of Europe, Israel, and the Asia Pacific.

Yucheng Technologies Limited provided IT software, solutions and services for state-owned commercial banks in the People's Republic of China.

Nippon Office Systems Ltd. provided IT services in Japan. Services include application system development, open source software, IT infrastructure services, and more.

Nihon Unisys, Ltd. provided information and communication technology solutions in Japan. It offers software development, system-related, and consulting services.

SinoCom Software Group Limited provided outsourcing software development and technical support services in the People's Republic of China and Japan.

Hitachi eBworx Sdn. Bhd. provided consulting and technology solutions in the banking sector in Malaysia and internationally.

iGATE Computer Systems Limited provided IT consulting, software development, and business process outsourcing sources primarily in North America, Europe, and rest of the Asia Pacific region.

Planet Soft Spólka Akcyjna provided professional IT outsourcing services to micro, small, and medium enterprises worldwide.

Logica plc provided business consulting, systems integration, and outsourcing services to various companies in Europe and beyond.

Info AG provided IT outsourcing and consulting services to medium-sized enterprises in Germany.

InfoVista S.A. designed, developed, and marketed software solutions for proactive service assurance in France, Europe, the Middle East, Africa, the Americas, and the Asia Pacific.

WorkPlace Systems International plc engaged in the development, supply, and implementation of software products and services for workforce management in Europe, North America, and Australia.

Quest Software, Inc. designed, developed, marketed, distributed, and supported enterprise systems management software products.

EXHIBIT 11 *(continued)*

ATS Corporation provided software and systems development, systems integration, information sharing and assurance, IT infrastructure and outsourcing, and IT and business consulting services primarily to government agencies in the United States.

Source: Capital IQ database, accessed October 2014.

EXHIBIT 12 Government Bond Yield Data as of 12/31/2012

		Bond Tenor			
Country	**Currency**	**1-year**	**3-year**	**5-year**	**10-year**
U.S.A.	USD	0.16%	0.36%	0.72%	1.78%
Argentina	USD	8.78%	12.48%	12.54%	-
Argentina	ARS	10.08%	6.49%	17.39%	-

Source: Compiled from Bloomberg, Thomson Reuters Datastream, U.S. Department of Treasury databases, accessed on October 2014.

EXHIBIT 13 U.S. IPO Returns

			Average 3-year Buy-and-hold Return	
Year	**Number of IPOs**	**Average First-day Return (EW)**	**IPOs**	**Market-adjusted**
2000	381	56.3%	-60.2%	-30.9%
2001	79	14.2%	17.8%	14.4%
2002	66	9.1%	68.6%	39.0%
2003	63	11.7%	34.0%	-7.8%
2004	173	12.3%	51.5%	6.9%
2005	160	10.2%	14.2%	2.6%
2006	157	12.1%	-28.8%	-11.2%
2007	159	14.0%	-16.5%	-0.5%
2008	21	6.4%	11.4%	8.0%
2009	41	9.8%	37.0%	-5.1%
2010	93	9.1%	38.6%	-7.3%
2011	81	13.3%	44.5%	1.4%
2012	93	17.9%	65.8%	30.1%

Source: Extracted from Jay R. Ritter's Website http://bear.warrington.ufl.edu/ritter/ipodata.htm, accessed October 2014.

Note: Market-adjusted returns are calculated as the buy-and-hold return on an IPO minus the compounded daily return on the CRSP value-weighted index of Amex, Nasdaq, and NYSE firms.

EXHIBIT 14 Share of Domestic and Foreign IPOs in the U.S. Market

Year	Number of IPOs	Domestic	Foreign Total	Foreign ADRs	% Foreign
2000	421	336	85	40	20.2%
2001	83	74	9	4	10.8%
2002	68	63	5	2	7.4%
2003	66	60	6	3	9.1%
2004	190	160	30	17	15.8%
2005	173	143	30	13	17.3%
2006	172	138	34	15	19.8%
2007	192	138	52	31	27.1%
2008	24	18	6	3	25.0%
2009	49	38	11	8	22.4%
2010	127	82	45	34	35.4%
2011	93	70	23	12	24.7%
2012	97	85	12	4	12.4%

Source: Extracted from Jay R. Ritter's Website http://bear.warrington.ufl.edu/ritter/ipodata.htm, accessed October 2014.

EXHIBIT 15 Investment Bank's Underwriting Fees in the U.S. IPO Market

Year	Number of IPOs	Gross Spreads Mean EW	Gross Spreads Mean PW	Gross Spreads Median	Gross Spreads =7%	Fraction with Multiple Bookrunners	Number of Managing UWs Mean	Number of Managing UWs Median
2000	381	6.9%	5.6%	7.0%	82.0%	7.1%	3.7	3.0
2001	79	6.6%	4.6%	7.0%	62.0%	19.0%	4.4	4.0
2002	66	6.7%	5.2%	7.0%	71.0%	28.8%	4.7	4.0
2003	63	7.0%	6.7%	7.0%	78.0%	31.7%	3.9	4.0
2004	173	6.8%	5.7%	7.0%	78.0%	37.0%	4.5	4.0
2005	160	6.7%	6.1%	7.0%	65.0%	50.6%	4.7	4.0
2006	157	6.8%	6.1%	7.0%	69.0%	54.1%	4.9	4.0
2007	159	6.7%	5.7%	7.0%	73.0%	60.4%	5.3	5.0
2008	21	6.4%	3.4%	7.0%	62.0%	76.2%	7.3	5.0
2009	41	6.4%	5.6%	7.0%	49.0%	85.4%	6.9	6.0
2010	93	6.7%	3.5%	7.0%	70.0%	82.8%	6.2	5.0
2011	81	6.4%	5.1%	7.0%	54.0%	87.7%	7.0	6.0
2012	93	6.7%	3.6%	7.0%	72.0%	91.4%	6.8	6.0

Source: Extracted from Jay R. Ritter's Website http://bear.warrington.ufl.edu/ritter/ipodata.htm, accessed October 2014.

EXHIBIT 16 Globant's Financials Forecast

Income Statement	2013A	2014E	2015E	2016E
Revenues	**158,324**	**197,087**	**240,840**	**293,825**
Cost of sales	96,198	114,166	140,651	170,418
Gross profit	**62,126**	**82,921**	**100,189**	**123,407**
SG&A	50,297	49,842	57,079	68,461
D&A	7,156	7,143	7,707	8,814
Stock based compensation	793	805	968	1,317
Other operating expense	9,579	1,337	-	-
Income from operations	**(5,699)**	**23,794**	**34,435**	**44,815**
Export settlement gains	29,577	9,756	5,100	3,300
Finance income	4,435	4,516	-	-
Interest expense	1,819	1,428	2,100	1,800
Foreign exchange loss and other financial expense	8,221	4,930	-	-
Other income	1,505	-	-	-
Other expense	-	33	-	-
Income before tax	**19,778**	**31,675**	**37,435**	**46,315**
Income tax	6,009	8,831	8,460	10,467
Net income	**13,769**	**22,844**	**28,975**	**35,848**
EBITDA	**32,539**	**40,660**	**47,242**	**56,929**

Cash Flow Statement	2013A	2014E	2015E	2016E
Net income	13,769	22,844	28,975	35,848
Income tax	6,538	8,831	8,460	10,467
Deferred income tax	(529)	(600)	(800)	(800)
Depreciation of PP&E	4,967	4,485	4,817	5,876
Amortization of intangible assets	2,190	2,659	2,890	2,938
Accrued interest	700	1,266	1,400	1,400
Other items	(18,725)	(5,629)	(3,090)	(1,290)
Profit before income tax expense adjusted for non-cash items	**8,910**	**33,856**	**42,652**	**54,439**
Changes in working capital:	(4,757)	(3,212)	(3,093)	(5,764)
Cash provided by operating activities	**4,153**	**30,644**	**39,559**	**48,675**
Income tax paid	(2,941)	(8,745)	(8,460)	(10,467)
Net cash provided by operating activities	**1,212**	**21,899**	**31,099**	**38,208**
Capex	(5,047)	(11,910)	(13,487)	(16,454)
Net acquisition/disposal	15,133	(4,120)	(5,738)	(6,480)
Other	(3,022)	-	-	-
Investing cash flow	**7,064**	**(16,030)**	**(19,225)**	**(22,934)**

Balance Sheet	2013A	2014E	2015E	2016E
Cash & cash equivalent	17,051	59,060	106,183	116,857
Accounts receivables	34,418	43,036	49,488	60,375
Inventory	-	-	-	-
Net fixed & other tangibles	23,827	29,563	36,126	44,074
Goodwill & intangibles	19,187	20,026	21,557	23,412
Financial & other assets	17,264	20,779	23,623	26,114
Total assets	**111,747**	**172,464**	**236,977**	**270,832**
Accounts payable	8,016	8,076	9,248	11,206
Short-term debt	-	-	-	-
Long-term debt	11,795	11,188	11,188	11,188
Provision & other liabilities	32,071	38,448	45,864	54,199
Total liabilities	**51,882**	**57,712**	**66,300**	**76,593**
Shareholder's equity	59,373	114,660	170,900	170,900
Minority interests	492	91	(222)	23,339
Total equity	**59,865**	**114,751**	**170,678**	**194,239**

Source: Compiled from Globant SA (GLOB) Citi August 2014 and Bloomberg database, accessed October 2014.

Note: $ in thousands. Fiscal year ends Dec.

CHAPTER 7.5

Luminar and the Rise of SPACs

Paul Gompers, Shai Bernstein,
Matt Wozny and Alex Gachanja

INTRODUCTION

Heena B. Serrano, Founder of Serrano Investment Advisors, had a difficult decision to make. Known as a leading star of the "SPAC Mafia," Serrano's hedge fund had invested $15 million in 2019 into the IPO of Gores Metropoulos, Inc. Gores Metropoulos was a special purpose acquisition company, or SPAC. SPACs were blank check companies formed for the purposes of finding and effectuating a merger with a target company within 2 years of its formation. SPACs had risen rapidly in popularity in the late 2010s as a back-door option for private, high-growth start-ups to go public. While in 2018, 34 SPACs raised $6.4 billion, in 2020 219 raised $72 billion, outpacing even traditional IPOs by more than $6 billion.[1]

Earlier in the month, the sponsor of the SPAC, who was chiefly responsible for finding and bringing a deal over the finish line, proposed to shareholders what it believed was an appropriate acquisition target. Luminar Technologies, a new-age LiDAR manufacturer for self-driving cars, would merge with the SPAC and thereby go public. An IPO shareholder, Serrano had the option either to redeem all of her shares to get back her full investment with an attractive return or to participate in the merger and remain a shareholder. In previous SPACs, sponsors had called her and enticed her with discounts and deals to remain after the merger. In this SPAC, no such call had come. As Serrano read through the memos prepared by her team of analysts, she wondered what she should do.

Luminar and the Rise of SPACs
by PAUL GOMPERS, SHAI BERNSTEIN, MATT WOZNY, ALEX GACHANJA,
case number 9-221-099 JUNE 22, 2021 © President and Fellows of Harvard College.

TRADITIONAL IPOS

Historically, the most attractive exit path for a startup to take was an initial public offering (IPO), the process of selling shares to the public for the first time. By going public, companies were able to gain better access to capital, which they needed for expansion, and liquidity, which their investors needed to provide returns to their respective limited partners. Over time, founders also took advantage of liquidity of public equity markets by selling some of their ownership.

To be a credible candidate for a traditional IPO, startups needed predictable revenue and historically positive profits, a public company-ready management team, and robust financial and compliance controls. After a decision to go public had been made, the process began with selecting an investment bank to serve as a lead underwriter for the offering. The underwriter managed the deal. In addition to providing advice and helping with all the necessary filing requirements, they were responsible for setting the valuation of the company at issuance, making the market for the firm's shares after the offering, and ensuring that the company would sell the "float," or its listed shares, at the offer price. If it did not, it promised to cover the difference.

To do its job, the underwriters used a "book building" process. First, they worked with the company to determine a credible price range for the offering. In addition to discounted cash flow analyses, they relied on a comparables analysis of recent IPOs to determine the offer price. Next, underwriters took the company's senior officers on a roadshow, a private promotion of the company to institutional investors. At the end of the roadshow, the underwriter received indications of interest from investors and adjusted the offer price based on the demand expressed.

Underwriters purchased shares from the listing company and sold them to investors on the day of the stock's debut. To protect themselves against a loss and ensure market liquidity, underwriters at times exercised a "greenshoe provision," which allowed them to issue up to 15% additional shares at the offer price.[2] Underwriters usually sold more shares in the offering than the company had allotted in the offering, i.e., they were naked short. If the price of the IPO remained stable and went up after 30 days, the underwriter covered their short position by exercising the greenshoe option. The lead underwriter typically had 30 days in which to exercise the greenshoe option. If the IPO started to trade down in price, the underwriter covered their naked short position by purchasing shares in the open market. These open market purchases had the effect of stabilizing the IPO share price. In return for their work in bringing companies public, underwriters were paid a fee, called an "underwriters' spread," typically in the range of 5 to 7 percent of the offering size.

The IPO process was not without its inefficiencies. Pre-existing shareholders were subject to a 180 day "lock-up" imposed by the underwriter, meaning insiders were unable to sell their shares for the first six months of trading. Regulatory and compliance costs associated with traditional IPOs greatly increased as a result of the Sarbanes-Oxley Act of 2002.[3] Finally, insiders often objected to the large share price increase on the first day of trading. Studies with data back to 1980 showed that, on average, IPO shares increased by 20% on their first day of trading.[4] This led many tech commentators to suggest that underwriters underpriced listing shares intentionally and left value on the table for the companies they represented, i.e., firms felt as if they could have raised more capital by selling the same number of shares at a higher price. By 2020, the most famous dissenter in the tech industry was Benchmark venture capitalist Bill Gurley, who complained that tech "had been on the bad end of a bad joke for about four decades now, in terms of how the traditional IPO process works."[5]

One proposed path of reform was direct listings, which Spotify and Slack undertook in 2018 and 2019, respectively. Direct listings differed from traditional IPOs in that no new stock was issued in an offering. By contrast, existing shareholder stock was auctioned on a public exchange. As a result, there was no 180-day lock-up period for existing investors and underwriters were not needed to engage in the book building process. Instead, companies hired capital advisors to communicate with institutional investors, offer forward looking guidance in advance of trading, and declare a reference price together with the hosting stock exchange. New regulations released by the SEC in August 2020 permitted companies opting for a direct listing to raise capital from the listing as well. Proponents for direct listings argued they were cheaper, faster, more transparent, and captured more value for the listing company.[6]

SPACS AS A SOLUTION

Special purpose acquisition companies, or SPACs for short, carried similar promises for companies wishing to go public. SPACs were blank check companies formed for the purposes of finding and merging with a private business, thereby bringing it public. Between 2018 and 2020, SPACs exploded as a means of taking a private high-growth company public. While in 2018, there were 34 SPACs raising $6.4 billion, in 2020 there were 219 raising $72 billion, outpacing even traditional IPOs by more than $6 billion.[7] SPACs had gained so much traction so quickly in the tech industry that commentators had begun labeling their growth a bubble. (See **Exhibit 1** for SPAC funding over time.)

The mechanics of a SPAC were complex and had five core steps. In the first step, a SPAC was formed by issuing stock and raising capital at $10 per share in an IPO. The median IPO proceeds for the 2019-2020 SPAC cohort was $220 million.[8] The SPAC then spent up to 2 years searching for and negotiating with an acquisition target. In the third step, a merger target was found and IPO shareholders decided whether to exercise their redemption rights (i.e., forcing the SPAC to repurchase their shares at $10) or not. Private investments in public equity ("PIPEs") were raised to replace any shareholders who exercised their redemption rights. Finally, a SPAC merged with the target company, bringing it public. (See **Exhibit 2** for the SPAC process and timeline.)

A SPAC was created by a sponsor. The majority of sponsors were private equity funds or senior officers of the world's largest publicly-listed companies. Sponsors worked with underwriters to bring SPACs public. Prior to the IPO, sponsors purchased SPAC shares or warrants as part of a commit. This commit served primarily to cover the underwriting fees of the IPO and all operating costs incurred during its search for an acquisition target. In addition, sponsors were allocated a sponsors' promote, or 20% of post-IPO equity. Sponsors, therefore, ended up with 20% of the SPAC for relatively little money. Over the next two years, sponsors had the chief responsibility of finding an appropriate acquisition target, convincing existing shareholders to stay on through the merger, bringing in required new PIPE investors, and closing the merger successfully. The promote served as compensation for their efforts throughout this process. After a successful merger, agreements usually locked up a sponsors' holdings for one year. A recent study examined the performance of SPACs and the return to various stakeholders.[9] Sponsors experienced a mean return on their investment in the SPAC of 393% and a median return of 202% when performance was measured after three months post-merger.

Investors in SPACs gravitated toward high quality sponsors.[10] Due to their extensive know-how and elaborate networks, high-quality sponsors were thought to be able to access the best targets and add additional value to those deals post-merger. Confidence in their prowess meant fewer SPAC investors would redeem at the time of a merger, reducing dilution. Their robust networks and high reputation made raising PIPEs easier and allowed them to raise more capital during the IPO process. While high quality sponsors had considerably higher returns than other sponsors, they still bore a large potential conflict of interest with IPO investors: they could generate a remarkable return for themselves even if the stock price declined and the merger target was relatively unattractive. On the other hand, they stood to make no money and to lose their investment in the SPAC if they did not find any target with which to merge within two years.

One apparent benefit of a SPAC for the private company target was that companies seeking to go public viewed the SPAC process as being less costly than a traditional IPO. To bring a SPAC public, underwriters were paid 2% of proceeds on average from the sponsor's commit. Only upon a successful merger were underwriters paid an additional 3.5%. For underwriters, SPACs had a unique advantage over IPOs that seemed to justify the reduced fee structure. Underwriters were common targets for shareholder lawsuits in traditional IPOs. But because there was little to disclose at the IPO of a SPAC, they were generally protected from Section 11 liability. In fact, there had not been a single lawsuit filed against SPAC underwriters in the past decade.[11] However, while underwriting fees seemed more amenable, most SPAC IPO investors exercised their redemption rights when the sponsor proposed a merger candidate. Academics pointed to this unique SPAC mechanism to suggest that the actual median underwriting fee was 16.3% for SPACs based upon the amount of capital that actually remained with the company post-merger.[12] Underwriters could also be paid additional fees to help secure PIPE investors needed to move ahead with a successful merger.

SPACs earned a reputation in the media as "poor man's private equity," in which average investors could participate actively in wealth creation. However, by 2020, 70% of SPAC IPO funding came from a group of hedge funds known as the SPAC Mafia. The SPAC Mafia were typically filed 13F forms (required for all 5% shareholders in public companies and funds with over $100 million in assets under management) and held at least 100,000 shares in 10 different SPACs that went public between 2010 and 2020.[13] SPAC IPO proceeds were placed in a trust and invested in Treasury notes for 2 years. As compensation for the illiquidity and as an incentive to make the IPO investment, SPAC shareholders were given redemption rights. These redemption rights allowed SPAC shareholders to redeem their shares at the IPO price ($10 per share) plus accumulated interest when a merger was proposed. While sponsors would offer private deals and discounts to keep existing SPAC IPO shareholders in through the merger, the majority took advantage of their redemption rights. The median redemption rate, or rate at which SPAC IPO investors opted to exercise their redemption rights, was 73% for the 2019-2020 merger cohort. Of those who redeemed, the divestment rate, or the percentage of a position an entity divested, was 98%.[14] As an added incentive to put their money into a SPAC, SPAC IPO shareholders were given warrants and rights. Warrants were call options created by a SPAC company for new stock. The warrants and rights did not expire even after SPAC IPO shareholders exercised their redemption rights, i.e., even if they redeemed their IPO shares for $10 plus accrued interest, they held onto their warrants.[15] As a result, the mean annualized return for redeeming SPAC IPO shareholders was 11.6% for what was essentially a risk-free investment.[16]

Commentators pointed to PIPEs, or private investments in public equity, as another material way in which SPACs were superior to the traditional IPO. To replenish the cash lost when shareholders redeemed prior to the merger, SPACs often raised PIPEs to ensure sufficient cash at the time of merger. Sponsors brought on new capital by way of PIPEs and new public shareholders. (In some instances, they also invested more of their own money.) Following rigorous nondisclosure agreements, prospective investors in PIPEs were brought over the wall and were provided confidential information that allowed them to do more thorough due diligence resulting in more accurate price discovery than was possible in a traditional IPO roadshow. Because of the strong signaling effect commitments from high quality PIPE investors would have on prospective public investors, about one-third of PIPE investors received discounts of 10 percent or more relative to the IPO share price. PIPE investors provided a median of 24.6% of total cash delivered to a target at the time of merger. (See **Exhibit 3** for SPAC Characteristics.)

Private companies merged with SPACs to go public for a variety of reasons. Underwriters typically had criteria in terms of revenues, market capitalization, profitability, etc. for which companies they would take public. As a result, many companies that did not meet those criteria had no other way to be become public. By negotiating with a SPAC, many target companies received financing they otherwise would not have obtained. In addition, going public via a SPAC only required negotiations with a single entity, unlike in a traditional IPO where road shows and pricing meetings typically involved a large number of new institutional investors. While fair value documents were included in prospectuses, they contained few if any forward-looking statements - they were not required. Commentators noted that mergers with SPACs had the potential to enable companies to go public faster than by more traditional methods. Finally, a point of friction for companies during a book-building process of a typical IPO was that valuation and share prices were often locked in. What was not locked on was the amount that would be raised. Although merger agreements often included minimum cash requirements, due to high redemption rates, SPACs were not always able to replenish cash available to meet the set minimum cash requirements. Nevertheless, the median post-merger market cap of a target was $500 million, with a median of $151.6 million. In contrast, a traditional IPO raised a median of $91 million in proceeds for companies.[17] If successful, the blank check company would de-SPAC and the target merged, bringing it public and marking the end of the SPAC.

SPACs were not without substantial challenges and costs to some of their stakeholders. While it was suggested that their personal commitments aligned sponsors to the performance of a company more closely than underwriters had been in a traditional IPO, sponsors risked losing everything if no merger went through. Their chief incentive was therefore a commitment to finding any deal, even if mediocre. Because of the promote, even a losing deal could generate substantial upside for a sponsor. The dilution experienced by most SPACs - 50.4% of its IPO proceeds - was staggering and was borne almost entirely by non-redeeming IPO shareholders and PIPE investors.[18] The post-merger public market performance of SPACs was also disappointing in the time periods that followed. In the 3 months after a merger, the median SPAC return was -14.5%, or a performance of -32.5% against returns anticipated for a company 3 months after an IPO. Twelve months after SPAC mergers had gone through successfully, their median return to shareholders joining at the merger was -65.3%. (See **Exhibit 4** for SPAC returns.)

LUMINAR TECHNOLOGIES

Company History

Austin Russell founded Luminar Technologies, an autonomous vehicle sensor and software company, at the age of 17. Russell spent his teenage years researching optics and photonics at Beckman Laser Institute at the University of California Irvine, where he became fascinated with building laser LiDAR systems used in self-driving cars that could "actually work and be safe."[19] In 2012, he incorporated the company, graduated high school, and later matriculated at Stanford University to study physics. However, he dropped out after six months to work on his business full-time after he was awarded the prestigious Thiel Fellowship, a $100,000 grant from Peter Thiel given to students to drop out of college.[20]

Luminar Technologies spent its first five years researching and building out its intellectual property. Like CEOs of many young enterprises, Russell had to find scrappy, creative solutions early on in his company's history. He moved back home to Southern California. He even brought on his uncle, an electrical engineer who his parents recommended as gifted in rapid prototyping, to support his operation.[21]

A key event in Luminar's development came when Jason Eichenholz, an experienced serial entrepreneur of various photonics technologies, joined the team as co-founder in May 2013. Eichenholz had been mentoring Russell while he had been in high school and later had acted in a consulting capacity for the business.[22] Upon joining, Eichenholz moved the company's headquarters to the Space Coast (Orlando, Florida), whose ecosystem of long-standing defense programs and pillar organizations like Lockheed Martin, Raytheon, L3 Systems, and NASA had created the highest concentration of LiDAR engineers in the world.[23] Luminar began to leverage Eichenholz's existing roots in the area to bring on top talent for research and development. At the time of the SPAC merger in 2020, Luminar Technologies had over 350 employees, 88 issued patents, and 80 pending patents in the US or abroad.[24]

Developing a LiDAR system meant significant research and development costs, opening up a manufacturing plant, and production of hardware that cost tens of thousands of dollars per unit. At first, Russell and his team put cash into the business themselves. To finance their ambitious operation, however, Russell soon turned to professional capital.[25] He first raised funds from the 1517 Fund, a venture capital firm backed by Peter Thiel. Over time, hedge funds, automotive corporate venture capital funds, and other venture funds joined in, with the most recent round of $184 million having been led by Alec Gores in September 2020.[26] By the time of the SPAC merger, Luminar Technologies had raised over $434 million in capital. (See **Exhibit 5** for a financing history of Luminar Technologies.)

Technology

Introduced in the 1960s to track satellites, light detection and ranging, or LiDAR, first gained consideration in the world of autonomous driving during the 2005 DARPA Grand Challenge. Eighteen months after no robot car could finish the track in the previous competition, Stanley, a Stanford vehicle that ran on a 2D LiDAR system, completed the 132 mile course and took home $2 million as prize money.[27] The majority of teams in future competitions would use LiDAR.[28]

LiDAR systems measured distances to objects by emitting light beams via lasers and calculating the time-of-flight until a reflection was returned. The combination of different sensors enabled LiDAR systems to map and respond to a dynamic, unpredictable environment in real-time. The core promise of LiDAR systems was that they could make Level 5, or full, autonomous driving possible.[29]

Nevertheless, they were constrained by cost, reflexivity, and range. Waymo famously paid $70,000 per vehicle for its early LiDAR system.[30] While startups projected to deliver a system as low as $250, at the time of the merger none were able to meet their ambitious customer promises. The system Waymo first used could process 1.3 million data points per second but could no longer be useful past a range of approximately 120 meters. LiDAR systems' poor reflection off of many materials encountered in an unpredictable environment led to lower resolution outputs and tracking ranges insufficient for a safe, autonomous automobile.

Luminar Technologies tackled these problems by building its hardware and perception software solutions from the ground up, i.e., chip level, for the automobile industry. Its full stack approach resulted in a three-dimensional, 1550 nanometer wavelength technology whose resolution approached that of a camera. Its first product, called Hydra, was a series of dynamically configurable dual-axis scan sensors that offered 200 points per square degree resolution, detected objects up to 500 meters away, and ran on under 40 Watts. The next version of their product, called Iris, promised improvements in weight, power, reliability, size, and cost. Its resolution was expected to increase by 50 percent, to 300 points per square degree, ensuring higher precision and promised to come at two price points: $1000 and $500.[31] (See **Exhibit 6** for photos of Luminar's products.)

Luminar Technologies primarily sold its design, manufacturing, and supporting software solutions to automobile OEMs. It entered into Strategic Partner Programs ("SSP"), promising to deliver products at a fixed price often in collaboration on an autonomous vehicle development program. In September 2017, Luminar Technologies signed a partnership with Toyota Research Institute. Audi AID selected to partner with Luminar in December 2019, citing its then industry-leading 250 meter effective range as the selling point. In May 2020, Volvo awarded Luminar the industry's first series production contract. It would build Luminar's technology into its global automobile platform starting in 2023. At the time of the merger, Luminar Technologies served 50 OEMs, including 7 of the top 10, who operated in the consumer, robotaxi, and trucking sectors of the automobile industry.[32]

Luminar Technologies net sales were $6.8 million in 2019 and approached $12 million in 2020. However, the company suffered significant operating losses of approximately $56 million in 2020. (See **Exhibit 7** for Luminar's historical financials.) At the same time, Luminar's forward-looking statements illustrated the company's high growth expectations. The company believed that by 2025 it would achieve $837 million in revenue. Most of this revenue was expected to come from the existing partner base. (See **Exhibit 8** for revenue projections from the merger presentation.) The company also expected to reach $531 million in gross profit and $365 million in EBITDA by 2025. (See **Exhibit 9** for gross profit and EBITDA projections from the merger presentation.) According to the S-4 document, Luminar Technologies expected that the total addressable market would grow from approximately $5 billion in 2020 to $150 billion by 2030. Adjacent markets such as aerospace, defense and smart cities would become increasingly relevant after that time.[33]

Going SPAC

Gores Metropoulos, Inc went public via an IPO in February 2019, raising $400 million in proceeds. The SPAC's sponsors were teams led by Alec Gores and Dean Metropoulos. Gores was a private equity investor who built his career making prominent leveraged buyouts of non-core businesses from Fortune 500 companies. Metropoulos, too, was a private equity investor who focused on buy-build transactions in the consumer brands sector. The two had collaborated before in 2016 when Gores had led the merger of his SPAC with Hostess Brands which had been privately owned by Metropoulos. Media reports attributed the subsequent explosion of interest in and growth of SPACs to the success that came from that merger.[34]

In late 2020, Gores Metropoulos, Inc. announced that they had found an appropriate target. They planned to include $400 million in cash in a reverse merger with Luminar Technologies at a market capitalization of $3.4 billion. This valuation also included an immediate financing round of $170 million which would be led by Gores and existing Luminar Technologies investors (referred to as series X).[35] Of course, these proceeds assumed that none of the Gores Metropoulos' stockholders exercised their redemption rights to receive cash from the trust account. The amount of cash remaining in the merged company would be reduced by the amount of cash used to satisfy any redemptions.

After the merger, the Series X investors would own 5% of the combined entity, the IPO stockholders would own another 11.8%, and Gores Metropoulos would own 3%. Together, they would own roughly 20% of the combined entity and pre-merger investors would own the remaining 80%, excluding the impact of warrants. (See **Exhibit 10** for pro forma post-merger share information and Exhibit 11 for post-merger projected ownership structure.)

By the time of Gores Metropoulos' announcement, the SPAC market had become particularly hot. SPACs appeared the preferred method of going public for companies involved in the future of mobility. Twenty two such companies went public via reversed mergers, and public valuations of electric vehicle businesses had risen by $800 billion. At the same time, while deal sizes in the private capital markets continued to rise, the number of venture capital transactions started to decline.[36]

Three direct competitors to Luminar Technologies - Velodyne, Aeva, and Ouster - had successfully completed their initial business combinations (i.e., SPAC merger) in the summer and fall of 2020, each achieving market capitalizations of over $1 billion and raising significant capital. (See **Exhibit 12** for SPACs in the EV market 2015-2020, **Exhibit 13** for a listing of various comparables, and **Exhibit 14** for venture capital investments in the LiDAR sector.)

CONCLUSION

Pouring over her analyst notes, Serrano knew that the mobility market's recent success could be a bubble. Were the growth expectations for Luminar Technologies reasonable? Would the promise of LiDAR justify the expected market size? Was this explosion of EV SPACs just a fad - the 2020 version of tulip mania?

Serrano was also wondering whether other SPAC IPO stockholders would choose to redeem their shares, and if so, how it would affect her position. In such a case, would the sponsor succeed in raising alternative capital through a PIPE? Would the sponsor have to offer significant discounts to the PIPE investors that would dilute her ownership?

Serrano glanced at the slides that Gores Metropoulos had presented to the SPAC IPO investors making the case that this was one ride that was not worth missing. While Serrano Investment Advisors had typically redeemed at the announcement of a SPAC merger and had been rewarded handsomely for that choice, she worried that this may represent a very different opportunity. The decision to hold or redeem was certainly not going to be easy.

NOTES

1 Jonathan Shieber "What's behind this year's boom in climate tech SPACs?" *Extra Crunch*, Dec. 29, 2020, https://techcrunch.com/2020/12/29/whats-behind-this-years-boom-in-climate-tech-spacs/?guccounter=1, accessed May 2021.
2 Although unknown to most investors, the term "greenshoe" was a nod to the Green Shoe Company, which went public in 1919 and was the first IPO to utilize a greenshoe option.
3 https://www.lw.com/thoughtLeadership/the-impact-of-sarbanes-oxley-on-ipos-and-high-yield-debt-issuers, accessed May 2021.
4 https://site.warrington.ufl.edu/ritter/files/IPOs-Underpricing.pdf, accessed May 2021.
5 Annie Palmer, "Tech investor Bill Gurley says IPOs have put Silicon Valley on 'bad end of a bad joke for about four decades,'" *CNBC*, Sept. 12, 2019, https://www.cnbc.com/2019/09/12/bill-gurley-says-ipos-put-silicon-valley-on-bad-end-of-a-bad-joke.html, accessed May 2021.
6 Jamie McGurk, "All about Direct Listings," *Andreessen Horowitz*, https://a16z.com/2019/07/02/direct-listings/, accessed May 2021.
7 Shieber "What's behind this year's boom in climate tech SPACs?"
8 Michael Klausner and Michael Ohlrogge, "A Sober Look at SPACs," Law and Economics Research Paper Series Working Paper No. 20-48, *Stanford Law School*, Oct. 2020, https://www-cdn.law.stanford.edu/wp-content/uploads/2021/01/SSRN-id3720919.pdf, accessed May 2021.

9 Klausner and Ohlrogge, "A Sober Look at SPACs."

10 "High quality sponsors" here are defined as meeting at least one of two criteria: (1) they're affiliated with a fund with at least $1 billion in assets under management or (2) they're a SPAC manager or a former CEO or senior officer for a Fortune 500 company.

11 More recently, the legal community observed that reduced liability was not so straightforward, highlighting the risk to sponsors. See "Rising Threat of Securities Liability for SPAC Sponsors" (https://corpgov.law.harvard.edu/2020/11/09/rising-threat-of-securities-liability-for-spac-sponsors/).

12 This calculation is the underwriting fee as a percent of non-redeemed share proceeds and takes dilution from investors redeeming at the merger into account. So if the underwriting fee for a SPAC is 5% and 50% of investors redeem their shares at the merger, the fee will in practice be 10% for the investors who remain.

13 Klausner and Ohlrogge, "A Sober Look at SPACs," page 13 definition.

14 Klausner and Ohlrogge, "A Sober Look at SPACs," page 13.

15 Klausner and Ohlrogge, "A Sober Look at SPACs," page 18.

16 The annualized return is calculated by counting the redemption price, any accumulated interest plus the market value of investors' warrants and rights at the time of the SPAC merger.

17 Anna Pinedo "Capital Formation Market Trends: IPOs And Follow-On Offerings" *Mondaq*, Mar. 3, 2020, https://www.mondaq.com/unitedstates/securities/897822/capital-formation-market-trends-ipos-and-follow-on-offerings, accessed May 2021.

18 Dilution costs are calculated as a percent of the cash delivered in a merger. If a SPAC delivered $1000 to a target, it would have borne $504 in dilution from a combination of the net promote, underwriting fee, and warrant plus rights costs.

19 "CEO at age twenty-two," *UCI Beckman Laser Institute,* Aug. 23, 2018, http://www.bli.uci.edu/ceo-at-age-twenty-two/, accessed May 2021.

20 Nilay Patel, "The 25-Year-Old Billionaire Building the Future of Self-Driving Cars," *The Verge*, Mar. 2, 2021, https://www.theverge.com/22298001/luminar-austin-russel-ceo-interview-self-driving-cars, accessed May 2021.

21 Patel, "The 25-Year-Old Billionaire Building the Future of Self-Driving Cars."

22 Patel, "The 25-Year-Old Billionaire Building the Future of Self-Driving Cars."

23 Alejandro Cremades, "Austin Russell On Starting His Business At 16 And Raising $250M To Make Self-Driving Cars A Reality," *alejandrocremades*.com, https://alejandrocremades.com/austin-russell/, accessed May 2021.

24 S-4 Filing, p. 265, https://www.sec.gov/Archives/edgar/data/1758057/000119312520245303/d48607ds4.htm, accessed May 2021.

25 Cremades, "Austin Russell On Starting His Business At 16 And Raising $250M To Make Self-Driving Cars A Reality."

26 Kia Kokalitcheva, "This 22-year-old CEO has raised $36M to improve self-driving cars," *Axios*, Apr. 13, 2017, https://bit.ly/3D1HUpH, accessed May 2021.

27 Steve Russell, "DARPA Grand Challenge Winner: Stanley the Robot!," *Popular Mechanics*, Jan. 9, 2006, https://www.popularmechanics.com/technology/robots/a393/2169012/, accessed May 2021.
28 Oliver Cameron, "An Introduction to LIDAR: The Key Self-Driving Car Sensor," *Voyage*, May 9, 2017, https://news.voyage.auto/an-introduction-to-lidar-the-key-self-driving-car-sensor-a7e405590cff, accessed May 2021.
29 James M. Anderson, et al. "Brief History and Current State of Autonomous Vehicles," *Autonomous Vehicle Technology: A Guide for Policymakers, RAND Corporation*, 2014, pp. 55–74. JSTOR, www.jstor.org/stable/10.7249/j.ctt5hhwgz.11. Accessed 12 May 2021
30 Ibid.
31 Kyle Wiggers, "Lidar startup Luminar raises $100 million, unveils Iris sensors," *VentureBeat*, Jul. 11, 2019, https://venturebeat.com/2019/07/11/lidar-startup-luminar-raises-100-million-unveils-iris-sensors/, accessed May 2021.
32 S-4, page 269, https://www.sec.gov/Archives/edgar/data/1758057/000119312520245303/d48607ds4.htm, accessed May 2021.
33 Ibid, page 238.
34 John Kell, "Hostess Brands Returns to Wall Street," *Fortune*, Nov. 7, 2016, https://fortune.com/2016/11/07/twinkies-hostess-brands-ipo/, accessed May 2021.
35 "Luminar, the Global Leader in Lidar Autonomous Driving Technology, to Be Listed on Nasdaq Through Merger With Gores Metropoulos," *Bloomberg*, August 24, 2020, https://www.bloomberg.com/press-releases/2020-08-24/luminar-the-global-leader-in-lidar-autonomous-driving-technology-to-be-listed-on-nasdaq-through-merger-with-gores-metropoulos, accessed May 2021.
36 Jeremy C. Owens and Tomi Kilgore "In One Chart: The explosion in electric-vehicle funding, valuation and trading," *MarketWatch*, Mar 15, 2021, https://www.marketwatch.com/story/in-one-chart-the-explosion-in-electric-vehicle-funding-valuation-and-trading-11615834956, accessed May 2021.

EXHIBIT 1 Number of SPAC and Operating Company IPOs

	Number of IPOs		Total Proceeds ($m)		Average Proceeds ($m)	
Year	SPAC	Operating	SPAC	Operating	SPAC	Operating
2010	2	91	104	29,822	52	328
2011	6	81	451	26,967	75	333
2012	9	93	475	31,112	53	335
2013	10	158	1,325	41,565	132	263
2014	11	206	1,555	42,200	141	205
2015	20	118	3,620	22,000	181	186
2016	13	75	3,224	12,518	248	167
2017	34	106	8,996	22,979	265	217
2018	46	134	9,935	33,467	216	250
2019	59	112	12,115	39,182	205	350
2020	248	165	75,300	61,900	304	375
Total	**458**	**1,339**	**117,099**	**363,711**	**256**	**272**

Source: Minmo Gahng, Jay Ritter, and Donghang Zhang, 2021, "SPACs," University of Florida Working Paper, https://ssrn.com/abstract=3775847, accessed May 2021.

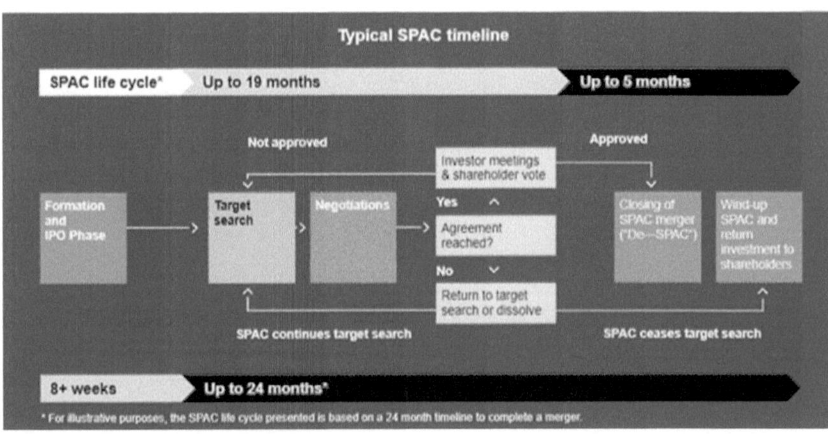

EXHIBIT 2 Typical SPAC Timeline
Source: "Typical SPAC Timeline." https://www.pwc.com/us/en/services/audit-assurance/accounting-advisory/spac-merger.html, accessed March 2021. © PwC. Not for further distribution without the prior written permission of PwC. PwC refers to the US member firm or one of its subsidiaries or affiliates, and may sometimes refer to the PwC network. Each member firm is a separate legal entity. Please see www.pwc.com/structure for further details.

EXHIBIT 3 Overview of SPAC Characteristics

	Median	25th Percentile	75th Percentile
IPO Proceeds ($M USD)	$220	$141	$328
Redemptions (% IPO Proceeds)	73%	18%	95%
Total Cash Delivered to Target in Merger ($M USD)	$151.6	$26	$353
Cash to Target as % IPO Proceeds	71.5%	16%	121%
Public SPAC Investors: % Total Cash Delivered	64.2%	28%	99%
3rd Party PIPE: % Total Cash Delivered	24.6%	0%	43%
Sponsor PIPE: % Total Cash Delivered	0%	0%	11%
Target Post-Merger Market Cap ($M USD)	$501.6	$321	$955
Post-Merger Shares (%) Held by All SPAC Shareholders (including sponsor)	34.5%	24%	50%
Post-Merger Shares (%) Held by Sponsor	11.7%	6%	15%

Source: Klausner, Michael D. and Ohlrogge, Michael and Ruan, Emily, "A Sober Look at SPACs" (October 28, 2020). Yale Journal on Regulation, Forthcoming, Stanford Law and Economics Olin Working Paper No. 559, NYU Law and Economics Research Paper No. 20-48, European Corporate Governance Institute – Finance Working Paper No. 746/2021, https://ssrn.com/abstract=3720919, accessed May 2021.

EXHIBIT 4 Post-Merger SPAC Returns (2019-2020 Merger Cohort)

	Three-Month			Six-Month			Twelve-Month		
	All	HQ	Non-HQ	All	HQ	Non-HQ	All	HQ	Non-HQ
Mean Return	-2.9%	31.5%	-38.8%	-12.3%	15.8%	-37.6%	-34.9%	-6.0%	-57.3%
Median Return	-14.5%	-4.6%	-46.9%	-23.8%	-15.9%	-43.0%	-65.3%	-34.6%	-66.3%
Mean Return (Excess over IPO Index)	-13.1%	25.1%	-53.0%	-33.0%	0.4%	-63.1%	-47.1%	-11.8%	-74.6%
Median Return (Excess over IPO Index)	-32.8%	7.1%	-52.1%	-43.2%	-31.0%	-56.3%	-56.5%	-54.8%	-89.9%
Mean Return (Excess over Russell 2000)	-1.3%	37.5%	-41.9%	-10.9%	22.5%	-41.0%	-21.5%	9.7%	-45.7%
Median Return (Excess over Russell 2000)	-16.1%	16.9%	-47.2%	-17.5%	-2.4%	-57.0%	-44.9%	-36.3%	-55.0%
N SPACs	47	24	23	38	18	20	16	7	9

Source: Klausner, Michael D. and Ohlrogge, Michael and Ruan, Emily, "A Sober Look at SPACs" (October 28, 2020). Yale Journal on Regulation, Forthcoming, Stanford Law and Economics Olin Working Paper No. 559, NYU Law and Economics Research Paper No. 20-48, European Corporate Governance Institute – Finance Working Paper No. 746/2021, https://ssrn.com/abstract=3720919, accessed May 2021.

EXHIBIT 5 Financing History of Luminar Technologies

5 Financing History of Luminar Technologies

Deal Type	Date	Amount	Raised to Date	Notable Investors
Corporate	30-Oct-2020	Undisclosed	$434.00 M	Daimler Trucks
Later Stage VC	8-Sep-2020	$184.00 M	$434.00 M	Volvo Car, Van Tuyl Companies, VectoIQ, Alec Gores
Later Stage VC	24-Jun-2019	$100.00 M	$250.00 M	Corning, Cornes Technologies and Corning Painted Post Agency
Early Stage VC	14-Jun-2018	$114.00 M	$150.00 M	Volvo Car and DVI Equity Partners
Debt - General	1-Sep-2017	Undisclosed	$36.00 M	SQN Venture Partners and Crescent Cove Capital Management
Seed Stage	1-Sep-2016	$36.00 M	$36.00 M	Canvas Ventures Fund, GVA Capital, 1517 Fund; Peter Thiel, Proioxis Ventures

Source: Created by casewriters using data from Pitchbook.

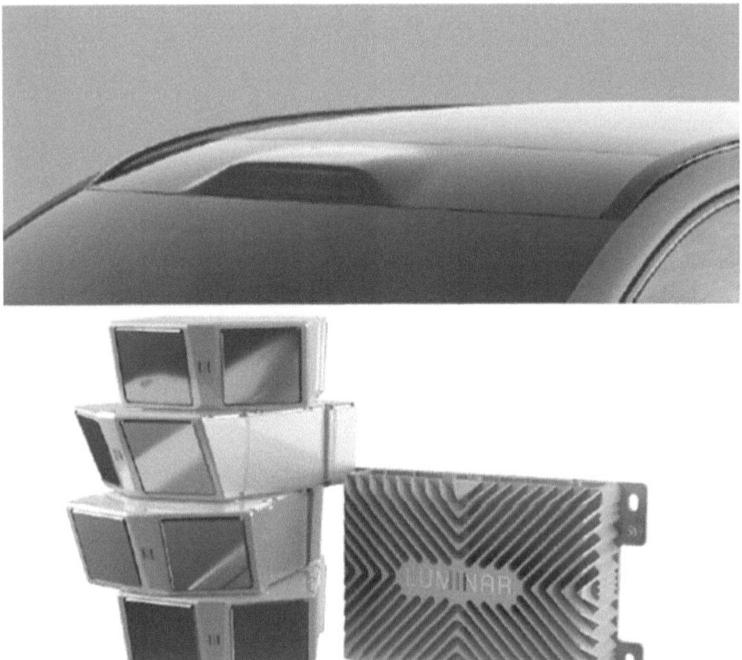

EXHIBIT 6 Luminar's Products
Source: Gores Metropoulos Inc. (2020). 2020 S-4 form, https://www.sec.gov/Archives/edgar/data/1758057/000119312520245303/d48607ds4.htm, accessed May 2021.

EXHIBIT 7 Luminar Technologies Financial Data

Income Statement

Income Statement

	For the six months ended June 30, 2020	2019	Change $	Change %
Net Sales	7,296	3,719	3,577	96%
Cost of sales	11,285	6,805	4,480	66%
Gross loss	(3,989)	(3,086)	(903)	29%
Selling and marketing expenses	3,075	2,121	954	45%
General and adminstrative expenses	9,505	8,059	1,446	18%
Research and development expenses	18,116	18,450	(334)	-2%
Operating loss	(34,685)	(31,716)	(2,969)	9%
Interest income	121	37	84	nm
Interest expense	(1,021)	(1,235)	214	-17%
Change in fair value of SAFE notes		(24,215)	24,215	nm
Change in fair value of warrant liabilities	(4,574)	(72)	(4,502)	nm
Loss of extinguishment of debt	(866)	(6124)	5,258	-86%
Other income	10	233	(223)	nm
Other expense	(1)	(3)	2	nm
Loss before income taxes	(41,016)	(63,095)	22,079	-35%
Income taxes	—	—	—	nm
Net loss	(41,016)	(63,095)	22,079	-35%
Net loss attributable to common stockholders, basic and diluted	(4.34)	(8.43)		
Weighted-average shares used in computing net loss per share attributable to common stockholders, basic and diluted	9,447,670	8,111,670		

EXHIBIT 7 *(continued)*

Balance Sheet

	As of June 30, 2020		Assuming No Redempt	Assuming Maximum Redemptions As of June 30, 2020
	Luminar (Hist	Gores (Historical)	Pro Forma Combined	Pro Forma Combined
ASSETS				
Current Assets				
Cash and cash equivalants	20,643	1,011	508,066	138,707
Restricted cash and cash equivalants	225	—	225	225
Marketable Securities	6,374	—	6,374	6,374
Accounts receivable, net	5,618	—	5,618	5,618
Inventories, net	4,961	—	4,961	4,961
Prepaids and other current assets	2,873	108	2,981	2,981
Total current assets	40,694	1,119	528,225	158,866
Non-current assets:				
Investments and cash held in Trust Account	—	406,398	—	—
Property and equipment, net	7,630	—	7,630	7,630
Goodwill	701	—	701	701
Deferred income tax	—	15	15	15
Other long-term assets	1,191	—	1,191	1,191
Total non-current assets	9,522	406,413	9,537	9,537
TOTAL ASSETS	**50,216**	**407,532**	**537,762**	**168,403**
LIABILITIES AND STOCKHOLDERS' EQUITY				
Accounts payable	3,553	—	3,553	3,553
Accured expenses and other current liabilities	5,544	86	5,544	5,544
State franchise tax accural	—	20	—	—
Current portion of long-term debt	3,948	—	—	492
Other current liabilities	593	195	788	788
Total current liabilities	13,638	301	9885	10,377
Non-current liabilities				
Deferred underwriting compensation	—	14,000	—	—
Long-term debt	32,602	—	—	28,217
Warrant liabilities	7,425	—	—	—
Other long-term liabilites	1,113	—	1,113	1,113
Total non-current liabilities	41,140	14,000	1,113	29,330
Total Liabilities	54,778	14,301	10,998	39,707
Common stock subject to possible redemption	—	387,135	—	—
Series A Preferred Stock	244,743	—	—	—
Seires X Preferred Stock	—	—	—	—
Stakeholder's equity (deficit)	—	—		
Preferred stock	—	—		
Founders' preferred stock	—	—		
Common stock	—			
Class A Stock			22	18
Class B Stock	—	—	10	10
Class F Stock	—	1	—	—
Additional paid-in capital	13,906	24	798,873	397,479
Treasury stock	—	—	—	—
Accumulated other comprehensive income	8	—	8	8
Retained earnings (accumulated deficit)	(263,219)	6,071	(272,149)	(268,819)
Total stakeholders' equity (deficit)	(249,305)	6,096	526,764	128,696
TOTAL LIABILITIES AND STOCKHOLDERS'S EQUITY (DEFICIT)	**50,216**	**407,532**	**537,762**	**168,403**

EXHIBIT 7 *(continued)*

Cash Flow Summary

	Year ended December 31		Six months ended June 30,	
	2019	2018	2020	2019
Net cash provided by (used in)				
Operating activities	(60,201.00)	(67,089.00)	(33,978.00)	(26,693.00)
Investing activities	(7,778.00)	(4,388.00)	(423.00)	(774.00)
Financing activities	85,457.00	67,919.00	27,964.00	80,366.00

Cash Flow Statement

	Six months ended June 30,	
	2020	2019
Cash flows from operating activities:		
Net loss	$(41,016)	$ (63,095)
Adjustments to reconcile net loss to net cash used in operating activities:		
Depreciation and amortization	1,241	1,136
Change in fair value of warrants and SAFE liabilities	4,574	24,287
Impairment of inventories	2,481	—
Loss on extinguishment of debt	866	6,124
Share-based compensation	3,413	1,170
Changes in operating assets and liabilities:		
Accounts receivable	(3,940)	2,143
Inventories	(3,440)	(2,524)
Other current assets	(1,049)	331
Other long-term assets	638	2
Accounts payable	92	3,135
Accrued liabilities	2,302	527
Other current liabilities	229	126
Other long-term liabilities	(369)	(55)
Net cash used in operating activities	(33,978)	(26,693)
Cash flows from investing activities:		
Proceeds from sale of marketable securities	285	—
Purchase of property and equipment	(708)	(774)
Net cash used in investing activities	(423)	(774)
Cash flows from financing activities:		
Settlement of SAFE notes	—	(5,609)
Principal payments on financing obligations	(3,843)	(4,719)
Proceeds from the issuance of debt	31,910	—
Proceeds from issuance of SAFE notes	—	37,379
Principal payments on capital leases	(108)	(26)
Proceeds from issuance of Series A Convertible Preferred stock	—	58,064
Proceeds from issuance of restricted common stock	9	61
Financing costs paid	—	(4,776)
Repurchase of Common Stock	(4)	(8)
Net cash provided by financing activities	27,964	80,366
Net increase (decrease) in cash and cash equivalents and restricted cash and cash equivalents	(6,437)	52,899
Beginning cash and cash equivalents and restricted cash and cash equivalents	27,305	9,827
Ending cash and cash equivalents and restricted cash and cash equivalents	$ 20,868	$ 62,726
Supplemental disclosures of cash flow information:		
Cash paid for interest	$ 1,328	$ 803
Supplemental disclosures of noncash investing and financing activities		
Conversion of Bridge Note to Series A Convertible Preferred stock	—	7,719
Conversion of SAFE notes into common stock	—	4,925
Conversion of SAFE notes into Series A Convertible Preferred stock	—	173,726
Assets acquired on capital leases	123	80
Purchases of property and equipment recorded in accounts payable and accrued liabilities	65	144

EXHIBIT 7 *(continued)*

Financial Projections

($ in millions)	2020E	2021E	2022E	2023E	2024E	2025E	2026E	2027E	2028E	2029E	2030E
Total Revenue	$15	$26	$35	$124	$418	$836	$1,399	$2,077	$2,894	$3,879	$5,056
Total Cost of Goods Sold	$22	$20	$23	$60	$164	$305	$488	$684	$945	$1,246	$1,587
Gross Profit	($7)	$6	$12	$63	$254	$531	$911	$1,394	$1,948	$2,633	$3,469
Operating Income	($72)	($95)	($100)	($71)	$102	$337	$678	$1,061	$1,490	$2,019	$2,673
Adjusted EBITDA	($61)	($90)	($88)	($51)	$126	$365	$707	$1,091	$1,520	$2,056	$2,717
Total Capital Expidentures	($4)	($26)	($33)	($39)	($18)	($21)	($31)	($32)	($38)	($46)	($58)
EBITDA less Capital Expidentures	($66)	($116)	($121)	($90)	$108	$344	$676	$1,059	$1,483	$2,010	$2,658
Change in Net Work Capital	($9)	($26)	($6)	$7	($24)	($55)	($76)	($92)	($109)	($136)	($165)

	Fiscal Year Ending December 31,											
($ in millions)	2020E	2021E	2022E	2023E	2024E	2025E	2026E	2027E	2028E	2029E	2030E	Terminal Year
Revenue	$8	$26	$35	$124	$418	$836	$1,399	$2,077	$2,894	$3,879	$5.06	$5,056
% Growth	-12%	68%	38%	250%	238%	100%	67%	48%	39%	34%	30%	
Adjusted EBITDA	($31)	($90)	($88)	($51)	$126	$365	$707	$1,091	$1,520	$2,056	$2,717	$2,717
Less: Depreciation and Amortization	(2.00)	(6.00)	(12.00)	(20.00)	(24.00)	(28.00)	(29.00)	(30.00)	(30.00)	(37.00)	(44.00)	(58.00)
Adjusted EBIT	($32)	($95)	($100)	($71)	$102	$337	$678	$1,061	$1,490	$2,019	$2,673	$2,658
Less: Taxes @25%	—	—	—	—	(25.00)	(84.00)	(170.00)	(265.00)	(373.00)	(505.00)	(668.00)	(665.00)
Plus: Depreciation and Amortization	2	6	12	20	24	28	29	30	30	37	44	58
Less: Change in Net Working Capital	(13.00)	(26.00)	(6.00)	7.00	(24.00)	(55.00)	(76.00)	(92.00)	(109.00)	(136.00)	(165.00)	(165.00)
Less: Capital Expidentures	(3.00)	(26.00)	(33.00)	(39.00)	(18.00)	(21.00)	(31.00)	(32.00)	(38.00)	(46.00)	(58.00)	(58.00)
Unlevered Free Cash Flow	($46)	($142)	($127)	($83)	$58	$206	$431	$702	$1,002	$1,370	$1,826	$1,829

Source: Gores Metropoulos Inc. (2020). 2020 S-4 form, https://www.sec.gov/Archives/edgar/data/1758057/000119312520245303/d48607ds4.htm, accessed May 2021.

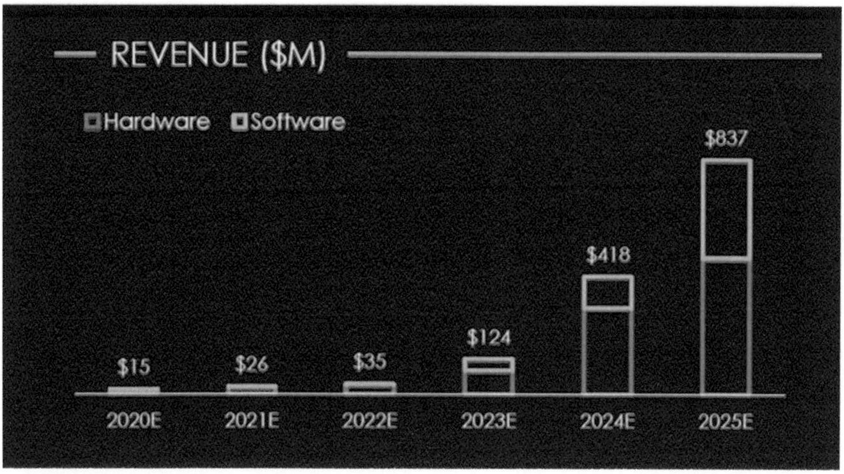

EXHIBIT 8 Revenue Projections
Source: Luminar Technologies Investor Presentation, November 2020, https://investors.luminartech.com/static-files/d5fe72a1-a244-4a39-bbe8-afe5c30a98ed, accessed May 2021.

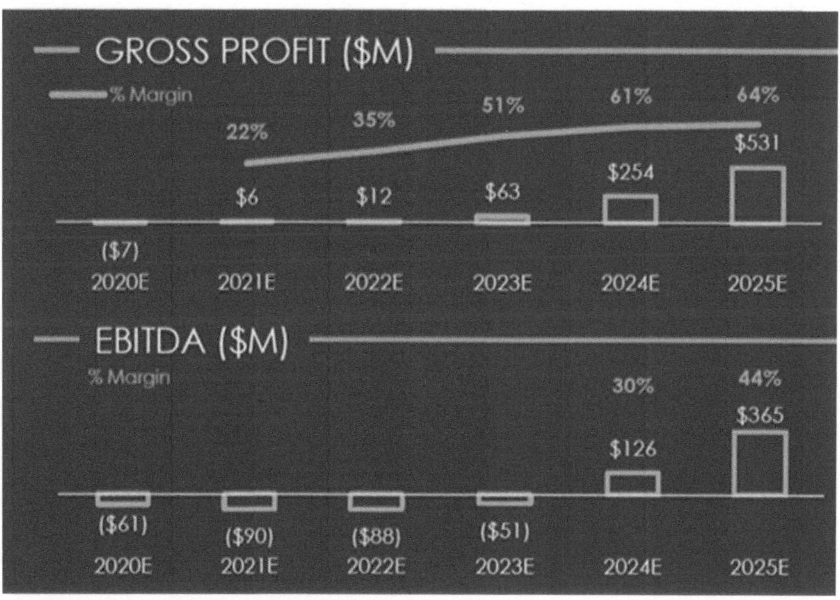

EXHIBIT 9 Profit and EBITDA Projections
Source: Luminar Technologies Investor Presentation, November 2020, https://investors.luminartech.com/static-files/d5fe72a1-a244-4a39-bbe8-afe5c30a98ed, accessed May 2021.

EXHIBIT 10 Comparative Share Information

a. As of and for the sixth months ended June 20, 2020

	Luminar (Historical)	Gores (Historical)	Combined Pro Forma: Assuming No Redemptions	Combined Pro Forma: Assuming Maximum Redemptions	Luminar Equivalent Per Share Pro Forma[2]: Assuming No Redemptions	Luminar Equivalent Per Share Pro Forma[2]: Assuming Maximum Redemptions
As of and for the six months ended June 30, 2020[3]						
Book Value per share[1]	$ (26.39)	$ 0.12	$ 1.64	$ 0.46	$ 22.27	$ 6.25
Weighted averages shares outstanding - basic and diluted	9,447,670					
Net loss per share - basic and diluted	$ (4.34)					
Weighted average shares outstanding of Class A Stock - basic and diluted		40,000,000	216,948,840	177,440,969	166,948,840	166,948,840
Net income (loss) per share of Class A Stock - basic and diluted		$ 0.02	$ (0.11)	$ (0.13)	$ (1.49)	$ (1.77)
Weighted average shares outstanding of Class F Stock - basic and diluted		10,000,000				
Net loss per share of Class F Stock - basic and diluted		$ (0.01)				
Weighted average shares outstanding of Class B Stock - basic and diluted			104,715,233	104,715,233	104,715,233	104,715,233
Net loss per share of Class B Stock - basic and diluted			$ (0.11)	$ (0.13)	$ (1.49)	$ (1.77)

b. For the year ended December 31, 2019

	Luminar (Historical)	Gores (Historical)	Combined Pro Forma: Assuming No Redemptions	Combined Pro Forma: Assuming Maximum Redemptions	Luminar Equivalent Per Share Pro Forma[2]: Assuming No Redemptions	Luminar Equivalent Per Share Pro Forma[2]: Assuming Maximum Redemptions
For the Year ended December 31, 2019[3]						
Weighted averages shares outstanding - basic and diluted	8,718,104					
Net loss per share - basic and diluted	$ (11.47)					
Weighted average shares outstanding of Class A Stock - basic and diluted		36,164,000	216,948,840	177,440,969	166,948,840	166,948,840
Net income (loss) per share of Class A Stock - basic and diluted		$ 0.16	$ (0.30)	$ (0.34)	$ (4.07)	$ (4.62)
Weighted average shares outstanding of Class F Stock - basic and diluted		10,162,656				
Net loss per share of Class F Stock - basic and diluted		$ (0.05)				
Weighted average shares outstanding of Class B Stock - basic and diluted			104,715,233	104,715,233	104,715,233	104,715,233
Net loss per share of Class B Stock - basic and diluted			$ (0.30)	$ (0.34)	$ (4.07)	$ (4.62)

(1) Book value per share = Total equity excluding preferred shares/shares outstanding
(2) The equivalent pro forma basic and diluted per share data for Luminar is calculated by multiplying the combined pro forma per share data by 13.5787, an estimate of the Per Share Company Stock Consideration.
(3) No cash dividends were declared during the periods presented.

Source: Gores Metropoulos Inc. (2020). 2020 S-4 form, https://www.sec.gov/Archives/edgar/data/1758057/000119312520245303/d48607ds4.htm, accessed May 2021.

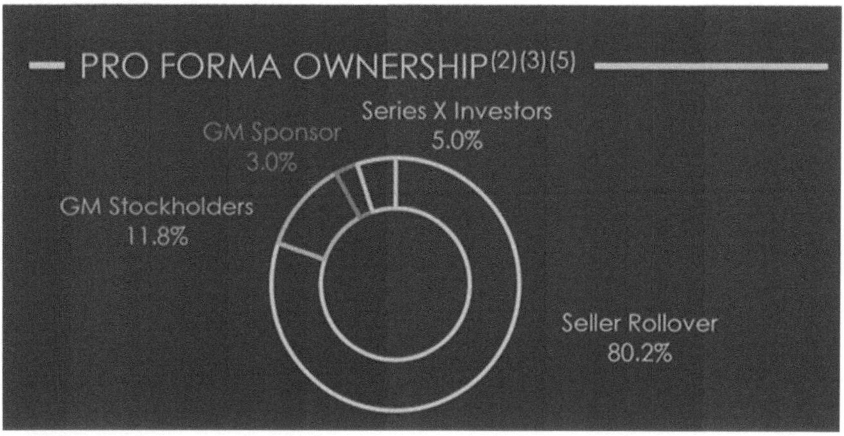

EXHIBIT 11 Ownership Structure
Source: Luminar Technologies Investor Presentation, November 2020, https://investors.luminartech.com/static-files/d5fe72a1-a244-4a39-bbe8-afe5c30a98ed, accessed May 2021.

The following diagram illustrates the ownership percentages and structure of the Post-Combination Company:

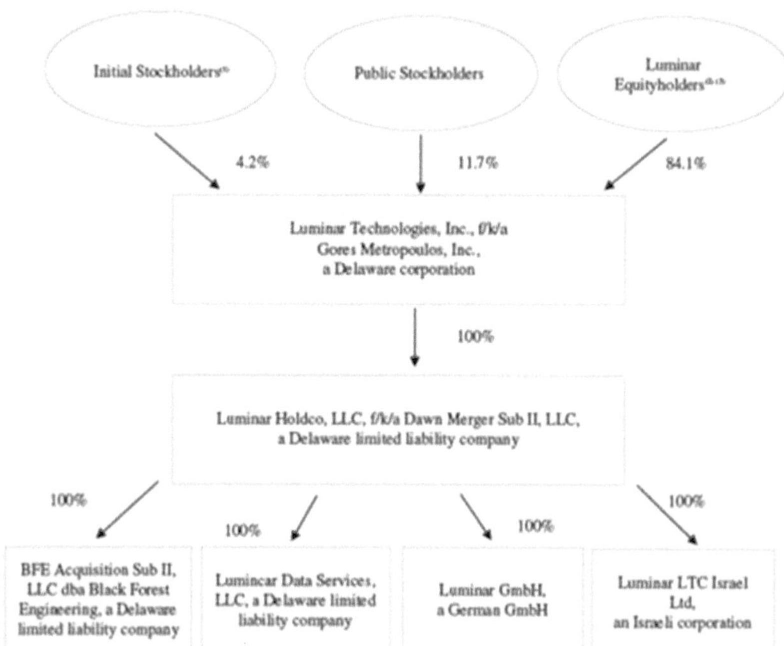

EXHIBIT 11 *(continued)*
Source: Gores Metropoulos Inc. (2020). 2020 S-4 form, https://www.sec.gov/Archives/edgar/data/1758057/000119312520245303/d48607ds4.htm, accessed May 2021.

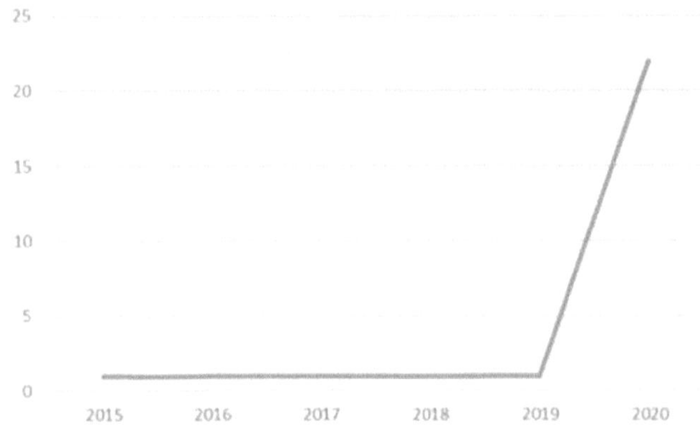

EXHIBIT 12 SPACs in EV Market
Source: Adapted by casewriter from Owens, Jeremy C., and Tomi Kilgore. "In One Chart: The Explosion in Electric-vehicle Funding, Valuation and Trading." MarketWatch. March 15, 2021. https://www.marketwatch.com/story/in-one-chart-the-explosion-in-electric-vehicle-funding-valuation-and-trading-11615834956, accessed April, 2021.

EXHIBIT 13 Luminar Comparables

a. Key privately backed lidar companies

Company	Total Capital Raised ($M)	Last Known Valuation ($M)
Innoviz Technologies	$264	$575
Luminar	$250	$900
Hesai	$231	$650
Velodyne Lidar	$225	$1,800
Surestar	$153	N/A
LeddarTech	$121	N/A
Aeva	$108	$460
Outser	$100	$212
Trilumina	$74	$103
AEye	$62	$220

*As of February 15, 2020
Source: Created by casewriters using data from Pitchbook.

EXHIBIT 13 *(continued)*

b. Multiples

Company Name	Similarity Score	Enterprise Value	Net Income after NCI	EBITDA (TTM)	Total Revenue (TTM)	EV(Daily)/Revenue	EV/Revenue (FQ)	EV/Revenue (FY)	EV/Revenue (TTM)	Date- Price Close	Stock Price	Market Cap
Luminar (NAS: LAZR)		6,884,628								13-Apr-2021	20.04	6,614,778
Veoneer (NYS: VNE)	99.69%	2,328,371	(545,000)	(398,000)	1,373,000	1.70	1.40	1.40	1.40	13-Apr-2021	25.40	2,668,371
Innoviz Technologies (NAS: INVZ)	98.16%				5,000					13-Apr-2021	11.00	
Aptiv (NYS: APTV)	97.24%	40,591,743	1,804,000	2,874,000	13,066,000	3.11	3.03	3.03	3.03	13-Apr-2021	141.20	38,716,743
Velodyne Lidar (NAS: VLDR)	96.02%	2,004,091	(149,864)	(145,422)	95,362	21.02	36.92	36.92	36.92	13-Apr-2021	13.46	2,344,375
Ambarella (NAS: AMBA)	95.71%	3,245,349	(59,786)	(45,336)	222,990	14.55	13.32	13.32	13.32	13-Apr-2021	102.21	3,675,621
Cognex (NAS: CGNX)	95.41%	14,545,637	176,186	213,414	811,020	17.93	18.03	18.03	18.03	13-Apr-2021	84.14	14,891,720
Gentex (NAS: GNTX)	95.10%	8,261,931	347,564	516,553	1,688,189	4.89	4.92	4.92	4.92	13-Apr-2021	35.51	8,712,467
Arlo Technologies (NYS: ARLO)	94.80%	309,548	(101,251)	(91,222)	357,154	0.87	1.24	1.24	1.24	13-Apr-2021	6.04	486,243
Wuhan Guide Infrared Company (SHE: 002414)	94.49%	7,869,577	111,536	117,406	358,894	21.93	26.18		26.18	13-Apr-2021	5.01	7,866,969
Keyence (TKS: 6861)	94.18%	103,471,546	1,710,728		4,843,973	21.36	26.56	13.74	26.56	13-Apr-2021	465.98	113,013,045

Source: Created by casewriters using data from Pitchbook.

EXHIBIT 14 Lidar VC Deal Activity

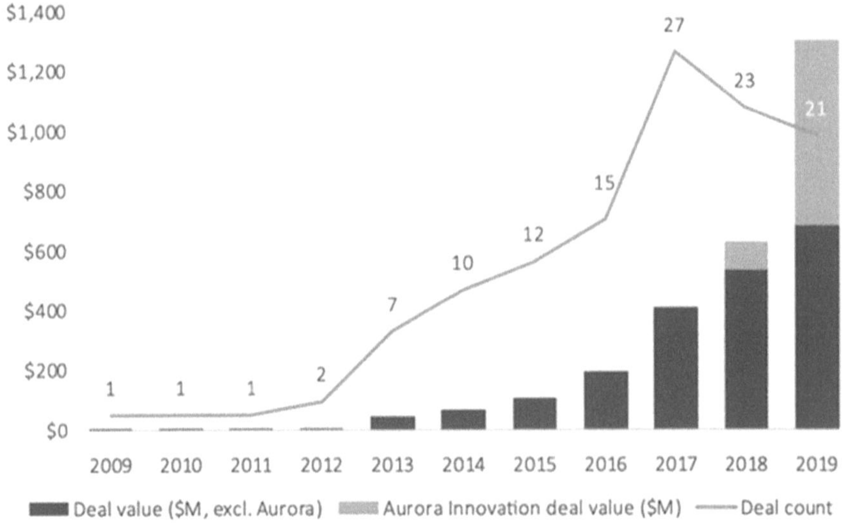

Source: Created by casewriters using data from Pitchbook.

INDEX

Page numbers in **bold** refer to tables and figures in **exhibit**.

www.ingramcontent.com/pod-product-compliance
Ingram Content Group UK Ltd.
Pitfield, Milton Keynes, MK11 3LW, UK
UKHW041830100926
8556IPUK00002B/97

9 781839 991486